MW01038656

THE INVENTION OF LAW IN THE WEST

THE INVENTION OF
LAW IN THE WEST

ALDO SCHIAVONE

Translated by Jeremy Carden and Antony Shugaar

THE BELKNAP PRESS OF
HARVARD UNIVERSITY PRESS
Cambridge, Massachusetts, and London, England
2012

First published in Italian as *Ius. L'invenzione del diritto in Occidente,*
© 2005 Giulio Einaudi Editore S.p.A.

Library of Congress Cataloging-in-Publication Data

Schiavone, Aldo.
[Ius. English]
The invention of law in the West / Aldo Schiavone ; translated by
Jeremy Carden and Antony Shugaar.
p.   cm.
Includes bibliographical references and index.
ISBN 978-0-674-04733-4 (alk. paper)
1. Roman law—History.   I. Carden, Jeremy.   II. Shugaar, Antony.   III. Title.
KJA147.S34513 2010
340.5'4—dc22   2009049333

Contents

Preface

The history of law—and in particular of ancient law—is a discipline which has never really taken root in America's university system and culture. There are various reasons for this absence, and an analysis of the causes would require a long discussion that it would be unwise even to begin here.

Europe, on the other hand, has a long tradition of such studies—in Germany, France, Italy, and in England as well: a tradition, however, that has been unable to regenerate itself, and so is almost everywhere in great difficulty, if not actually dying out. We have thus long since been in the hands of generations of jurists, often with great operational responsibilities, for whom Roman law, or even medieval and early modern law, are nothing more than an extremely blurred image, impossible to bring into focus. It is a lack, though, which deprives us of an important point of view—a depth of perspective on the past when it comes to law—precisely at the moment in which it is most required.

The world awaiting us—and that is already beginning to unfold before our eyes—is more than ever in need of a new legal order, just as it needs a new politics and a new ethics. Building these systems of rules – the norms of a still untested worldwide equality, and of a universal measure of our individual lives and sociality – is the great task we must face. Yet we will not be capable of performing it if we have forgotten where we come from, if we are unable to view the past with that mixture of critical reflection and fitting acknowledgment which alone will permit us to really think the new.

Law is, in its specificity, an invention of the West, which would not otherwise be what it is. Its birth leads us to the heart of a truly impressive experience, that of the first "world" empire in the history of humanity—the Roman empire—and its extraordinary and thus far unequalled talent for generating order from power; and not only crushing force, dominion, asymmetry. It is not possible to conceive an adequate and mature relationship between law and life, rules and needs, and a world order which no longer takes the form of an empire—the great theme of our future, and of America's future—without going back to reconsider that remote beginning.

I have attempted to write a book that is not just for specialists—though I am fully aware it is not an easy book, lying as it does at the intersection between two very arduous fields of studies: legal history and Roman history. Wherever possible, I have tried to bring to the fore the men and the settings lying behind the concepts. To present a warm history not frozen by abstractions. It is a complex story, but one which I believe still involves us all: and I have endeavored to tell it as directly as I could. The reader will judge whether I have succeeded.

The English edition of this book would not have been possible without the support of a small group of people to whom I owe a warm vote of thanks. Firstly, to my translators, Antony Shugaar and Jeremy Carden, who rose magnificently to the difficult task of translating my complex Italian, respecting all its peculiarities and shades of meaning—and in particular to the latter, for his patience and attention over the long days spent working on the final revision of the manuscript. Then, to Sharmila Sen, and the editorial team at Harvard University Press, for the helpfulness, professionalism and intelligence with which they followed the preparation of the text. Finally, and above all, to Glen Bowersock, who originally had the idea to translate the book into English: my debt to his friendship and generosity never ceases to grow.

THE INVENTION OF LAW IN THE WEST

I

The Tradition and the History

I

Roman Law and the Modern West

I.

Our story begins with a book, which will never be lost from sight: a set of writings that the West has tirelessly continued to reflect upon and discuss over the ages. It will be like a journey that remains almost entirely within the realm of this one work—extraordinarily rich in concepts and history—and will take us into largely unexplored territory.

Law is a social and mental form that has invaded modernity, quickly becoming an essential component of our lives—and it is a form invented by the ancient Romans. Such a radical attribution may come as a surprise. Of course, every human society, however basic, cannot get by without establishing a set of rules for itself, which we may call "law" (historians and anthropologists frequently use the term). Yet in doing this we essentially resort to a kind of assimilation by analogy, overlaying a well-known concept onto remote experiences when we believe it possible to discern in those distant realities aspects that can be associated with a more familiar idea. And so while we freely talk about Mesopotamian law, and Egyptian, Greek, or (to move beyond the ancient world) Hawaiian or Aztec law, it was Roman law alone that provided the paradigm enabling us to recognize as "legal" the prescriptive practices that were originally integral parts of radically different contexts and systems—theological apparatuses with varying links to royalty, kinship ties, and political institutions. However, it was only in Rome that the ordering inevitably found in any human community was subjected at an early point to a strict specialization, in turn transformed into a strongly grounded social technology, which identified, once and for all, the juridical function and its experts, the "jurists" (a word unknown to any ancient language but Latin), detaching them from any other cultural production or institutional center—from religion, morals, or even politics—and endowing them with a clear, autonomous, and definitive identity. From then on, law would be seen in every depiction and image, even the simplest and most unassuming, as something entirely apart—a compact, impenetrable corpus—and would always be distinguished by the delineating of regulatory devices with a special and powerful rationality. Its separateness came to be regarded as a peculiar feature of the West: around this isolation an extraordinary ideological discourse quickly took shape to recast it as "independence" and "neutrality"—of norms, procedures, judges—making it one of the underlying values of our civilization.

Over the past one and a half thousand years, all that is known of this decisive heritage has by and large been found gathered into a single group of writings, which during the Renaissance began to be called the *Corpus iuris civilis:* a name that remains in use today.

In the beginning, then, was the text: lone, multiform, austere—and it was a text that came from the East. It was composed shortly after the turn of the sixth century A.D. by a small group of experts at the behest of Justinian I—a man of many talents, the subject of memorable portraits from figures as disparate as Procopius and Gibbon—who ruled over the Byzantine part of the Roman empire, the only one to have survived the catastrophe that engulfed Italy and the other regions in the West.[1]

The dimensions of the *Corpus* are impressive but not overwhelming: it occupied, with the accompanying philological apparatus, three volumes, amounting to a little over 2,000 dense pages, in a classic Berlin edition published in the late nineteenth century.[2] It consists of four distinct units: the *Codex,* the *Digesta,* the *Institutiones,* and the *Novellae.* These titles (especially the first three) would become universally renowned.

At the time when it was compiled in the offices of the imperial court, legal studies were enjoying a revival in the East, which probably started at the turn of the fifth century, following a period of crisis that, in the middle of the third century, had put an end to the golden age of Roman law. If we fail to keep in mind this background of renewed activity, the astonishing rapidity with which the project was completed becomes inexplicable.[3]

Twentieth-century historians have often described the perspective of Byzantine culture in the fifth and sixth centuries as "classicist," also to contrast it with the "vulgarism" that would mark the life and the understanding of law in the western part of the empire during the period of its dissolution: a zealous preservation of the ancient, in the face of an unstoppable slide into loss and decay.[4] We should, however, take great care neither to apply such labels too rigidly nor to attribute excessive importance to them. After all, a genuinely thorough evaluation of the work done by the eastern schools of legal studies prior to Justinian has still to to be attempted. Nonetheless, we can be sure that the debate and research taking place in those circles were based on a solid revival of a relationship with the ancient masters—and in particular with the eminent jurists who lived in the second and third centuries—albeit in the terms of an unequal and unbalanced dialogue, dominated by the authority of ancient writers, and by a sense of deep veneration for that distant and glorious past.

It was in this climate of stimuli and ideas that Justinian developed his project. The initiative was linked to a political vision of strategic import and universalist scope that called for the military reconquest of Italy, the reunification of the Mediterranean, and the restoration of a united empire—objectives that for the most part were actually attained, but only briefly: history had started to take another path.

The program developed the tendency toward codification that should be considered the most important new aspect of the legal experience of late antiquity, a trend that had already produced the Theodosian compilation at the turn of the fifth century. It proceeded in stages, and it is impossible to say whether the redactors initially had a clear picture of the scale of the entire project. Certainly, they could not have foreseen its incredible destiny—perhaps an unrivaled example of the heterogenesis of ends.

Justinian had begun by ordering, in 528, a new collection of "constitutions" (that is, of normative measures issued by the emperors in a variety of forms) extending from the age of Hadrian to his own time: an ample *codex* (as this type of compendium had long been called) that was meant to replace three previous collections—the *Gregorian Code,* the *Hermogenian Code,* and the *Theodosian Code*—and to bring order to the mass of legislation accumulated over the centuries.[5] The year after this project had been completed, the emperor put his minister Tribonian—an intellectual and a statesman of the first rank[6]—in charge of a commission with a far more ambitious task: that of editing a vast collection of texts, which were to have the value of governing law, drawn systematically from throughout the most important writings of the ancient jurists (from Quintus Mucius Scaevola, who lived at the turn of the first century B.C., all the way to Hermogenian and Arcadius Carisius, at the end of the third century), and arranging them by subject within a broad, clearly defined framework (though it actually turned out to be very rough and ready, reelaborating in an uncertain manner old sequences that were already present in legal literature, which had originally served purposes quite different from that of supporting the weight of a full-fledged codification).

Nothing of the sort had ever been attempted before. The goal was highly ambitious: to remodel the thought of the ancient masters in the form of a codified body of law (in the modern sense of the word, though the lexicon of late antiquity assigned the term *codex* only to collections of imperial constitutions), so as to incorporate, in a coherent fashion and within a solid and applicable structure, the old *iura* (as the works of jurists of the past were called) and the new *leges* (that is, the constitutions of the emperors), in the regenerated legal order that Justinian wished to reconstruct around his own well-established autocracy.

2.

> We therefore command you to read and work upon the books dealing with Roman law, written by those learned men of old to whom the most revered emperors gave authority to compose and interpret the laws, so that the whole substance may be extracted from them . . . Since this material will have been composed by the supreme indulgence of the Deity, it is necessary to set it out in a most handsome work, consecrating as it were a fitting and most holy temple of justice, and to distribute the whole law into fifty

books and distinct titles, taking as a model both of our *Codex* of *constitutiones* [enactments] and of the Perpetual Edict, in such a way as may seem convenient to you, so that nothing may be capable of being left outside the finished work already mentioned, but that in these fifty books the entire ancient law—having accumulated in a disorderly fashion for fourteen hundred years, and now made clear by us—may be as if defended by a wall and leave nothing outside itself. All the jurists will have equal weight and no superior authority will be preserved for any author, since not all are regarded as either better or worse in all respects, but only some in particular respects.[7]

It is the emperor himself writing here, describing and explaining his project:: the date was December 530, and the *Digesta,* the most substantial and important part of the *Corpus iuris,* whose composition still holds a number of mysteries, were taking form. In the approach set out by Justinian, they were to serve both as a code and an anthology, an intrinsic ambiguity which, as we shall see, was destined to produce incalculable consequences.

What came to the fore was above all the aspect of the code, which expressed the absolutist and centralizing nature of the imperial government structure, dating back at least as far as the reign of Diocletian. In fact from the start the work assumed the characteristics of a full-blown normative text, designed to ensure juridical certainty and reliability for Byzantine society and its bureaucratic machinery in the wake of the chaos of the preceding periods. The *Digesta* were completed in December 533. Just six months earlier, a massive fleet had set out to reconquer the Mediterranean; in September the imperial army had landed in Africa, immediately retaking possession of Carthage. Arms and law, then, as if a conscious effort was being made to renew a connection that had been crucial to the triumph of Rome.

The emperor's glowing description reveals the idea of a majestic totalization of the Roman legal experience, without any gaps or flaws, ideally presented as the attainment of full maturity: "the whole law . . . nothing may be capable of being left outside the finished work already mentioned . . . the entire ancient law . . . leave nothing outside itself"—the wave of rhetoric betrays a proud confidence that this project constituted the culmination of an unprecedented journey ("for fourteen hundred years"), where at long last the

wisdom and farsightedness of the emperor could become a privileged instrument of divine providence for completing a plan for perfection and salvation.

This perspective could be advanced because the *Digesta* (the title means
"systematic collection")[8] were more than just a code of laws. They were not
the expression of a contemporary lawmaker setting out to regulate the society in which he lived. Through them light was once again shed on the authority and wisdom of the ancient jurists. Their writings dominated the stage:
in the course of its activities the commission appointed by Justinian would
make use of more than 200 treatises and monographs by some forty authors who had lived over a period of four centuries—a collation that had no
precedent.[9]

The texts, which had originally been amassed in relatively compact clus-
ters—in accordance with procedures that probably antedated the composition of the *Digesta* themselves and are still the subject of discussion today[10]—
were disaggregated one by one by the skilled and discerning commissioners.
Only a relatively small proportion of fragments (about 9,000) wound up being included in the collection. The result was an exceptional literary and juridical mosaic. Byzantine art's vocation for this kind of composition was, in
those years, a reflection of the same idea, incorporating diffuse, Neoplatonic
and in particular Plotinian motifs: the attainment and the contemplation of
the truth of the whole, of oneness, as a redemption made possible by the
actuation of a divine plan in opposition to the chaotic and deceptive multiplicity of human life and experience (this is the significance of Justinian's reference to the "disorderly" quality of history, in contrast with the compact
transparency of the codifying order).[11] Rather than a "classicist" culture, there
emerged a sort of providentialism with antihistorical and metaphysical leanings, which brought together past and present above time in the name of a
superior and revelatory rationality: that of the whole, of the totality, which
God's favor had finally made it possible to achieve.

Beneath the profile of the "code," the anthology structure thus appears:
fifty books, grouped into seven parts, and in all but three books a rigid division into titles, containing, one after another, with no editorial linkage or
transition whatever, the fragments extracted from the works of the chosen
jurists.[12] Varying in length from a few words to entire pages, and preceded by
the name of the author and of the source text, they were filled with prescrip-

tions and doctrines, and arranged in long sequences whose internal order is not always clear, but was meant to convey, wherever possible, the impression of a unified discourse.

The anthology model served not merely to enliven the recollection of the past and to stir the memory. The primary aim was to save it. From the middle years of the third century onward the transmission of Roman legal literature had encountered severe difficulties, yet another indicator of the scale of the catastrophe looming over the ancient world and its culture. In the space of just a few decades, an irreparable fissure had opened up: the depths of the disaster into which Roman legal knowledge had plummeted in the aftermath of the Severan age emerged first and foremost as a radical crisis in the preservation of texts. The original versions of the works of the most important jurists—hundreds of them, by about a hundred authors, in accordance with a strict canon of authoritativeness established between the second and third centuries—were on the brink of vanishing due to a shortage of new copies, together with a lack of interest in preparing and circulating them, as those writings had fallen out of the vital circuits of a world of law increasingly dominated by imperial legislation. They had suddenly become incomprehensible and rarely if ever usable in tribunals and in offices, both because of the intrinsic difficulties of mastering so complex a literary universe, and as a consequence of the dismal level of preparation of judges, lawyers, and bureaucrats—the threshold of qualifications for the study of the law had sunk dramatically, especially in the western regions.

An intellectual legacy painstakingly built up over the centuries by the empire's cultural elites was thus in great and imminent danger. Although the situation had improved from the middle of the fifth century onward, especially in the eastern provinces, the risk that it might disappear altogether had certainly not been averted. When Justinian's commissioners embarked on their task, there were only a very few copies of even the best-known works in the finest libraries of Berytus (Beirut) and Constantinople (more will be said about their philological condition shortly). There was already no trace of some of the texts, including certain very important ones, and so these could not be included in the collection. We cannot say what would have happened had Justinian not intervened, but it is by no means far-fetched to think that everything might have been definitively lost. In any case, the fact remains that after the publication of the *Digesta* the chain of transmission was entirely broken; the contents of the new collection remained almost the sole links to a universe that had otherwise vanished into thin air: swallowed up, along with so much of the rest of Greek and Latin culture—from philosophy and poetry to theater and history—in the black hole that the collapse of the ancient world had opened up in the path of the West.

3.

The wholesale rescue carried out by Justinian, however, came at a very high, twofold cost.

Above all, it had demanded a drastic process of selection. As we have seen, the writings of the ancient jurists had not been recovered in their entirety, and indeed not even in any substantial proportion with respect to the originals. The fragments that survive in the *Digesta* are the result of an arbitrary choice—certainly not haphazard, but equally surely made in accordance with criteria that differed greatly from those that a historian of today or, for example, a nineteenth-century professor, would have employed were he or she obliged to undertake the same operation. In our understanding of the legal thought of the ancient world, we are pinned to a single point of view— that of Justinian. We know of the existence of a vast garden, but we must be satisfied with the narrow glimpse of it that we are allowed to see through a single window.

Nor did the Byzantine editors stop here. They also reserved for themselves the right to introduce undeclared modifications into the fragments they were preserving wherever they felt that there was some shortcoming in the thought of the author being copied—for any of a wide range of reasons— in terms of the needs of the times; and Justinian himself, in his presentation of the results of the work done, did not hesitate to emphasize the scope of the interventions, in order to exalt the importance of the achievement:[13] not a mere transcription, but a full-scale updating and adaptation of ancient doctrines to the new conditions of the empire.

The second cost was that the salvaged fragments received an imprint entirely alien to them: the model of the code. It was chosen in order to allow a practical, normative utilization of the *Digesta,* and without doubt greatly facilitated the modern diffusion and expansion of what remained of Roman law, preserving it in a format that would ensure its (relative) manageability and usability in a broad array of diverse contexts. Still, it was the furthest form imaginable from the original characteristics of the Roman legal experience, which during the centuries of its maturity had always steered well clear of any notions of codification (though fully aware of the possibility), finally accepted only in the wake of the great crisis of the third century in the heart of late antiquity.

The code form—the only one through which Roman law has been handed down to us—was at once a sturdy container and a radically distorting mirror, which altered the authentic elements of that culture at the very same time that it played a decisive role in keeping alive its memory. Within it, the real process of ancient legal thought was both guarded and destroyed. While essential documents were at least partially saved, the links and contexts each of them had actually developed in were erased, and the texts were enveloped in a mesh of relations that differed sharply from the original weft and weave in which they had first come into being. The new network was entirely contrived, dictated by the normative fabric and equilibrium of the codification. The structure of the individual writings and the specific profiles of each author seemed to disintegrate just as fundamental aspects and doctrines were being conserved, so as to form, with the recovered threads, the prescriptive weft of another text—a code—that nonetheless continued to reveal in every line the particular quality of the materials from which it had been composed.

The *Digesta* and the entire *Corpus iuris* would enjoy a spectacular success. They would contribute to the establishment of the very idea of the West, or at least its civic rationality, formed over the course of modernity by integrating within it two major devices: the Greek paradigm of politics as popular sovereignty and the principle that public legislation is equal for all, and the Roman paradigm of law as conformity with a self-sustaining system of rules defined by reason. Antiquity had developed these two models in a largely independent manner. Only modern Europe would ultimately and laboriously succeed in combining them, in an attempt to join together law and democracy, legal order and popular sovereignty: a complex process with still open and far from certain outcomes. On the one hand, there was the Greek idea of basing the public space upon a constitutional architecture that was an expression of the supremacy of the assembly and the equality of all citizens before the law; and at the same time of resolving the power of the rulers in the transparency and verifiability of their actions. On the other hand, there was the Roman vocation for capturing bare life—in terms of the relations between private individuals—within the protocols and the parameters of verifiable and regulatory procedures, in a network of measures and conceptual formalities that were the subject of a specific, strongly grounded branch of knowledge—legal science—conceived as an analytic approach to power and its rational normalization.

The trajectory of ancient legal thought, then, places us in the presence of a phenomenon of vast duration and basically universal scope. An extremely dry body of knowledge, harsh and difficult, in every age directly accessible only to a small circle of specialists, has managed to shape our basic common sense, and has been deposited in deep layers of extensive and shared mindsets, from the end of the medieval world—the age of the *Divine Comedy* and of Giotto—right up to the era of the American and French Revolutions, the triumph of capitalism and the bourgeoisie, ultimately lapping at the central years of the twentieth century. In the geography of modern legal systems— in the complicated physics of their structures—the finely calibrated mechanisms and austere principles of that order deriving from a distant past would be summoned to play a decisive role, almost through to the present day: a particularly tenacious layer of concepts and practices that would extend to those political and institutional laboratories of whose creations we are the direct heirs.

4.

Although knowledge of the *Codex* (in its second edition, drawn up in November 534), of the *Institutiones* (a brief handbook for teaching, composed with the use of literary sources from the second and third centuries), and the *Novellae* (a collection of constitutions issued by Justinian himself) did survive with a certain unbroken continuity,[14] the *Digesta,* which represented the most valuable and important portion of the entire compilation, the only part that directly featured the thinking of the great Roman jurists, were largely lost from view in Europe throughout the high Middle Ages, though it would be inappropriate to talk in terms of a complete disappearance as such.[15] Corresponding to their failure to take hold as a code for Byzantine society—for a number of reasons, also linked to the difficulties of transplanting a Latin text to a Greek-speaking world—was the dimming of knowledge of them in the West: another substantial indication of the traumatic fracture of history in this part of the world.

The *Digesta* were rediscovered by scholars in Bologna who, toward the end of the eleventh century, began to work on a copy of what was known as the *Vulgata*. Their example constituted the first assemblage that would eventually lead to the foundation of the universities: in the new institution, the study of Roman law immediately won recognition as a discipline on a footing almost equal to that of theology, and an autonomy that protected it from any excessively strict religious intrusion. The text that was utilized derived indirectly—there is no longer any doubt about this—from an older manuscript, the *Littera Florentina* (probably dating from the sixth century), which arrived in Italy through unknown means, and was housed first in Pisa and later in Florence (hence the name), in the Laurentian Library, where it is still held today.

Since then, for more than eight centuries, the *Digesta* have been the focus of uninterrupted attention, which has established a neo-Roman legal model at the foundations of the modern world, through a process that began in the revived cities of medieval Italy and eventually reached the heart of bourgeois Europe.

The interest in Roman law was not only theoretical and intellectual in nature. It also (and often primarily) had a practical orientation—involving judges, lawyers, and notaries—directed toward the adoption of the *Corpus iuris* in the concrete praxis of courts and bureaucracies: after all, the subject was law, not philosophy. In short, the *Digesta* immediately found a placement, from the Middle Ages on, at that cardinal point of intersection between norms and life, between rules and behaviors, a crucial testing ground for the new civilization then coming into existence: the definitive institutional and cultural consecration of the legal order as a separate and specialized technique of governing social relations, established in an autonomous space, though abutting onto the sphere occupied by political power, in an unbroken contiguity bristling with complicity and tension.

Innumerable studies have been written on this topic. And the doctrines of the Roman jurists, anchored to fragments of the *Digesta* as if to articles of a code that really had been composed by a lawmaker outside of time, have long appeared, in the ideological discourse that followed and conditioned their influence and popularity, as so many depositaries of infallible principles, capable of shielding law in modern civil societies from the pressure of politics and the unprecedented harshness of the class conflicts before and after the growth of capitalism and the Industrial Revolution. They were like the tables of an authentic science for social control, which on all occasions succeeded in treating its own incandescent material without allowing it to be a source of perturbation, instead freezing it within the forms of universally acceptable schemes.

We are accustomed to distinguishing between a "continental" model—dominated by the great French, German, and Italian triptych—where we can detect a stronger and more visible presence of ancient law, and an English example (and in time, with a number of significant variations, an American one) in which that influence was exercised in a less direct manner. But we should not forget that in the English and Scottish world as well, from Bracton to Hobbes, to the circle of Smith, right up to Bentham and Austin, the influence of the *Corpus iuris* would still manage to exert its influence in a thousand different ways. While it is distinctly possible that the reasons for its success in France, Italy, and Germany should in some sense be linked to the peculiar nature of the relationship established in those countries between surviving relics of the ancien régime and the consolidated use of Roman law as an antidote to the residual but tenacious force of feudal legal systems.

Still, we should not allow ourselves to be hypnotized by this continuity. The revived fortunes of Roman law would take on, everywhere in Europe, a quite distinct character: almost invariably the most significant periods—in the fourteenth, sixteenth, and nineteenth centuries—would correspond with the affirmation of fundamental legal innovations, though they always appeared in the ambiguous guise of simple reelaborations of the ancient models, in accordance with a style of disjunction typical of the history of the West. Whenever elements of Greco-Roman culture were recovered, in art, politics, religion, philosophy, and the symbologies of collective life, there was an inevitable and unfailing tendency to use them as vehicles for content that was for the most part quite new, thereby marking an essential discontinuity.

In the exceptional endurance of ancient law into modern times, in an almost inextricable intertwining of tradition and innovation, then, there flows before our eyes the entire history of Europe, albeit in an unconventional sequence, marked by three different forms of the neo-Roman renascence.

The first, which included the glossators, the jurist-theologians who constructed canon law, and the fourteenth-century theorists of the sovereignty of the Italian *comuni*, coincided with the great period of exegesis: a reappropriation of the literal significance of the texts of the *Corpus iuris,* in which the categories and analytical schemes of Roman legal thought were brought back to light in a detailed manner. The second, ranging from the humanists to the scholars of the new political science, the English jurists who debated civil liberty, all the way up to the French and German Enlightenment, ran through the dissolution of the medieval order and the construction of the nation-states, a period marked by the spread of the Romanistic paradigm beyond the ambit of private law, becoming the foundation of the *ius publicum Europaeum* and the modern doctrine of natural law, divided up at an early stage into a multiplicity of orientations, all of them, however, built around the belief that the law of the *Corpus iuris* represented an unrivaled model of natural and civil rationality, if not an expression of an authentic and immutable juridical metaphysics.

The third form—though in many ways the most important for our purposes—involves the age of revolutions and the bourgeois-Romanist codifications in France, Italy, and Germany, including the German system of civil law (known as "Pandectism," in honor of Roman law), and the years surrounding the First World War. The central role played by ancient law was justified in this context by the use of a new discourse, which might be described as that of "classical time."[16] The Roman legal experience was no longer viewed as the revealed rationality of a natural law fixed for eternity, but as the historical outcome of an unrivaled operative method containing within it the secret of law, which modern science could do nothing other than imitate. This preeminence made the Roman jurists appear as absolute protagonists of the legal "classicism" of the West, in a period in which the concept of the classical, ranging from the history of art to the various histories of literature, was enjoying its greatest success; and legal science, first romantic and later positivist, would likewise contribute to the diffusion of that model: ancient culture as a measure of the progress of the moderns.

A comparison, in some cases implicit and only roughly sketched out, in others expressed and articulated to the point of crystallizing into a successful metaphor, accompanied this last phase of the European life of Roman law. It reflected the idea that in the knowledge and the wisdom of ancient authors the enunciation of doctrines and the silent interplay of principles were intrinsically similar to the mechanisms of mathematical calculation. "They calculate with their concepts," it is said of the Roman jurists in a famous text by Savigny.[17] It was this analogy that best described the supposed infallibility of the methods of "classical" jurisprudence—the belief, in other words, that there was a compelling likeness between Roman legal thought and the canons of what had been viewed in the period from the seventeenth to the nineteenth centuries as by definition the most objective and rigorous science: when Savigny was writing, the infinitesimal calculus had been in existence for less than a century, and Kant had just finished studying its implications. It was believed that the unveiling of the secret content in the resemblance was the path to take in constructing a full-fledged "social mathematics," indispensable for any compliance with the primary task of modern legal reason: the construction of a system of "maxims" and "fundamental principles" that were not "arbitrary," but connected in a "real" fashion to a set of preestablished measures and proportions.[18] This image of jurists as mathematicians accompanied the culmination of the modern presence of Roman law: the age of its connection with bourgeois individualism, in the effort to build on a Roman foundation a universally acceptable form of legal syntax, capable of orienting the whole of modernity.

In a Berlin preparing to lead Germany's national unification, Savigny could still therefore entitle the chief work of his maturity—a great treatise on private law that would greatly influence later generations—*System des heutigen römischen Rechts,* or "System of Modern Roman Law,"[19] in which the sharp juxtaposition of two differing chronological determinations immediately betrayed the author's programmatic intent: to suggest the existence, in the field of law, of an authentic short circuit between the past and the present, between the subjectivity of the ancients and the individualism of the moderns, through which the historic time of Roman legal thought ("classical time") was definitively abstracted from the particular context, and was made to coincide with the development of human civilization itself. And in post-unification Germany, the law of the *Digesta,* albeit filtered through an impressive mass of interpretive work by professors and judges, did in fact remain in force until the end of the nineteenth century.

At about the same time in Victorian London, Henry Sumner Maine, at the peak of an eminent career, began his most famous book, *Ancient Law,* with a judgment of Roman law as "the staple of the civil institutions by which modern society is even now controlled";[20] and in the heart of the twentieth century, a perceptive American jurist could still devote two volumes to an admiring description of the widespread presence of the *Corpus iuris* "in the modern world."[21]

5.

This very long arc—roughly 1,000 years—gradually dipped over the course of the twentieth century; the decline, already discernable to some degree in the Europe of the late 1920s—let us say, after Max Weber and after Hans Kelsen's Viennese writings or, if one prefers, with the advent of the totalitarian regimes—was increasingly evident in the post-war period, becoming manifest during the 1960s and even more accentuated in the era of "global law," marking a genuine break with the past. It is perhaps too early to make any categorical judgments, but there is every sign that it has exited for good.

The explanations for the eclipse are complex, and it is not the task of this story to analyze them. Without a doubt, though, there is compelling evidence that links this disappearance to the exhaustion of a function and a role: the development of a formal legal order built around the figures of property and the contract, interpreted as concepts so powerful that their form could even pervade the categories of sovereignty and liberty.

And the fact remains that in any case we are now in the presence of the first generations of legal experts and professionals—French, English, German, and Dutch (not to mention American)—some of them with major roles of responsibility, who no longer refer to a unitary model of legal education, and for whom the *Corpus iuris* is nothing more than a name lost in the void, to which no associations can be made other than a series of vague and nebu-lous notions. In Italy and Spain, things are moving in a slightly different direc-tion, though close inspection will reveal that this is more apparent than real, and is perhaps more a matter of delay than anything else.

This situation may lead to a series of unpredictable consequences, at a time when the economic and political scenarios unfolding before us are pos-ing in entirely new and unfamiliar terms the problem of relations between state organizations, world society, and normative order, and seem to be open-ing up vast areas of life that law is no longer capable of governing and disci-plining, at least in the ways that we have known until now. It does, however, allow us to acquire a point of view that is advantageous in historiographic terms: that of finally being able to observe from outside and from a distance a heritage that has conditioned us all for so long, and which has so tenaciously continued to form part of our horizons. It does not appear that scholars of Roman law have yet managed to find a way of exploiting this new possibility, wrapped up as they are in nostalgia and regret for their lost standing.

This book, on the other hand, will attempt to do just that.

2

History Rediscovered

I.

The *Digesta* were composed to challenge time. With their creation, Roman law already broke away entirely from the world that had originally produced them and began a new and ambiguous life in which the reworking of the past would continually become an instrument for the birth of new forms. Its "actualizations," to use an expression that was common among Italian [*attualizzazione*] and German [*Aktualisierung*] specialists,[1] did not commence, as is commonly thought, in the late Middle Ages; the first—and decisive—one was actually the project realized by Justinian, which in turn made all the others possible. The decontextualizing treatment of the fragments transcribed in the *Digesta* was in fact an initial but complete step in that process of uprooting Roman legal thought from its original setting and history which medieval and modern interpreters would continue to carry out upon those same texts, reading them in continuity with Justinian's editors in order to ensure ever new and more perfected reutilizations.

The progressive stages of this estrangement—a genuine and systematic destruction of historicity—carried out continuously from the late eleventh century through the turn of the twentieth, constitutes what we now call the "Romanist tradition" in the legal experience of the West. The imposing body of work thus accumulated has had a peculiar consequence: it has constantly shielded Justinian's compilation from the consideration of historians, consigning it exclusively to the care of jurists. Only during the brief interlude of the so-called Italian and French legal humanism—let's say from Valla to Cujas (Cujacius)—can a different attitude be identified, as a more specifically historiographic approach gained ground in the study of the *Corpus iuris*.[2] Thereafter, with its growing vigor and specialization, legal studies departed once and for all from the domain of historical and antiquarian research: it is the distance that, in European culture, separates Gibbon and Niebuhr from Hugo and Savigny. Entirely preoccupied by their concern to actualize, the gaze of the Romanists-jurists moved right away from the nascent historiography on classical antiquity, never to reconverge.

The studies of Roman law were not therefore part of the intellectual currents within which European ancient history research would take form. They were irresistibly and solely attracted by the relationship with the new legal science that they themselves were helping to shape. On the other side of the fence, in the most significant modern reconstructions of the history of Rome, up to Rostovtzeff, or Syme, or Mazzarino, the ancient jurists were relegated to an elusive and unfocused marginal role. There are two isolated exceptions to this general tendency: Godefroy, the perceptive interpreter of the *Theodosian Code*,[3] and Gibbon, who provided a concise but invaluable account of the development of Roman law in the celebrated forty-fourth chapter of his *Decline and Fall of the Roman Empire*. The only other person perhaps worthy of mention, for certain brilliant and fleeting flashes of intuition, is Vico, who, in a 1731 addition to the first edition of his *Scienza nuova*, was already wondering "why jurisprudence developed only in one place on earth, among the Romans,"[4] a useful and long-forgotten observation that we shall have occasion to pick up on later.

Even Mommsen, who besides being a jurist of the very first rank was also a gifted philologist and historian, always kept his fields of interest quite separate (as Savigny had in his way), a practice that subsequently made him the target of a witheringly sarcastic critique by Dilthey.[5] The disjuncture is still clearly reflected in the educational structure of European and American universities: Roman law is taught exclusively, if at all, in law schools, and has never managed to penetrate into those of the classics.

The resulting situation was decidedly singular: the more modern law celebrated the importance of the Roman heritage for the whole of Western civilization, the more the actual historical reconstruction of that culture, of its real conditions of existence—conceptual, social, and political—and the consequences of its development, was neglected by scholars of ancient history. And, as we have said, the jurists were utterly incapable of seeing it as well. Absorbed as they were in the problem of "actualization," of the modern re-use of Roman law, they studied it with the (justifiable) view that it was a substantially governing, or, as it is usually described, "positive" body of law, often reducing the Roman legal experience to the sole, misleading dimension of a codified system, and therefore to Justinian's perspective alone. They viewed the *Digesta* as a normative text to be fine-tuned, updated, and applied, or in any case as a source of rules and guidelines for the present day—and not as a document through which, if carefully disassembled and deciphered, the variegated map, however full of lacunae, of an exceptional intellectual itinerary was still clearly discernible. They focused on the code, failing to consider the anthology. And even in cases where they did turn their attention to history, it was in a subsidiary and extrinsic manner, and almost exclusively in order to reconstruct institutional and political frameworks, without ever plumbing the depths of Roman legal thought.

For the entire nineteenth century—the great century of history, but also a decisive era for the definition of modern legal science—this fracture grew wider and wider: on the one hand, the Romanist tradition, (almost) entirely wedged into the field of legal studies, intent—especially in Italy and in Germany—on establishing neo-Roman foundations for the national legal systems then developing in Europe; on the other hand, studies in antiquity, which had no perception of the real importance of law and legal wisdom in the unfolding of Roman history.

Neither the "Historical School" of Savigny and Puchta nor the immense body of philological and historiographic work done by Mommsen succeeded in reducing the terms of the schism: the former was confined to a minor-key historicism, too feeble to overcome the problems that faced it, rapidly converted into a conservative apologia of Roman law and of the mission of the jurist in defiance of the overweening ambitions of revolutionary codes; the latter, substantially incapable of melding together law and history, order and becoming.

Between the Romanist tradition and the historical understanding of Ro-

man law there thus developed a radical incompatibility, which would ultimately condition all of European culture. Unquestionably, over the course
of the twentieth century, following the promulgation of the German code of
civil law, which began to undercut many of the assumptions at the heart
of actualization, and with the end of the "national" period of study of Roman law—vainly contested by Jhering, in the name of a more directly universalist apologia of ancient jurisprudence—something quite visibly changed. In
Italy after Scialoia and Bonfante, in Germany after Pandectism, and to an
even greater extent in both countries with the advent of Fascism and Nazism—substantially hostile to neo-Roman legal conceptions, deemed to be
overly compromised by liberal individualism—various different attempts
were made in the field of Romanist studies to engage with history (more will
be said about this later). But without ever really succeeding in shaking off the
weight of tradition. Barring a few exceptions, its scholars fundamentally
lacked the essential tools of historical research; their background, culture,
and interests remained exclusively legal, not historiographic. They posed elementary or poorly formulated questions, and were unwilling to tackle the
real problems; they operated with an uncritical faith, adopting an improvised
philology full of prejudices.

It was only in the second half of the twentieth century, especially from
the mid-1960s on, that, brusquely confronted with changes in contemporary
legal systems and science so great as to undermine any residual hope of a
return to actualization, more determined efforts were made throughout
Europe to seek new horizons—though perhaps still with excessive timidity.
Some significant results were obtained, however, largely thanks to the pioneering work of Italian academics, without whom an account like this one
would be impossible.

But the task is fraught with difficulty. Legal historiography, if undertaken
in a serious manner, and not in the facile and mechanical way that prompted
the justifiable sarcasm of Fritz Schulz,[6] is clearly an arduous and thorny endeavor: the relationship between law and history is intrinsically challenging,
and for a variety of reasons, some of which are theoretical (a point that does
not usually receive due attention and will be considered shortly).

At the center of Western consciousness, around a decisive element in its
formation—the genesis and original structure of its legal vocation—there
continued to be an unexpected and surprising void of knowledge: a deep and

vast zone of shadow, all the more serious because the changes we must consider demand a profound reflection on the meaning of our own past, and the substance and quality of our roots. These questions have to be addressed if we are to think once again, without the compromises or bad determinism of times past, in terms of a possible—and perhaps more necessary than ever—critique of modern legal reason: in the sense of Kant, even more than that of Marx, though this too is far from being untopical.

It is now time for this gap to be filled, restoring to the thought of the Roman jurists—from which everything developed—the traits and characteristics belonging to them; for us to reconsider their thinking no longer with a view to imitating and drawing upon it, but to better understand—and help to understand—where we come from, what we were, and how we have been shaped.

Certainly, to restore those old writings to their place in history is a complex endeavor, but it is the only way to rescue what would become a crucial feature of the West from misunderstandings and mythologies that can no longer be accepted.

2.

On the one hand, then, there is the Romanist tradition: a glorious lesson, the source of the modern form of law, but intrinsically incapable of historicizing its own content, because it was entirely consumed with constructing their duration beyond antiquity; interested solely in excavating in the *Digesta* along the traces of the code, not of the anthology; intent, in its finest hour, on developing, upon Roman foundations, a general "dogmatics" of law as a universal prerequisite for thinking about all legal phenomena (the word, much used until recently by many European jurists, betrays the medieval contiguity between theology and jurisprudence).

On the other hand is the historical understanding of ancient law, alone capable of showing—in legal terms—ourselves to ourselves: which nonetheless, in order to be truly equal to the task, must throw off the mantle of Romanist tradition and (re)construct its object of inquiry in, so to speak, its original nudity, restored completely to its own time.

But are the remains preserved in the *Digesta* and in the other parts of the *Corpus iuris* sufficient to allow us to achieve such an aim? Or must we resign ourselves to the idea that the distortions and mutilations produced by the Byzantines in their textual assembly and editing will always prevent us from seeing beyond the view that they decided to impose upon us once and for all?

In the eyes of Justinian's commissioners, the history of Roman jurisprudence must have seemed a substantially monolithic block, endowed with an essential cohesion all its own, despite what they considered to be the inevitable disorder of history and time. Those learned men viewed it in terms of a total finalism—as a long and magnificent (though inevitably chaotic) preparation of the providential "codicistic" outcome. Unless we imagine them as being driven by such a set of beliefs, the entire project that inspired the creation of the *Digesta*—the reduction of four centuries of thought to the unity of a single text, as if all the authors who formed part of this mosaic could actually be blended together into a single mind and a single voice—becomes entirely incomprehensible.

Underlying this conception was a not entirely misguided idea, but the intuition it contained was only half-correct, combining as it did an acute perception and a serious error of evaluation. The element of truth corresponded to the effective existence of a compact framework of methods, concepts, and paradigms that could be traced throughout the history and course of Roman legal thought, at least from the late republican age onward—the persistence, in other words, of an analytical style that took shape definitively during the great sea change of the first century B.C., and was never abandoned. A distinct and recognizable imprint, which had made that body of knowledge unique among ancient cultures, and Roman law a prescriptive paradigm of absolute originality.

The error lay in the concealment of the equally fundamental fact that a network of diversity, of non-coinciding lines, tendencies, orientations, personalities, intellectual disputes, and conflicting powers—hidden and yet not entirely erased by the composition of the *Digesta*—gradually developed around that uniform nucleus from the very beginning, the thorough understanding of which was no less important for a proper grasp of the whole than the exact determination of the points of unity.

Obviously, the presentation of a proper and accurate balance between stable features and specific differences did not form part of the program of the Byzantine masters: the compilation of the *Digesta,* dominated by the idea of the construction of the code through the homogeneity of the mosaic, does nothing to render this directly. But if we fail to focus clearly upon this tension, even the authentic compactness of the thought of the jurists ends up appearing in an almost metaphysical light, as the plan of a rationality that was, in its own way, definitive, beyond time and history. Indeed, as we have seen, that is precisely how it seemed for so long to the modern tradition, deceived by Justinian's perspective: all the way up to Savigny, who would unhesitatingly go so far as to describe the Roman jurists as "fungible personalities"[7]—though the idea was first expressed by Valla[8]—where particular subjectivities joined together in subscribing to a shared scientific project: a glaring betrayal of its historicism, in the name of the discovery of a higher scientificity and a "mathematized" purity of law.

3.

In order to start moving in the correct direction, we must make an effort to completely reverse the point of view, to play the compositional sequence of the *Digesta* backwards, forgetting the code and dismantling the mosaic piece by piece, then reconstructing the anthology not in accordance with the systematic layout that was imposed upon it, but rather by gathering the single pieces author by author and work by work, bringing to light the original position of each text, so as ultimately to reassemble, as far as possible, the intellectual profile of each jurist recorded in the collection.

This task of restoration was actually undertaken from a closely textual point of view at the end of the nineteenth century by a great—and lone—German scholar, Otto Lenel, who, given the technical means available to him, worked with rare competence and attention, and displayed an exceptional ability to anticipate future trends.[9] An overall interpretation of his findings has yet to be carried out (and also, at this point, some necessary revision, using modern information management tools and taking into account the historiographic and philological progress of the last century).

A fair-minded reading of the general framework provided by Lenel's research is astonishing: lightly veiled by the superficial uniformity of a style that adhered consciously to a rigid model of communication, as well as a conceptual formalism and a narrowness of argumentation that tended to re-cur in a number of fundamental parameters, it is as if the unpredictable and jagged silhouettes of an entire lost continent were suddenly to reemerge from the mist into which they had long ago vanished.

But are we really sure that what stands before us is a reliable vision?

Setting out from the statements of Justinian himself concerning the vast array of interventions undertaken by his commissioners upon the texts re-produced, scholars of Roman law from the end of the nineteenth century through the first three decades of the twentieth, especially in Germany and Italy, came to the conclusion that it was necessary to make a systematic dis-tinction in the *Digesta* between two different layers of writing: the perilously thin one of the authors to whom each fragment was attributed; and that of Justinian's editors, who, by concealing, omitting, condensing, deforming, and shifting, supposedly created a welter in which the authentic and the superim-posed (the so-called interpolations) became increasingly intertwined.

The opening of this new research perspective had a number of explana-tions, including the diffusion of the canons and techniques of late-Romantic and then positivist philology. Up to that point, the primary task of the nine-teenth century Romanist tradition had been—as we have seen—the classicist and bourgeois modernization of Roman law. But when, during the years be-fore and after the German codification, that path started to become less and less certain, and scholars began to sense the need to reestablish some contact with the realm of historical research, the possibility of identifying two dis-tinct levels of composition in the *Digesta*, assignable to different eras—the Byzantine age and the one extending from Augustus to Diocletian, which unified in a single block all the authors present in the anthology—seemed like an eminently acceptable way of reintroducing the dimensions of time and movement into a field of studies that had till then substantially excluded them.

Suddenly the apparently lost historic depth of Roman law seemed to come back into sight, enabling an internal understanding of its development and transformations. Thus was born the myth of a "classical" law (to use the term that was assigned, in accordance with Savigny's paradigm, to the layer of writing believed to be original; and here the adjective also took on the meaning of "authentic," in keeping with a semantic slippage that was quite common in those years): a reality that could be recovered only by taking a razor to the documents, in an attempt to free them from the alterations that the Byzantine commissioners were thought to have encrusted around them. Nor was it merely a question of philology: the separation of a "pure" legal form from its "altered" version presupposed a severely discriminating historical judgment regarding the specificity of the legal content involved, which accompanied the confident certainty of a no less drastic gap in the history of the texts.

Today we can safely say that this was a blinding error, encouraged by a flawed historiography as well as by an inadequate philology. The hunt for interpolations was not the correct route to serious historical understanding. Through that method, it was impossible to attain anything more than an extrinsic and simplified reconstruction of Roman law, which in the final analysis continued to be entrapped by the Byzantine outlook and the Romanist tradition that had perpetuated it, and relied on an elementary stratigraphy organized around the counterpoint between the "classical" and the Justinianic. And the philology that supposedly justified such a degree of reductionism was (as we have said) weak and improvised, seriously behind the times with respect to the most important achievements in textual criticism during those same years: its critical airiness astonished Giorgio Pasquali.[10] To tell the truth, there were those who even then harbored doubts: Mitteis, de Francisci, Levy, and certainly Arangio-Ruiz. But at least until the 1950s, interpolationism remained the dominant point of reference.

Over the past few decades, however, thanks to the development of more mature and up-to-date critical methods, we have been far more cautious about the real scale of Justinian's interventions. Having set aside the cumbersome classicist prejudice, we came to realize that we did not actually possess any substantial evidence to support most of the suspicions advanced by the preceding generations of scholars. Seemingly evident interpolations proved, in virtually every case, to be nothing more than conceptual and stylistic peculiarities of the original authors, entirely explicable when not measured with the criteria of an abstract canon of linguistic and cultural purity. And even the Romanists finally adopted, in the criticism of the texts, the fundamental methodological maxim that a more conservative reading is by and large to be preferred in the absence of decisive evidence to the contrary. Even when there must have been modifications, it is quite probable, in the majority of cases, that the alterations made by Justinian's compilers were not destined to result in major distortions of the jurists' thought, or of their fundamental stylistic canons.

4.

It was possible, though, to consider a different option: that the texts of the *Digesta* might reveal the presence of another kind of corruption produced before the compilation, from the time of the first editions all the way up to the composition of the versions utilized by the Byzantine commissioners; and, what's more, that certain works, attributed by Justinian's editors to authors from the second and third centuries A.D. (especially from the Severan age), and included as such in the collection, were nothing other than full-fledged counterfeits, fabricated much later, and published under the name of an ancient master.

So it came to be hypothesized that there may be a third layer of writing in the *Digesta,* besides the authentic and the Justinian ones, attributable to "post-classical" interventions (as scholars would soon begin to say) which might have been made consciously—abridgements, simplifications, updatings, summaries, and falsifications—or involuntarily—oversights, mechanical errors of transcription, misunderstandings, notes of commentary inadvertently inserted into the body of the original text—by publishers who reissued, over the course of time, the work that was finally given to the editors of the *Corpus iuris.* In the most complete and up-to-date formulation of this theory—proposed by an important German Romanist, Franz Wieacker, at the turn of the 1960s[11]—the crisis that started around the end of the third century in the transmission of Roman legal literature coincided with an era of profound and substantial modifications to that group of texts, nonetheless destined to resist and survive.

The demonstration proposed by Wieacker, much like the reconstruction of the history of the culture and the manuscript tradition that accompanied it,[12] has not yet been fully evaluated, including the idea that the age of alterations should be considered to have been concentrated between the end of the third and the beginning of the fourth century, up to the time of Constantine, and that from then on there was an almost complete stabilization. But the core of the thesis—with the possibility of a major reworking, in particular of the Severan texts (by far the most widely used ones in the *Digesta*), right from the first "postclassical" editions—refers for its justifications to the heart of the interpolationist methods, and at this point shares their implausibility.

It is certainly true that in the history of Roman legal thought the dynamics of textual transmission are linked very closely to the conceptual history of the content handed down. And it is equally unquestionable that criticism of the texts—an unavoidable task, because it would be a serious error to think that abandoning interpolationist prejudices means forgoing the opportunity to analyze the constitution of documents—makes no sense unless it is inserted into a complete history of the transmission of each writing, from its first edition all the way up to Justinian. Just as, last of all, it can certainly be agreed that the great works of Roman legal literature ended up, for many long decades from the third into the fourth centuries—let us say, between the Gordians and Constantine—in a maelstrom.

But to acknowledge this set of elements does not necessarily require us to accept as inevitable the existence of a dense network of substantial alterations, or of a systematic falsification of entire works, or even a programmatic rewriting of the originals. To believe that would mean perpetuating a classicist prejudice, transplanted from an old world of studies into the fabric of new research. And one fact in particular should be made clear immediately. If, in principle, we cannot rule out by any means the presence of manipulations by editors in the late antique copies, a fair analysis, and in particular all the comparisons—illuminating in the few cases possible—between and among independent textual traditions, lead us to believe that, even where they may have taken place, those interventions hardly ever modified the substantial structure of the author's thoughts, and that moreover the entirely falsified texts are far fewer in number than was suggested by Wieacker (to say nothing of Schulz).[13]

Without doubt there exist apocryphal works from the third and fourth centuries, and the post-Severan editors certainly were no strangers to the idea of intervening in the texts to which they had access: the most important problem for them remained the readability of the writing, not its philological precision or accuracy. But to distort the doctrine of an ancient master was, even in cultural contexts marked by a profound crisis, an operation of quite questionable value; we must yield to this eventuality only in cases of very serious incoherence or inconsistency for which no other explanation seems to be possible—and that almost never happens.

In reality, what seemed like a dense blanket of alterations and fakes—which would have presupposed, above all, an enormous amount of work in a culturally rarefied age—is increasingly revealing itself, beneath the microscope of more careful verification, to be nothing more than a fairly tenuous veil, which only very rarely prevents us from engaging directly with the thought of the original authors. We can assume, then, that the editions of the works utilized for the composition of the *Digesta* were on the whole reliable, with largely correct attributions, marked though they may have been by cuts, summarizations, and minor modifications.

The textual foundations upon which we are relying are therefore reasonably solid: our understanding is clearly patchy, based as it is almost solely upon Justinian's selection, and at times our reconstructions are only supported by clues and conjecture, but that, for the historian, is all part of the game.

3

The Jurists in Rome

I.

From Justinian's perspective, like that of the medieval and modern tradition, one thing was taken completely for granted: the most significant part of the Roman legal culture was to be found in the activity of the jurists, which essentially—but not exclusively—concerned what nowadays we would call "private law" and "civil trial" law.

This representation is accurate, even though the central role of private law that it sets forth warrants some explanation. Certainly, alongside the jurisprudential work, the history of Rome also featured a significant presence of legislation, of which substantial remains still survive: ranging from the Twelve Tables, dating back to the heart of the archaic era, to the measures approved, during the republican and Augustan periods, by the votes of popular assemblies, and all the way to the complex typology of the imperial constitutions. And a role of no less importance—to say nothing of the regulatory activity of the senate—was played by the praetorian edict, a text which gradually become stratified through an unbroken and gradual process of work that involved, year by year, hundreds of serving magistrates, from at least the third century B.C. right up until the definitive stabilization ordered by Hadrian.

So varied an articulation, however, never operated concretely outside the dense network of prescriptions, interpretations, and integrations that juris-prudence would in time weave around it. The Romans themselves were per-fectly aware of this. "Law cannot exist unless there is some jurist who can improve it from day to day," wrote Pomponius around the middle of the sec-ond century,[1] when that model had already begun to slip into crisis.

Roman jurists, then, were not just the learned men or the scientists of law. For a considerable portion of their history, they were also its chief build-ers and producers: a professional category of experts working for dozens of generations, following a path that had never before been pursued.

The age that witnessed the greatest flourishing of ancient legal culture—from the end of the second century B.C. to the opening decades of the third century, prior to the great crisis—thus coincided almost completely with the period of the definitive establishment of what we would call a "jurispruden-tial law": a legal order concentrated to a decisive degree, though not totally, in the hands of a compact group of specialists, who carried out their activi-ties independently of whether they held public offices. In other words, they performed their task not as magistrates of the Roman people (during the re-publican era) or as functionaries serving the emperor (during the principate), though they almost always wound up becoming magistrates of the republic and, later, advisers or even ministers of the *princeps*: and that aspect was not without significance. Rather, they were jurists as private citizens—albeit within more or less narrow elites—provided there was that burst of self-iden-tification described, once again by Pomponius, as *fiducia sui,* or self-faith:[2] if they felt and recognized themselves to be masters of a prestigious body of knowledge, the *iuris scientia* (as Cicero would have said[3]), a competence that made its proponents the guardians of the ordering of the city and then, ad-mittedly in a less direct fashion, of a vast empire.

What we generally think of as "Roman law" is therefore first and fore-most their creation. A "living law of custom,"[4] case-based and guided by ex-perts: much closer, in its mature configuration, to modern English and (in a number of ways) to American law—even though they are devoid in their de-velopment of a Romanist tradition comparable to that found in continental Europe—than to French law after the codification under Napoleon, or to Ital-ian law subsequent to the codification of 1865.

When the central role of the work of jurisprudence began to fade over the course of the third century and the creation of norms increasingly, and to a quite unprecedented degree, became a bureaucratic and legislative affair, the whole of Roman law entered an irreversible zone of shadow. The establishment of a more specifically state-oriented dimension within it marked the definitive crisis of that experience.

2.

The jurists were, then, the chief protagonists of Roman legal culture. But their acknowledged role, which has never been called into doubt, did not prevent the complete eclipse of their profiles in the modern tradition. This was a paradoxical outcome, the effect of another distortion brought about by Justinian's codification. Since the *Digesta* were to appear for so many years as a code, and not as an anthology, over the centuries the constituent texts would not only be viewed (almost always) outside of any historical perspective, but also in a light that compromised the perception of their very quality. They would be seen not for what they truly were—fragments of literary works that needed to be reintegrated into their original context, as historians do with every other aspect of ancient cultures when faced with incomplete and gap-riddled transmissions—but rather as well-framed and carefully sorted articles of a unitary legislative apparatus. What really mattered was not the provenance (at best of marginal concern) but the normative structure to interpret.

The prescriptive aspect present in those writings—for example, the rules governing the obligations of the purchaser in a sale, the usufruct system of property, or the responsibility for the non-fulfillment of a contract—was always considered much more important than reconstructing the background of philosophical and political ideas, and even the legal theory or policy they expressed and might still reveal. The flow of interactions between analytical models and power relations that constituted the microphysics of those discourses; the logical structures they subtended; the web of reasoning and argumentation techniques developed; the intellectual genealogies that had enveloped and linked the discourses to the history of their own knowledge and those of other ancient disciplines (philosophy, rhetoric, historiography, medicine); the scope and significance of the works to which those texts had originally belonged; the authors' convictions concerning their own roles and tasks, still discernable in those documents though frequently only in the form of clues; the tissue of interference between legal constructions, political forms, and economic organization—this whole universe was constantly ignored, and with it, the tangle of themes that tend to arise in research when it comes to describing the movements and paths of knowledge with respect to the emergence and modification of the social relations that run through and (in part) determine it.

Nor was there an ability to bring the real crux of the matter into focus, the unresolved issue that the thinking of the Roman jurists has continued to pose for us ever since it first began to take shape: the question concerning the conditions and modalities that engendered and oriented the development of its fundamental conceptual paradigms, together with the problem of deciphering elements that can explain characteristic traits and attitudes—in short, what made the legal reasoning of the West what it was.

Instead, tradition always placed normative frameworks at the center of investigation, in the vacuum of their abstract functioning rather than the culture that had produced them; the "institutes" of private law (as it is customary to say, employing a term that comes to us from the organicism of the nineteenth century, first Romantic and then positivist), spectral protagonists of an endless bibliography, and not the jurists—flesh, blood, and ideas—in their specific and concrete individuality. Incredible though it may seem, we have masses of research about Roman praedial leases or servitudes, but not a single monograph on the books by Ulpian *Ad edictum,* or on the books by Paul *Ad Sabinum* (to mention just a pair of crucial authors and texts, which we shall encounter again in these pages), nor on their conceptual contents or their textual traditions—nothing at all.

And even when the study of Roman law in the twentieth century attempted to introduce some history into its horizons by distinguishing between "classical," "postclassical," and "Justinian," those schemes were strictly used to construct an image of "classical law" as a piece of timeless architecture, with no appreciable movement inside it. The jurists' personalities continued to be invisible, canceled by the dogma of their complete "fungibility": a prejudice that once again absolutized Justinian's perspective and, at the same time, the outlook of the Romanist tradition that had accepted it as unmodifiable. Efforts were made to emerge from the shadows of the past, but without ever being truly capable of entering the territory of historical research.

It must be said that this distortion has a more complex explanation, which places its origin well beyond the bounds of historiography, despite its evident areas of weakness. In an attempt to identify it, we will draw on an important study.

Not even the sole Romanist study devoted to an overall reconstruction of Roman jurisprudence in the twentieth century was able to extricate itself from the blind alley of the tradition to which it belonged: the *History of Roman Legal Science* by Fritz Schulz, published in Oxford in 1946, has exerted a great influence over studies of Roman law, and can still aid our understanding.

Schulz was a reader of Weber, one of the very few non-Romanist scholars that he cited, alongside Croce, Dilthey, Ranke, Huizinga, and a handful of others.[5] The concepts of "vocation" and "scholarliness," which appear together right from the start of the *History of Roman Legal Science,* have a distinctly Weberian ring; and Schulz himself acknowledges it explicitly, citing the second, 1925, edition of *Economy and Society.*[6] It is likely that Weber's influence was even more extensive: the ordering sequence of Schulz's *History*—pontifical, aristocratic, bureaucratic jurisprudence—seems indeed to rework the Weberian distinction between charismatic power, traditional power, and rational-bureaucratic power.[7]

But in Weber the utilization of the scheme linking together vocation, specialization, and science was completely dominated by the relationship, established at the outset, between legal knowledge and political power: specifically, "the influence of the form of political authority on the formal aspect of the law."[8] The whole "sociology of the law" in *Economy and Society* is constructed around the connection between the development of legal techniques in a "formal" and "rational" sense, transformations of political power, and shifts in economic structures.[9] An integrated field of research was delineated that combined legal theory (and history), the sociology of political power, and economic analysis of great significance in terms of its theoretical presuppositions and historiographic potential.

However, nothing survives of this framework in Schulz. His categories are merely a pale shadow of the ones adopted by Weber. There is no longer any allusion to the relationship between the morphologies of (political) power and models of legal thought. Politics (to say nothing of economics) literally vanish. The transformation of Roman legal thought into a conceptually powerful intellectual practice—a development that had incalculable consequences—is reduced to a vague and blurry description, which does no more than invoke the relationship between the "natural and national energy" of Roman wisdom and Hellenistic culture.[10] Moving further and further away from Weber the more he seemed to draw on him, Schulz presented a simplified history disconcertingly frozen in an extrinsic examination of literary genres—without ever realizing even the importance of the nexus between the forms of thought and the forms of communication—restricted as it was by the myths of the Romanist tradition in the nineteenth and twentieth centuries: the idea of the "classical," cultivated through the exercise of a devastating interpolationist critique, and the prejudice concerning the absolute indistinguishability of the personalities of the individual authors mentioned in the *Digesta*. No effort was made to build up any kind of profile of the Roman jurists, who continued to appear as cardboard cut-outs, the absent protagonists of an evasive and disappointing reconstruction which we have read over and over again with a mounting sense of frustrated impatience.

The *History of Roman Legal Science* was written in a tragic time, by an exile who had fled from a country devastated by Nazism and the war. It is plausible that in those conditions the idea of politics and power, and their connections to law, may have been inextricably bound up in Schulz's mind with images of violence and the crushing abuse of power; and that it was disturbing for him to unearth, in the history of Roman jurisprudence, and thus at the foundations of European legal knowledge, the very same relations and ties between law and politics that in their contemporary expression could appear to him only as evil aberrations. Perhaps this unresolved trauma encouraged him— despite Weber—to erase from the early history of legal science in the West any presence that might be evocative of shadows and contaminations. The great culture of law had necessarily to be presented, from its Roman beginnings, as an untouchable and all-redeeming space somehow removed from history and politics, in which to celebrate the continuity of an impersonal, coldly mathematicizing knowledge. A vast tradition of German scholarship, from Savigny and Jhering to Windscheid and Laband, pushed him toward the pursuit of this mythical "neutrality," accepted even by Kelsen, which Schulz relied on with absolute faith. Admittedly, Carl Schmitt did not take refuge in the same persuasions, and as a jurist and a historian he looked to Weber (and to his own present) with different eyes and a different sense of disquiet.[11] But here we are on the opposing front of a lacerating split, a division through which blood was shed—and we are not speaking metaphorically.

The silences and the hiatuses of the *History of Roman Legal Science* can thus be seen as a web of repressed notions and unconscious allusions; and perhaps we must learn to read that text as a work which, aside from its chilliness of expression, clearly bears the marks and the anguish of a terrible era. No different, after all, from how Arnaldo Momigliano—he too in exile at Oxford—helped us to understand another important book, written in almost the same years: *The Roman Revolution,* by Ronald Syme, in which the seizure of power by Octavian Augustus and the establishment of the principate were described with Mussolini's coup d'état and the advent of the Fascist regime still vividly in mind.[12]

But Schulz's forgoing of the historicization of his own field of inquiry, in complete adherence to the line followed by the Romanist tradition, was accompanied by an intense focus upon a new aspect which he arrived at more by developing Savigny than by studying Weber. It was the discovery of what he defined as an intrinsic feature of Roman legal wisdom, the tendency to "isolate" its object of study,[13] an elegant interpretation which enabled him to emphasize, however approximately, an essential characteristic to which little attention had previously been paid: the establishment of such thought as a set of techniques grounded in the particular conditions existing in the culture of the age; as a separate and remote body of knowledge intended to cast a dissecting and detached gaze upon the world, in a quest for invisible relations and proportions, between things and between people. Such a stance wound up opacifying legal science in the eyes of contemporaries, plunging it into a rigorously specialized and almost initiatory dimension; distant, after Cicero —who fully grasped this aspect well ahead of his time—from the interest of the great figures of the age, who generally treated it in a distracted and super-

ficial fashion, albeit frequently with some degree of mannered admiration—
from Livy to Apuleius, from Virgil to Ovid, Petronius, Seneca, and Quintilian. Only rarely did the veil part to reveal something genuinely fresh and
lively: the jurist Cecilius Africanus caught in a subtle discussion with the philosopher Favorinus in a passage by Aulus Gellius;[14] an extraordinarily well-
informed description of Aristo in a letter by Pliny;[15] several observations by
Tacitus;[16] and little more than that. In general, in the mirror held up by the
educated, the philosophers, the historians, and the erudite men of Latin culture, legal matters were perceived as a distant world—an isolation that was
both its greatness and its downfall.

We are touching on a crucial point here, which relates to the very essence
of law: a motif that would be repeated and become increasingly common
throughout modern culture, and which would condition the entire Romanist
tradition and the weak historiography that grew out of it. In Schulz, the refusal of an historical approach and the discovery of the isolation in which the
Roman jurists situated their wisdom revealed themselves to be two aspects of
the same problem, which moved forward apace and oriented the direction of
his research in the years of his maturity, to a far greater degree than he himself ever seems to have realized. What was concealed behind the tangle of issues? Sketching out a response will allow us to find the explanation that we
are seeking.

3.

Unfailingly, in the story of the West, the more law has developed its function
as an ordering and measuring apparatus capable of completely formalizing
life—the nucleus of the heritage of antiquity, deeply rooted in the construction of modern systems—the more it has tended to distance from itself the
dimensions of history and mutation. This inclination goes back a long way.
Between *nomos* and *chronos*—between rule and time—there was, from the
very origins of Western thought, a reciprocal exclusion: the intrinsic vocation
of order, its telos, is to halt the process of becoming. If the norm and the rule
are perceived as a "revealing of being"—as is stated literally in Plato,[17] and
less explicitly but just as forcefully in the Roman jurists, who would make
great conceptual efforts to construct an authentic ontology of prescriptiveness—their dimension is that of unlimited duration, not that of transforma-

tion; time is, with respect to them, pure destruction, external and irremediable negativity: this is a familiar theme in the context of a millenarian line of philosophy, from *The Republic* of Plato to Heidegger's *Being and Time*.[18]

Tracing back through history this formalized and extreme figure of the "legal," constructed for the first time by the Romans, is a profoundly daunting task. It is a question of deciphering the content hidden deep within the inner structures of normativity—the history canceled by the form—and of bringing it back up to the surface, into the light of day. That is the obstacle where all legal historicism from Savigny onwards has ultimately come unstuck. And it is surely no accident that it is only in Hegel, Marx, and Weber (and later in Schmitt and Foucault)—the great critics of the historicity of the moderns—that we can find some ideas pointing us in the correct direction. It is for this precise reason that Schulz himself was able to write that "although the ambiguous term 'development' is a favourite with legal historians, they rarely give us more than accounts of ready-made legal rules chronologically arranged. 'Et puis . . . et puis . . . il y a beaucoup de "puis" dans cette histoire'":[19] We would hardly have expected such a sharp comment from him.

It is now clear why the difficulty we have identified is not attributable merely to a problem of historiography, to a cultural and academic separation between the scholars of ancient history and the historians of law, as Arnaldo Momigliano must have believed deep down when he declared the end of legal historiography as an independent discipline in the historical sciences.[20]

If it is still so complicated to place the Roman jurists at the center of their time, to reintegrate their thought into the context of the culture and the civilization that produced it, the problem—as Schulz helps us again to understand—is that we are in the presence not only of a historiographic deformation but also of something bound up with a real and effective scission. More specifically, it relates precisely to the self-isolation of ancient legal wisdom as a historical consequence of the "morphological" exclusion between the planes of temporality and normativity, which kicked in immediately after law began to be organized as a specialized technique of social regulation disintegrated from the original incorporation within other sets of functions and systems of ideas.

In brief, if the (modern) historiographic view developed in a weak and uncoordinated manner, it was also (though not only) because its object was already irremediably disconnected—and this fracture at the heart of the Ro-

man experience is the very origin of the establishment of Western legal reason as a separate and special mode of analysis.

The ways in which such an outcome was achieved, how the isolation of
law as a measuring and ordering technique originally came about, and how it
was transmitted to modernity—everything Schulz failed to see—is precisely
what will form the basis of our investigations.

4.

Roman jurisprudential law was an order with a fluid, changing surface, in
continual movement: a reality that the frozen mosaic of the *Digesta* might
cover over but could not eliminate entirely. The shared core of a scientific and
preceptive paradigm that had been very precociously developed was constantly riven by polemics, disagreements, and divergent solutions.

Partly due to this intrinsic instability, and for many other reasons besides—both political and cultural, as well as more strictly technical and practical—the law of the jurists was never really the law of the whole empire,
neither in a horizontal, geopolitical sense, nor in a vertical, social sense. It
never became, without mediation, the law of the vast, outlying territories
under Roman dominion, from the Red Sea to the Atlantic Ocean; nor, by the
same token, in Italy and in Rome itself, was it the law of all the layers of the
population, of the entire social body.

The law of the jurists always remained an extremely circumscribed model
in terms of its effective range of application, but carried great prestige and a
potent charge of exemplarity: a bright, luminous center around which there
gravitated a stellar myriad of minor and local legal systems—about which,
with few exceptions, very little is known nowadays[21]— sometimes lacking
any formal recognition but sustained by great material effectiveness, which
assumed it as a distant and unattainable point of reference that still had to
be taken into account, even if only in a rough and ready manner. It was the
law of a relatively restricted elite, which had, however, consolidated immense
power and politically unified the world.

The activity of jurisprudence had developed entirely within the heart of
this state of supremacy, and would now be incomprehensible if we did not
trace it back to the everyday exercise of a hegemony that it itself helped so
greatly to construct. And the jurists themselves frequently became embroiled

in the management and the problems of a world government, even though their science seems almost never to have left the slightest trace of such involvement, and they managed to avoid being shackled by an excessively close bond between legal learning and political action. On the contrary, they were capable of defending the isolation of their knowledge also in this respect, rebalancing it every time as a technique capable of self-legitimation well beyond the underpinnings of political power, even though it was entirely constructed right next to it, and of developing around its own argumentations a shield that was difficult to pierce, with the capacity of conferring upon legal rationality a strong basis, that might—at least to a certain degree—protect it from excessively heavy pressures. And in turn, politics would always find itself in need of alliances and compromises with jurisprudence, in which the relative balance of powers was determined by the conditions prevailing at any given time.

We can draw together the entire history of Roman legal thought around three pictures, which will serve as a backdrop to our investigation. In each of them, a different type of protagonist emerges: an archaic priest; a republican nobleman; a great specialist who worked in the milieux of the *princeps* and the court, rising to high office in the imperial government.

The time has come to begin telling that story.

II

The Birth of a Technique

4

Origins

Let us imagine for a moment that it were possible to ask an educated man living at the time of Cicero or Augustus—someone from imperial Rome, accustomed to reading in Greek and Latin and reflecting on the history of his institutions—what the earliest layers that had shaped the law of his city were. We can have little doubt about the nature of his response. In all probability he would mention the tradition of the pontifices on the one hand and the Twelve Tables on the other, thereby connecting, in line with a point of view common to the age, two elements that the cultural memory of the Roman aristocracy had for many centuries integrated into a single canon, that of the *ius civile,* the majestic and venerable root of all the Roman legal systems.

Two thousand years on, our perspective is much the same: pontifices and decemviral legislation are still the fundamental points of reference for historians when attempting to describe the origins of what would become the Roman legal experience. Unfortunately, however, only faint and indirect signs now remain of the early activity of the pontifices. Their wisdom was exclusively oral, as was the memory of it that was then handed down, and little or nothing is known about the one piece of written evidence that may have given an account of it in fairly authentic terms, namely the *Tripertita* by Sextus Aelius, composed at the beginning of the second century B.C.[1]

As for the Twelve Tables, which were, by contrast, a written text, we are able to reconstruct only a version riddled with gaps, and in a Latin not as archaic as the original must have been, given that the vocabulary of the Twelve Tables often proved obscure even to jurists and the learned during the late republic.[2]

Of one thing, however, we can be certain: the legislation of the Twelve Tables should be regarded as dating from a later period than a core already established in earlier times. And we can feel equally sure that this early crystallization should be related to the duties then performed by the pontifices, a collegium of priests whose traces date back to the very beginnings of the city.

The Romans who lived centuries later had no hesitation in identifying this original nucleus as *ius:* they rightly believed it was already called that by their distant ancestors. In fact, the word had very remote origins, and the absence of corresponding terms in the Greek of the classical and Hellenistic eras—with respect to the significance it acquired during the republican period—made it a venerable and ancient token of the distinctiveness of Roman history.

We should, however, take great care not to be deceived by the duration of the sign, overlooking the changes in its meanings: in earlier periods, *ius* did not evoke the same ideas that would have come to mind, using the identical word, to a Roman from the late republic or the principate, much less the notions that might occur to someone nowadays in connection with the word "law." In fact, it is precisely the overly casual use of this term, summarily employed as a translation of the archaic significance of *ius,* that has led to a great many misunderstandings and distortions, which even historians of the first rank have stumbled over. In the pages that follow, we shall try to avoid the traps posed by this asymmetry between the enduring presence of the word and the shift in the ideas and things denoted by it.

2.

The origins of Rome, and the reconstruction of the situations and events that determined and accompanied the foundation of the city, have been the subject of one of the most absorbing and impassioned historiographic debates of the 1900s. The century which commenced with a radical positivist skepticism about the stories elaborated by the ancient tradition, which justified a critique of sources—of Cicero, Livy, Dionysius of Halicarnassus, Plutarch—irremediably unbelieving of any reconstruction they might have proposed of Roman antiquity, drew to a close with a general admission that those narrative materials do not depict implausible scenarios but rather events and characters that deserve to be considered with great attention and an open mind, if not perhaps with absolute faith.[3]

It would take too long, and be irrelevant to the scope of this book, to describe what caused such an outcome, which involved a complete turn-around in methodological approach and, all things considered, a marked change in the very idea of what it means to write history. On the one hand, the field was occupied by a positivist dogmatism in which "arbitrary skepticism towards the tradition" of Roman historiography accompanied "an equally arbitrary credulity about its own conjectures,"[4] to the point of developing a desperately destructive critique of the sources. At the opposite extreme, there were passionate investigations in the fields of archaeological stratigraphy, linguistics, and religious history, suspended between land, words, and rites, which sought "to explore more than to prove,"[5] and did not hesitate to venture far beyond the barrier established, in the view of a great many scholars, by the seventh century B.C. At the same time they made great efforts to include, classify, and decipher even the slightest trace, fragment of stone and scrap of language, with the excavation techniques and the analysis of clues alone often tending to be taken as complete metaphors for the craft of the historian, projected toward increasingly profound depths of time.

Between these two extremes, one could trace, over decades of debate, the articulation of a whole series of intermediate positions, variously motivated: just to remain in Italy, from De Sanctis in *Storia dei Romani* and *La leggenda della lupa e gemelli,* to Fraccaro in the essay on the monarchic age, Momigliano in the *Interim Report,* and Gabba in *Problemi di metodo.*[6] And we can easily delve even further back. Hegel's heated dispute with Niebuhr, at the turn of the nineteenth century, fully targeted the reconstruction of Roman archaism entrusted to the *Römische Geschichte,* and destined almost immediately to become a classic of European academic historiography.[7] Niebuhr came from a context that combined the new Romantic philology with

the erudite legacy of the French and German eighteenth century, but his perspective was a bellwether of many approaches which would later be adopted
by the positivist movement. In the *Lectures on the Philosophy of History*, in
which he developed his critique, Hegel's horizons were quite different:[8] he
attempted to reestablish threads of meaning along a path leading from East
to West, which he saw as having been clumsily severed in the intrusive hands
of investigators blinded by presumptuous methods and with no taste for abstraction and concept. It would not be until Dilthey, Weber, and the development of the more modern school of archeological, linguistic, and religious-
anthropological research that the philosopher's lesson was saved from
oblivion, and we learned how to bring back to life settings, episodes, and connections that were thought to have been lost entirely.

The requirements of our account are such that we can do no more than
touch on this welter of issues. But following just a single trail will enable us
to uncover some elements of decisive importance for the subsequent course
of our story.

Rome is the city of the ancient Mediterranean that preserved in the period
of its maturity—through a network of memories, traditions, and relics—the
greatest amount of information about its own origins. That is certainly no
accident: the imperial supremacy continually drew on and reworked memory, as it required an adequate background of myth and history to give depth
to its own grandeur. The belief that all this represented nothing more than an
accumulation of inventions and falsifications with no relation to actual events
is less and less justified. The institutional, social, and economic status of the
city during the middle republican age—the earliest one that we are able to
investigate reliably, according to the hypercritical approach in vogue at the
turn of the twentieth century—points, through a mass of clues, to a prior
weft of forms and events that we can (at least partially) bring to light and interpret. Failure to do so would be to abandon any attempt to piece together
the traits of a genesis that is crucial for understanding those later developments about which we seem to know more, but which would be intrinsically
indecipherable unless measured against their earliest antecedents. And this is
also—and primarily—true of law.

But how then can we make use of the richness of Roman memory? And within what limits can we consider legitimate a "symptomatic reading" of our sources—be they the ruins of a wall, the fragments of a legend, or the precepts of a ritual crystallized in a tradition or in a norm?

In principle, it cannot be denied that interpretation on the basis of clues is an effective tool that it would be unwise to reject a priori. The problem is how far we should venture in making use of this method: that is, to evaluate to what extent the conjectures it produces are capable of verifying a conservative reading of the Roman tradition, of inserting narrative threads and ancient memories into a larger grid of relations, causalities, correspondences, and traces that would otherwise have remained unobserved.

Latium was a densely populated region from the Bronze Age onwards, at least by the demographic standards of the Mediterranean: a crossroads for trade and the intermingling of cultures. Many sites were suitable for the development of more structured dwelling patterns and communities. One in particular was located in a narrow area not far from the sea, delineated by a short chain of hills overlooking an oxbow curve in the Tiber, where there had been a certain continuity of settlement since the middle of the second millennium. The presence of a tiny island midstream made it easy to cross the river, and a nexus of exchanges and commerce had formed, encouraged by the convenient ford, the proximity of the sea, and the importance of the salt trade. The area was at once open and circumscribed—with forests, swamps, huts, and small cultivated fields—and was developed especially in the zone stretching from the Tiber to the three hills closest to it: the Capitoline, the Palatine, and the Aventine. And there had also built up there a significant network of sanctuaries, a no less essential element of connectivity at the time.

This is the context in which Rome came into being. When that was, we cannot say with any certainty. Nor can we confidently link the event to a qualitative leap in the fabric of the settlements—to something comparable to an authentic urban foundation—rather than to a slow and progressive stratification of elements. The response also depends on what we understand by the word "city," sticking of course to the range of meanings it held in ancient times. Still, it is possible that a significant event may have occurred sometime around the middle of the eighth century B.C., the period indicated by the tradition most generally accepted by the ancients. Different reconstructions, which shift the date of the event to the final decades of the seventh, or perhaps even to the first few decades of the sixth century, seem less persuasive.[9] We should not, however, forget that the formation of an urban environment, from an architectural point of view (city walls, buildings), no less than that of its institutional and social ties, need not necessarily have coincided with the establishment, within its bounds, of a fully political organization (in the sense of the Greek-style city state). This incorrect identification underlies and explains a great many misunderstandings, as much as faintly nominalist attempts to distinguish the "pre-urban" and "proto-urban" phases that supposedly preceded the actual birth of Rome. "City" and "politics" should not be placed together as if they were the two invariable terms of a genetically demonstrable equation. Undoubtedly, in the Mediterranean area the connection did exist by and large, but it was found for the most part as a tendential outcome of the processes of foundation, rather than as an original and basic datum. Where a city springs up, sooner or later political relationships will develop within it, but by no means can it be said that, for an urban space to be established and begin to function, a specifically political fabric must already be in place: this happened in Rome no earlier than the last part of the seventh century, while it is almost certain that by then a city nucleus had already existed for some time. It was sufficient for a shared social and cultural mesh to come into being, and that this network should produce a certain centralization of power. In the origins of Rome, the decisive role in the attainment of this threshold was played by the structures and dynamics of family ties, by the associated aristocratic selection, and above all by the diffusion of shared religious practices (what Andrea Carandini, following in Dumézil's footsteps, called "the theological unification of the habitat")[10] —complemented, in all likelihood, by the royal charisma of some fortunate military leader. Nothing less, but also nothing more.[11]

The historiography, the archeology, and the anthropology of recent decades have shed a good deal of light on the importance, in Tyrrhenian-Etruscan social organization, but also in that of the Latins and Sabines in the ninth and the eighth centuries, of religious bonds —the real prepolitical fabric of the community—and of kinship ties (extended families and, to an even

greater degree, groups of families with a shared forefather, welded together
to form clan structures known in archaic Latin as *gens,* while *pater* was the
term for the head of each family nucleus, a word that soon came to indicate
both the hierarchy of power within the family and the primacy of the male
reproductive function, as in any other patriarchal and patrilinear society).[12]

The gentilitial system manifested quite early as an elitist tendency, documented by the opulent consumption patterns of certain clans and by the acquisition of tastes and behavioral models of Greek and eastern origin. The
eighth century was a time of prosperity and growth for the western Mediterranean, with a resumption of relations between the Tyrrhenian basin and
the Aegean Sea, the development of colonial settlements in southern Italy
and in Sicily, and the fairly extensive spread of cultural elements that we
might describe as Homeric. In the case of Rome, the impetus toward aristocratic selection was probably also accentuated by the effects of the wars between armed bands that were so frequent in Latium during that period, and
which continually spawned heroes and adventurers (just as sapiential practices linked to religious cults produced priests), perhaps even outside the gentilitial bonds. The figure identified by the celebrated Roman foundation myth
as the father of the city—a character named Romulus—allows us to glimpse,
albeit through the ins and outs of a very elaborate saga, all the characteristics
of one of these individuals: a warrior chieftain "without family," and therefore attributable to a direct divine descent, capable of murdering his brother
—and hence breaking all blood ties—in order to affirm the inviolability of
the new space and the new community that he had just established.[13]

3.

The first urban nucleus, then, took shape within a fragile, fluid, but clearly
delineated network of functions: cults, weapons, *gentes,* use of the land, both
family-oriented, on the part of each *pater* with his group, and collective, undertaken by the entire community. Socialization through clan relations and
oligarchic differentiation left an indelible mark upon the formation of the
city, at the center of which it is possible to discern a primitive aristocracy
striving to consolidate itself in a highly insecure environment, continually
subjected to the traumas of violent and sudden upheavals: enemy raids, food

shortages, epidemics, difficulties in matrimonial exchanges, which sexual ta-
boos rigorously demanded be exogamous. An aptitude for combat and competition, talent in cult practices, and extensive blood ties were the prerequisites for hard-earned supremacies.

The mental forms of this world are extremely difficult to investigate. The
first problem that arises when we attempt to make out its features might be
described as a sort of "interdiction of genesis": a phenomenon that historians
frequently encounter when they explore Mediterranean origins (Greek ones,
for example), and which helps to make structural explanations almost always
preferable to evolutionary ones. However far into the past we may try to cast
our gaze, we are unable to identify, even in an indirect manner, a genuine
"nascent state," the elementary and as yet unintegrated seeds of developments still to come.

Of course, there was not the slightest scrap of writing in Rome prior to
the decades around 550 B.C., and even after that, for the whole of the fifth and
fourth centuries, what we have is exceedingly rare and desperately fragmentary.[14] However much we may investigate these texts and attempt to
go back in time, we always wind up encountering, as our final point of
arrival, the reference to an already cohesive and compact cluster of mental
habits, persuasions, and beliefs: in short, the dense latticework of a fully
formed structure, not the precarious instability of a crystallization that had
just begun.

Not even archeological research—to which we owe so great a debt for
our new knowledge about archaic Rome—can offer us much help in this case.
It allows us to ascertain a network of facts—urbanistic, economic, and social—and sheds some light on the chronology and specific unfolding of certain events, especially in relation to cults, the acquisition of goods and technologies, and the organization of the community. But it cannot indicate, if
not in the vaguest and most approximate ways, the quality, the connections,
and the dynamics underlying the frameworks of thought that were being developed within these contexts.

It is possible to suppose that the solidity and the substance with which the
primitive world of ideas relating to the city presents itself to our modern eyes
is also the product of a distortion wrought by historians and antiquarians—
extraordinary constructors of the proto-Roman tradition—working between
the end of the third century B.C. and the years of Augustus: from Fabius Pic-

tor to Verrius Flaccus. But we have many reasons to believe that the reelaborations and even the inventions of those learned men reflected memories and
motifs that appeared genuinely remote to them, and in which the essential
traits of a solid Roman cultural identity already seemed to be fully established
and acquired. In other words, that what we have described as the "interdiction of genesis" affected ancient reconstructions no less than it now screens
the view of modern historians.

We can do nothing other than acknowledge this. The image of compactness that continues to surface in our documentation should be considered to
a certain extent as an original trait, and not merely as the product of a subsequent overlay. Operating in a somewhat different realm of conjecture to the
one we are proposing, Dumézil claimed to identify in such a characteristic a
sort of tendency to "think according to systems," proper to every primary
mental experience, in particular in the Indo-European world.[15] There is no
reason to go down this treacherous path with him. Comparative linguistics is
one of the glories of modern research, but its findings become exceedingly
unreliable when we mechanically project its results onto the history of mentalities and institutions; and it is likely that the great French scholar—who
was certainly correct in preferring a structural interpretation of archaic religion to a diachronic one—tended in this case to generalize and to broaden an
element clearly identifiable with great force and evidence only in a strictly
Latin context.

But in any case there can be no doubt that we must be willing to recognize, in the most ancient layer of Roman culture, the presence of a tenacious
disciplining and ordering pressure; of an imprint that appeared to have the
power of an apparatus on the boundary between history and anthropology;
a mental scheme that operated almost as the genetic code of the entire urban
world. We shall shortly formulate a hypothesis about the type of conditioning, as it were environmental, that could have prompted such a characterized
and invasive response. In any case it led the early protagonists of community
life to filter reality through a mesh of symmetries and symbolic correspondences; like an original ritualistic and systemic paradigm, with ceremonious-
ness appearing to be the prerequisite for all equilibriums, which irradiated
out over every mental construct, and not just religious ones: the initial figures
in the history of Rome—Romulus and Numa—are, above all, in the memory
of the city, two founders of social taxonomies and canons of worship. What's

more, the whole of very early Roman history, in the mirror of later tradition, from the early annalistic tradition to the antiquarianism and historiography of the Augustan age, reflects the dominant presence of a mentality that took delight in rigorous distributive geometries. Remaining for now just with institutional profiles, suffice it to consider the ratio between tribes and *curiae* (3:30), in an organization that all surviving testimony agrees should be regarded as highly prominent, and which existed alongside the gentilitial system; the division of the three oldest tribes, Ramnes, Tities, Luceres, all divided into *Primi* and *Secundi,* on the basis of a scheme that led to the symmetrical selection of six vestals, according to the accounts of Varro and Festus;[16] the theological framework erected around the so-called pre-Capitoline triad of Jove, Mars, and Quirinus (in these examples, there is always either the number three or numbers divisible by three: an element that we will also find underlying other bodies of archaic ritual and distributions, with an unmistakable magical component); or the rigorous hierarchy of the primitive "Septimontium" in the account of Marcus Antistius Labeo.[17]

In actual fact, such a tendency cannot be considered peculiar to Rome alone: we find it both in Greek settings and in the eastern Mediterranean. What is typical of the Roman situation is its intensity, and especially the depth of its roots, destined to enjoy a lengthy history, albeit with numerous adaptations and transpositions.

Soon enough this mentality would manifest itself via two levels of communication, closely combined and yet not completely intermingled: the principal, if not entirely exclusive, core notions of the entire archaic Roman culture. In all the accounts available to us—from Cicero to Varro, and then on to Livy, to Dionysius, to Plutarch, and to the jurists who were so passionately interested in archaic Roman culture, such as Labeo and Pomponius—there is complete agreement on their identification, all the more significant in that it is confirmed by findings in archeological and linguistic research. We can describe them as cognition of the divine and cognition of *ius.* The quality of the tie that linked the two fields, and the shared vocation expressed in them, relate back to the earlier existence—which we are supposing—of the single and indistinct ordering drive we have attempted to describe, and that we may consider to have already been active when the community first came into being.

This reference—and the conjecture that underpins it—is not intended to hold any mechanically evolutionistic implications. But the contiguity of traits between the two elements in question—the divine and *ius*—fully visible from our earliest documentation onward, establishes a tie that can hardly have failed to express itself on the historical plane. The hypothesis just set forth should therefore be considered as nothing more than the genealogical transcription of an unquestionable morphological relation.[18]

We can attempt to represent the peculiarity we are trying to describe as a synchronic projection along two axes—vertical and horizontal—of the same, and constant, regulatory overdetermination. Running upward, it marked the relationship with deities imagined to be tremendously irascible, always to be treated with the greatest prudence: this was the theologization of divine wrath of which Assmann speaks, widespread throughout the eastern Mediterranean all the way to Mesopotamia.[19] But in our case, its weight was probably accentuated by the influence of a collective psychology strongly affected by specific local conditions. An echo of this exceptionality would carry all the way through to the observation of Polybius, many centuries later, about the continuous "tragedifying" of the Roman religion, astonishing to a Greek mind;[20] and it is on this foundation that the skeleton of Roman civic religiosity would take form, with its distinctively social and cultic character: "religion, that is, in reverence for the gods," as Cicero would later write.[21]

Horizontally, the same impulse invaded and disciplined the relations of equal reciprocity among the heads of family (*par*, a monosyllabic archaic term that may have been of Etruscan origin, indicated the parity of each member in peasant-warrior communities as early as the first Iron Age).[22] And it would become the specific terrain of *ius*—a field that the Roman mind would never completely identify with the powers of the king, reserving it instead for the practice, in some way sovereign, of the *patres*, directly dependent only upon religious ties that did not coincide with the domain of royalty. This was the original germ or generative nucleus of the autonomous regulation of a "private" dimension of community life (*privus* is also an archaic term), where the family and patrimonial prerequisites of citizenship were elaborated quite distinctly from the political order—a phenomenon not to be found, in these terms, in any other Mediterranean society, and destined to create a path that would have extraordinary consequences.

4.

Religion, then, as a set of cultic attitudes, and alongside it, determined by the same mental mechanism, a first layer of prescriptions likewise linked to the divine, but already to some degree vaguely distinguishable from it, and referring only to the "horizontal" plane of human behaviors and peer relations among the heads of family within the community, in a connection-disjunction pervading the whole collective sentiment: it is no accident that until the fourth century B.C. all of the sparse surviving remains of archaic writing would be attributable with some certainty to these two spheres alone.[23]

The power of the tie—which endured throughout the republican age—should come as no surprise. Once again, this same combination of religiosity and prescriptivity—though usually linked to the royal function—can be found elsewhere, in Mediterranean settings and in the Near East; and it is no less explicit and invasive, even in the diversity of religious practices and their mental and social diffusion. In Egypt, for instance, in a hymn to Amun dating from the fourteenth or thirteenth century B.C., we come across the following: "the two lips of the lord are your shrine. Your majesty is within: he pronounces on earth what you have decided."[24] Or, though less evidently, in Mesopotamia, in the precepts preserved on the stele of the Babylonian king Hammurabi.[25] Or again, in ancient Israel, where the intertwining would be reflected in the construction of monotheism and would even end up influencing the writing of crucial sections of the Bible, from Exodus to Deuteronomy;[26] but in this case, unlike the Roman situation, it was part of the theological elaboration of a no less highly structured moral life experience, giving rise to a sort of precocious "sacralization of ethics."[27] And finally, in Greece, clearly identifiable in the mythical and ritual-magical substrate of many precepts and normative complexes dating from the archaic and classical eras.[28]

In describing, in Rome as elsewhere, the more strictly normative aspect of this recurrent integration, it would be inappropriate and rashly premature to use the word "law" (even though historians are accustomed to doing so).[29] The function we indicate with this term still appears here to be too deeply incorporated within entirely different cultural and institutional systems—either religious or of kinship—for it to be used meaningfully; even though we should not forget that *ius* is in any case a term that alludes from the very outset to a prescriptive specificity unknown elsewhere, which began to emerge with original features during the very early history of Rome, with the existence of the word immediately betraying the precocious flowering of the thing—albeit of something that was not the "law" we know, or the *ius* of the more mature Roman civilization.

In an attempt to resolve partially similar difficulties, Gernet made use, in some of his studies, of the notion of "pre-law";[30] and that concept, which in truth has not received much attention, might prove useful, so long as it does not cause us to lose the perception that we are in the presence—respectively in Greek and in Roman archaism—of forms of religiously dominated social regulation destined to develop in markedly different ways, with outcomes in Greece far removed from those that would lead, in Rome, to the birth of a rigorously "legal" cultural and institutional dimension: of a *ius,* that is, in the middle- and late-republican meaning of the word.

In this sense, the Roman situation achieved an ineradicable singularity. It would be the only one in the ancient world where the production of rules of social behavior—the creation of *ius* in the still archaic sense of the term— once it began to break away in a more definitive manner from the domain of religion, would not be entirely integrated within the model of politics and legislation, as in Greece, where the presence of statutes as forms of political command would soon become the mark of the fully achieved and complete secularization of the urban societies.[31] Instead, it would remain in the hands of a restricted circle of wise men, who would build around it a technical and exclusive body of knowledge, which could be distinguished at a fairly early point from both religious and political experience.

In a moment we will relate the most plausible modes of this division, which the stratigraphy of the Roman legal orders from the third to second centuries B.C. allows us to reconstruct, at least in general terms. But before doing so, let's briefly focus once again on the initial situation, characterized by the almost complete fusion of the two elements—the religious and the prescriptive. What can still be seen here?

The cultural context of early Roman archaism (probably extending from the eighth into the sixth centuries B.C.) already seems—from the clues available to us—quite different from that which must have characterized Greek religiosity in roughly the same period, despite the not inconsiderable amount of contact between the two worlds. An attempt to explain the difference would take us down dangerous paths that are not worth exploring here. But without doubt there is a clear and unmistakable distance. In place of an extraordinary mythological, and then cosmogonic, imagination, from which would spring, as of the sixth century, the first great speculative body of knowledge in the West—from Heraclitus to Parmenides and Plato—we find ourselves in the presence, in the Roman case, of a type of transfiguration of reality in which theological invention and the animistic imagination were totally dominated by the ideation and the staging of a multiform cascade of deities and rituals. Scrupulous respect for every ceremony was considered indispensable for establishing a sort of relationship of reciprocity with the supernatural powers (the only kind regarded as beneficial and reassuring), whose management was rigorously controlled by a priestly structure that bore no resemblance to anything that ever existed in Greece.[32]

It is hard to say whether or not these aspects should be considered, in turn, as nothing more than the product of the repression or abrasion of a previous phase of mythical creation, as Dumézil still believes.[33] And it is certainly also possible to think of myths and rites as dynamic elements of a single mental circuit—as opposed to an irreversible passage from myth to ritual (or even an inverse process, as for instance posited by Mauss)[34]—which can be traced back to a single scheme of primary religiosity in which, it might be supposed, the original forms of the sacred took shape, cultic practices were established, physical space was organized, a historical temporality introduced, and a rough sketch of social life delineated.[35]

In any case, in the context of Roman archaism, the relationship between mythical creation and the development of rituals and formulas—the latter also present in Greek thought, though it seems to have been superseded very early on without leaving much trace—immediately became completely weighted in the direction of the rite, the stereotype, the precept that acquired a peculiar and irresistible coercive power. It was a condition that came very close to that of a genuine prescriptive syndrome, entirely absent in the context of archaic Greece: the human sphere and the supersensible one of the divine, perceived through magical manifestations, appeared to be enclosed in a network of rituals—dense, constraining, and, in a certain sense, even obsessive. The human and natural world was chopped up and explored with an almost feverishly analytic approach—still quite clear to Varro—in an attempt to protect even the most minor functions of everyday life through the presence of specific gods and of ceremonies capable of appeasing them. We are reminded of the observation made by Sarpi, that "for the ripening of an ear of wheat, ten [gods] are required." Every *numen*, every divine power, had a specific task, and it was necessary to turn to them at the appropriate time, and with the proper supplications. "The pontifices used to say that for every act a special god is set," wrote Servius Grammaticus in the fourth century A.D.; and Latin preserves a noun and a verb, *indigitamenta* and *indigitare*, both probably very ancient, to indicate the litanies in which the deities were named one by one, along with the functions attributed to each.[36]

As soon as it was formulated, each ritual acquired an alienated and irrevocable objectivity, according to a projection common to many cultures, including Mediterranean ones: it crushed the very minds that had elaborated it. But its scrupulous and literal respect proved amply remunerative—it was an observance that gave the community faith and equilibrium.

We have already said that in its early life Rome was surrounded by dangers and enemies, isolated by the hostility of the Latins, Sabines, and Etruscans. It was a city that was at the same time threatened and open, a precariously multiethnic crossroads, exposed and in great peril; the memory of these difficulties would later be reflected in the myth of a "Trojan" derivation, irreducibly foreign with respect to the context where it had been transplanted.[37] And it is therefore possible to consider the proliferation of ritualistic and systemic fantasy as nothing other than a stabilizing response to the environmentally induced need to exorcise the danger—perceived as devastating—of the violence and chaos that not only surrounded the community, but might also penetrate it at any moment: the order of ritual against the overwhelming and ever present force of disintegration.

The unremitting focus on the expiatory victim in the primary rite of sacrifice, the cultural construction of the *sacer*—"that which is due to a deity," also in the sense of "that which is killable" and is therefore "cursed," as Festus explains very well[38]—could be considered in this context as a founding element of all the ritualistic-magical phenomenology emerging from the depths of Roman history, and of which so many traces can still be seen in what has survived of the Twelve Tables. A ceremonial that was then multiplied endlessly, and in countless variants, inasmuch as it was capable—through the memory and the evocation of the blood once shed—of raising a barrier between the city and the risk of annihilation.[39] This would explain why ritual thought in Rome would always lie at the foundation of religious experience and all prescriptive and ordering practices. It was the community as a whole that, by establishing a symbolic order capable of systematically involving both gods and men, disciplined, pacified, reconciled, measured, against the paroxysm of destructive violence. In this way we would really touch the point of origin, the generative element of all the history we are recounting here, where mental predispositions and historical events meshed together to form a definitive web.

Upon this basis, a complex network of ceremonial customs thereafter came into being, which we can describe as secondary or derived with respect to the original figure that we have just hypothesized: the hand that takes and gives; the wand that affirms power, or the step backward that cedes it; the word that pronounces the oath or the invocation, or else creates an obligation toward one's peer. These gestures and formulas were destined to fix the behaviors of heads of family during the most important episodes in their lives as "private persons," and the republican legal orders still contain evident relics, handed down virtually intact over the course of time and very well documented for us (Latin is one of the Indo-European languages that has best preserved its very ancient stock of vocabulary). Each of them—like a fossil—represents, so to speak, with its very being, proof of its own origins: such as establishing a marriage, making a will, contracting a debt, conveying an animal or a parcel of land.[40] Failing to respect these ceremonial practices meant breaking the order of the community and the network of its symbolic equilibria, placing oneself outside the protection of the gods, and therefore of *ius*.

The origins of this word (its earliest spelling must have been *ious*) and its first meaning, have been endlessly debated by modern historians:[41] as with *sacer*—a term that can already be found in the writings of the Lapis Niger[42]— and the pair *fas/nefas* ("that which is licit" and "that which is illicit" for the will of the gods; literally: that which is in conformity or not with the divine word),[43] which probably indicated, in its original distinction with respect to *ius,* the first rough attempt to separate the divine plane from the human one in the archaic mentality. It is probably possible to link *ius* with *yaos* and **yaus,* and to trace its origin back to Vedic and Iranian strata; the semantic field that would emerge in this way links the term to the representation of a state of conformity in accordance with the prescriptions of rites. The corresponding verb is *iurare,* to swear; the formal relation is certain, because the Latin for *giuramento* ("oath" in Italian) is *ius iurandum;* and the connection is explained precisely with the original significance of *ius* as a "formula of conformity," whereby *ius iurandum* was, literally, the "formula to be formulated," while *sacramentum*—another very ancient word that we always translate into Italian as *giuramento*—indicated instead the result that was obtained by pronouncing the "formula to be formulated": that is, the "consecrating oneself" *(sacrare)* of those who swore an oath before the gods.[44]

It is in any case certain that the earliest experience evoked on the horizon of *ius*—an array of ritual compliances midway between the human and the divine—played from the very beginning an essential role in the social and power relations of the community, and that the continuity between men and gods in the ordering that it indicated contributed decisively to the establishment of the oldest symbolic framework of the city.

A careful deciphering of the legal thought and the religious experience of the middle and late republican eras fully reveals the traces of this genesis: the formalistic layout that still dominated them would be inexplicable if we were unable to conjecture a beginning like the one described; once again, the origins are betrayed in the very form of things.

Certainly, by the time of imperial Rome that which had once been presented as an irresistible psychological conditioning had become nothing more than a cultural model protected by the power of tradition, and no longer implied any direct emotional participation. And yet, just the existence of a powerful original mental pressure, filtered and readapted but not erased by the passage of time, could explain the obstinate intersection, through the entire republican age, of hermeneutic paradigms lying somewhere between legal "prudence" and religious caution, between the rigidity of the *ius civile* and the ritualistic unremittingness of the sacral prescriptions. In both fields, it was easy to uncover the very same proliferation of verbal subtleties, the same attention to detail, to extrinsic sequences of behaviors, to the magical manipulation of time, to formulas, and to rites.

On the terrain of religion, this complex armature, dissociated from the very beginning from the perception of any moral interiority, would end up becoming fossilized and result in the suffocating, in contexts shaped by more mature inner needs, of the ancient imagination, and in the separation of the traditional cults from both the popular and the aristocratic sensibility. That burdensome prescriptive welter would appear as intrinsically devoid of any scope for evolving—a cold, dead body. And it would spell the end of the republican religion.

But the presence of the same imprint would have a radically different outcome in the context of legal wisdom, just as it would in the religion of ancient Israel: regenerated, in the first case, by integration into a universe of rules that increasingly had to come to terms with a complex imperial reality; and invigorated, in the second, by continual contact with an ethical elaboration of great power. From this point of view, the case of Israel appears in a certain way to be a mirror image of the Roman one. The ritualistic-prescriptive syndrome had at first been similar, but in Israel the evolutionary force developed entirely on the side of a religiosity shot through with morals, and an autonomous legal function never came into existence, suffocated as it was by the monotheistic theology; in Rome, by contrast, the development would take place entirely in the progressively secular area of social regulation, while religious practice was abandoned to inevitable fossilization.

It is now more and more evident that the specificity of the Roman situation did not emerge so much from the peculiar aspects of the original mental structure—even though here, too, as we have seen, intensely specific elements were probably present as well, dictated by historical conditions—as from its early and successful transposition beyond the boundaries of the divine into the space of *ius,* increasingly perceived as separate and unique. What was original, then, was not so much the characteristics of the archaic syndrome as their intensity and subsequent evolutionary history. And the consuming interest in prescriptive practices, placed in contact, through the wisdom of its experts, with the sheer substance of the social world and the new political and economic realities of a city in a phase of rapid expansion, would soon lead to the forming of an extraordinarily lively and subtle intellectual tradition: a sort of concrete rationalism, fully deployed in the third and second centuries B.C., and in its turn rich in further potential. Far from constituting a useless stumbling block, the persistence of a substantial archaic imprint in the more mature products of Roman legal knowledge would lead instead to its success and particularity, marking its style and essence in a definitive manner.

5

Kings, Priests, Wise Men

Chief among them all is the king, then the flamen Dialis, followed
by the flamen Martialis, and then in fourth place the flamen Quirinalis, and in the fifth place the pontifex maximus. And therefore
in the benches the king can sit above all others; the flamen Dialis
above those of Mars and Quirinus; the flamen Martialis above the
last named; and all of them above the pontifex. The king because
he is the most powerful; the flamen Dialis because he is the universal priest, called "Dium"; the flamen Martialis because Mars is
the father of the founder of the city; the flamen Quirinalis because Quirinus arrived from Curi to be associated with the power
of Rome; the pontifex maximus because he is considered to be
judge and arbiter of all things, divine and human.[1]

Sextus Pompeius Festus is writing here, probably in the middle of the
second century. He was copying and summarizing from Verrius Flaccus, the
antiquarian of the Augustan age, whose work is a gold mine of information
about early Roman antiquity.[2] The text concerns the hierarchy of the priests
(the *ordo sacerdotum*), in a ceremonial configuration dating from the monar-

chic era, at the very beginning of the city's life. It is hard to doubt that we are actually in the presence of a recollection of a much older tradition, capable of rendering up to us an authentic fragment of the first pattern of organization in Rome. On this issue, it is reasonable to take Dumézil's observations as conclusive.[3]

What we are given is a complete outline of the hierarchy of powers and functions at the top of the community. The fact that the entire structure, including the *rex*, mentioned at the beginning of the sequence, appears under a unified nomenclature, offers confirmation of the existence, in this period, of a sort of original "unitary mechanism" of king and priests: the key to the entire pre-Etruscan phase of Rome. It was a system that integrated military clan power (the *rex*), direct depiction of deities (the flamines as living statues of the leading gods, Jove, Mars, and Quirinus), and a prescriptive-ritualistic wisdom (that of the pontifices) within a single order, characterized by the all-pervading role of religious experience. The relations of power lay at the intersections between the ritual ordering and realistic acknowledgment of the supremacy of a military commander, a warlord (who emerged during the conflict between armed bands upon which Arnaldo Momigliano focused).[4] Nothing other than this fragile but already fairly distinct equilibrium is expressed in the dualism of the pairing *rex–flamen Dialis* ("potentissimus . . . universi mundi sacerdos"), in which the symbolic significance of the representation was concentrated. Archaic religiosity once again revealed all of its unifying potential. Together with the power and the charisma of the king, it held together the nascent city and enabled integration between *gentes* and *curiae* (about which we are by no means devoid of information; only a state-oriented prejudice could persuade us to discard the decisive testimony of Laelius Felix, handed down by Gellius, concerning relations between *curiae, centuriae,* and tribes, or to ignore the comparativist observation made by Dionysius on the similarities between the Roman *curia* and the Greek *phratria,* pointing indisputably to a link between the organization of the *curia* and pre-city family ties; to say nothing of certain duties of the *comitia curiata* during the republican age—*adrogationes,* solemn wills—which still bear traces of the ancient functions of safeguarding the patrilinear lines of descent).[5]

The existence of an early division of duties between kings and priests, in any case subject to considerable variations according to the differences in the figures who held a position of regality—physical strength, relative youth, and skill and aptitude at combat for the kings; ritualistic talent, cultic memory, and transfigurative capacities for the priesthood—did not, however, entail a rigorous distinction between functions, unthinkable in that context. The profile of the first kings (tradition records that there were four before the arrival of the Etruscans—Romulus, Numa Pompilius, Tullius Hostilius, and Ancus Marcius—but the actual number must have been far higher) would not be conceivable unless it were further endowed with magical and religious attributes. Indeed, the relation between royalty and sacrality—widespread in the Mediterranean area and investigated in modern historical and anthropological research from Frazer onwards[6]—well documented, in the case of Rome, by the survival, well into the republican era, of the presence of a singular figure, the *rex sacrorum,*[7] would become a constant in the whole of European history: even Christianity would ultimately rework it in a penetrating and creative way right up to the dawn of the modern age.[8]

Through the activity of the priests, religiosity took form in a continual shift between strictly cultic experience and magical practices, without any discontinuity between the two levels: from the cult of the dead to the consecration of fire, and the magical rites that emerge distinctly in many archaic traces, memory of which survived into the historical era—as in the ceremonies of the *fratres Arvales,* or in the *Fordicidia,* or in the war dances of military consecration.[9] Around these shared rituals performed for the benefit of all the *patres*—no less than through the deeds of the commanders—the collective life of the city took shape. The very idea of a "public" space—understood in a material, physical sense as well—actually developed in Rome as the experience of a ceremonial and religious space.

2.

We are not in a position to reconstruct, in even a minimally reliable way, the formation of the various priestly circles, which must already have been fully functioning during the monarchic era: flamines, pontifices, augurs, and vestals (a female priesthood established at the center of a rigidly patriarchal and patrilinear society).[10] But we do possess a wealth of clues pointing to an early specialization of duties among the various structures; and there is plenty to support the idea that there was an accentuated and old difference between the sacrificial and symbolic ritual roles attributed to the flamines and the sapiential functions acquired by the pontifices.[11] The wisdom of the latter bore a powerful connotation of social utility: the oracular prescriptiveness of their pronouncements—handed down through an unequivocal tradition—ensured good relations between the gods and the community, and tended in any case to assure an immediate benefit for the *patres,* through a process that acquired the features of a marked refounding, in a distinctly civic setting, of the old gentilitial religion.[12] The preexisting legacy of Latin myths—in part already tainted by Greek and Etruscan influences—was now reinterpreted in a Roman context; it was exactly that "mythical disintegration" discussed by some scholars, and which very possibly may have encouraged the transposition beyond the boundaries of the sacred of models and mental schemes that were originally formed solely in reference to the magic-religious imagination.[13] And it is on this aspect that we should now focus.

The anthropomorphization of the deities was complete by the middle of the eighth century B.C. It did not, however, result in a tangled mass. Here, too, however far back we may try to look, we once again find ourselves in the presence of something that resembles a coherent and clearly defined "theological structure." At the summit is the archaic triad, Jove, Mars, and Quirinus, which was only later replaced by the better-known Capitoline triad: Jove, Juno, and Minerva.

It is very likely that Dumézil's well known and widely discussed reconstruction, which linked each of the figures of the first triad to the symbolic representation of a "social function" perceived by the community as quite distinct from the others, is schematic to a degree that no comparative analysis can ever justify, and should therefore be rejected (on this hypothesis, Jove indicates "sovereignty with its magical and juridical aspects, and a sort of maximal expression of the sacred," while Mars represents war and warriors, and Quirinus agriculture and peasants).[14] This in no way detracts from the fact that the radical critique leveled by Momigliano against the French scholar, according to which all of his research, and in particular his trifunctional model, does absolutely nothing to help us to understand archaic Roman history, is harsh to the point of being implausible.[15] It is unquestionably correct to refuse to accept that separate social groups (priests, warriors, peasants) corresponded to the "three functions," but even Dumézil himself wound up admitting this.[16] And it is equally true that behind each archaic tripartition we cannot claim to find a trifunctional structure. But these observations do nothing to undermine the great achievement of having identified, in the depths of the Roman mentality, the presence of a self-regulated ordering scheme, based in turn on the reelaboration of elements of social and psychological experience that remain shrouded in shadow for us, but can be linked in some way to the original ritualistic syndrome and the needs to which it attempted to respond. Just as, on the other hand, it is plausible to glimpse in the figure of "pre-Capitoline" Jove the presence of a particular tension between the anthropomorphic representation of the supreme deity and the unitary construction of the city through religion and the declaring of *ius*.[17]

In Festus' words, however, there is still more. In them we find allusions to a twofold role of the pontifex maximus (the priest in charge of the collegium, made up originally of three and later of five members), which reflects and confirms that dual projection—toward the gods and toward men—that was identified as the first hint at diversification in the unitary web of regulatory overdetermination underlying the Roman mentality, perfectly expressed by the age-old pair of *fas-ius* that survived up to the time of Plautus, who used it as an ancient stereotype.[18] Even though the distinction may not be clearly placed in time, and it is expressed in a formula that was probably fairly late ("judge and arbiter of all things, divine and human"—"iudex atque arbiter habetur rerum divinarum humanarumque"), there can be no doubt that Festus was implicitly projecting it far into the past, because he used its content as a justification for the extremely ancient importance of the priest about whom he was speaking (the expression would later be transformed almost into a cliché, and we find it intact in Ulpian, though no longer referring to the priests, but directly to the jurists, their successors, at least in the perspective adopted by the Severan master).[19]

The pontifices thus appear in the city's memory as the wise men of the community, the depositories and interpreters of all its most important reserves of knowledge, according to an attribution of duties common to many

ancient societies, as was evident to the attentive eye of Polybius.[20] It is difficult to imagine that the concentration in their hands of such crucial tasks was
merely the result of a belated "pontifical revolution," which supposedly took
place over the course of the fourth century, and of which, moreover, there is
no trace in the sources.[21] There is no need to conjecture the existence of such
an event; and for that matter a relative specialization of functions is a trait
that surfaces in the earliest institutional and mental stratigraphy of the city.
The processes of social differentiation, with the tendency toward the formation of restricted elites—a feature common to all the Tyrrhenian communities beginning in the ninth and eighth centuries B.C.[22]—entailed inevitable
projections on the cultural plane: they fixed in the nascent gentilitial aristocracies ("vos patricios solos gentem habere"—"you alone are of noble birth"—
as Livy had Decius Mus say in a famous speech)[23] the depositories of functions that were essential for the collective life: that of magical and religious
regulation and the one linked to military command. The prescriptive attitude
therefore never came on the scene as the spontaneous production of the
mental experience of the community, but rather as an attribute of a restricted
group of wise men—the pontifices, selected from the ranks of the most powerful *gentes*—capable of offering a concrete sense of completion to a latent
collective psychological condition: the syndrome was projected from the very
beginning into the form of a secret and exclusive body of knowledge.

The intertwining of the planes between "divine" and "human" things,
and their common civic horizons, thus revealed themselves to be the dominant sign within the pontifical activity: the vertical relationships between
gods and men, and the horizontal ones among the *patres*—which also entailed
the active presence of the divine—were elaborated on the basis of the same
culture, reflecting the same attitudes: a ritualistic propensity and verbal caution dominated both, and shifted continually from one field to another. The
ceremonial contractualization of relationships with the deities, rites (sacrificial and otherwise) as protection against their wrath, became formulaic symmetries in dealings between heads of family, networks of reciprocity assured
by gestural and verbal behaviors designed to attain the same objective: harmony with the supernatural and peaceful coexistence among the *patres* were
essential values in a community with constantly precarious equilibria. Underlying it all was a repetition of the same scheme: there could be no peace, ei-

ther theological or social, without the enactment of the rite. Outside there always loomed the imminent shadow of devastating violence.

3.

The basic structure of the early city changed irreversibly under the weight of the radical shift of the sixth century: the great Etruscan period of Rome. Probably, if we were better informed about how the successor was chosen following the death of the *rex,* we would be able to venture more reliable conjectures about its beginnings. But we are not: and the hypothesis—albeit fascinating—that the investiture of the new king took place through the involvement of female figures, in a mysterious counterpoint to the gentilitial patrilineal succession, remains nothing more than a vague possibility.[24] At any rate, however the Etruscan kings took possession of Rome, all the documentation available to us—from archeology to the annalistic tradition—confronts us with a radical qualitative leap.

The transformation that relates most closely to our tale is the one concerning what we may call the birth of politics in Rome, rendered evident by the first weakening of kinship structures, replaced by ties that were more properly bonds of citizenship. These, in their turn, were favored by the adoption of a new military organization, introduced into Italy by the Etruscans, which was much more rational and effective than the old pattern of fighting in armed gentilitial bands. This was the hoplite system: masses of footsoldiers armed with spears, recruited according to a civic belongingness progressively constructed on the basis of an identity between the warrior who fought, the citizen who participated in the assembly, and the landowner who cultivated and produced. The polysemy of the word *centuria* clearly reproduced the bond; in fact it indicated simultaneously a military unit, a voting unit in the assembly, and a unit of measurement of land.[25] From then on, the unitary mechanism of king and priests exalted and protected by the magical and sacral shell, would dwindle in importance, although it did remain a prominent element. The new equilibrium shifted onto the axis—no longer mystical or gentilitial, but more properly political—between king and army (which would soon become the assembly of citizens under arms).

The Servian reform (albeit only in its original nucleus, datable to the sixth century B.C.)²⁶ and the development of the centuriate city, "the great Rome of the Tarquins,"²⁷ characterize the shift. It is not without significance, however, that already a republican tradition should present Servius Tullius as the founder of Roman liberties, in a line of thought whereby *libertas* was the constituent element of politics in the city.²⁸

With the ordering by *centuriae*—even in its first rough version—there was an intensification of power at the center of the community along new lines with respect to those glimpsed in the eighth and seventh centuries: and this change—at once cultural and institutional—was perhaps the single most significant contribution of the Etruscan presence, which was destined to leave an ineradicable mark on the history of Rome. The result would be not only the formation of a new kind of fighting man but, in a narrower sense, of citizens, now detached from their old clan ties and outside the circles of the *curiae*. The liberation of these energies, and their reference to a military machine that imposed discipline, cooperation, and much more incisive centers of command than the gentilitial ones, reinforced the community and regenerated the figure of the *rex*: the unitary status of the city redefined itself around a more centralized and mature configuration, an expression of a change in the balance of powers.

From this point of view, the reform was also an attempt to bring the early monarchy up to date with the more fully developed social articulation of the sixth century, which could no longer be brought within the limited framework of the clans. But the centurial army, precisely because it linked the operation of the military machine with the economic and social role of the single combatants, emphasizing their importance and responsibility, was no longer merely a fighting force. It was, at least potentially, also an assembly, in keeping with a transposition already well known in the Greek experience. And an assembly that decides and elects—albeit within limits that were very restrictive at the outset—is already a political body, just as its internal workings from then on would be political, and likewise the tie first with the king, and later with the republican magistrates.²⁹

The public dimension was now no longer reducible exclusively to the religious space, but increasingly referred to the functions of the army and the assembly. Religion of course remained decisive, but gradually became part of a different and a more complex game. It was no longer a totalizing element, but started to feel the secular influence of politics. The entire priestly structure was swept by the wind of change, and the original hierarchy, as documented by Festus, began to wane. Communion with the deities was no longer in itself sufficient to determine the importance of the ministers of the cult. What became prevalent was another type of social function linked to their tasks and duties. It was the concentration of knowledge that now gave power and prominence, more than the pure symbolic representation of the deities. The role of the pontifices thus emerged into the foreground, with respect to that of the flamines—their "revolution" was nothing if not wholly induced by politics.

The new context accentuated the division between the two values that we have identified and which Festus underscores: *res divinae* and *res humanae* tended from now on to become increasingly distinct, while still maintaining—in the mentality of the priests who preserved the exclusivity on both, and also in the collective one of the people—an exceedingly dense network of interactions. Although *ius* continued to be protected and enveloped by an aura of religiosity and magic, it began to be perceived as the product of a civil knowledge—by this point profoundly integrated into the body of the *civitas*—which organized itself in keeping with distinctive and special criteria.

We are not able to establish how much rational thought—admittedly, as we have defined it, a concrete rationality without concepts and abstractions —went into the talent of the pontifices, with respect to the originally prevalent presence of thought dominated by forms of magical associationism and pervasive ritualism. But we can suppose with some grounds for support that the new context favored the development of models, albeit in embryonic form, of empirical realism and distributive calculation; and that this opened new paths for the attention of the men of wisdom.

Politics, therefore, did not come into being in Rome on its own. Just as it was immediately flanked, in Ionia, Athens, and Magna Graecia, by philosophy, the direct successor to the mythical and cosmogonic thought of the earliest archaic religiosity, in Rome it was accompanied by another entirely original cognitive practice, descended from an ancient line of religious thought, though one with different characteristics from its Greek counterpart. A sphere of knowledge that demanded for itself the social regulation of the familial and patrimonial—and therefore "private"—prerequisites of the "political" citizenship of the *patres,* and which organized, according to distinctive modules, a mentality and an already rich, deeply layered cultural fabric: the initial core of a full-fledged technique of *ius,* of a *iuris prudentia* (as the phrase very soon became), recognizable as such, with a specific and unmistakable style all of its own. And just as, at least from the sixth century, Greek politics would have been inconceivable without its philosophy, likewise Roman politics could not have survived without its *ius.*

6

Rituals and Prescriptions

I.

In the memory of late-republican culture the wisdom of the ancient pontifices was associated above all with their role as guardians of the *mos*, the religious and social customs of the ancestors.[1] Another important piece of testimony by Festus enables us to confidently place this other ancient monosyllabic word (which can be translated as "habit," "custom," "usage") back at the very heart of the archaic mentality: "Ritus est mos comprobatus in administrandis sacrificiis" ("the rite is the approved practice in the administration of sacrifice").[2] Two elements stand out immediately: the connection between rite and sacrifice (already noted, and significantly confirmed here), and that between rite and custom. The *mos* is revealed as lying at the foundation of the mechanism of ceremonial transfiguration that we saw invading very early Roman thought, the exclusive domain of the priests ("in administrandis sacrificiis"), and expressed with great emphasis in the sapiential construction of the *sacer*.

The pontifices were also repositories of the calendar, containing predictions of the full moons, the new moons, and the *dies fasti*, and therefore exerted a decisive social control over time; of the formulaic sequences of the prayers and ritual invocations directed toward the gods; and probably, starting sometime around 600 B.C., of writing itself. Furthermore, they kept a record of the history of the city, including important events such as famines, epidemics, battles, eclipses, the names of the kings (and later those of the magistrates); and they took part in the *comitia calata,* the assemblies of the *curiae* at which fundamental acts of community life were carried out, such as wills or instances of arrogation (the definitive submission of a *pater* to the power of another *pater*).³

Their pronouncements immediately acquired an irrevocable objectivity. Observance conferred power: in fact it allowed those who respected them a total participation in the sphere of the sacred and the magical, which, it was thought, protected and rendered invincible those capable of understanding the signs and secrets, and of complying with their indications.

We can say that *ius,* then, was tradition (*mos*) in its most strictly preceptive sense. It is impossible to say how the manipulation of these memories took place, how social practice and religious imagination were mixed together: the components were the product, in turn, of a lengthy process of sedimentation that is almost completely inaccessible to us. Without a doubt, the perception of a temporality marked by repetition (the same that can be found in magical astrology) must have played a decisive role in this context. The *mos* featured as the symbolic transfiguration of this experience, which became rite, rule, and *ius* ("mos est ritus"): it enabled a normalization of the present—a reduction of its uncertainties and traumas—endowing it with a self-confirming measure of its own continuity, reducing it to something archetypal and repeatable. This is the origin of what we are accustomed to describe as Roman "conservatism": the use (and invention) of repetition and duration as forms of reassurance in the face of the chaotic multiformity of life; the weight of tradition as against the volatile lightness and riskiness of unprecedented decisions and behaviors.⁴

We also know that the pronouncement of the prescriptions dictated by the pontifices took a particular form, which would remain impressed upon the entire successive development of Roman legal culture. They were nothing other than "responses" formulated by the pontifices in a typically oracular style—revelations of secret truths, unquestionable and unmotivated—to questions from the *patres,* who wanted to know what *ius* was in a particular circumstance; that is to say, what verbal and gestural conduct (the rite) should be adopted when performing essential operations in dealings between family groups: claiming power over a person or thing *(manus:* the first verbal representation of dominion was expressed in the symbol of a grasping hand); conveying of property *(mancipium),* formulating a will, entering into marriage, making a bond whereby a free man formally came under the power of his creditor until he could pay off his debt *(nexum).* This was the model that would later—in republican legal language—be termed the *responsum:* a style of authoritarian communication of great importance in the life of the archaic city, through which a hidden wisdom would exert an ordering and regulatory influence according to a scheme destined to become one of the most important paradigms of Roman aristocratic sociality.

In this case too, the form was not original. We can in fact find something similar in the Greek world, associated with the notions of *themis* and *themisthes,* which allude to the verdicts of a king-priest who, when questioned, responded in an oracular manner;[5] but it was only in Rome that such a modality, instead of being replaced by other regulatory models, experienced a quite unique development and elaboration.

The *responsa* constituted the city's living rules, the crystallized and symbolic projection of its social relations—at first relatively elementary and still dominated by gentilitial family ties, and then, in the Etruscan period, increasingly articulated and complex. Responding to the questions of the *patres* became a fundamental task for the pontifices. What particularly required the protection of the sacerdotal pronouncements were mechanisms of patrilinearity, economic reciprocity, and matrimonial exchange. Cognition of *ius* did not appear elsewhere, nor did it have meaning other than in solving concrete problems and meeting the particular needs of the community.

However, the *responsa* did not establish general norms. They were valid only for the issue raised in the submitted question—another characteristic destined to leave a decisive mark. And yet they were not forgotten. Their memory was entrusted to the pontifical collegium, which preserved it from generation to generation. Every new question presented by the *patres* was compared above all with possible precedents, with the deposited mass of previously expressed opinions. Through the filter of a very restricted group, a potentially new body of wisdom began to accrue with respect to the resources of the archaic mentality. Intrinsically case-based, preceptive, and punctiform (an opinion for every question), it was the first, authentic nucleus of *ius*, and we can still identify some of its coordinates.

The point of departure should be considered the realization that we are in the presence—until the end of the third century B.C.—of a tradition that was almost entirely oral. This characteristic relates to the entire cultural structure of Roman society in the first few centuries of the city's life. Orality was not, in that context, an extrinsic aspect of the thought it was transmitting, a pure medium without consequences for the communicated content. As in all ancient civilizations, and not only archaic ones, it played a constituent role, impinging heavily on the knowledge therein expressed, on its quality and style. Plato was well aware of this.[6]

We should primarily focus on the nexus between words and power: a very close relationship, which the practice of *ius* exalted and expanded.[7] The archaic mind concentrated to a far greater degree upon verbal pronouncements than on the objects evoked by them. The signs themselves appeared to be concrete beings, no less than the reality perceived through the senses. The experience of *ius* never referred directly to the facts. These only emerged in the linguistic and gestural constructions created to reproduce them, in the symbolic transfiguration that successfully fixed, in the immobility of the rite, the fluid and continuous sequence of life, making it possible to link it to the sphere of the divine: of the *fas*, of the *sacer*. The control exerted by the pontifices over the choice of words to be pronounced, over their sequence, over the rhythm of the language, served to trigger a contact with the supernatural and with the magical; but it also wound up holding powerful sway over the shaping of the collective mentality, and on the very form of social relations. The stricter its exercise, the more it became exclusive from the point of view of power. The verbal and gestural symbolizations, fixed in a rigid manner, were transformed into precise techniques for ordering the community's sociality.[8]

We can therefore understand why, in the mirror of the more highly developed late-republican sensibility, the whole archaic experience of *ius* should ultimately appear as a world completely shackled by an unacceptable framework of petrified clauses: what had once been a living body of knowledge had by this point become a technique oriented toward pure conservatism.[9]

An oral wisdom that was so deeply impregnated with religious rituality tended inevitably to focus on the utterance of words that gave power, as genuine magical formulas. "Uti lingua nuncupassit, ita ius esto"—"as the tongue declared, so it will be ius"—as the Twelve Tables recite in connection with the declarations that accompanied the rituals with which one ceded the *manus* (power) over a good, clearly harking back to a far older tradition, certainly pontifical in origin, and not referring only to *mancipium:* this is precisely what, in oral cultures—even those not belonging to Mediterranean antiquity—we identify as the formulaic character of solemn acts, and the performative value of the language employed.[10] The objective was a sort of static equilibrium, based on memory and the repetition of the typical. And it is no accident that memory would be the distinguishing feature of the traditional model of the jurisconsult later outlined in a famous text by Cicero.[11]

We should also underscore the relationship between orality and event. Orality has no conceptual architecture—no complex description in terms of causal links—and instead focuses on the single episode, captured through the words that represent it. In the wisdom of the pontifices, the event was, properly speaking, the "response" and the occasion that had determined it. The words of the submitter's question; and the words of the learned priest, who prescribed by responding. To preserve the knowledge of *ius* according to events (through chains of memorized *responsa*) and not by concepts presented itself as a solution without any alternative: and it would become a long-lived custom, even when, centuries later, legal thought learned to make use of far more elaborate techniques and schemes.

2.

In the "response," the opinion of the sage sprang from observation of the case in question, through the voice that described it. The thought developed in the context of the urgency of the situation requiring attention. The first model of knowledge of *ius* was a mental organization, "by events" (later, by types of events), of the ritual prescriptions that were to guide the action of the *patres* in the community.

For a long time, right into the heart of the republican era, the "responses" would be remembered along with the name of the questioner.[12] They expressed a wisdom that was in its way based on clues, semiotic—a sort of "prophecy on the past," in which ritual practice steeped in magic was com-

bined with the empirical and measuring rationality of the new political institutions introduced by the Servian reform. In examining the question submitted to him, the pontifex focused on the details, on the sign, that only to a
trained mind could become revelatory and guide the "response." It was in
any case necessary to situate every action within the framework of the *mos;*
to identify the rite that could take it into the sphere of *ius.* Times, behaviors,
precedents, repetitions, and magical spells; gestures, whether omitted or performed; words, whether stated or left unsaid; instruments, objects, roles, and
technologies indispensable for the rituals: the wand, the piece of bronze, the
scales, the weigher, the witnesses. A diagnostic type of investigation developed, centered upon the special relationship with the particular, the tendency
toward the concatenation of signs that we can first identify in roughly the
same period in the logical thread—much better documented—of the Greek
medical texts of the clinical tradition. Between the archaic thought of *ius* and
Greek medical wisdom prior or extraneous to the shift toward anatomical
practice there is something more than just a vague resemblance. There is the
common framework of a similar concrete rationality focusing on the detail,
the clue, the event: rituals and diseases, social relations and human bodies as
sets of signs to be exhibited or deciphered.[13]

The survival of the pontifices' verdicts—which were not motivated, inasmuch as they were manifestations of a secret talent and capacity, and any
failure to comply would not even be punished directly by the city powers, but
would simply plunge the transgressor into an abyss of shame[14]—was linked
to the existence of a delicate relationship between the event that was memorized in its unrepeatable individuality, and the search for its potential prescriptive typification (in other words, the possibility that it might, in turn, generate *mos*). This tension determined the lifetime of the response. A bond was
established between typificability and continuity, between the empirical con-
servation of identity and the already partly abstract observation of quantities: a relationship likewise destined to live on in the history of Roman legal
thought, in the form of a profound integration between *scientia* and *prudentia,* between *ars* and *usus* (to say it with Cicero), between *episteme* and *phronesis* in the terms of Greek philosophical conceptualization.[15]

But alongside this first cognitive nucleus, the pontifical wisdom of *ius*
gradually began to acquire another trait, which would have just as many consequences. In the context of the city's institutions, it established itself as in-

trinsically nondiscriminatory with respect to the various subjects of the post-gentilitial community: its precepts defined models of gestural and verbal behavior that could be used in an egalitarian manner by patricians and plebe-ians. Its only point of reference was the social actions of the individual *patres* of the community. Everyone could make use of it, so long as he was a citizen. Its measure was the same personalizing, molecular one that we find in the centurial rationality, and in the development of the parceled ownership of land. Inequality manifested itself in the exclusively pontifical, and therefore patrician, concentration of knowledge of *ius,* and so of all prescriptive power; not in the constructive rationality that guided the elaboration of the re-sponses.

It was thus inevitable that wisdom of this sort would come into contact with political conflicts and issues: concentrated within it was the power of an essential ordering, which the government of the centuriate city could not do without—and at least from the end of the sixth century on, we must attempt to trace it in this new context.

Servius' reform did not save the monarchy, but it nonetheless survived the catastrophe of the Tarquins. It is probable that the old gentilitial aristocracies, in the decades following the establishment of the republic (for which the date offered by Roman tradition, the end of the sixth century, seems the most plausible), sought to annul its effects, both military and political, and to rein-troduce the ancient model of wars fought by armed bands: what memory survives of the battle of the river Cremera points precisely in this direc-tion.[16] But the ensuing disaster helped to protect the centuriate organiza-tion—showing that its new criteria were by this point essential if further de-feats were to be avoided—making it clear that the principal challenge facing the aristocratic groups was their political renewal, and not the return to their old gentilitial shells.

For that matter, it was not merely a military issue. The progress made in the sixth century had created in Rome a social and economic stratification that it would have been impossible—especially in the period of serious diffi-culties (in production, demographic levels, and even of food supply) follow-ing the birth of the republic—to channel back into the ancient pattern of gentilitial subordination. The end of the monarchy (whatever the nature of the magistracy that immediately replaced it), the breakdown of the system based exclusively on family ties, the economic crisis, the development of political relations through the centurial assembly, all came together to bring about a situation that had never been seen in the history of the city: a harsh conflict between two opposing groups, to which the new institutional framework as much as the antagonism of diverse interests gave a form and substance that it would be misleading to describe as "class-based" in the modern sense, but which was in any case destined to persist. On one side was an aristocracy moving toward a no longer exclusively gentilitial organization of its power, which was attempting to redefine its "patrician" nature in political terms. On the other was an array of nonaristocratic groups lying outside the system of gentilitial kinship, united by the bond of a shared "plebeian" identification.

The conflict, though extended and acute, did not lead to the disintegration of the city: on the contrary, it completed and rendered integral its politicization, bringing about the consolidation of those organizational elements that the centuriate model had always carried with it.

Right from the city's first beginnings, the space occupied by the community had been split into sections, divided up, and shared out: the three tribes, the thirty *curiae,* and the *bina iugera* of the individual assignment of land, which the saga of Romulus attributed to the founder himself.[17] Some of the numbers may be the product of later influences, but we have no reason to doubt that the idea of the fractioning, of the symmetrical breakdown of groups and areas of land, goes back to very early times— the "quantitative" counterpart of the original prescriptive syndrome.

Implanted onto this mesh was the measuring tendency of the new politics, and of the mentality that accompanied it. Each and every citizen-soldier was weighed up, evaluated, and slotted into a position. The classificatory predisposition established itself as the authentic criterion of order for the new republican culture. It was capable of assessing each member of the community, irrespective of gentilitial affiliation, and assigning him to his rightful place in a whole that was perceived—though not yet conceptualized—as an organic totality.

The establishment of this particular organizational paradigm, though initially opposed, did not replace the old magical-religious world that had till then dominated the city. Republican politics and the culture of the city's early community were instead integrated into a whole in which centuriate rationality and the apparatuses and customs of the original gentilitial religiosity coexisted. The oscillations of this equilibrium mapped power shifts in the city. The stubborn efforts of the patrician groups to reserve for themselves access to the sacerdotal collegia—and in particular to wisdom and to pontifical practices—represented a defense of a cultic and prescriptive exclusivity that in any case made it possible to delimit and restrict the potentially subversive effects of the excessively free spread of politics.

And for its part, the new Servian structure, probably from the very outset, but certainly once the republic had been established, was never just a patrician model. It was undoubtedly fuelled by an aristocratic form of thought, according to which differences in wealth had a decisive importance; but its boundaries never coincided with those of the old landowning culture of the *gentes:* the strongest groups of the stratified plebeian structure immediately found a place in it, with a degree of adherence that would ultimately have consequences of great importance. The political rationality of the army and of the centuriate assembly was an oligarchical, not a gentilitial, paradigm. The ideas that moved it were already potentially the fabric of a new aristocracy, which would lead to the great patrician-plebeian compromise, still a long way off in the fifth century, but then increasingly well defined and successful, and destined to mark the republican stabilization beginning around the year 300 B.C.

There thus began to take shape the pattern of an interaction between politics, religion, and knowledge of *ius* that would have a major influence on the entire history of the Roman republic. The more the sphere of politics expanded, the less pervasive would be the weight of religion and of the gentilitial kinship ties. And the relative contraction of the magical-religious world, already perceptible in the fifth century, and increasingly accentuated from then on, would for its own part mark the irresistible expansion of *ius,* the unrivaled regulator of the familial and patrimonial requirements of citizenship. Beginning at the turn of the third century, this would acquire the features of a body of knowledge that was a repository of a normative function now perceived to be distinct and self-sufficient, though still an integral part of the oligarchy's political dominance. The ancient interrelationship between the sacred and *ius* was flanked and then slowly replaced by a different alliance, which became fully operative over the course of the third century, between legal knowledge and the secular power of the new aristocracy, while religion would come under significant pressure from politics.

But the rhythms of these dynamics would always be anything but transparent. Synchronic combinations would tend to prevail over linear sequences, and for a long time there would be gray areas, enveloped in shadow, confusion, and tension. Even when the archaic religious imagination had exhausted all its creative power, the contiguity with the world of *ius* would continue to manifest itself in the form of a massive jurisprudentialization of traditional religion (by this point, a reverse mirror image of the original supremacy of religious culture), which would accompany its political contamination and lead to the consolidation of a full-fledged *ius pontificium*: cultivated by Quintus Fabius Maximus Servilianus, in the heart of the second century B.C., by Servius Sulpicius Rufus, toward the end of the republic, who would reiterate programmatically the link with the *ius civile*, by Trebatius Testa, and by Varro, to say nothing of the analogous phenomenon of "augural law."[18]

The Roman pantheon also expanded and became stabilized, accepting with increasing willingness the presence of the Greek deities. A network of temples sprang up round the Capitoline triad, through which the gods took up residence in the center of Rome, alongside the citizens. The new situation emphasized the change in the social role of the priests: the religious scene was less and less occupied by the living symbols of the deities, making way for those who were depositories of a vast patrimony of knowledge. Much more than the priest-statues, it was the priest-sages who dominated the scene: masters of the sacred and of rites, but also stern controllers of the investiture of the republican magistrates—subject to the approval of the gods—of which they remained nearly absolute arbiters. The integration of the divine into the political took place through the transfer onto the new terrain of all the weight of the archaic ceremonial ritualism: just as the rest of society was changing, the antiquity of religion, safeguarded by its ministers, was becoming the supreme guarantee of the continuity of power, and of its proper use.

But where the transformation of the city would have the most important consequences would be in the other area of pontifical wisdom: in the production of *ius*. The priests were now faced by a social world riven by radical tensions, intensified by the claims of the plebs, which had to be addressed in some way. What was called into question was not so much the patrician exclusivity of the pontifical collegium, but the very idea—the authentic Roman peculiarity—that the ordering of the entire city had to be filtered through the oracular prescriptions of an exclusive and secret wisdom. It did not necessarily have to be like that. The reality of the Mediterranean at the end of the sixth and the beginning of the fifth century offered different solutions. Another example was offered by Greece: that of "legislation" as an expression of political command, which had taken root with the spread of writing and then with the democratic wave. And in Rome, too, a new contest was about to begin, with unpredictable results.

7

The Model of Statutory Law

The fifth and fourth centuries can be considered the laboratory of the republic: a lengthy and difficult transition from the fall of the monarchy up to the final consolidation of the new institutional order.

In this sense, we should avoid offering a merely regressive interpretation of the crisis in the fifth century. In those years, despite everything, the foundations of the republic were laid, and the military-expansionist mechanism that would later be so effective was first introduced.

With varying fortunes, two ideas of institutions and of power faced off throughout the century, both in some way ascribable to the new Servian rationality, but still divided according to a diametrical opposition that drew on the political dialectic of many Greek cities of the time. The later Roman tradition, which emerged under the influence of the subsequent oligarchic normalization, would attempt to soften the radical nature of the contrast, fragmenting the account into a sequence of clashes, some of them quite bitter, but episodic and circumscribed in their scope. Nonetheless it was unable to entirely conceal the real scale of the conflict.[1]

The first of the models revolved around the attempt, by the old gentilitial groups, to restore an intransigent primacy, albeit beyond the traditional clan relations: this was what Gaetano de Sanctis called the *serrata* ("lockout") of the "patriciate."[2] The second undertaking must have appeared, even to its own protagonists, and at least at the outset, to be more vague and uncertain. Its aim was to challenge the preeminence of the patriciate and to project the plebeian masses more forcefully upon the political stage. However, it gradually splintered into two distinct versions, as may reasonably be conjectured on the basis of available information. In one, there emerged what we might define as a democratic orientation (thinking of contemporary developments in the Greek *poleis* in Attica, the Aegean, and Sicily), which sought to institute, in the heart of the republic, the power of control of a plebeian assembly based on universal male suffrage; at the same time, more or less openly "tyrannical" solutions were not entirely excluded, in line with a well-known demagogic drift in the affairs of the ancient democracies. The other version, far less drastic and increasingly successful from the end of the fifth century onwards, called for the possibility of a compromise between the patriciate (or at least a significant part thereof) and the plebeian elites, and the consequential formation of a new oligarchic bloc, with a fairly broad social base, capable of putting an end to the period of conflict, and of giving the city a unified and "temperate" government.[3]

From the middle of the fifth century on, the line of patrician intransigence crumbled quite rapidly in the face of plebeian successes, and the mediating idea of an oligarchic alliance began to take shape. But around the year 300, the mirage of a radical and probably "tyrannical" democracy was still so powerful that it even attracted prominent figures from among the most ancient sections of the patriciate: only in this context do the role of Appius Claudius Caecus and the events linked to the Ogulnian plebiscite find their proper significance. And on the other hand, the specter of a democracy that was (from their point of view) subversive—and of a possible convergence and unity between tyrants and people—would continue for many years to haunt the optimates, long after the struggles of this period were over: it would be a recurring fear for the nobility until the time of Catiline, and, in many ways, all the way through to that of Caesar himself.[4]

In any case it was not until the opening decades of the third century B.C. that the conflicts of the early republican age can be said to be definitively over, with the advent of a long period of aristocratic stabilization which continued through to the years of the Gracchi and the formation of a world empire. Its establishment would lead to the extraordinary expansion of the city, the great fortunes of the republic, and the very birth of the legend of Rome. But before all this happened, the conflict would be long and harsh, and things could easily have turned out very differently.

2.

The most important episode in the struggle had a profound impact on the history of *ius*. It was the sudden and enigmatic one that led, around the middle of the fifth century, to the legislation of the Twelve Tables. The collective memory of the aristocracy, which founded what we might call the "republican canon," later entrusted to the historiography and antiquarian studies active between the second century and the Augustan age—upon which we almost exclusively depend—would attempt in many ways (as in other, less crucial cases) to conceal the traumatic character of the radical shift, devoted as it was to constructing as continuous and teleological an account as possible of Roman history, in which everything was to converge in an orderly manner toward future greatness. It was a vision which, as regards the Twelve Tables, even Pomponius still had good reason to accept (he is the only jurist to provide us with a concise account of the event).[5] Even so, with just a little effort, the depth of the rift still emerges clearly.

With a precocity that itself proved decisive, in the wake of the events of those years, the city was faced with two equally well-defined hypotheses of regulatory organization and social ordering: two alternative models of sovereignty, we might say. One was based on the specifically Roman paradigm of *ius*, the other on the Greek and Mediterranean one of the *lex*. It is not unreasonable to claim that this confrontation would have incalculable consequences: on it would depend the invention of the "form of law" in the subsequent development of the West.

According to the narrative core of the annalistic tradition, variously taken from Polybius, Cicero, Livy, Dionysius, Diodorus, and Pomponius—about which nineteenth- and twentieth-century historians have had occasion to express often serious doubts, though its basic reliability is no longer in question—the Twelve Tables were composed between 451 and 450 B.C. by a de-cemviral collegium that was largely (or exclusively) patrician, which had been appointed to govern the republic—as all the other magistracies had been sus-pended—and to draw up laws that were to be placed solemnly in the center of the city.⁶ There are still a number of highly controversial details, especially in relation to the events of 450 and the composition of the collegium in this second year, and the end of the mandate of the decemviri in 449, but we can overlook these issues here.

And we can be quite certain about another point as well: that from the very outset, a key word was associated with the work of the decemviri: *lex,* a term that appeared very early on in the Latin lexicon, though perhaps not as early as *ius, fas,* or *mos.* Its etymology has posed as many problems as those other mysterious monosyllabic words. But it is certainly correct to link its original meaning to an act of *imperium* of the city's political power: a com-mand that lay on a plane intrinsically distinct from the religious ordering of the priests, intended to operate at a different, more strictly human level of community life, and for this reason endowed with the force of a coercive sanction (in contrast with the pontifical *responsa,* which in a sense did not need one).

In the language used in Rome during the fifth century B.C., then, *lex* had the same value that, in the Greek world of the time, was attached to another important word in our story: *nomos.*⁷ But for the latter—and it is essential not to forget this—it was a recently acquired significance, not an element rooted in the origins of Greek experience. In that culture the first semantic field of the term oscillated instead around the identification of a religious rituality, or a customary principle, or even a moral precept: and it is in these senses that *nomos* is found in texts by Hesiod, Archilochus, Theognis, and Alcaeus (but not in Homer, who seemed not to be familiar with it, except perhaps on one occasion);⁸ the contiguous words are *themis* and *thesmos* (respectively, the pre-scription given by the priest-king, an oracular pronouncement; and the rules governing relations among families or, in a later period, and in a more generic sense, justice). In older Latin we would have to render the concept variously as *mos,* or perhaps as *ius* in its original meaning, but not as *lex.* When, instead, in archaic Greece, and also in Athens, one wanted to indicate with greater precision commands issued by the king, mostly in his capacity as an interme-diary of divine will, it was customary to use, besides *themis,* the word *thesmos,* which recurs in Homer, and can also be found later in reference to the laws of Draco and Solon.⁹ But from the end of the sixth and throughout the fifth century B.C., *thesmos* became less common (just as the oracular meaning of *themis* began to die out), and finally vanished entirely around the year 450. *Nomos* completely took its place, in the new meaning, imposed by the democratic impulse that was gaining ground in those decades, which championed the idea of an entirely human "law (dictated by) politics," of a bringer of equality, of *isonomia* (another key term: "the loveliest word of them all," as Herodotus famously put it);¹⁰ and this was probably already the case as from the reforms of Cleisthenes, which might well have introduced both terms into the Athenian political lexicon.¹¹

In the fifth century, then, the word *nomos* was charged with ideological connotations. It indicated a paradigm of sovereignty, because its significance was closely associated with the experience of democracy (as would happen, for instance, in Demosthenes),¹² as with that of writing—no less essential in that context—as a vehicle of political communication (thus, among others, in Euripides' *Supplicants*).¹³ This led to the formation of an indissoluble triad— law, writing, secularity—capable of setting the certainty of knowability and of stability against the arbitrariness of a religious or customary rule that could be manipulated as desired by those in power—an apparatus that may also have contained a distinctly antimonarchic value; in fact the "excarnation" of the precept through its graphic representation presupposed the disintegration of the figure of the king-priest, guarantor and mystical founder, through his own person, of every social rule.¹⁴

This is precisely the meaning—no less ideological—of *lex* in the Rome of those same years, or at most a few decades later, and it can reasonably be supposed that the word spread precisely as a way of translating the new political notion of *nomos*, for which there was no adequate corresponding term in Latin (and *ius* certainly could not have performed the task). However, there was a decisive difference in context. In Greece the invention of the law as "excarnate" political command was not opposed, in the social disciplinary practices developed up until then, by anything of similar cultural or institutional strength. There were just the residues of a declining royalty that still contained a confusing mix of religious and prescriptive aspects. As a result, it quickly became the exclusive point of reference for every development in this field, and the subject, in the new philosophy, of a great ethical and metaphysical debate—another indication of the absolute preeminence of politics, able to integrate everything else within it. In Rome, on the other hand, when some sectors of the city attempted to impose the same model, they immediately ran up against something firm, hard, and consolidated: an alternative experience that already had great substance, was capable of reforming itself and even of acquiring a progressively secular dimension of its own—the paradigm of *ius*.

No Indo-European comparativism or reckless extension of the concept of law can ever obscure this essential fact, rendered evident by the manifestation of a clear and unprecedented asymmetry in the respective vocabularies of Greek and Latin. In the mid-fifth century B.C. there was already an ineradicable Roman specificity in the forms of social regulation, which could no longer be aligned with any Mediterranean context: neither with ancient religious practices (more or less commingled with mechanisms of regality, widespread in Egypt and Mesopotamia and also in the very origins of Greek and Italic cultures), nor with the new power of written and "excarnate" political law. Instead it was something intrinsically different and solitary. A structure capable of activating around itself a new type of knowledge unrelated to the mentalities of the past, but able instead to break progressively away from them, and to take on the profile of a previously unseen set of techniques. In fact, it would be when the horizon of significances of *nomos*, polarized at this point by the reference to political law, began to be transformed, and the experience of *ius* started to break away from its exclusively religious matrix— roughly around the same time, between the end of the sixth and the middle of the fifth century—that *ius* became substantially untranslatable into Greek: the absence of the thing inevitably brought with it the absence of the name.

It is likely, however, that the word *lex* was not introduced into Rome for the first time in association with the Twelve Tables. Traces exist, in the memory of the historiographical and antiquarian tradition, of *leges sacratae* dating to the earliest years of the republic. These were measures approved by plebeian groups in their own assembly *(concilia),* and imposed by force upon the city as a whole, according to which anyone who used force to prevent the magistrates of the plebs from exercising their role as guarantors was to be considered *sacer—sacer esto,* killable insofar as they were excluded from the community.[15] In this case as well, the texts in question would have been written ones (and this is highly plausible) linked to the social conflicts—the same context that we find for the Twelve Tables. Nor should the connection with the religious plane, so evident in the reference to *sacer,* be considered disturbing; it can be interpreted as an attempt to protect the new and still fragile political command from the ingrained mechanisms of the earliest civic mentality. It is a connection that would crop up in the Twelve Tables as well, though the formula also recurs in the provision transcribed on the stele known as the Lapis Niger. And if the latter actually does prove to be datable to the late monarchic period, we will have found the missing link, in the use of this clause, between Etruscan royalty and the very earliest republican legislation.[16]

It is very difficult to go any further back, and in any case the advent of the *lex* cannot be shifted to a period prior to the first diffusion of writing in the city, which took place in the last part of the sixth century. According to a tradition that formed during the republican age, royal commands, known as *leges regiae*—laws of the king,[17] had been issued even earlier than that, not one but two collections of which were reputedly in circulation during the sixth century. The first was assembled by Servius Tullius, and included norms from the times of Romulus and Numa Pompilius, while the second one, dating from the age of Tarquinius Superbus (or Tarquin the Proud, the last king, at the end of the sixth century), was attributed to a certain Sextus Papirius (perhaps a pontifex maximus), who is said to have collected all the laws from the royal age in a work titled *Ius Papirianum,* though the versions of Pomponius and Dionysius differ on a number of far from secondary points.[18]

In principle, we cannot rule out the existence of provisions relating to Etruscan royalty, nor can we exclude that they might immediately have been called *lex* (in this case, the Latin word would have been a translation of *thesmos* rather than of *nomos*). Ascertaining what they contained would be an arduous task, though—perhaps the structure of family ties (marriage, paternity), regulations governing funerals, the suppression of crime (parricide).[19]

But even if we give credence to this hypothesis, the idea of the collection and the complete edition must be a much later one, and only referable to the monarchic age by projecting backwards a much more recent work. Certainly, a collection of ancient *leges* must have been well known in the first century B.C., most probably dating from the earliest predecemviral republican age, perhaps even from the late monarchic period, identified as the *Ius Papirianum* (a definition that was perfectly plausible for that era). Perhaps already familiar to Cassius Hemina and Licinius Macer, it was commented upon during the Augustan age by the man of learning Granius Flaccus, and quite likely wound up in the hands of Massurius Sabinus, during the reign of Tiberius, and it is possible that it was consulted by Julius Paulus as late as the turn of the third century A.D.[20] Still, it must have been a text prepared no earlier than the third or the second century B.C., whose composition must be linked to the publication of the pontifical *Annals*—around the middle of the second century B.C.— and which also contained very early provisions, by this point customarily referred to as *leges*; their written form reached the publisher through a tradition that remains unknown to us, and was probably not unreliable, though modernized with respect to the originals, at least in terms of the language.[21]

It is equally hard to believe that these *leges* had been approved, at the time of their issuance, by the *comitia curiata,* as the historians of the Augustan era vainly insist. This is obviously yet another projection, which backdated to the monarchic period—even as far as Romulus!—the typically republican model of the relationship between the *lex* and assembly (centurial or tribunal). In reality, not only were the so-called *leges regiae* never approved by any assembly, neither were the Twelve Tables. At the very most, they may have been read aloud before the assembly so as to inform the community. The only conceivable relationship in the archaic age remains that between the *lex* and supreme political authority: the magistracy; the decemviri; and, in certain exceptional cases, the plebeian assembly, an expression of a power that was both subversive and, in its way, sovereign. Only later would this original link be transformed into the one—destined to enjoy very long-lived and partly ideological fortunes—between the people (in its comitial expression) and the *lex* (by this point, *lex publica,* that is, "of the people").[22]

3.

Behind the novelty of the Twelve Tables, clearly visible and unconcealed by tradition, lay plebeian pressure. The intent was clear: to decisively split the axis along which every form of regulation of the city's social existence had been constructed until then—from the *ritus* to the pontifices to *ius*. The aim was to replace the intrinsically aristocratic form of the *responsum,* inherited from the earliest gentilitial origins of the city, with—as in Greece—that of the *lex*, oriented toward *isonomia* if not fully toward democracy. With a set of rules established once and for all, stabilized and rendered knowable by means of writing. From now on it would be the city as a whole, through the text of its laws ("invented to speak to all men at all times in one and the same voice," as Cicero would later write, clearly grasping its isonomic value),[23] that would stand as guarantor of the behavior of its own citizens, no longer entrusting each and every precept to the manipulation of remote customs and the memory of an inaccessible circle of priests (so the city could be "endowed with laws," as Pomponius would write some six centuries later).[24] Between the community and its *mores*—and between social discipline and religious experience—there now loomed the secular shadow of a lawmaker accepted by the populace. The recourse to writing—the Twelve Tables were carved in wood or engraved in bronze—accentuated to an even greater degree the implications of the break: from a secret *ius* to an officially proclaimed *lex* (in accordance with one of the nuances of meaning of the word itself).[25] Throughout the fourth century B.C., a clear thread can be identified in Roman affairs between writing, social discipline, and politics, as had occurred in the Greek experience shortly previous to this: the written word as opposed to an exclusivist and arbitrary use of patrician orality; the pervasiveness of the legislator's authority as opposed to the oligarchic attempt to avoid the transparent regulation of a significant portion of the city's life.

It is hard to dispute that the idea of this major shift reached the plebs through Greek influences. Historians continue to discuss the reliability of reports that Rome sent out embassies on this occasion to Greece or Magna Graecia, as recalled by Livy and by Dionysius and, following in their footsteps, by Lucius Annaeus Florus, Pliny the Elder and Younger, Ammianus Marcellinus, Symmachus, Augustine, and Isidore of Seville, but unmentioned by Polybius, Cicero, and Diodorus (while Pomponius writes about assistance offered to the decemviral collegium by Hermodorus of Ephesus, a Greek exile, philosopher, and lawmaker who was a friend of Heraclitus).[26] In reality, though, pinning down this detail is of relatively little importance. Whether true or false, it has an unmistakable symbolic value in the memory of it preserved by tradition, and that is precisely how we should interpret it: as the factual transcription of an unquestionable cultural connection that linked the plebeian movement and its objectives to the legislative, isonomic, and, in some respects, openly democratic wave that swept through Greece and its colonies from the Aegean to southern Italy at the end of the sixth and the beginning of the fifth century. Where else could plebeian leaders have possibly derived the idea of a legislation that, at a single blow, and in just two years, would redefine, on foundations entirely extraneous to the history of Rome, the terms of civil coexistence in the city? And what can we reasonably imagine lay behind the plebeian extremism of the fifth century if not notions and programs arriving from that other far from distant world? It was a complex cluster of ideas and examples that helped to conceive a design to transform the newborn republic into something along the lines of a "radical democracy," constructed around the primacy of an assembly where the views of each individual carried equal weight (obviously providing the individual in question was a free male citizen, and the context was that of the *concilia* of the plebs, where in any case votes were cast by tribe)—the most advanced solution ever attempted in ancient societies, though it had been condemned as both dangerous and ill-considered by the dominant current of Greek political thought itself.[27]

Against such a background, what clearly emerges is the directly antipontifical character of the legislation of the decemviri. And it is highly singular that a substantial portion of modern historiography has obstinately refused to acknowledge the salient nature of this datum.[28] The fact that Roman tradition does not report it explicitly proves absolutely nothing. Indeed, it would have been surprising if it had. What we have described as the "republican canon" in fact tended to conceal this sort of rift, just as it hid, for instance, the Etruscan hegemony over Rome, which is no less certain a fact. The Twelve Tables had by this point become fully integrated into the channel of the *ius civile,* and it was possible to emphasize a continuist analysis of Roman legal and institutional history: a substantially apologetic and reconciliatory interpretation that has proved irresistibly attractive even to modern legal historiography, also little inclined to find at the origins of Roman law anything other than the uniform beginnings of a magnificent course of events, rather than the contrasts and alternatives indicative of a far more tortuous and problematic path.[29]

In addition to this, the Roman tradition itself was incapable of concealing the fact—illuminating in its own right—that pontifices were not part of the decemviral collegium, even though it was dominated by patricians—a decidedly strange exclusion, if we consider that the priests were the city's leading experts on the issues covered by the legislative intervention. But evidently the goal of the legislation was to reduce, if not completely eliminate, pontifical control over Roman life, at a time when all the institutional structures had been called into question, and the force of the plebeian demands was threatening to split the city in two. And it is evident that a project of this sort—supported both by the plebeian elite and by the segment of the patriciate which, for various reasons, favored a compromise—could not involve the direct participation of the pontifices. To think the opposite, to believe that the pontifical collegium could suddenly have generated a framework of ideas that was absolutely different from the ones it had hitherto produced and followed, and that an authentic alternative paradigm of sovereignty might have affirmed itself—writing, where oral tradition had previously prevailed; public proclamation, where secrecy had previously been the rule; certain and equal rules for one and all, where there had previously been case-by-case prescriptivity not subject to any control—is outside the bounds of any historic plausibility. The truth is that Rome was a divided city at the time—"two states had been created out of one" as Livy pointed out in a telling metaphor[30]—and in the harsh conflict two cultures were facing off, expressions of two contrasting ideas of the republic. The model of *ius* and that of *lex* were quite manifestly at opposite extremes.

Nor is this interpretation in any way hampered by the hard-to-contest fact that the collegium of the decemviri—at least in its original makeup, the one about which we know most—did not have any plebeian members.[31] This can be explained by the peculiar nature of the task assigned to the magistrates. The transcription into legislative form of the pontifical *ius* was too difficult an undertaking for anyone belonging to the plebs, presupposing as it did a sophisticated body of knowledge that until then had been the exclusive preserve of patrician families. The plebs simply lacked the cultural prerequisites to complete the task—until then the gentilial policy of exclusion had proved effective. It was inevitable that they should resort to their first alliances, turning to those sections of the patriciate willing to make a substantial concession—an isonomic legislation—but certainly not yet willing to sweep away the contents of the ancient *ius* from the city's mental horizons, nor to renounce all its privileges. This explains the persistence of discriminatory regulations, such as the prohibition of *connubium* (the possibility of marriage between patricians and plebeians), though this was lifted a short while later,[32] or servitude for debtors *(nexum),* which would not be abolished for another century or so.[33]

At first, the plebeian pressure seemed to be successful. The legislation was passed, and it was applied as the supreme regulation of civic life (there is some confusion over the enactment of the last two tables, but we can over-look this point).[34]

We have incomplete but not entirely vague information about the con-tent. The original of the tables was lost in the fire that devastated Rome in 390 B.C., in the wake of the invasion by the Gauls, and diffusion in the last centuries of the republic was based on the edition produced, at the turn of the third century B.C., by Sextus Aelius Paetus Catus in the *Tripertita* (none-theless, there can be no doubt that he had access to a faithful version: it was the one on display in the Forum that had been lost, not the copies preserved in the archives of the pontifices).[35] His work formed the basis for all the com-mentaries by successive jurists, from Labeo to Gaius; the latter was still work-ing on it in the heart of Hadrian's era, and he was not alone in doing so.[36]

Despite the fame and respect that the text enjoyed—Cicero recalls that in his day it was normal for boys to learn it by heart[37]—the literal meaning of many of the words found in it were unclear even to the late-republican anti-quarians and jurists, as we have mentioned, notwithstanding the moderniza-tions (more a question of spelling than vocabulary, and which certainly did not touch the normative content) that the original text underwent in the edi-tion produced by Sextus Aelius.

Stylistically, the prescriptions had the character of rhythmic prose (Cicero speaks of them as a *carmen),*[38] and although they were not in "meter" as such, the words were arranged in binary or ternary sequences of components that facilitated their recitation and memorization, and in some cases even made it easier to interpret them. They were relatively simple and generalized rules, in sharp and intentional contrast, we may assume, with the particularistic and point-like aspect of the precepts contained in the pontifical responses: a brief phrase, often in the form of a hypothetical premise introduced by an "if" *(si)*, in which an event would be described in a bare-bones typical configuration, followed, as if by inevitable consequence, by the rule itself, whose binding character was expressed through an imperative.[39]

The Twelve Tables were nothing like a "constitutional charter," and we are fairly certain that they did not specify the structure of the republic (functions of the assemblies, tasks of the magistracies, and so forth). A passage from Livy gives us a glimpse, presenting them as "the fountain-head of all public and private law,"[40] but we must be able to grasp the emphasis of the statement—once again in line with the "republican canon"—without expecting to assign a literal meaning; nor, most importantly, should we take the reference to "public law" in the modern sense of the expression: here *ius publicum* probably meant merely *ius* based on *leges publicae,* to which the historian had just in fact made reference, also in the same context.[41]

It is, however, possible that in the Twelve Tables there were references—and not necessarily chance ones—to rules that limited the powers of the city's political rulers: for instance, the principle that no citizen could be sentenced to death without a trial in the presence of the centurial assembly ("de capite civis nisi per maximum comitiatum ne ferunt"),[42] or the provision for an appeal to the populace *(provocatio)* against an order from a magistrate who had exercised his authority *(imperium)* in an arbitrary or abusive manner.

But the purpose of the legislation was not to define these aspects, the profile of which had evidently been consigned to the outcome of the clash then under way, but instead to cover the ground that until that point had been the exclusive domain of the pontifical collegium, namely the field of family and property relations, in order to regulate potential conflicts of interest among citizens. It interfered, therefore, in a programmatic manner with the sphere of *ius*—with the discipline of the "private" fabric of the community, where the prerequisites of citizenship were constructed—by removing its anchorage to the *responsa.* Rather than introducing substantial new developments with respect to the preceding prescriptions—and not even in a way that was particularly favorable to the plebs: this was no emancipatory legislation—the Twelve Tables served to shift the axis of reference from one power to another: from the pontifices to the lawmakers. From this time on, the priests themselves would be obliged to respect the laws in formulating their *responsa.* This is the meaning of Livy's observation concerning the "equality of *ius* for all, both high and low" as the primary duty of the decemviri,[43] as well as of Dionysius' remark—quoted later by Pomponius in reference to Appius Claudius—concerning the "gathering and transcribing," by magistrates, of precepts predating the legislation.[44] Evidently it was not a matter of intervening on their content, changing, that is, the relationship between rules and *mos* in order to modify the intrinsic rationality of the prescriptions, but rather a case of ensuring they were not pronounced in a form that seemed to bear, intrinsically inscribed within its very structure, the germ of inequality and abuse.

4.

It is not even possible to reconstruct the order of the topics dealt with in the different tables with any precision or certainty. The best guide to some idea of the sequence continues to be Gaius' six-book commentary (perhaps one for every two tables), some thirty fragments of which survive in the *Digesta* (too little is known about Labeo's commentary to be able to deduce anything substantive).[45] But one point remains unquestionable: the text brought together for the first time many of the words *(verba)* theretofore prescribed by the priests for performing rituals essential to relations between citizens. The prerogatives of the *paterfamilias* were determined in specific situations (Dionysius offers a reliable list: the head of the family could imprison his children, beat them, force them to work on his property, sell them, or kill them),[46] reaffirming the authoritative character of the archaic family, a Roman peculiarity that would continue to attract the attention of jurists many centuries later. But it was also established that if the father abused his power of temporary sale, after the third mancipation the son would become free ("si pater | filium || ter | uenum du[uit] || filius | a patre || liber | esto").[47] The text established the rules of succession in the event of the *pater* dying intestate: "if [someone] dies without having made a will and has no *sui heredes* [that is, people, subject to his *patria potestas,* as it would later be called], the closest relative on the male side [*adgnatus proximus*] will have his family [also in the sense of his property]. If there is no *adgnatus proximus,* the members of the same *gens* will have his family."[48]

The Twelve Tables regulated the carrying out of solemn acts linked to the relationships of exchange and reciprocity among the family groups, accomplished through the ritual of the bronze and the scales: *mancipium* (mancipation) and *nexum* (a ceremony through which a *pater* submitted himself or another subject who was in his power—*manus*—to the power of another *pater*): "whenever a solemn act of submission or of passage of the *manus* takes place, as the tongue declared, so it will be ius."[49] Within the context of the ritual staging was a reiteration of the value, which we would now describe as performative, of words, whose sound was still charged with magical evocations. This was true for another solemn act as well, to which the Twelve Tables must have made reference, the *sponsio*: a contextual exchange of formulaic questions and answers between creditor and debtor that constituted a bond for the one making the promise.[50]

Also covered were cases involving the ownership of estates and buildings: boundaries; damage from rainwater;[51] the right of passage through farmland belonging to others. Other norms—these may have been plebeian in inspiration—regulated the details of the performance of funeral ceremonies, limiting the display of luxurious costumes and furnishings: there could be no more than ten tibia players; it was forbidden to pour a great deal of wine into the grave, or to cover the corpse with long wreaths.[52] Likewise, in the Greece of the fifth century, the disciplining of funerals was located at a crucial intersection between aristocratic traditions and the new democracy—there is more than one reference to this in *Antigone*.[53] An identical plebeian orientation can be glimpsed in the provision allowing anyone to intervene in the executive procedure against a proletarian-debtor (*proletarius,* probably by metathesis from *protelarius,* the "migrant," in opposition to the *adsiduus,* the "resident-owner"),[54] to halt the action of the creditor and oblige him to prove that his demands were well founded, or in the detailed regulations governing the operations permitted to creditors with respect to a defaulting debtor (which could extend to the dismemberment of the debtor's body, ritually ripped to shreds and shared out among the creditors—*partis secanto*).[55]

A significant amount of space was devoted to what successive jurists would call the punishment of crimes and murders. There emerged a delicate moment of transition from private vendetta to the regime of the *poena* (a very ancient word, whose original meaning connects it to the "payment of the blood price"):[56] it was in turn still suspended between the sanction for religious transgression—to strike out, that is, at an act that might have broken the harmony between the city and its deities (and the person found responsible thus became *sacer,* one who could be killed by anyone)—and a now-secular form of repression, inflicted by the collectivity on anyone disturbing the social order. While recourse to vendetta still continued to be envisioned—"if a lesion was caused, and there was no agreement, then the *lex talionis* will come into effect"[57]—the content of the regulation, notable for its emphasis upon the possibility of a nonritual reconciliation among the parties ("ni cum eo pacit"),[58] was a deferment, pure and simple, to the naked violence of life, barely mitigated by the requirement of a certain degree of proportionality: we are here, as it were, close to the degree zero of prescriptivity.

We also know that punishment was meted out not only to the murderer *(parricidas)*[59] and the traitor to his own community *(perduellio),*[60] both of whom were sentenced to death, but also to false witnesses (hurled from the Tarpeian Rock)[61] or uncooperative witnesses (with a ritual endowed with a magical character, the *obvagulatio*);[62] to those who deliberately set fire to a house or to sheaves of grain that might be close to a house (bound, whipped, and burned at the stake);[63] to those who performed magic against the crops of others, either to destroy them or to lure them into their own fields (in either case, the penalty was death);[64] to those who grazed their own livestock by night on fields belonging to others (sacrificed to Ceres, if pubescent; otherwise, whipped and sentenced to a fine of double the damage done);[65] to those who threatened with magical incantations ("malum carmen incantassit") the life or the health of others (once again, the sentence was death).[66] As for theft, the victim could kill the thief, if he caught him red-handed by night ("if he committed theft by night, if he murdered, he will be struck down according to *ius*").[67] Otherwise, there were various possibilities, which set limits upon the reaction of the victim of the theft, up to and including the hypothesis of an agreement between the thief and his victim, as we learn reliably from Ulpian, who perhaps followed Labeo.[68]

Finally, we are certain that the Tables—along with the earliest forms of trial (which we would call penal) to be held in the presence of the assembly (mentioned earlier with reference to crimes that entailed the death of the guilty party: situations, so to speak, not subject to *ius,* but consigned to the realm of politics and its rules)[69]—also regulated what we might define as a civil procedure, intended to resolve property disagreements between citizens. This would later be called by jurists *per legis actionem* or simply (and probably in an earlier era) *lege agere:* expressions in which *agere* and *actio* indicated the "going to judgment" of someone who believed that he had been harmed (later, in technical language, *actio*—"action" or "suit"—would identify the right to proceed to the presence of a magistrate in order to ensure that one's claims were respected, and *actor*—like the English "actor"—whoever brought a lawsuit), while *lege* or *legis* referred in fact to the Twelve Tables, which had regulated that mechanism. [70]

It is all too easy to imagine that in this case as well the legislators chose not to innovate, and instead limited themselves to setting down in the written text a procedure that was at least in part already in existence. It is harder to establish how far back it dated: perhaps all the way to the Etruscan monarchy, which developed an interventionist royalty and may have assigned to the *rex* on a regular basis the task of resolving certain types of disagreements, relating, for instance to the power *(manus)* over a particularly valuable good (a plot of land, a domestic animal, a very rare slave), or the existence of a relationship of personal submission *(nexum)*. This would thus have existed alongside the oracular work of the pontifices to prevent an indiscriminate recourse to self-protection from undermining the ties of the community. We have seen, after all, that it was precisely around the need to ward off violence and instability that the entire first mental horizon of the city was probably constructed.[71]

As far as we know, thanks especially to the account by Gaius,[72] who, as the author of a commentary on the Twelve Tables, was certainly well informed, there emerged in these procedures the same world, hovering between religiosity, magic, and an early secular prescriptivity, that we saw as a dominant element in the composition of all the decemviral legislation. Its purpose was to replace the physical clash between contending parties with a ritual, defused and symbolic staging of it.

The oldest such form—which served as a model with respect to those introduced by the Twelve Tables, or added with subsequent laws[73]—would be called "by consecration" (*agere sacramento,* or *legis actio sacramenti,* known to us in two versions, according to whether the dispute was over the ownership of property or the existence of a debt);[74] the others are known to us as "by request of judge or arbiter," "by imposition of the hand," "by taking of a security," and "by injunction."[75]

Everything took place in two well-defined contexts. In the first, which the jurists would call *in iure,* "within *ius,*" involving the presence of a magistrate of the republic endowed with *imperium* (originally, perhaps, the presence of the *rex* himself; from the fourth century onward, certainly the presence of a praetor), the litigants stylized their behavior and words (*certa verba*, "words established once and for all") in accordance with the ritual prescriptions. One wrong word or gesture would break the (still) magic circle of *ius* and automatically lead to the losing of the case; according to one early *responsum*, it was sufficient to say "vines" instead of "trees," and all would be lost.[76] The opposing claims were reduced to rigidly preestablished formulas, to be staged before the attentive eye of the magistrate, who presided over the ceremony. In the procedure "by consecration" (*sacramentum*), the parties challenged each other to a sort of bet, which would oblige the losing party to pay a heavy restitution to the community. Once this ritual had been completed, the disagreement no longer existed, except in the context of its symbolic transfiguration: the two quarreling parties, with all their reasons and all their force, both social and physical, had now been transformed into actors performing a ritual, in which each played symmetrically opposing roles. The possibility of violence had thus once again been warded off and kept safely outside of the community.

In the second context, described by the jurists as *apud iudicem*, "in the presence of a judge," the magistrate (or the king) had vanished: there were no longer ceremonies to be celebrated or supervised. Instead there entered onto the stage a citizen serving as judge and arbiter (an influential man, we may suppose, though in no way involved in declaring *ius*). It was his responsibility to determine who was in the right and who was in the wrong. But his investigation into the actual circumstances that had led to the dispute was drastically circumscribed: he could only establish whether the actual letter of the words spoken by the rival parties in the presence of the magistrate (or king) corresponded to a verifiable state of affairs. Whoever departed from it lost.

These few elements already suffice to embody an entire world. Reflected in the Twelve Tables is the image of a harsh peasant society, controlled by the closed ranks of an aristocracy of rigorously patrilinear and patriarchal lineage, undergoing a process of transition from a community still dominated by clan ties toward a more specifically political structure organized around a series of core family groups constituting a multitude of economic cells that were by and large self-sustaining—for the most part, agriculture, but also some primitive manufacturing—though already involved to some extent in mechanisms of trade.[77] Deep in the minds of its inhabitants was a dark foundation of terror and nighttime visions (the punishments prescribed by the Twelve Tables were often harsher if the crimes were committed in the dark), nourished equally by vivid memories of violence, spell-casting, and blood, and by an objectively difficult present always capable of threatening the very existence of the city. An omnivorous body of ritual—perhaps originally constructed around a primary and founding practice of sacrifice, managed by a narrow group of wise priests—attempted to discharge these tensions in the context of a contractualized religiosity, prescriptive and ordering, which chopped up life, so as to exorcise its many perils, into a myriad of acts behind each of which lay concealed a supernatural power that needed to be appeased with an appropriate rite: an order that soon shifted from the plane of relations with the gods to the plane of relations among human beings. When plebeians later tried to replace the model of *ius* with the model of the *lex,* it was the prescriptive form of the normative process that changed, not its contents, much less its symbolic backdrops: and that is why the memory of the new aristocracy—what we have described as the "republican canon"—by handing down to us substantial fragments of that ancient legislative monument, allows us once again to sketch out, through those relics, a sort of original cultural archeology of the city and its earliest normative fabric.

Viewed not necessarily through modern eyes, but even just those accustomed to the mature Roman law of the late-republican era or of the principate, the Twelve Tables appear to be a rough and ready and loose-knit assemblage, an expression of an ancient archaism (and that is precisely how they were judged even by the troubled intellectuals of Hadrian's time, who looked back on them with chilly disengagement):[78] we are as far as can be imagined from any idea of codification that is not only not modern, but not even typical of late antiquity. And yet the Twelve Tables contributed decisively to the crystallization of the first civil statute of Roman society, unequaled and unrivaled in the other experiences of antiquity. They managed to impress—albeit provisionally—the magnetic force of the isonomic law upon a regulation that was by tradition distinct from royalty and later from politics, but without having the time to eliminate its specific aspects, allusive to the original condition of heads of family as the protagonists of a direct relationship, mediated only by the wisdom of the priests, with the deities and with their order. And it is for this reason that the generative nucleus of Western law, even though it may have passed through the filter of the lawgiver, has continued to bear engraved upon it a dual and connected determination: an irreducible sapiential presence, and the reference to a social material and to a fabric of egalitarian rules with an unmistakable and already clearly defined "private" aspect.

8

The *Logos* of the Republic

I.

If the plebeian design really had prevailed, the ensuing sea change would have had incalculable consequences. The whole history of Rome would have been different, and certainly so too would its legal history. The city would have acquired the features of a democratic *polis*, and the definitive shift of the production of *ius* from the pontifices to the realm of legislation (first decemviral and then completely comitial) would have ultimately triggered a decisive transformation in the forms of sovereignty. Of course, we cannot say what exactly would have happened at this juncture, but probably the disciplining of relations among the *patres* would have lost its sapiential character and been handed over—as in the Greek cities—to the mechanisms of politics and of the people's juries, swayed by oratorical practices. We might have had, as in Athens, rhetoric in the place of jurisprudence.

But none of this happened. In order to explain the course of events, we should think not so much of the patrician reaction (or at least of that portion of the patriciate that was opposed to the initiative of the decemvirate), felt almost immediately, perhaps as early as 449,[1] as of reasons that can be described as cultural, or rather as belonging to the social history of ideas.

The Twelve Tables were a complex document for the Rome of that period. Unlike the legislative corpuses of the Greek cities, they were the expression of a stratified and already highly elaborated knowledge. They set forth, often in an elliptical fashion, general hypotheses (this trait of generality was a fixed point in the isonomic program, in contrast with the form of the response: *privilegia ne inroganto*—"no law of personal exception shall be proposed," ordered one of their prescriptions,[2] and "general" would remain the adjective assigned to *lex* in a celebrated definition from the Augustan age).[3] In order to be applied effectively to real situations, the laws had to be read, understood, and interpreted. But the secular (or in any case nonpontifical) culture of the city—to say nothing of the strictly plebeian one—was not capable of the intellectual effort required for these operations: that is, to transform a success of principle into an effective turning point in the life of the community. This shortcoming was decisive, and it alone explains what then happened.

Unanimity of tradition confirms that the priests immediately returned to the center of the stage. Their intervention proved indispensable in ensuring the very survival of the legislation. It was only through their pronouncements that the Twelve Tables succeeded in performing the disciplinary function for which they had been passed. The writing revealed the full extent of its ambiguity: although it brought with it both equality and certainty, it also contained a complexity of expression that always had to be clarified, evaluated, and transposed from the generality of the prescriptions to the concrete nature of the case at hand, of the situation to be regulated.

In a very brief time, the pontifices thus became the sole guardians of a text that they had not helped to create, and the introduction of which they had in all likelihood viewed with no great favor.

On this point as well, the Roman memory is in no doubt: "for many centuries the civil law was [...] known only to the Pontiffs," wrote Valerius Maximus;[4] and Livy spoke of a *ius* "in penetralibus pontificum"—"among the secrets of the pontifices";[5] to say nothing of the others, from Cicero[6] to Pomponius.[7] The Twelve Tables therefore soon ceased to enjoy any autonomous existence. Through their exegetic labors, expressed once again in the customary form of the *responsa,* the priests quickly took complete control of *ius,* enveloping it within the explicatory and adaptive web of their pronouncements. The text was still afforded the highest respect, and its dictates surrounded by veneration. But the more this happened, the more the novelty it represented was substantially absorbed, sterilized, and integrated into the context of pontifical practice. It was the priests who invented a new form of will, alternative to and more advantageous than the one issued before the *curiae,* utilizing in a creative way the age-old ritual of the bronze and the scales.[8] They were the ones who transformed the provision in the Twelve Tables that prevented the parent from replicating the sale of offspring into bondage (mention has already been made of this) into the model of an act of emancipation, ensuring definitive freedom from the *manus* of the father (and the same was true of adoption). And the priests were also responsible for disciplining the essential modes of practice of family cults.[9] Between the *lex* and *responsum* it was the latter that once again prevailed in real terms as the generative element of *ius.* And so it would be for centuries.

The rapid thwarting of the autonomous power of the laws, totally caught up in the force field exerted by the hermeneutic techniques of the pontifices, was accompanied by the precocious and very clear definition of the most important feature of what the Roman legal world was about to become, and one of the essential traits of the whole Roman experience: the supremacy of the knowledge of experts over the norms passed by the city's political institutions. In this way a strong correspondence was established: on the one hand the almost exclusive concentration of *ius* around the "private" structure of community life, reaffirming the original connection between the disciplining of family and property and of patriarchal sovereignty; and on the other hand, the increasing identification of *ius* with a set of practices removed from the direct domain of the political activity of assemblies, magistrates, or the senate.

The oligarchic face of Roman society was thus restored, even though it was less narrowly patrician in composition. Hopes of establishing a "plebeian democracy" faded as the elites of groups that had originally been excluded from the patriciate system were gradually integrated into it, giving rise to the new nobility that from then on would lead the republic.

Over the fourth century, in the wake of the compromise enabling the plebeians to participate in the government of the community but definitively sanctioned the oligarchic form of the political order (what Polybius would judge to be an extraordinary dovetailing of forces, which, in his view, had been set at odds rather than brought together in Greek history),[10] the Roman experience of *ius* gradually acquired the characteristics that would eventually lead to what we have called "jurisprudential law": built, that is, around the particular knowledge of men to whom society, under the leadership of the aristocracy, had entrusted the task of dictating the rules of coexistence among citizens, and not around the form of a "general" law approved by the assembly or imposed by a tyrant, as prescribed by the most important constitutional models of the Greek experience. It was a path that contained the signs of a conflict and of an alternative, and of a consciously oligarchic and antidemocratic choice.

With an astonishing precocity, this page of Roman archaicity offers an early anticipation—sketchy but quite distinct—of a guiding motif, almost a common thread, of the entire development of law in the West: the polarity between a model based on laws (statutes) and one grounded in custom (cases), shaped and guided by jurists (and tribunals). This diversity, as we have seen, originally entailed a contrast between two different hypotheses of sovereignty, one based on the supremacy of politics and its institutions, the other on the primacy of a class of experts and specialists, who would later, in the modern world, be professors, notaries, judges, and lawyers. This dualism would reemerge on various occasions in Europe in the late Middle Ages and the Renaissance, and in France it would accompany the formation of the nation-state. In a memorable passage, singularly overlooked by historians, Hegel would revive it in the heart of modernity, and in the midst of a radical polemic:

> The particular form of bad conscience which betrays itself in the vainglorious eloquence of this superficial philosophy may be remarked on here; for in the first place, it is precisely where it is at its *most spiritless* that it has most to say about *spirit*, where its talk is driest and most lifeless that it is freest with the words "life" and "enliven," and where it shows the utmost selfishness of empty arrogance that it most often refers to the "people." But the distinctive mark which it carries on its brow is its hatred of statutory law. That law and ethics, and the actual world of law and the ethi-

cal, are grasped by means of *thought* and give themselves the form of rationality—namely universality and determinacy—by means of thought, all this, *the statutory law,* is what that feeling which reserves the faculty to do as it pleases, that conscience which identifies law with subjective conviction, justifiably regards as the main enemy. The form of law seen as *duty* and statutory *law* is felt by it to be a *dead, cold letter* and a *shackle;* for it does not recognize itself in statutory law, and thereby does not recognize its own freedom in it, because statutory law is the reason of the thing [*Sache*] and reason does not allow feeling to warm itself in the glow of its own particularity [*Partikularitat*]. Statutory law is therefore . . . the chief shibboleth by which the false brethren and friends of the so-called "people" give themselves away.[11]

Hegel was writing in 1821, and although he does not name him explicitly, the target of these scathing observations is the work of Savigny and of his "Historical School," a firm advocate of a paradigm of jurisprudential law for Germany and opposed to the intrusion of the legislations that continued to spread across Europe, driven by the winds of revolution and the Napoleonic codification, despite the restoration in continental Europe.

According to Hegel, there is no correspondence in Savigny between ideas and words, but a ruinous dissonance. Three key terms of the program of the Historic School, steeped in the Romantic idiom—"life," "spirit," and "people" —are isolated as signs of this disquieting subversion. When they are used in that line of thought, says Hegel, we should understand the meaning to be their opposite: the reversal reveals confusion and deceit, ethical and logical disorder. The crucial point, however, is the idea of statutory law. Savigny and his followers, in their hostility to any possible notion of codification, interpret that form solely as a "shackle," as an alien and external power, to which they counterpose the "feeling which reserves the faculty to do as it pleases," identifying law only with "subjective conviction" (of the class of jurists). The result is a fracture without any scope for mediation. At the opposite extreme, it is only in statutory law, according to Hegel, that law and reason can be made to coincide, because it alone embodies at once "universality" and "determinacy." Once the mask has fallen, it is finally possible to distinguish "the false brethren and friends of the so-called 'people'": in the overwhelming force of the attack, the divergence reveals itself to be not merely doctrinal but also political. There resurface, irreconcilable, precisely as we first saw them, the two models of sovereignty. The sarcasm of that "so-called" is merciless. A truly adequate relationship between general will and science, and between reason and law, cannot be forged, in Hegel's view, by the partial and subjective elaboration of the jurists. They do not reflect the spirit of the people, as Savigny tries to claim; instead they defend a false version, which bends it to the particular intellectual traditions of a class clinging to its privileges. Authentic universality can be found only in the form of a general statutory law (and of the state that presupposes it, at least in the modern world).[12]

Hegel's interpretation undoubtedly distorted Savigny's position,[13] but even if we consider it cautiously, the basic terms of the contrast continue to direct us back to the theme that had already been discovered in archaic Rome —now illuminated by the light of a powerful reflection, at an important juncture of European history and in a surprising interplay of reflected images between the ancient and the modern.

We must nonetheless refrain from the temptation to read this sort of symmetry as a kind of constant or invariance that, irrespective of the times and circumstances, ends up becoming established between statutory law and democratic construction on the one hand (when the law is connected with the direct expression of the "universal" will and not of the monarch's autocracy), and jurisprudential law and oligarchic closure on the other. In England, a customary law directed by jurists and the courts would give rise to a network of civil liberties unrivaled anywhere in Europe; and later, in America (albeit in a mixed model, with an accentuated presence of legislation), it would accompany the first example of mass democracy in history.

Nor can we forget that the success of one paradigm over another would have incomparably different consequences in antiquity and in the modern world. While in antiquity the unlimited establishment of statutory law would prevent (as was the case in Greece), wherever it took root, the birth of an autonomous juridical function and an authentic legal science, this would never happen in modern Europe, where the medieval and Renaissance reelaboration of the Roman legacy had cultural and social outcomes (the formation of professional classes, intellectual and institutional traditions, the organization of studies) of such importance that an eventuality of this kind was impossible.

We need to look in another direction if we want to find the key to the correspondence.

In modern experience the legislative model would never monopolize the path to democracy—as undoubtedly happened in antiquity—but instead has tended to establish itself in relation to the political dismantling of "ancien régime" structures or in any case of legal and social ties inherited from a more or less remote past (which is why it was praised by Hegel): both when the operation was carried out by triumphant bourgeois revolutions, in situations where the cultural and political experience of a relationship between revolution and the people had taken root, as in France; and when the battle against the particularistic relics of bygone eras was waged only by state structures that took form belatedly and with difficulty, with a more or less open authoritarianism—as in Germany and Italy at the turn of the twentieth century. In short, in its every manifestation, whether ancient or modern, it appeared as the product of the subjective prevalence of political command and its project, which attempted to halt the reproduction within already established forms of existing social and power relations.

In contrast, the jurisprudential, customary model would accompany historical conditions marked by the establishment of the primacy of social continuity, and of the hegemonies produced along with it, over the influence of politics and its interventions; and it would always develop in situations of relative, long-term stability rather than of conflict and rupture.

If we enter into this order of ideas, we can see where the astonishingly anticipatory nature of the Roman experience revealed its exemplarity—what we might call an original or genealogical paradigmicity—even though, of course, the scenario of antiquity—social subjects, patterns of ideas and mentality, political and economic forces—is incommensurable with any modern context. The scheme that first made its appearance there, and which would never be eradicated, was something truly ground-breaking. It links the establishment of regulations arising from the knowledge of classes or groups (represented first by a circle of priests, and later by real jurists) with the actuality of a cultural and social practice that we could describe as the reduction of politics and its command, whatever form it might take, in the face of the pressures and needs of bare life and its powerful impulses; while it connects the domain of statutory law to the inverse need, which can be defined as the hypertrophy of political rule, in the face of social formations (or a part thereof) that required rules and directives to cling on to in order to break with the past and acquire a new substance.

In the ancient world, the choice between the two models determined, in the contexts of Rome and Greece, the birth or the absence of law as an independent cultural and social function. In modernity—with the now-guaranteed autonomous presence of a legal form—it would entail consequences that were in appearance less radical, but in effect, from the point of view of the history of legal systems and institutions, no less substantial in scope.[14]

2.

Between the end of the fourth and the beginning of the third century B.C., the image of the wise priest as a protagonist in the production of *ius* began to fade, if not actually to vanish, and its place was taken by that of the wise noble (Roman tradition used the term *nobilitas*—nobility—for the new social bloc, which we can consider to have been formed by around the middle of the fourth century, when the most important plebeian families were regularly admitted to the consulship, and whose institutional organ was the senate). Giving *responsa* began to be viewed as an aristocratic prerogative, linked to the primacy of the new ruling groups, and no longer directly and exclusively related to religious practice: an attitude that was now an integral part of the predominance of an oligarchy. The authoritativeness of the response was no longer rooted in religion and sacrality. It began to be based on a cluster of notions and cognitive habits that by the end of the fourth century must already have appeared to be almost entirely "civil" (though still broadly identified with the pontifical tradition), but not for that reason any less austere and respectable in the eyes of citizens: its mastery was the exclusive preserve of influential men involved in governing the republic, though associated less and less with sacerdotal functions. The pontifices who continued to give responses must also have had to take account of the parameters of this new rationality, which required behavior different from that of an earlier time, and was poorly served by the style of the old oracularity shrouded in the sacred and the magical.

The new tie between legal knowledge and political hegemony, entirely contained within the history of the leading families of the republican *nobilitas*, was, however, very different in appearance to the archaic integration still influenced by the city's early religiosity. They were now two distinct, non-overlapping spheres, albeit expressions of the same supremacy and even though knowledge of *ius* continued to be viewed exclusively as a nonisolable aspect of a fundamentally unitary aristocratic education, which encompassed, on the same plane, other disciplines and other duties: from oratory to the military arts, political experience, religious wisdom, and the physical aptitude for combat. But the knowledge of *ius* was already associated with experts, *prudentes* for whom wisdom in their chosen field and the activity of giving responses could become an authentic "civil militia," as Cicero would later write;[15] and legal practice, along with nobility of blood (being born into a senatorial family) and a military career, would always remain the best way to obtain a consulship.

The shift from religion toward politics of the locus of power enveloping *ius* would ultimately modify its constituent features. But more time would elapse before it became possible to discern any significant mutation. Evidently, there were hermeneutic refinements and accumulations of new experiences, but no precocious changes in the fundamental cognitive parameters. In the middle of the third century, we are still in the presence of an almost exclusively oral tradition, deeply rooted in the cultural and social specificities of the city's very early history: a wisdom of words and signs, which tended to remain within the bounds of formulaic modules, and to preserve substantially archaic schemes in interpreting *mores* and *leges* to obtain appropriate rules for the cases that citizens submitted to their experts.

The aristocratic orality continued to bear the hallmark of the old pontifical secrecy. But it was a contested orality. It would perhaps be rash, in the context of the republican institutional systems and the political struggle taking place within them—in which it is difficult to identify any authentically popular pressures—to use the adjective "democratic" to describe those orientations. But in any case it is reasonable to suppose that the presence of writing, wherever it is possible to ascertain its existence up to the middle of the second century, always betrayed an intent to diffuse legal knowledge outside the circle of the aristocracy, or in any case an impulse toward a less rigorously exclusive understanding of it.

The nature of the alternative explains the structure of the first two works on *ius* about which we still have any reliable accounts; they were composed at the turn of the third century, and their construction appears to be linked to contingent problems of political struggle. The architecture of these isolated texts—little islands of writing still lost in an ocean of orality—immediately betray their essential function: to divulge, or, one might even say, to reveal or reappropriate norms and formulas that the renewed supremacy of the pontifices had placed out of the community's view; and not works designed to explore or develop the field of knowledge to which they belonged. The written word was not intended or was not yet able to break the oral tradition as an intrinsic and constituent characteristic of *ius*. The aim was only to undermine, temporarily, and within clearly delimited contexts, its political purpose and objective.

We can be certain that what ultimately became Roman legal literature began with *De usurpationibus,* by Appius Claudius Caecus, a member of the same Claudian *gens* to which the chief of the legislators of the Twelve Tables had belonged, censor in 312 B.C., consul in 307 and in 296, and responsible for building the road that bore his name; a figure whom it is difficult to pin down, and perhaps the very first person to write in prose in Latin.[16]

Nothing of his text has survived, and it probably no longer figured among the most significant interests, both antiquarian and legal, of intellectuals in the late-republican period: certainly, it was no longer possible to consult it as early as the second century A.D.[17]

It is quite likely that it was a collection of trial formulas taken from the pontifical repertoires: a sequence of abbreviations and formulaic clauses relating to the *lege agere*—on which we know Appius must have worked—that had until then been the exclusive domain of the pontifical collegium.[18]

According to an ancient story, also mentioned by Cicero and by Pomponius, one of Appius' scribes, Gnaeus Flavius, the son of a freedman, after Appius himself "had written out these actions-at-law," stole the text and "passed it over to the people"; its subsequent circulation gave rise to the so-called *ius Flavianum.*[19] But it is also conceivable that the text that wound up in the hands of the "people" was nothing other than a copy of *De usurpationibus,* and that therefore the *ius Flavianum* should be identified with the contents of the work by Appius. There remains the difficulty of the title. That, too, however, can be overcome by giving *usurpatio* the meaning of *frequens usus*—"frequent use," referring to the *certa verba* of the actions—or else by attributing to it the meaning of "abuse" (actions to obtain a judgment against the abuses perpetrated by others): both of which would be perfectly compatible with the activities of the censor.[20]

It is also quite likely that the idea of the theft by Gnaeus Flavius was invented by a tradition that was at once pro-Claudian and close to the *nobilitas*—still in line with what we are describing as the "republican canon," the goal of which was to soften the antipontifical (and antiaristocratic) connotations of Appius' initiative, and that it is therefore necessary to consider it as unreliable. It is better to suppose that the content of *De usurpationibus* was not made public through the betrayal of a scribe, but was written with the intention of placing it before other eyes than those in the pontifical collegium: and that Gnaeus Flavius should merely be considered the instrument of a strategy decided upon entirely by the censor himself.

It would also have been an understandable decision in the context of the tumultuous Roman political scene at the end of the fourth century.[21] The line of the patrician-plebeian compromise, although it had already attained substantive objectives (first and foremost, the admission of plebeians to the consulship, as from 367 B.C., with the passing of the Licinian-Sextian laws), was anything but uncontested. And perhaps the most significant alternative, in those years, was represented precisely by the political views of Appius, which the republican tradition described in apparently contradictory terms, because it was difficult to fit them into its narrative canon.[22] In his thinking there was some kind of a return to the plan for "plebeian democracy" that had been confounded by the substantial failure of the paradigm of sovereignty proposed by the Twelve Tables. The project could now also count on the support of the urban plebeians—the *turba* or *factio forensis* mentioned by Livy in connection with Gnaeus Flavius[23]—and relied on the new mercantile and pro-expansionist classes as well: the "knights" (the *equites*), as they would thereafter be described in the nomenclature of the Roman orders, which distinguished them rigidly from the nobility.[24] At the center of this program there was once again the hypothesis of an assembly-based supremacy of the plebs through the councils, appropriately guided by the charismatic, if not actually "tyrannical," presence of prestigious figures—such as Appius Clau-dius himself—who had fled, as it were, both from the extremist patrician camp and from those favorable to the compromise with the plebeian elites.

Once again, this radically antioligarchic solution would come to nothing. But its presence alone can explain the twofold battle of Appius, who was ob-stinately engaged on what appear to be opposing fronts: on the one hand, with the publication of the *De usurpationibus,* against pontifical arrogance; but on another front, he was also against admitting plebeians into the colle-gium of priests, which he must (rightly) have seen as the completion of the oligarchic and antipopular design, and of the welding together of the patrici-ate and the plebeian elites.

Among the groups most hostile to the plans of Appius were the Ogul-nii—an important plebeian family originally from Chiusi and of distant Etrus-can descent, animated by Greek ideas, and on this occasion allied with the *gens* Fabia, one of the most prestigious of the patriciate.[25] And it was in fact an Ogulnian, Gnaeus Ogulnius, tribune of the plebs for 300 B.C., who ar-ranged for the passage in that year of a plebiscite granting plebeians access to the pontificate:[26] the measure, despite its apparently antipatrician character, would wind up reinforcing the patrician-plebeian alliance, further cementing the interests of the new oligarchy.

It was the alternative design to the one which had succeeded in establish-ing the legislation of the Twelve Tables that proved definitively victorious: not to introduce a different model of sovereignty—based on councils and plebiscites—in place of the patrician one, but rather to integrate itself within it, fully sharing its oligarchic logic, even if mitigated by reference to a broader social base.

The writing of *ius*—linked to a political approach that had been defeated a second time—was once again ushered offstage, and so it remained for the rest of the third century. The pontifical reaction would in short order nullify all of Appius' efforts, as had already happened with the Twelve Tables.

> A certain clerk, Gnaeus Flavius, was found who . . . published the calendar enabling the people to learn the court days, and plucked the plumage of their wisdom from the canny jurisconsults them-selves. And so these men, enraged because they were afraid that legal action could be conducted without their assistance, once the

scheme of days was published and made a matter of common knowledge, invented certain legal formulae that they might still have a part in every case.[27]

This is Cicero speaking here, in the *Pro Murena,* in a context in which, for reasons linked to the rhetorical occasion, he was attempting to speak as badly as he could of the jurists. But this does not make his testimony—which is echoed elsewhere, in the *De oratore,* in *De republica,* and in a letter to Atticus[28]—of any less value: in it, we find again, quite clearly, the now-familiar contrast between an oral, secret form of knowledge *(sapientia)* and revelatory writing. It was not the priests who were called directly into question, but rather, in more general terms, the "jurisconsults" because Cicero was well aware that at the end of the fourth and the beginning of the third century the pontifical collegium no longer monopolized the knowledge of *ius;* but this change had not yet undercut its exclusive and secret character.

And yet the entry of the plebs into the pontifical circle paved the way for a turning point. What's more, the city itself was changing, emerging definitively from its archaism. The middle years of the third century, during which the first clash with Carthage took place, in connection with the resumption of a powerful expansionist thrust northward, as well as toward the Greek-colonized south of Italy, saw the delineation of a set of elements that would soon lead to the creation of a wholly new context. The conquests "enriched" the republic for the first time: Quintus Fabius Pictor's observation referred to the consequences of the Roman occupation of Sabina, beginning in 290, but we can take it as indicative of a more general tendency in that period.[29] And the military campaigns were not limited to the acquisition of new lands. The proceeds generated by the military machine triggered irreversible changes, ranging from an increase in trade with the first substantial accumulation of commercial capital, to the spread of a stable Roman coinage, and the spectacular increase in the number of slaves (certainly many hundreds of thousands, before the end of the century), with ensuing and significant changes in production; to say nothing of marked demographic growth and the consequential transformation of the city's architectural shape.

Around all this, politics and the institutional set-up were also mutating. The granting of equal importance to the plebeian deliberations and the laws voted upon by the centurial assembly[30] put a definitive end, after the Ogul-

nian plebiscite, to the age-old conflict that had marked the whole of early republican history. The new nobility (or at least a sizable part of it), which had
already begun to acquire an imperial behavior and mentality, quickly divided
into a promercantile and expansionist political orientation, which would soon
find in the Scipios its most prestigious leaders; and another alignment which
continued to see the future of Rome as contained within narrower horizons,
and did not want to break the tie between the aristocracy and the old peasant
world of small landowners that had, until then, constituted the social foundation of the republic.[31]

Prompted by new requirements, the culture of the ruling groups also
changed. How to combine in the most profitable manner possible for the
landowning classes the abundance of land and the abundance of slaves; how
to construct a set of measures that would best ensure evermore intense mercantile traffic, but without abandoning the Roman traditions; how best to organize the military machine and efficiently govern the conquered territories—it was around these themes that the horizons were defined of an
aristocratic rationality increasingly secular and open to Greek and Mediterranean influences now entirely detached from their old plebeian connotations.

3.

According to the account of Pomponius[32]—which we have no reason to
doubt—in those same years, again around the middle of the third century,
Tiberius Coruncanius, a pontifex maximus from a plebeian family, who took
office in 254 B.C. (he had served as consul in 280: the pontificate now frequently rounded off a successful political career), was the first to make a
"public profession" of his knowledge of *ius*, violating its secrecy: one of his
responses is recorded by Pliny.[33] He had ties to the Ogulnii, and, like them, he
was not distant from the Greek "wisdom," according to an observation by
Cicero.[34] Perhaps he was following a path that others before him had attempted to blaze, though with less success: it is possible to interpret in this
sense the reference by Pomponius to P. Sempronius Sophus, consul in 304 and
censor in 300—the year of the Ogulnian plebiscite—who also seems to have
been influenced by Greek philosophy.[35]

Pomponius' observation contains an evident trace of the change: whereas half a century earlier, the isolated and opposed composition of a text—which, according to a revelatory tradition, had actually been stolen from the author—had proved unsuccessful, there was now, against a transformed background of ideas and relations, a change of style within the collegium of the priests, probably connected to the new plebeian presence.

A different model of the pontifical role now became established, far less tightly bound up with the archaic religious traditions, and closer to a body of civil knowledge suited to the changing needs of the city: an image perfectly reflected in the Ciceronian portrait of Coruncanius intently "tracing out for the citizens the lines of *ius*,"[36] or resolving in an entirely secular manner what would later appear as the delicate relations between "civil law" and "pontifical law" with regard to family cults;[37] a figure endowed with a "wisdom" *(prudentia)* cultivated "to the last breath."[38]

And some sixty years after the pontificate of T. Coruncanius, writing appeared once again in the history of *ius*. It was reintroduced this time by another nobleman of plebeian origin, Sextus Aelius Paetus Catus, consul in 198 B.C., censor in 194 (his father, a candidate for the consulship for 217, had been killed a year later at the battle of Cannae, with a substantial part of his family), a friend of Scipio Africanus, and greatly admired by Ennius.[39] The work —now lost except for a handful of citations by Cicero, Gellius, and two jurists of the principate[40]—is mentioned by Pomponius, who knew it very well, under the name *Tripertita*: in it he even saw "the origins of *ius*" *(cunabula iuris)*.[41] This is probably an exaggerated judgment, just as too close a connection— which the *Enchiridion* seems to suggest in a veiled manner—with the *De usurpationibus* can be misleading.[42] Sextus Aelius was working in a very different context from that of Appius Claudius, and it would be difficult to identify any directly antipontifical content in his work, one century after the Ogulnii, and decades after Coruncanius. However, we can still imagine there was a political motivation: a text intended to carefully reappropriate a "democratic" legislative tradition whose presence was now less clearly evident in a city on its way to becoming increasingly Mediterranean and imperial.

It is difficult to establish the link between the work that Pomponius called the *Tripertita* and what, in another section of the *Enchiridion*, he called the *ius Aelianum*, closely following the formulation used for Gnaeus Flavius.[43] Certainly, however, in this new book as well, the need to transmit with precision trial formularies referring to the *lege agere*, interpretive maxims consolidated by the authority of the sacerdotal pronouncements and the literal tone itself of the decemviral norms, was far greater than the presence of an autonomous reelaboration of the material developed by the author, isolable from the body of knowledge and the legislative elements that were being reproposed. The novelty of the *Tripertita* was perhaps the order in which the content was organized (according to one strong hypothesis, the three parts of the book contained, respectively, a version of the Twelve Tables, in an edition that was orthographically and, in some cases, also lexically updated with respect to the original, but absolutely faithful in the prescriptive contents; a sort of summa of the pontifical interpretation of the provisions of the laws, as it had been stratified and selected over the previous two centuries; and finally, the *certa verba* of the *lege agere*).[44] The triadic structure alluded to in the title seems to contain philosophical echoes of Greek origin (unless it should be interpreted as a reference to motifs of Roman archaism), and it was destined to spark enduring resonances.

The *responsa*—once pontifical, now also pronounced by aristocratic experts—constituted the prescriptive skeleton of relations among the citizens. And yet they continued not to establish general rules. Their utterance, in a certain sense, consumed them entirely. They lasted only as long as their actuation, which continued to have no sanction—nor were they any longer covered, except to the smallest degree, by the sacrality of religion—but was linked only to the respect for the civil prestige of the figure who issued them: a bond that was in any case very strong in a still very cohesive society. Their memory was zealously preserved by the tradition of the experts, through a learning process that took place within aristocratic families and provided guidance in choosing the most appropriate rule from among the multiplicity of cases examined, in a continuous linkage of resemblances between past and present. Any decision to depart from the already-established and to propose an innovative solution required long and hard consideration. It was in any case necessary to channel every situation into the groove traced by the rituals of the ancient *mores* and the norms of the Twelve Tables, as reelaborated through the pontifical interpretation of the fifth and fourth centuries.

Taken as a whole, these prescriptions—which throughout the third century still did not crystallize in any other context than the memory and wisdom of the experts—would constitute the bedrock of the entire republican legal system, and was called, probably beginning in the second century B.C., *ius civile.* And here, finally, it is possible to translate *ius* with the word "law," and therefore "civil law," in the sense of "law of the citizens" (Roman citizens). It now appeared, as reflected in the culture of the time, to be an autonomous legal system, detached from religious customs but also distinct from politics, yet capable of giving power (*potentia,* as Cicero would later say)[45] to those who mastered it. Grounded in a cognitive practice that oscillated between *prudentia* and *sapientia,* to use Cicero's vocabulary once again,[46] it was endowed with rules of its own and was capable of producing a consolidated technique lying midway between precepts and their conceptualization, but with operative protocols that were already quite strict and binding.

Its normative range pertained chiefly to the status of persons in the network of kinship ties, questions of inheritance, forms of ownership of land and other goods, both movable and immovable—buildings, animals, slaves, agricultural and artisanal products, tools—and their circulation, forms of personal bondage arising from the contracting of debts, certain illicit behaviors, and the civil trial *(lege agere)* regulated by the Twelve Tables: the developments of the original "horizontal" network linking families, no longer subject to the intervention of royalty and of civic power.

We can distinguish three layers in its composition, even if, from the Roman perspective, it was perceived as a single homogeneous block. The first—and oldest—comprised the archaic *mores,* reworked by the early sacerdotal tradition. The second consisted of the law of the Twelve Tables—including its procedural aspects—reflected in the mirror of pontifical interpretation. The third, more recent, layer was made up of the *responsa* of the new secular *iuris prudentes,* around which the entire construction revolved. Centuries later, in the retrospective view of Pomponius, the prevalence of their work appeared particularly imposing, and he was able, without hesitation, to make *ius civile* correspond directly with the oral interpretation of the jurisconsults.[47]

The new figure of the aristocratic expert was not yet completely identifiable with that of the "jurist" in the professional sense that the word would later acquire. The vocation could not yet be defined as a specialized aptitude with respect to the civil and political heart of the city. And above all, it would long remain linked, in a delicate relationship of conjunction and disjunction, to the exercise of political power: it was not possible to be a jurist without having at some time held political office in the republic; and for that matter, in order to serve as praetor, an essential step in the *cursus honorum,* the ascent toward the consulship, it was necessary to possess legal competence.

At least during the period extending from Sextus Aelius to Servius Sulpicius Rufus, consul in 51 B.C., the connection had the force of an unquestionable bond. Giving *responsa* was an invaluable service to the collectivity, every bit as important as leading an army to victory in battle. And those who devoted themselves to it deserved for that very reason to rank among the city's leading citizens. Their knowledge was a "civil doctrine"—*civilis scientia,* as Cicero would also write[48]—which could not be acquired without hard work, a sense of vocation, and a rigorous grounding.

The legal discipline, consisting as it did of memory, a capacity to orient oneself in the tangle of similarities and differences between cases, an inventive aptitude, acuity in perceiving clues and causal links, a sense of tradition, perfect mastery of the appropriate language for expressing rules calibrated to the millimeter, and an ability to quickly evaluate the interests at play, had by now become decidedly technical. But the practice of it did not separate, indeed it exalted, the aristocratic propensity for public life and the exercise of command. The meeting point was represented by political action—the leading magistracies, the proconsulships outside Italy in the first overseas conquests, the senate—as a hub around which there revolved, without any possibility of escape, the self-recognition of the nobility. The force of that association is what created the connective structure holding together, in a single framework, the wisdom and expertise upon which the primacy of the great oligarchic families was based. Legal knowledge—albeit within the autonomy of its function—was still an integral part of this network; in some respects, it was already the most advanced discipline, but its complexity did not prevent its integration, had not yet broken—and this would remain the case until the crisis of the republic—the underlying unity of the aristocratic rationality.

The jurisconsults of this period were not just occupied in giving responses. The image that the Roman culture of a slightly later period would form of this activity included, alongside that of *respondere,* at least two other responsibilities, fixed, in a stereotype destined to become famous, by two more verbs: *cavere* (advise) and *agere* (act in a lawsuit).[49] The first verb indicated the work of advising and consulting that the experts performed free of charge on behalf of citizens, not only those of equal social standing (all aristocratic commitments were characterized by gratuitousness, in a world in which paid labor was pejoratively regarded as servile), who were protected and guided in finding their way through the web of restrictions that the *ius civile* had extended over the behavior of everyday life (selling a parcel of land, emancipating a son, manumitting a slave, contracting matrimony). The second verb referred to assistance given during the *in iure* stage of a civil trial: first in the *lege agere,* then in the so-called formulary phase (we shall return to this topic shortly). This collection of tasks clearly described the primacy of legal knowledge, and not merely with respect to the formation of *ius,* but in republican social interaction as a whole: the community life of the city was fully reflected in its constructions and pronouncements.

4.

Cicero's thought in *De republica* and in *De oratore*—the two great treatises of his maturity—offers a clear and faithful mirror of the essential nature of this supremacy, and of the delicacy of the links that it entailed.

The *De republica* is the great text of the Roman civil conscience, rethought in a moment of extreme turmoil and crisis in the lead-up to the final clash between Caesar and Pompey, and while the streets of Rome were awash with blood due to factional violence that even made it impossible to hold the elections for the consulship.[50] The underlying thread of its structure is a description of a people taking form and constructing, through republican political participation, its identity; of a people that was becoming State, we might say, if the modernization implied by the use of that word were not to some degree misleading: the same content that Machiavelli (who obviously never read Cicero's *De republica*) would later find in the account of Livy.

The understanding of *ius* was an essential element in this overview, a real driving force behind the entire process. The whole of the first book at least needs to be borne in mind, but here it is sufficient to recall just two brief passages. Very near the beginning of the dialogue, we read:

For there is no principle enunciated by the philosophers—at least none that is just and honorable—that has not been discovered and established by those who have drawn up the laws of States. For whence comes our sense of duty? From whom do we obtain the principles of religion? Whence comes the law of nations, or even that law of ours which is called "civil"? Whence justice, respect of the word given, the sense of fairness? Whence decency, self-restraint, fear of disgrace, eagerness for praise and honour? Whence comes endurance amid toils and dangers? I say, from those men who, when these things had been inculcated by a system of training, either confirmed them by custom or else enforced them by statutes.[51]

The topic is the relationship between jurists and philosophers, between law and philosophy: a motif that, to tell the truth, was not particularly beloved by the Roman jurists, but which was nonetheless destined to reemerge, centuries later and in a completely different context, in a crucial passage of Ulpian's thought. Even though the subject is apparently general in nature (*in civitatibus* . . .), Rome alone is the true locus of the comparison. Greek philosophy and Roman legal wisdom: these are the terms of the comparison that Cicero's words summoned up without any possibility of doubt in the minds of his readers (about 1800 years later, Vico offered the same observation, though not even the great Neapolitan philosopher could have known the *De republica*).[52] And Roman knowledge emerged from the judgment in a position not only of absolute parity with respect to that of the (Greek) philosophers, but even in a kind of superiority: it was a primacy of civil reason with respect to the siren songs of pure theory. *Ius* was presented no differently than as the *logos* of the republic, and as the foundation of its virtue: a *logos* that was not solely thought, but which, as a disciplining reason, had the advantage of being embodied in normative order and social regulation ("ius aut gentium . . . aut civile"); in faithfulness to the gods and the cults ("unde pietas . . . a quibus religio?"—"est enim pietas iustitia adversum deos," Cicero would later write in *De natura deorum*);[53] and in moral temper ("unde in laboribus et periculis fortitudo?"); in ethical principle ("unde pudor, continentia?"). In brief, of having founded a society of the strong and just: a conviction in which the idealization of the republic, albeit from a point of view that remained substantially faithful to the aristocratic canon, accompanied the dramatic experience of its irreversible crisis.

In the image forming before us, the republican city is constructed and lives entirely around law and its emblematic words: besides *ius,* there is mention of *fides, iustitia, aequitas*—we shall encounter them all during our tale. Shortly after, Cicero reiterates this central role in the clearest imaginable terms:

> The republic, said Scipio Africanus, is that which belongs to the people. But a people is not any collection of human beings brought together in any sort of way, but the union of a multitude aggregated by a consensus about law and the common good.[54]

The republic therefore absorbs within it the people, and in some manner identifies with it (this nexus belongs to the thinking of those years: in Ateius Capito we find it, from another point of view, in the elucidation of the relationship between the people and the law).[55] But which people? The conception that emerges in Cicero might be described as strongly organicist: a classic of aristocratic thought, but here reproposed with a new accent, more attentive to the complexity of the social universe of the first century B.C., and the new emerging classes. In order for the people to become a republic, it is not enough to have a multitude; it is necessary for this mass to be intrinsically structured and cohesive; that there be a generally agreed system of regulation, and a widespread perception of the common good. Law, *ius,* in its multiple manifestations—*ius civile, ius gentium, fides, aequitas, iustitia*—and in its historic connections with religion—*religio, pietas*—is the warp and weft of this fabric; the keystone of the entire construction: without a people there is no republic, but without law a people cannot have an identity.

And yet there is no law without its experts ("ab iis qui haec disciplinis informata"). The *De republica* presents us with the first conceptualization of that most durable aristocratic topos which makes jurists the "natural" representatives of the will of the people in the creation of law; a motif that would surface frequently in European thought, and of which we have seen a highly polemical echo in the words of Hegel. Cicero offers us, as it were, an archeology of that motif. In fact he emphasizes its integrating and organicist aspect, exactly as Savigny would later do; Hegel would denounce its insuppressible

THE BIRTH OF A TECHNIQUE

oligarchic content (a class of specialists who claimed to represent a generic and undifferentiated populace: an aspect that perhaps did not entirely escape the notice of Cicero himself, and which nonetheless fitted in perfectly with what we have defined as the "republican canon").

But in the same years, alongside this entirely political and sociological formulation, which instilled law into the profound sentiment of the community, Cicero delineated another model as well, in which the cognition of *ius* clearly appeared to be a technique and a specialization, linked to a mode of reflection and a practice that were by this point quite distinct with respect to civic action as a whole. We must now turn to the *De oratore,* where the author outlines the figure of the ideal statesman:

> But if we were inquiring who is he that has devoted his experience, knowledge and enthusiasm to the guidance of the republic, I should define him thus: 'Whoever knows and uses everything by which the advantage of the republic is secured and developed, is the man to be deemed the helmsman, and the originator of national policy,' and I should tell of Publius Lentulus that illustrious leader, of Tiberius Gracchus the elder, Quintus Metellus, Publius Africanus, Gaius Laelius, and countless others, some from our community and some from abroad.

He then moves on to that of the jurist:

> If again the question were, who is rightly described as learned in the law, I should say it is the man who is an expert in the statutes, and in the customary law observed by individuals as members of the community, and who is qualified to advise, direct the course of a lawsuit, and safeguard a client, and in this class I should refer to Sextus Aelius, Manius Manilius and Publius Mucius.[56]

In this perspective rulers and jurists already performed different functions, each with their own canons, and they made reference to two distinct galleries of great figures. Their roles were certainly contiguous, and yet all the same possible to separate. And it should be noted that the three jurists who are mentioned (in the fiction of the dialogue it is Antonius who is speaking) had all been consuls—and therefore politicians of the first order—in full compliance with the aristocratic tradition (Sextus Aelius, as we have said, in 198, M. Manilius in 149, and Publius Mucius in 133). But this was no longer enough, in Cicero's view, to overlap and blur the boundaries: his memory— the city's cultural memory—now identified those figures only (or at least primarily) as men of law, viewing the significance of their lives in terms of a vocation *(respondere, cavere, agere)* that was reckoned to absorb any other public function, however prestigious, in which they might have served. They represented, in the retrospective gaze of Cicero, specialization in its nascent state.

This fragile equilibrium between isolation and integration, placed in the spotlight with such great lucidity in the Ciceronian treatises (the *De republica* more in the direction of an integrated vision; the *De oratore* tending toward the new specialization), was not to last long, and would be swept away by great changes. Already at the time of the *De oratore* it was a trait that belonged more to the city's past than to its tormented present; and Cicero himself, while he was writing, was probably fully aware of that fact. Still, throughout the entire second century, that connection would occupy a central place in the course of crucial events.

III

Science, Forms, Dominion

I. Preservation and Change in the Age of Conquest

9

Ius civile and the Praetors:
The Idea of Fairness

I.

The resumed influence of the pontifices, followed by the definitive establishment of the jurisprudential model, did not cancel the *lex* paradigm from the
Roman experience. Indeed, it can safely be said that its importance was actually reinforced during the republican age, following the consolidation of
the relationship between statutory law and the assembly (tribunal or centuriate), which was destined to become an essential component of the equilibrium between assemblies, magistracies, and the senate that would characterize the finest period of the republic.

But the legislative activity—fairly limited in quantitative terms, given that
no more than a few hundred measures were passed in the whole republican
period—did not concern, with a few rare exceptions, the themes that fell
within the ambit of the *ius civile,* by now identified with the social disciplining
of the city.[1] From this point of view the example of the Twelve Tables was
not followed. The boundaries of the jurists' activities also marked the usually
impassable limits for the *lex populi* or *lex publica,* as it soon came to be called.
The fields attributed to it were different: the regulation of relations between

citizens and political power; the functioning of the assemblies, the senate, the magistracies, and the priesthoods; the organization of cults; the municipal and provincial administrative systems; the apportionment of land; and the repression of crime.

The separation wound up creating a latent dualism between *ius* and *lex,* never explicitly theorized but nonetheless perceived by Roman culture as a peculiar and characteristic element of its institutional reality. *Ius* expressed the original nucleus—sapiential and aristocratic—of Roman civic ordering: the collective belief, radiating out from the hegemony of the *nobilitas,* that a sense of measure in the "horizontal" and equal relations among the *cives* ("private" heads of family) was based on the rules of an ancient practice, once intermingled with religion and cult rituality, but now endowed with techniques and autonomous protocols that needed to be attended to and preserved by special talents.

Lex, on the other hand, linked as it was to the will of the assembly and of the magistrate who convened and presided over it, represented the regulatory presence of the "rule of the people" *(iussum populi)* considered to be essential in republican governance, although the people in question were organized in a strict hierarchy, which continued to relegate the less well-off to a very marginal civic role, and were still divided up according to their census class, with the complete exclusion of women and slaves (the latter soon numbering millions). But it was a normative function that restricted itself to the public sphere of community life, having ceded to the jurists—who acted outside of any institutional power, any magisterial *imperium,* supported only by the authority of their own personal standing and rank—the territory in which the economic and family premises of citizenship, understood as the autonomous "private" identity of each head of family, were built and reproduced.

This distinction should not, however, be taken as a rigid antinomy: rather, perhaps, as a strong tendency, a relatively flexible but firm bond, not to universalize the nexus between people and the law—or between the law and magistrates—as had happened in the Greek experience (and as would occur in many systems in modern Europe), but to consider it as just one part, albeit important, of the ways in which the city regulated the coexistence of its members. A model to be constantly set alongside another and no-less-decisive disciplining form, that of the pronouncements of the jurists in which the tradition of the *ius civile* found expression. *Lex* and *responsum*—the general com-

mand of the people gathered in an assembly and the particular pronouncement of the case-based knowledge of the experts—thus became the two
parameters, distinct but not diametrically opposed, of a prescriptive continuity whose coherence did not rely upon any external mechanism, much less
upon any explicit constitutional principle, but on the substantial organic unity
of a pattern of aristocratic government for a long time without any alternative, even in the moments of most acute crisis. The production of *ius* thus
became, in the middle centuries of the republic, an essential element of the
hegemony of the *nobilitas,* and of the ability of the leading families to maintain a high degree of social cohesion around their primacy. Indeed, they
ended up appearing, through the knowledge administered by their jurists, as
the depositaries of the rules that maintained the social fabric (the Romans
used the term *civile*) of political citizenship: the conduct of family life, mechanisms for the transmission of property to heirs, the paradigms of the ownership and circulation of goods, the rules disciplining trials—in short, order
in the city. This was precisely the "civil militia" about which Cicero spoke,
entirely comparable with its non-metaphorical counterpart on the field of
battle, through which those same families figured, with the deeds of their
generals, as the protagonists of the republic's military fortunes.

But the division of roles between *ius* and *lex*—civil discipline and political
rule—was not without its exceptions. During the republican age it is possible
to identify a limited number of *leges*—no more than thirty or so, over the
course of more than four centuries—that deliberately invaded the territory
of *ius.* When it happened, we are always in the presence of *plebiscita* (if one
excludes measures prompted by Augustan interventionism): small tears in
the fabric of *ius,* in each case brought about by the force of popular pressure,
which demanded a directly political response in circumstances that mirrored,
though on a smaller and less traumatic scale, the situation that had led to the
Twelve Tables.[2]

Thus, between the fourth and the third centuries, there was a Lex Poetelia Papiria, concerning the abolition of the *nexum* (debtor's servitude, which
particularly affected the most economically vulnerable plebeian families);[3] a
Lex Aquilia, on wrongful damage;[4] a Lex Cincia, relating to donations;[5] and
later, between the third and first centuries, a Lex Furia about wills;[6] a Lex
Atilia about guardianship;[7] a Lex Plautia about violence;[8] a Lex Falcidia about
legacies;[9] and a Lex Aebutia about formulary procedure.[10] These laws, which

were never formally published following the vote of the assembly that approved the proposals of the magistrate, but were recopied by scribes from the text preserved in the Erarium (Public Treasury) or in the Temple of Ceres, were immediately subjected to the incessant interpretative work of the jurists. They succeeded in appropriating their dictates entirely, integrating them into their own tradition of knowledge in much the same way as had been done, in an earlier era, with the Twelve Tables. Thus they too became part of the *ius civile:* small fragments of institutional writing in a space controlled by a completely different form of normativity.

2.

The progressive detachment of a knowledge of *ius* from pontifical practice, and the consolidation of its technical framework, accompanied—with numerous reciprocal implications—another phenomenon of great importance in the story we are recounting here: the establishment of the role of a magistracy as a crucial element of innovation and change.

With the stabilization of the republican order, from the fourth century onward, performance of the jurisdictional function had become concentrated in the hands of the praetors, senior magistrates who ranked just below the consuls. As regards civil trials, they were expected to administer them solely on the basis of the *lege agere:* it was said then that *ius dicebant*—"they pronounced law [in disputes]"—from which the technical term *iuris dictio,* "jurisdiction," later derived.

This highly rigid procedure was (as we have seen) the quintessence of the intertwining of ritualism, prescriptivity, and magical projections that had dominated the origins of the archaic *ius,* and reflected a pattern of beliefs and customs that were less and less in step with the cultural climate and the reality of life in the republican city, which was beginning to look elsewhere in Italy and across the sea, and was becoming increasingly crowded with traders, ships (which sailed up the river to the foot of the Aventine Hill), goods, and slaves. The pontifical perspective was an increasingly out-of-date depiction of a vanishing world. Every attempt to reconcile its models with the new social and economic realities could only be achieved through a further complication of its already burdensome verbal rituals: it was the "excessive technicality" that would still be cited by Gaius as the cause of an intolerable degeneration.[11] The pontifices and the aristocratic sages had tried to introduce some adaptations, for instance, by extending the original scheme of the *lege agere sacramento,* first of all to the protection of praedial servitudes and later of usufruct, when these new rights over things began to be separated from the undifferentiated paradigm of archaic property. A few other steps forward came about through the comitial legislation: with the Lex Silia (certainly before 204 B.C.), which protected cash credits through the newer and less formalistic *agere per condictionem;* or with the Lex Calpurnia, which further extended this type of protection. But these were limited interventions incapable of solving the problem.

In the meanwhile, however, another path was being opened up to deal with the transformations, at first (probably) in an entirely fortuitous fashion, driven by the urgency of circumstances, but then in a more lucid and conscious manner. The new development was introduced through the sedimentation of parallel and overlapping rules, where the changes did not erase the old, but instead coexisted alongside it, slowly swallowing it up: a way of proceeding that would prove to be a cornerstone of the more mature Roman intellectual identity, heir to that fear of the new and of the discontinuous whose origin lay, as we have discovered, in the archaic mentality. In this work the magistrates always had the jurists at their side, in a collaboration that took place entirely within the aristocratic leadership and which succeeded in integrating different functions, competences, and talents into a substantially unitary practice of government.

The praetors were careful not to abolish the *lege agere*—for that matter, they would not even have had the power to do so—which survived for centuries thereafter, all the way up to the age of Augustus. Instead, they allowed it to slide into anachronism, while flanking it with another type of civil trial, to which citizens could resort for a progressively wider range of cases—a system organized on an entirely different basis.

All magistrates had the faculty, in the exercise of their duties, to issue communications to the populace: the so-called *ius edicendi,*[12] the power to issue edicts *(edicta),* pronouncements—originally verbal, later written—directed to citizens as a whole. Taking advantage of this possibility, the praetors began to announce that, in particular circumstances, for those litigants willing to request it, they would not administer justice—perform the *iuris dictio* —according to the ancient rules of the *lege agere.* Instead they would adopt a

new type of procedure, no longer based upon rituals and the symbolic constructions of the *certa verba,* but upon formulas put together and agreed upon
(*concepta verba,* as they would later be called)[13] on a case to case basis by the
parties involved and by the magistrate (perhaps with the assistance of jurists),
working together to identify the best way of expressing the opposing interests involved in the controversy: the affirmation or denial of a debt, the ownership of a slave or a shipment of wheat, the restitution of a sum of money.

We do not know exactly when this custom began, or what form it took at
first. It may date as far back as the end of the fourth century, and it is also possible that it was based in part on the scheme of the procedure *per iudicis arbitrive postulationem,* the most flexible form envisaged by the *lege agere.*[14] What
we do know for certain is that it originally pertained only to disputes between
Romans and foreigners who did not enjoy *ius commercii,* that is, the right to
trade with Romans in accordance with the rules of the *ius civile*: trade relations that the praetor should not have had to deal with, but which it would
have been politically undesirable to leave outside of his jurisdiction.

It is also certain that the development of the custom received decisive
impetus from the introduction, with a *lex* enacted in 242 B.C.—just before the
victorious conclusion of the First Punic War—of a *praetor peregrinus* (praetor for foreigners), which doubled the previously unitary functions of the
magistracy, envisaging a new figure to deal exclusively with disputes arising
between Roman citizens and foreigners, or between foreigners only—merchants, in the vast majority of cases.[15]

From its early beginnings Rome had been a place of congregation, exchange, and trade. In the heart of the third century, the accentuation of its
Mediterranean profile further emphasized this ancient role, and it is easy to
imagine the new praetorship—which from the outset applied only the trial
forms *per concepta verba*—as both a cause and an effect of the strengthening
of a broad network of maritime exchanges, with Sicily, Africa, and the eastern Mediterranean. This was the republic deploying its own *ius*—its best and
most powerful instrument of social control—in defense of the new economy,
for which the protection of the magistrates, accompanied by the attention of
the jurists, would soon become an essential driving force, in turn deriving
from it decisive elements of transformation and enrichment.

The jurisdictional proceeding still remained split into two parts, as in the
past, and a clear division was retained between the function of the magistrate

and the effective judgment of the dispute, between the *iuris dictio* and the ascertaining of the facts for the purpose of issuing a verdict. This fracture was associated with an indelible and original characteristic of the Roman experience, which enclosed the cognition of *ius*—both on the part of the praetor and on the part of the expert respondent—in a solely verbal universe—words in exchange for words—suspended midway between the weight of the facts and the virtuality of the pronouncements (a paradoxical condition, if we think about the well-known commonplace of the "concreteness" of the ancient jurists).

Every evaluation on the merits of the matter remained, as before, the responsibility of a private judge. But now, *in iure* what was performed was no longer an unchangeable ritual tied to the enactment of its own symbolism. Instead, a sort of elastic and informal agreement was constructed between the magistrate and the litigants, united by their search for a formulation that made it possible to define the opposing claims in terms that would allow for the exercise of a *iuris dictio* that was far more in line with the reality of the needs involved.

3.

It was a subversive innovation, but presented in the opaque forms of an expedient, as a technical mechanism in the exercising of a broadly discretional power. A change contained within a framework of drastically diametrical oppositions that would mark, also in other fields, the entire history of Rome, and which reveal one of its intrinsic characteristics: the capacity to hold together, alongside each other, opposing ideas and practices, ensuring that their encounter did not peter out into a sterile and paralyzing elision of opposites, did not lead to the reciprocal canceling out of the interests at stake, but instead produced combinations that would open up new paths unknown to other ancient civilizations. Various examples lie before us: the ethnic isolation—to the point of estrangement—of the originality and the superiority of the Roman and Latin component with respect to the rest of Italy (and of the world), together with the almost limitless predisposition to absorb and assimilate different peoples and cultures. Or the incomparable and long-cultivated vocation for imperial dominion and exploitation, but also the impulse to build a network of regional autonomies and a policy of enhancing the role of local leadership that has never been equaled in the history of the West. Or, again, the massive, intensive, and unprecedented reliance upon slavery, accompanied by the very common practice of manumission, which transformed at a single stroke, with the solitary and irrevocable decision of any master, a slave into a citizen of the hegemonic community. And in our case, the most exaggerated ritualism together with the most ductile and co-operative flexibility.[16]

The pronouncements of the magistrates were thus linked directly to the new horizons of the republic: to the transformation of its sensibility, the development of its economy—increasingly trade- and slave-oriented—and its growing influence in Italy and in the Mediterranean. From then on, and certainly from the middle of the third century B.C. onwards, year by year the edicts of the praetors would become almost the manifesto of a society that was changing and moving toward empire, and of a governing class which, while not cancelling any aspect of its own past, was capable of keeping pace with change: like the standard-bearer of a new way of thinking, even though it existed in a culture that would never renounce a tough and demanding relationship between rituality and prescriptivity, between rules and ceremonial typification.

Throughout the third century, and probably also the second and perhaps into the beginning of the first, the praetors would continue to issue jurisdictional edicts in a fairly episodic and fragmentary manner. Whenever the search for *concepta verba* for the resolution of a dispute managed to crystallize into a typical formula, such as could also be utilized in future cases, this became the subject of an edict, with which the magistrate declared—though without being formally required to respect the commitment—that it would be adopted in all comparable situations that might subsequently arise.

In all likelihood, it was not until sometime in the second or first century B.C. that the praetors first acquired the custom of regularly issuing, at the beginning of their term of office—which lasted for one year, like the consuls—an edict of, let us say, a general nature. Valid for the duration of their incumbency, it contained all the trial formulas that they intended to employ. From that time on, every new magistrate would take the text of his predecessor and, with the help of jurist advisors if he himself was not particularly well versed in *ius,* would make any additions or modifications judged to be appropriate (predictions of new *actiones,* or of other trial-related tools, a more appropriate or comprehensive rewriting of formulas that were already well known, and so forth) and would then present it. This progressive work continued without abate for more than a century, a combined effort that was certainly clearly visible to Cicero, when he wrote, around the middle of the first century, that the edict of the praetor (in the singular) was to be considered a sort of *lex annua,* which was just as important for the law of the city as the Twelve Tables had once been.[17]

4.

But they were not only trial regulations. The *ius civile*—like the *legis actiones*—was, taken as a whole, a body of law applicable only to Romans: its exclusivity revealed once again the origin of its precepts, which had emerged from the core of a religious experience that was also rigorously linked to Rome's civic identity. As we have seen, in the middle of the third century republican ruling groups decided to break out from this cage and to use the technique of *ius* in order to provide regular legal protection for that part of the city's life that fell outside of the realm of tradition, but which was acquiring increasing importance: the web of transactions with foreign merchants, until then summarily governed by ancient Mediterranean customs that had accrued between Phoenicians, Carthaginians, Greeks, and the Romans themselves, but still without any stable jurisdictional protection.

The praetors, probably even before the year 242, thus began to regard as pertinent for the purposes of their *iuris dictio*—and therefore envisioning *concepta verba* in the eventuality of disputes between the parties—commercial transactions entered into in ways that lay outside the bounds of the traditional rituals, and which could not therefore be protected by the *lege agere.*

The magistrates were chosen from the same aristocratic ruling groups that were the protagonists of imperial expansion. Their attention was fully focused on the new demands of the world that was taking shape: a social formation produced by the impetuous drive for expansion in the age between the first two Punic Wars, following the conquest of Samnium and the fall of Tarentum, when large landholdings began to replace the small peasant properties, slave labor became an increasingly dominant feature of the agricultural landscape, and relatively intense trade, in the hands of an ambitious and enterprising class of profiteers—merchants, tax farmers: the core of the equestrian order—very often linked to the nobility (though not infrequently in a highly competitive way), at other times in a more openly conflictual relationship, began to result in the accumulation of substantial amounts of capital, destined sooner or later to be reinvested in new concentrations in land ownership.[18]

The praetors—both urban and peregrine—worked on two fronts: one more strictly concerned with property-related issues of the traditional Roman citizenry, the other oriented toward the new requirements of mercantile development, and therefore toward the Mediterranean trade circuits. On the one hand, they began to deal with situations, involving only Roman citizens, that represented further dents in the ritualism of acts already governed by the *ius civile:* for instance, assigning ownership of the property of a deceased head of family to whoever he had indicated as his heir in a will that lacked the formal requisites of the ancient ceremony with the bronze and the scales (according to the traditional *ius,* the assignment would have been null and void); or else refusing to grant an action *(denegatio actionis)* to someone who would have had the right to it according to the rituals of the *ius civile,* where that person's behavior did not appear, given the de facto circumstances, worthy of protection.

On the other hand, they envisioned formulary *actiones* to protect claims arising from transactions completely extraneous to the *ius civile,* originally between Roman citizens and foreign merchants, but soon extended also to those between Roman citizens alone. Examples include cases of exchanges—not always simultaneous—of money for goods to transfer full control of them outside of any ritual; of offering something for rent, allowing the leaseholder to make use of it for a certain period with the obligation to render it when the deadline expired; and just a little later, the establishment of a partnership in order to perform a common undertaking; or of the carrying out of a commission by one party at the request of another *(mandator):* a precise typology, which would constitute—in part thanks to the successive conceptualizations of the jurists—the nucleus of a full-fledged Roman "business law," later defined as *ius gentium:*[19] law, that is, inspired by principles for which it was presumed there was (or could be) a consensus on the part of all the peoples of the Mediterranean, and quite distinct from the specificity of the Roman civil law tradition.

And yet the perspective of the magistrates, we should not forget, was merely—given the limitations of their power—that of the trial. Their task was to administer civil justice, not to create *ius:* the latter function was entrusted in an autonomous manner to the tradition preserved by the experts, who, in interpreting it, adapted and transformed *ius* in a continuity that could only be interrupted by the external intervention of a *lex* (which, as we have seen, after the Twelve Tables happened only very rarely). The praetors could, in the exercise of their office, request the collaboration of jurists, but they could not act in their place. To grant an action was not the same as giving a response. And yet, by deciding, through the concession of an *actio,* to provide trial protection for claims and expectations arising from relationships outside the rules of *ius civile,* the magistrates wound up, even if only indirectly, recognizing new rights and thus ultimately producing new *ius* entirely unfettered from the past—often inspired by mercantile practices which, though equally archaic, had nothing in common with the symbolic and ritual framework that had shaped the mental landscape of early Rome.

Scholars have devoted a great deal of time and energy in attempting to describe, in terms that would be acceptable to a modern jurist, this continual shift of planes from procedure to substantive law. One explanation consisted of making use of the well-known distinction in nineteenth-century continental legal science between the (procedural) action and the (substantive) subjective right: the Roman praetors, operating as they did exclusively in a trial-based context, focused on the former element, allowing actions (the protection of a trial) without previously acknowledged (by the *ius civile*) subjective rights.

In reality, descriptions of this sort serve only to satisfy a need to systematize that has nothing to do with historical interpretation. The only datum from within Roman experience to which we can refer is the distinction, certainly present as early as the third century, between a *ius* based on the tradition preserved by the aristocratic experts, and distantly related to the Twelve Tables, and ordering produced solely through the *iuris dictio* of the magistrate—and precisely in connection with that function also called, as a result of lexical and semantic attraction, *ius*—consisting entirely of *actiones,* each with its own formula linked to the typification of a case. A *ius* made up of actions, alongside the *ius* of the *responsa,* founded on the power of the praetors and not upon tradition; a *ius* that the jurists would later call *ius honorarium* or *ius praetorium,* dependent, that is, upon the *honos* (the office) held on an annual basis by the magistrate.

The dialectic between the *ius civile* and the *ius honorarium* would determine the shape, from the third to the first centuries B.C., of the core of Roman law that is most familiar to us (albeit seen through the distorting lens of the *Digesta*): law made up of cases and actions, constructed day by day through the very long collaboration between magistrates and jurists in the final centuries of the republic, destined to acquire its most complete form in the elaboration of legal thought in the principate. But the outlook of the more mature jurisprudence—the one we know best—would be intensely retrospective, so to speak, *post festum.* It would appear to be a point of view that illuminated a process of germination already complete when it was at work: the unitary and synthetic presentation—made possible by the deployment of very powerful conceptual schemata—of a concluded experience, originally far more fluid, polycentric, and indeterminate. Our modern vision, bound as it is primarily to this latter-day angle of observation, finds it difficult to recognize, in the compositional outlines of an order that the great Hadrianic and Severan masters would render practically monumental, the traces and the fossilized remains of the previous magmatic process. In the designs of those authors—of, say, a Julian, a Gaius, not to mention Paul or Ulpian—the ancient polarity of the Roman legal order dissolved into a harmony of lines and interpretations in which everything appeared to be solid and compositionally reconciled: the projection of this image of completeness would contribute not insignificantly to the mythical status of "classical" law.

But the original dualism, in the period of its earliest and most fervid development, must have had much more dissonant features. It was not, however, an opposition between different legal systems: this is another modern distortion, of positivist derivation, and is entirely alien to Roman legal culture. Rather, there was an alternation of positions—to some extent radically different and potentially conflicting—within the continuity of a single path, a single web, represented by the life of the city itself, captured from the standpoint of its social discipline, the course of its *ius* and its *iuris dictio.*

And as with other polarities to which we referred earlier, the dualism be-

tween *ius civile* and *ius honorarium* (to use the names established by later jurisprudence) also did not express a political or social contrast. Behind it we can
see nothing that refers to the partisan antagonisms that had marked republican history, nothing similar to the original alternative between *ius* and *lex*.
The two viewpoints emerged from the same milieux, and were often sustained by the same men—magistrates and jurists—at different but contiguous phases of their activity: the same praetor decided, case by case and in the
context of his professional discretion, whether to apply the Twelve Tables or
to opt for the trial formula that had been established by his predecessor, and
thus effectively to acknowledge a claim that was entirely inadmissible for the
ius civile. It was what might be called a functional dualism, corresponding to
the morphology of a society and a culture that had no difficulty in identifying
with them: a symmetry in which, through its law, the entire history of Rome
revealed (as we shall see) one of its most profound and hidden traits. [20]

5.

When they chose to depart from the *ius civile,* and to administer justice on
the basis of their own edicts, the praetors wound up adhering to a number of
guiding principles that had already been developed between the third and the
second century, and which would become, in legal thinking, equally crucial
points in the development of Roman law. Naturally, they were never set forth
explicitly, nor did successive thought formulate them in any systematic and
direct fashion. Nonetheless, we can identify them quite clearly (and indeed
we shall come across them again later).

First and foremost, consensualism, that is to say, acknowledgment of the
agreement between the parties (*consensus,* according to a term that was consolidated in the third and second centuries; later, *conventio; pactum,* according
to an earlier term, perhaps with a different semantic nuance), however manifested, provided it was demonstrable, and expressed, at least as early as the
turn of the first century, within the context of a typology of relations rigorously envisioned in the edicts: the one that was forming, through the interpretation of jurists, around the praetorian granting of actions "of the pur-
chased" and "of the sold," "of hiring" and "of the hired," "in defense of the
partner" and "of the mandate," and which would lead to the jurisprudential

formation of the corresponding contractual schemes of sale, hire, partnership, and mandate.

Then there was reciprocity, later conceptualized in a strand of jurisprudence around the notions of *synallagma* and *ultro citroque obligatio* (obligation on one side and the other), according to which, in a transaction, an economically onerous performance already discharged by one of the parties to the contract should be matched by a symmetrical performance on the part of the other party, or at least its financial equivalent.[21] Another principle was the idea of "good faith" (*bona fides,* already in the republican legal language), where the reference to *bonum* betrayed the distinctly aristocratic and proprietary reelaboration—according to the perceptive intuition of Nietzsche—of the more ancient *fides,* the faith one is capable of radiating; from the point of view of the praetor, this meant a commitment to a reliable and trustworthy form of behavior, based on the Roman tradition, as a way of limiting "Mediterranean" mercantile cunning.[22]

Finally, and in many ways the most important of all, "fairness" (*aequum,* according to attestations from the middle republican era): a criterion whereby, in the assessment of a case for trial purposes, the literal application of the *ius civile* could be set aside in favor of a more flexible measure that was better suited to the interests and values at stake: "since it is often the case that, though a man is liable at civil law, his condemnation in an action would be inequitable," according to the carefully chosen words of Gaius,[23] who often liked to present as present-day productions legal constructions that were much older than the mature Antonine age.

It is worth looking more closely at this latter notion, because of the implications it would have, and a good point of departure for doing so is the text by Gaius that we have just mentioned.

As we have seen, the jurist organized his discourse by exhibiting a possible (and paradoxical) coincidence between (civil) law and the inequitable (*ius civile* and *iniquum*), imagining, that is, the existence of *ius* that might prove to be the opposite of *aequum*: it was to correct this aberrant outcome (he explained) that the praetor intervened. This was not an original piece of reasoning: indeed its presence was an indication of the great antiquity of the conceptual (and perhaps even narrative) materials that Gaius was employing in this circumstance. And the idea that law could be perverted into injustice—the central core of the argumentation—was the most well-worn of them all. The first formulation known to us extends very far back in time, again to the second century B.C., to a verse by Terence: "ius summum saepe summast malitia"—"the height of law is often the height of malice"[24]—a line that, given the way in which it was introduced into the dialogue of his play *Heautontimorumenos (The Self-Tormentor),* seems to preserve and convey the flavor of an already familiar concept ("it's true what they say," affirms the character who utters it immediately beforehand).[25] It is possible that here Terence was reworking Greek motifs (he was probably drawing on Menander, but in that case these would be reflections which emerged in cultural contexts that were not comparable, and with quite different meanings).[26] It is certain in any case that the Latin author translated what he perhaps read in the model, presenting it in terms that must have sounded profoundly familiar to the Roman public. And that is precisely how—almost as if it were a cliché or a commonplace, a *tritum proverbium*—the maxim was repeated, more than a century later, by Cicero, in a famous passage from the *De officiis:* "summum ius, summa iniuria"—"the height of law, the height of injustice."[27] We do not know whether this formulation, not devoid of elegance and focused entirely on the counterpoint between *ius* and *iniuria* (with the two terms in reciprocal lexical and semantic reversal), is due to an original stylistic construction, or instead literally reproduces (as Cicero attempts to convey) a timeworn play on words, well consolidated in an old tradition midway between folklore and learned wisdom. In the two versions—one by Terence, the other from the *De officiis*—both the expression *summum ius* and the repetition of the adjective (*summum . . . summa*) are stable, while what changes is the substantive used in contrast with *ius: malitia* in one case, *iniuria*—more elegantly—in the other. But the idea that was being expressed appeared in both contexts as the legacy of an unquestionable and very ancient experience. And it is again in these terms, finally, that we find the maxim in a text by Columella, shortly after the middle of the first century A.D.: "nam summum ius antiqui summam putabant crucem" ("the ancients considered the height of the law to be the height of torment").[28] Once again, only the second noun changes with respect to the preceding formulations—now the choice was to use *crux*—while the content remains the same, and is explicitly referred to an unspecified but ancient tradition.

But in the name of what principle, of what violation of reasonableness, was *ius* criticized so forcefully?

Let us return for a moment to Gaius and Cicero. The former offered a specific indication: the praetor intervened with the means at his disposal (in this case, an *exceptio*—exception—in favor of the defendant to reject the claim of the plaintiff, because the outcome that would otherwise have been attained in accordance with the *ius civile* would have been "inequitable"; and this would happen for example, Gaius continued, if someone were condemned to repay a sum of money that he had never actually received in the first place, despite a solemn promise to that effect (according to the ritualism of the *ius civile,* the obligation of repayment was incurred from the moment the promise was uttered, with no consideration of whether the money was actually delivered—let us recall the words of the Twelve Tables: "uti lingua nuncupassit, ita ius esto"); or if someone who had made a certain pact was suddenly asked to fulfill it, despite the fact that the creditor had made an agreement with him, promising to desist for a certain time from the exercise of his claim (a simple informal agreement could not modify an obligation that had been established in accordance with the rituals of the *ius civile*).[29] According to Gaius, then, who was drawing on a much older point of view, "iniquity" meant the enrichment of one party without a justified social or economic reason, but merely in compliance with the ancient rituals. The (possible) connection between ritualism and iniquity, however, is not without remedy; it is broken by the intrusion of an alternative view, which is not satisfied by the respect of words and gestures, but focuses instead on the substance of matters: it is precisely this that dispels iniquity, but not to make way for *ius,* which vanishes at the same time, but for something new and previously unconceived, which is the genuine and hidden driving force behind Gaius' explanation: the respect of "fairness."

Cicero had already moved in the same direction, though in that context he did not even name the principle, despite being very well acquainted with it (as we shall see). "Wrongs often arise also through chicanery and an oversubtle interpretation of the law" ("existunt etiam saepe iniuriae calumnia quadam et nimis callida iuris interpretatione"), he wrote in the passage of *De officiis* to introduce his version of the maxim, before giving as an example the case of a general, who, having agreed to a truce of thirty "days," then proceeded to lay waste to enemy territory "by night," considering himself fully authorized to do so in accordance with the letter of the treaty.[30] What was at issue here was now, rather than ritualism, the verbalistic subtleties of the jurisprudence of pontifical tradition, and the *lege agere* that derived therefrom: here, one had only to make a slight slip, saying "vines" instead of "trees," to lose a case. The orientation, however, was the same as the one that later crops up in the account by Gaius: in both texts we are abruptly confronted with the break-up of the magical-religious world of Roman archaism—which had survived in a formulaic structure that changes in the city had stripped of almost all justification—which freed up an entirely unprecedented outlook. It was the awareness, finally, of the substance of relations, and no longer merely their symbolic guise—long considered to be both indispensable and highly retributive—that permitted the critique of a *ius* imprisoned within its own past, on the basis of a balanced and concrete rationality that had never hitherto been tested in such an explicit and direct manner on the plane of social ordering.

The new style had a guiding idea, a date, and a protagonist. The first was identified, as we have mentioned, with the notion of *aequum* (which Gaius only gives us a glimpse of in his text). As for the date, we find ourselves once again in the period between the third and the second century: it is in the context of a small group of documents dating from this period that the word makes its first appearance. And it always comes up—in a coincidence so glaring that it would be difficult to understate it—alongside *ius* or (in one case) with *lex.*

Let us begin with Ennius, in some verses handed down by Nonius: "id ego ius atque aecum fecisse expedibo atque eloquar" (this is Apollo speaking, in the *Eumenides:* "I shall explain and say that he [Orestes] did that in accordance with *ius* and *aecum*");[31] and "Melius est virtute ius: nam saepe virtutem mali / nanciscuntur: ius atque aecum se a malis spernit procul" ("Better than valor is *ius:* for often wicked men may stumble upon valor; but *ius* and *aequum* always ward off the wicked from themselves": a fragment from

[149]

The Ransom of Hector).[32] Then there is Plautus, in the *Menaechmi* (or *The Twin Brothers*): "qui neque leges neque aequom bonum usquam colunt / sollicitos patronos habent" ("Who [among the clients] fails to respect either laws or *aequum bonum* must have zealous patrons").[33] And again, in the words of Epignomus in the *Stichus:* "et ius et aequom postulas: sumas, Stiche" ("your request is in keeping with *ius* and *aequum.* Go ahead, Stichus").[34] And finally, Terence, again in the *Heautontimorumenos:* "Quid cum illis agas, qui neque ius neque bonum atque aequom sciunt?" ("What can you do with people who know nothing either of *ius* or of *bonum* and *aequum?*" says Chremes).[35]

What is striking about all the texts is the stereotypical value of the pair. At the end of the third century, it must have been used topically, in a Latin that might not have been particularly learned—those speaking, both in Plautus and in Terence, are certainly characters of less than impressive culture, simple men[36]—to succinctly and effectively describe an element about whose identity we can have little or no doubt: the set of rules that guided the social behavior of the collectivity—we would undoubtedly say the world of law—inasmuch as it was a complex of norms and values. Evidently, to indicate this function in its entirety, which, as we have seen, was in those very same years increasingly positioning itself as something distinct and specific in the Roman perception, the word *ius* on its own was no longer sufficient. It needed to be complemented with a second noun capable of evoking another level of rules, distinct from but not in opposition to the first: a modality that was new (there had been no trace of it until then), but in some way already crystallized, and endowed with what might be described as an institutional relevance of its own, able to create, with *ius,* a bipartite but homogeneous totality.

And who was the head of this new order? The text of the *Menaechmi*—testimony that we should take very seriously—offers us an unmistakable identification. After the verse quoted above ("Who [among the clients] fails to respect either laws or *aequum bonum* must have zealous patrons"), Chremes continues his description of the crowded throng of unscrupulous clients. "What has been entrusted to them, they deny to have been so entrusted; men full of litigation, rapacious, and fraudulent; who have acquired their property either by usury or by perjury; their whole pleasure is in litigation. When the day for trial is appointed, at the same time it is mentioned to their patrons, in order that they may plead for them, about what they have done amiss. Before the people, or before the praetor, or before a private judge, is the cause tried."[37] The symmetry could not be any more clear and evident. At the beginning of the passage, Chremes has mentioned the laws and *bonum et aequum:* those who fail to respect them end badly, and must have "zealous patrons," with a first, veiled reference to the trial ambit where, in fact, the intervention of the patrons would need to take place. Thereafter the allusion becomes more explicit, and in perfect correspondence with the initial indication of the *leges* and the *bonum et aequum,* there is an indication of the places where the unworthy men who failed to respect that sphere would end up: either a criminal trial before the popular assembly, governed in fact by *leges,* starting with the Twelve Tables ("aut ad populum . . ."); or else a civil trial— to which evidently the previous reference to *bonum et aequum* is directed—indicated here, with absolute technical precision, in its two constituent phases ("aut in iure aut ad iudicem"); and for that matter immediately before that Chremes uses the expression *ubi dicitur dies,* which reiterates precisely the formula—*diei dictio*—through which the accused was ordered to appear on a certain date before the assembly of the people for judgment (the *contio*).[38]

In the language used by Plautus—and, we may safely assume, in that of Ennius and Terence as well—the reference to *aequum* must have represented an eloquent way of connoting, through the evocation of its most innovative aspect, a set of rules and evaluations different and complementary to those indicated by *ius,* and which found its institutional anchor in the praetorian jurisdiction: formulary procedure; nascent consensualism; attention to the reciprocity of performances; good faith as a measure of the behavior of the parties. The praetors, then, and they alone, were the protagonists of the new style of disciplining rationality summarized figuratively by the invocation of *aequum.*

We also know that in the republican age formulas of the new type of trial existed in which the magistrate explicitly inserted a clause whereby the sentence would be limited to "quantum . . . aequum iudici videbitur"—"as much as seems fair to the judge"—according to the text of the *actio iniuriarium* (an action for injurious behavior, also including minor bodily harm), which has survived through the memory of a jurist from the Augustan age, Fabius Mela, later quoted by Ulpian: probably the earliest trial scheme with a direct reference to *aequum.*[39] Evidently, however, in the common perception, as reflected in the language of Ennius, Plautus, and Terence, the meaning of the term went well beyond these specific aspects. The word must have appeared instead as emblematic of a newer and more flexible ordering, better suited to the demands of a growing community, capable of combining the intrinsic case-based vocation of the Roman prescriptive experience (an original trait that was never abandoned) with a closer and more realistic assessment of the interests and requirements at stake in given circumstances: an important driving force behind the erosion of the ritualistic skeleton of a *ius civile* still entirely based upon the Twelve Tables and the pontifical interpretation; a *ius* whose rigorous respect might result (according to a widely shared belief) in the most blatant wrong.

In this sense, *aequum* expressed in its original semantic field—which can be rendered as "the equal," "the balanced," or "the leveled"—a mental form that also dated far back into the culture of the city (as we have noted), updated and revived by the new times: the tendency toward the practice of redistribution, to social symmetry, to a community equilibrium. It did not greatly alter the Roman legal reality with respect to its archaic roots, but it did reflect a tendency, no less ancient than the one expressed by the term *ius* (the ritualistic prescription as the order of the world), which nonetheless had not yet succeeded in manifesting itself with equal force on the plane of a social ordering completely infused with ritual customs.[40]

As we have already seen in part, alongside *aequum* there also frequently appeared, in Latin usage in the republican age, the other neuter *bonum,* combined with the first term in still unstable sequences: in addition to the texts mentioned above we must add another dozen or so, also from Plautus and Terence.[41] There is no need here to consider the presence of this second word also in the original content of the procedural formulas that made reference to *aequum.* Suffice it to point out that one datum does not appear ever to have been contradicted: the early formation, around the sequence, of an expressive stereotypy extensively documented in the literature (we have just encountered it), that would certainly be difficult to explain except as a reflection of a rapidly consolidating technical language. The range of meanings that were thus evoked was in any case linked to the representation of a point of view—proper to the praetorian jurisdiction—congruent with factual situations, with particular circumstances, with the concrete analysis of each case instead of its ritual stylization, with the contingent equilibriums to be respected or restored, as a silent or explicit alternative to a *ius (civile)* incapable of extricating itself from its own ceremonial, verbal, and gestural schemes.

The distinction between *ius* and *aequum* was not, however, destined to become established. It would last as long as *ius* was identified only with the *ius civile* of the pontifical tradition. But soon this would no longer be the case, and already toward the end of the second century B.C. the praetorian jurisdiction was perceived as also being capable of creating *ius,* even though different from that of the civil law tradition, and limited only to the context of actions. *Ius honorarium,* as it began to be called, was a system of rules reliant upon the edicts of the magistrates, which the incessant interpretative activity of the jurists through their *responsa* linked, by means of a subtle process of disjunction and connection, to the old structure of the *ius civile,* also considered from a perspective less and less tied to archaic conceptions, and yet not entirely forgetful of the past.

And when, at the beginning of the first century B.C., the earliest Roman treatise of rhetoric presented, in an important passage to which we shall return, a description of the "parts of the law"—the first to be found in Roman culture ("Constat autem [ius] ex his partibus . . .")—*aequum et bonum* readily and unproblematically figured as one of the components of the whole:[42] the *ius civile* no longer constituted the entire field of *ius,* nor was *aequum* a world apart *(ius ac aequum);* instead, both formed part of a totality, which we can by now safely describe as the Roman legal order, within which they indicated the poles of a dialectic between rigidity and flexibility that would endure right up until its mature integration into the thought of the Severan jurists.

In this development, even the maxim concerning the *summum ius summa iniuria* lost much of its original critical force. Already when Cicero adopted it, it must no longer have regarded the whole world of *ius,* in the name of a different disciplining principle, but rather expressed a general warning inviting jurists not to rely upon an overly rigorous consequentiality or on excessively literal interpretations: a message, as we shall see, to which great attention would be paid.

10

Orality and Writing

I.

Scholars customarily consider the 40s and 30s of the second century B.C. as a crucial period in the history of Rome. It was the age in which the aristocratic leadership's will to empire—following the annihilation of Carthage and the definitive occupation of Greece—assumed the definitive traits of world domination.

In the confident and effective picture painted by Polybius, who was writing after 146 B.C., progress over the course of time meant nothing other, in the affairs of the Romans, than the acquisition of new territories. The historian made conscious use of a Thucydidean scheme, testing it out on a far broader stage than that of classical Greece: behind the formation of any great power, there must necessarily be a firm aspiration to conquest. And he had no doubt that, between 220 and 168 B.C.—the fifty-three decisive years of his account, from the onset of the Second Punic War until the Macedonian disaster of Pydna—Rome had already embarked upon a project that aimed at worldwide hegemony, which would ultimately lead to the birth of a universal historiography: "but ever since this date history has been an organic whole, and the affairs of Italy have been interlinked with those of Africa, those of Asia with those of Greece, and all have one and the same end."[1]

And in fact, something really had changed in the mechanism of Roman expansionism. The impulse to wage war had now become more important than attaining the original objective, namely security, the need for which had dominated the city from the moment of its foundation, and had shaped its earliest mentality in such a decisive manner. The dogged search for protected areas, on land and sea, was yielding to a very different pressure. Conquest was beginning to become a sort of collective conditioned response, a good thing in itself, a value that became self-justifying in the culture and the ethical and political system of society as a whole. Not just in the behavior of a no-bility increasingly conditioned by the "lust for glory"[2]—the Roman aristoc-racy was, from its earliest origins, a warrior aristocracy: "warfare was almost continuous then," as Cicero later put it[3]—but also in that of the lower social classes, in the masses of disfranchised citizens—impoverished peasants up-rooted from a rural landscape now dominated by large landholdings—which increasingly swelled the ranks of what was well on the way to becoming a fully professional army.

The definitive consolidation of the imperial perspective, however, was not all that filled the horizons of the period; other phenomena of no less im-portance—by and large, themselves consequences of the process of expan-sion—began to invade the public stage. The most significant developments concerned the institutional framework. The fabric of the oligarchic compro-mise, which had provided the city with an exceptionally solid foundation for its expansion into the rest of Italy and across the sea, began to crumble under the weight of pressures too great for such a reality. The year 133 B.C., with the tribuneship of Tiberius Gracchus, marked the beginning of the "hundred-year revolution"[4] that was destined to rock the very foundations of the repub-lican system.

The proceeds from the conquests were increasingly determining the shape of Roman social and political history. In the Athens of the second half of the fifth century B.C, control of the seas had contributed to the preserva-tion of democracy. In Rome, on the other hand, the empire definitively sepa-rated the aristocracy and the populace, shattering the cohesion that had been constructed with the end of the plebeian conflicts; it destroyed the pattern of small peasant landholdings—which had been the foundation of the repub-lic—crushing it beneath the weight of war corvée and the competition from large estates worked by slaves. The result was widespread unemployment, which assumed massive dimensions in the large coastal cities and the capital, where the uprooted rural population sought shelter. But empire also brought with it opportunities for promotion and upward social mobility to an extent unknown to the rest of the ancient world, and for the formation—both in Italy and in the provinces—of new landowning classes, which exchanged pledges of loyalty for material prosperity. And it also permitted the maintenance (especially in the capital) of a network of public assistance that allowed the new proletariat to exchange political consensus for bare-bones survival: a vote in the *comitia,* in return for bread and circuses.[5]

But in those decades, in the same places and the same aristocratic milieus, another, less visible but nonetheless equally decisive transformation was taking place. The prestigious body of legal knowledge—an integral part and a prominent element of the hegemonic system of the *nobilitas*—was entering its season of great change, powered no less by the vehement capacity for innovation manifested in the praetors' edicts, with which jurisprudence continually had to deal, than by the ever more pressing crisis of the political order inherited from a lengthy tradition.

The convergence of these different series of events—the rise to world power, the crisis of the social bloc that had brought about the success of the republic, and the transformation of legal knowledge—was no coincidence: they were linked by a subterranean and as yet unexplored connection, which we must attempt to uncover.

The awareness of the change—that something memorable had happened for Roman legal culture in those years—was very ancient. It can already be found in the more mature jurisprudential thinking of the middle years of the principate. And the figure we must turn to in this context, whom we have already had cause to mention and shall encounter again later, is Sextus Pomponius, who lived between the age of Hadrian and that of the *Divi fratres.* He wrote a book that was entirely atypical for Roman legal literature: entitled the *Enchiridion,* meaning "manual" or "breviary," it was possibly a single volume, or perhaps more extensive in length. Justinian's compilers, who were able to read it through an extremely tortuous textual tradition, reproduced several large sections of it in the *Digesta.*[6] The singularity of the work—which makes it exceptional for us—is its shaping of a perspective that was otherwise almost entirely absent from ancient culture: an account of the history of jurisprudence and of Roman legal systems, which Pomponius related, however summarily, from the earliest origins of the city to his own times.

In truth it was a fairly unimpressive sort of historiography, halfway between a chronicle and a compilation of anecdotes. The profile it offered was almost entirely extrinsic to the vicissitudes of legal thought being evoked, though not devoid of significance. It mentioned names and public careers, biographical details, the titles and size of works, in keeping with a taste and a style related to some extent to the intellectuals active in the reign of Hadrian; but there was almost no reference to the content of the work of the jurists mentioned, or to the role played by their doctrines in the elaboration of a centuries-old knowledge.

Nonetheless, there are occasional breaks in this silence, where the bare and monotonous prose of the *Enchiridion* allows us to hear a voice with a more absorbing tale to tell. They reveal some assessments of merit that would have been quite clear to a leading jurist like Pomponius. Of particular interest to us are three specific observations—brief flashes of light in a long sequence of gray—all of which are in the section devoted to the history of jurisprudence between the middle of the second century B.C. and the years of Augustus.

The first involves three figures active after 150 B.C., Junius Brutus, Manius Manilius, and Publius Mucius Scaevola, who, Pomponius says, "consolidated the *ius civile*."[7] The second refers to the son of Publius Mucius, Quintus, who "first established the civil law in genera."[8] The third and last one concerns Marcus Antistius Labeo, the famous jurist from the Augustan age mentioned earlier, who introduced "a great many new innovations."[9] *Fundare, primus constituere, plurima innovare:* running through the different judgments we can perceive a single and deeply rooted conviction: in the context of a history of legal thought attentive to the content of the knowledge under consideration—Pomponius seems to be trying to say—the age to which these figures belonged should be seen as the century of the great sea change.

Nothing more is to be gleaned from the *Enchiridion*, at least in this respect; although other evidence does suggest the existence of a widespread belief in the jurisprudence of the principate that a decisive qualitative leap had taken place between the second and the first centuries B.C., which had reduced the preceding periods, from the point of view of law, to little more than an extended period of prehistory, albeit valued and revered—a conviction that survived right through to Justinian's editors, who went no further back in their compilation than the work of Quintus Mucius. But what the ancient authors never did was to try to describe the constituent features of this radical change. They took a significant perception of change for granted, absorbed it into their working practice, but they never really gave an account of it.

Pomponius had seen things correctly: the intellectual revolution that marked the birth of the new legal thought really did coincide with the biography of certain leading figures in the jurisprudence of the late republican period and the very beginning of the principate. Most of them, following the *Enchiridion*, have already been mentioned: Publius Mucius Scaevola, his son Quintus, Servius Sulpicius Rufus (also significantly cited by Pomponius), and Antistius Labeo. They were not the conscious protagonists of a unified project. They worked in different directions, under the influence of different pressures and needs. But they did so in accordance with specific modalities determined by the conditions of the era, with the experience of each being inherited and evaluated by the following generation, and utilized within the context of a more complex paradigm. The entire web could thus be seen by a retrospective gaze as the profile of a single design

Yet these men did not just devote their lives to the study of law. They were also, in keeping with republican custom, magistrates and aristocratic members of government; and the meaning of their intellectual choices is incomprehensible if we fail to take into account their uninterrupted involvement in politics.

In the years from the Gracchan failure to Augustus' seizure of power, the major aristocratic families found themselves faced with a crucial question of ideological and political identity. The problem was how to reconcile the new developments of the imperial reality, some of them profoundly disturbing, with the institutional and cultural models elaborated by a long tradition, the abandonment of which—as events themselves often seemed to impose—was perceived as ruinous.

The jurists were at the heart of this tension. They were, in many ways, the custodians of the past: the *ius civile,* which lived on in their responses, was part and parcel of the very history of the city. Through their collective memory, the ancient *mores* continued to speak, and the remote legislator of the Twelve Tables continued to be heard. But they were also—given the peculiar nature of their position of command, and the jurisdiction that all of them, as praetors (and some of them also as promagistrates), had had the opportunity to exercise—the ones who more than anyone else could perceive and grasp the changes that were being produced, and to which they themselves were contributing in no small measure. In their education and training, there were always two fundamental tenets: nothing should violate tradition, but nor should anything lie outside of a body of knowledge capable of dictating rules suited to the needs of the present. Up to a certain point, the dialectic between *ius civile* and edicts seemed to be an adequate response. But from the turn of the first century onwards, the precipitous rush of events and the transformation of the city under the overwhelming weight of empire appeared to open up a menacing, and even insuperable, fracture between loyalty to received canons and the new demands pouring in from every direction.

Concentrated into the few decades from the end of the Social War, and coinciding with the culmination of expansion, was Sulla's constitutional and administrative reorganization; the urbanization of south-central and Cisalpine Italy (where the phenomenon took the form of an imposing rationalization of the territory, destined to leave a millennial mark); Pompey's feats in the East and on the seas; Spartacus and the last great slave revolt; Caesar's conquest of Gaul, through to the outcome of the civil war and the Augustan peace: a feverish and ineluctable *"prestissimo"* without parallel in ancient history.[10]

The crisis of the nobility and the disintegration of the political set-up and the social bloc that supported them had deep-rooted causes, linked both to the shortsightedness and the political mediocrity of the chief exponents of the aristocratic elite (excluding Sulla and, to a certain extent, Pompey), and, above all, to the consequences of expansion and conquest. To say nothing of the problem of sheer size: Roman assemblies—like all those of antiquity—operated on the principle of direct representation. There was no form of delegation: they were based on the personal participation of citizens, who voted on laws and elected magistrates. This arrangement presupposed that the boundaries of the republic extended little further than the capital. So it had been for centuries. But when, in the wake of the Social War, the polis grew to embrace virtually all of peninsular Italy, the system broke down, consigning the *comitia* to a restricted minority of residents and of the privileged (who could afford the cost of lengthy journeys).[11]

Suddenly faced by this shift in scale, the old senatorial ruling group was never capable of conceiving its own role in terms of an authentic Italic community, and often it even refused to accept any form of integration of the new city elites that had become established from southern Italy to the Po valley in the north. The conditioned reflex remained the closing of oligarchic ranks, the tightening of class circles, in defense of an exclusivity of power that was by that point no longer sustainable.

The economic model based on the cycle of war-exploitation-tenders-profits-(further)war, and on the intertwining ties between the redistributive intervention of government bodies and market circuits had led, in Italy, to the accumulation of substantial resources: land, slave labor, financial liquidity, and technical knowledge. But it had also propelled onto the stage for the first time—in part as a result of mechanisms of social mobility offered by the new forms of military recruitment—the forces, ambitions, expectations, and needs of groups, classes, and milieus, both in Rome and in Italy, which were demanding access, recognition, and power: a context that was well beyond the capacity of the aristocratic networks to control.

The history of the struggle between the various late-republican factions, from the Gracchi to Caesar, offers us the surprising image of a ferocious clash of political groups that can all to some degree be traced back to the disintegration of the unified fabric of the nobility, which did not have any authentic political ideas or any concrete, contrasting programs. A fight for power in which it is impossible to find either the broad sweep of big themes or a trace of any true alternatives. It is not our task here to explain the origin of this lack: we are in any case in the presence of a deep-rooted characteristic, dating back in part to the persistence of a tenacious and substantial oligarchic imprint found deep within the whole course of Roman history, in contrast with that of Athens (or, with far more specific class connotations, that of medieval Florence), where the long and radical strife between the nobles and the demos (between *magnati* and *popolani* in the case of Florence) culminated in a conflict that the modern sensibility would find it much easier to grasp.[12] Nor did the *equites* and the new Italic middle classes truly manage to establish themselves as a distinct and recognizable presence, much less to become—above all in cultural terms—something comparable to a modern bourgeoisie, even though they had developed certain elements of such a class.[13]

The harshness of the conflict thus seemed to close in upon itself: there was never the prospect of an authentic way out, of a clear innovation in the set-up of power and the composition of the ruling groups. Everything flowed together in a single direction without alternatives, clearly detectable in the work of Sallust, who extolled it as a sort of negative anthropology of political action: "only a few prefer liberty; most seek nothing more than just masters," we read in the *Histories*.[14] The naturalistic scheme of Aristotle's *Politics*—"There is he who rules by nature, and he who is ruled"[15]—was reinterpreted in the light of a bitter and pessimistic historicization.

In the end, the city would find an answer. As a result, disintegration and chaos—the much-feared consequences of the *res novae,* the "new developments" that so terrified the majority of aristocrats—were averted. The brilliance of the Augustan solution consisted precisely in transforming the absolute fragility of the alternatives into the strong point of the adopted strategy. If there had been no space for a design based on new social protagonists, external to the aristocratic bloc, the only feasible path was to promote and organize a skillful "passive revolution" of the old ruling classes.[16] It required a willingness to give up some old privileges and powers, to be cautiously open to the new Italic elites—the local aristocracies, not the landowning middle classes—and to accept, in the new figure of the *princeps,* a leadership that was substantially elevated above the traditional noble and equestrian "orders," as well as the senate itself. The aim was to regenerate, in the eyes of the urban popular masses, the army, and even the Italic municipalities and the most important provincial circles, the legitimation of an ancient superiority, without ever really calling it into discussion, obtaining peace and security in exchange for the lost prerogatives.[17]

The jurists were totally involved in this effort to contain and dampen the new developments that emerged over the course of the first century, and they helped in a decisive way to establish the paradigms of the neoaristocratic stabilization. The intellectual revolution of which they were the protagonists had this significance as well. But the process—in some ways grandiose—of absorbing and adapting all the impulses and pressures within confines that ensured the survival and, in a certain sense, even the further growth of the imperial system was anything but painless. It devastated at least two generations of the old class of republican government, those who came onto the scene between Marius and Caesar: Quintus Mucius Scaevola and Servius Sulpicius Rufus would certainly have known something about it. Lives were physically consumed, and unrealistic political hypotheses swept away. But it also appropriated its remarkably rich laboratory of experiences, attempts, and models, bending it to new and more complex ends that had not even been glimpsed at the outset—the closest thing to modernity that the ancient world had ever produced—obtaining the constructive elements of a new equilibrium among the classes, of a previously unseen constitutional set-up, of a more advanced and complex relationship between politics and areas of knowledge, and, as far as law was concerned, between ordering and knowledge, between disciplining and episteme.

Unless viewed carefully against the backdrop of such a setting, the entire history of jurisprudence from Publius Mucius to Labeo runs the risk of remaining indecipherable. It speaks to us of the relatively sudden attainment of a radical qualitative leap, which managed to merge in an original manner with the reelaborations of the old sapiential tradition, in an intertwining that would remain one of the most distinctive features of the whole of Roman legal thought. And it reveals to us the earliest establishment, in Western history, of jurists as a professional class, invested with distinct and recognizable interests and values: still, of course, an expression of the dominant elites, but not directly identifiable with the groups in power and then with the circles of the *princeps* himself.

On various occasions during all this, the renewal of the cultural fabric upon which it was working was experienced by jurisprudence as a lacerating disconnection from the dramatic developments of the political situation. Quintus Mucius Scaevola was probably the last to believe a synthesis was possible between studies and politics, in keeping with the parameters of the old aristocratic rationality. After him, specialist-based progress and hope in an outcome that might result in the reestablishment of the city's original institutions and hierarchies parted company. The trauma of this division still made a profound impact on the life of Labeo, with whom the cycle of change came to an end, and who, in his lifetime, witnessed the definitive triumph of Augustus.

2.

The first part of our story is also that of a family, the Mucii Scaevola: of Publius Mucius Scaevola and his son Quintus Mucius Scaevola.

Members of the ancient plebeian nobility, the Mucii had long seen their finest men rise frequently to the highest magistracies of the republic.[18] And Publius Mucius Scaevola, praetor in 179 B.C. and consul in 175, fathered, around 180, the Publius Mucius that interests us here.[19] His career was every bit as brilliant as those of his father and his uncle, but his consulship came at a difficult time: 133 B.C., the year of Tiberius Gracchus.

Relations with the tribune were anything but straightforward: the decisions made by Publius in that intricate situation are perhaps tinged with uncertainty and ambiguity. Nonetheless, his prestige—at least among the most important aristocratic groups—was not tarnished, and from 130 on he held the office of pontifex maximus, the culmination of a long career in the heart of the republic.[20]

In addition to and even more than politics, his life was filled by legal knowledge, this too part of a family tradition: for nearly a century the Mucii Scaevola had cultivated a knowledge of *ius*, and publicly offered responses.[21] Publius was the greatest expert in law of his time: an exemplary figure, as we have seen, in the gallery of illustrious men depicted by Cicero in his *De republica*.

In the *Enchiridion*, Pomponius mentions his name with great emphasis: "After these men [the two Catos, Cato the Censor and Marcus Porcius Cato Licinianus, who were also father and son] came Publius Mucius and Brutus and Manilius, who consolidated the *ius civile*."[22]

It is a peremptory yet highly enigmatic judgment, which has puzzled historians over the years. It clearly alludes to a new phase in legal knowledge, destined even centuries later to be viewed as a fundamental transition. But what exactly did it consist of, and how did it come about?

Only a few faint traces of Publius Mucius' thought can be pieced together today, all of them mediated by subsequent authors: a quotation from Labeo; another text by Pomponius; a passage from Aulus Gellius; one from the *Rhetorica ad Herennium;* and finally a brief chain of testimony in Cicero.[23]

But we do know with absolute certainty that Publius wrote a work—not a very long one—dedicated to the *ius civile,* from which many of the citations mentioned here come. And it is the composition of this text, and the choice that underlies it, to which we must now turn our attention.

When Publius Mucius produced the ten books of his opus (or *libelli*, little books, according to the designation found in Cicero, and adopted by Pomponius),[24] Roman legal knowledge was still, as we have seen, marked by a great poverty of texts. It was around 140 B.C.., and until then writing had cropped up only rarely in the legal tradition, associated in any case with particular circumstances, as had been the case with *De usurpationibus,* and then for the *Tripertita.* But in the middle of the second century, there was a sudden increase. Cato's books on the *ius civile* appeared—we cannot be sure whether this was Cato the Censor, or, as is perhaps more likely, his son, Cato Licinianus, who died in 152 B.C., prior to the death of his father, just after being elected praetor but before he could take office (both were interested in *ius,* and wrote about it in roughly the same period)—a little before the work of Publius.[25] The writings of the two other figures mentioned by Pomponius also appeared: three books by Brutus and seven by Manilius.[26]

Little more than a century later, when Antistius Labeo wrote his commentary on the praetor's edict, Roman legal literature already had a history of its own. All the genres that were to characterize its entire course had been created: the treatise on *ius civile,* by Quintus Mucius; the great case-study anthology composed in the school of Servius by Alphenus Varus and Aufidius Namusa; the commentary on the edict, first with Servius, and later with Ofilius and Labeo.[27] And the latter already had to engage with a textual universe so complex that it was regularly necessary to tackle problems of selection and citation with respect to previous authors. In less than a century and a half, a complete literarization of Roman legal knowledge took place: a phenomenon that it is impossible to separate from the simultaneous transformation of the content itself. They are the two traits of the same change. And it is in the work of Publius Mucius that we can first find them together, albeit in an embryonic form.

In his writing, as in that of Brutus (some doubt may perhaps remain for Manilius),[28] the material utilized consisted of records of the *responsa* given orally by the author. For the first time, the duration over time of jurists' opinions was entrusted to the new method of communication; the relationship with oral memory began to give way to the new space of textuality.

But the change brought to the surface another major problem that must have traversed jurisprudence—even if at a subterranean level—at the end of the second and the beginning of the first century B.C.: how to endow legal knowledge with all the advantages of writing, without losing the legacy of centuries of orality. The unwritten culture of tradition, first pontifical and later secular, appeared to the aristocratic sensibility of the mid-second century as being far from weak thought, albeit inadequate at times. It was necessary to preserve its ancient richness, channeling it into new forms. This was a theme with distant roots: it had already been, in its own manner, a Platonic motif. "For this invention will produce forgetfulness in the minds of those who learn to use it, because they will not practice their memory. They trust in writing, produced by external characters which are no part of themselves," we read in the *Phaedrus*,[29] where an argument is employed that was to resurface with every major change in communication technology, from the invention of printing to the computer revolution: the route that we are retracing in the development of legal knowledge was certainly not a new one in ancient thought. Nor, for that matter, was the literarization of jurisprudence an isolated phenomenon in Roman culture: it grew in the context of an impetuous development of writing, which accompanied the Hellenistic wave that spread with the encouragement of important aristocratic circles, and ranged from historiography to poetry and rhetoric.[30] Rome rapidly filled with libraries and books, even though only in the case of *ius*—the supremely Roman wisdom— did the new form of communication have to engage with a significant background, which had adopted orality as its constituent characteristic: and that determined a very particular transition.

With Publius Mucius, Brutus, and Manilius (and probably with Cato himself) the figure of a new kind of jurist began to take shape: from the scanty documentation we have managed to gather, we can intuit the appearance of a genuinely analytical mode of thought, however laboriously attained. Writing finally appeared as an internalized technique, not subordinate to orality and to its formulaic rules—as was still the case in Appius Claudius and Sextus Aelius—but instead at the service of the development and valorization of personalities with an autonomous profile, who consciously tended to break away and distinguish themselves from the background represented by tradition. Writing was now the medium for a maturation of the wisdom that it expressed, linked to the establishment of a knowledge that had become too complex to remain enclosed within the old horizons of the past.

In the books of Cato—there are at least fifteen—the recipients of the *responsa* were still remembered with their names.[31] Evoking the figures of the questioners had more than a marginal significance. The specific memory of the request for an opinion pointed to the interweaving between the aristocratic families and the entire collectivity that constituted the very essence of the republic, at least as conceived by the nobility. And it served to prevent the shift to writing from causing the factual background of the knowledge thus evoked from fading with time: the written word was not intended to erase the civic contextualization of the issue discernable in the response.

But even within this framework, the figure of the author stood out with an unprecedented clarity. The admittedly minimal fragments that survive are sufficient to identify the traces of a body of work that would still be quite familiar to the jurisprudence of the principate: from Celsus, who cites Cato with precision, to Paul, active in the Severan age and to whom we owe another fairly precise recollection, all the way up to Ulpian.[32]

The effect of time and of the changes it wrought with respect to the validity and the interpretation of specific legal acts (a will or a promise of payment) is the common point of reference of two responses.[33] One in particular, extremely restrictive, according to which the invalidity of a legacy at the time of its formulation (for instance, because the property that was meant to be bequeathed was not part of the testator's estate) could not be amended by any event subsequent to the preparation of the will, was widely followed, to the point that it became paradigmatic.[34] Subsequent jurisprudence, probably in the period between Labeo and Celsus, would call it the *regula Catoniana,* projecting upon it a model—that of the *regula iuris*—which emerged (as we shall see) only much later.[35] But the anachronism is revealing: the original formulation (reported by Celsus) revealed a capacity of expression and interpretative generalization that was well situated in the culture of the period, which placed them without excessive contrivance at the beginning of a process of development that was just beginning to take shape (and, likewise, the other opinion, cited by Paulus, probably ended with the construction of a maxim).[36]

It is hard to understand why, if his work contained so many significant new ideas, Cato's name was not included by Pomponius among the figures who "consolidated" the *ius civile*. The answer cannot be anything other than hypothetical. Much of what Pomponius knew about the earliest jurisprudence reached him through the filter of the books *Iuris civilis*, by Quintus Mucius Scaevola, an authentic milestone of republican legal studies. This did not exclude the possibility of direct readings, when the texts were still available, but in any case Pomponius found in the work of Quintus Mucius, which he had studied closely, a reliable guide for evaluating what was alive and what was dead in that ancient tradition: a criterion for order and judgment. Yet whereas there is some evidence to suggest that in the work of Quintus Mucius there must have been a significant presence of the opinions of Brutus, Manilius, and his father Publius (and probably also of Sextus Aelius himself, who was much admired by Pomponius), we cannot say the same thing about the books of Cato; in fact, while the majority of the later citations of doctrines by the first three jurists have an origin that links them to the books of civil law by Mucius rather than to a direct reading of the originals, the faint traces of Cato seem to be absolutely independent of this intermediate source.[37]

It is reasonable, then, to suppose the existence of a sort of evaluative "Mucian canon" of the previous jurisprudence, faithfully reproduced by Pomponius (and perhaps even earlier by Labeo), in which Cato did not figure, in contrast with Brutus, Manilius, and Publius Mucius (and perhaps Sextus Aelius, whom Pomponius must have read directly). The reason for the exclusion can once again be conjectured in keeping with what we know. Cato's work—despite the traces of novelty it contained, which certainly would not have escaped Mucius—must have appeared to him as still lying outside the debate that had sprung up, relatively suddenly, in the 40s of the second century, and which he saw as centering upon the figure of his father. The books of Cato—perhaps a heterogeneous agglomeration of materials and not just his responses, which would explain its size, unusual for the times— remained outside this circuit; and they must have seemed an unsuccessful hodgepodge of the old and the new, suspended between Sextus Aelius and

Publius Mucius. And Quintus excluded them, preferring to link, when necessary, his father's generation directly to Sextus Aelius.

The three books by Marcus Junius Brutus—son of the consul of the same name who held office in 178 B.C., and himself praetor around 140[38]—are dialogic in nature: a choice that was never made again in the entire history of Roman jurisprudence.[39]

The dialogue was of the Varronian and not the Ciceronian variety: inside the packaging of the literary genre, the narrative content was not entirely reelaborated stylistically.[40] The work was crammed with characters: besides Brutus, there were, as in Cato, the names of those who had submitted the questions prompting the *responsa,* reframed in the written text as examples for his son (who was also a character in the dialogue).[41] The locations were also recorded, a different one for each book: Privernus, Albanus, Tivoli.[42]

It is quite likely that in this case as well, behind the idea of the dialogue, there was also a desire to keep alive the link with the old customs of the oral tradition, even though we cannot rule out Hellenistic, and possibly Peripatetic, influences.[43] Doctrines set forth in this work were still mentioned later by writers such as Cicero, Labeo, Gellius, Ulpian, Paul, and Modestinus.[44] Almost always, in these citations, the name of Brutus does not crop up on its own but together with that of Manilius or one of the Mucii (Publius or Quintus) or both.[45] Only in two cases is the jurist mentioned in solitude, by Ulpian: in one, Brutus discusses a problem relating to the application of the Lex Aquilia concerning damage to property; in the other, the topic examined concerns the regime of usufruct, a notion that at the time had only recently been consolidated in the Roman legal experience.[46] And once again we are in the presence of a general interpretative criterion, which attempted to discipline the intersection between a relatively new juridical figure, whose outlines were still fluid, and the practice of slavery, which was then developing to an incomparable degree.

The child born to a female slave did not belong to her usufructuary, said Brutus, because the fruit of a slave woman cannot include another slave (the question had also been discussed by Manilius and Publius Mucius, who, according to Cicero, took a differing view).[47] Ulpian called this formulation a *sententia,* a maxim—the word also used, as an alternative to *regula,* to indicate the principle developed by Cato. And in fact it was the same world that emerged: a jurisprudence that was seeking to equip itself with more powerful analytical instruments and operative methods, capable of embracing synthetically, through the shaping of a single discipline, entire families of cases.

The work of Manilius is more difficult to assess, also with regard to the relationship between his two known writings. About ten short citations survive,[48] too small a collection to evaluate the novelty of his thinking. One exception might be found in a short phrase about *nexum,* transcribed by Varro, perhaps the first attempt at a systematizing definition to be found in Roman legal thought: *"nexum . . .* those things which are done by bronze and scales, including property transfers"[49] (we shall have more to say about this below, in reference to Quintus Mucius, who did not approve of the Manilian approach, to which instead Aelius Gallus subscribed).[50] But the text is ambiguous, and it is difficult to conclude much from it alone: Manilius unified what the Twelve Tables had already brought together, and it is somewhat arbitrary to glimpse in this brief fragment a classificatory method that was a precursor of the studies in legal logic that would characterize first-century thought.

We may, however, state with confidence that the most advanced response came from the work of Publius Mucius. It can be supposed that the position of the interlocking series of *responsa* in the sequence of his books was not casual, but corresponded instead to some criterion that it is impossible for us to reconstruct; and the hypothesis that the order was inspired by that of the Twelve Tables remains unprovable.[51] What is certain is that there is no dialogic framework or naming of questioners in the transcription of the opinions.

In none of the traceable citations is there any reference to a specific work, so it is impossible to link with any certainty even one of the fragments to the composition of the *Decem libelli* about which Cicero and Pomponius write. Two elements in particular are striking in this small cluster of documents. The first is the notable presence of signs of debate between jurists—of *ius controversum,* as it would be technically known at a later date—that suggests a strong personal characterization of the work of Publius: a new development linked, as we have seen, to the adoption of writing, and which must have contributed to the formation of the "Mucian canon." Doctrinal disagreements are quite evident with respect to the retroactivity of the Lex Atinia, the legal regime of the *partus ancillae,* and the case of the imprisonment of Hostilius Mancinus; and perhaps may also be discerned in the question linked to the riots following the death of Tiberius Gracchus.[52]

The second element is the presence of a definition, the oldest together with the Manilian text on *nexum:* that of *ambitus aedium,* a notion dating back to the Twelve Tables: "Publius Scaevola has said that the *ambitus* of a house is only that space which is covered by a roof put up to protect a party wall, from which roof the water flows into the home of the man who has put up the roof."[53] The aim was probably to restrict the original meaning of *ambitus,* in connection with changes in urban building patterns and dwelling practices. The technical precision deployed by the jurist linked the meaning of the words to purely functional parameters: interpretation was by this point capable of detaching the normative element from the shell of tradition, handing it over to the logical force of the response alone.

3.

The introduction of writing had not been an isolated change within the body of legal knowledge. On the one hand, with the generation of Publius Mucius—and already, earlier, with Cato—a different kind of relationship began to be delineated between case and response, in which the expert's opinion tended not to be restricted to the specific nature of the question, but to lie on a broader disciplinary plane; and this path would then lead to the revolution of Quintus Mucius, of Servius, and of Labeo. On the other hand, a more complex ethics of jurisprudence as a "civil wisdom" was taking form, alongside other disciplines, inspired by different morals of persuasion and truth, with respect to the older city traditions.

A passage in *De oratore* reflects this increasing degree of intellectual and social complexity. In Cicero's fiction, Antonius is speaking:

> I ask then, of what service was legal knowledge to an orator in
> those cases, when that jurist was bound to come off victorious,
> who had been upheld, not by his own dexterity but by a strang-

er's, that is to say, not by legal knowledge but by eloquence? Often too have I heard how, when Publius Crassus was a candidate for the aedileship, and Servius Galba, his senior and a past consul, was in attendance upon him, having arranged a marriage between his son Gaius and the daughter of Crassus, a certain country-man approached Crassus to obtain his opinion: he took Crassus apart and laid the facts before him, but brought away from him advice that was more correct than conformable to his interest; whereupon Galba, noting his chagrin, accosted him by name, inquiring what the question was on which he had consulted Crassus. Having heard the client's tale and observing his agitation, 'I see,' said he, 'that Crassus was preoccupied and distracted when he advised you': he then seized Crassus himself by the hand and asked, 'How now, whatever entered your head to suggest such an opinion?' Upon this the other, with the assurance of profound knowledge, repeated that the position was as he had advised and the point unarguable. Galba, however, sportively and with varied and manifold illustrations, brought forward a number of analogies, and urged many considerations in favour of equity as against rigid law, and it is related that Crassus, being no match for him in discussion—though ranked among the accomplished, Crassus came nowhere near Galba—, took refuge in authorities, and pointed out his own statement both in the works of his brother Publius Mucius, and in the text-book of Sextus Aelius, yet after all admitted that Galba's argument seemed to him persuasive, and very near the truth.[54]

In this account, two different narrative layers coexist. The first is derived from the source that Cicero utilized to reconstruct the anecdote, which we can identify as the "autobiography" of P. Rutilius Rufus, consul in 105, orator, and legal expert—"a learned man devoted to philosophy" (he had been a pupil of Panaetius of Rhodes), closely tied to the Mucii (as a young man he had studied under Publius, whose home he had frequented assiduously).[55] The second layer, overlaid on the first, can be traced directly to the author of the *De oratore*.

The episode served a twofold function in the context of the dialogue.

First and foremost, it served to justify the apologia for the rhetorical talent of Servius Sulpicio Galba, consul in 144, who without being particularly versed in the study of law, had managed to prevail, in an exquisitely juristic discussion, over none other than Publius Licinius Crassus Dives Mucianus, consul in 131 and the brother of Publius Mucius Scaevola, as well as being himself a renowned expert in law ("the best speaker of all the jurisconsults," in the view of Pomponius).[56] Moreover, it allowed Cicero to construct, albeit with some contrivance, a precedent to the famous "causa Curiana" (a celebrated trial in which Quintus Mucius took part), linking the polemic between Galba and Mucianus with the opposition between *ius* and *aequitas* (we have already discussed its origin, but in the late republican age it was charged with partly new significance, about which more will be said in due course).[57]

It is quite likely, on the other hand, that in the Rutilian source used by Cicero, the recollection of the episode served a completely different and in some ways contrasting purpose. The objective may have been to cast a negative light on Galba's rhetorical opportunism, as opposed to Mucianus' rigorous correctness. It is however precisely this original meaning, which compared rhetoric and jurisprudence, that was so extremely significant. It testifies, in an indirect but unequivocal manner, to the existence and the complete cultural legitimacy, as early as the last few decades of the second century and within the same aristocratic groups, of two models of response, both defendable and justifiable, though on different planes: one "true" (with respect to the traditions of civic legal knowledge), the other built according to the interests to be protected (*ad suam rem accomodatum*).

What were being weighed one against another here were two paradigms of truth, dependent upon the recourse to clearly distinct techniques: legal knowledge on the one hand, and oratorical ability—though not entirely devoid of a grounding in law—on the other. And what was invoked and in all likelihood valued by Rutilius must have been the ethical foundation of the autonomy of legal knowledge, as compared to considerations of political opportunity and convenience. The behavior of Mucianus and Galba was based, in the stylized version of the account, on opposing notions of the duties and the functions of an aristocratic sage: that of a quest for the "truth," conducted rigorously within the context of a legal tradition conceived of as autonomous and powerfully legitimizing; and, in contrast, that of a willingness to construct the responses on the basis of a reckless assessment of the interests at play, including those of the responding jurist—in this case, the coinciding advantages of the peasant-elector and the aristocrat-candidate (and it was onto the roots of this contrast that Cicero rather unperceptively grafted the reference to *aequitas*).

But it would be a mistake to read this disagreement in terms of a clear contrast between the old and the new. If we look carefully, both positions can be seen to be reflections of the adjustments of aristocratic rationality in the face of the new reality of Rome as an imperial and world power. Galba's position was evidently veined with a possibilistic and utilitarian relativism that was very sensitive to the cultural climate of the age, the new forms of knowledge that had recently arrived from Greece and to the new ways of conducting politics. But the position of Mucianus—possibly emphasized by Rutilius and soft-pedaled by Cicero, to whose writing we probably owe the uncertain and ambiguously conciliatory denouement of the story—was every bit its equal. In it we can glimpse (at least as Rutilius must have presented it) an intuition of a new bond between the logic and the ethics of the response, between the rigor of legal knowledge and the moral and civil prestige that derived therefrom, which went beyond contingent interests to occupy a plane of greater intellectual autonomy with respect to oratorial techniques of persuasion. This was in keeping with a hypothesis and a program of the supremacy of legal reason that Rutilius must have learned from the Mucii (especially from Quintus), and which had guided his life, even in the most difficult moments.

The understanding of the *ius civile,* which writing was beginning to establish on new foundations, had by this point acquired a justification that was completely detached from its ancient pontifical origins. The separation from religion was by now complete. And we can still see Publius Mucius intent on constructing the terms of the new relationship. The intermediary, once again, is Cicero, in a passage from the *De legibus:* "How often"—says the son of Publius [that is, Quintus Mucius]—"have I heard my father say that no one could be a good pontiff without a knowledge of the civil law."[58]

In that observation—almost a warning—we see the atmosphere of the times. The old hierarchy of knowledge and functions, whose genesis and history we have followed, was by this point completely overturned: it was no longer the pontifical practice that served as the foundation of the understanding of civil law; rather it was the legal doctrine that justified the pontifical role. There began to gain ground an entirely secularized image of sacerdotal duties, though still anchored to a model of aristocratic education that remained unitary and all-encompassing.

The need to observe the pontificate—from which the first *ius* of the city had developed—in a different light emerges clearly from another labor undertaken by Publius Mucius: his edition, prepared around 130, of the *Annals of the pontifices*—the *Annales maximi*.[59] It was a decision that had broken a long custom of secrecy, and in a certain sense marked the end of an era: an imposing work (eighty books, the result of a collation of different sources), to which Brutus may also have contributed, as might be deduced from a flimsy but significant piece of testimony from Varro.[60] If this was the case, we would once again have discovered the two jurists working together, once again through the construction of a text, on the shaping of a new relationship between the republic and the memory of its most distant past.

II. The Building of Legal Science:
From Quintus Mucius to Servius and Cicero

II

The Quest for Order

I.

It is impossible to reconstruct in any detail a profile of the legal education of Quintus Mucius Scaevola, the son of Publius born around 140 B.C., in the same years in which the *Decem libelli* probably first saw the light of day. The meager biographical data we can count on does not take us beyond the remains of his works, not datable with any precision, and an indication of the periods of his magistracies, some of which—his praetorship, in 98, and the proconsulship of Asia (whose dates are not certain)—are closely associated with the practice of law.[1]

Several decades on from his father's generation, writing had become firmly established in jurisprudential activity, and Quintus Mucius devoted himself to it with unprecedented intensity. The ordering power of the written word had already emerged with the works of Publius, Brutus, and Manilius. But the literization of the whole of Roman culture was now becoming very marked, prompting a radical adaptation in the sphere of legal thought as well. This requirement would take the guise of a new necessity: a recapitulation of the city's legal past in a clear and unequivocal form; a synthesis of the entire tradition in a single work.

This demand for textuality in the face of the magmatic sedimentation of the *ius civile* stemmed also from comparison with what was taking place in the everyday running of the republic's most vital institutions: with the edicts of the praetors and the other magistrates in the capital and in the provinces, with the *leges rogatae* in the *comitia* or the *leges datae* in the municipal communities. Everywhere a pervasive and indissoluble relationship was being established and diffused between writing and normativity, in a way that Rome had not experienced since the time of the Twelve Tables. And that is to say nothing of the inevitable drawing of parallels with other fields of culture, which were being influenced by a wave of books arriving from Greece and from the libraries of Mediterranean Hellenism.

It was in this climate that the eighteen books of the *Iuris civilis* came into being—Quintus Mucius' most important work, to which his name and reputation are closely tied, and very well known in later culture, which unanimously considered it to be the first great document of Roman legal thought. But none of it has survived to the present day, at least under the author's name, through Justinian's *Digesta,* and it is quite likely that not even a single copy existed any longer in the Byzantine libraries—a gap that unfortunately extends to nearly all the output of Quintus Mucius. We are not even certain of the titles of his works; we can safely identify only two of them, without knowing whether they were the only ones: the *Iuris civilis* and a short composition entitled *Horoi,* or "definitions."[2]

The compilers of the *Digesta* did, however, make fairly extensive use of a thirty-nine-book commentary by Pomponius on the work regarding the *ius civile*, employing over a hundred fragments.[3] The text was organized into a series of lemmata, as was customary in the literary tradition of jurisprudence from the Augustan age onward. In it was reproduced, book after book, the original text by Mucius, dissected into extracts (lemmata), which were followed by Pomponius' commentary, in a dovetailing that we shall have occasion to study more closely. This allows us to form a fairly accurate idea of what the overall structure of Mucius' work must have been like, when, that is, it does not put us in direct contact with the original text as transcribed by Pomponius; and it renders the historiographic situation less precarious. In addition to this commentary, detailed quotations of the doctrines of Mucius can be found in about thirty texts by other jurists present in the *Digesta*, ranging from Labeo to Celsus, Julian, Paul, and Ulpian.[4]

The *Horoi,* on the other hand, must have been available for reading in the

Byzantine libraries. The *Digesta* include six passages—the only fragments directly attributable to the jurist.[5] Outside Justinian's compilation, Mucius' views are recalled by Cicero, Varro, Gellius, and Gaius,[6] further extremely useful testimony which helps to provide a more solid foundation for our understanding of his work.

But now we must focus on the *Iuris civilis*. They were probably composed, at least in their final form, in the years after 95 B.C.—the date of the consulship of Mucius—when the relative tranquility of the pontifical collegium (which the jurist had entered after 95, attaining the position of pontifex maximus no earlier than 89) sheltered him from the burden of excessive direct responsibilities.[7] It is possible that he completed them before the final and difficult period of his life, in the wake of the attempt on his life in 86 B.C. in which he was wounded (he actually died in 82, killed by assassins under the orders of the consul Gaius Marius Minor, and his body thrown into the Tiber).[8]

In writing the work, he must have drawn on all of his experience as a respondent: an activity to which he had dedicated himself, in accordance with the family tradition, with a degree of commitment that would help to increase his prestige.[9] Nonetheless, we are in the presence of something more complex than a simple collection of responses, as the *Decem libelli* of Publius had been. The case-study approach was not abandoned, and served as a unifying thread for the entire discourse. But within it Mucius tended to pursue a more ambitious goal: it was the first attempt to carry out a complete survey—albeit from a very specific point of view—of the principal themes that the jurisprudential tradition assigned to the *ius civile*.

This decision inevitably raised compositional issues about how to arrange the treated material, a problem that had not been resolved—or only in a manner that now appeared inadequate—either in the *Decem libelli* by his father Publius, or in the works by Brutus and Manilius, to say nothing of the by-now-obsolete *Tripertita* by Aelius.

We can therefore consider the order of the *ius civile* as the authentic code of Mucius' writings: the most important key of his textuality. There is an evident allusion to this primary position in the previously mentioned judgment of Pomponius:[10] we need to stop and weigh up the sense of the *constituit*—to provide foundations, structure, stability—before moving on to evaluate the *generatim* that usually attracts the attention of scholars. And without neglecting that *redigendo*, which clearly suggested a "gathering" and an "ordering": it was the whole of the *ius civile* that was being brought together in the eighteen books of a work that the words of Pomponius reveal to have been similar to a full-fledged treatise, the first in all Roman legal literature.

When Quintus Mucius was writing, he already had a complex history behind him: the Twelve Tables, the pontifical interpretation, that of the aristocracy, Sextus Aelius, the first texts of the generation preceding his own, and the normative web arising out of the intermingling of the civil law tradition with the edicts of the praetors. How could this tangle be unraveled?

There is more than one piece of evidence to suggest that Quintus Mucius attempted to solve the problem by arranging his materials, whenever possible, in three distinct layers: the Twelve Tables, Sextus Aelius, and the books by Publius and the other authors cited together with him by Pomponius. And it is a procedural method of this kind that gave rise to an impression of a historicizing perspective in his analyses, as sometimes emerges in the works of modern scholars.[11] The fact that this expository criterion does not appear clearly in the lemmata transcribed by Pomponius in his commentary is simply an indication of the full-scale editing job carried out by the latter with regard to the more ancient master.

But Quintus Mucius did not stop here. He also introduced a different kind of structure, very effective though apparently only extrinsic: he arranged his material into *capita,* "chapters," conferring on the account of the *ius civile* a measure and a cadence capable of becoming, in the minds of readers, a genuine expository canon:

> You made fun of me yesterday over our wine for saying it was a disputed point whether an heir could lawfully prosecute on a charge of theft committed before he succeeded to the property. So, although I had returned home comfortably mellow and at a late hour, I nevertheless marked the section [*caput*] in which this question is discussed, and I have sent you a correct copy of it, so as to convince you that the opinion held, according to you, by no one, was held by Sectus Aelius, Manius Manilius, and Marcus Brutus; all the same, I agree with Scaevola and Testa.[12]

Cicero's quick letter to the young Trebatius Testa (later a respected and skillful jurist, the teacher of Labeo and a friend of Augustus)[13] provides a savory sketch of Roman intellectual conviviality, through the depiction in sequence of two small nocturnal scenes: the first, a lively discussion over dinner; the second, a silent and solitary transcription (if we skip over the likely presence of a slave copyist), once back at home, among his own books.

What Cicero found for his interlocutor is nothing less than a passage from the sixteenth of the *Libri iuris civilis* by Quintus Mucius, in which we know the jurist dealt with theft.[14] The words used for the reference cast a ray of light on the structure of the work. It is inconceivable that Cicero would have used so precise—and indeed, in a certain sense, technical—a term as *caput* without there having existed an objective and immediately recognizable correspondence in the text by Mucius. Evidently, the *capita* must have been the ordering structure of the text: the molds within which the entire *ius civile* was consolidated and enclosed.

In the late-republican legal lexicon—which now had a fairly well-defined uniformity—*caput* referred unequivocally to the form of the *lex*. *Capita legis* is an expression used by Cicero himself, and denoted, in its common meaning, the parts of a *lex publica* and the successive articulation of its provisions.[15] The word, then, had a distinctly systematic and normative tone and nuance: constructing a jurisprudential text in a series of *capita* meant giving it, in some way, a cadence that punctuated its prescriptions, endowing them with the incisiveness of the magistrate's *rogationes*. In short, it served to remove the *ius civile* from its intrinsically fluid condition, and conferred upon it a solidity and a certainty that it had never before enjoyed.

Further confirmation that we are successfully unearthing the authentic ordering scheme of the books of the *Iuris civilis* comes from the title—quoted by Gellius—used by later tradition to refer to a work by Servius Sulpicius Rufus specifically devoted to a critique of the Mucian oeuvre. The first, and incidentally, highly polemical, commentary written by a jurist about the work of one of his predecessors (we shall have occasion to return to this matter), it was called the *reprehensa Scaevolae capita*, "the refuted chapters of Scaevola," in which the observations of Servius must have reflected the structure of the text under discussion. Though not a systematic and detailed critique of all the Mucian *capita*, all the criticisms were arranged in accordance with the work to which they refer, already probably known to his contemporaries as the *capita Scaevolae,* or, by antonomasia, *capita iuris civilis;*[16] which would sat-isfactorily explain the formulation of the reference in the letter to Trebatius ("id caput . . ," with no further specifications).

It would be unwise to assume that every *caput* contained an account of a legal dispute, of the type evoked by Cicero.[17] It is likely, on the other hand, that a principle of the *ius civile* resulting from the Mucian elaboration was stated in each, and constructed through a markedly case-based analysis (this emerges clearly from the lemmata transcribed in the commentary of Pompo-nius), accompanied, when necessary, by the citation (or the refutation) of the previous authors. We can therefore intuit the development of a certain ten-sion, previously unknown, between the typification of the case and the for-mulation of the prescription. This polarity was encouraged on the one hand (the case-based approach) by the ancient sapiential tradition of jurisprudence, and on the other (the regulatory aspect) by the use of the new instruments of logic employed by Mucius. In the lemmata found in the commentary of Pomponius (though the task of fully identifying them has yet to be under-taken), the separation of the general character of the prescriptions from the more narrowly case-based profiles emerges with relative clarity, despite the alterations overlaying the original text.[18]

The Roman jurists were to engage in an uninterrupted dialogue with the past of their discipline—a link that appears to be one of the great constants of ancient legal thought. It defined the peculiar historic time of the intellectual endeavor of an entire class, ensuring continuity from generation to gen-eration.

Despite this tendency, of the whole course of republican jurisprudence until Quintus Mucius, and including the work of Publius and the other au-thors mentioned with him in the *Enchiridion,* later jurists would preserve only a vague and blurry memory, as if of an irretrievably remote past unrelated to the shared legacy of doctrines, and whose faded recollection only just brought to the surface the trace of an isolated name or an opinion detached from any larger context. In the body of legal literature that has survived to the present day, the theses and doctrines of authors prior to Quintus Mucius (Sextus Aelius, Cato, Brutus, Manilius, and P. Mucius) are explicitly cited no more than about fifteen occasions in all, and very few of these references suggest a direct reading of the original texts.[19] It was a lost world.

With the *Libri iuris civilis,* everything changed. Their diffusion up to the time of the Severan jurisprudence was extensive and consolidated. Just a few decades after their publication, Servius made them the exclusive subject of an important and innovative critical work.[20] In the years between Augustus and Tiberius, Sabinus used them as a starting point for a compendium that was in turn destined to leave an enduring mark.[21] And in the second century A.D. three jurists treated the books in considerable depth: Laelius Felix (although nothing is known about his writings, with which Paul may have been familiar), Gaius (probably with a lemmatic exposition, though about this we can also say nothing), and Pomponius, in the large-scale work we have just mentioned.[22] And there were not just commentaries. The name of Quintus Mucius crops up, as we have said, dozens of times in the remains of Roman legal literature, proof that, at least from Labeo onward—but certainly already with Servius himself—there was a widespread awareness that his work marked a turning point, the beginning of the historic time of the great jurisprudence.

The passage of a few decades from the age of Publius Mucius—let us say, the years between the forties of the second century B.C. and the nineties of the first century B.C.—cannot alone explain so marked a change. We are not in the presence of an unbroken progression, but of a veritable qualitative leap: a mutation that would be incorporated permanently not only in the work of the Roman jurists, but in the very form of law in the West.

2.

Let us return to Pomponius' short but thoughtful evaluation:

> After these [the adepts of P. Mucius, of Brutus, of Manilius, and their contemporaries, minor figures in our story: Publius Rutilius Rufus, whom we have already encountered, Paulus Virginius, Quintus Tubero, Sextus Pompeius, Celius Antipater, and Publius Licinius Crassus Mucianus, who we have also mentioned], Quintus Mucius, the son of Publius, pontifex maximus, first established the civil law in genera, gathering it together in eighteen books.[23]

The time has come to explore the central core of this account: the reference to the type of logical foundation of Mucius' thought. It was a new analytical structure for legal thought, identified in the articulation of the content according to the modules of division by genera and species.

We know that this was a very familiar paradigm to Quintus Mucius, who also drew on it outside of the sphere of legal knowledge; indeed, a thorough acquaintance with it formed part of the customary framework of aristocratic culture between the second and first century B.C.[24]

The model had been developed in a comprehensive way for the first time in two of Plato's dialogues—the *Sophist* and the *Statesman*—and it was connected to the very foundation of dialectics and ontology ("Shall we not say that the division of things by classes and the avoidance of the belief that the same class is another, or another the same, belongs to the science of dialectic?").[25] In those texts there appeared for the first time a terminology— centered on the notion of *diairesis,* division—that would be preserved for centuries, and would lie at the foundation of the Roman translations and re-adaptations. But in the passage from Plato to Aristotle a decisive shift had taken place: dialectic, which represented the highest and most profound level of knowledge, was transformed into a form of logic subordinate to and less important than the scientificity of demonstrable knowledge. Detached from its original context, diairesis survived as a simple descriptive method (a comparison of Plato's *Sophist* and Aristotle's *Rhetoric* will make this immediately clear). While codifying in a definitive manner its use, though with oscillations which would still be reflected in the work of Cicero, to say nothing of the writers of late antiquity, Aristotle attributed to it only a minor role, far from the decisive points of his conceptual system: nothing more than a useful technique in rhetorical persuasion, or in the classification of ethics and the natural sciences.[26] The logical studies of the Stoics would not alter this picture in any substantial way. Diairesis, however, was not forgotten; Chrysippus devoted attention to it, and, after him, Diogenes of Babylon, the philosopher who with Carneades took part in the Athenian embassy to Rome in 155 B.C.[27] It would continue to be used in rhetorical literature as well: we find it in the treatise of Hermagoras, also around the middle of the second century B.C, and later, almost in the same years as Quintus Mucius, the author of the *Rhetorica ad Herennium* made extensive use of it.[28]

Quintus Mucius, who was not unfamiliar with Greek, enjoyed direct access to these texts. The majority were in the massive library of Perseus of Macedon, transported to Rome in 167 B.C., after the Battle of Pydna, by Aemilius Paulus—such a vast number of books had never before been seen in the capital—and then used by the circle of Scipio Aemilianus,[29] a milieu that was certainly familiar to the Mucii. Furthermore, even aside from the suggestion of this bibliographic trace, there can be no question that there was a more-than-superficial penetration of Greek philosophy within a significant part of the Roman ruling classes, beginning with the earliest years of the second century: a work like that of Cassius Hemina quite clearly presupposes it.[30] And for the more recent output—which Perseus' library could not have included—there were direct contacts and the reading opportunities these offered.

In the same years the circulation of the work of Hermagoras, which in all likelihood was available to Quintus Mucius, led to a growing knowledge of rhetoric. Many of the cultural disputes that divided the republican nobility were linked to the history of the establishment of this discipline in Rome. A particularly bitter moment in this story was the closure, in the year 92, of the first school of rhetoric in Latin, which had been founded by Plotius Gallus, a follower of Marius—an initiative taken by the censor Lucius Licinius Crassus, a colleague of Quintus Mucius in the consulship of 95, and the author, with him, of the law against the Italics.[31]

But why did Quintus Mucius decide to employ the diairetic method so extensively, to the point of making it the distinguishing feature of his entire treatise, at least in the eyes of Pomponius? The customary response is to refer generally to the intellectual climate of the time, to which a couple of generations of jurists were not indifferent: a parenthesis brought about by the spread of a kind of fashion.[32]

It is an unsatisfactory interpretation, to say the least, and fails to consider an essential point: the connection between the use of diairesis and the quality of the knowledge first developed by means of those models; that is, the logical form through which, beginning with Quintus Mucius and his innovations, the experience of law was constructed and conceived. If we do not keep our gaze fixed firmly on this interrelationship, we will lose the thread of any plausible interpretation. And we must not just take care to avoid the old fallacy that led to a mechanical distinction between Greek "method" and Roman "content,"[33] but also a far more serious and subtle risk: that of measuring the

work of the Roman jurists by the criteria employed to evaluate the philosophical and epistemological debate from Plato to late Stoicism, influenced
only by the superficial trace of certain evident debts of jurisprudence to philosophy, and by the sporadic contiguity of terms and categories. If we go
down this path, we are forced to the conclusion that there was a dramatic
impoverishment of the logical pattern of classical thought when it passed
from the philosophers to the jurists, and that the work of jurisprudence was
an irremediably minor discipline lacking any theoretical vocation. But this
would be unfounded—however many times it may have been reiterated, to
the point of becoming a historiographical commonplace.[34]

In reality, what was involved was neither reduction nor impoverishment,
nor a simple and superficial transposition of methodology, devoid of any particularly substantial significance. Instead it was a delicate and crucial process
of integration, which managed to project Roman legal knowledge beyond
previously attained horizons, without ever losing the sense of a very strong
identity—in a certain sense, revolutionizing it in order to complete it. The
end result would be the birth of a new way of conceiving law, which would
transmute its protocols into those of a science without equal in antiquity, no
less compact and conceptually dense than the great classical philosophy. An
achievement by virtue of which it would from that time on always be potentially possible to establish a distance between "juridical" regulation and naked
acts of will on the part of constituted powers—albeit bound, to a greater or
lesser degree in different circumstances, by tradition, by the weight of a certain technicalness, or by respect for other ties—and to consign them to the
rigorous syntax, impersonal and formalized, of abstract acts of knowledge.

3.

Let us consider the sequence of topics treated by Mucius. The essential lines
can still be reconstructed today, thanks especially to the commentary by
Pomponius. An overall view of them prompts two considerations. First and
foremost, there is a marked ancientness about the fundamental thematic
cores, many of which can actually be traced back to the prescriptions of the
Twelve Tables and to the earliest jurisprudence. Moreover, it is clearly impossible to deduce from the succession of subjects the presence of any systematic organization according to genera and species. If a diairetic approach had

been adopted for the general layout of the books of the *Iuris civilis,* it would necessarily have become evident in the possibility of linking one theme to another within the context of a unified and all-encompassing classification. But that is not the case; nor is it reasonable to suppose that this lack is attributable merely to a difficulty in fully exploiting the new instruments. Indeed, the intensity with which they are used in connection with specific themes shows that Mucius was able to deploy them with confidence. What's more, the jurist must have been familiar with examples in Hellenistic literature of a general, comprehensive organization based on such models. If Quintus Mucius had decided to go down that road, the result might have been more or less satisfactory, but certainly we would now be exploring outcomes far removed from the sequence that can be glimpsed today. If the order of the books of the *Iuris civilis* reveals no sign of such a development, this can only be the product of a deliberate choice: a conscious refusal to make use of the ordering device past a well-established limit.

We can thus begin to discern the existence of a precise relationship, in Mucius' treatise, between the diaeretic method and the overall order: a relation whose peculiarity casts light on both the quality and scope of the new logic, and on the weight and substance of the system that incorporated it without being transformed by it.

But in those years there were some who viewed things very differently.

Less than forty years later, in 55 B.C., Cicero, in the first book of his *De oratore,* in a passage that the fiction of the dialogue attributes to Lucius Licinius Crassus, delineated what in his opinion were the tasks of a legal knowledge finally in step with the times through which the city was living:

> After the formulas of actions at law had been first published by
> Gnaeus Flavius, there were none able to organize these matters
> [the *cognitio iuris,* the knowledge of law] organically, shaping
> them into genera. For nothing can be reduced to system unless
> the man who has mastered the subject, of which he would orga-
> nize a system, already possesses the special knowledge requisite
> to enable him, out of particulars not yet embodied in a system, to

construct one. I see that, in my desire to be brief, I have spoken a little obscurely, but I will try to express myself, if I can, in clearer terms . . . Nearly all the elements that have now been reduced to systems were once without order or correlation: in music, for example, rhythms, sounds and measures; in geometry, lines, figures, dimensions and magnitudes, in astronomy, the revolution of the sky, the rising, setting and movement of heavenly bodies; in literature, the study of poets, the learning of histories, the explanation of words and proper intonation in speaking them; and lastly in this very theory of oratory, invention, style, arrangement, memory and delivery, once seemed to all men things unknown and widely separate one from another. And so a certain system was called in from outside, derived from another definite sphere, which philosophers arrogate wholly to themselves, in order that it might give coherence to things so far disconnected and sundered, and bind them into a unitary rational form. Let the goal then of civil law be defined as the preservation, in the concerns and disputes of citizens, of a uniform criteria founded on statute and custom. We must next distinguish the genera, restricting these to a small fixed number. Now a genus is that which embraces two or more species, resembling one another in some common property while differing in some peculiarity. And species are subdivisions, ranged under those genera from which they spring; while all names, whether of genera or species, must be so defined as to show the significance of each. A definition of course I may describe as a concise and accurate statement of the attributes belonging to the thing we would define. I would therefore append illustrations to what I have said, were I not mindful of the quality of the hearers of this discourse: as it is, I will briefly summarize my plan. For if I am permitted to do what I have long been projecting, or if someone else anticipates me, preoccupied as I am, or does the work when I am dead, first dividing the entire civil law into genera, which are very few, and next distributing what I may call the sub-divisions of those genera, and after that making plain by definition the proper significance of each, then you will have a complete system of civil law, magnificent and copious but neither inaccessible nor mysterious. And yet in the meantime, while these disconnected materials are being assembled, a man may, by culling even at random and gathering from every quarter, become filled with a tolerable knowledge of the civil law.[35]

The text is loaded with a considerable theoretical tension, which explains its evidently laborious style.

The critical meditation on the state of legal knowledge was profoundly motivated in Cicero. We have already seen that he recognized in *ius* the very *logos* of the republic, but it was precisely the acknowledgment of this preeminence, and an exact evaluation of the crucial tasks jurisprudence had already taken on in the city, that engendered his dissatisfaction with certain aspects of it that still appeared to be inadequate: a worthless legacy of tradition.

His observations immediately paved the way for a kind of full-blown gnoseology, from the point of view of the theoretical foundation of all knowledge, which was made to coincide with the attainment of the system. There is no truth without system, Cicero is saying here: the discourse on the state of legal knowledge *(cognitio iuris)* could thus readily slide into a reflection on the foundation of any kind of knowledge. The shift took place through two progressive reductions. First, every field of knowledge was observed only with respect to the foundation of the system *(ars)*. And then, in order to construct the latter, it was deemed indispensable to be in possession of a specific technique *(scientia)* elaborated and preserved by philosophy. In this way, *ars* and *scientia,* the system and the instruments for achieving it, enclosed within a purely methodological horizon the problem of all developments in knowledge. Everything was reduced to the possession of a resolutory method, external to the content of the specific disciplines, but capable of transforming them: a topos of ancient rationalism.

It was based on a very marked contrast. On the one hand, the purely historical development of any line of knowledge—geometry, music, astronomy, law—where each notion was overlaid upon the others in a haphazard and unrelated way, without links and without mediation, just in the sequence in which they were progressively learned. On the other hand there was systematic order, where each piece of information was placed within a unitary model that disrupted the chronological seriality, reworking it in the frame-

work of a structure capable of bringing out its implicit cognitive potentiali-
ties: diairesis—here described in the version that Cicero himself would later
theorize in the *Topica,* borrowing freely from Aristotle—as *partitio.*[36]

The antecedents of such a position, clarified with an entirely new completeness in Latin, are not hard to identify; they lead back to currents of ideas
within the elaborations of middle Stoicism. It must have figured, even before
Cicero, as a fairly easily identifiable point of reference—even though it was
almost certainly expressed in a more nebulous way—in the intellectual climate of Rome at the turn of the first century. From this point of view, setting
the dialogue almost forty years prior to its actual composition must not have
been seen as a major problem. In the literary fiction, Crassus voiced his considerations one day in September of the year 91: a time that was not very distant from when Quintus Mucius must have been particularly busy with the
composition of his most important work.

We do not know whether the books of the *Iuris civilis* had already been
published by that date, and if therefore Cicero composed his dialogue assuming that Crassus, as he was speaking, knew the writings of Mucius. But one
thing is certain: the program that Cicero attributed to Crassus was not the
one to which Quintus Mucius had adhered, but represented the decisive step
in the direction that the jurist had decided not to follow—and Cicero must
have been well aware of this.

The polemical efficacy of the text thus reveals its actual target: nothing
other than the work of Mucius, although it was never mentioned directly;
and the impact was enhanced by the evidence that the goals announced by
Crassus, which can easily be placed as far back as the 90s, were still unachieved
in the 50s.

The testimony of *De oratore* thus serves not only to ascertain the existence of an alternative position, in clear contrast with that of Mucius; it demonstrates that the possibility excluded by the jurist manifestly formed part of
the intellectual legacy of his generation, and it illuminates the full extent of
the problematic nature of the choice. In those years, there really were two
paths open to the aristocratic legal knowledge: two different ways of responding to the new developments of the times.

We cannot say what would have happened if the orientation expounded
by Cicero had ultimately prevailed. It was, however, a substantially unrealistic
hypothesis: the tradition of the jurists—the specificity of their civil order-

ing—was by this point too strong and deep-rooted for its constituent elements to be swept away in favor of a wholesale standardization in compliance with the canons of Hellenistic encyclopedism. It is quite likely for that matter that Cicero's lost juridical work, the *De iure civili in artem redigendo*—a revealing title—reflected this intrinsic fragility. The complete silence with which it was immediately enveloped by the jurists—they would never have considered the work's author to be one of their own—sealed its early fate; and its rapid disappearance once again sheds light on the radicalness of the clash and its outcome.[37]

Quintus Mucius, on the other hand, had followed a different path: he projected a different model upon his work, less linear than the one set forth in *De oratore,* but much better suited to the characteristics of legal knowledge. The choice induced him to undertake a difficult mediation. He was willing to introduce a new logical order into the *ius civile,* but he then brought it to a halt at the threshold of the construction of an overall system, adopting it only for the arrangement of topics within the books and the *capita.* In the tension that was thus created, it was already possible to glimpse the proposal of a new equilibrium, at once theoretical and communicative, which for centuries to come would underpin the successive developments of Roman legal thought.

Nine years later, in *Brutus,* written in 46 B.C., almost at the end of his life, Cicero returned to the theme, and his assessment now involved explicit reference to the figure and work of Quintus Mucius. Indeed, this time he presented a full-scale profile of him both as jurist and as orator. At a certain point, the account abandons the style of a mannered eulogy, and expresses a terse judgment of his intellectual activity:

> At this Brutus said: "Do you mean to say that you place our
> Servius even above Quintus Scaevola?" "Yes, Brutus," I replied, "I
> would put it this way: Scaevola, and many others too, had great
> practical knowledge of the civil law; Servius alone had a scientific
> understanding of it. This he could never have attained through
> knowledge of the law alone had he not acquired in addition that
> science which teaches to divide a whole into its component parts,

sets forth and defines the latent and implicit, interprets and makes clear the obscure; which first recognizes the ambiguous and then distinguishes; which applies in short a rule or measure for adjudging truth and falsehood, for determining what conclusions follow from what premises, and what do not. This science, the most important of all, he brought to bear on all that had been put together by others without system, whether in the form of legal opinions or in actual trials." "I suppose you mean logic," said he. "Quite right," I replied; "but to this he joined a knowledge of letters and a finished style of speaking, as can be seen from his writings, which are without equal."[38]

It is Cicero himself who is speaking in the dialogue: author and character coincide. The persistence of the same key word found in the text of *De oratore—ars*—should not deceive us. Cicero's outlook was very different to the one he had held in 55. Nine years had not passed in vain.[39] Concealed behind the identical term is a marked conceptual change. Otherwise, the entire discourse would be inexplicable, and his judgment of Servius completely unjustified.

Ars no longer denoted the system, as in the *De oratore:* there is no more mention of this. The word's consolidated polysemy in late-republican Latin now enabled it to signify the technical and specialized knowledge of a given discipline, without any particular accentuation of the systematic aspects. There was not an authentic semantic change, just a shift in tonality within the same layer of meaning. *Ars* still translated something that lay, in Greek, between *technē* and *epistēmē:* in the *De oratore,* it underscored the systemic implications; in *Brutus,* the more generically gnoseological aspect.

Legal knowledge was no longer measured in terms of whether it achieved a desired systematization, but in accordance with its ability to incorporate an analytical mechanism—that of the Stoic dialectic and no longer just of diairesis—capable in any case of transforming it. The option of 55 had not been explicitly overturned: it had only been set to one side and virtually ignored (the reasons will become clear shortly). However, the conviction that it was impossible to carry out a fully and properly scientific transformation of legal knowledge without the intervention of an external contribution, which unfailingly referred to the field of philosophy, was preserved and reiterated.

THE QUEST FOR ORDER

But Cicero was now judging the work of the jurists by, as it were, assuming their point of view, without worrying about assigning to them a task—the construction of the system—that they appeared unwilling to espouse. He weighed up the history of jurisprudence in the previous fifty years, as personified by its two leading figures, Mucius and Servius. And Cicero had no doubts: the work of Mucius still did not merit a completely positive evaluation, even leaving aside the question of the system. It was therefore deemed not to have attained a scientific understanding of law, as was the work of all those who had had *usus* of *ius* and not *ars*. The establishment of legal science was linked exclusively to Servius. And it was solely in connection with his doctrine, and with the complexity of the analytical processes to be found in his responses, that—here and not in the text of 55—the category of "dialectic" was applied.

Cicero's dissent, thinly veiled in the *De oratore*—perhaps for reasons linked to the literary fiction—was fully displayed in *Brutus*. At first sight, his position would appear to be the reverse of what would ultimately be the appraisal of Pomponius and (as we have observed) of all later jurisprudence. In reality, he was probably playing a more subtle game. Cicero could not have been unaware of the importance of the innovations made by Quintus Mucius, and the significance of the role of diairetic instruments in his work, and consequently of the undeniable proximity between the jurist's position and his own in believing that the intervention of an external logic was in any case indispensable to bring Roman legal knowledge up to date with the times. In his *Pro Caecina,* for that matter, as we shall see, that work had already been taken greatly into account, albeit implicitly.[40] But Cicero now polemically downplayed the points of convergence, because it seemed to him that Quintus Mucius—in comparison with Servius—had not attained the threshold of a genuine transformation, and that he was, on the whole, still too much in debt to a tradition from which Servius appeared to be entirely liberated (we shall later see the degree to which this view was actually justified).

Tradition, history: it was precisely this development to which Crassus had denied all rationality (with a polemical excess that may not have fully reflected Cicero's thought, but was part of the literary game). And yet it was the elaboration of this and its associated implications, to which Quintus Mucius proved to be particularly faithful: against the risks of an excessively Hellenizing normalization, destructive of a distinctive trait to which the very supremacy of Rome was linked (Servius would also successfully avoid this danger, but Cicero rightly perceived his attitude as being less indebted to the past).

The use of diairetic frames within the books and the *capita* was thus combined with a delicate work of connection between new logic and ancient history: a complex mediation, which also concealed other and more profound implications, and which is the core of Mucius' work.

We cannot say to what degree the overall order of the books of the *Iuris civilis*, though unprecedented, might not be to some extent dependent upon models already present in Roman legal culture: the Twelve Tables, the Aelian scheme, the sequences present in Cato or in Publius Mucius, or even in the ancient oral memorization of chains of *responsa*. But it can be affirmed with reasonable confidence that its structure not only did not correspond to a diairetic framework (as Cicero would have wanted), but that it did not even possess any autonomous constructive and systematic organization.

It is not to logic that we need to turn (in the ancient sense of the word), but instead, once again, to history. The rationale underlying the Mucian order was not in fact identified with any adhesion to a classificatory method, but rather with the progressive stratification itself of *ius* in the city, and with the functional hierarchies of Roman society, as they must still have appeared at the high point of the republic, prior to the great changes between the third and second centuries. At the center were issues relating to the family, seen as the specific site of germination of the entire social life of the community and as an essential presupposition of citizenship. Preservation of the family over time was of paramount importance, and hence: wills, legacies, legitimate succession. Then there were the powers of the *pater* with respect to the condition of those subordinate to him: guardianship, manumissions, *patria potestas*. And then the exercise of the other powers of the head of the family, referring to particular functions: mancipations, possession, usucaption, and servitudes. Around this axis were a few other figures, in some cases dating far back into the past, grouped according to topical affinity: stipulations, unlawful damage governed by the Lex Aquilia, *consortium*, partnership, *postliminium*, *condictio*, sale, theft. A world of relations, as we have already observed, with a markedly archaizing imprint far removed from the overwhelming changes brought about by the imperial conquests. The cases that Mucius cited in relation to these thematic nodes only confirm that impression. They are composed almost exclusively of depictions of things and artifacts (plows, trees, lumber, water, ditches), animals (oxen, mares, rams), individuals (stable grooms, pruners) that were typical of the world of the peasantry and small farmers. The existence of significant mercantile networks, large concentrations of slaves, substantial accumulations of commercial capital, and so on seemed not to impinge on this world; a context, in short, that we could describe as even less developed than the one that had served as the background to the agricultural handbook of Cato the Elder; in other words: a mirror of a Rome that was vanishing.

But against such a social backdrop, presented according to a perspective that emphasized its archaizing imprint, Quintus Mucius had not hesitated to undertake something quite new. The detailed and fine-grained utilization of diairetic mechanisms within the specific themes treated, along with the organization into *capita*, already radically changed the form of the traditional perception of the *ius civile*. But the author did not stop here. These new developments introduced another, even more decisive one. Let us now attempt to understand what direction it took.

12

The New Paradigm:
Abstraction and Formalism

I.

Two ordering patterns coexisted, then, in Mucius' books: the one determining the overall sequence, a reflection of the development of the *ius civile* in the city (and which had provoked Cicero's dissatisfaction through the words of Crassus); and the one governing the treatment of individual topics, centered on the use of diaeresis (and which explained the judgment of Pomponius). A citation from Gaius and one from Paul, referring to guardianship and possession, provide solid confirmation, albeit only as a sample, of how diffuse the intertwining of the genera must have been within the *capita:*[1] a complete reading of the treatise, if that were still possible, would probably reveal no less a presence of these models than that which we can observe by examining the pages of the *Rhetorica ad Herennium*.

It is clear that the significance of a compositional scheme applied in such an extensive manner cannot be evaluated solely from the point of view of the failure to construct the system (as the character of Crassus essentially does in Cicero's dialogue), but must also, indeed primarily, be measured with respect to the impact of the new criteria on the specific legal items subjected to Mucius' analysis.

If we stick to this perspective, a new horizon immediately opens up. We discover, in fact, that the diairetic approach invariably required, in each and every application, one essential prerequisite: the attainment of a solid level of abstraction in relation to the knowledge concerned. It is impossible to arrange horses or oratory qualities according to genera and species unless one possesses an abstract idea of horseness or oratory; and this necessarily had to hold good for legal notions as well: the breakdown of their constituent elements always presupposed the abstraction of the concepts from which one set out.

In the Platonic dialectic, the link was evident on what we might call a genetic level: the introduction of the division by genus was intrinsically tied to the development of a previously existing ontological foundation. Likewise, in Aristotle, in the Stoic tradition, and in that of Hellenistic encyclopedism, the dependency was not denied: in individual disciplines, abstraction was always a logical and historical prerequisite for diairesis.[2]

But this condition was by no means obvious in the legal field, prior to the change effected by Mucius. Here, everything from the work of the pontifices to the jurisprudence of the second century evinced the effort of an arduous and still incomplete process of building constructions capable of moving beyond the rigidly case-based character of *ius*. The extension of the decemviral norm on *furtum* undertaken by Brutus (then adopted by Quintus Mucius himself), or the definitions of *ambitus aedium* and *nexum* constructed by Publius Mucius and Manilius offer (as we have seen) precious testimony to this difficult journey.[3]

Certainly, viewed retrospectively, we can confidently state that, by the end of the second century, all the principal core elements of Roman private law had already been roughly shaped through the prolonged exercise of an increasingly refined technique, and with close collaboration between jurists and praetors: rights concerning objects and commodities, obligations, and the law of succession.[4] But their substantive presence was only manifested in the discipline of individual responses, in the specific rationality of cases resolved and actions allowed (or refused), in concrete aspects of social and economic life, and not in the interconnection of a homogeneous web of unitary categories and conceptual figures. Even the hypothetical formulations found in the Twelve Tables and in subsequent legislation ("if this . . . then it will be that . . .") pointed in the same direction: and yet we should not forget that in their dictates, they never moved beyond the enunciation of a case, however typified (the thief, the murderer, the *pater* who uttered a formula or presented a suit . . .); and the same happened in the writing of the edicts, at least up until the first century.

It was only with Mucius that the picture changed drastically. This simply must be acknowledged: the achievement of abstraction and concepts developed, in Roman legal thought, not before, but in conjunction with, the use of diairetic models. In such a context, its priority was logical, not historical. From this point of view, the position of Quintus Mucius was by no means comparable to that of the master of *Rhetorica ad Herennium*: jurisprudence was not rhetoric—behind it there is no sign of a Hermagoras.

We must therefore consider abstraction, and not diaeresis, as the core of the new ideas introduced by Mucius. The *constituere generatim* of Pomponius' evaluation can thus assume a broader significance than simply an allusion to a classificatory method taken for granted outside the field of legal knowledge. It is an indicator that necessarily leads (without abstraction there can be no diaeresis) to the earliest formation of an entirely new analytical approach in which the *ius civile* was for the first time presented through a network of concepts distributed in diairetic schemes whose pervasiveness appears to be an unmistakable token of a corresponding expansion of the realm of abstraction. Within them, *caput* by *caput,* were arranged series of cases obtained directly from the personal activity of giving responses or from the tradition of the discipline. Some traces can still be discerned today.

What, then, did it mean to conceive *ius civile* in abstract terms?

The explanation is anything but simple, and has far-reaching ramifications, as is always the case when in the explosion of an event preceded by the patient work of history there precipitate a shower of consequences that we are unaccustomed to seeing as linked but which are connected on various levels.

In effect, the concepts developed by Mucius and, following him, by the whole of Roman jurisprudence, were entirely particular, and in no way resembled those employed in Greek philosophy for centuries. Their point of reference was neither nature nor man's inner universe nor the modes of ethics and politics, but instead the structure of "private" sociality in a now well-developed civic setting moving toward a full-blown imperial dimension. They stemmed from the capacity to separate analytically—in other words, to render abstract—the functional forms of the relationships taken into consideration by *ius*—exchanges, belongings, obligations, claims, powers, subjects, and actions—from the living material that made them up, and to endow them with a wholly autonomous existence, detached from the concrete determinations that constituted their content in reality (those goods, that asset, that citizen, that performance, that procedural behavior, that set of interests), and which had theretofore only allowed a sort of empirical typification of similarities. Consequently, the legal ordering could be linked in a direct and synthetic manner to the formal scheme thus obtained and to the functional equilibria that it expressed, rather than depending merely upon the evaluation of the multiplicity of cases that society's growing complexity inevitably rendered elusive. No longer a myriad of situations in which buyers and sellers were only recognized *a posteriori,* and to whom the procedural actions "of sale" and "of purchase" could be linked. But instead an abstract paradigm of sale as an exchange functional to the transfer of goods for a price, accompanied once and for all by a whole series of rules that defined the reciprocal obligations of the subjects involved in a transaction, the violation of which triggered the right to jurisdictional protection through the exercising of an action.

Every form thus developed would have its own (legal) name: to attribute it was to acknowledge its separate existence; and the names—in the thinking of those who assigned them—reflected the (juridical) existence of things and were an immediate consequence of their truth. Without doubt, as we have just said, the stylization of cases brought about by republican jurisprudence (and outlined as early as the Twelve Tables) already pointed in this direction: and it might well be considered as a sort of "zero degree"—common also to many other ancient legislative experiences—with respect to the subsequent process of abstraction. But the shift wrought by Mucius made it possible to start a decisive change: the first construction of law capable of taking on an entirely formal dimension—in the sense that from its point of view, nothing else could be seen except the abstract dimension of the relations considered by it—to which was linked the deployment of a specific "practical," calculating, and quantitative rationality.

We have seen that Rome had already long attributed to *ius* a disciplining function "excarnated" not only from religion, but also from politics, and that the ensuing isolation had accentuated the technical and specialized aspect of this knowledge: first grafted onto the trunk of early religious rituality (the technique of *ius* as knowledge and social manipulation of rites), later consolidated in the practice of responses in increasingly complex conditions, but in any case associable with a sort of secularized ritualism perfectly absorbed by the republican culture.

Now, however, a new separation was taking place, this time within the shaping of law itself. Abstract thought led to the beginnings of a detachment of *ius,* in the minds of its interpreters, not only from the social and institutional spheres that were historically contiguous to it—as had happened in the past with religion and, to some degree, politics—but also from the concrete actuality of life to which it referred: needs, conflicts, interests, power relationships—in other words, the reality in which it was immersed. In this way, a cognitive barrier arose between *ius* and the world, and precisely at the time when imperial expansion, now nearing its peak, placed the governing groups of the republic at the center of previously inconceivable pressures and strains.

Nonetheless, the distance was an ambiguous one, which did not distract the jurists from their operative function: it did not turn them into philosophers, but into the protagonists of an untested social technology, and made them capable of performing their duties in an extraordinarily more effective manner. The self-isolation of the custodians of *ius* in a universe made up solely of forms, proportions, defined and hidden compatibilities, released an immense ordering force, exerting an incomparable grip upon the reality of life, placed (provisionally) to one side only to master it better. There began to be established the taxing protocols of a technique of social control that would enjoy an enduring and unrivaled success.

Cicero would realize this immediately.

Stressing the explosive nature of the new development introduced by Mucius should not, however, lead us to break the innumerable threads linking it to a sometimes very remote past. We have just spoken of the undeniable bonds with those methods of stylization of cases that Roman legal thought had elaborated for centuries. But perhaps we need to go even further back, and that is to the very point from which our account first started: from the ritualistic syndrome that we found invading (and explaining) all Roman archaism.[5] In that original state of mind there was a sign—intellectual and social—that we must not miss, and which can be tracked without interruption in the successive developments of Roman history. There too a sort of scission had been made, albeit an elementary one, steeped in magical thinking: the continual prevalence of the verbal and gestural shell enveloping the behavior of the *patres* over the material content expressed on a given occasion; the almost obsessive attention to the symbology of the rite, of the stereotypy, with respect to the substance of the relation in question.

We can reasonably consider that aptitude—not typically Roman, but exercised in Rome with a very particular level of intensity—as the historical manifestation of a sort of first-degree formalism, weak and surface level, associated with entirely unique conditions, but destined—through a lengthy evolutionary path that would keep its cultural memory vividly alive—never to be completely erased in the history of *ius*. And I believe there is good reason to suppose that the tenacity of such preservation went even further; to the point of permeating, in a completely different situation, into the genesis of the second paradigm of formalism, this time strong and profound, which we are currently attempting to reconstruct. Though undoubtedly arising in far more advanced historical circumstances, and linked not to the elaboration of a ritual but to the discovery of a new episteme, it was still in some way mindful of that remote precedent.

The genealogical hypothesis we are attempting to tease out is a subtle yet pressing one, based on a connection motivated both historically and morphologically: the possibility that the memory of very early ritualism—maintained in far more mature intellectual milieus—acted in such a way as to predispose legal thought to the breaking down of forms for disciplining and normative ends that was Mucius' great discovery; that it established a sort of precedent, something like a cultural and mental matrix. The common trait, or we might even say the anthropological constant, in both the archaic and the late-republican situation, was the Roman tendency to isolate the typical and repeatable aspect of each relation—the simple gestural and verbal shell, or its functional paradigm.

It is only a trace: and yet, if we have followed it correctly, we will once again come face to face with one of the primary features of the whole history of the West.[6]

There is more, however. The abstract concepts constructed through the formalizing gaze of the jurists would not be viewed, from Mucius onward, merely as categories of thought. They were also seen, in an increasingly defined manner, as figures of being, as real entities endowed with life of their own and an inescapable objectivity, which legal knowledge limited itself to mirroring, in a sort of adaptation of the intellect to the thing. Savigny, good Kantian that he was, grasped the difference, and in a celebrated passage mentioned earlier, describes this attitude very well, the implications of which were, incredibly, overlooked in subsequent historical studies.[7] Whether directly Platonic (ideas as essences) and Aristotelian (dualism between form and content, and the metaphysical priority of form) influences were at play is something we cannot say.[8] But certainly in the epistemic revolution of Roman thought it was the whole of Greek classical philosophy that came together to contribute to the great change.

Legal concepts could thus acquire a value that made law an authentic form of metaphysics, albeit a highly particular one, exclusively devoted to the transformation of abstract schemes of social relations into figures of being, where the concrete experience of life was reduced to one of a defined number of archetypal models: a full-fledged ontology, which established itself as the motor of any development of *ius*. A restricted group of forms—obligation, contract, ownership, possession, guardianship, usufruct, servitudes, pledge, stipulation, loan, deposit, inheritance, legacy, sale, hire, partnership, but also equity, fraud, good faith, error, and so forth—made familiar to us by centuries of use would from then on become the protagonists on an invisible and in a certain sense spectral stage, yet capable of exerting a decisive influence upon the concrete reality of life, which ultimately appeared devoid of (legal) meaning outside of that contact. The great invention of Roman thought began to be revealed in its successful combination, within a single circuit, of the quest for a rigorous legal order and the discovery of a metaphysics that justified it from an ontological rather than an ethical point of view. From then on, the legal rule would appear to be nothing other than an act of knowledge, and not of will; an adaptation of thought to being, the result of a cognitive operation that was rationally controllable in every phase and entirely free from personal will, abuse, and dominion: and this was happening precisely when the Roman aristocracy had managed, as the result of an extraordinary desire for strength, to concentrate around it an enormous power and a previously unknown capacity to project it onto a world stage.[9]

From then on, the path leading to law would pass through the realm of legal science. Law was consigned to the principles of a new intellectual practice, which with its protocols would contribute decisively to forming the epistemological frame of all social knowledge, and which modernity would not hesitate to call "science," the generator of a logic that succeeded in combining positivity and abstraction—from the concrete nature of the case to the power of the rule-determining concept, and then back to the case, but now enlightened by the disciplining abstraction, and therefore regulated by the norm.[10] It would immediately shut itself away in a world marked by a temporality of its own, filled with essences forever equal to themselves (the form of a sale is laid down just once, and remains defined solely by the structure established through the functional relations between purchaser, seller, goods, price, and exchange), self-subsistent and immutable but still susceptible to the acquisition of an endless array of new attributes and qualities (the obligations of the seller or those of the purchaser, or the characteristics of the goods can be described in an increasingly analytical manner, taking into account an ever increasing number of hypotheses and circumstances), in a technically limitless interplay of predications and specifications that in turn constitutes sociality.[11]

The ontologization of legal concepts would soon become total, and the essences transformed into indispensable presuppositions for each and every normative experience, absolute conditions for conceiving of the "private" fabric of our lives: a sort of "a priori" of law, capable of extraordinarily effective syntheses of empirical experience. (The expression is used intentionally: although basically describable in the terms of classical Greek philosophy, the originality of the epistemic model developed by Roman legal thought—and its capacity to combine abstraction and realism—does not exclude, as was pointed out earlier, a potentially "a prioristic" interpretation of forms: something midway between Plato, Aristotle, and a sort of Kantian precognition.[12])

In truth, in the actual process of their genesis, between Quintus Mucius and Servius, the breaking down of the forms away from the concrete content of the relations had preceded the appearance of the ontology: the construction of juridical entities would be a result of the new formalism. But then, once the legal figures had been elaborated as pure essences, in the constructivism of the jurists the functional forms of the relationships would wind up appearing as nothing more than the reflection, the effect of an obligatory perception, of an accurate vision of the entity. "Law is the revealing of being," writes Plato in the *Minos*, and we might say that the working program of the Roman jurists seems almost to have been foretold in this statement. Their deep-rooted sense of realism did not exclude acknowledgment of a sort of ontological primacy (the combination may have been informed by the teachings of the Stoics, but it was certainly also quite closely linked to the Roman conception of *ius*). It was however (as we noted earlier) a metaphysics that hypostatized abstractions of "private" sociality—deduced, therefore, from the economy and from family ties: land, slaves, patriarchal family structures, subjectivity of status, imperial trade—and not from nature, from the mind, or from the "political" form of the community. This decisive difference encompasses both the distance and the close proximity that separate and join together, in a continual play of concealment and references—extending from Cicero to Ulpian—Roman jurisprudence and Greek philosophy.[13]

2.

The surviving fragments of Mucius' work clearly retain the traces that mark the opening of the new space. Among the fragments that best lend themselves to our conceptual archeology, a prominent position is occupied by those relating to contracts. This is the beginning of a thread that will run through the rest of this book, since the formation of the doctrines of contract law will be considered here as privileged terrain for reconstructing the thought of the jurists. Such a choice is not a belated tribute to a distortion pertaining to the modern tradition, which has often tended to inflate the importance of reflection on the theme of obligations and contracts with respect to the whole of the Roman legal experience, given the centrality acquired by these figures in systems and codifications around the turn of the nineteenth century. Rather it stems from the consideration that, quite aside from the position these topics occupied on the map of ancient legal thought (which in any case varied from jurist to jurist), there was a gradual accrual around these arguments, from Quintus Mucius to Ulpian, of the analytically richest and most important part of the new logic that we are discovering as the great invention of jurisprudence.

The concentration was not the product of chance. Obligations and contracts regulated the interplay of trade dealings, which in turn constituted the most advanced sector—albeit not the most important in purely quantitative terms—of the entire imperial economy, even though it would always remain a world dominated more by personal relations than by markets.[14] We have previously seen, in another context, how the new developments introduced by the opening of the praetorian jurisdiction to foreigners had encouraged the first significant expansion of overseas trade networks in the wake of the new military conquests.[15] But the decisive connection would be made only later, when, between the mercantile networks of the now entirely Roman Mediterranean—a sea of cargo, slaves, merchants, and money unlike anything that had ever existed in antiquity—and the qualitative leap forward of late-republican legal thought, it became possible to discover convincing and revelatory symmetries.

Formalism was the key to the link: the crucial nexus between the mercantile development of the economy and the original features of law. From the perspective of the antiquarian interest of Severan jurisprudence, the establishment of a generalized relationship between goods and money as a substitute of the archaic one that created a direct contact between the use value of the goods without the mediation of money, as was the case in simple bartering, would have appeared to be an event of great and significant scope, destined to mark a profound change in the legal schemes that defined those mechanisms. Paul grasped the difference with extreme clarity. In the bartering of goods for other goods there was no formal specification of subjects and things, present in the relationship only with an absolute lack of differentiation: "For there was once a time when money did not exist and no such terms as 'merchandise' and 'price' were known; rather did every man barter what was useless to him for what was useful, according to the exigencies of his current needs."[16] By contrast, in the more mature sale something quite different took place, according to Paul. It could exist and claim to be such only if the elements that formed it were formally characterized by the role assigned to them in the abstract configuration that the mercantile circulation

of goods was able to assume by virtue of the presence of a universal equivalent such as money ("aequalitas quantitatis," as the jurist literally wrote). In
this case, "it is one thing to sell, another to buy; one person again is vendor
and the other, purchaser; and, in the same way, the price is one thing, the object of sale, another; but, in bartering, one cannot discern which party is vendor and which, purchaser."[17] It was, then, that particular type of formalization—an economic one—already implicit in the exchange of goods for
money, that underlay the corresponding juridical abstraction that led to the
construing of the concept of sale. This modality of relation enacted through
the medium of money necessarily included the existence of precise determinations, which derived solely from the form of the exchange. Paul expressed
himself with a very literal clarity on this point: once money had made its decisive appearance, what we might define as the material aspect of the relationship no longer counted ("when you had something which I wanted, and
I, for my part, had something that you were willing to accept"),[18] just the role
that each subject or thing was assigned through their reciprocal qualification
in the formalized mechanism of exchange: "it is one thing to sell, another to
buy . . . the price is one thing, the object of sale, another." In this case, the juridical ontology did nothing more than to project onto a plane of social metaphysics (the abstract scheme of the *emptio-venditio*) what it found already prepared on the terrain of the economy. A bridge had been built between legal
forms and the technical-economic artificiality of life that would never be interrupted.

Paul's reasoning was of powerful significance in the story we are recounting here. But it was Quintus Mucius who had first blazed the path. Of course,
he had not developed an authentic doctrine of contracts; that would come
only later. What's more, the structure of his work—leaving aside other
considerations—would have prevented him from doing so. And yet in his
thinking it is possible to make out quite distinctly the basic lines of a unitary
project.

The pertinent text is a Mucian lemmata preserved in the fourth book of
Pomponius' commentary on the *Iuris civilis*:

> In whichever way something is contracted, in the same way it
> should also be resolved. So that if we contract by the delivery of a
> thing, it should be resolved by the delivery of the thing: when we

make a loan, it must be resolved through repayment of the same amount. And when we contract something through the utterance of words, the obligation must be resolved either by the utterance of words or by delivery of a thing: by words, when one declares to have received from he who promised; by thing, when what was promised is given. Equally, when there is contracted a purchase or a sale or a hiring, since they can be contracted by bare consent, they can also be resolved by consent to the contrary effect.[19]

Even though the name of Mucius does not appear, and the passage in the *Digesta* seems to be directly attributed to Pomponius, we can confidently regard it as a fragment from the original writings of the republican jurist. In thirteen fragments of Pomponius' work, Justinian's compilers are more careful in their attributions, introducing the Mucian lemmata with "Quintus Mucius writes," and the comment with "Pomponius."[20] In another hundred or so cases, however—and this is one of them—the *Digesta* omits all explicit distinctions between lemma and commentary, and we must rely upon an analysis of the textual structure. To do this it would be useful to draw on an overall framework of evaluative criteria, but unfortunately we do not possess a unitary critical reading of Pomponius' text.[21] Here, however, there can be no doubt: the manifest stylistic roughness of the writing, which recalls that of other lemmata whose derivation from Mucius is incontrovertible thanks to the preservation of the jurist's name in Justinian's edition,[22] and even a few slight incongruences, betray the massive effort required to successfully conceive the formulation of a legal discipline through a scheme that had never previously been attempted: to describe in accordance with general principles something that had hitherto been only a dispersive mass of cases and specific rules. This condition could not have been that of Pomponius. And in fact, when the Antonine jurist himself addresses these same issues, probably quite mindful of Mucius' formulation, there is a much greater degree of confidence in his discourse. A passage from the second book of the *Enchiridion* (or possibly from the *Liber singularis regularum,* a work that was probably composed under the influence of Mucius' *Horoi*) allows us to make a conclusive comparison: "A verbal obligation is resolved either naturally or at civil law; naturally, as with payment, or when the object of the stipulation ceases to exist without fault on the part of the promissor; at civil law, by a formal release or when the roles of promissor and stipulator vest in the same person."[23] And for that matter Sabinus, in his *Ius civile,* written with a clear awareness of the treatise by Mucius, reformulates with quite a different level of elegance the principle first expressed by the republican master: "Nothing is so natural as to dissolve something in the same way as that in which it is put together. So a verbal obligation is verbally dissolved. The obligation of bare consent is dissolved by contrary consent," we read in a lemma transcribed by Ulpian.[24]

Instead the Latin in the Mucian text is rough and laborious. In it we can perceive the halting quality of a language not yet familiarized with the conceptual threshold that, all the same, it was finally attaining: it would not be until the writings of Cicero and Servius that the adaptation can be considered complete. For now, we are discernibly short of the objective: the impression—identical with that which is often transmitted by the *Rhetorica ad Herennium*—is in some way akin to German philosophical prose prior to Kant.

Nor can we find any significant evidence that the fragment underwent substantial alterations in its successive transcriptions. Admittedly, it is quite probable that the original version also contained a reference to *contrahere litteris* (that is, to bonds established through the entering of the debt in the account books of the *paterfamilias*): a modality that was well known to Cicero, and which Quintus Mucius was unlikely to have forgotten to record, but which Justinian's editors tended programmatically to erase from the fragments they were utilizing. And it is also likely that in the final phrase, we should correct (from "by dissent" to "by consent") an innocuous and glaring error of a copyist.[25] But it is difficult to imagine that the compilers or even Pomponius himself intervened to introduce substantial modifications. Certainly, the latter did not hesitate to bend Mucius' texts to some extent, and we may reasonably suppose that the resulting lemmata were the product of careful editing (cuts, stitching, perhaps the occasional stylistic tweaking) designed to facilitate the commentary. However, this must not have involved full-scale rewriting.

Let us first consider the introductory phrases: "Prout quidque contractum est, ita et solvi debet." Mucius wrote them in the initial section of his work, between the second and the third book. He was writing about legacies, and it is probable that the classification of the *genera legatorum* was in fact one of the products of his work on this theme.[26] We cannot say with any certainty what link made it possible to effect the transition from the topic he was dealing with to a more generalized point of reference such as the one in question: the hypothesis advanced by Otto Lenel, who identified the connection as a possible analysis of the *liberatio legata*—the formula with which one obtained the extinction of a debt encumbering the patrimony of the legatee—from which the jurist would have arrived at a more all-inclusive framework, remains anything but certain.[27]

Whatever the context of his thinking might have been, though, it definitely must have had a broader scope, in counterpoint with the occasion that had provoked it. From then on, this sudden interruption of the examination of a case or, in any event, of a more restricted notion, followed by the insertion—even in connection with the slimmest of lexical links—of an overall viewpoint or a general rule would become a typical mode of procedure in Roman jurisprudence, indicative of the coexistence, in its working horizons, of two paradigms: the case-based one, arranged by events, and the one arranged by concepts.

Mucius' exordium was charged with a unifying tension that already placed it outside the realm of tradition. The point of departure was not internal to the customary jurisprudential interpretation, even in the terms in which it had been updated by the generation of Publius Mucius. It was already properly speaking an abstract concept, a first ontological outline: the notion of *quidque contractum*—of "anything contracted."

The lexical choice places us in the presence of one of the oldest (if not absolutely the most ancient) uses of the verb *contrahere* in a legal text.[28] And the word—quite recent by comparison with very remote terms such as *agere, gerere,* and *facere*[29]—immediately became the mark of an ambitious project, a unitary representation for a sequence of situations that the development of *ius* had presented as disjointed, each with its own history and its own particular rules: the *stipulatio,* the loan, the purchase, the sale, the bookkeeping entry. The attempt was feasible on two conditions. The first was that the field of observation not be enclosed within the context of a vision fragmented into a multiplicity of cases and actions, capable at the very best of perceiving in a nebulous manner the emergence of certain typologies: the entering into an undertaking through the delivery of a thing, or the utterance of words, or the recording of a debt in a bookkeeping register, or bare consent. The second was the availability of the general ideas of "obligation" and of "contracting," as formal schemes entirely detached from the modes in which they might concretely manifest themselves.

Both of these conditions had already been achieved by Mucius: the discovery of abstraction allowed him to attain an unprecedented point of view, from which wholly new syntheses became possible. And it also enabled him to conceptualize the notions of obligation and of contracting as separate and empty forms, devoid of any specific content referring to a single class of economic or legal operations (a loan or a stipulation, a sale or a bookkeeping entry).

In truth, the concept of *obligatio* appears in the text more than anything else as an established premise—as the fruit of an already completed elaboration—rather than as an element yet to be constructed, while all the attention seems to be concentrated on the idea of "contracting." Still, its presence, albeit in a (so to speak) lateral collocation, probably presents us with another decisive Mucian invention. The jurist certainly made use of the verb *obligari*, and Cicero for that matter was familiar with the substantive *obligatio* (not found in the *Rhetorica ad Herennium*), a term it is hard to imagine he was the first to introduce. The array of possibilities for the birth of the word (and of its concept) thus narrows considerably, and it is probable that it was precisely in the books of *Iuris civilis* that the word was employed for the first time in the strong sense of an immaterial legal bond: as the abstract form of debt and liability between private subjects, made conceivable by the diffusion of exchanges and by the system of edictal actions designed to protect them (nor can we fail to note that here the concept of *obligatio* was placed alongside that of *solvere,* in a connection that would surface again in a famous definition, probably attributable to Gaius, who in turn utilized Mucian material).[30]

As we have already said, the stylistic choices betrayed the effort behind these achievements. The *quidque*—"anything"—that precedes the verbal participle demonstrates at once the necessity and the difficulty that the jurist perceived in underscoring the totalizing generic nature of the *contractum*—"that which has been contracted"—with respect to any clearly defined content. Its being conceived, in fact, as a pure form of relationships, each of which would then be determined in its singularity by the events of social and economic life, and by the legal rules that had been constructed alongside them. The category did not yet identify the contract found in thinking from Labeo to Ulpian, which we shall encounter later; it would only be the transformation of the verbal form into the corresponding substantive that marked the completion of the ontological path. But even though this result would only emerge in the subsequent development, the presence of an initial nucleus of formalization can already be detected in the text of Mucius. The contents of relevant segments of the civic legal experience thereby emerged transformed. The existence of a hidden morphology was revealed, with major implications of a normative character: from then on, it would become possible to formulate authentic *regulae* (*horoi,* as Mucius preferred to put it), general normative principles that disciplined, in a unitary manner and through a single concept, apparently distant spheres of reality that had once been impossible to compare, associated—in this circumstance—by their common recurrence in mercantile exchanges.[31]

The category of the *quidque contractum* was nonetheless only a starting point, though a decisive and original one. It was presented by Mucius within the context of a more complex apparatus, which linked the two clearly distinct notions of *contrahere* and *solvere.* It can not be excluded that the elaboration of the principle set forth by the jurist might have been the product of the extension of an older discipline, concerning the relationship between the constitution and the dissolution of noxal liability. We know that Mucius had worked on the notion of *nexum,* reviewing the earlier Manilian definition, which, probably still under the influence of the Twelve Tables, also included within it the *mancipatio,* dividing and separating the two figures, despite the repetition of the same rituality.[32] The instrument that made possible the splitting up of the decemviral prescriptions was, once again, the concept of *obligatio* as an abstract bond of liability—which increasingly appears to be the authentic hidden impulse of this whole area of Mucius' thinking. *Nexum* should encompass, according to the jurist, only obligatory relationships, and not property transfers: "Manilius writes that *nexum* are all those things which are done by bronze and scales, including property transfers; Mucius, on the contrary, all those things which are done by bronze and scales in order to enter into an obligation, except property transfers," as we learn from Varro.[33]

We are therefore in the presence of the first formulation in conceptual terms of an original feature of the entire Roman legal experience: the distinction between obligatory relationships, conceived as personal bonds between subjects, and property relationships, represented as an exclusive, immediate, and direct power of the person over the thing.

It is certain in any case that the equation of *contrahere* and *solvere* marked a shift from all previous formulations. It was constructed through the comparison of two concepts, which now became two full-fledged categories: the idea of contracting, and the idea of dissolving. The nexus that joined them was purely logical. Once the form of the *contrahere* had been elaborated in abstraction, it was measured, so to speak, against its opposite. The pair proved capable of representing within a purely formal trajectory an entire range of legal relations in the compass of their interaction, from the moment of their establishment to the point of their conclusion.

Nonetheless the link between the two categories did not establish a rigorous symmetry. The counterpoint of the interplay between the *prout* ("in whichever way . . .") and the *ita et* ("in the same way . . .") indicated only the necessity of the connection, without imposing any rigid correspondence. And it was precisely the description of the interweaving of these possibilities that opened the way to the second part of Mucius' discourse.

Indeed, the examples of behavior that resolved the obligatory relationship were presented in accordance with a precise classification, which broke down the elements included within the concept of *quidque contractum*. And even if there was no explicit reference to the division by genera, there can be no doubt that the model was in point of fact a diaeretic scheme, which divided the abstract totality of the *contractum* into distinct parts, each with its own characteristics, but all of them with a shared reference to the founding category.

There thus emerged the specific junction linking abstraction and diaeresis in the construction of the books of the *Iuris civilis*. The attainment of an abstract dimension (in the case in question, the linked notions of *contrahere* and *solvere*) was the immediate condition for the application of diaeretic techniques, while the latter proved to be an essential instrument for mastering the diverse array of legal segments that the new ontology contained within itself. And so the module that conveyed the sequence of examples (*veluti cum . . . et cum . . . veluti cum . . . veluti cum . . .*) split the unity of the *quidque contractum* according to whether, in it, there had been identified an act of giving, or an oral promise, or else (if we can rely on what we have supposed concerning the integration of the text) a written undertaking. A relationship contracted *re* could be resolved *re;* a contract *verbis* could be resolved *re* or *verbis.*

We cannot rule out that some of these statements already circulated in the jurisprudential interpretations of the second century. And it is possible that Mucius himself might have worked elsewhere on orderings that could be considered as preludes to his model: perhaps, for instance, the one, reported by Cicero, that distinguished three conditions for presenting the *actio certae creditae pecuniae* (an action for the restitution of a sum of money): the existence of an act of giving, a stipulation, or an entry in the account books, in keeping with a scheme that closely mirrors the one just examined (provided, that is, Cicero was not here copying Mucius himself).[34] Certainly, however, the overall pattern was absolutely original, a framing that was destined to enjoy lasting success in the history of contract theories. We shall have occasion to come back to this later.

Let us return now to our text. A clear break marks the beginning of the last part. Mucius was attempting to work into that same concept—the symmetry between *contrahere* and *solvere*—alongside the traditional ways of establishing liability foreseen by the *ius civile*, also the new figures recognized by the praetor, and based on consent: in all of them there was a contracting, in all of them there was an obliging. But the transition took place only with evident fatigue (and this reveals the unquestionable Mucian provenance of this part of the writing as well: Pomponius, more than two centuries later, would have no such difficulty). In the first place, to affirm the new symmetry a shift was made from the level of necessity *(debet)* to the plane of possibility *(potest)*. Moreover, reference was no longer made, as had previously been the case, to whole typologies *(contrahere re,* or *verbis)*, but instead there were indicated, quite distinctly, two of the relations that could be established through bare consent, without any mention of a more general *contrahere consensu;* indeed, there was a division of the sale into its structural elements *(emptio* and *venditio*, purchase and sale), continuing, that is, to have as a point of reference not so much the unitary (abstract) figure, as yet not entirely in focus, but the distinct actions placed in the edict to protect the two sides of the obligation: the *actio empti* and the *actio venditi.* Clearly, we are still short of a complete conceptualization of the category of the *obligationes consensu contractae* ("obligation by consent") Quintus Mucius restricted himself to observing the existence of a decisive functional point of contact between the types of obligation that he had already examined, and two specific relations based on bare consent *(consensu nudo)*: there was a *contrahere* in these cases as well, albeit one attained in a different manner; and here too the equation of *contrahere* and *solvere* held good.

In this way, admittedly with a certain degree of effort, through the elaboration of an abstract form, acts from the ancient heritage of the *ius civile* and new transactions recognized by the praetor—the past and the present of *ius,* distant in the traditional topical organization of the subjects—were reconducted within a shared paradigm. The diversity of the schemes based upon consent, though carefully underscored, did not prevent them from being classified within the same model. The result was made possible by an original process of fusion between the civil law tradition and praetorian innovations, from then on a part of legal thought: a way of bringing together, through the abstraction of formal connections, what the city's history had presented as separate and diverse. The connective force of the concepts transformed the ancient *ius civile* at the very moment in which it was confronted with the new edictal figures, rendering it capable of dealing with the needs of the society before it.

The close proximity between figures of *ius* and new edictal schemes, enabled by the elaboration of abstract concepts with a totalizing function, opened up unexplored perspectives. One of those concerned the possibility of describing in a unitary fashion the rules establishing the importance and the limits to be recognized with regard to the statements of the author of a legal act, even if expressed in ways that departed from customary practice. The fact that in relations based on bare consent there was plenty of scope for the free realization of the parties' wishes was a product of the particular structure of those transactions. But what might have happened, for instance, in a property transfer, or in a stipulation?

It was a problem that did not exist for the old civil law ritualism: in that context, everything was reduced to strict observance of the prescribed words and gestures, and the effects could be only those that had been rigorously established in advance: there was no room for any different acknowledgment of the wishes involved (and it was also an impediment of this sort that in some cases, in the general perception, turned the *summum ius* into a *summa iniuria*).[35] But now the thrust of consensualism and its integration within a broader conceptual framework contributed to breaking down the barrier of that ancient exteriority, and a new perspective began to gain ground, namely that, quite irrespective of the rituals, the will of the subjects could in some manner be expressed, and should be taken into account in precisely measuring the effects of the act performed. Once again, the abstractions of legal thought reflected concrete phenomena and behavior: commercial reality demanded that even the schemes regulated by the old civil law tradition, but now utilized for the requirements of the new world of trade, be able to adapt to the change.

And it is precisely on an issue linked to this theme that we find Quintus Mucius once again at work:

> No one can procure an advantage for a third party, either through
> an agreement or by adding a clause to an act, or through a stipu-
> lation.[36]

The extract comes from a longer passage in the *Liber singularis horon,* a Mucian work from which the compilers of the *Digesta* drew a handful of fragments.[37] It can be identified without hesitation as the writing of Mucius (even if we cannot rule out the possibility that the sequence of statements in which we now find it inserted in the *Digesta* was only a sort of collage put together by Justinian's editors).[38] Ontology and *horoi,* forms and maxims, developed along a single line: here as in the books of the *Iuris civilis* it was the construction of abstract concepts that allowed the formulation of general rules, which established genuine principles, capable of recomposing in an organic manner the multiform normative reality.

We cannot say what criterion guided the exposition in the original structure of Mucius' work, but nothing bars us from thinking that it repeated that of the *Iuris civilis,* of which the *Horoi* must have been a sort of synthetic recapitulation.

In our text the jurist's perspective no longer led him to consider just relationships forming part of the scheme of *contrahere* and *obligatio,* but any act with legal consequences—whether that was an otherwise undefined agreement, a clause tagged onto a typical figure (a sale or a mancipation with bronze and scales, for instance), or a stipulation. The three typologies indicated—*paciscendo, legem dicendo, stipulando*—figured as authentic categories within which Mucius included the indication of every possible legal activity undertaken by a subject legitimately capable of carrying it out *(quisquam)*. The difference between obligatory relationships and property transfer acts was set aside: the *legem dicere*—adding a clause—could refer equally to a consensual contract or to an act transferring property of an asset. The objective was to determine the boundaries of private power in all of its various manifestations. The limits were defined by the impossibility of unilaterally affecting the patrimonial situation of a third party: the model that emerged in the background of this rule—a universe of subjects equal by law, where everyone's legal position was evaluated against the measure of a rigorous symmetry—had distant points of reference, where the ancient political traditions of the city and more recent influences of Greek and Hellenistic philosophical thought came together.

Nor should we be surprised by the use of the term *pacisci* ("to agree") instead of *contrahere*: the latter term, as we have seen, did not refer in Mucius' view to the sphere of consensualism alone, while it is precisely to this that the jurist wished to allude, indicating it in the most exclusive and comprehensive manner possible, in keeping with a usage that we already find in the *Rhetorica ad Herennium;*[39] whereas the *legem dicere* had, so to speak, a transverse value, inasmuch as it could be applied both to "contractual" relationships and to deeds of transfer of rights to material things.

3.

The presence of the new episteme was not an exceptional episode in the *Iuris civilis,* but constituted the background against which the entire work was constructed. A mosaic of fragments that has fortunately been preserved allows us to follow, in the process of composition of an entire section of the treatise, the thin yet visible thread of this fabric.

The context is the fourteenth book (in Pomponius' commentary, the corresponding books are the thirty-fifth and the thirty-sixth), which appears to be devoted (perhaps entirely) to an analysis of the notion of *societas* (partnership),[40] a very important figure in the social and economic life of first-century Rome, regulated by the edictal activity of the praetor and whose transformations would mark the progressive expansion of the Italic economy. Once again, the subject was extraneous to the traditional patrimony of the *ius civile*, and Quintus Mucius could have excluded it from his examination. But instead he decided to deal with it, though in a very particular manner, attempting as far as possible to maintain the link between the scheme of the new consensual contract and an old institution of the archaic legal experience (and this, truly, was a topos of civil law): the *consortium ercto non cito* (a grouping of coheirs, who, upon the death of the *pater*, continued to manage the family estate without partitioning it).[41]

It is very likely that Quintus Mucius started precisely from the ancient *consortium* (which had become unusual in his time) to arrive at the consensual partnership, thereby keeping faith with his own archaizing tendency.[42] There are various clues to suggest this. The first is that Gaius—whose dependence upon a tradition that can be traced back directly to Mucius we have previously mentioned—in his description of the regulations of consensual partnership included a classification articulated around at least two "genera of partnership." One was "of the law of peoples," that is to say, consensual partnership (*quae consensu contrahitur nudo*: and the reference to the *ius gentium* was obvious in this age in connection with consensual contracts), while the other *(aliud genus)* was "proper to Roman citizens," and that is, the *consortium*. Such an arrangement cannot possibly be attributed to Gaius, in an era when the memory of this ancient institution was only a pale erudite reminiscence. Its roots go further back in time, in keeping with the elements combined in it (archaic *consortium*, consensual partnership, diaeretic scheme): to an age that, while it may already have been familiar with the use of diaeretic models and the practice of consensual partnership, had not yet entirely lost the experience of the *consortium*; and thus precisely to the age of Quintus Mucius, the only years where all the three elements can be placed.[43] If one adds that in a section of Pomponius' commentary, again with reference to the fourteenth book of the *Iuris civilis* and in which there is a clear trace of Mucius, mention is made of a *societas quae in consensu consistit*, with an implicit allusion to the existence of a different type, not based on consensus, the hypothesis that the distinction between the "two genera" should be attributed to the thought of Mucius acquires quite considerable weight.[44]

If this is so, then we must believe that the authentic point of departure was not even the *consortium,* but a unifying concept of *societas:* an ontological construction, to which we should relate—though probably only in an implicit manner—the distinction between the two genera. And the substance of the common reference must have been identified by Mucius in the discovery, in both figures, of the joint entitlement of a property right, combined with the aspect of the shared management of the assets—a viewpoint that the jurist would stick to firmly in the subsequent development of his reasoning.

But even in these terms, comparison between the new consensual *societas* and the old *consortium* was far from easy: it still required, to become possible, a revision of the archaic institution to make it compatible with the more recent model, and the associated elaboration of a concept of "part" (until then nonexistent) as an ideal share in a joint ownership. And in fact we know that Quintus Mucius specifically devoted himself to both of these tasks. Another lemmata in his *Libri iuris civilis,* preserved by Pomponius and also likely to have come from the fourteenth book, shows the jurist intently working to place the fraternal consortium within the scheme of joint ownership according to ideal shares (by "parts": and here we see the return of the theme of joint entitlement);[45] while a citation from Paul faithfully reports the Mucian idea of *pars:* "Quintus Mucius writes that "part" refers to an asset before it has been divided: and in fact what is ours after having been divided belongs to us entirely and not in part."[46]

Once the ancient institution had been thus redesignated, its link with the consensual *societas* became virtually obligatory; and the most immediate connection could not fail to take the form of the figure of the *societas omnium bonorum,* the "partnership of all assets"—probably the original model of a partnership based on consensus—through which the partners pooled their assets in a common fund. And once again we can see Mucius devoting himself to this theme, still in the fourteenth book of the *Iuris civilis,* probably after treating consortium, but before moving on to an analysis of the other types of partnerships deriving from mercantile practice and recognized by the praetor, though he did quickly get to them as well in the same context.[47]

What first attracted his attention was the disciplining of the so-called *questuaria* partnership (for the acquisition of profits), a very important model in the mechanisms of accumulation of commercial capital between the second and first centuries. The jurist was the first to dedicate attention to its conceptual construction, and his work would be completed by successive authors, especially Sabinus, operating in the same line of thought.[48] Mucius probably continued to employ diaeretic distinctions, which led him to underscore the differences of regime between "partnerships of all assets" and *questuaria* partnerships: another surviving fragment of his thinking reveals his determination to maintain the inadmissibility of the conferment of inheritances, legacies, and donations in the patrimony of this last type of partnership, evidently in contrast with what applied to "partnerships of all assets."[49] Nor can we rule out that there was already in the writings of Mucius several of those elements that would later form the central focus of the analysis of Sabinus, both concerning the definition of "profit" *(quaestus)*, and with respect to another distinction, which isolated with greater precision those types of partnership defined by "a single business transaction" (including the *questuaria* partnership).

But Quintus Mucius was also engaged with issues regarding the normative discipline of the new figure. And it was in this context that he ventured to conceive—again, in the same book—a solution that triggered a celebrated dispute. Gaius tells us:

> There has been a great dispute as to whether a partnership is possible on the terms that one of the partners should have a larger share in profits than in losses. Q. Mucius considered this to be against the nature of partnership, but Servius Sulpicius, whose opinion has prevailed, held that not only is partnership possible on these terms, but even on the terms that one partner shall bear no share of losses and yet have a share in profits, on the supposition that his services are considered so valuable that it is fair that he should be admitted to partnership on such terms.[50]

There can be no doubt that the basic reason underpinning the thesis of Mucius (even if we wanted to exclude the authenticity of the reference to the *natura societatis,* which might be the product of a lexical and argumentative choice that was not original) refers back to a faithful adherence to a rigidly property-based idea of the partnership relation: the only possible approach, if one wished to hold together, within a single paradigm, consortium and consensual partnership. Profits and losses therefore could not fail to reflect the proportional nature of the patrimonial contributions: any other possibility would have been a violation of that principle, which constituted for Mucius the foundation of the very essence of the partnership as an ontological scheme (*natura societatis*: even if it is not Mucian, there can be no doubt that the expression perfectly captured the master's thought). The price paid in the name of this conception could only be the sacrifice of all autonomous evaluation of the professional activity of one of the parties, albeit reflected in a specific expression of the will of the contracting parties: *opera eius*—the professional activity of the partner; here lies the core of the controversy, as is clear from the motivation of Servius' opposing opinion, to which we shall return. The profile of the *questuaria* partnership must have been rigorously derived from the prevalence, in all types of partnership, of the aspect of the joint ownership of the assets forming part of the partnership—and it is on this element alone that Mucius based his position. It was enough for Servius to depart from this scheme to succeed easily in overturning the entire body of reasoning.

Like the text on *contrahere*, so too the conceptual framework of the entire fourteenth book reveals the presence of that same underlying theme. Constantly, and with crystalline clarity, we see delineated the architecture of an articulated movement of forms that determined the structure of the entire treatise. And now we can identify a further element, which had not previously emerged with similar evidence. The ontological design that made it possible to link the ancient consortium to the more recent consensual partnership proved an original way of preserving a solid relationship of continuity between the past and the present in the *ius* of the city: the diaeretic connections mediated and to a certain extent annulled on the plane of abstraction the discontinuities that had inevitably been produced on the terrain of historical development. Only the elaboration of an abstract form of partnership enabled the preservation of comparisons that were otherwise impossible: and this was the only condition that allowed the tradition of the *ius civile* to succeed once again in becoming the measure of a present now in flight from the old canons and their restrictions.

4.

Not always, in Mucius, did the horizon of the concepts develop from the basis of an edictal norm or from a figure of the *ius civile*. In some cases it opened onto a completely different space. An example of this can be found in a passage of the third book of Cicero's *De officiis:*

> It was Quintus Scaevola, the pontifex maximus, who used to attach the greatest importance to all questions of arbitration to which the formula was appended "as good faith requires"; and he held that the expression "good faith" had a very extensive application, for it was employed in guardianships and partnerships, in trusts and mandates, in buying and selling, in hiring and letting—in a word, in all the transactions on which the social relations of daily life depend; in these questions of arbitration, he said, the principal task of the judge was to decide the extent of each party's obligation to the other, especially when, as often happens, the defendant also presents claims.[51]

We are here in the presence of the mature elaboration of a crucial category of the Western legal tradition, to whose genesis we have already referred: "good faith." We cannot directly ascribe the content of the citation to the *Iuris civilis* or to the *Horoi*. We know in fact that outside of (and probably before) these two works, Quintus Mucius had had occasion to reflect on this notion, with which he had been concerned in his edict as proconsul of Asia (a magistracy that he may have held in the year 94): a text that had struck Cicero as an exemplary document in the administration of provincial communities.[52] It is, however, likely that the jurist took these elaborations into account in the treatise (in which good faith was in any case discussed),[53] even if we are not able to say where and to what purpose.

In terms of the logical schemes employed, it would seem that we are once again in the presence of a construction that we have already learned to recognize: a series of different figures, considered from the point of view of their trial protection (the separation of the actions explains the division between purchase and sale and between *locatio*—hire—and *conductio*—letting—

which we have previously encountered), were joined together by the discovery of a common element, which served as a point of reference for the classification. Nor should we even rule out that in this case too in the original writing the identification of the concept was accompanied by the use of diaeretic models to support the ensuing systematization.

There was, however, an important new development. The unifying form was no longer the ontological projection of a legal relationship, as in the case of *contrahere* or of *societas,* but rather the formalization of an ethical trait, established to prescriptively define a model of behavior.

The word *fides*—originally the capacity to instill trust, the reliability of a *pater* in the eyes of his peers or subordinates (clients, for instance, or freedmen), his credibility; later and more generically, the faith placed in a person with whom one has dealings—formed part of a small group of terms defining certain fundamental ethical-political characteristics of republican culture as early as the third century (and for some of them it would be quite natural to suppose an even more ancient presence), such as *salus* (prosperity, safety), *spes* (hope), *virtus* (virtue), *pietas* (piety), *pax* (peace).[54] Its history is linked to the cultural archeology of the city, within the context of which it described the tendency toward stability, compactness, and reciprocally unequivocal behavior that can be considered the other aspect of the ritualistic prescriptivity diffused by archaic religiosity.

This was the foundation upon which the work of jurisprudence and the normative practice of the praetors had been based since the second century, attempting a typification of personal conduct in order to assess it in a trial, probably also in connection with the early idea of *aequum*. Thus, *fides* was transformed into the *ex fide bona* clause added to some actions of the formulary procedure—especially in relation to the new contractual schemes derived from Mediterranean mercantile practice—and indeed it is possible that the appearance of the neuter *bonum* alongside the older *aequum* should be linked to the use of the same adjective along with *fides*: a redundancy that in both cases would reveal the aristocratic pressure on the two notions, which thus became more socially connotated, and would characterize the early stereotypy of stylemes.

But in Mucius' design this orientation was the point of departure for a further step. Good faith now appeared as the founding category of a wide-ranging classification, which referred to others present in the books of the

Iuris civilis: it had been transmuted into an abstraction (it was Quintus Mucius who, in all likelihood, had written "manat latissime"—"wide scope"), in the quantifiable measure of an ought-to-be: transfiguring a reference dense with historicity and exactitude into a scheme devoid of content, in a paradigm that the judges would be obliged in each case to fill with concreteness. In this way, formalism did not open out from within to a positive ethic, but reduced it to its own logic, transforming it into an abstract imperative for conformity, which would then have to be fleshed out by its interpreter.[55]

In Pomponius' commentary on the *Iuris civilis* of Mucius we find a precise example of this construction:

> In all transactions which have been entered into, whether they be
> of good faith or not, if some error should occur, so that, say, the
> buyer or hirer understands one thing, and the party who con-
> tracts with them another, the transaction is of no effect. And the
> same answer must also be given if a partnership is entered into,
> so that if the parties form different views, the one understanding
> one thing and the other another, that partnership based on the
> consent of the parties is of no effect.[56]

It is a text we have just encountered. The writing still reveals traces of what we have learned to recognize in the republican jurist, with the reference to the consensual partnership as a nonexhaustive typology of all forms of partnership. The theme explored here is the need to evaluate the intentions of the subjects in a transaction ("the buyer or hirer understands one thing . . .") with respect to the possible occurrence of an "error," considered to be an element sufficient to render the completed act void.

There can be no question that the discourse, insofar as we can read it today, is the result of a stratification of texts, in which, overlaid upon an original Mucian nucleus there is an analysis by Pomponius, and in all likelihood other interventions by editors of late antiquity, or even by Justinian's compilers. The culmination of this process is the stable establishment of the legal gaze in the interiority of the agents: it is their will and not merely the materiality of the acts undertaken that was important for the purpose of producing legal effects. But it is probable that the regulatory pattern was first started by Mucius: a further blow to the verbalistic framework of the *ius civile,* already long since and irreversibly undermined.[57] The rule that the evaluation of intentionality was not be considered limited only to contracts included within the concept of good faith (whose actions contained the *ex fide bona* clause), but was to refer to every type of contractual activity, probably constituted a non-Mucian extension. Even so, its premise—the connection between good faith and error, and perhaps the very conceptualization of this latter notion—should be regarded as being already present in the books of the *Iuris civilis*.[58]

In them good faith reappears as a general category, a point of discrimination within which it was possible to lay down innovative rules. Starting from there, the successive stage of development (probably from Pomponius on) would build a classification of the entire phenomenology of *contrahere* (contracting: *in omnibus negotiis contrahendis*) in keeping with that already set forth by Mucius. But now the stated principle went beyond the original distinction based on good faith, underscoring that this was not to represent a barrier against the extension of the discipline, which was understood to take in the whole contractual range.[59] All that was excluded were wills (to say nothing of the *mancipationes,* which Mucius had also considered to lie outside the realm of obligations), in which it was not possible to identify any *contrahere,* and the will of the testator was not destined to coincide with that of other partners: and we know, from a celebrated trial in which Mucius took part, that in this case the jurist's opinion had been far more restrictive.[60]

Once again we have seen that the disciplining capacity of forms meant for Mucius the possibility of joining together civic antiquity and new times, and of carrying on orienting society through the accumulation of past knowledge and the revival from an ontological perspective of the original republican values.

In truth, and this has become very clear to us, the *Iuris civilis* books must have been particularly charged with this tension between past and present. The real motivation for maintaining the plan of exposition in keeping with the traditional order, and for recollecting the more archaic features of the city's legal experience, is now apparent: the refusal to enclose *ius* within the dimension of a system deduced only logically, which would have erased memory and the space of the ancient institutions. Conducted instead within well-defined limits, the force of the new conceptual forms did not eliminate the past, but helped to recover it. Ontological contiguity took the place of social and historic discontinuity, creating a new link: something similar to a historic time specific to *ius,* the rhythm of its duration.[61]

And yet in the development of that tension something else could also be detected. A contradiction that determined the fate of the republican aristocracy, caught as it was between the need to remain bound to a tradition which, though compromised, was alone capable of preserving the system of power upon which it depended, and the force of the changes brought about by the unprecedented success of its own will to power.

In the midst of the crisis, which would end up dramatically destroying his own life, Quintus Mucius proposed—as the great repository of an essential and prestigious body of knowledge—a solution based on a far-from-simple compromise. In the face of a menacing future, he reiterated the primacy of the old *ius civile* as a way of measuring the present—the entire history of the nobility was reflected in this defense—but he grounded it on an unmatched renewal that would enable it to deal with the new tasks imposed by the extraordinary imperial transformation.

The political attempt to preserve intact the primacy of the senatorial class was destined to fail. But the new legal thought being incubated within the context of that strategy would completely surpass the horizon of events that had witnessed its formation, and would make an indelible mark on an extraordinarily long path.

13

An Aristocratic Theology

At the end of a prestigious career and in the final years of his life (certainly not earlier than 89), Quintus Mucius rose to the office of pontifex maximus, like his father before him.[1] The exercising of the role was not without intellectual consequences (as it had not been for Publius, publisher of the *Annales*), but was accompanied by reflection on the meaning and value of religious tradition in that difficult period of great change.

A surviving trace of this thought, very late but no less important for its specificity and for the world it reveals, can be found in the fourth book of Augustine's *De civitate Dei:*

> It is recorded that the learned pontiff Scaevola maintained that three kinds of gods are handed down to us—one by the poets, another by the philosophers and a third by those who are at the head of the city's community. He says that the first class is trifling, because the poets invent many disgraceful stories about the gods; the second is not suited to citizens, because it includes some superfluous doctrines and some also that it is harmful for the people

to know. As for the superfluous doctrines there need be no great controversy, for, as the jurists are wont to say, "Superfluous things do no harm." But what are the doctrines that are harmful when made known to the crowd? It is such statements as these, he says: "That Hercules, Aesculapius, Castor, and Pollux, are not gods, for it is related by the learned that they were men and passed on from the mortal state." And what more? "That society has not the true images of those who are really gods, because the true God has neither sex nor age nor well-defined bodily parts."[2]

In the passage by Augustine the reference to the ancient master is constructed in a way that conveys to the reader the impression of the literal accuracy of the quotation. And yet the idea that he had direct knowledge of one of Mucius' writings can be ruled out with almost absolute certainty. The most plausible hypothesis is that Augustine drew upon an intermediate source, and the array of texts used in the early books of *De civitate* makes it possible to identify this link in Varro's antiquarian output: his *Antiquitates* or, more probably, a brief but erudite dialogue, the *Curio de cultu deorum*. In both cases, it was a link worthy of trust, even though we cannot make any conjectures about the work by Mucius that lay at the origin of Varro's transcription.[3]

Of course this reliability does not authorize us to mechanically delineate, in Augustine's writing, the clear outlines of a Mucian nucleus entirely distinguishable from the larger text that preserved it, and it is only by starting with Augustine's overall plan—whose intentions permeate the passage that was quoted—that we can hope to recover the original thinking of the pontifex. Nonetheless we shall try, as far as possible, to keep the two levels separate: the plane of analysis attributable to Mucius, and that of its use by Augustine.

The structure of the text, as can be seen at first glance, appears once again to be that of a classification in genera, which ordered according to a triadic scheme—the procedure customarily adopted for the books of the *Iuris civilis*. We can be certain, however, that the pontifex was not the first to come up with the idea of such an arrangement. After being used by Mucius, the tripartite model resurfaces (albeit with substantial differences) in Varro and is utilized, again with important variants, by Dio Chrysostom, Plutarch, Aëtius, and Eusebius, for whom it is hard to imagine reciprocal influences on this point, much less a shared Mucian or Varronian genealogy.[4] The most plausible hypothesis is to suppose the existence of a common archetype, dating to a relatively early period, from which to trace both the tradition of Mucius and Varro, and the later (and reciprocally independent) one of the authors just cited: a nucleus that formed in a period no later than the beginning of the first century B.C. (probably already in the second), and almost certainly of Stoic derivation—perhaps a doctrine prior to Panaetius of Rhodes himself, and going back to ancient Stoicism, though it is quite likely that it was due to the latter's work in particular that it was subsequently introduced into Roman milieus close to the Scipionic Circle, and reached Mucius from there.[5]

We are also able to intuit the original course of the classification: it must have been limited to a listing of the three different forms without a hierarchical order; the first outline of such a criterion can perhaps be traced back only to the contribution of Panaetius. At the most, it is possible to attribute to the older notion—based on the testimony of Plutarch—the acknowledgment of a disagreement among poets, philosophers, and legislators (those whom Mucius interprets, with a keen eye on the aristocratic aspect so intrinsic to the history of Rome, in the sense of the *principes civitatis*). And it is also likely, as can be deduced from the text by Aëtius, that the earliest nucleus accentuated, with respect to the universality of the poets and the philosophers, the particular qualities of the third genera, closely connected to the normative customs of each community.[6]

2.

But Mucius did not place the three genera on the same plane. After some introductory remarks, in a passage we can take to be original, he severely criticized the first two perspectives: in his view, the value of the traditions of the poets and philosophers was to be measured against that of the *principes civitatis,* the hub around which the entire construction revolved. In this way he ended up proposing a new tripartite division, no longer ordered on parallel planes, but structured hierarchically to stress the primacy of just one of its component elements.

That this was the criterion underpinning the entire discussion can be seen in the critique of the tradition of philosophy, rejected solely because it "is not suited to citizens": evidently, it is that which is suitable to the *civitates*—later subtly exchanged with their *principes*—that determines the judgment regarding philosophers and poets. In this light, even the "disgraceful stories" of the first genera could not be judged as such except in relation to the same outlook. The intrusion of a differing point of view thus overturned the traditional classification. But what explained the novelty, and what were the underlying motivations?

The critique of poetry was brisk and radical: "trifling." The style once again is almost literally reminiscent of the *Rhetorica ad Herennium,* in which, with reference to the two kinds of "defective arguments," it is said that "one can be refuted by the adversary, and so belongs to the cause proper; the other, as it is trifling, does not need to be refuted": and one might well suppose that we are in the presence of the traces of a reading.[7] But the content of the Mucian observation went even further.

The role of poetry as a path to truth, and particularly toward religious truth, was a theme that, by Mucius' time, had already pervaded all of ancient culture. Disputes about the wisdom of the poets had stratified into a complex web of attitudes, ranging from the harsh Platonic rejection to the more cautious Aristotelian, and later Stoic, position, which strove to incorporate within its own vision of physics and ethics, through a careful allegorical interpretation, much of archaic and classical poetry, from Homer to the tragic poets.[8] But the firmness of the jurist's position was determined above all by other elements more closely bound up with the customs of the Roman aristocracy. Until the beginning of the first century, in fact, experience of poetry had been almost entirely extraneous to the nobility's model of living. "The Roman people were better trusted with trouble than with leisure. Not that he [Appius Claudius] was unaware of how pleasant is a state of tranquility but because he saw that powerful empires are roused by disturbance to energetic action but lulled into sloth by excessive peace and quiet": Valerius Maximus thus summarized the remote thought of Appius Claudius, in the golden age of the republic, between the fourth and the third centuries, and it may be that in his writing there also surfaced the shadow of a quotation from Ennius.[9] It was an entire world that mirrored itself in an implacable ideology of action, where all knowledge was measured in no other way than in terms of its practical purpose. Shortly thereafter, Quintus Caecilius Metellus, consul in 206 and a member of one of the republic's leading families, stuck to the same line:

> Q. Metellus, in the panegyric that he delivered at the obsequies
> of his father Lucius Metellus the pontiff, who had been Consul
> twice, Dictator, Master of the Horse and Land-commissioner,
> and who was the first person who led a procession of elephants in
> a triumph, having captured them in the first Punic War, has left it
> in writing that his father had achieved the ten greatest and high-
> est objects in the pursuit of which wise men pass their lives: for
> he had made it his aim to be a first-class warrior, a supreme orator
> and a very brave commander, to have the direction of operations
> of the utmost importance, to occupy the highest magistracies,
> to acquire supreme wisdom, to be deemed a most authoritative
> member of the senate, to obtain great wealth in an honorable
> way, to leave many children, and to achieve supreme distinction
> amongst citizens.[10]

The art of war, the conducting of important enterprises, the attainment of the most important magistracies, the accumulation of wealth (though "in an honorable way": it was possible to detect the scornful attitude of the big landowners toward the new but already well-established merchant classes)[11] firmly placed the value of *sapientia,* "wisdom," within the context of a life entirely dedicated to action: it is impossible not to think of the knowledge of *ius,* implicitly evoked by Metellus; but even it was subject to this sort of primacy of action, and indeed was perfectly integrated within it.

And it was precisely in the context of loyalty to such an attitude that an outright hostility to poetry would later manifest itself, when changing times already encouraged a nostalgic evocation of the past, in the presence of a degeneration in behavior and lifestyles (this too was the empire) that became the focus of unqualified reprobation. "Besides this, in the same work of Cato, I recall also these scattered and cursory remarks: 'It was the custom,' says he, 'to dress becomingly in the forum, and with the bare minimum at home. They paid more for horses than for cooks. The practice of the poetic art was not deemed suitable for men of honor. If anyone devoted himself to it, or frequented banquets, he was called a parasitic ruffian.'" This is Gellius quoting from the *Carmen de moribus:*[12] poetry was here compared without hesitation to gluttony and dissolute behavior, and associated with the polemic against luxury—one of the favorite themes of the political debate of the period, with remote plebeian origins. Cato for that matter had no reservations on the point: "Indeed, human life is very like iron. If you use it, it wears out; if you do not, it is nevertheless consumed by rust. In the same way we see men worn out by toil; if you toil not, sluggishness and torpor are more injurious than toil." Once again, it is Gellius who is quoting,[13] and his recollection is intertwined with a maxim mentioned by Columella, and likewise attributed to Cato: "To do nothing teaches one to do evil."[14]

But the unambiguousness of this testimony should not deceive us. It reflected an important but not undisputed orientation among the nobility of the middle period of the republic: Cato's shots were aimed at stiff adversaries. Alongside the tradition we might describe as Claudian-Catonian, there had developed, toward the end of the third century, and then throughout the whole of the second, trends that were certainly less hostile to the work of poets, and, more in general, indicative of a different valuation of the relationship between civil action and the contemplative life, and of less austere and archaizing styles of behavior.

As always happens in these cases, differences on the plane of ideas pointed to rifts in other fields as well. The transformation and decline of the old peasant structure under the pressure of the new slaveholding, agrarian, and mercantile web—the result of the imperial drive—and the formation of a much more complex social stratification led to demands and discontinuities that could no longer be reconciled in the political and cultural compactness of the ancient nobility. Any depiction of the intellectual and moral world of the Roman ruling groups between the third and second centuries must necessarily abandon any attempt at a unitary reconstruction. The Pythagorizing mysticism of Scipio Africanus, his relations with Ennius (though Cato himself was familiar with the poet as well, a circumstance we should not overlook if we do not want to erase the complexity of the positions that emerged over his long lifetime),[15] the philo-Hellenism of important families like the Aemilii, the circle of Scipio Aemilianus and the moderate cosmopolitan and imperialist rationalism practiced there, certainly offered better possibilities for the formation of more open-minded attitudes toward the work of poets, as compared to those dictated by a moralism that could easily appear both archaic and obsolete.[16]

And so when Quintus Mucius described poetry as trifling (even though he was only referring to the relationship with theology), behind him lay a cultural history that was neither single-voiced nor homogeneous. His contemporaries were about to witness the flourishing of a group of "new" poets (as Cicero would call them, without much sympathy),[17] and he himself lived to see the childhood of Catullus and the adolescence of Lucretius. His position did not reflect a straightforward acceptance of an unopposed point of view, but was a clear-cut choice on an issue that was keenly felt by his entire generation, and which entailed important questions in the taking of ideological and, in the final analysis, political sides.

3.

From poets to philosophers: thus we come to the core of Mucius' thought. His negative judgment makes a further specification: "superfluous doctrines" and "some also that it is harmful for the people to know": a breakdown—doubtless original with respect to the Greek model—that continued to proceed according to diaeretic patterns. As regards the first part, his criticism drew on and directly referred to a maxim of the ancient hermeneutic wisdom accumulated by the jurists: "Superfluous things do no harm." It was in all likelihood a reference to the work of jurisprudence between the third and the second centuries, and in particular to the interpretation of writings that documented the existence of a will carried out with the rite of the bronze and the scales. A clue pointing to this is offered by a text from the *Horoi*, which we can consider as symmetrical to what Augustine reports: "Those things which are written in a will in such a way that they cannot be understood are as if they were not written."[18] The stated rule sprang from the same culture that had formulated the principle cited in *De civitate*: the incomprehensible, like the superfluous, could not impede the validity of a will if everything else was in order. The same principle resurfaced later in a discussion between Trebatius and Labeo, in relation to a condition attached to a legacy, and was then adopted by the Severan jurisprudence, with Paul and Ulpian, and finally found its latest formulation, and with lexical choices almost identical to those seen in Augustine, in a text from the *Pauli sententiae,* at the turn of the fourth century.[19]

Having cleared the field, Mucius could now touch on the point that most interested him: the analysis of that which, in the theological tradition of the philosophers, was best kept from the people. All the previous distinctions served no other purpose than to carefully isolate this theme: it was here that Mucius played his final and decisive hand. The text, from this point on, seems to take on a dialogic course, possibly closely mirroring the stylistic framework of the Varronian source.

Mucius singled out two different blocks of doctrines in philosophy, both equally pernicious. The criterion for this further division will become clear later. For now let's focus on the first of the two blocks: the line of thought according to which certain gods, far from always having been such, actually lived and died as human beings. The pontifex avoided identifying the authors of this doctrine, but the milieu in which it had developed must have been well known to him, and is fairly easy for us to reconstruct. It once again led back to a Stoic orientation—Stoicism is the dominant frame for the entire text— that linked the origin of certain gods to a phenomenon of deification of hero-benefactors: a very old theory, already familiar to the Greek rationalism of the fifth century, close to the psychologistic skepticism of Critias, and most likely formulated already by Prodicus, during the time of Socrates.[20] Stoic thought would soon pick up on and redevelop this notion. Perseus, a follower of Zeno, explicitly referred to the teachings of Prodicus: "What Prodicus wrote does not appear unlikely, namely, that foods and other things useful to man were once considered deities and were worshipped; and later the discoverers of food, of shelter, and of the various arts, were deified, among them Demeter and Dionysus," we read in a fragment that has come down to us from Philodemus.[21]

The belief would then remain a fixed point in successive Stoic thought: a passage from Aëtius offers reliable confirmation.[22] And probably it was through the mediation of Panaetius that it was diffused in Roman circles. On the other hand, Euhemerism itself, accepted by Ennius and filtered, through him, into the circle of Scipio Africanus, had linked heroes and deities in a perspective very close to the one evoked by Mucius: Cicero himself, in a passage from the *De natura deorum,* would mention Prodicus, Ennius, and Euhemerus in the same breath for a common orientation on religious issues; Stoic philosophy and Euhemeristic reminiscences mingled together in the fabric of the aristocratic intellectual rationality.[23]

In the examples given by Mucius, the gods named—Hercules, Aesculapius, Castor, and Pollux—were among the most popular deities of the republican religion. Their veneration is rooted in memories and legends in which family traditions, the history of the city, and religious practices all contributed to form the collective cultural memory. The cult of Hercules should perhaps be traced back to the early receptiveness of the Romans to the influence of the settlements of Magna Graecia: first of all in a small temple near the Porta Trigemina, along the Via Ostiense, between the Aventine and the Tiber; later, adopted and promoted by a patrician family, the Potitii, at a private altar, the Ara Maxima, in the Boarian Forum. Public recognition came in the fourth century, probably due to the intervention of Appius Claudius: from a position opposed to the acceptance of this cultual practice there sprang up the legend of a divine vendetta that supposedly led to the extinction of the Potitii and the blinding of Cato the Censor.[24] The interpretation of the *Libri Sibillini,* or Sibylline Books, on the other hand, lay at the origin of the cult of Aesculapius, in the wake of the epidemic of 293 B.C. According to a widespread tradition, the serpent—symbol of the divinity—transported to Rome from Epidaurus in 291 escaped from the ship in which it was being housed and hid on Tiber Island (Insula Tiberina): and it was there, in 289 B.C., that a temple was dedicated to it.[25]

The veneration of the Dioscuri seems to have been linked to the Battle of Lake Regillus and the ensuing establishment of Roman hegemony over the Latin cities: a decisive event in the history of the early republican era; the two gods were said to have hurried to Rome to announce the success of the day's fighting, and to have watered their tired horses at the *lacus Iuturnae,* at the foot of the Palatine Hill, where a famous temple was erected in their honor in 484 B.C. next to that of Vesta; rebuilt on numerous occasions, some traces of it still survive.[26]

About forty years after Mucius, Cicero would take the Stoic and Euhemeristic doctrine about the deification of heroes for granted, mentioning it in connection with the same gods named by the pontifex: "Human experience moreover and general custom have made it a practice to raise up into the sky those illustrious men who distinguished themselves in procuring

benefits. This is the origin of Hercules, of Castor and Pollux, of Aesculapius,"
he has Lucilius Balbus—the proponent of the Stoic ideas—say in the *De natura
deorum*.[27] And in the *De legibus*, while describing an ideal model of religious
legislation, to which he tried to give the language and style of the Twelve
Tables, he adopted the same doctrine as the foundation of one of the precepts: "They shall worship as gods both those who have always been regarded
as dwellers in heaven, and also those whose merits have admitted them to
heaven; Hercules, Liber, Aesculapius, Castor, Pollux, Quirinus."[28] In his view,
therefore, the theory of the divine metamorphosis of heroes was an unquestionable tenet, not just in learned circles, but also in the popular sensibility,
appearing not only in the words of a sage like Lucilius Balbus, but also among
the very principles of a "religious constitution" of the city, an expression of
deep-rooted collective sentiments.

It is a position that poses a delicate problem. Without underestimating
the transformations that Roman religiosity underwent in the years between
Mucius and Cicero, as it began to slide toward an irreversible crisis (the Cotta
of *De natura deorum* represented a type of pontifex who would still have been
unimaginable at the end of the second century), it is nonetheless hard to believe that the doctrine of deified heroes, a widely held and uncontroversial
opinion between 50 and 40 B.C., should have been considered just a few decades earlier merely as a topic for private discussions among philosophers,
and for that matter with potentially subversive connotations. It seems much
more plausible to suppose that by the end of the first century the idea had already circulated to the point that it now influenced fairly broad social circles.
In that case we should view Mucius' reference to the risks of its mass diffusion as being more of an acknowledgment of a dangerous state of affairs
than of a possibility that could still be warded off.

If this is the case (and everything points in that direction), the analysis of
the pontifex acquires a meaning not perceptible at first glance. It would thus
no longer appear to be the rejection of a doctrine posing a threat to a religious tradition with a different orientation, but an attempt to trace back to a
learned and philosophical origin what had become a widely held opinion, in
order to clearly show the hidden dangers attached to it. Mucius knew perfectly well that attributing a human origin to certain deities did not diminish
their popular credibility at all: and this, what's more, in an era marked by the
breakdown of the old protorepublican religious patrimony. What he must

have really feared lay in another direction: the possibility of conceiving the deifications of heroes not only as events from the distant past, but rather as phenomena that might occur in the present as well. If the popular sensibility and learned thinking both accepted that such things really had taken place in the remote past, this belief might also influence perceptions of more recent episodes in republican history, and be transformed into a powerful instrument of political action. Even now popular heroes might be divinized in the imagination of the plebs (or of the soldiers), with the additional sanction of a philosophical legitimation. In this case, the power and prestige of certain families of the nobility, or even, in the worst of cases, of a "homo novus" at the head of a rampant and victorious fighting force, might swell out of all proportion. And these were not imaginary risks: the increasing professionalization and proletarianization of the army made these perils all too real. For that matter, part of the aristocracy was proving to be anything but immune to such ideas: a more or less subterranean tendency that would extend from Scipio Africanus' Pythagorean "mysticism" all the way through to Caesar. And that is to say nothing of men like Marius, from outside the ranks of the aristocracy, but with a dazzling military career behind him (made possible by the new organization of the command structure) consecrated by a charismatic relationship with his troops.[29] The more conservative sectors of the aristocracy had not been slow to perceive this danger: the disagreement between Scipio and Cato was partly the result of a clash deriving from the manifestation of these tendencies.[30] And these disputes probably even underlay the scandal of the discovery of the false books of Numa (the legendary second king of Rome, who lived on in cultural memory as the founder of the city's religious institutions), in 181, and the ensuing drastic reaction of the praetor Petilius, who was probably close to Cato.[31]

It is a well-founded hypothesis that the texts the magistrate ordered to be burnt made extensive reference to the deification of heroes, and that for this reason most of their content threatened to "subvert religion," and so it was not "opportune that they should be read and preserved" (according to Livy's account).[32] It is reasonable to suppose that only the risk of them being used for political purposes—just as the falsification that led to their "discovery" had been political—can explain the radical reaction by the authorities.

With this previous history, and in an undoubtedly more difficult moment, with all the shadows that Marius' dizzying ascent had cast on the power sys-

tem of the nobility, it comes as no surprise if it seemed to Mucius that a possible union of popular beliefs and philosophical doctrine on such a delicate
issue, fraught with potential consequences, might set in motion a dangerous
slide for the aristocratic institutions.

It was, in short, the encounter between Stoic thought and a new popular
sensibility—in a much less close-knit situation than the cultural and political
landscape of the turn of the second century, which had absorbed the repression of the Bacchanals and the destruction of the false books of Numa—that
created a context which in the eyes of the pontifex was threatening and unacceptable. Once again, faced by the troubles of his time, Mucius had no hesitation in reproposing the points of reference of his own ideal horizon. No denial of philosophy, but something to be kept well enclosed within learned
circles; a religiosity solidly based on traditional beliefs, and, in displaying
agreement between the gods and the city, an expression of the social concord
within the republic.

There was also a second core of doctrines whose divulgation was judged to
be harmful: Mucius' discourse thus moved toward its conclusion, still preserving its dialogic form. This thought too referred generically to the
"learned." But there is little difficulty in once again attributing to it a Stoic
origin.

The criticism of anthropomorphism ("the true God has neither sex nor
age nor well-defined bodily parts," though it is possible that here Augustine's
style was overlaid upon the formulation of Mucius-Varro) had run through
the whole of ancient and middle Stoicism, from Zeno to Chrysippus. And
Panaetius had certainly not been extraneous to it either, albeit with moderation; nor, after him, did Posidonius refrain from it.[33] Nonetheless it is probable that Mucius primarily had in mind the radicalization that such perspectives might undergo, if not prudently mediated, in theories of a reckless and
subversive skepticism. What worried him was not evidently the question of
the truth or falsehood of the notion, but its consequence for the religious ordering of the republic: a sudden crisis in the representations of the deities
underpinning the entire Roman temple system.

It is clear at this point that the criterion with which Quintus Mucius had

distinguished between the two doctrines in question had little to do with issues of a philosophical nature, but corresponded instead to a distinction between various types of dangers that, when welded together with popular sentiment, would be created for the aristocratic order. According to a highly
plausible reconstruction, the false books of Numa had also expressed strong
criticisms of anthropomorphism, and this would contribute greatly to their
fate.[34] But in any case, the attitudes of Petilius and Mucius can be seen to have
been guided by the same persuasion: two political responses in defense of a
religion also perceived as being completely political, put at risk first by an obscure falsification based on an ancient legend, and later by the perils of a possibly subversive use of a dominant philosophy, which threatened to converge
dangerously with the imagination and the sometimes uncontrollable reac-
tions of masses disoriented and unsettled by the times.

4.

Concerning the third genus—the tradition about the gods handed down by
the rulers of the city—Mucius, at least in Augustine's quotation, says not a
word. But we have already seen that this point constituted the real ordering
criterion of the entire classification, which broke the original parallelism in
order to introduce a new subordination of the first two elements to the
third.

And in fact the genus of philosophers and that of the *principes civitatis*
seem to be completely dovetailed. The point of view reflected in the tradition of the erudite never existed on its own, in a well-defined and separate
sphere: it appeared at the same time as its criticism, conducted in the name of
a different perspective, endowed with an irresistible force which obliterated
the previous one. It is only by keeping our eyes on this twofold movement—
the formation and disappearance of two fields of visibility, one of the philosophers and the other of the *principes*—that Mucius' thinking becomes fully
comprehensible. In this alternation, the religion of civic communities was
made to coincide with that of their optimates: the political rulers of the city
were also the depositories of the collective religion. In the identification, it is
the aristocratic nucleus of the history of Rome in its entirety that reveals itself, fully illuminated, and with it, the significance of religion as civil bond
and political tie. The *civitas* existed in the hardworking and anonymous activ-

ity of the people and in the organic design of its *principes:* the life of the republic had become, in them, political act, religious practice, creation of *ius.*

It is evident that the pontifex had no arguments capable of undermining the Stoic doctrines: nor, probably, did he have any desire to do so. He replaced the evaluative criterion of philosophical truth with that of political harmfulness. Augustine was perfectly aware of this when he commented: "the pontifex does not wish these ideas to become popular; all the same, he does not deem them to be false":[35] and indeed it was precisely the possibility of drawing this conclusion that prompted him to make this lengthy quotation. Thus (correctly) interpreted, Mucius' thought fitted in perfectly with Augustine's aims in the passage that restored it to us. The demonstrative purpose of the Christian philosopher, namely to emphasize the contradictions of pagan religion, meshed perfectly with the reasoning of the ancient pontifex, and underscored its most distinctive traits with clarity and ease.

We should nonetheless avoid construing Mucius' position in terms of a sharp contrast between politics and philosophy, according to a scheme that would recur frequently in the history of modernity. The perspective of the pontifex was not in fact that of a contrast between two separate spheres, with the primacy of one over the other. Rather it was a defense of that aristocratic rationality, still understood as the overall image of society and its values that we have already had occasion to describe and whose early formation we have carefully traced. Its coherence derived to a great extent from the very position of social and political dominance of the class that expressed it.

This idea had shaped and produced the representation of self, of its tasks, and of its bodies of knowledge—above all the knowledge of *ius*—that had been maintained by the majority of the nobility of the second century. It was a vision inherited, albeit with some adjustments, from the old republican world of the late fourth and early third century: a solid and compact conception, like the social and political relationships expressed in that context, but which had proved capable of adapting to change and to the early establishment of a Mediterranean hegemony. It had in fact been able to produce—as we have seen—the great legal transformations linked to the exercising of praetorian jurisdiction, and had invented with extreme ductility the government organization of the provinces. Behind it was a relatively small elite, though not yet a closed one; at least until the middle of the second century many "new men" were admitted to it, from Q. Publilius Philo and M. Curius

Dentatus to C. Fabricius Luscinus.[36] It was only later, not before the war with Hannibal, that the closing of ranks of the nobility would begin, a phenomenon that would characterize the rest of republican history.[37]

But at the same time that vision inevitably tended to block social dynamics and political relations around a now dated model of agrarian revenue, still centered on small and medium-sized peasant landholdings, coupled with a relatively limited presence of commercial capital and slave labor. The aristocratic rationality—at least in its historic nucleus—was hard pushed, beyond a certain limit, to transform itself into a full-fledged imperial rationality.

On the other hand, the expansionist drive, which became increasingly marked over the course of the second century, kept introducing elements that could not be controlled within traditional contexts: the formation of new agricultural relations, dominated by the latifundia and the slaveholding estates; the development of large-scale trade networks, together with the acquisition by the whole economic structure of that distinctive dual character— production for the market and for subsistence, intertwined in the same circuits—which it would then preserve for centuries; the formation of new classes, both as a consequence of the proletarization of entire sectors of the ancient peasant social base, and in connection with a different valuing and redistribution of wealth, no longer perceived just through the static landholding model but also through the more dynamic one of money; the weakening of institutional forms, by now deprived of their functional prerequisites.[38] The very same nobility that had aspired to and built the empire was now unable to support the burden without forgoing at least part of its identity and power.

In the face of the new wave of transformations, the most deep-rooted parameters of aristocratic rationality tended to remain substantially rigid. They idealized the past in an attempt to nail the present to it and to throttle the impulses toward change: the program expressed therein would be summed up in a particularly apt verse by Ennius: "in the customs and in the men of a long-ago time rests the fortune of Rome."[39]

And yet, already in the middle of the second century, and then in the first, under the weight of massive pressure, compromises and modifications took place that were destined to change, at least in part, the mentality of the dominant classes: the new power of money began to be interpreted no longer just from the pessimistic and typically aristocratic viewpoint of a limitless growth of corruption, even though nothing emerged that was fully comparable to the protocapitalist ethic of reinvestment and productivity. Now, besides the intractably conservative groups, there came into being a stable and partially renewed aristocracy ready to make concessions required by the times and by the very existence of the empire. Reckonings were made with Greek culture in a spirit of prudent acceptance, provided that there was no real threat of a radical critique of the foundations of Roman political power and of the relative strengths that it reflected. This primarily was the threat that Cato had opposed, and it was thanks to a mediation basically suggested by the Censor's own orientations that men like Polybius and Panaetius (all friends of Scipio Aemilianus) became an integral part of the new aristocratic culture in the last part of the second century.[40] The work of Publius Mucius and of the other jurists of his generation always formed part of a search for such an equilibrium.

But this path would soon prove inadequate as well. Once again, elements of rupture prevailed over ones tending to recompose the cultural and political framework. The definitive breakdown, after Sulla, of the power system of the nobility would irreversibly disassociate the old aristocratic and the new imperial rationality: the stage was set for the dramatic crisis of the central years of the first century.

The thought of Quintus Mucius—both legal and theological—was entirely consumed by the effort to find an acceptable synthesis between these contrasting impulses. He had carried on the work of his father, opening a new perspective on the knowledge of *ius*. But even in the revolutionary use of abstract concepts and the invention of formalism, he continued to present the past as a guide to the present. He evaluated the power of the new philosophy, but longed to confine it within a space away from politics. In short, he still imagined a cultural model that could master the new realities without denying them, but also without renouncing the bonds with the past; that was capable of bending the world to a design that did not stop taking antiquity as its measure.

Mucius therefore did not wish to discuss philosophy as such—the rationalist Stoicism of Panaetius, of Polybius, and of Scipio Aemilianus—nor did he wish to forgo the power of the new legal concepts and their logic. He wished only to reaffirm the limits of philosophical investigation and of the legal science that was coming into being, in relation to an overall conception of culture and the republic of which the nobility was to remain the depository, and whose final end was neither truth nor the limitless acquisition of power, but only the preservation and justification of the ancient city and its institutions. His religious thought reflected with extraordinary transparency this inborn ambiguity. What emerged from it—as Augustine clearly grasped —was a singular theory of a double truth, incomprehensible to us without taking account of the complex of conditions that determined it.[41]

About forty years later, the classification of knowledge concerning the deities was re-proposed by Varro, in a passage from the *Antiquitates,* as we learn once again from Augustine in the *De civitate Dei* (though on this point there is also the testimony of Tertullian):

> Next, what is the significance of his [Varro's] saying that there are three kinds of theology, that is, of the science concerning the gods? Of these one is called mythical, another physical, and the third, civil. . . Then he continues: "They call the theology that is used chiefly by poets 'mythical,' that used by philosophers, 'physical,' and that used by the people, 'civil.'"[42]

Varro no longer speaks of traditions concerning the gods, but instead of a genuine science, theology. His entire discourse focuses on the development and systematizing of a critical form of knowledge, the *ratio de diis*. And moreover, in place of the Mucian *principes civitatis,* there is reference to the people taken as a whole—an authentic reintegration of the social body—with a substantially greater respect for the original Greek model.

These two changes were connected. If the chief and privileged point of view was that of the "science concerning the gods," then it was no longer solely the knowledge of the *principes* that was decisive in the construction of a "civil theology," but rather that of the people as a whole. And, indeed, in the lengthy quotation taken from the *Antiquitates,* Augustine affirmed that in Varro's view the "third kind" regarded "that which citizens in cities, and especially the priests, ought to know and to administer": citizens and priests together. It should come as no surprise, then, that the relationship between the three genera—the central theme of Mucius' thought—appeared to have changed profoundly. Let's continue to listen to Augustine:

> Finally, when our renowned author [Varro] was trying to distin-
> guish the civil theology from the mythical and the natural, as be-
> ing a third and special kind, he wished it to be understood that it
> is rather a combination of the other two kinds, and not one sepa-
> rate from both. For he says that the writings of the poets are too
> low to serve as a guide for the people, while the writings of the
> philosophers are too high for them to investigate safely.[43]

The perspective of Mucius— it is inconceivable that Varro was not familiar it—had been entirely ignored. No alternating points of view, no double
truth. But the two theologies—that of the poets and that of the philosophers—combined to create a civil persuasion with which both the people and
men of learning could identify; and from Augustine's quote as a whole it was
clear that Varro was inclined to consider the theology of the philosophers as
the most important: a preference that was perfectly in keeping with the construction of a science of the deities. The three different traditions about the
gods had become an equal number of categories designed to arrange the
sources of a purely doctrinal knowledge; and the most significant of these
could be none other than the one best suited to a similar order of discourse—
that of the philosophers.

An openly rationalist scheme without any political constraints now
bound together philosophy and theology, in a pattern that seemed to have
forgotten all of Mucius' concerns. And it is remarkable that the causes of
those fears—the deification of heroes and the critique of anthropomorphism
—were actually viewed in a positive light by Varro (as they had been accepted
by Cicero).[44] His belief concerning the aniconism of early Roman religion
and his favorable orientation toward the deification of heroes (explicitly regarded as a possibility in the present as well) overturned the general picture
and the shadows so feared by the pontifex. The crisis of the old system of
power and of its culture—the *Antiquitates* appeared in 47 and were dedicated
to Caesar—was by this point capable of engendering reflection on crucial
themes of the old republican order centered on content that was wholly different from that of Mucius. That such a distance, albeit within the apparent

continuity of the model of reference, not only concealed two different sensibilities, but was also an indication of phenomena of much broader significance, is unmistakably evident. In this case as well, only the modification of social and political equilibriums can explain the multiplicity of responses that, for a single issue, emerged on the terrain of ideas. And the description of the relationship between these changes and the history of culture is the only one capable of fully revealing the very meaning of those ideas.

14

A Separate Reason:
Entities, Rules, Cases

The combined use of abstraction and diaeretic schemes had given the work of Quintus Mucius a sweep otherwise unknown to the legal literature of the second century. In the *Iuris civilis* books the development of the formal dimension of law had led to the creation of an order of writing that had never previously been attempted, the premise for the formation of a stylistic and scientific canon. Through it, the words and constructions of *ius,* transformed into concepts and integrated within the context of complex and rigorously deductive argumentative frameworks, became nodes for the radiation of rules in which the order of the discourse established itself as a legal order of the world and as a mapping of sociality. The presupposition of this integration was assured by the metamorphosis of law from an act of will into an act of knowledge: a transition that had been prepared by the progressive technicization of republican jurisprudence, and then completed by the intellectual revolution of the first century.

Nonetheless, the ancient rockbed of the Roman tradition was not abandoned. The persistence of the case-orientated character of legal knowledge, which refused on the one hand the formation of a system, and on the other the regular recourse to the paradigm of the *lex,* definitively stabilized the intrinsic pluralism of a prescriptive mechanism which, even though it had learned to use the powerful instrument of abstraction, was unwilling to subject itself to the standardizing force of universal commands, but required each time—in the examination of every case—the renewal of the contact between order and life, between disciplining and events.

As we have seen, this alternative—the law of the State or the knowledge of experts—would be inherited by modernity, and now seems to be presenting itself once again, with very different mechanisms compared to those at play in antiquity, in the definition of a legal order of the world market: state regulations or self-governance entrusted to the protocols of a globalized science and praxis. But the model of dualism was already a wholly Roman phenomenon.

It is likely that in the decades following the death of Quintus Mucius the pressure—cultural and, in the end, directly political as well—on legal thought to assume the full guise of a Hellenistic science, finally enclosed within a system (*in artem redactum*), must have become even heavier. The Cicero of the *De oratore* and of the lost work on civil law voiced this need with conviction: otherwise, the discourse of Crassus in the text of 55 B.C. would be incomprehensible, and a whole context of ideas and promptings would be rendered obscure or misunderstood.

The fact that this path was never actually taken is due for the most part to the choices made by Servius . Although he decisively abandoned Mucius' persistent tendency to blend legal knowledge into the framework of the old aristocratic rationality, he did completely accept the antisystematic perspective of his predecessor, and the constant effort to combine abstract concepts and case-oriented knowledge.

Indeed, it was the oeuvre of Servius that constituted the greatest departure from the aims described by Cicero: the primacy attributed to his work over that of Mucius in *Brutus* was, as we have seen, merely the result of a change in attitude on Cicero's part, and not a tribute ascribable to a shared perspective. Servius had actually also abandoned the idea of a complete exposition of the *ius civile:* his literary models pointed in an entirely different direction.

The number of fragments we can rely on in attempting to piece together the views of Servius is not vast, but there are certainly more than for Mucius.

Not a single text in the *Digesta* features the name of Servius in its inscription. He is, however, mentioned repeatedly, and often with great precision, in writings by other authors, from Labeo to Ulpian.[1] And outside Justinian's compilation, there are various citations by Gaius, Gellius, Festus, and Quintilian, to say nothing of a great many references in Cicero.[2]

The *Digesta* also include seventy-six texts taken from the *Digesta* of Alphenus Varus, the first to write a work with that title, and the most important, along with Aulus Ofilius, of the pupils of Servius.[3] Alphenus reproduced a great deal of Servius' thought, and with particular faithfulness, enabling us to regard it as a full-blown edition, with commentary, of the responses of the master himself.[4] Unfortunately, in Justinian's transcription, the name of Servius has almost invariably been lost, and there are considerable problems (as happened for Mucius with respect to Pomponius) in isolating the authentic Servian core from the notes that Alphenus frequently added to it.[5] Nonetheless they are all passages that revolve around theses and themes of Servius, and can therefore be used with some degree of reliability for a reconstruction of his ideas.

The jurist, for his part, had produced a lot: 180 books, according to what we are told by Pomponius, almost all of them consisting of collections of responses.[6] This is the most voluminous corpus of republican jurisprudence: evidently, in a single generation, the writing of *ius* had progressed greatly, assuming a literary dimension and communicative status that made such a remarkable output possible.

Even though the final composition of the work was compressed into a few years, it reflected the study and commitment of an entire lifetime—no less difficult than that of Mucius—or at least of the last three decades, from the mid-70s until the death of the jurist in 43.[7] Over this long period Servius had developed the weft of Mucius' logical endeavors into an even closer connection with the Greek and Hellenistic speculative apparatus, freeing it from any archaizing leanings, and steering it away definitively from any temptation to systematize. Through a close comparison that soon became almost legendary, he would tease out all the potential of Mucius' thought, orienting it in an even more clear-cut direction. And it was especially in his weaving together of case examination and ontological forms that he displayed the force of his talents most fully. His knowledge always tended to be organized in a dimension marked by the presence of the individual and the detail, as in the ancient tradition of responses, but transfigured now by the presence of the concept. It was a combination that thereafter characterized the best that Roman jurisprudence would produce: an analytical model still judged incomparable by Savigny, who pursued at length the mirage of a new, modern identity of legal theory and practice; not the constructivism of a "dogmatics" lost within itself, but a play of concepts entirely resolved in the regulating of cases—and nothing outside of that.[8]

Let us consider the texts of Alphenus as a whole. Nearly all the cases described relate to a society with a widespread pattern of trade circuits, with a strong mercantile imprint. In more than twenty of the cases, the issue revolves around one of the new "contractual" schemes (according to Mucius' description) introduced by the praetor, and then defined in those years as figures of *ius gentium* (sale, hire, partnership, mandate)—an unprecedented degree of attention in jurisprudence.[9] Around the middle of the second century, a collection of formularies had been drawn up by Manius Manilius,[10] but drawing parallels with Servius would be improper. Manilius worked toward immediate and exclusively practical goals, and did nothing more than record the customs of the marketplace. Servius reelaborated around those themes the entire tradition of legal knowledge.

A much more solid comparison can be made with Quintus Mucius. But here too the reversal in perspective appears complete: the small-scale peasant society that so attracted the pontifex seems to have been forgotten. And yet nothing so very decisive had happened over the previous few decades to justify such a marked change. Nor can we put it down to diversity in personal experiences. Servius, quaestor in Ostia in 74,[11] would certainly have had an opportunity to see what Mediterranean trade had become, and the complexity of the operations required simply to keep the city supplied with food: just consider, for instance, that estimated annual wheat consumption was over 200 kilograms per person, and that the population was almost one million inhabitants.[12] But Quintus Mucius, proconsul in Asia,[13] had also been in a good position to observe the outdatedness of the small-farmer memories evoked by the aristocratic tradition.

The point is that we are in the presence of a further demonstration that

Mucius had intentionally archaized the content of the *ius civile*. The whole thrust of his interpretative endeavour was to stress the unbroken continuity between the new legal figures of the Mediterranean world and the older civic institutions: *consortium* and consensual partnership, *stipulatio* and contracts of the *ius gentium, fides* and obligations.

Servius had not inherited this constraint. That is not to say that he did not look to the past, but his eyes were not those of Mucius. For him the link with antiquity was built on other foundations. Completely absent was any faith that the past could be a potential model for the present. Certain aspects of traditionalism did remain in his thought, some of them quite substantial, but they were not anymore the exclusive center of an invasive and totalizing aristocratic rationality.

Imperial society, no longer viewed through the lens of the ancient *mores,* now appeared as a world undergoing a radical transformation. We are in the heart of the Roman slaveholding and mercantile boom, at the culmination of a wave of expansion without precedent in the ancient economies: a process of growth still tied to limits and contradictions that kept it from creating the foundations for an authentic capitalistic liftoff, but sufficiently powerful to achieve a level of performance long unrivaled in the West: new farming estates, with impressive standards of productivity; manufactories created exclusively for the production of commodities; large quantities of slave labor; a spectacular accumulation of public and private money; urban centers supported by magnificent building programs; trade networks that had created an interdependent grid of markets extending across the entire Mediterranean; opulent levels of consumption, though concentrated among tiny elites.[14] The crisis was political, inherent to the institutional system and the ruling groups, and did not concern the economy; indeed, in many ways it was a product of the economic growth. Servius was well aware of this.

2.

Several merchants had poured their grain into Saufeius' ship, stowing it all together; Saufeius had returned to one of them his share of the grain from the joint load, and then the ship foundered. It was asked whether the other merchants could sue the ship owner for their share of the grain with an action for the misappropriation of cargo. Servius responded that there are two genera of hired things, insofar as either there is the obligation to return the same object received, as when clothes are entrusted to the care of a laundryman, or to return an object of the same kind, as when purified silver is given to a craftsman to make vessels or gold to make rings.

In the former case, the thing remains its owner's; in the latter, it is transformed into a simple credit. The rule is the same for the deposit: If someone deposits a sum of money in such a way that he does not hand it over enclosed in a box or under seal, but counts it out, the depositee owes nothing except to pay an equivalent amount. According to what seems to be the case, the wheat is construed as becoming Saufeius' and as being validly handed over. But if each person's wheat had been separately enclosed within partitions or baskets or in a different vat, so that each person's could be distinguished, we cannot exchange one cargo for another, and so each person, remaining the owner of the grain returned to just one of them, could claim it. And so, according to Servius, it is not possible to approve an action for the misappropriation of cargo, since either the goods handed over to the ship owner were of the same kind that they immediately became his property, and the merchant therefore just had a credit, in which case the cargo is evidently not being pilfered, because it belonged to the ship owner; or, the same thing that was handed over is to be returned, in which case the hirer [merchant] can bring an action for theft, and so the action for misappropriation is superfluous. But if the grain had been handed over such that it could be repaid in kind, the contractor [the ship owner] is liable to the extent of his fault, since one is liable for fault in a matter contracted by both parties for their mutual benefit; but it is scarcely fault that he returned some grain to only one person, since he had to return it to somebody first, even though he thereby advantaged this person more than the others.[15]

Roman imperial society takes on form with extraordinary clarity in these lines, in which Alphenus Varus records a response by Servius. Ships and grain, shipowners and merchants; and then shipwrecks, and badly stowed cargo: commercial routines and sloppy behavior; laundrymen and depositories of money on the verge of becoming bankers (though that threshold would never truly be crossed); entrepreneurial practices and technological fragility; customs we might call "modern," and typically ancient uncertainties: in short, Rome.

The language is more mature than that of Mucius, with stylistically effective solutions, though one can still discern all the laborious effort of a conceptual elaboration without any consolidated models. And at the same time, looming impressively, the new law: a welter of abstract figures and dialectic schemes; an authentic ontology of actuality. It began with the distinction between two types of "hired things" (an absolutely new development, we must believe, to which we will return); and immediately afterward the analogy that linked them to the figure of the deposit, due to the recurrence there of the same formal paradigm; and then we find the difference between the rights of property and of credit, on which depended the pursuability of different actions; hence a first construction of the concept of contractual bilaterality (which, as we shall see, was reworked by Labeo); last of all, the notion of blame.

Underlying it is a quantitative idea of law as a relation of order and as reciprocal measure; a principle of universal commensurability identical with what we find in early Greek science—number, music, astronomy—a sort of geometry, but applied to social materiality rather than to physical magnitudes, having reduced this, as the Greeks had those, to pure forms.[16] It was in fact the process of formalization that made it possible to consign the qualitative aspect of life to the quantities of law, preventing it from remaining immeasurable, in an unrelated opposition of its elements, but enabling the jurist to value the measure of *ius,* its "quantum," we might say, which is present in every subjective situation: the normative fabric thus proved to be an elastic, infinitely divisible, structure. Legal entities existed solely and exclusively in their measurability; but, in such a connection, they replaced real relationships, since they had themselves become real. The ship owner and the merchants and the tangle of their contrasting interests, though evoked with great attention, disappeared; in their place there was now hire and deposit, blame and contractual responsibility.

An entirely calculable space, defined by a knowable and rational order, substituted life and dictated its rules: which in our case freed the ship owner from the action against him, because it was based on the presupposition that the merchants held rights of ownership, which they had lost once the grain was loaded since it had become impossible to distinguish between different batches of wheat. Therefore we are outside the sphere of *dominium* (property) but within that of *contrahere* (contracting) and between the two—property, contract—the Roman aristocractic mentality, heir to a remote tradition, raised an insurmountable wall, reflected and formalized by *ius*. A passage from *Timaeus* comes to mind: the dominion of intelligence over necessity as the genesis of the cosmos, wrote Plato;[17] here, instead, the primacy of a disciplining rationality guided by science over the abitrariness of opposing subjective wills, as a founding element of social order.

But the quantitative revolution, already begun by Mucius and completed by Servius, did not eliminate the qualitative and clue-based analysis of the problem to be resolved; it just redefined its boundaries and scope, subordinating them to the presence of a different point of view. In the preservation and refinement of this combinatorial aptitude, the retention of the case-based character of legal knowledge revealed all its importance. The intertwining of the two kinds of logic—quantitative formalism and attention to the detail—appears with great clarity in the text we have just read. It was the way in which the grain had been loaded that decided the outcome: a minor detail, conjuring up ropes and timber, worked its way in among the concepts and the analogies, and determined everything.

Let's look at another case:

> Some mules were pulling two loaded carts up the Capitoline Hill.
> The muleteers were holding up the rear of the front cart so the
> mules could haul it more easily, but suddenly it started to roll
> backward. The muleteers, seeing that they would be caught be-
> tween the two carts, leaped out of its path, and it rolled back and
> struck the rear cart, which careened down the hill and ran over
> someone's slave boy. The owner of the boy requested a response
> about whom he should sue. I replied that law already lay entirely
> in the circumstances of the case. In fact, if the drivers who were
> supporting the front cart had got out of the way of their own ac-
> cord and that had been the reason why the mules could not take

the weight of the cart and had been pulled back by it, no action could be brought against the owner of the mules, but action could be taken on the basis of the Lex Aquilia against the muleteers who should have supported the cart. And in fact, no less wrongful is he who provokes damage by voluntarily letting go of something in such circumstances that it hits someone else: like he who fails to restrain an ass he is driving after having excited it, or like he who throws a missile or anything else from his hand in such a way as to cause injury. But if the mules, in shying, had moved backwards, and the drivers had left the cart for fear of being crushed, no action would lie against them; but action should be brought against the owner of the mules. And if neither the mules nor the drivers had anything to do with the event, but the mules just could not take the weight or if in trying to do so they had slipped and fallen and the cart had then rolled down the hill and the men behind it could not support the weight, there would be no action either against the owner or against the drivers. What is certain, however things went, is that no action could be brought against the owner of the mules pulling the cart behind, because they did not deliberately go backwards but as a result of being struck.[18]

The background here is the city—a small city, one might well say, but perhaps what is intentionally small is only the scene portrayed—with its historic hills and its maze of alleys and lanes. The reasoning centered entirely upon a laconic statement: "I replied that law already lay entirely in the circumstances of the case," a crystal-clear aphorism for a type of knowledge that did not deny its semiotic, clue-based vocation. The investigative regime had, however, changed radically with respect to tradition: under its lens, there were no longer any rituals to be checked word by word, no magical signs to be verified, even if the focus on the individuality of the event remained. Now the discipline continued to be inscribed within the material deployment of the event, because it was observed in the light of the concept (in the present case, that of damage envisaged by the Lex Aquilia) and could be cut up into its most elementary particles, through a highly lucid analytical deconstruction: segments of actions, gestures, intentions, and variants; and each one bore the logical necessity of a different response and regulation. This marked the birth of legal diagnostics, which medieval scholars would sum up with the renowned motto "Give me the fact, I'll give you the law,"[19] and which modern practice would consecrate in the variegated talent of generations and generations of lawyers. The normative element—the Lex Aquilia on loss, a monument of republican legislation, which had been long integrated by jurisprudence into the corpus of the *ius civile*[20]—was subjected to very strong interpretative pressure, in order to decide on the admissibility of the action that derived. Once again, as in the preceding text, an analogical scheme was adopted, followed by the explanation of a network of causality, described with implacable precision: a carefully calibrated intertwining of ontological inquiry and empirical analysis that would always be found in Servius' writing, elsewhere expressed in a careful counterpoint between the study of a case and the formulation of a definition, such as those of "fraud" and "guardianship,"[21] considered exemplary by later jurisprudence.

3.

In at least twenty-six texts of Alphenus' *Digesta,* at the center of the economic issue underlying the legal problem, we find the presence of a slave.[22] This is a very high proportion, probably unique in the history of jurisprudence: the Roman law of slavery saw the establishment of doctrines that would then remain fundamental. It is as if Servius had discovered the pervasiveness and essentiality of slave production in the reality of his own world. We shall return to the significance—anything but obvious—of this observation. For the moment let us attempt to isolate certain aspects of the jurist's perspective.

There is no doubt that in Servius' eyes a slave was above all else a human machine, a thing, a commodity—"a speaking tool"—in keeping with a tradition that had its theoretical foundation in Aristotle and was borne out in the everyday life of a centuries-old Mediterranean practice.[23] But this condition of pure thingness, though accepted as an unquestionable state of affairs, appeared in an unexpectedly ambiguous light: no longer as a circumstance that allowed a total exploitation of slave labor, but also as a brake, a limit, an obstacle to be avoided, in order to permit combinations between the skills of the workforce and trade and production circuits, which the classical form of chattel slavery would not have permitted.

We can consider the years from the middle of the second century B.C. through to Augustus as the golden age of the Roman slave system: as far as we are able to deduce, at the end of this period, roughly one-third of the population of Italy were slaves.[24] The praetors responsible for the administration of civil justice, in close collaboration with the jurists, kept a watchful eye on this astonishing development, attempting to grasp its decisive implications: the result of their work led to a kind of commercial law of slavery that was unparalleled in any other slaveholding society, ancient or modern.[25] Their objective was to integrate—as far as seemed possible without calling into question the bond of personal subordination—the organization of slavery with a valorization of the labor of the enslaved, which could only be achieved by conceding ample forms of autonomy, midway between fact and law. Slavery thus came to be disciplined by a sort of dual regime: one that continued to be based on the binding force of dependency, and another that referred to a limited but nonetheless disruptive subjectivity—patrimonial and commercial—on the part of slaves, a sort of permanent state of exception, valid as long as one remained within the spheres of production and markets. This twofold discipline—"status" of subjection and contractual autonomy[26]—wound up modifying not only the relationships between slaves and third parties, but even those between slaves and masters, penetrating, that is, into the very heart of the relationship of dependency. As far as we know, Servius was the first to conceptualize the phenomenon, and to employ a formal device to account for this particular condition. In a response, once again published by Alphenus Varus, we read:

> A person leased land to a slave of his for cultivation and provided
> him with some oxen, but as the oxen proved unsuitable, he told
> the slave to sell them and to buy replacements with the money he
> got for them. The slave sold the oxen and bought replacements
> but became insolvent without paying the person he bought them
> from. That person now claimed the price of the oxen from the
> master by means of an action "on the *peculium*" or for "benefit
> taken," the master still having possession of the oxen in respect
> of which the money was sought. He [Servius] responded that it
> did not seem to form part of the *peculium,* if not the balance
> remaining after deducting what the slave owed the master; it

seemed clear that the oxen had become part of the master's property, but they had cost the master the value of the previous oxen, so he should be held liable only to the extent that the replacements were more valuable.[27]

If we were to take as the sole point of reference the relationship of dependency between master and slave, the case giving rise to this question would have been unthinkable. The slave was totally subject to the master's will, and could not enter into any form of exchange with him that had any significance for *ius*. And yet both Servius and Alphenus took the existence of such a relationship for granted, and in defining it they did not hesitate to use a verb that placed it in the formal scheme of the *res locata*. This was a conceptually subversive qualification, in which slave and master figured as distinct subjects, facing off against one another on a plane of abstract equality. Though restricted to well-defined limits, and only with regard to transactions in progress, the formal determinations induced by the legal models of exchange—the ambit of the work of Mucius and Servius'—overlapped with and prevailed over those of the relationship of dependency: "A person leased land to a slave of his"—"servo suo locavit." The contrast could not be expressed more effectively; they truly were two opposite worlds that had come face to face: the discriminating one of "status" and the inclusive one of the "contract."[28]

There can be no doubt that we are in the presence of what we might call an extreme use of the concept of *res locata;* certainly neither Servius nor Alphenus would ever have thought that from such a hire there could derive for the slave any entitlement to an action against his master. Nonetheless, the use of such an exacting terminology (which would endure over time: Papinian, almost two centuries later, would write about a slave who "se locaverit"— that is, had given his labor in hire to his master)[29] could not in any way appear casual. Indeed it reflected a very clear choice: to construct in an analogical fashion, as far as seemed possible, the economic relations between slave and master as a relationship between free men, on every occasion in which the developments of the new economy, and the need to enhance the value of the slave's abilities, intervened to modify the typical and traditional structure of the relationship of dependency. And we have already seen that the use of analogy formed part of Servius' hermeneutic procedure: alongside the cases just explored, we should add at least one text by Ulpian, recording a response of the jurist in which he suggested the concession of a new action "on the example" of an already-existing one.[30]

But the Servian account did not speak only of hire. In the course of the events, we see the slave selling and buying, receiving sums and failing to pay them, and then becoming insolvent. None of this was rare in that time. In the context of a broad and detailed series of cases—recorded not only by Servius—we find slaves commanding ships, running shops, and administering estates. A subtle civil trial technique invented by the praetors enabled the assignment of responsibility for these business dealings to the master, without however entirely canceling the role played in them by the slave. The expedient consisted in indicating the name of the slave in the part of the formula in which the events were described, and the name of the master when it came to the issue of conviction or acquittal: a manipulation carried out at the very margins of *ius,* utilizing all of its ancient and shrewd ritualistic wisdom, a sort of exchange within the conducting of the trial that in some way made it possible, albeit obliquely, to incorporate personal dependency and participation in commercial networks into the slave's activity.[31]

In our text, Servius evokes two of the most important of these legal actions, elaborated by magistrates between the second and first centuries B.C.: the one "on enrichment without cause" *(de in rem verso)* and the other "within the limitations of peculium" *(de peculio).* The latter referred to a practice that was by this time well established: the existence of property that belonged de facto to the slave *(peculium)* and which might consist of money or various goods—even other slaves—that in principle belonged to the master, but was actually managed freely by the slave, so much so that it could even be used to buy his freedom.[32] The determination of its exact magnitude could prove to be an essential factor in the dynamics of the trial: and indeed Servius devoted himself to that task with great care, as we learn not only from the response we are examining here. In fact, Ulpian wrote: "Everything owed by the slave to the master is deducted before the *peculium* is valued."[33] Servius, to this definition, "adds that one must also deduct anything owed by the slave to people in the master's power, as this too is admittedly due to the master."[34] We cannot say with certainty who was the first to formulate the definition mentioned by Ulpian, to which Servius "adds" a second part. But it is certain that it literally echoed the Servian rule just encountered ("it did not seem to form part of the *peculium,* if not the balance remaining after deducting what the slave owed the master").[35] Nor for that matter did Ulpian state that the first part of the definition was not by Servius; he limited himself to noting that something had subsequently been added to that formulation. Moreover, he had just transcribed, quoting second-hand from the *Digesta* by Celsus, a definition of *peculium* that was very similar to the one he would report a little later, but with a significant completion, this time attributing it, in accordance with his source, to Quintus Aelius Tubero the Younger, a pupil of Ofilius, and therefore subsequent to Servius, but nonetheless educated and trained in the same milieu: certainly, a thought that showed continuity with respect to the master's first pronouncement.[36] We may therefore conclude that Ulpian reproduced, in the same context, in close proximity and with a degree of confusion, two very similar definitions of *peculium,* assigning the first to Tubero, and indicating his intermediate source (Celsus); and presenting the second as anonymous, but with an "addition" by Servius. In reality it is probable that also in the second case he was indebted to the intermediation of Celsus, and that in the overlapping of the two names of Servius and Tubero read in Celsus, he chose to assign to Servius only the second part of the definition, presenting it as an addition.

It is clear in any case from this group of texts that Servius had worked to achieve a genuine doctrinal organization of the patrimonial relations between slave and master. We should add to the documents just mentioned at least two other important responses transcribed by Alphenus, one of which mentions the notion of *pactum*—a key word in late-republican legal experience—to indicate an agreement between a slave and his master.[37]

But what attracts our attention more than anything else is a response transcribed by Aufidius Namusa, another of Servius' pupils, which was later quoted by Labeo and then found its way into a work by Javolenus Priscus:

> A master left his slave five gold pieces thus: "Let my heir give to my slave, Stichus, whose freedom I have directed in my will, the five gold pieces which I owe him by my accounts." Namusa reports Servius to have been of opinion that there was no legacy to the slave, because a master could owe nothing to his slave.[38]

The legal recognition of economic relationships within the bond of slavery ran up against an insurmountable asymmetry. The admission of a debt on the part of the master counted for nothing, even if it was certified in his accounting books: to accept its existence in terms of *ius* would have meant pushing the analogy to the point of accepting the possibility of an obligation on the master's part toward the slave. If such a step had been taken, one of the fundamental presuppositions of the whole slaveholding mechanism, and therefore of the entire society of the time, would have been swept aside. The fact that the binding force of dependency appeared, in the context of Servius' reasoning, only as a limit and an obstacle to the legal qualification of economic relationships completely integrated into everyday life is an indication of the degree to which the jurist's thinking was capable of capturing graphically ("which I owe him . . . because a master could owe nothing . . .") the sharpest contradiction that the growth of trade had introduced into the fabric of a society based on slavery: the contrast between the desirability of valorizing productive forces, which would have required the setting aside of personal relationships of dependency, and the presence of a generalized form, without any practicable alternatives, of chattel slavery.[39] It was probably the dim perception of this antinomy that placed the institution of slavery at the crucial point and, at the same time, at the extreme margin of that world—at once the principal condition of its very existence, and an impassable boundary with respect to its further development—that attracted Servius and oriented his thought and analyses.[40]

In appearance it seemed that not much was required for the decisive step to be taken, and for slavery to dissolve, as it were, from within, destroyed by a sort of precapitalist maturing of economic networks, accompanied and encouraged by a vigilant and precursory legal reflection: and on certain occasions, Servius really does seem to be on the brink of that threshold. But that jump was never made, and Roman slavery did not slip into a gentle transition toward dominant forms of free wage labor. It was also a question of numbers: the new developments introduced by the praetors and reelaborated by the jurists concerned only a minority—albeit the focus of great attention—of the millions of slaves who lived in Italy between the age of the Gracchi and the time of Augustus. The outlook of the great majority of them, divided between the prison dormitories of the villas and the latifundia, the damnation of the mines—the sight of which would so appall Posidonius[41]—or the grinding drudgery of the most humiliating domestic duties in the city, would never extend beyond pure survival.

Over a few generations the creative and brilliant excogitations of the jurists would thus end up in a blind alley. In order to continue, what was needed were social, economic, and cultural foundations that it was impossible for that world to provide. Later jurisprudence would not cancel out the results that had been achieved; instead, it would perfect and organize them.[42] But there would be no further steps forward of any significance: and every time the legislation of the princes, particularly in the second century A.D., looked favorably upon the condition of the slaves, this would happen because of a generically philanthropic attitude—dictated by dominant beliefs—and not for strictly economic considerations.[43] Quite different, however, had been the intentions that led the republican jurists down the path of their inventions, dictated solely by considerations of functional efficiency with a view to the profits of the masters, and by the pursuit of an economic rationality that, while not rejecting slaveholding, reconfigured its structures to achieve a valorization of the productive forces compatible with the preservation of the given structure: a result that the new law made possible, and which no doubt contained within it the seeds of a culture already in some way protocapitalist, but without there emerging a class capable of taking possession of and developing it.[44]

4.

The legal disciplining of imperial commercial activity centered, as we have seen, on the contractual paradigms defined in that age of *ius gentium*, relatively recent in a consolidated set-up. They had already been the focus of extensive reflection by Mucius, and Servius, in turn, further elaborated that thought, guiding it toward outcomes unseen or ruled out by Mucius. One case once again concerned the *res locata*: Mucius, who certainly must have been familiar with both the terminology and the concept, believed that he should not recognize this figure in the example of a quantity of gold delivered to a goldsmith so he could make jewelry. The response was faithfully transcribed by Pomponius in his commentary: the gold was "given," not "hired";[45] in the Mucian doctrine, *res locata* ("thing hired") was therefore only that which could be restored in its original form, and not in that obtained through the artisan's work. Entirely different was Servius' solution. In the response concerning the ship of Saufeius we saw that the jurist claimed the existence of "two genera" of *res locata* (here as elsewhere, he also made free use of diaeretic schemes): only in the first hypothesis was the same identical thing returned; in the second one, something of the same kind (and, probably intentionally, Servius repeated the example as was used in the response of Mucius: gold given to a craftsman to be made into rings).[46] Certainly, this was still entirely bound up with a materialist conception of the *res locata,* without arriving at the notion of the "hired work," constructed later by Labeo.[47] Nonetheless, the usefulness of the new discipline was easy to perceive: it was not merely a conceptual requirement that motivated Servius. By applying his scheme, both the work of the artisan and the restitution of the thing were covered by a single action, with greater certainty in terms of their protection. Whereas previously the only option had been to resort to a complex duplication of procedures, one for the material supplied, and another for the labor performed, now instead Servius' attention, concentrated on valuing the skills of the artisans (laundryman, goldsmith, mason), used the logical power of the new conceptual instruments to simplify the rules, all to the advantage of that small world of enterprises whose network enveloped the city, transforming its customs and habits.

The same logic explained the polemic—this time not implicit—with Mucius over the issue of *societas* (partnership) to which we have already made reference, and that can be reconstructed through two lengthy citations by Gaius and Paul.[48] As we have seen, Quintus Mucius remained anchored to a rigidly property-based construction of the partnership structure: the inevitable price to be paid in order to hold together, within the same form, consensual partnership and the ancient fraternal consortium. He was therefore not capable of adequately evaluating a situation in which the professional activity of one of the partners might be so important for achieving the goal of the partnership that he "shall bear no share of losses and yet have a share in profits."[49] Servius, on the other hand, unrestrained by any of Mucius' requirements, could easily envision a reverse solution, based on a solely consensualist idea of the partnership contract, capable of reflecting an assessment that adhered to the realities of the professions and the technical expertise. "On the supposition that his services are considered so valuable that it is fair that he should be admitted to partnership on such terms," he said with reference to the privileged partner.[50] Technical skills and expertise now had a precisely calculable monetary value. "For a man's services are often as valuable as money," as Gaius in fact concluded his account:[51] this might be a comment by Gaius himself, rather than a Servian maxim, but it is of little importance. It was in any case Servius' idea that emerged quite unambiguously.

Paul noted that the exposition of the controversy formed part of the *notata Mucii,* or the *Reprehensa Scaevolae capita* (in the title handed down by Gellius):[52] the text, as we know, that Servius devoted entirely to the critical revision of Mucian thought. We know almost nothing else about it,[53] but certainly the difference of views on partnership went well beyond the bounds of a simple learned controversy: in it, we truly see the clash of two realities, which were being riven by a definitive rupture.

The pursuit of a legal knowledge no longer rooted in a traditionalist political certainty did not erase in Servius a keen sensitivity toward the past, but it also included a perception of change and a capacity to accept it.

The memory of lost things demanded the gaze and love of an antiquarian: an attitude that developed in Rome along with the crisis of the nobility. And free from any actualizing temptation, Servius was fully capable of becoming an antiquarian, like other great erudite men of the late republic. As a jurist, he looked above all at the Twelve Tables. We do not know if he ever wrote a commentary on the laws (as Labeo would do, after him).[54] But certainly in a series of citations by Festus,[55] we can see him intent on rescuing the literal meaning of those ancient norms, composed in a Latin by then almost incomprehensible. And so he even explained the archaic words, as if he were translating them: *noxia, sarcito, pedem struit, sanates, vindiciae.*[56] Sometimes (though not in relation to the Twelve Tables) he himself did not know what they meant, and he turned to the greatest antiquarian of his time, to Varro, to ask, for instance, what on earth was the meaning of *favisae Capitolinae.*[57]

Besides these more narrowly lexicographic interests, of which other traces also survive,[58] Servius was not immune to a subtle curiosity about the establishment and workings of remote institutions of the Latin world. From what we are able to reconstruct, his monographic work *De dotibus* ("On Dowries") still read by Neratius and Gellius,[59] must have been rich in information on such matters. There was also a detailed depiction of the ceremonial of *sponsalia*—betrothal—as conducted "in the part of Italy known as Latium": "One who wished to take a wife, says he, demanded of him [the head of the bride's family] from whom she was to be received a formal promise that she would be given in marriage. The man who was to take the woman to wife made a corresponding promise. That contract, based upon promises given and received, was called *sponsalia*, or 'betrothal.'"[60] In this description, Servius found occasion to make use of the substantive *contractus*—"contract": and this is the first documented use of the term, which was destined to become emblematic of Western legal history (in Mucius we only found the presence of the verbal participle: *quidque contractum*). The new term—though it appeared in a context unrelated to the regulation of mercantile exchanges—indicated the taking of a decisive step toward the construction of a fully realized ontological form capable of representing the abstract existence of a symmetrical legal bond between formally equal subjects, irrespective of the concrete social content arising in the relationship: a figure that from then on would play an essential role in the conceptual baggage of every jurist and thereafter, in modernity, of every political or social scientist.

But what attracted Servius' interest with particular intensity were the mechanism and the effect of the change—of the *mutatio,* as he wrote, employing a word that was also dear to Cicero and perhaps used for the first time by Terence[61]—on the habits of citizens and the customs of the community, paving the way for the gradualist and sociologizing "historicism" particular to a part of Roman legal thought, from Sextus Caecilius Africanus to Gaius and Paul.[62] He analytically observed the domain of the family and its network of relations: a sphere of old certainties, the heart of the Roman social fabric. Here too the passage of time was producing its effects. Customary domestic terms could now change meaning and indicate new objects. This happened with *penus* (provisions stored in the home), redefined, once again in disagreement with Mucius.[63] But above all with household utensils,[64] a term with which heads of family might describe an array of things. We would need to examine, Servius explained, the domestic inventories to find out what objects the *pater* was accustomed to describe with that name (the case concerned a legacy), unless he arbitrarily used the term to refer to objects that, by unanimous agreement, could not be said to be covered by the word. The growth and diversification of consumption tended to shatter the semantic clarity of terms; on the other hand, the quest for significance in relation to the uses of individual speakers could not go so far as to throw into crisis the social usage of the language, in keeping with a tradition of thought very familiar to Servius.[65]

And it was not merely a question of words. The jurist observed that the passage of time and changes in customs was also modifying an ancient and important relationship in the organization of the Roman family: that of the former master with his former slave, or, to use the Latin terms, the *patronus* with his *libertus*. As we read in Ulpian:

> This edict [on the property of freedmen] has been put forward by the praetor for the purpose of regulating the degree of respect which freedmen are to have with respect to their patrons. For, as Servius observes, in former times [patrons] were accustomed to make the most severe demands on their freedmen, that is, to repay the enormous privilege conferred on freedmen when they are brought out of slavery to Roman *civitas*. And indeed Rutilius was the first praetor to proclaim that he would not allow a patron more than an action for services and partnership, namely, where a pledge has been made, so that where a freedman did not give what was owed to his patron, the latter would be admitted to partnership in his assets. Later praetors promised patrons right of ownership of a fixed part [of the freedman's property]; it was evidently the model of partnership that had led to the concession of this share with the result that what the freedman had to offer in his lifetime in the name of partnership, he likewise had to give after his death.[66]

The representation of the change led Servius to adopt an evolutionary perspective regarding the discipline in question: a small cross-section of the history of the edict, according to a scheme that jurisprudence was not often to repeat. The exposition was organized around three distinct phases, marked by an equal number of stylistic breaks: "in former times . . . And indeed Rutilius was the first praetor to proclaim . . . Later praetors . . ." The transformation of the relationship between master and freedman had taken place entirely through its progressive commercialization. The "severe demands" reflected the customs of an era during which there were no limitations on what could be required of a freedman, because nothing, in a slave society, was comparable to the gift of liberty: "the value of freedom extends to infinity," as Labeo would put it a little later, in a tone probably veined with polemic and nostalgia.[67] But Rutilius—whom we have already come across in a Ciceronian account[68]—had replaced a solely ideal and qualitative, and therefore incommensurable, evaluation with an economic unit of measurement, the criterion of a quantification. What was emerging was a mercantile model: each thing had a price. And at the same time, that of the new law: the idea of exact measure and calculation that must accompany every demand, in order for it to be executed in a predefined manner, without violating the position and the certainties of others—the quantification of money prepared the quantification of law. And so the relationship between master and freedman could not merely be left to the (prejuridical) *fides* and to the *mores*, but instead was to be constructed by analogy, taking as a point of reference typical figures of commercial life: performance of services, contracts of partnership. The reference to the *imago societatis* (model of partnership) evoked the same hermeneutic mechanism we discovered in connection with the action conceded *ad exemplum* of another already envisaged one. *Ius*, then, was capable, inasmuch as it was a network of abstract concepts, of developing in accordance with an intrinsic logic, which it was up to the interpreter to discover and bring to light: we are at the origins of the ontological organicism that would later mark, also through medieval theology, the whole of continental European legal culture.[69]

From the observation of the changes in customs and institutions in the city, Servius moved on to an analysis of the very concept of "change," of how it came about and interacted with that which endured, with "permanence":

> The case was put that several of the judges appointed for the same trial had been excused after the case had had a hearing, and others had been put in their place. The question was whether the replacement of individual judges had resulted in the same case or a different court. I replied that not merely if one or two, but even if all had been changed, the case and the court both still remained the same as they had been before. And this was not the only ex-

ample of a thing's being considered the same after its parts had been changed, but there were many others too. For a legion too was held to be the same although many of its members had been killed and others had been put in their place. The people too was thought to be the same at the present time as it had been a hundred years ago, although no one was now alive from that period. Likewise, if a ship had been repaired so often that no plank remained the same as the old had been, it was nevertheless considered to be the same ship. For if anyone thought that a thing became a different one when its parts were changed, it would follow from this reasoning that we ourselves would not be the same as we were a year ago, because, as the philosophers said, the extremely tiny particles of which we were made up daily left our bodies and others came from outside to take their place. Therefore, it must be recognized that as long as the form of a thing remains the same, so does the thing continue to be the same.[70]

In the past some doubt was cast on the authenticity of this text, even to the extent of suspecting that it was largely the result of a later rewriting.[71] In reality, in few other cases as here, in the *Digesta* of Alphenus, is it possible to discover the language and the intellectual world of Servius. Unmistakably his—truly just like a signature—are a number of stylistic solutions such as the slightly redundant syntactic development, irresistibly reminiscent of the first letter, which we shall examine shortly: "non modo si . . . sed et si . . . tamen et; in hoc solum . . . sed et in multis; quod si quis . . . fore ut; propterea quod . . . quapropter."[72] Also typical is the use of *existimari*, repeated no fewer than three times.[73] Also undeniably his is the scheme of the analogy—which here resurfaces in the sequence of court, legion, the people, ship, body—combined with the recourse to argumentation *ab absurdo*. And as if these were not enough, the reference to the ship as a whole also recurs elsewhere in Alphenus' *Digesta*.[74]

Though subject to the flow of continual changes—the planks of a ship, the soldiers of a legion, the citizens of a people, the atoms of our body (in this last example there is an unmistakable Epicurean and Lucretian reference)—a proper *episteme* should be capable of identifying the nonmaterialist and entirely ideal crystallization of stability and permanence, and of building on it. In the space defined by these coordinates—change and identity—for a rationality accustomed to the vortex of transformations, but not dragged along by it, the possibility emerged of elaborating a positive social knowledge: the cognition and study of permanencies, removed by the representational capacities of the concepts from the precarious nature and fallibility of the phenomenalist and naturalistic appearance. Of a nature that—as would happen later in the letters as well—always included the Lucretian motif of death and dissipation: behind the literally Aristotelian persistence of the "forms"—the *species,* as the jurist wrote—planks deteriorated physically, citizens and soldiers died, and the particles of the human body continually dissolved.

For Servius, law was immune from this perpetual materialistic catastrophe: it constituted a whole where it was possible to find certainties. In its ontological transcription it would reveal itself, to a jurist capable of penetrating its secrets, as something intimately and permanently organized—an organic whole—to the point of enabling the analogical integration—from within— of the prescriptive fabric. And the image of *ius* as a structure endowed with a reason of its own emerged quite clearly again in another response:

> All interested parties can present an action for exhibition [of a thing]. But someone inquired whether this action could affect the exhibition of his opponent's accounts, in whose exhibition he had a great interest. The reply was that the civil law should not be interpreted in a captious manner nor its words forced, but it is opportune to consider the spirit of every statement. For by the same reasoning, a student of some discipline could say that it was in his interest for such-and-such books to be exhibited for him, because if they were exhibited, he would be more knowledgeable and better when he had read them.[75]

It was therefore necessary to discover the *mens*—the spirit—of the law in order to understand it properly. The literal meaning of its formulations could be deceptive: the words should be understood as signs of a concealed reason.

Behind an evident rhetorical echo, almost certainly Ciceronian (though Servius himself was no mean orator),[76] there appeared the idea of a *ius* that could only reveal its full consistency and coherence if investigated in depth with adequate instruments. The hermeneutic style of the new jurists was taking shape. The discovery of a rationality contained within the object studied, and which developed in concert with its complete ontological formalization, constituting its substrate, became an implicit and powerful source of self-legitimation for those interpreters capable of analyzing it. Now separate from the model of aristocratic rationality, which lay in ruins, jurisprudence began to create for itself a framework of persuasions and methods that made it into a body of knowledge with hard-to-falsify procedures: an austere discipline for great specialists, which demanded the vocation of a lifetime.

Transformed in these terms, it is clear why Servius felt that jurisprudence had no need of the systematics offered by Hellenistic encyclopedism, still aspired to by Cicero in the *De oratore,* nor, any longer, of a treatise like that of Mucius. The unity was entirely contained in the internal structure of the object—of the *res,* in the language of Servius—and of the methods with which it was investigated. It had no need to be expressed in an extrinsic frame as well, in a communicative canon. From the pupils of Servius, from the edition of the master's responses, in fact, there sprang a literary genre, the *Digesta,* destined to enjoy a great fortune until the second century A.D., and which was, from the point of view of Hellenistic panopticism, as nonsystematic an approach as could be imagined. Not the predisposed circularity of a closed structure, but rather a manifold and unpredictable combinatorial intertwining of threads that are variously knotted and unraveled. An open universe, with transient, soft boundaries, constantly in motion. A vast chart, bearing the marks of countless events, all governed by the same reason: in the model of Servius and Alphenus, sequences of cases that illustrate a problem, like polyptychs.

And alongside the *Digesta* the other great literary model of Roman jurisprudence took shape with Servius: the commentary on the praetor's edict, then immediately adopted by Ofilius and Labeo.

In truth Servius' *Ad Brutum,* in just two books, was perhaps more of a first contribution to consolidating texts elaborated year after year by the magistrates than a full-fledged commentary.[77] But it was once again a mark of interest in the new times. In that unadorned judicial program, which was continually being rewritten, there was, if one could only manage to decipher it, a new history of the city, just as the very ancient one could still be seen reflected in the Twelve Tables (the comparison, as we know, was Ciceronian),[78] which Servius continued to read word by word. The urgency of new tasks and more complex responsibilities intersected for him with the preservation of outmoded traditions, in a world that had never before been so rich and diverse, but precisely because of that overwhelmed by the collapse of a politics that was now inadequate and incapable of offering prospects in keeping with the forces and potential it itself had succeeded in constructing.

15

Politics and Destiny

I.

The year 45 B.C. began for Servius in relative tranquility. He was in Athens, where he was detained by the commitments involved in the proconsulship of Achaea, with which Caesar had unexpectedly entrusted him before leaving for Africa at the end of 47.[1]

Like many Roman aristocrats of his generation, Servius was familiar with Athens and Greece. He spoke the language, and on the threshold of adulthood he had spent a lengthy period of study there. Now he had returned, practically an old man (at least in terms of the Roman idea of life), marked by the experiences of his long engagement in intellectual and political affairs: he was about sixty years old.[2]

From Athens, sheltered but not excluded, the elderly consul watched Caesar consolidating his autocratic power, and the final melting away of Pompey's forces: the outcome of the second African campaign, the tragic death of Cato, the events in Rome during 46, the spectacular beginning of the second Spanish expedition in the winter of the following year. In brief, the irremediable end—the "sunset," as Cicero had once written to him—of his republic.[3]

Here, absorbed in his quite demanding administrative duties, he might

have felt he had put some distance on the terrible events of 49, when everything was collapsing around him, and he had appeared to Cicero (who may
have been exaggerating, though only to a degree, in the pitiless description he
sent to Atticus) as exhausted, frightened, and distraught—a man upon whom
it was no longer possible to count.[4]

And perhaps retrospectively, as a voluntary exile absorbed in his studies at
Samos, his choice not to reject the benevolence of Caesar (a favor probably
given in part out of sincere respect, but also as the result of political calculation), and instead to accept the unexpected assignment in Greece, might have
seemed much less reckless and increasingly opportune.[5] It had in any case
been a decision made with some hesitation, and troubled Servius for a long
time, even afterwards, in Athens, if as late as the middle of 46 he wrote that
he regretted it; and Cicero, in response, deemed it useful to express his whole-
hearted approval.[6] But the distance from Rome weighed heavily on Servius,
and he spoke of his far-off home with open nostalgia.[7]

Still, correspondence and news arrived from Rome regularly. For the
whole of 46, Cicero had sent him letters of recommendation for Roman merchants who wanted to extend their trade networks to include Greece.[8] At the
beginning of March, he received some far from happy news. Once again it
concerned Cicero: his beloved daughter, Tullia, just a little over thirty, was
dead.

Servius knew her well. Between 51 and 50 his son had been one of her
suitors.[9] Though still young, she had already been married twice (which at
the time was not uncommon among the nobility), to Gnaeus Piso, quaestor
in 58, who died the following year; and to Furius Crassipes, quaestor in 51,
whom she divorced in the same year.[10] Initially the prospect of a tie appeared
to jibe well with the strategies of the two families: it would have strengthened an important bond, following the unpleasant episode of the *Pro Murena*.[11]
Moreover, Servilia, Cato's influential and widely respected sister, seemed to
be a major supporter of the union.[12] But then nothing came of it, and Tullia
married, as must have been her personal preference, Publius Cornelius Dola-
bella—tribune in 47, debt-ridden and with a dissolute past—whom she divorced at the end of 46. Shortly afterwards, in February of 45, she died suddenly, perhaps as a result of complications following a birth.[13]

Her death was a big blow for Cicero, who retreated for some time to As-
tura; and it was there, around the middle of March, that Servius sent him a

long letter, which we can still read in its entirety (a real piece of luck) in
Cicero's epistolary collection:

> When I received the news of your daughter Tullia's death, I was
> indeed as much grieved and distressed as I was bound to be, and
> looked upon it as a calamity in which I shared. For, if I had been
> at home, I should not have failed to be at your side, and should
> have made my sorrow plain to you face to face. That kind of con-
> solation involves much distress and pain, because the relations
> and friends, whose part it is to offer it, are themselves overcome
> by an equal sorrow. They cannot attempt it without many tears,
> so that they seem to require consolation themselves rather than
> to be able to afford it to others. Still I have decided to set down
> briefly for your benefit such thoughts as have occurred to my
> mind, not because I suppose them to be unknown to you, but be-
> cause your sorrow may perhaps hinder you from being so keenly
> alive to them.
>
> Why is it that a private grief should agitate you so deeply?
> Think how fortune has hitherto dealt with us. Reflect that we
> have had snatched from us what ought to be no less dear to hu-
> man beings than their children—country, honor, rank, every po-
> litical distinction. What additional wound to your feelings could
> be inflicted by this particular loss? Or where is the heart that
> should not by this time have lost all sensibility and learned to re-
> gard everything else as of minor importance? Is it on her account,
> pray, that you sorrow? How many times have you recurred to the
> thought—and I have often been struck with the same idea—that
> in times like these theirs is far from being the worst fate to whom
> it has been granted to exchange life for a painless death? Now
> what was there at such an epoch that could greatly tempt her to
> live? What scope, what hope, what heart's solace? That she might
> spend her life with some young and distinguished husband? How
> impossible for a man of your rank to select from the present gen-
> eration of young men a son-in-law, to whose honor you might
> think yourself safe in trusting your child! Was it that she might
> bear children to cheer her with the sight of their vigorous youth?

who might by their own character maintain the position handed down to them by their parent, might be expected to stand for the offices in their order, might exercise their freedom in supporting their friends? What single one of these prospects has not been taken away before it was given? But, it will be said, after all it is an evil to lose one's children. Yes, it is: only it is a worse one to endure and submit to the present state of things.

I wish to mention to you a circumstance which gave me no common consolation, on the chance of its also proving capable of diminishing your sorrow. On my voyage from Asia, as I was sailing from Aegina toward Megara, I began to survey the localities that were on every side of me. Behind me was Aegina, in front Megara, on my right Piraeus, on my left Corinth: towns which at one time were most flourishing, but now lay before my eyes in ruin and decay. I began to reflect to myself thus: "Hah! do we mannikins feel rebellious if one of us perishes or is killed—we whose life ought to be still shorter—when the corpses of so many towns lie in helpless ruin? Will you please, Servius, restrain yourself and recollect that you are born a mortal man?" Believe me, I was no little strengthened by that reflection. Now take the trouble, if you agree with me, to put this thought before your eyes. Not long ago all those most illustrious men perished at one blow: the empire of the Roman people suffered that huge loss: all the provinces were shaken to their foundations. If you have become the poorer by the frail spirit of one poor girl, are you agitated thus violently? If she had not died now, she would yet have had to die a few years hence, for she was mortal born. You, too, withdraw soul and thought from such things, and rather remember those which become the part you have played in life: that she lived as long as life had anything to give her; that her life outlasted that of the Republic; that she lived to see you—her own father—praetor, consul, and augur; that she married young men of the highest rank; that she had enjoyed nearly every possible blessing; that, when the Republic fell, she departed from life. What fault have you or she to find with fortune on this score? In fine, do not forget that you are Cicero, and a man accustomed to instruct and advise others; and do not imitate bad physicians, who in the diseases of others profess to understand the art of healing, but are unable to prescribe for themselves. Rather suggest to yourself and bring home to your own mind the very maxims which you are accustomed to impress upon others. There is no sorrow beyond the power of time at length to diminish and soften: it is a reflection on you that you should wait for this period, and not rather anticipate that result by the aid of your wisdom. But if there is any consciousness still existing in the world below, such was her love for you and her dutiful affection for all her family, that she certainly does not wish you to act as you are acting. Grant this to her—your lost one! Grant it to your friends and comrades who mourn with you in your sorrow! Grant it to your country, that if the need arises she may have the use of your services and advice.

Finally—since we are reduced by fortune to the necessity of taking precautions on this point also—do not allow anyone to think that you are mourning not so much for your daughter as for the state of public affairs and the victory of others. I am ashamed to say any more to you on this subject, lest I should appear to distrust your wisdom. Therefore I will make only one suggestion before bringing my letter to an end. We have seen you on many occasions bear good fortune with a noble dignity which greatly enhanced your fame: now is the time for you to convince us that you are able to bear bad fortune equally well, and that it does not appear to you to be a heavier burden than you ought to think it. I would not have this be the only one of all the virtues that you do not possess.

As far as I am concerned, when I learn that your mind is more composed, I will write you an account of what is going on here, and of the condition of the province. Farewell.[14]

The sole documents of one of the most important jurists in Roman culture that have reached us in their original version—the only ones by Servius still definitely readable according to the order of his own thoughts—are quite unrelated to the world of law. But these pages constitute a rarity for another reason as well: they may be the only surviving pages by an ancient jurist, in which he discusses something other than his own discipline. An original and strict choice in favor of specialization and self-isolation, emphasized over time by a particularly scarce textual transmission, has limited our knowledge of those authors to nothing more than a few snippets of their technical writings: they can only have consisted of their doctrines. All the rest (if there was anything else) has been pulverized by the dissipating power of history, which is also made up of emptiness and silence.

In our case, however, for just a fleeting moment, a countenance and an age resurface; and we are given the opportunity to cast a backward glance.

In this first letter, Servius subjected his writing to an intense and readily discernable stylistic elaboration. It moved in the direction of an evident and very conscious archaism: of vocabulary, stylistic elements, and syntactic usages. This is a choice that we should evaluate carefully. First of all, the stylistic archaism did not entail by any means a symmetry of the content. The idea of a complete correspondence between linguistic form and cultural substance is modern, and quite foreign to ancient models.[15] In Servius' writing, in fact, we can see the establishment of a diametrical opposition between the urgency of the subject matter, closely tied to the present, and stylistic structures, which instead tended to reflect a tradition. In years close to the time of Servius, Sallust operated in much the same way.[16]

It would be difficult to identify with any precision the references of this archaizing taste: perhaps Ennius, Plautus, and Terence, if it is true, as Quintilian recounts, that Servius read a great deal of poetry;[17] but also historic and annalistic prose, and probably Cato, whom Servius imitated in certain, often clearly synonymous, redundancies.

Certainly, drawing on such an old tradition of language helped to ensure a level of expression that never abandoned the measure and tone of austere solemnity: of that *gravitas* which Cicero, in his portrait of Servius in the *Ninth Philippic*, identified as the most important aspect of the jurist's personality.[18] The Sallustian monographs once again come to mind: in this short text by Servius, as in those, the choice of such a strict communicative register never became monotonous and lifeless uniformity. Even within very restrictive compositional confines, the author displayed his skill in touching the notes of pathos (in the compelling series of questions, under whose hammering refrain the existential fabric of an entire generation seemed to be collapsing) and to make refined use of the language of epic poetry (in the sudden and beautiful opening: "Ex Asia rediens . . .").

Thus is created an expressive model that it is inconceivable to consider an invention of the moment: Servius was following his own well-established working method; in the legal texts, for that matter, we have repeatedly found traces of the same literary inclination. And this way of writing—not without alternatives in those years—was already in itself a signal and a message. It represented the strongest and most visible point of conjunction and loyalty to a sociality and a culture it was undesirable to lose, in the very moment when the pressure of the new was becoming more powerful.

But the debt to the past finished here. In a communicative canon that we have discovered to be so extremely guarded, there are emotions and states of mind that had nothing to do with the aristocratic tradition: crystallized therein is a surprising, lucid, and disenchanted pessimism, unremitting and indeed almost devoid of hope.

It was a condition that had nothing of the literary or topical. Certainly, the "consolatory" genre ("genus hoc consolationis")[19] was a model well known to schools—for instance, the academic one—with which Servius must have been familiar. And yet he did not resort to the string of commonplaces in which this type of composition usually wallowed. His theme was in reality only paradoxically "consolatory": by now no grief could do anything to worsen the tragedy into which they had been plunged. The thread of his thought developed entirely out of that initial line: "Think how fortune has hitherto dealt with us": it was entirely bound up with the present, and with a catastrophic reading of the institutional crisis. Its contemporaneity prevented any cooling of the content. Roughly sketched out within the structures of an exhortative argumentation, there emerged the living emotional material, barely controlled by the closed composure of the vocabulary and syntax.

The tragedy was, in a highly concentrated form, a political tragedy, and politics was experienced as an all-encompassing fact, in perfect correspondence with the aristocratic experience. The disaster affected the whole collectivity, but it weighed on the lives of individuals no less than more personal suffering: "we have had snatched from us what ought to be no less dear to human beings than their children." Precisely as its collapse was being perceived, the primacy of the republican model ("country, honor, rank, every political distinction") was reaffirmed as a value that was in a certain sense absolute. Outside of that, there was no possibility, no haven: "What scope, what hope, what heart's solace?" The power of the text—if we can say so without falling into an excessively modernizing psychological transcription—its burden of despair, lay entirely in the emphasis that accompanied the description of the republican order, observed from the point of view of its irreversible end: "What single one of these prospects has not been taken away before it was given?" What had been the fullness of time now returned only as an unattainable dream, whose vision did not comfort, but only increased the torment: "Was it that she might bear children to cheer her with the sight of their vigorous youth? who might by their own character maintain the position handed down to them by their parent, might be expected to stand for the offices in their order, might exercise their freedom in supporting their friends?"

The disconsolate acknowledgment of the end of the republic segued directly to the other theme upon which Servius' pessimism was focused: the—Lucretian—one of death. What had died was, above all, the republic itself, represented, through a barely indicated metaphor, as a body that could "fall," in the same manner in which a person could expire (writing to Servius a few years earlier, in 49, Cicero had used the same word, in connection with the same subject, but constructing a less violent metaphor: "occidenti rei publicae," he had said, "the sunset of the republic").[20]

This end so afflicted spirits and ravaged hopes that a desirable fate could even become that of not outliving it: "when the Republic fell, she departed from life." The present—the time of catastrophe and chaos, in opposition to the past, when all things proceeded "in their order"—eliminated any possibility of an acceptable personal destiny, to the point of presenting, as a hypothesis worthy of consideration, the idea of suicide, the thought that "in times like these theirs is far from being the worst fate to whom it has been granted to exchange life for a painless death." Behind the severity of the language there is no stiff rhetorical contrivance, no empty emotional hyperbole. Cato the Younger really had taken his own life, less than a year before.[21] Servius was talking about a possibility that was well within the experience of his class and milieu.

Still, the image of a single person's death, suggested—in some sense dictated—by the death of the republic, was not limited to the recognition of this dramatic but also desirable identity of personal and political destiny (to live

"as long as the Republic"): the institutions of the city, at one with their custodians. Servius' gaze went further: the tragedy was taking place against a
vaster, even a cosmic background. The motif that united the different planes
was once again that of a reflection on death. (And it should be said, albeit
with caution, that in a stratigraphy of the text, above and beyond the stylistic
effort and the political despair, this omnivorous presence of death, of its foreshadowing, of the staging of a desire for it, is the most profound aspect that
can be glimpsed: the most hidden code of this writing.)

The outlook was at once personal and metaphysical: the fragility of human life, destined in any case to break (this is almost obsessively repeated
three times in quick succession: ". . . we whose life ought to be still shorter";
"recollect that you are born a mortal man"; "she was mortal born"), irresistibly evoked the decline and fall of cities (Aegina, Megara, Piraeus, and
Corinth). Though such ideas were anything but new, they were presented in
an original combination. The effect was one of a geometry of pessimism and
death, built in a series of ever larger circumferences, set one within the other.
In the center lay the ruins of politics, the disaster of the republic that had rendered vain the existence of entire generations, to the point that it had become
desirable to exchange life for death: an extreme state of mind, but a contingent one, linked to specific occurrences. Then the circle of negativity wid-
ened: it was the very life of man, well beyond the experiences of the present,
that revealed itself as nothing more than an ephemeral event, destined inevitably to vanish into nothingness. But this destiny was no longer that of the
single man; it was also—and the circle grew ever larger—that of his works, of
his most enduring constructions: walls and cities and projects. If there could
be any "consolation," it consisted solely of always keeping "before your eyes"
this sort of interlocking combination: a general entropy of death in which
the ruins of one's own time were shrunk to a smaller scale, and thus acquired
a more tolerable dimension. Nothing could be hoped for beyond this. Servius
looks, with a skepticism barely veiled by the discretion imposed by circumstances—and perhaps by a respect for the difference of opinion publicly manifested by Cicero—to the possibility of a life after death ("if there is any consciousness still existing in the world below . . .").

Nonetheless, not even in these conditions was he capable of entirely renouncing the prospect of action—a stubborn persistence of the old aristo-

cratic mentality—and the idea, certainly contradictory but evidently deeply rooted, that not everything was lost and something could still be done. Immediately after saying that death was not after all the worst of misfortunes, he immediately began to urge Cicero not to succumb to pain, but instead to remain vigilant, so that "if the need arises, [the fatherland] may have the use of your services and advice." The dissonance of this observation with respect to the text as a whole—almost an unconscious slip—is an indicator that pessimism was for Servius a mental condition that was not the result of his intellectual background, but rather something that came later in the course of his life, and not in an unalloyed form. It was now an invasive presence, and yet still quite conflicted with respect to an earlier education of reason and the passions that had been built upon values and certainties that were far more deeply rooted in the mental history of the aristocracy, but now reduced to nothing more than the barely perceptible phantom of a world and an episode that had been definitively broken.

2.

About two and a half months after the first letter, on the last day of May, Servius wrote again to Cicero from Athens. Once again the subject was a death. But this time it was Servius who announced it:

> Although I know that the news which I am about to tell you will be painful to you, yet since you cannot be unprepared for any of the casualties which happen to all of us by nature or chance, I have thought it proper to send you a circumstantial account of what has just taken place. I came by sea from Epidaurus to Piraeus on the 22nd instant, where I stayed all that day to enjoy the company of my colleague Marcellus. The next day I parted from him, intending to go from Athens into Boeotia, in order to finish what remained of my jurisdiction. He was preparing, as he said, to sail for Italy. On the day following, about four o'clock in the morning, when I was about to set out from Athens, his friend, P. Posthumius, came to tell me that Marcellus had been stabbed by his companion P. Magius Cilo after supper, having received two

wounds, one in his stomach, the other in his head, near the ear, but that he hoped still he might recover. That Magius had then killed himself; and that Marcellus had sent him to inform me of what had happened, and to desire that I would bring some physicians to him. I collected some, and proceeded with them before break of day; but when I was come near Piraeus, a servant of Acidinus met me with a note from his master, to acquaint me that Marcellus had expired a little before day. Thus perished by the ruthless hand of a most detestable assassin this illustrious man. He whom his enemies had spared out of respect for his virtues received his death from the hand of a friend. I proceeded, however, to his pavilion, where I found two of his freedmen and a few of his slaves. All the rest, they said, had fled in the greatest terror, dreading the consequences of the murder of their master. I was obliged to carry his body with me into the city, in the same litter in which I came, and by my own servants, where I provided as splendid a funeral for him as Athens could supply; but I could not prevail with the Athenians to allow a place for his interment within the city walls, which, they said, they were forbidden by their religion to permit; but they readily granted what was the next honor: permission to bury him in any of the gymnasia I might choose for the purpose. I selected a place, therefore, the noblest in the world, the school of the Academy. There I consumed his body, and took care that the Athenians should erect a marble monument to him on the same place. Thus have I faithfully performed to him, living and dead, every duty that could be required at the hands of him who was his colleague, and his relation. Farewell.[22]

The text is not as rich and elaborate as the preceding one, with a depth of style and content that is certainly less substantial, even if the more significant features of the March letter seem to recur in a basically unchanged state here.

Almost the whole missive is a description—as if in real time—of an obscure episode: the murder (and there were those who suspected it was a hired killing) of Marcus Claudius Marcellus, who had been a colleague of Servius in the consulship of 51.[23] The prose is entirely given over to the narrative: Sallust comes to mind once again, or the commentaries of Caesar.

It is all the more surprising and intriguing then that a text crammed with actions and facts—places, times, itineraries, names, details—should open, albeit as if it were a parenthesis, with a further existential and metaphysical reflection, formulated in the at once spare and scorching tone of a truth that cannot be contradicted: "any of the casualties which happen to all of us by nature or chance." We see, undiluted, all the pessimism of the March letter, but now there is no longer the vehicle of the present and its political disaster. The thought touches straight away and directly on the entirety of human destiny. What is present, once again, is death—or, to be precise, the event that brings it about: nocturnal and absolutely unexpected ("about four o'clock in the morning . . . after supper"), paradoxical ("He whom his enemies had spared out of respect for his virtues received his death from the hand of a friend"), inexplicable (at least for Servius as he wrote, and he did not even wish to make any conjecture). And there is a definitive lack of faith in the possibility of understanding within what chain of causality and ends the existence of men is inscribed, entrusted to powers that elude all control. One can only depict their effects, record the external mechanisms of events. Servius uses the singular conjugation of the verb for these forces *(dominatur),* as if to emphasize that the two elements—chance and nature—act with respect to us ("in nobis") as if one. There is no polarity between them: they are bound together inextricably. Nature is completely veined by chance; in the stylistic combination, it is the latter that takes on the semantically and conceptually more powerful function.

Chance, nature. Two words laden with meaning, even in the joint usage selected by Servius: two terms in which Greek culture had invested so much of itself, and to which quite diverse ideas and images had been consigned.[24] Servius, a man of letters, a jurist, and in a sense himself a philosopher, was certainly familiar with their representational capacity and the elliptical force of their combined use.

In the context of the letter, they unquestionably revealed a strong agnostic inclination with regard to the actions of men and the overall meaning of their history. It is a motif that recalls the March text. And even if there is not an implicit radically skeptical conviction—the two letters do not allow us to deduce this—we are still quite distant from the teleological providentialism that a lengthy tradition of thought had situated in the more intellectually open spheres of the imperial nobility from the circle of Aemilianus onwards: the culture of Polybius, of Panaetius, of Antiochus, and, to a certain degree, of Philo: the one that had fostered, from the middle years of the second century on, Roman aristocratic rationality, and which still formed the background to Mucius' thought. [25] And we are also very distant from Cicero himself: not merely from the Cicero who had resorted without hesitation to the most intransigent dogmatism of an Antiochus, but also from the more doubtful and intimist Cicero of a work such as the *Fourteenth Philippic*. [26] What can be glimpsed in the Servian aphorism is an underlying layer of relativist radicalism, feeding on motifs that suggest meditations linked to the Greek materialist physics of Democritean origin (for that matter, a materialist nucleus—in the sense in which it is possible to use that adjective with reference to ancient culture—survived even in the thought of Posidonius, to say nothing of Hipparchus: and in fact it was Rhodes that Servius had visited). [27] A layer that here is practically laid bare, and which constituted the implicit presupposition of the March letter.

In truth, tendencies that could be defined as negative thought were never entirely extraneous to the realm of Greek reflection as it encountered the Roman world. But the aristocratic mentality—even the part most sensitive and open to new developments—had always succeeded in expunging them from their own universe of ideas, in a quest rather for intermediate solutions that might render compatible the absorption of certain forms of Stoic or Academic critical thought, with the rational justification of the primacy of Rome in the world, and of the senatorial tradition in the city. The crisis now seemed to have overturned the terms of this mediation. And under the weight of the emotional pressure there emerged ideas, memories of readings, perceptions of reality and of history that had previously been canceled by the choice of rejection, if not actually repression.

We cannot say with any certainty whether Servius had carefully read Lucretius. Probably, considering that Cicero was definitely familiar with him, and since he was very much at home with poetry. But perhaps it is not even that important to ascertain whether he had or not. There is a whole cultural climate here, a new intellectual openness encouraged by the crisis, irrespective of a precise textual genealogy. Physical materialism and negative thought were already linked in the Greek experience. The drama of the present prompted Servius to turn his gaze there, and when he did, he found a rich seam of ideas and thoughts that pointed in a direction that was certainly not far from the thinking of Lucretius.

It would nonetheless be inconceivable to transpose mechanically the state of mind of the two letters from the year 45 to the background of the jurist's entire life. He had a long public career behind him; for over a decade he had pursued the consulship, which he obtained only relatively late; he had perfected his grasp of legal studies more and more, dedicating himself with great passion to the activity of respondent. It is entirely plausible that with the passage of time he did not always observe the world with the same eyes: to the point that on many occasions he wound up believing that the die had not yet been cast, that not everything had already been decided, and for the worst. The rapid succession of shifting and confused political situations would in turn have favored these oscillations. We are left, however, with the impression that the texts of 45 still in some manner flung their own shadow over the past. It would be difficult to enclose them in a small corner, in a fold of Servius' life history. The pessimism filling them betrays a gestation that was too complex to be just the result of a momentary crisis, or of a sudden moment of disheartenment. Above all, those first few months of the year 45 had not been particularly demanding: a period of meditation and work rather than of anxiety.

Servius must instead have developed his vision over a considerable length of time, and not without inner conflict. It is much more plausible that the two letters should be regarded as the culmination of a long process of thought, despite the education he had received, and which was fuelled by bitter confirmation: an entire period that coincided with the "sunset" of the republic.

But he had also gradually developed an exceptional legal culture, entirely within and beyond the context of the great sea change brought about by Mucius. The political disaster and the ensuing pessimism had done nothing to prevent—indeed might even have encouraged—the pursuit of this vocation, and the idea that in the circumscribed but decisive field of *ius* it was possible to construct a rigorous and rational body of knowledge, the inheritance of a prestigious past. This led to the severance of an ancient bond that Quintus

Mucius had attempted to preserve. But at the same time a new prospect opened up. Political disenchantment, a pessimistic inclination, and faith in one's own studies could—albeit painfully—coexist. The letters thus became the biographical outcome and the first testimony of a scission which would still have been unthinkable in the years of Mucius—a scission that was destined to endure.

16

Legitimacy and Power:
The Doctrine of Natural Law

I.

The "scientific" revolution had stamped the seal of formalism on the Roman legal experience. The disciplining power in the field of private relations among citizens, the exclusive province of an elite of experts selected by an ancient tradition, had definitively transformed its decisions from acts of will (expressions of a power that was first religious and later dependent upon aristocratic supremacy) into acts of knowledge and of the application of a science.

This sea change, though relatively sudden, was the outcome of a very lengthy preparatory process. Behind it lay not only the progressive technicization of legal knowledge over the course of the republican age, but also the all-pervasive influence of archaic ritualism, which had predisposed the Roman cultural sensibility to the prevailing, in the eyes of the jurists, of a symbolic, idealized, and quite separate transfiguration of social relations—a sort of prehistory, or, if you will, a degree zero of formalism—over the hard concreteness of their material content.[1] The affirmation of the principle of fair-

ness, partly due to the acceptance of ancient Mediterranean mercantile practices, had never really eliminated this attitude, but instead had integrated it
into a sort of dialectic, in which the initially ritualistic and later fully formal
aspect would always remain the key element.

And yet those acts of knowledge would never be innocent. They substituted bare life with an ontological projection of it which rendered absolute
relations that were historically determined, in turn an expression of hierarchies and powers:[2] ownership as unlimited rule over men and things; mercantile exchange insofar as it was reciprocity mediated by money; the civil trial as
a moment of transformation of the legal bond *(obligari)* into the imposition
of an encumbrance *(dare oportere,* as the jurists would later put it); the very
indifference of legal evaluation with respect to political judgment.

The rules of *ius,* following the great transformation, would from then
on be the product of a kind of constant reduction of sociality to a frame of
forms presented, as we have seen, in a twofold light—in an ambiguity of status that was at once the great limitation and the theoretical greatness of the
Roman jurists—both as abstract conditions for the thinkability of all normative articulation—a sort of transcendental analytics, an "a priori" syntax of
the relationship between powers and (private) subjects—and, equally, as authentic ontological constructions, endowed with an objective and metaphysical existence: a presence that imposed upon reason a continuous effort at adaptation, constituting first and foremost the truth of law.[3]

Underlying all this was the deep-rooted idea—also derived from an ancient and remote precedent—that reality, both the sensory and the metaphysical and theological kind, could be entirely interpreted through relations of
order, and that nothing could be more gratifying than to observe them so as
to establish regularities. Splendidly summarized by Saint Paul,[4] this point of
view ran throughout the history of Roman culture, and was clearly reflected,
albeit in an embryonic form, by the original "quantitative" and hierarchical
aspect of the centuriate ordering; to say nothing of the many ritualistic symmetries of the archaic religiosity.[5]

But it was only the unprecedented accumulation of power deriving from
the growth of the empire that created, in institutional and social terms, the
critical mass required to bring about the sea change, to nudge those remote
premises toward a sudden paradigm shift. The full unfolding of a world
power—when Servius was writing, Roman armies were everywhere, from

the English Channel to the Rhine and the Black Sea—brought with it a need for rules, for discipline, for a standardization beyond anything that had ever been attempted. It was not just a matter of constitutional structures, which were still largely outside the orbit of *ius:* in this field the republic was able to respond by producing from its own ruins the new regime of the principate. To a greater extent, it was a question of social order and measure: not of *politeia,* but of *taxis* (to use the word employed by Aelius Aristides),[6] also a constituent element of the "pax romana." The change that had permitted the transformation of *ius* from will to knowledge had not been merely a revolution of conceptual schemes. It had made its prescriptive models the point where knowledge and dominion came together and fused, each reinforced, if not actually rendered possible, by the presence of the other; and had made the separation (both ideological and, to a certain extent, real) the sole form of their connection.

Ius did not impinge directly upon the institutional order of the empire, which relied on other foundations for its effectiveness and justification. It was, as we know, an intrinsically "private" rather than "public" law: the juridicization of the political order would be a uniquely modern process.[7] But the capacity to irradiate its culture, at the end of the republic, was vast: and it wound up irresistibly linking Roman political supremacy to an idea of harmony and discipline that the revolution of formalism rendered potentially universal. The objective was not to impose a single law on the entire empire: centuries would pass before such a possibility could even be conceived, and it was never really achieved.[8] Instead, it was to adapt an ancient normative wisdom so it could guide a set of governmental practices—in the capital, in an Italy Romanized by municipalization, and in the provinces (especially with regard to the administration of justice: a central and very delicate task), which were not meant to be reduced to an undifferentiated unity, but which still required an unequivocal point of reference; and at the same time to find a criterion that might illuminate and explain from within such an extraordinary concentration of power and force.[9] This last problem—bridging the gap between supremacy and its justification—was (as we shall see) an issue that concerned Cicero; and it had provided the indispensable momentum enabling the transformation of *ius* from will to knowledge, in a situation where no further obstacles existed to Roman supremacy, which began confusedly to be perceived as boundless.

Power and order, knowledge and dominion, with the invention of formalism serving as a hinge. From the perspective we are proposing, the story of Rome offers us the archeology of a crucial relationship—the full implications and scope of which it has become possible to evaluate in the most recent period of modernity—providing us with a version elaborated through extremely coherent and effective conceptual schemes that have pervaded the course of Western history.[10]

Admittedly, the response of Roman thought—to deal with the problem by constructing a formal order capable of obscuring the non-innocence of its choices and their dependence on the constituted structures of concrete life, and to present itself as a separate and self-founding rationality—did not really resolve matters, as history would prove: formalism, even when it extended beyond the narrow limits imposed by the social conditions of ancient experience, would nonetheless leave open a number of dramatic problems; and the law—in the configuration deriving from Roman law—would inevitably reveal itself, irrespective of all ideological self-representations, to be the instrument of far from neutral choices, and much too structurally dependent on politics and the economy not to be conditioned by them.[11] But its paradigm would appear in any case to be the product of a different discourse, not immediately reducible to government or state power, the product of a rationality regulated by a complex of proportions and equilibriums that guided its path, freezing it into a network of calculations and preestablished compatibilities: it was, in short, the birth of legality, not as simple conformity with norms, but rather as a science and a tradition capable of incorporating and interpreting laws within its own confines, and of giving them sense and meaning.

The acquisition of formalism would, however, come at a high cost—and the time has come to find out what it was.

2.

Let us return again to Cicero: the legitimation of imperial power—a dominant motif in the culture of governing groups in the late republic—is an invaluable key to deciphering his political and legal thinking. He would pursue his objective by following, over the course of the years, two main paths: the reaffirmation of law as a separate kind of rationality with respect to political and economic power, and the representation of the Roman legal experience in terms of the doctrine of natural law.

We can begin by exploring the first of these:

> For he who thinks the civil law is to be despised, he is tearing asunder the bonds, not only of all courts of justice, but of all usefulness and of our common life; but he who finds fault with the interpreters of the law, if he says that they are ignorant of the law, is only disparaging the men, and not the civil law itself. If he thinks we ought not to be guided by learned men, then he is not injuring the men, but he is undermining the laws and justice. So that you must feel that nothing is to be maintained in a state with such care as the civil law. In truth, if this is taken away, it is not possible for anyone to feel certain about what is his own property or what belongs to another; there is no measure of equality valid for all. Therefore in other disputes and trials, when the question at issue is whether a thing has been done or not, whether what is alleged be true or false, and when false witnesses are sometimes suborned, and false documents foisted in, it is possible that sometimes a virtuous judge may be led into error by a seemingly honorable and probable pretense, or that an opportunity may be given to a dishonest judge of appearing to be guided by the witnesses, or by the documents produced, although in reality he has knowingly given a wrong decision. In the law there is nothing of this sort, O judges: there are no forged documents, no dishonest witnesses; even that overgrown power, which has sway in this state, is dormant with respect to cases of this sort; it has no means of attacking the judge, or of moving a finger. For this can be said to a judge by some man who is not so scrupulous as he is influential; "Decide, I pray you, that this has been done or planned; give credit to this witness; establish the genuineness of these documents";—but this cannot be said, "Decide that if a man has a posthumous son born to him, his will is not thereby invalidated; decide that a thing is due which a woman has promised without the sanction of her trustee." There is no opening for transactions of this sort, nor for anyone's power or influence . . .

For, indeed, what is the civil law? A thing which can neither be bent by influence, nor broken down by power, nor adulterated by corruption; which, if it be, I will not say overwhelmed, but even neglected or carelessly upheld, there will then be no ground for anyone to feel sure either that he possesses anything or that he shall leave anything to his children. For what is the advantage of having a house or a farm left one by one's father, or in any way legitimately acquired, if it be uncertain whether you will be able to retain those things which are yours by every right of property? if law be but little fortified? if nothing can be upheld by public and civil law, in opposition to the influence of any powerful man? What is the advantage, I say, of having a farm, if all the laws which have been most properly laid down by our ancestors about boundaries, about possessions, and water, and roads, may all be disturbed and changed in any manner? Believe me, every one of you has received a greater inheritance in respect of his property, from justice and from the laws than from those from whom he received the property itself. For it can happen, in consequence of anybody's will, that a farm may come to me; but it cannot be ensured to me, except by the civil law, that I shall be able to retain what has become my own. A farm can be left me by my father, but the enjoyment of the farm—that is to say, freedom from all anxiety and danger of lawsuits—is left to me not by my father, but by the laws. An aqueduct, a supply of water, a road, a right of way, comes from my father, but the ratified possession of all these things is derived from the civil law. Wherefore you ought to maintain and preserve that public inheritance of law which you have received from your ancestors with no less care than your private patrimony and property, not only because this last is fenced around and protected by the civil law, but also because if a man loses his patrimony, it is only an individual who suffers, but if the law be lost, the disaster affects the whole community.[12]

Here we are in the *Pro Caecina,* delivered possibly in 69 B.C.—and certainly earlier than 67[13]—by a Cicero who was still quite young. And we should not allow ourselves to be deceived by the studied archaism of the examples: the ancient rustic servitudes, the *mancipium,* old rules of the law of succession, the veiled references to the Twelve Tables.[14] It is mere window-dressing, nothing more than a patina of antiquity useful to intimidate and seduce his audience, when it was *ius* that occupied center stage. Behind the façade a quite different material was taking shape, and the perspective was much more up-to-date and current.

We can consider this text as the foundational locus of Western discourse on the neutrality of law, suspended since then midway between reality and myth, science and ideology. A twofold dissociation pervades his writing, that between the world of *ius* and the world of facts, and the one between law and power (in all its specific forms, political, social, and economic: *potentia, gratia, pecunia*—a total semantic coverage, in a relentless onslaught of repetitions). The world of facts appears to be dominated by ambiguity, by arbitrariness, by false appearances: witnesses may be truthful or false; the judges (that is, the private judges, those involved in the second phase of the formulary procedure, not the jurists) may be acting in good or in bad faith; and documents may be authentic or manipulated. The pervasiveness of this deceptive and deceitful light has a very specific origin: the inequality among citizens, the differences in their condition. All archaism has vanished. The fracture is a product of the empire and the opportunities created by the times. Unprecedented powers now controlled society without scruple: "ista quae dominatur in civitate potentia." It sounds like Sallust: occupying the scene is the overwhelming "modernity" of the new Rome, perceived moralistically as degeneration, decay, the sundering of social ties and ancient aristocratic bonds.

Standing against this is the solitary and unique bulwark of law. There is undoubtedly a touch of emphasis here. It is after all a harangue. But the oratorical technique was based on a widespread perception. This really is what *ius* appeared to be for many people in Rome during those years: a point of reference and a salvation.

But law would have been unable to perform its task had it not succeeded in establishing itself as an autonomous and literally untouchable space, determined by its own criteria. Its force stemmed from its capacity to separate itself: the spontaneous and original bond between *ius* and people that Cicero himself would later idealize so effectively in the *De republica* (as we have seen)[15] to describe the orderings of the city in their nascent state, could now no longer be evoked, devoured as it was by change.

And yet the isolation of *ius* in no way diminished its effectiveness: indeed, it increased it, becoming a presupposition of its very existence, reproduced materially in the incipient social separation of the class of its experts. The split—theoretical and sociological—was depicted as two spheres facing off against each other: that of society (of the *civitas*), and that of the legal tradition regenerated by the rationality of its interpreters, custodians of its new condition and, at the same time, of its memory. Where the law extends, there is no way of "moving a finger." This was the birth of the dialectic between law and politics. And the technique of the jurists was a form of knowledge that in turn conferred power: elsewhere Cicero would say this explicitly.[16] But it was, in this representation, a beneficial power. While in society there prevailed privilege and the abuse of power, *ius* imposed, where it operated, a general principle of uniformity: a "measure of equality valid for all," capable of acting as an order and a value (a point of view that Cicero would stick to firmly: in the *De oratore* he wrote of an "aequabilitatis conservatio"—a "maintenance of equality"—as the very "end" of civil law).[17] The isonomic motif returned, no longer referring to *lex*, however, but to *ius*. The new formalism could exalt and now render transparent this leaning toward equality (which developed an ancient tendency, as we stressed earlier), placing it in opposition to the new imbalances of an increasingly articulated and complex imperial world. It reduced private power—political, social, economic—into the network of symmetries and calculations of a reason capable of challenging, in the name of order, the disproportion of force, to sterilize rather than to eliminate it, transcribing it into a sequence of formal relationships: it is in this sense that we spoke about the new science of Mucius and of Servius as a form of analytics of relations between subjects and powers. Cicero, who could see the transformed heart of jurisprudence (at the time of this oration, Servius was already at work, the books of Quintus Mucius had been published several decades earlier, and those of Publius more than seventy years before), focused upon it an attentive and inspired gaze that accompanied him in the composition of the great treatises of his maturity.

3.

The legitimation of *ius* could, however, also take another path, parallel to the first: that of its "naturalization."

The idea that nature contained a regularity and a measure that could guide the actions of men was Greek in origin, and arrived in Rome from Greece, where it had experienced a lengthy period of gestation: the Greek words were *physis* and *nomos:* nature and the law.[18] The philosophical tradition had assigned various meanings to *physis,* in a line that might be defined as the progressive metaphysical dematerialization of the notion, already identifiable in Heraclitus, to the point of giving it the sense of constituent reason of the universe, of the ordering principle of the cosmos[19] (it would then be the Roman jurists themselves, from Servius to Paul, who were the great ancient rematerializers of nature, scrutinized with eyes attentive to the phenomenology of its weight and physicality, for the implications they might have for social life and its regulation).[20]

It was along such a course that *physis* had first met *nomos*—already in its meaning of an "excarnated" and secular law—and the encounter had given rise to a number of classic themes in Greek political speculation at the intersection between poetry, historiography, and philosophy: from the problematic relationship between the written (positive) law and the unwritten (natural) law, to the concept of "sovereign law"—of *nomos basileus*—superordinate with respect to the power of governors themselves, in a line of thought that dated back to the *Gorgias* and to the *Politics,* and which was certainly familiar to the Roman culture of the first century.[21] But it is not on these developments—which have been extensively studied[22]—that we must now focus, but rather upon a decisive difference between the Greek context and the Roman assimilation, the understanding of which leads us back to what we have called "the price of formalism."

When the connection between *physis* and *nomos* crystallized in Athens, let's say between the fifth and fourth centuries, there was no existing legal specialization or any authentic experience of law, but only, on the one hand, statutes as political command (an absolutely predominant form of social regulation—an authentic model of sovereignty—entirely immersed in the culture of the orators who interpreted it), and, on the other, ethical and metaphysical thought, ranging from the Sophists (and Heraclitus) to Aristotle, who were passionately interested in morality in the civic horizon of the *polis:* in other words, nothing other than rhetoric and philosophy.[23] This led to a framing of the discussion in terms of a relationship between the (written) laws of the city and the (unwritten but natural) laws of morality; and therefore to an early consideration of the relationship of "justice" to the political order, and of the conformity of political laws to the natural order: a major theme that would run throughout Greek culture, at least from the Sophists to middle Stoicism, resulting in the composition of extraordinary texts, from the *Antigone* to the *Apology of Socrates.*[24]

In Rome, on the other hand, when these ideas began to circulate, they were faced not by a philosophical tradition (which was only just coming into being, with the work of Lucretius and Cicero), nor by the *lex* as a prevalent figure of civic regulation, but the wisdom of the jurists, the *ius civile*, the edict: a different model of sovereignty in the regulation of private relations. They therefore had to be measured on a terrain already influenced by a hard and demanding layer of technicalness, which was coming to its formal culmination precisely at that time: an outcome that moved law and its science away from every content-based evaluation of social relations, enclosing them instead in a vision that only emphasized the respect for a network of quantitative measurements indifferent to moral doubt—the sole perspective ensuring the separation from political and economic power that was stressed so greatly by Cicero.

It was for this reason that the Roman jurists would always prefer not to speak of "justice": the word is almost never found in their writings. *Ius* was something else: conformity with the protocols of a ritualistic tradition regenerated by technicalness and by science. Ethics had been excluded from the very outset (just as it had been from religion). Republican virtue identified it—outside of any relativistic possibility—with the very solidity of the social bond and with the primacy of the community with respect to its components: it was a cultural and anthropological presupposition for the construction of *ius*, not the object of an intellectual debate or of a positive prescription. When this moral backdrop began to crumble away in the midst of the crisis between the second and first centuries, it would already be too late. The revolution of formalism was already crystallizing that original split for good, transforming into an abstract legal ought-to-be—devoid of all content, even civic—what had once been a concrete historical characteristic; and the imperial public ethics would be identified with pure conformity to the *ius* established by the jurists (and later by the *princeps*): outside this it was now difficult to see anything else—with the sole exception of Seneca, perhaps, as Hegel would clearly grasp.[25]

The two paradigms of the law *(nomos)* and of *ius* had therefore developed in quite different directions: the former toward an engagement with a substantive idea of justice, consigned to ethical reflection in the shadow of politics and a "public" experience of social regulation, but without any legal specialization; the latter, toward an outcome in which the long-prepared completion of formalism entrusted it to a rigorous and powerful science, also tendentially isonomic, but eluding all "political" control, and separate from those ethical workshops in which Greek culture had traced a path that would not be lost. Justice (as the respect for a shared and superior moral law, however open it might remain to discussion) and legality (as formal compliance with a scientifically constructed order) were about to diverge along two separate paths in the course of Western history, just like their paradigms of reference: politics and law. We have still not managed to completely join them together:[26] the successful establishment of formalism had required the excavation of an abyss around it.

But the Roman jurists were nonetheless conscious of "fairness," originally opposed to, and later assimilated within, the context of *ius*: the consequence of their first Mediterranean and imperial broadening of horizons.[27] When the new wave of Greek influence arrived, they—in the midst of the transformation of their knowledge, partly resulting from the assimilation of the very same foreign philosophy that had produced the debate about the law and justice—did not reject it entirely, but chose instead to integrate it into the conceptual framework they already had and which they were in the process of reelaborating. In a sense, then, they repeated the operation carried out between the third and second centuries, the chief protagonist of which had been the office of the praetor. They did not renounce any aspect of their formal framework—this by now was their identity—but they tried to reconcile it with a vision of *ius* in which there was space for other, more substantive, elements. The old idea of fairness lent itself to this purpose, provided it was possible to give it a new image backed by more robust and up-to-date theoretical foundations. And that is exactly what they did. The result was the birth of the Roman doctrine of natural law.

The first trace of the impact can be found, not in a legal text, but in a passage of the *Rhetorica ad Herennium:* "The constituent departments [of law], then, are the following: nature, statute, custom, the "thing judged," the "fair and good," and "agreement."[28] We are in the presence of the earliest definition of *ius* to emerge in Roman culture, already sketched out on two other occasions in the same work—technically a *partitio,* in keeping with the scheme employed later by Cicero in the *Topica*—and probably taken from a rhetorical precept.[29] We cannot say whether a jurist of the time would have shared the notion (it would be intriguing to think that it might have a Mucian foundation: his *Iuris civilis* books had appeared roughly a decade earlier, and must by then have become essential reading). While the reference to the statutes (the Twelve Tables above all), to custom (in the sense of the *mores* and their jurisprudential interpretation), to the thing judged, or *res iudicata* (the sentences issued at the conclusion of a case, whose pronunciation precluded any reexamination of what had been decided: it should be remembered that a rhetorician is writing here, with an inevitable attention to the trial), and to the "fair and good" comes as no surprise, the same cannot be said of the reference to nature and agreement (that is, consensus among the parties). We shall return to the second element later.[30] But how can we explain the presence of the first one?

It is possible that here the author was simply copying a Greek model: indeed, in the *Nicomachean Ethics* and in the *Rhetoric* we see the same sequence that articulates the definition in the Roman treatise.[31] But is it credible to believe that it was reproduced without some connection to the elaboration of the jurists? It seems unlikely. And if there is a link, who should we be thinking of? Quintus Mucius comes to mind once again: his familiarity with Greek culture cannot be disputed, and it is not unreasonable to imagine that what would later become the Gaian idea of *naturalis ratio* might reflect a remote foundation attributable to the republican jurist.[32] Perhaps the best hypothesis is to suppose that whoever came up with the scheme in question was aware both of Greek sources and of a reference to be found in Roman circles, which served for a construction that did not faithfully reproduce the opinion of the jurists, but adopted from a rhetorical point of view traces and elements that can be found in their doctrines.

In any case, we cannot yet speak in terms of of an authentic paradigm of natural law: above all, the justification for mentioning nature in the *Rhetorica ad Herennium* was limited to a simple reference to the duties deriving from consanguinity in kinship ties.[33] Only with Cicero would the decisive step be taken, in the context of his efforts— pursued between 55 and 44, drawing on ideas from the *Rhetorica ad Herennium* and more generally the teachings of rhetoric—to establish a philosophical foundation for Roman positive law, freeing it from the specificity of its earliest history. His attempt to achieve a degree of delocalization and universalization was likewise suggested by the imperial experience, the reflection of a culture that was striving to transcribe, not only through the revolution of formalism, the ancient *logos* of the city into a knowledge capable of regulating the world rationally, without losing its own original characteristics. "Then you do not think that the science of law is to be derived from the praetor's edict, as the majority do now, or from the Twelve Tables, as people used to think, but from the deepest mysteries of philosophy?" Atticus asks Cicero in the *De legibus*.[34] Going beyond the historic continuity of *ius,* so well described in the reference to the Twelve Tables and the edict, the role of the original source was now played by the *intima philosophia*. The idea took the place of history; and there emerged the hypothesis of constructing a sort of ordering without a sovereign and without any specific territorial (we would say "national") reference, justified only by a common philosophy, unanimously shared because it was inscribed in the reason of all men. Again there were echoes of the ancient doctrine of the *nomos basileus*— of the statute as king—now presupposed as a foundation for a universal law.[35] "With respect to the true principle of justice, many learned men have maintained that it springs from the law, and, as far as I know, correctly so, if the law is, as they themselves define it, the highest reason, implanted in nature, which commands what ought to be done, and forbids the contrary. This reason, when firmly fixed and fully developed in men's minds, is the law." Once again it is Cicero speaking here, still in the *De legibus*,[36] the great theoretical text of ancient natural law. Nature has within itself an irresistible normative vocation, innately inscribed in human reason: the law (but in the Roman sense of *ius*) is nothing other than the translation of this natural human order, oriented toward what is good.

In Greek culture, and in the Stoic thought of which Cicero was particularly mindful here, the naturalistic scheme had often served as the basis for an alternative to written laws, in order to create the possibility of a critique of the positive order: the moral rule, in opposition to political command. This, however, was not Cicero's viewpoint. The Roman reception—conditioned by the twofold presence of *ius* and the empire—steered well away not only from any possible use that might be construed as subversive, but even merely critical of this paradigm (just as it rejected, on the other hand, and for the same reasons, any relativistic refusal of the idea of natural law: a similar position, attributed to Carneades, is treated in the *De republica* with a detachment tinged with scorn).[37] The perspective was quite different: not a criticism of positive law, but its full legitimation—through the discovery of a transcendent foundation for it—in the face of highly complex administrative tasks, requiring difficult comparisons:

> Even if the lot had made you governor of Africans, or of Spaniards, or of Gauls—uncivilized and barbarous nations—it would still have been your duty as a man of feeling to attend to their needs, and to dedicate yourself to their interests and protection. But when the men we rule are of a race that not only consider themselves to be perfectly civil, but also believe they have brought civilization to others, we are bound to repay, above all things, what we received from them. For I shall not be ashamed to go so far—especially as my life and achievements have been such as to exclude any suspicion of sloth or frivolity—as to confess that, whatever we have accomplished we owe to those studies and principles which have been transmitted to us in Greek literature and schools of thought. Wherefore, over and above the loyal respect of obligations which is due to all men, we have a special duty to that race of men: as they have been our masters, we must be willing to repay what we have learnt from them.[38]

This is still Cicero, writing to his brother Quintus, in 59, about the renewal of his Asian proconsulship; and what emerges in his words is a full-fledged cultural anthropology of imperial conquest and domination. The Roman west and east posed different problems, each requiring attention in equal measure. In the west there was empty space and barbarism, in the east a great civilization, and the work of the imperial magistrates—jurisdictional edicts, administration, government—had to model itself on this fact and adapt accordingly. In the east, it was necessary to "repay what we have learnt": the problem of the legitimation of the empire was looming ever larger.

A power with no further obstacles to its progress tends to be a source of order; and if the order is based not only on force, but also on consensus—as dictated by the realism of conquerors capable of filling the role—it requires knowledge, skill, and techniques able to portray it as the result of a superior and advantageous point of view; of transforming itself from a fact of history into a design of reason. The culture of the Roman ruling groups at the end of the republic was certainly learning all this, and Cicero himself had a strong and substantial idea of what it meant to rule the world; in the *De republica,* he would provide an incisive and effective representation, when, reworking an Aristotelian metaphor, he compared imperial dominion to the control exercised by the mind over the body: "The power of kings, of generals, of magistrates, of fathers, and of peoples, rules their citizens and allies as the mind rules bodies."[39]

But the problem could not be stated only in philosophical terms. From the Roman standpoint, it was first and foremost a legal question. If the *ius* of the city was to perform this new universal function—to endow the social control stemming from political dominion with a content of law and a rational foundation—it would not be enough to express a theoretical principle; it would instead be necessary to come up with operative tools. Formalism had elaborated a number of powerful instruments, but its calculative and quantitative reasoning might not suffice on its own, just as, in its time, the old ritualism of the *ius civile* had not been enough for the city. The paradigm of natural law could usefully be set alongside it, offering a criterion capable of compensating for its rigidity and of expanding its outlook to include evaluations that were otherwise external to the horizons of *ius.* There was a need, however, to translate Roman law into a category genuinely capable of shaping legal practice in the various parts of the empire, of extracting *ius* from a purely philosophical investigation of what was "just," consigning it to a disciplining rationality that had already found its essential points of reference. And that is why we see the return, in a more modern version, of the idea of fairness.

4.

We must return once again to the *Rhetorica ad Herennium,* to a passage from the third book: "Justice is the equity that gives to each his own right, for the dignity of all."[40] The two words that open it are an almost absolute novelty. *Iustitia* can be found prior to this only in a passage from Terence, in the restricted sense of "prudence," "wisdom," "measure," as opposed to "foolishness."[41] *Aequitas* (equity) has not appeared at all; previously we have come across *aequum*, a neuter serving as a substantive (which we have translated as fair, fairness).[42] Now the joint use shed reciprocal light on the meaning of the two terms. They served to introduce into the Roman intellectual world a more complex notion, somewhere between rhetoric, philosophy, and law, the concept of a universal principle of equilibrium and measure, of what we might call proprietary proportionality: this latter formula is a Ciceronian topos ("gives to each his own") recurring continually from the *De inventione* to the *De republica* and the *De officiis*[43]—which went beyond (though without contradicting) the reality of the *ius civitatis*.

The word "justice" can be abandoned to its destiny for now: it was immediately dropped by the jurists, who rigorously expunged it from their vocabulary and their theoretical baggage (we have briefly explained why) until it made a spectacular comeback, which we shall examine later.[44] Let's concentrate instead on "equity." Its meaning cannot be made to coincide with the *aequum* (fair, fairness) documented in Plautus; overlaid on that ancient value a new and broader meaning had now been stratified (otherwise the definition of the *Rhetorica ad Herennium* would not have held together), which translated the Greek model of the *epieikeia* (according to a well-established hypothesis, the root of *eoika* is the same one identifiable in *aequum*) as it had developed over time—not without some oscillation—in Aristotle, from the *Nicomachean Ethics* to the *Rhetoric,* where we read: "unlike written laws, *epieikes* always remains the same and never changes."[45]

The *Rhetorica ad Herennium* perfectly reveals this double meaning: while in the definition of *ius* just mentioned, *aequum et bonum* only figured as a part of the concept of law (evidently here the author was referring to the original sense of the expression, namely "flexibility" and "adherence to the concrete case," as he himself clarified shortly thereafter, speaking of a "new law," constituted in consideration "of the circumstances and the dignity of men"),[46] it would be impossible to reduce the meaning of *aequitas* (equity) just to this, identified as it was with that of a "justice" (a translation of the Greek terms *dike* and *dikaiosyne*) based upon the "giving to each his own," that is, with a principle of universal scope—with an evident Stoic origin—capable of embracing not a specific part of *ius,* but its entirety.[47]

Let us be perfectly clear, however: the original value of *aequum* (fair, fairness)—the one assigned to its alternative use with respect to civil law rituality—would never fade away. Late-republican rhetoric and philosophy re-elaborated it in depth, and this can still be clearly glimpsed in Cicero, for instance in the *Pro Caecina* ("If people argue speciously about the literal meaning of written or uttered words, and, as it is customary to say, about the most narrow and inflexible law, it is usual to oppose this kind of iniquity with the name and dignity of the fair and good"),[48] or in the praise of Lucius Crassus in the *Brutus* ("in handling questions whether of the civil law or of the fair and good he was fertile in argument and in analogies," with the direct display of the ancient dualism between *ius civile* and *aequum et bonum*).[49] But its significance went deeper. The innovative features that had been specific to the praetorian jurisdiction spread into the work of later jurisprudence: the idea emerged—between rhetoric and legal thought—of a normative canon distinguished by ductility and social utility, shaped by the interpretation of the jurists and by the hermeneutics that supported it, and integrated within the new formalism, rendered congruent with concrete situations and their circumstances.

This intrinsic polysemy—which we should understand not as a diametrical opposition, but rather as a shift between relatively contiguous semantic fields, albeit distinct and not entirely overlapping—would be fully accepted by Cicero. In the *Topica* the two meanings were set side by side in a studied symmetry. The former, older and more restricted, returned in a text that we may consider a mature reelaboration of the definition of law present in the *Rhetorica ad Herennium* —"as if one said that the civil law consists of statutes, *senatusconsulta*, sentences passed into judgment, jurisprudential authority, magistrates' edicts, customs, and equity"[50]—where the thinking of the jurists seemed to be taken into greater account, and a scheme was drawn up that would form the basis for the definition of *ius* as proposed by the Sabinian tradition, which reached Gaius, and different from the model utilized in a parallel fashion by Pomponius in the *Enchiridion*.[51] In place of the "good and fair" we find directly here the corresponding substantive (*aequitas*, equity), but in the same position as a particular element, isolable within a general *partition* of *ius*.

The second meaning appears in a slightly earlier passage: "Civil law is equity established for those who belong to the same city, for the purpose of obtaining what is theirs."[52] Here equity is identified with the totality of the *ius civile* (as in the *Pro Caecina*, and something similar had already happened in the *De oratore*);[53] and the assimilation obliges us to understand it as a general paradigm, capable of imprinting itself on the entire formation of law. And there is more in this text. Identification—once we assign to the word a value close to that of the Aristotelian *epieikeia*—determined a sort of universalistic transcription of Roman positive law, which was Cicero's real objective: a purpose underlying the *De legibus,* and which returns in several significant passages of the *Partitiones oratoriae.*[54]

But for Cicero this second form of equity also had an unquestionable basis in natural law, and it is a point to which he would always hold firm: from the *De inventione* (where in his reelaboration of the definition of *iustitia* offered in the *Rhetorica ad Herennium,* although he never named equity directly, he alluded to a "natural" origin—*ab natura profectum*—of the principle of *sui cuique tribuere* or "giving to each his own");[55] to the *Partitiones oratoriae,* in which he spoke of aspects of *aequitas* that were common to nature and to law ("communia naturae atque legis"; but here he means *lex* in the sense of *ius,* as is made abundantly clear immediately afterward);[56] and once again in the *De legibus,* where the entire argumentation is clustered around the outlining of the triad *natura lex aequitas:*[57] the supreme reason of *lex* reflects a principle of nature, and *lex* expresses in its turn a universal rule of justice called *aequitas,* which consists in giving to each his own.

It would be once again in a text of the *Topica* that both of these aspects— the polysemy of *aequitas* and the natural law foundation of its newest meaning—were definitively affirmed:

> But when the discussion is about what is fair and unfair, all the topics of equity are brought together. These are divided in a two-fold manner, depending on whether they regard nature or a positive rule. Nature has two parts: to give to each his own, and the right to punish a wrong. Equity, which consists of a positive rule, is in three parts: one part rests on statutes; one depends on agreements; the third is confirmed by the antiquity of custom.[58]

We are at a crossroads. The ambiguous value of *aequitas* in the late-republican language here receives its most evident seal, which leads to a crucial distinction: there is an *aequitas* that refers to nature, based on the principle—a genuine Ciceronian leitmotif—of giving to each his own—property and redistribution—and another that is internal to positive law: a difference that will have its sequel, as we shall see.

These are the beginnings of the doctrine of natural law, and at the same time the transubstantiation of Roman law, elevated, through an exaltation of its original proprietary nucleus, to the status of universal principle of justice. The circle closes: the rule of the world could therefore perfectly well be a Roman rule.

It was in such a framework, centering entirely on the notion of *aequitas* and its transfiguration in terms of natural law, that the jurists operated from the late republic into the early principate. We have already said there is no evidence to suggest Mucius should be included in the context we have outlined, though the possibility cannot be completely excluded. Two protagonists of this work can, however, be identified with certainty: Aquilius Gallus—an adept of Mucius, praetor in 66 B.C., who died sometime after 55—and Servius, his pupil in Cercina.[59]

Yet again our guide is Cicero. Let's start with Aquilius: "Wherefore I will say this, that too much weight cannot be given to the authority of a man [Aquilius] whose wisdom the Roman people has been able to discover in the prudence of the advice and not in deceptions; of a man who has never separated from equity the reason of civil law."[60] The praise comes from the *Pro Caecina,* and the reference to *aequitas*—not as an alternative to the *ius civile,* but incorporated within a common reason—is too specific to imagine that it lacked correspondences in the thinking of the jurist. For that matter, Aquilius' definition of fraud (in connection with the trial formula he proposed),[61] based on the distinction between fiction and substance in the behavior maintained by the parties in the realization of a juridical act, is the signal of a line of thought that is openly in contrast with the old verbal and gestural ritualism, oriented toward an evaluation of the effective correctness of the subjects involved—and therefore in the same direction indicated by the *bonum et aequum.*[62]

But it had been Servius who brought about the shift:

> Nor will there be unrecorded an admirable and marvelous and
> almost god-like knowledge in the interpretation of the laws, and

in explaining the principles of equity. All men of every age who
in this community have understood jurisprudence, were they
brought into one place, would not be comparable with Servius
Sulpicius. For he was no greater a master of law than of justice;
and thus he always referred provisions derived from statutes and
from the civil law to a standard of lenient interpretation and equity; nor did he seek to set actions on foot rather than to do away
with controversy.[63]

The above comes from the celebrated portrait produced by Cicero on the
occasion of his friend's death, which dominates the *Ninth Philippic,* and it is
an extraordinarily vivid Servius that is conjured up. His doctrine deserved to
be judged "almost god-like" precisely because of his skill in "explaining the
principles of equity." And this made it possible to say of him that he cultivated "justice" no less than "law": an essential point for Cicero, who emphasized this exceptional conjunction of two spheres related in an increasingly
problematic manner, and also an observation whose polemic value can easily
be discerned (the point of view was not that of a jurist) with respect to a discipline that displayed a complete lack of interest in the great questions of
moral philosophy. *Ius, iustitia, aequitas* thus once again figured together, and
for the last time until Ulpian,[64] brought together to describe an exceptional
personality, the authentic interpreter of a profound—though thwarted—requirement of the imperial age: the reconjunction of legality and legitimation,
of ethics and formalism.

In a stylistically effective crescendo, the attainment of *aequitas* was finally
presented as the true objective of all of Servius' work: the entire Roman legal
order *(leges—ius civile)* was gathered together in the ambit of this concept.

It is possible Cicero was exaggerating, and that his perspective on Servius'
work did not coincide with that of the jurists. But not to a very great degree:
those who listened to him must have been well aware of what he was talking
about. And, for that matter, there is no shortage of confirmation: indeed, we
find *aequum* as a criterion of Servian doctrines in the polemic with Mucius
about the regime of consensual partnership (as we have seen);[65] in a citation
from Paul concerning imprisonment during wartime;[66] and in a text by Alphenus used to justify the concession of a trial exception.[67] Instead, we need
to ask whether the *aequitas* evoked by Cicero was still the *aequum (et bonum)*

of the republican tradition, or whether it was not already the other one oriented toward natural law. Probably Cicero was consciously playing on the polysemy of the word—which for him had become a central idea of the new imperial and cosmopolitan humanism—in order to underscore philosophical resonances that were perhaps not entirely explicit in the work of Servius. But the fact remains that the jurists were preparing to accept the distinction envisaged in the *Topica,* and to develop a concept of equity with a declared basis in natural law. We learn this from Labeo, through a citation in Ulpian:

> Consider the case: a slave manumitted in the will, fraudulently prevents, after the death of his master and before acceptance of the inheritance, something from the estate coming into the hands of the heir. Against him, now free, a "useful" action for twofold will lie against him for a year. This action, as Labeo wrote, contains a natural rather than a civil equity: and certainly it is fair by nature that he should not go unpunished who was made the bolder by the expectation that, as he judged, he could not be punished as a slave by reason of his imminent free status nor yet be condemned as a freeman because he had stolen from the inheritance.[68]

The hypothesis centered upon the condition of a slave manumitted by a will, during the evaluation of the inheritance: he was not yet a free man, but he no longer had (and never would have again) a master. How should his fraudulent behavior be punished, if it took place during this sort of legal nontime? Ulpian recalled Labeo having commented on the "useful" action issued by the praetor to emerge from this quandary (construed, that is, by adapting to the circumstances of the case a not strictly corresponding trial formula): it was based, according to Labeo, on an equity that was more "natural" than "civil"; and in fact Ulpian added (we cannot say whether he was again drawing upon Labeo) that it was "fair by nature" that someone who committed an offense should not go unpunished, and should not be able to count on the impossibility of prosecuting him either as a freeman or as a slave.

We have no reason to question the accuracy of the reference; the scheme that emerges in it, centering on the opposition between *aequitas civilis* and *aequitas naturalis,* is, in fact, from Ulpian's point of view, a conceptual fossil (to say nothing of the doctrines of late antiquity), and it shows its age in an unmistakable manner: no jurist after Labeo ever employed it again: subsequent thinkers would be familiar only with *aequitas naturalis* or simply *aequitas,* with no further specifications. But it accurately reflected the classification delineated in the *Topica,* with the *aequitas civilis* in place of (but with the same value as) the Ciceronian *aequitas instituta.*[69] In the case discussed by Labeo, the latter could be of no help: the rules of the positive order were precisely what had created the conundrum. On that occasion, natural equity had offered aid, supporting the decision to concede a new action: it demanded that those responsible be punished in any case ("ulciscendi ius," in the words of Cicero, which were carefully paraphrased by Labeo or by Ulpian: "natura aequum est non esse impunitum eum . . .").

With Servius and Labeo we are therefore at the point of juncture between the rhetorical and philosophical tradition and the work of the jurists: the natural law paradigm, often filtered through the idea of equity, and in any case always restricted to a horizon of prescriptive operativeness, would become, from then on—even without having ever been theorized directly—one of the threads of the jurists' thinking, through to the conclusive affirmation by Ulpian, and one of the founding elements of the universalistic perspective that, during the principate, jurisprudence would pursue with increasing consistency, as a definitive legitimation of its choices and its practice.

IV

In the Heart of the Empire

I. The Compromise and the Alliance:
From Labeo to Gaius and Pomponius

17

Hermeneutics and the Politics of Law

I.

The middle years of the life of Antistius Labeo coincided with those of the principate of Augustus, with the establishment of the new order which, following the death of Caesar, ended the crisis of the aristocratic republic.[1]

It was an epilogue the jurist would never approve, viewing it instead with the nostalgic gaze of a republican attached to the political past of the city and its ideals. His father, Pacuvius, had taken part in the conspiracy against Caesar, and at Philippi had been killed, at his own command, by one of his slaves.[2] Labeo's hostility toward Augustus was never in doubt, in the name of an aristocratic intransigence unwilling to give up some of his power and privileges in order to reopen his salons (to borrow the effective image used by Ronald Syme).[3]

But the moderation he showed in refraining from pushing opposition to the extreme of an irreparable rupture intersected with that of the *princeps* in tackling the conflict with prudence: the result was a precarious yet decisive equilibrium, destined to orient the delicate transition from the republican paradigm of a substantial identification of the jurists with the governing class, to a previously unseen collaboration between rulers and jurisprudence—allied but distinct—that would later characterize the very highest offices of the empire. The point of engagement was, on the one hand (that of Labeo), the choice never to explicitly contest the constitutional foundation of the new political set-up, though still indirectly calling it into question; on the other (that of Augustus), the decision to accept the primacy of jurisprudence in creating *ius,* though also flanked by significant comitial legislation regarding marriage and civil trials, and attempting to some extent to influence the activity of jurists through the management of the so-called *ius respondendi* (more will be said about this later): but without showing any sign of yielding to the idea—anything but unthinkable—of transforming the principate into a full-blown normative autocracy.[4]

The compromise would later be evaluated positively by Tacitus, who in a brief but incisive portrait of Labeo praised his "uncorrupted liberty" and his reputation, more splendid than that of the other great jurist (and rival) of those years, Ateius Capito—a man of undisputed learning and talent, but scathingly deemed in the *Annals* to subservient to the new power.[5] Labeo's cult of freedom (which the jurist considered, as we have seen, to be of "infinite" worth[6]) was, however, open to alternative and sometimes less glowing judgments than that of Tacitus. Capito himself, who wrote about it in a letter recalled by Gellius, obviously saw things in a very different light: "In one of the letters of Ateius Capito I read that Antistius Labeo was exceedingly learned in the laws and customs of the Roman people and in civil law. But, he said, 'that man was driven by an excessive and mad love of freedom, to such a degree that, although the divine Augustus was then emperor and was ruling the republic, Labeo regarded nothing as confirmed and valid other than what he had found to be sanctioned and decided in Roman antiquity.'"[7] Here the "freedom" that "drove" Labeo (but that also "troubled" him: the choice of that verb—*agitare*—was full of sly malice) appeared unquestionably disproportionate, and the term of comparison was the attitude toward Augustus—truly, for Capito, the tongue always turned to the aching tooth. When the *princeps* was already in the fullness of his powers and functions, wrote Capito—and his prose really does seem to bow to the overwhelming majesty of the new power, with more than a touch of the "obsequity" that would irritate Tacitus—Labeo did not hesitate to state that nothing had a foundation for him unless it found a correspondence in the ancient memories of the city: where certainly there was no mention of the principate, just a deep-seated aversion to tyrants and to all forms of reign.

It is a significant piece of testimony, despite the evident partiality. In its mirror, Labeo's behavior was perhaps reflected with malignant emphasis, but not completely distorted. The memory of antiquity—the punctilious respect for its details—was used by him in a subtly ideological manner, as we can clearly see in the anecdote related immediately afterwards by Capito, and once again reported by Gellius: "'When ([Capito says]) the tribunes of the plebs had been appealed to by a woman against Labeo and had sent to him at Gallianum bidding him come and answer the woman's charge, he ordered the messenger to return and say to the tribunes that they had the right to summon neither him nor anyone else, since according to the usage of our forefathers the tribunes of the plebs had the power of arrest, but not of summons; that they might therefore come and order his arrest, but they did not have the right to summon him when absent.'"[8] The republican order was based not on a written text, but only on consolidated practices, a literal interpretation of which could serve as an effective means to undercut the new developments of the present: while Labeo probably avoided making any direct pronouncements on them, they were rendered fragile and diminished through comparison with the weight and the authority of the past. (All the same, things were complex: Augustus also knew how to revive the *mores* to his own advantage; in his own way, he too was an "inventor" of traditions, and he took pleasure in presenting himself as a restorer.) There was, then, no explicit criticism of the principate: it stopped just short—the final step would never be taken. And it was in this restricted space—in which we should also position Labeo's rejection of the consulship offered to him by Augustus[9]— that the path to compromise was opened up.

Prior to Labeo, in the years between Caesar's solitary rule to the fall of Antony, the last generation of republican jurists, just after Servius—that of Aulus Ofilius, Aufidius Namusa, Aulus Cascellius, Alphenus Varus (the publisher of the Servian responses), Quintus Aelius Tubero, and Trebatius Testa[10]—had all contributed to the consolidation of the great results of the Mucian and Servian elaborations and the quest for a new and previously unexplored relationship with political power. Until then, the link between knowledge of *ius* and aristocratic hegemony had been entirely unconcealed and visible, with the former completely incorporated into the totalizing rationality of the latter. But the revolution of formalism had coincided with the crisis of this model; the nexus between the new science—separate and specialized—and the new political power became increasingly complicated and (in some ways) hidden, giving rise to an arduous process of mediation. Upon the ruins of the old aristocratic bloc, and concomittant to the new isolation of the knowledge of *ius*, there was the emergence of a "professional" class of jurists as a distinct social body: it was the politics of law that was coming into being, as a locus of compromise between powers (and groups) by now quite diverse, though obliged to take part in an unbroken dialogue.

From the very beginning, however, it did not have a linear course. And within the Servian school itself (though all those jurists had dealings with Servius, as they did with Cicero) a number of distinct projects took shape, including some oriented toward giving space to the idea, previously rejected by Mucius before it had even been completely formulated, and subsequently dismissed by Servius as well, of a legal science standardized through an overall diaeretic approach, and of a jurisprudence remodeled in terms of a Hellenistic body of doctrine. And it is quite possible that this revival of systematizing hypotheses—to a substantial extent alternatives to the triumph of Mucian and Servian case-based rationality—was favored, in those years, by the so-called Caesarian codifying project, about which we are informed by Suetonius and by Isidore of Seville: a design possibly imbued with autocratic and orientalizing overtones, in line with Caesar's final inclinations before the Ides of March.[11] And perhaps this is the explanation for Cicero's shift between *De oratore* and *Brutus:* what in 55 B.C. must still have seemed to him a merely cultural requirement, by 46 must have appeared to be contaminated by an absolutely unacceptable political option, with the danger of being interpreted as approval of Caesar's policy. In the circumstances, it was far better to hold on tight to the tradition of the jurists.[12]

Aulus Ofilius—a pupil of Servius but very close to Caesar—was perhaps the most deeply involved in those designs. He had been one of the masters of Labeo (who, however, had also studied under Trebatius, and had learned from Tubero and Alphenus). The aim of his *Iuris partiti* books[13] was probably to rewrite the *ius civile* in a markedly systematic fashion (his *partitiones* must have had a quite different ordering force from the Mucian *capita*): an echo of the attempt can still be glimpsed in the judgment of Pomponius,[14] even though later jurisprudence, clearly opposed to such an approach, would erase almost all memory of this work, as would also be the case for the comparable *De iure civili in artem redigendo* by Cicero[15]— the two texts were in all likelihood the closest to the *Rhetorica ad Herennium* (from a diaeretic point of view) of anything produced by Roman legal thought.

A greater fortune would be in store for Ofilius' commentary on the edict, despite being written with the same intent. But in this case, he was in tune with the much more deeply felt need for a substantial consolidation and reordering of the edictal text, following the impetuous development of the preceding period; an objective that was probably achieved (we will talk about this shortly), and which would render possible, several decades later, Labeo's most mature treatise.[16]

In Ofilius' output there is also a *De legibus:* and once again we are in the presence of a piece of writing evidently intended to be an ordering collection (the Ciceronian title should not deceive us here):[17] to the point that we might imagine the entire triptych—*Libri iuris partiti, Ad edictum,* and *De legibus*—as a sort of preparation for Caesar's project, through which the three major normative layers of the city's experience—the *ius civile,* the edict, and the comitial legislation—were subjected to an initial systematizing pressure, in view of further intervention that would be no longer jurisprudential but directly political in nature.

But these were ephemeral ideas: the assassination of Caesar (who, besides Ofilius, had certainly had jurists of his own, probably, among the most prominent, Alphenus Varus and Trebatius Testa)[18] would immediately sweep them away, allowing the Mucian-Servian line of thought to prevail once and for all. When we find Labeo at work, the trail was clearly and definitively marked.

2.

The detail recounted by Pomponius that Labeo apparently spent six months of the year in Rome, engaged in his work as a respondent, and the rest of the time well away from the city, in his country villa, devoting himself exclusively to writing and studying,[19] was a perfect reflection, whatever its biographical credibility, of the new status of the Roman intelligentsia, following the crisis and decline of the old aristocratic rationality. The detachment of different branches of knowledge from their previous identification with the exercising of political hegemony enhanced the potential for theoretical developments, and reinforced their autonomous standing. Of course, the transformations took distinct paths: historiography away from rhetoric, and the latter from grammar or philosophy, each in relation to its own particular tradition. And it was precisely in the fracture brought about by this division that the first Roman "intellectuals," in a sense not all that distant from the modern meaning of the word, were formed, Sallust, Servius, Cicero himself, and Labeo: all of them compromised by the collapse of the old ruling groups; all of them, in one way or another, politically finished.[20]

Legal knowledge nonetheless maintained a quite separate position in the new geography of knowledge. It continued to define the privileged locus of a power—the force of a disciplining science, constituent of the social order—even though it was by this point separable, both in common perceptions and in reality, from the direct practice of politics and of the magistracies. The span of time from Publius Mucius to Servius and Cicero had proved decisive in this sense. Operating in what was now a different context, dominated by the success of the Augustan revolution, Labeo was able to gather together and reelaborate the results of previous generations, in an attempt to establish a more thoroughly articulated relationship between the work of the jurists and the new—and triumphant—politics. Turning to his studies as a response to the crisis became an instrument of resistance against a mode of government to which he did not subscribe. And the Servian invention of a rationality within law, which it was the interpreter's task to explore and bring to light, acquired a new meaning: not just the route to founding a fully scientific legal knowledge, but a vehicle for preserving the autonomy of law as well, capable also of growing and developing outside a political system of which it did not approve.

But it would be a mistake to look at those years solely from the point of view of what was new. Legal thought also changed because it managed to establish and reinforce a nondestructive relationship with the most ancient traditions of its own past. It achieved, and not paradoxically, a revolution-in-conservation, as always happens with paradigm shifts in the human sciences; and in this case also in accordance with the inherent style of the whole of Roman history.[21]

Observed from the perspective of continuity with its own roots, and not merely that of the change it admittedly succeeded in bringing about, the jurisprudence of the first century wound up presenting many points of contact with other aspects of Roman culture in the period. The specific element in common appears to have been the problem of how to adapt to the new times the complex fabric of traditions that had long been an essential component of civic life, but which now appeared increasingly adrift at the center of a world empire. Of how, that is, to defend the city's cultural specificity—still perceived in many ways as the reason for its superiority and success—from the risk of a syncretistic and relativistic dissolution: an outcome that was quite possible, after the expansion in knowledge, in spatial bounds, and in interaction resulting from the age of conquest.

Viewed in this light, the formal revolution in Roman legal thought also seems to have been an extraordinary opportunity to regenerate the very oldest traditions: to salvage the original underlying features of the archaic understanding of *ius*. Ultimately, this is exactly what the combination of the ontological paradigm and the case-based model had been; to say nothing of the enduring presence, albeit transfigured, of a remote imprint of archaic ritualism.

It would therefore be misleading to divide the jurists and intellectuals who debated the changes in legal knowledge into conservatives and innovators: in fact they all moved within a horizon that contained both these points of view. All that distinguished them were the forms of reelaboration of the past that they sought to achieve. We can consider Quintus Mucius, Servius, and Cicero to be the great protagonists of the discussion. One generation later, in a political context that had by then become stabilized, and while Labeo was active, it can be said to have been concluded, and Roman legal thought had definitively fixed the relationship with the original characteristics of its own history. The role played by Cicero in all this was unique. He appears as the defender of a thesis that was quite distinct from that of Mucius and Servius, but also as an indispensable source for an understanding of their thought. However, it would be a mistake to place him at the head of a current of ideas totally at odds with those of Mucius (though Crassus' position in the *De oratore* had radical and hypercritical overtones). Rather, they were different interpreters—in terms of culture, background, ideal and political horizons—of the same need: to give the city and the empire the measure of a new textuality and a new episteme of law.

For their own part, Mucius and Servius displayed a point of substantial convergence, albeit in the context of a diversity that cannot be underestimated, and which soon became, in later thought, a symbolic element of that crucial and troubled period. For both, the past of jurisprudence looked like a case-based paradigm that had become stratified over time, and was not to be discarded: of an empirically and tendentially qualitative model of prescriptive rationality, entrusted to the exemplarity of the response. To remain faithful to that hermeneutic style, and to succeed in combining it with the construction of an ontology and of formal law, without allowing the power of the new concepts to absorb and destroy the old cognitive schemes, was their great shared objective.

But barely beyond this common goal, their paths divided. For Mucius, tradition was something else as well; it acted as an explicit political bond, and weighed as more than just an option on behalf of a particular style of analysis; in Servius, on the other hand, it translated exclusively into a choice of method, and no longer had any directly political value.

Labeo never met Servius, but knew his writings well, and was able to evaluate his example with absolute clarity. The situation was however changing rapidly. A new phase was starting in the relationship between law and politics. The *princeps* cautiously tried to concentrate around his role the functions that were decisive for governing the empire. Law, even though it did not directly influence the constitutional framework, lay at the center of the chessboard: a dense network of magistracies—Roman, municipal, and provincial—assigned to control the jurisdiction adopted its guidelines in their edicts, making it the hub of the social regulation not only of the city but also of the most important part of the whole imperial community.[22] And the jurists, who were beginning to identify more with their shared specialization than with their (still) common origins in the ranks of the senatorial nobility, were called upon to choose and to take sides.

Pomponius (as we have seen) presented Labeo as the protagonist of a great renewal.[23] The loyalty to Roman antiquity emphasized so polemically by Capito is not in contrast with this judgment. Traditionalism and innovation were in effect two traits that Labeo managed to hold together without difficulty. The attachment to the past must have characterized above all his attitude toward the republican order—we might say his constitutional thought outside of the sphere of *ius,* though not entirely extraneous to its diffusion—and was employed as a weapon that was always potentially turned against the decisions of Augustus. The innovations, on the other hand, concerned the more strictly technical and specialized aspects of law, whose jurisprudential character he wanted at all costs to protect and reinforce with respect to the new political set-up.

3.

The boldest and most significant novelty of all of Labeo's thinking—as far as we can ascertain—regarded a doctrine in the field of contracts: this marks the reemergence of an underlying thread whose importance we have previously explained, and in relation to which we have already taken the measure of Mucius' work.

The *Iuris civilis* books sketched out—developing the symmetry between the forms of *contrahere* (contracting) and of *solvere* (resolving)—a pattern of descriptive categories of the entire phenomenology of obligations deriving from licit acts, present in the late-republican experience: ranging from the most ancient ones, realized through the utterance of certain words *(verbis)* or the delivery of something *(re)*, to the more recent ones, based solely upon an agreement between the parties, in whatever way it might be manifested *(consensu)*.[24]

It was the initial core of a classification destined to enjoy great and long-lasting fortune—but which took for granted the existence of an insuperable limitation: that in order to establish obligatory relationships sanctioned by *ius* it was necessary to have recourse to one of the acts required without exception by the civil law tradition (stipulation, loan, account-book entry, and little more), or else one of the figures indicated by the praetors in their edicts through the recognition of corresponding actions (purchase and sale, hiring and letting, partnership and mandate), and by this point (after Cicero) defined as belonging to the *ius gentium,* inasmuch as they could be traced back to the acceptance of ancient Mediterranean practices, incorporated into the Roman models of reciprocity and good faith ("Since Aulus Agerius sold to Numerius Negidius the slave in question, with regard to everything in compliance with that relationship Numerius Negidius must do or give on behalf of Aulus Agerius in accordance with good faith, let the judge Gaius Aquilius condemn Numerius Negidius with respect to Aulus Agerius; if it does not so appear, let him be acquitted": thus ran the formula protecting sale).

Modern jurists define the existence of such a bond as the rule of "typicality": no obligation can be established without an act specifically provided for by law. This was a principle destined to be swept away by the European legal systems—and especially by the individualistic bourgeois incorporation of Roman law—which would replace it with the opposing one of contractual liberty. The will of the subjects obliges the parties contracting through whatever type of legal scheme they consider to be suited to their interests, provided it is not in violation of a norm: the keystone of the legal order of the capitalist market.

It is difficult to exactly pinpoint the origin of the Roman preclusion; it was rooted in the invasiveness of archaic ritualism: no effect could derive from *ius* that did not have a correspondence in a verbal or gestural behavior already previously established and prescribed by the *mores.*

But the problem of somehow overcoming such a barrier would not have to wait for modern times to be raised; commercial development in the empire between the second and first centuries B.C. had already made manifest the need for legal protection of those types of trade mechanism not included among the few categories prefigured by the *ius civile* or by the edict: the only ones considered by Mucius. And yet the pressure would never be sufficiently strong or long-lasting to bring about a complete breakthrough, to the point of attaining stable recognition of full contractual autonomy.

The difficulty was both social and cultural. The economic drive—without a real industrial take-off behind it—would prove to be too intrinsically fragile to force any decisive breaks with tradition.[25] Nor for that matter did legal thought ever elaborate a theory of subjectivity capable of withstanding the burden of a drastic individualistic shift:[26] in the whole course of Roman history through to the Byzantine era, the capacity to completely resolve the formalism of exchange, realized through the universal equivalent of money (which had been clearly glimpsed by Paul), in the recognition just of consent between the parties as sufficient for the determination of the legal effects, would never be completely affirmed.[27]

This resistance demands careful interpretation. It probably sheds light on the persistence, in the depths of the conceptualizations of Roman legal thought, of a kernel element not entirely reelaborated within the abstract paradigm of the bare will of subjects rendered equal in their indistinct nature. The conceptually unresolved trace of the concrete material substance of trade in a world not dominated by the market; and therefore perceived in part as still lying outside the serial and quantitative formalism intrinsic to the circulation of goods: like a structure to be linked in its specificity, in order to produce effects on the plane of law, to the prior existence of a legal qualification that would correspond (of a contractual *nomen*, as the jurists would later say); a need that in its turn was an echo of a time when there was no *ius* except in the presence of a ceremonial and ritualistic typification.[28]

And yet attempts were made to shatter this bloc. The most significant one also proved to be the shortest-lived: a relatively brief moment in which the obstacle seemed to have been overcome, and the prospect emerged of a radical and "modern" solution.

It was linked to the (rather mysterious) history of the edict "on pacts" (*de pactis),* introduced by a praetor whose name we cannot identify, in an age not very distant from that of Quintus Mucius.[29] They were the years of the Roman "economic miracle," when the impetus of large-scale trade must have become increasingly strong so as to impose mature legal solutions suitable for the needs of the new reality.[30]

We do not know exactly what this text envisaged: the history of the edict before its "codification" by Salvius Julianus is enveloped in an obscurity that is very difficult to dispel. The fact remains that the choice of words itself appears quite significant: *pactum* was, with the verb *pacisci,* used as far back as the Twelve Tables, the most important term in the vocabulary of Roman consensualism, with a technical meaning—that of an "agreement" not endowed with a specific ritual, but which *ius* could in some way take into account—prior to the terminologies that spread later.[31] And it is also certain that equally powerful was the enunciation in which that word was included. Reconstructed through Ulpian, it must originally have run more or less as follows: "I will enforce pacts agreed between parties which have been made neither maliciously nor in contravention of a statute, plebiscite, or decree of the senate; nor as a fraud on any of these" (but perhaps there was also a reference to the prohibition of violence).[32]

It is therefore all the more surprising that in Julian's version, after this solemn declaration, only a single form of legal protection was foreseen: an "exception deriving from the pact," which did not serve to protect any agreement established outside of the schemes envisaged by *ius,* but could be proposed only by someone who had already been sued, to freeze the lawsuit brought against him, and to ensure the implementation of a clause featured in the margins of a typical contract with reference to which the plaintiff requested compliance (for instance a sale with the addition of a pact in which the purchaser promised not to ask the price before a certain date).[33]

The gap is inexplicable except as the outcome of a transformation that in the age of Hadrian (and of Ulpian) had drastically reduced the normative scope of this edict, turning it into a kind of fossil of a then abandoned evolutionary line. Evidently the praetor must originally have foreseen—in relation to the unequivocal general scope of his declaration, which by now floated like an inert relic in Ulpian's prose—other far more effective means for safeguarding agreements he had recognized: full-fledged atypical actions *(arbitria)* based on his discretional power—this was the praetorian jurisdiction's period of greatest creativity—and with a reference to good faith, in part similar to the formulas that governed the schemes of sale, hire, partnership, and mandate.

This reconstruction is not merely circumstantial. We are in fact able to assemble a sequence of late-republican documents in which the *pactum* figures unquestionably—and with great prominence—among the acts that can fully constitute legal bonds: a fact that does not correspond at all with the state of *ius* from Labeo onward. We can begin with two texts that we have already encountered: the passage of Mucius on *pacisci*—in which the latter is assimilated to the *legem dicere* and to "stipulating," in keeping with a perspective unthinkable at the time of Julian's edict—and the definition of law in the *Rhetorica ad Herennium,* where the *pactum* even features as one of the *partes iuris* (and how could it have attained such a position if it were not capable of fully determining legal effects?).[34] Then there is a series of Ciceronian documents, from the *Pro Caecina* ("What statute, what resolution of the senate, what edict of a magistrate, what diplomatic treaty or agreement, or—to return to men's private affairs—what will, what judicial formula of stipulation or of established pact cannot be misunderstood or distorted, if we wished to reduce things to the letter of the words, ignoring the intent, the reasonableness and the will of those who wrote them?");[35] to the *De inventione* ("A pact is that which is considered to be so just by those who make it that it acquires significance for the law");[36] the *De officiis* ("The question arises also whether pacts and promises must always be kept, 'when,' in the language of the praetors' edicts, 'they have not been secured through force or fraud'"—with a full quotation of the edict);[37] the *Partitiones oratoriae* ("Among the written texts, some are private, others public: public, such as the statute, the decree of the senate, the treaty; private, such as the testamentary tables, the established pact, the stipulation");[38] and the *Letters to Atticus* ("In fact, Pomptinus, according to the established pact, had already left . . .").[39] And we can conclude with a text of Servius-Alphenus (the previously discussed one about the slave who made an agreement with his master to be given his liberty in exchange for a sum of money),[40] and another by Seneca the Elder (written in a later period than the one being considered here, but taken from a work largely composed of materials from the late-republican era: "Acts performed under threat or under violence are not valid. Established pacts made in compliance with the laws are valid."[41]

It is impossible to explain away these statements by claiming that the term *pactum* is adopted therein to indicate the contracts of *ius gentium*. Any such hypothesis would be completely unfounded: *pactum* in these uses describes a vast and indeterminate notion, possibly in some cases inclusive of consensual contracts, but certainly much broader than just that group.[42] Moreover, in the *Pro Caecina* there is an allusion to a *formula pacti conventi* that unmistakably suggests the existence of jurisdictional protection through schemes lacking a specific contractual name.[43] There is no alternative but to admit that between the final years of Mucius and the age of Servius and Alphenus, alongside the "typical" consensualism of the contracts of the *ius gentium* (protected by formulas endowed with *nomen*), there developed, albeit in a fluid manner that had not yet been entirely conceptualized by the jurisprudence, an "atypical" consensualism which had emerged on the crest of the wave of economic growth. It was protected by the praetor in an edict whose outlines remain unclear, on the basis of his own discretional powers and taking advantage of the flexibility of the formulary procedure at the moment of its greatest creative impulse.[44]

It would not have required a great deal, at this point, to move definitively beyond typicality, and to transform the edict *de pactis* into an authentic charter of Roman contractual liberty. But that path was never taken. As in other situations, late-republican history (not only legal) presents its most peculiar aspect, that of a laboratory of a "modernity" that was barely delineated and then immediately dropped: perspectives, solutions, ideas, intellectual and social practices on the brink of emerging from antiquity, only to fall back into it, unfailingly and forever.[45]

It is difficult to say what broke the consensualist evolutionary line; certainly there was a consolidated legal tradition that opposed it, which saw in typicality a reaffirmation of a framework of customs and references not to be lost (an orientation which may have crossed the mind of Mucius himself, possibly faced with the first draft of the edict in question).[46] And certainly, as we said, there was no cultural elaboration capable of supporting the weight of the change: something similar to a fully individualistic construction of legal subjectivity, which might combine into a unitary vision the tendency to place greater emphasis on intentionality in the interpretation of legal acts carried out in accordance with the old schemes of the *ius civile* (especially stipulations and wills), with the drive toward full legal protection of agreements that did not fit into typical models. Nor were there groups and circles capable of putting these points of view on the agenda of the time: the social and intellectual evanescence of Rome's merchant classes, which would never succeed in giving rise to anything like a "bourgeois" context, is unquestionable and determinant.[47]

But it is probable that the decisive blow came with a new institutional development: the promulgation, in 17 B.C., by the decision of Augustus, of a Lex Iulia on private trials, which conclusively regulated the formulary procedure, sanctioning the definitive end of the *legis actiones*.[48] The measure significantly reduced the magistrate's autonomy, establishing a rigid civil law typicality of actions, each with its own precise denomination. Thus was created a binding symmetry between the "names" of the actions and the "names" of the acts being protected. It was an important step toward the stabilization of the text of the edict; but it was also a drastic obstacle to the possibility of recognizing agreements freely entered into by parties without a corresponding form in the edictal schemes. The difficulty might also be described as "technical," but behind it we can clearly glimpse the congenital fragility of an entire social and cultural world: the other face of the Roman "miracle."[49]

4.

The institutional closure did not, however, sweep away the substantive problem. And it would for that matter have been impossible, after decades of relatively broad contractual freedom, to return to a strict regime of typicality: the repercussions on the realities of commercial activity would have been too marked.

But other ways had to be found to ensure a good level of legal protection, even if outside the bounds of the edictal names. On the one hand, it was possible to attempt to redesignate transactions not expressly envisioned by the edict (without *nomen,* as the saying became) so as to bring them under the wing of the existing models in the *ius civile* or in the *ius gentium,* making use of subtle techniques of assimilation and adaptation. On the other, a solution was devised that succeeded in protecting the new relationships by recognizing the legal qualification not for the consensus as such, but for the reciprocity of the economic functions that were performed: that looked not at the moment of the agreement but at the effective intersection of the obligations and compliance by the contracting parties. It was a construction that was at the same time innovative and in line with the Roman normative and commercial experience, and which would represent an important development in the history of legal thought. And it was one of the inventions for which Labeo would above all be known.

Once again we are indebted to Ulpian—to a passage from his eleventh book *Ad edictum*—for a precise recollection of this doctrine:

> Labeo in his first book on the urban praetor defined which things are done by means of an *agere,* which are done through a *gerere,* and which through a *contrahere:* and he [defines] "act" as a word of general scope, inclusive of when one acts either with words, or through things, as in a stipulation or in a payment in cash; "contract," on the other hand, is a reciprocal obligation, what the Greeks call a *synallagma,* such as sale, hire, and partnership; "deed" is the operation carried out without the use of words.[50]

There is no reason to doubt the basic soundness of the text, both as regards possible alterations in late antiquity and its transcription by Justinian's compilers. Ulpian was also directly familiar with Labeo, whose commentary on the edict he rightly saw as the foundation of a literary tradition that, through similar works by Pedius and Pomponius, would come down to him.[51] He was particularly attracted by the writings that he called Labeonian "definitions" (we cannot say whether their author also used this word): he cited, for instance, those of "wanderer,"[52] "public place,"[53] "malice or fraud,"[54] "attendant,"[55] and "*ostentum* [sign]."[56]

It is difficult to say whether, in transmitting the citation we are looking at here, he went to the original, or if he simply—as happened on other occasions—transcribed it from Pomponius. The latter was, in turn, a faithful and careful reader of Labeo, drawing heavily on him, and who he saw (as we shall have an opportunity to appreciate) as a guiding star for the course of jurisprudence.[57] But everything suggests we are in the presence of a well-preserved passage of the earlier jurist's original thinking.

Labeo's *Ad edictum* was not used in Justinian's *Digesta* (nor were the commentaries *Ad Edictum* by Pedius and Pomponius). What we can attribute to him—actually quite a lot—comes to us from some 200 citations by later authors, almost all of them from Paul and Ulpian, but also Neratius, Celsus, Gellius, Venuleius, and Callistratus.[58] And there are still too many things we do not know about the work—the years in which Labeo wrote it, the ties between these dates and the period marking the consolidation of his hostility toward the principate, even the expository structures of the work, both in relation to the state of the text of the edict in that period, and with regard to the previous commentary by Ofilius—to have any hope of restoring the fragment in question to the context in which it must have belonged.[59]

It is certain in any case that the points of departure for Labeo's analysis were lexical terms taken from the text of the edict of the urban praetor that the jurist was studying, and which he was probably commenting upon in a lemmatic fashion—*agantur, gerantur, contrahantur*—although it is also possible that the jurist had found in the edict only two, or even only one, of the words he was examining, and that he introduced the other two himself to compare them with the first. But while there is no doubt about the theme treated by Ulpian when he inserted his reference to Labeo—the comment on the edict concerning the invalidity of acts performed under duress[60]—we are not at all certain about what topic induced Labeo to propose his "definition." It might conceivably be the same as Ulpian's, despite the disparity of the locations— the eleventh book for the Severan jurist, the first for Labeo—if we suppose (as would be correct) for the Augustan age a different structure of the edict from that of Julian: faint but not insignificant clues seem to point precisely in that direction.

Labeo was not concerned with reconstructing the meaning of the verbs in the language of the edict. He moved quite freely with respect to the text he was examining, and perhaps also with the intention of critiquing its choices. He was interested in the ontological relationship between the forms identified, not in the literal meaning of the terms, adopting a hermeneutic criterion that we have already observed in the work of Servius.[61] Otherwise he would probably have been forced to conclude that there was not much of a difference between those words, and that the edict muddled much more than it distinguished.

In late-republican legal Latin, *agere* and *gerere* were words marked by long use: both were sufficiently flexible to overlap in everyday legal language.[62]

The same, as we know, could not be said for *contrahere:* the term was certainly less worn, and was used to indicate the objective establishment of a relationship, an intersection, an exchange, rather than emphasizing the moment of the agreement underlying the relationship, as *pacisci* and *convenire* did. And it was with this meaning that the verb must have been employed, though not frequently, in the vocabulary of the edict, and which had appeared, as a full-blown category, in the thinking of Mucius.[63] Immediately afterwards came the transition to the noun: we have observed traces of it in the language of Servius.[64]

There can be no doubt that Labeo's approach was conditioned by these antecedents, and that his entire analysis was intended to develop the preceding elaboration, albeit on another level. His first problem was to distinguish the meaning of *contrahere* from other terms close to it in late-republican legal language, overturning the position of Mucius, who had made it a concept of general scope, the center of an overall description.

He therefore gave *agere* a generic significance, though it remained limited to the old acts of the *ius civile,* while *gerere* was explained in specific contrast with the other verb, by means of an unusual restriction of its semantic field, perhaps on the basis of its most remote meanings. In this way he cleared the stage for an innovative definition of *contractum*—the real center of his whole discourse—capable of taking on a conceptual value oriented in a previously unseen direction. His viewpoint emphasized the moment of exchange, of the objective intersection of undertakings (a point of view that may already have been foreshadowed by Servius, but not by Mucius).[65] He maintained the firm connection with the concept of obligation, provided it was reciprocal, and identified a symmetrically and objectively bilateral tie.

Everything rested on this identification. The heart of Labeo's paradigm was based on the reciprocity binding together the subjects involved in the contracting (*ultro citroque;* literally: "on this side and that"; a scheme that would recur in the *Ad edictum*).[66] And to reiterate the point even more forcefully, Labeo introduced a new element: the *synallagma* (Greek words crop up on various occasions in the jurist's writing: the culture of the time did not hesitate to use them when Latin seemed to lack an adequate form of expression for a new conceptual development someone wished to introduce).[67]

There is no doubt that concealed behind the generic nature of the reference lay very precise memories, not unknown to the jurist's readers: *synal-*

lagma was an erudite and infrequent term. One usage in particular clearly leads us to Aristotle, to a passage from the fifth book of the *Nicomachean Ethics*. The philosopher is analyzing the concept of "justice" *(dikaiosyne)* with the diaeretic-descriptive method forming part of the original nucleus of the treatise, devoted to the construction of the civil ethics that we have already discussed. Aristotle distinguished general justice from specific justice, dividing the latter into two kinds: distributive, which "consists of the apportionment of honors, wealth, and all other divisible things to those who form part of the citizenry"; and corrective, which consists of "the discipline of social relations" *(en tois synallagmasi diorthotikon)*.

> Of this there are two divisions; of social relationships some are voluntary and others involuntary—voluntary such as sale, purchase, lending at interest, pledging, lending without interest, depositing, and letting (they are called voluntary because the origin of these relations is voluntary), while of the involuntary some are secret, such as theft, adultery, poisoning, procuring, enticement of slaves, treacherous murder, false witness, and others are violent, such as assault, imprisonment, murder, robbery, maiming, slander, insult.[68]

Synallagma served here to indicate the objectively bilateral relationship between two subjects, independent of their will (which might be present or entirely lacking, as the philosopher explained in detail): it established a modality of community life. We are a long way here from any genuinely legal construction: social anatomy (an Aristotelian talent), not theory of law. The examples adopted to illustrate the two-part division were taken directly from commercial practice or from criminal cases as understood in common sense terms, without any further formal elaboration: they had uncertain and very rough boundaries. An enormous distance separated them from the rigorous analytics of Roman legal figures. In the field reserved for *ius* the parts were reversed, with respect to philosophy. The jurists there held the place occupied in the latter by Plato and Aristotle: the side of concepts and forms; while the Greek masters were unable to progress beyond a barely sketched empiricism. This text alone is sufficient to describe the abyss separating them from Roman thought.[69]

The difference did not concern Labeo. He was interested in what Aristotle had constructed before the threshold of law: a logical scheme that described a relational syntax based on bilaterality, so as to link to this idea the ontology of contracting. To complete the legal formalization of his paradigm he could draw on something quite different: the Roman model of *obligatio*. The bare bilaterality of the relationship *(synallagma)*, in order to become *contractum*, would have to be determined by both sides *(ultro citroque)* through a bond that constituted an obligation. Greek philosophy could help to clarify the interplay of the forms, but the talent for legal abstraction was already entirely Roman.

Labeo was very familiar with Aristotle. Recently Andronicus of Rhodes had brought out in Rome a major edition of the philosopher's achromatic corpus,[70] which was certainly owned (at least in part) by Cicero. It was as a result of perusing these books that Trebatius first attempted to explore the *Topics*, without understanding a great deal.[71] And if Trebatius read it, how could Labeo not have done?

A number of other passages in the *Ad edictum* suggest that Labeo devoted particular attention to the *Nicomachean Ethics*. The first can be found in a text of Paul: "By hire of *opus* Labeo says that by these words is meant that work which the Greeks call *apotelesma* not that which they call *ergon*, that is, some completed product of an executed work."[72] The citation of the Severan jurist reproduced, as we know, another important moment of Labeo's thought: the construction of the concept of *opus locatum*, in which a significant role was played by the comparison between the two Greek terms—one of which was used only very rarely. Interestingly, in two passages from the *Nicomachean Ethics* we find the combined use of precisely these terms, in contexts such as to allow Labeo to easily deduce the difference he had underscored: "We must therefore say that every virtue, in accordance with the object of which it is a virtue, perfects it [*apotelei*] and makes good its labor [*ergon*]";[73] and also: "labor [*ergon*] is accomplished [*apoteleitai*] through wisdom and ethical virtue."[74]

In another passage, Labeo offered an important clarification regarding the definition of *metus*, duress. In this case, we are able to read him through Ulpian: "Labeo says that duress is to be understood not as any alarm whatever, but as fear of a greater evil."[75] And Aristotle, while analyzing, at the beginning of the third book of the *Nicomachean Ethics*, the concepts of "voluntary acts" and "involuntary acts"—in a text that should be linked to the text previously examined—and describing a series of behaviors that could be qualified as involuntary, referred to those performed "out of fear of a greater evil":[76] a model of expression identical to that used by Labeo.

There is sufficient reason to consider the derivation well founded. And having ascertained the plausibility of the reading, it can be hypothesized that for Labeo the notion of *synallagma* must actually have been the key enabling him to formulate the idea of the contract as *ultro citroque obligatio,* even if the Roman category represented an entirely original specification of the Greek scheme, and if in the writing of the *Ad edictum* the relationship that the two concepts must have had originally appears to have been reversed, and the *ultro citroque obligatio* proved to be independent of the Greek example, evoked solely as a subsequent support for reference and confirmation.

5.

Labeo's definition concluded with a series of examples, which also seemed to hark back stylistically to the text of the *Nicomachean Ethics,* and more probably to the Mucian precedent as well. And it is precisely the solution to the problem posed by this last step that will allow us to grasp the most important implication of the whole analysis. The reference to the relations of the *ius gentium,* which a fairly well-consolidated tradition already defined as "contracts," did not in itself present any obscure points: in the three figures mentioned, the evident presence of an *ultro citroque obligatio* as the constituent form of the scheme cannot be called into discussion. The difficulty comes from another direction: from the need to understand whether Labeo considered those examples to be exhaustive of the category of the contract—whether, that is, they constituted a limited set, respecting the principle of typicality—or whether instead they simply represented the beginning of an open sequence.

In the first case—if Labeo intended the *ultro citroque obligatio* to be limited to the consensualism already typified by the *ius gentium*—the scope of his thinking would have to be reduced to a simple clarification concerning the structure of those relationships alone, with no broader perspective. But in that case the entire construction would be rendered inexplicable. Why should the jurist have broken up the unitary structure of the classification by Mucius, who had also included under the concept of *contrahere* relationships established *verbis* or *re?* What would there have been to gain—theoretically or practically—from unhinging that elaboration to limit the category of *contrahere* to the ambit of the figures of the *ius gentium,* and probably not even of all of them, since the exclusion of mandate had been no accident?[77] And finally, why, if Labeo's goal really was to describe just the figures of the *ius gentium,* would he have decided not to mention the element of consensuality—which by then had become the most distinctive feature of those relationships—and instead to emphasize so forcefully only the aspect of objective bilaterality and of the *ultro citroque obligatio?*

If, however, we think of the alternative solution—that the reference to the three contracts of the *ius gentium* had a merely exemplary function—everything appears in a different light, and all the choices make sense.

Labeo had elaborated a much narrower category of *contrahere* than the one proposed by Mucius—leaving out of it the relations established *verbis* or *re*—because he was pursuing a new and more advanced objective: an extended use of the ontology of contracting, not only to better reelaborate and discipline figures already envisaged in the civil law and edictal tradition, but also in order to construct a limitlessly extendable paradigm, which, setting out from the identification of a form present in relations already protected by *ius,* could serve as an analogical model (be taken *ad exemplum,* as Servius used to say)[78] for the legal qualification of new figures of mercantile exchange, even in the absence of a specific edictal provision, and after the end of the most innovative experience of the edict on pacts. From this point of view, it makes perfect sense that the jurist should have concentrated on the contracts of the *ius gentium* and that, despite this, he should have focused entirely on the paradigm of the intersection of obligations, and not on consensus. He was proposing, for the legal recognition of the new relationships, the same path that, centuries earlier, had led to the progressive qualification of sale, of hire, and of partnership, that is to say, of the nucleus that had engendered Roman commercial law: to set out—as the praetor had done—from the objective existence of the exchange, of the reciprocity of obligations and their performance in accordance with the ancient Mediterranean practices, and to protect the reliability *(bona fides)* of these operations, and then go on to the identification of consensus as an essential and determining element, though with the necessity of its reduction to predetermined types. If the form of their essence—reciprocity as the basis of trust—could be isolated within those first schemes, and if it could be projected in an ontology, then the way was open for that procedure to be repeated, without the restriction of new and specific edictal provisions. It did not represent the complete overcoming of the barrier of typicality, as would have been ensured by a direct recognition of legal effects deriving from the bare consent of the parties; aside from the will of the subjects, it was still necessary to identify a structure that, though transfigured into a form, somehow related back to the material nature of the exchange. The path based entirely on consensus—the route attempted by the edict on pacts—had proven to be impracticable. But the alternative solution kept open a breach, and satisfied demands and expectations that, even if they had been unable to impose and defend more "modern" outcomes, were not, however, completely expendable.

That Labeo had moved in the direction we are reconstructing here is shown not only by considerations pertaining to the internal consistency of his analysis, but also by some unequivocal items of testimony. The first comes from his *Posteriores*—published posthumously, and used by Justinian's compilers through an epitome made of it by Javolenus between the end of the first and the beginning of the second century A.D.: "No one can be regarded as having sold a thing, the ownership of which the parties do not intend to pass to the purchaser; this is either a case of hire or some other kind of contract."[79] Labeo (there are excellent reasons to attribute this text to him, and not to his epitomizer)[80] was examining a particular relationship of exchange in which the transfer of an asset took place without there being a transfer of ownership. Such a transaction could not, in the jurist's view, fall within the model of sale—because otherwise the economic function underlying that scheme would have been completely clouded—but instead had to be qualified either as hire or as "some other kind of contract," for which no *nomen* was available. This is a decisive notation: evidently Labeo considered contractual genres to be an open series, subject only to the principle of the *ultro citroque obligatio*.

From the *Posteriores* let's return to the *Ad edictum*, again through the mediation of Ulpian: "You asked me to give you money on loan; I did not have the money, but gave you an object for you to sell and use the price of. If you did not sell it or did sell it but did not receive the money as a loan, it is safer, as

Labeo says, to bring an *actio praescriptis verbis,* as if the transaction of a specific contract had been concluded between us."[81] The case under examination was quite close to the form later typified by jurisprudence in the model of *aestimatum,* or valuation, protected by a special *actio aestimatoria.* If we take as a point of reference Ulpian's account in the thirty-second book *Ad edictum* on the introduction of this new means of protection,[82] Labeo's proposal seems to be a decisive foreshadowing of it, capable of orienting it toward the birth of the new action: about which, however, the jurist said nothing, merely suggesting the advisability of acting *praescriptis verbis.* (We shall have more to say on this shortly. The jurist judges this remedy to be "safer"; the alternative, not explicitly indicated in the version of the text that has survived, was in all likelihood the action of mandate). And in any case, the concluding argumentation, formulated with a certain degree of circumspection, clearly reiterated Labeo's idea that the types of contract did not have to coincide with those expressly indicated in the edict, but rather depended on an ontological form in which the ordering capacity of the entire phenomenology (the objective pursued by Mucius) was sacrificed on behalf of a definition of essence, the analogical grounds for an open series of identifications.

The recognition of new contractual types meant, first of all, the possibility of their specific procedural protection. This, in the end, had been the obstacle against which, following the Lex Iulia concerning private trials, the programs of the edict on pacts had foundered. Labeo managed to elegantly circumvent the difficulty with a highly creative strategem: he suggested making use of what he called (as we have just seen) *agere praescriptis verbis,* that is, a formula conceded on a case by case basis by the praetor (and therefore defined as *in factum*), the opening of which was to be preceded by a *praescriptio* (a "pre-scripture," or pre-writing) indicating the circumstances for which the praetor was being asked to intervene (in the case in question: the existence of a reciprocal obligation that was taken to constitute a contract), followed thereafter, as was the rule, by an *intentio* (the part of the formula in which the claims of the plaintiff were set forth, along with, in some cases, the counterdeductions of the defendant), which would have as its content a request that was not precisely quantified (*incerta:* "all that the defendant must give, do, and guarantee"),[83] and without indicating the name of any specific action, but conceived as a point of law (*in ius:* because reciprocity analogically constituted true obligations) and in accordance with good faith (the reference to which was also a consequence of the analogical extension of the contracts of the *ius gentium*). The rule of typicality was safe: no new actions were created, use was just made of a formula constructed on the example of other typical actions; and the procedural use of *praescriptiones* was attested as early as the age of Cicero, and was common in the practice of the first century A.D.[84] Labeo therefore was not inventing anything new; he was merely proposing its extension onto a new terrain; and in any case he was careful not to define the procedure as a new "action": this result would not be reached until much later.[85]

Another Labeonian text, also transcribed by Ulpian, reaffirmed the line followed by the jurist: "Labeo writes that if you have sold me a library on the condition that the Capua magistrates in turn sell me a site on which to house it, and, through my own fault, I do not seek a site from the magistrates, there is no question that it is possible to act *praescriptis verbis*."[86] The specific aspects of the case ensured that the failure to hand over the land made it impossible to have recourse to the action of sale (although Ulpian was not of this opinion). Labeo, however, felt that there was a reciprocal obligation, and therefore a contractual scheme different from that of sale, which could be protected by employing a formula *praescriptis verbis*. Once again there was the same reasoning observed in the preceding text, where, what's more, the reference to this type of *agere* was directly linked to the definition of a new relationship as "contract"; and the combination of the two pieces of testimony allows us to observe in its entirety the overall conceptual framework drawn up by Labeo: identification of a transactional scheme not foreseen by the edict; its "contractual" qualification through an analogical comparison with the schemes of the *ius gentium* and the discovery of an *ultro citroque obligatio* in its structure; and the consequent procedural protection by means of an *agere praescriptis verbis*.

The achievements of the formal revolution emerge with great clarity in Labeo's thought: the establishment of an ontology guided by a rigorous and consistent legal rationalism—the first one to manifest itself to such a complete extent.

Rationalism can be seen, first of all, in the very need to "define." Then there was the use, with great conviction, of analogy (which Labeo also employed in his grammatical studies)[87] as a guiding principle capable of directing the growth of his knowledge and its disciplining force. Finally, the faith—with and beyond Servius —in the organic and wholly formalized deployment of *ius* around conceptual schemes that entirely contained it, predetermining its lines of development even outside the other normative offices of the *res publica*—the popular assemblies, the magistracies—now subject to direct pressure from the *princeps*. The recourse to equity—both "civil" and "natural"—that we have witnessed in Labeo did nothing to alter this paradigm: instead it completed it, integrating flexibility and nature—a nature not dominated by chance but by reason—within a single overall design, under the control of the interpreter.

In a stimulating book, Peter Stein hypothesizes that Labeo, perfectly aware of the implications of his work, qualified for the first time as "rules"—perhaps translating from Mucius—his normative solutions, reserving the term "definition" for his descriptive statements.[88] Whether or not this idea is credible, it is certain that the jurist must have fully grasped the importance and value of his method, capable as it was of establishing a new relationship between interpretation and normative text, as well as presenting on new foundations the traditional primacy of jurisprudence, contending with the new political power for the monopoly on legal innovation (hence the sense of the reference to "innovate" present in Pomponius' judgment).

It is hard not to see in this position a certain resistance to the pressure that the Augustan principate had begun to exert on jurisprudence. The autonomy of legal knowledge defended by Labeo—enhanced by the construction of an increasingly complex theoretical organism—aimed instead to subordinate all normative activity to the intellectual authority of the jurists. The web of concepts that now governed their expertise constituted the almost definitive fabric of a great new science that the governing power had to take into account, making compromises in which the reciprocal balance of forces would be determined from case to case by the conditions prevailing in a given moment.

Thus began—precisely in that period and in that context—the uninterrupted dialogue between law and politics that would constitute, despite the continuous change of situations and events, one of the great motifs of Western history. A relationship that from this point forward we should not consider as intrinsically unequal, one that forced a helpless science to measure itself against a far more combative interlocutor with a tendency to abuse its power. But rather as a face-off between a body of knowledge itself girded with power—the power that derives from the production and control of techniques capable of disciplining the world and legitimizing those rules in the very act of establishing them, precisely because they were presented as the expression of a separate and self-referential rationality—and a political set-up that certainly could claim to have the monopoly on force and the concrete capacity to use it, and yet could no longer manage them beyond a certain point without the sanction of law, and without principles justified by an authoritative and intransigent science.

18

The Definition of Characteristics

The commentary on the edict, as we know, was not Labeo's only work, although in all likelihood it remained his most important and widely read one. Even if we discount two isolated claims that the jurist was the author of books of letters and responses,[1] we can attribute to him with certainty at least three other writings (according to Pomponius, he left some 400 scrolls):[2] a commentary on the Twelve Tables, of which only a few citations in Gellius survive (possibly an exercise in legal antiquarianism of, let's say, a Servian type, in which it would be unwise to exclude an ideological intent: a recovery of Roman archaism polemically different from the kind of restoration praised by Augustan propaganda),[3] and two texts, one dealing with problems and definitions, and the other an anthology of cases, the *Pithana*[4] and the *Libri posteriores,*[5] the latter published posthumously. In both, the order of exposition must have adopted Mucian sequences. In the *Pithana* (literally: "things – maxims – persuasive," or perhaps we might better say "plausible"), composed by and large after 18 B.C., and published one book at a time; the Greek title, which alluded in various ways to the choice of the *Horoi,* reflected far more than just a generic philosophic inclination—an option with influences from Aristotle and the Stoics of Megara.[6] It also revealed Labeo's effort to construct in an exemplary manner, through a careful assembly of maxims and problems, the syntax of a model of reasoning that was the mature product of the revolution of formalism: a full-fledged epistemological paradigm of legal knowledge, enclosed in a highly developed interplay of abstractions, capable of ensuring the formulation of maxims that were difficult to disprove. Greek philosophy was only a laboratory from which to draw on freely in order to attain entirely independent results, on the plane of another science.[7]

In the *Posteriores* the more markedly theoretical interests gave way to arguments oriented toward the relationship with tradition and engagement with previous authors (though set against a background of considerable thematic heterogeneity), with Trebatius on the one hand, and Ofilius, Servius, and Quintus Mucius from another perspective. In little more than a century, the literarization of Roman legal knowledge had produced impressive results, and Labeo must have had to master a textual universe already so complex and composite as to pose not insignificant problems in selecting and ordering citations.

From a narrowly political point of view, the tenacious opposition to the principate of Augustus had of course been completely unsuccessful. But being thwarted did not result in Labeo's defeat, much less the marginalization of his work. In fact, in his untiring efforts to rein in the new power and to defend the prerogatives of the aristocratic jurisprudence, he had succeeded in forging and strengthening a model of a jurist who made the autonomy of his practice and the directly normative value of the solutions he proposed a refined and effective instrument against any danger that the eminently jurisprudential nature of Roman law might be clouded, as well as any changes in the ancient equilibria.

The persistence of the Labeonian model is one of the most significant elements in any account of the history of legal knowledge throughout the first century A.D., as well as for some of the second, at least until the turning point that came with Julian. We do not know to what extent Labeo was aware of the importance of his proposal and the favor it would meet. But it is safe to say that he was not a loser; and his constant commitment to writing, in the seclusion of his country villa, may indicate some perception of a task that cannot be measured in terms of a single lifetime or of individual political for-tunes.

The success of his line did not, all the same, entail for the generations that followed any involvement in the original hostility toward the principate. This trait was not transmitted, in part thanks to the caution of Augustus, who immediately abandoned any Caesarian program in the field of law, and surrounded himself with jurists—Trebatius and Ateius Capito above all—who were certainly not proponents of any project that might prove subver-sive of the ancient jurisprudential primacy. The very institution of the *ius respondendi ex auctoritate principis*—a concession through which Augustus re-inforced with his own authority the value of the responses of certain authors that he chose himself, and which wound up having a controlling and discrim-inating effect on a task that had always been at the heart of the social function of jurisprudence—was used with such discretion, also to bring order to an activity that really had long been in a state of confusion, that no serious reac-tions were provoked.[8]

And so it happened that, after Augustus, in political contexts in which the principate increasingly appeared to be a solution without alternatives, the un-questionable attraction of Labeo's exemplarity shed its contingent ideologi-cal frame, and was reworked in order to delineate the boundaries of a historic compromise that jurisprudence sought to maintain for more than a century. In the silent agreement that the jurists would make with the power of the *princeps,* they guaranteed the new institution loyalty and collaboration (albeit with varying degrees of conviction and adherence, depending on different personal inclinations and shifts in political circumstances), receiving in ex-change a substantial assurance that the traditional "jurisprudential" hierarchy in the production of law would be preserved. The *princeps* chose for the mo-ment not to assume the role of legislator, but instead to himself become a jurist among jurists—or what has been called a "respondent" *princeps*.

This was not, however, a linear process. We can consider much of the first century—in particular the years between the death of Augustus and that of Nero, but probably also the age of Domitian—as a difficult period in the story we are recounting: an era of shadows and obstacles, dispelled only by a few brief periods of tranquility. Many traces immediately appear to be significant: a certain rarefaction of truly important figures and works, both as regards the flourishing of talents between the late republic and the Augustan principate, and with respect to the period that would dawn later, with the work of great jurists ranging from Nerva to the Severans; an extreme dearth of biographical information; convergent indications in the ancient tradition, from Tacitus to Suetonius, and from Seneca to Pomponius:

> Soon after this Cocceius Nerva, one of the Emperor's constant companions, a man learned in all law, human and divine, unassailed in his position, and in full health of body, made up his mind to die. When Tiberius heard of it, he came and sat beside him, inquired of him his reasons, and implored him not to carry out his design; impressing upon him at last how distressing it would be to himself, and how damaging to his reputation, if his nearest friend were to escape from life without cause. Nerva declined all conversation, and persisted in his abstinence from food. Those who knew his mind best reported that his inner view of the evils of the *res publica* had filled him with terror and indignation, and he had, in indignation and fear, while he was as yet unscathed, yet unassailed, decided for an honorable death.[9]

> With regard to the jurists too, as if intending to do away with any practice of their science, [Caligula] often threatened that he would see to it, by heaven, that no one other than himself could give responses any more.[10]

> The jurists [after the death of Claudius] came crawling out of their dark corners, pale and thin, with hardly a breath in their bodies, as though just coming to life again.[11]

> He [Gaius Cassius Longinus] was consul along with Quartinus in Tiberius' time, and was considered a great authority by citizens right up until the emperor banished him. Exiled by him to Sardinia, before his death he was recalled by Vespasian.[12]

> And from that time [after Augustus] this concession [the *ius publice respondendi*] began to be sought as a privilege.[13]

Different voices, all developing the same theme. Opened, in Tacitus' deeply felt evocation, by the exquisitely political suicide of Nerva: the most prominent jurist of his generation, consul in 22, a committed Labeonian, and, like him, a republican in spirit (he may also have inspired the tormented republicanism of the early Tiberius), whose doctrines were still cited by Paul and Ulpian.[14] A death "unassailed," an extreme testimonial of rigor and intransigence in the face of the collapse of a governmental action whose unworthiness—for someone who had been so close to the *princeps*—could not be escaped: those truly were the worst years, in the wake of the crisis of 31 and the death of Sejanus.

Next comes the highly vivid portrait of an exasperated and wrathful Caligula—as far away as can be imagined from the calculated prudence of Augustus, who had been faced with the likes of Labeo—in Suetonius' colorful account: with the *princeps* attempting to shake off the troublesome jurists, and his temptation to simply eliminate them entirely, replacing their intolerable presence with his singular self. Those same jurists whom Seneca described with pitiless irony—in an exaggeration both effective and grotesque —as pale and unkempt (they were not all like Nerva), emerging from the shadows in which they had concealed themselves, finally reassured by the death of Claudius. And finally the laconic notation (in keeping with his style) of Pomponius, with a reference to the exile inflicted by Nero on the very prestigious Cassius Longinus, who had survived unharmed the principates of Tiberius, Caligula, and Claudius. Scenes and memories that all reflect, from various angles and with different sensibilities, what we can consider to be the atmosphere around the middle of the first century: a sort of topos suspended between historiography, literature, and legal studies, which preserved the memory of a general deterioration of relations and of increasing confrontation, putting jurisprudence into an uneasy position if not actually with its back to the wall.

Read against such a background, the last, very brief Pomponian notation takes on no small significance. The author was sketching out, again in the *Enchiridion,* the history of the *ius respondendi*. The institution had undergone, in his view, a varied and uneven development; he seemed to appreciate the original idea of Augustus, subsequently taken up by Hadrian, which was (in his assessment) intended to renew and restore the prestige of the jurists. But he did not fail to observe that between those two moments there had been an interval of enfeeblement (if not actually of degeneration), in which *ius respondendi* was no longer obtained on the basis of the talent and authority possessed by illustrious figures, who had earned them in their own field of expertise, but instead was conceded graciously (as a "privilege") by the *princeps* to those faithful to him, with no consideration of achieved merits. The period of darkness underlined by Pomponius coincided precisely with the age identified previously, with the middle of the first century: the death of Nerva, the wrath of Caligula, the fears of Claudius' time, and the exiles inflicted by Nero constituted the chain of events that could explain the decline of the *ius respondendi,* reduced to the occasional concession of a privilege, which was no longer determined by the recognition of great personalities.

2.

It is hard to ascertain to what degree the decay of the governmental function that wore away for long periods at the Julian-Claudian principate actually undermined the delicate equilibrium set up by Labeo. Overall, the terms of the solution seem to have withstood the test, and indeed contributed to reinforcing the vocation of jurisprudence as specialization, as well as its establishment as a separate circle. The dominant trait was caution, what in the *Apocolocyntosis* was presented as flight and cowardice (and probably really was in some cases). It was an attitude that even Cassius Longinus did not entirely forgo: though he was the figure who stood out most, he too chose silence and reticence on a number of occasions.

In reality, a tendency of genuine hostility toward the principate—something akin to a republican current of opposition—never emerged in those years. The jurists (at least the most important ones) did try to follow the action of the government, if not to support it. The relationship between intellectuals and power took on dimensions and tones that were unprecedented for the ancient world: Seneca's personal example and his philosophical research illuminated the scene with what was the only authentic Roman contribution to building a public ethics, prior to the work of Ulpian;[15] thereafter the field was entirely dominated by the formalism of legal discourse. But the outlook was one of collaboration, albeit within a network of guarantees, and not of resistance.

And the jurists were divided among themselves as well, sometimes passionately so, though without ever renouncing a certain group solidarity. Grafted onto the shared basis just mentioned were a variety of choices of a technical-legal no less than a political-legal nature. In the period between the middle of the first century A.D. and the central years of the second, jurisprudence seems to have itself distinguished internally—as happened by tradition in philosophical, rhetorical, medical, or grammatical studies—at least two "schools": the "Sabinian" and the "Proculian" (from the names of two figures whom we shall discuss immediately, though the origin of the division should actually be traced back to the much earlier rivalry between Capito and Labeo). It is highly probable that the distinction carried less weight than we might be persuaded to think by reading Gaius and Pomponius (our sources for nearly all the information that we have on this point), and that it should be considered only as an interpretative model proposed by the two authors in order to provide a summary overall view, but destined to be discarded in the transition from handbooks (the *Enchiridion* and the *Institutiones*) to more in-depth works.[16] The fact remains that every attempt to ascribe the diversity between the two groups to unequivocal political or scientific attitudes (the Proculians as favorable to the principate, the Sabinians as philo-republicans, for instance), does not stand up to careful examination.[17] What we are faced with is merely a diverse array of personal orientations, mediated by weak and nebulous affiliations, set within a common attempt to preserve, in a period of difficulty and danger, a professional independence threatened by the recurrence of repressive and "tyrannical" episodes capable of bringing about an early and unexpected crisis of regime.

Three figures in particular attract attention: Sabinus, Cassius, and Proculus (although the first and the third appear not to have been deemed worthy by Tacitus of even a single mention: from the viewpoint of an entirely political historiography such as his, the grayness of caution—that did not even deserve to be considered—was the sole color of these personages). From a strictly legal perspective, Sabinus appears to be the most significant figure: his most important work—a short composition concerning the *ius civile* in just three books—led in fact to the definitive stabilization of this field and the construction of a text that would become the chief point of reference both for the major civil law commentaries of Pomponius, Paul, and Ulpian and (probably) for the handbook by Gaius.[18] The backdrop to his work was a fairly limited set of dealings, of no great political or cultural prominence, with Sejanus and Tiberius: relations that outlived the suicide of Nerva (who Sabinus did not like) and that are clearly testified to by the concession of the *ius re-*

spondendi.[19] He also wrote a commentary on the edict (although all that survives is a citation by Paul: it was not destined to enjoy a great fortune)[20] and some other minor writings, including an antiquarian text titled *Memorialia,* perhaps with radically different motivations from those that we have identified in Labeo's thought.[21]

We may in fact consider Sabinus—who came from the equestrian order, had no great family fortune to support him, and was therefore biographically distant from all aristocratic ideals—to be the authentic anti-Labeo of the first century. Obviously, he did not contest the legacy of the scientific revolution, or the technical and specialist depth that the author of the *Ad edictum* and the *Pithana* had brought to legal analysis, or even a now inalienable separation of law from political power: in this sense, none of the later jurists could have claimed not to be Labeonian. But besides rejecting any ideological involvement hostile to the principate, and remaining loyal to the alliance already supported (with Augustus) by Capito and Trebatius, Sabinus denied with great conviction that the autonomy of jurisprudence could venture—as Labeo had held, making it a crucial element of his thought—so far as to assert a direct normative value for the rules it introduced. This must have been a distinguishing feature of the politics of law in those decades, and Sabinus took a clear stand. First of all, he rejected Labeo's doctrine of the contract as reciprocal obligation and the possibility of its analogical extension, choosing instead to repropose and develop Mucius' classification, inasmuch as it was descriptive of existing law. Moreover, he did not hesitate to go further, disputing the very foundation of Labeo's theory:

> A rule is something which briefly describes how a thing is. The law may not be derived from a rule, but a rule must arise from the law as it is. By means of a rule, therefore, a brief description of things is handed down and, as Sabinus says, is, as it were, a summary of the case [the *causae coniectio,* a phase in the trial debate], which loses its force as soon as it becomes in any way defective.[22]

The fragment comes from a commentary by Paul on the work of Plautius, a jurist from the late first century A.D. not utilized by Justinian's compilers;[23] and it is likely that, on the whole, it bears witness to Sabinus' thought more than being a literal transcription of it. Certain elements, however, are unquestionable. Above all, the first part of the text, even if it is not taken directly from Sabinus, must have reflected his doctrine; otherwise the subsequent reference—in evident continuity with the preceding statements—would have been entirely incongruous coming from Plautius, who was an attentive reader of the quoted master. Second, the enunciation of the most important point—"The law may not be derived from a rule, but . . ."—is formulated as an exhortation, which contains an explicit reference to an opposing hypothesis, hinted at and then immediately overturned into its very opposite; and the unnamed interlocutor in this polemic could have been none other than Labeo, whose thought moved in quite a different direction: an adversary on the same level as Sabinus, though perhaps too elevated for Plautius. Finally, the function of the rule in this doctrine was based on a model that lay right at the center of Sabinus' work: descriptive completeness guided by "brevity." The effort to achieve a synthesis of the civil law tradition had in fact been the chief impulse of the jurist's work, as the expository thread of the *Iuris civilis* books confirms beyond any doubt.

In response to Labeo's proposal, Sabinus delineated a completely different hierarchy of tasks and goals for jurisprudence: a change to which at least two orders of ideas must have contributed. One was the abandonment of the more demanding implications of Labeonian (and perhaps also Servian) rationalism. The other was an awareness of the need to attain a redistribution of roles in the relationships between jurists and the constitutional functions more directly controlled by the *princeps*: to begin, that is, to define, perhaps with greater realism, though without being tantamount to surrender, the terms of the compromise that Labeo had so strenuously attempted to establish in the conditions of his time.

Sabinus enjoyed a very long life: he survived unscathed the final grim phase of the Tiberian age, which, as we have seen, proved fatal to Nerva, who chose to follow the *princeps* into isolation on Capri; he witnessed, to the best of our knowledge without negative consequences, the decline of the classicist dreams of the time of Augustus, and we find him (probably) still at work in the early years of the principate of Nero.[24] Political convulsions hindered the consolidation of the compromise between jurists and the *princeps*; and for that matter the portion of Labeonism that had already been assimilated by jurisprudence prevented an excessively subordinate attitude from taking root: it was probably this subterranean resistance that provoked the outburst by Caligula mentioned by Suetonius. The early years of the principate of Nero seemed to offer some rays of hope, but the illusion was short-lived; in 65 A.D. the repression struck at the most prestigious of Sabinus' pupils: Gaius Cassius Longinus, an aristocrat steeped in pro-republican culture, a descendant of Quintus Aelius Tubero and Servius Sulpicius Rufus.[25] Cassius, young, brilliant, very much in the public eye in Tiberius' time, and close to Sejanus, had already experienced some difficult moments in the final phase of Caligula's rule, at the end of 41, and had made a cautious alliance with Claudius. Relations with Nero immediately became tense,[26] as testified by an invaluable passage from the *Annals*.

Tacitus was recounting the murder, in 61, of Pedanius Secondus—of noble Roman-Spanish lineage, a life of career success and power—which took place, in obscure circumstances, in his magnificent Roman residence, at the hand of a slave (perhaps because the master capriciously denied the slave his liberty, after a price had already been agreed, or else due to torrid sexual rivalry: this too was part of domestic life in imperial Rome).[27] Probably at the behest of the *princeps* himself, the senate assumed control of the trial, bringing it within its own jurisdiction. According to an ancient prescription, confirmed by the Silanian senatorial decree of 10 A.D., in a case of the murder of a master in his own home, all the slaves who lived with him were to be tortured and executed. The atrocious reasoning behind this law—"the slave is no easy chattel," Plato had written[28]—would be reflected in the detached prose of Ulpian, who commented about it some two centuries later: "no home can be safe except if slaves are compelled, under threat of death, to guard their masters both from members of the household and from outsiders."[29] A kind of implacable objective responsibility hung over those unfortunates, obliging them to become the most ferocious guardians of the safety of their masters; they would pay with their lives for any shortcomings in vigilance.

But in the case of the murder of Pedanius, the strict application of the law would have led to terrible consequences. There were 400 slaves living in the home of the murdered man ("under the same roof," as the decree of the senate read),[30] which would require mass torture and executions, certainly resulting in the sacrifice of many "innocent lives" (as Tacitus wrote).[31] Even allowing for the suspicion that the murderer might not have acted alone, and that the complicity involved might suggest a genuine servile conspiracy, indiscriminate punishment would have to be meted out to a vast number of slaves, who could not possibly, even with the maximum diligence, have known about and been able to thwart it. Their number certainly included women and children.

Among the senators there must have been a certain body of opinion in favor of a lenient approach. It is likely that Nero himself would not have been displeased by a solution that avoided a bloodbath: the plebs of the capital, whose animosity he did not want to incur, had displayed unusual favor toward the slaves.[32] And Seneca—whom Nero still had at his side—certainly supported a far less intransigent model of relations between masters and slaves: a line of thought expressed soon afterwards in one of the letters to Lucilius.[33]

On the day of the trial debate, it was none other than Cassius Longinus who stood up to speak. His speech made history. Tacitus reports, reliably—though probably with some reelaboration—the essential elements. The jurist spoke passionately in favor of a rigorous application of the law, and thus for a guilty sentence: it was not possible to preserve slavery without recourse to terror, he claimed. But it is the beginning of his speech which interests us for now:

> I have frequently, Conscript Fathers, made one of this body, when demands were being presented for new senatorial decrees in contravention of the principles and the legislation of our fathers. And from me there came no opposition—not because I doubted that, whatever the issue, the provision made for it in the past was the better conceived and the more correct, and that, where revision took place, the alteration was for the worse; but because I had no wish to seem to be exalting my own branch of study by an overstrained affection for ancient usage.[34]

Cassius admitted his previous reticence, but justified the meaning behind it. His opposition to the new developments was head-on and programmatic:

aristocratic traditionalism and legal knowledge ("my branch of study") were united in a direct and total bond. Everything that changed what was ancient could do nothing but make it worse. The same attitude as Labeo's seems to be resurfacing ("Labeo regarded nothing as confirmed and valid other than what he had found to be sanctioned and decided in Roman antiquity"),[35] once again as an implicit criticism, if not of the principate itself, then at the very least of its normative initiatives. And indeed all the reasons for Cassius' dissent could be traced back to Labeonian ideas: protection of the autonomy of jurisprudence, polemic against the explosion of imperial intervention, and a strong revival of the memory of antiquity. Still, the web of ties linking them was different: Labeo distinguished between respect for the republican political past and changes in legal science: the defense of tradition was limited to constitutional matters; innovations were in fact indispensable, precisely in order to protect the ancient hierarchies of aristocratic power. For Cassius, on the other hand, the exaltation of antiquity embraced the entire field of law, and itself became the foundation for the autonomy of legal studies; a sort of short circuit that we will also find in another great Labeonian author: Neratius Priscus.[36] A radicalism was emerging that perhaps did not even entirely spare his friend Sabinus (whom he also protected), if we are to assign a significance to Cassius' decision to move away from the master's synthesis, to return—in his most important work, the last one about the *ius civile* not to be presented in the form of a commentary upon Quintus Mucius or upon Sabinus—to an exposition of Mucian dimensions (and in accordance with a non-Sabinian order, which is very difficult to explain). But Sabinus was followed (and perhaps specifically cited) by Cassius in many doctrines—including the anti-Labeonian one concerning contracts[37]—and his traditionalism seems to have been closely linked to the Sabinian idea that law could be entirely summarized in a brief sequence of maxims. The difference must have been more to do with the assessment of the descriptive capacity of the rules rather than the underlying convictions of the master. And in any case the fact remains that roughly two-thirds of the citations from Cassius present in later jurisprudence link his name to that of Sabinus, without there being a single recorded case of disagreement; while a continual conflict emerges—though with a few significant exceptions—with Nerva and Proculus.[38]

Now, however, we must look at the conclusion of the speech in the senate:

'But some innocent lives will be lost!'—Even so; for when every tenth man of the routed army drops beneath the club, the lot falls on the brave as well. Every great example contains something unfair, which is meted out to single persons in the name of the common good. [39]

Cassius took for granted the sacrifice of the innocent. And to make it acceptable, he deployed two concepts, which were dramatically linked: the "unfair" and "common good" (*utilitas publica:* which should not be understood as "reason of state"—a completely misleading interpretation—but as an expression of the contrast between "the people"—*publicus*—and "single persons": the influence of Mucius is detectable here, and, perhaps, a more narrowly constitutional outlook, that of Ateius Capito).[40] But how should we interpret the first word? Here too we need to find the trace of a polemic. The overwhelming force of the term—"unfair"—pronounced in the senate, and by an important jurist, was destined to hit hard and leave a lasting mark.

It was easy to identify the adversaries: proponents of "fairness"; supporters of the line of thinking lying between rhetoric, philosophy, and law which, as we have seen, by developing a theme present since the heart of the third century, and clearly reflected in the *summum ius, summa iniuria,* had constructed a paradigm of equity—"civil" and "natural" in the reflection of Cicero and Labeo—at the intersection between Greek classics and Roman tradition.[41] Though there is not a particularly rich body of testimony for the first century A.D., we have no reason to doubt that this elaboration continued uninterrupted, especially with regard to the idea of equity as a flexible, moderate law measured in relation to the demands of concrete situations. As far as we know, at least once Cassius himself (with Sabinus) had not hesitated to make recourse to it.[42]

In his view, in any case, the possibility of a fair law ran up against an insurmountable boundary. It could not neglect to protect the common good, of the interests of the people as both organization and as system—of the people, in short, as the political subject that had constructed the *res publica.* And that was not all. Cassius did not view the two criteria—equity and the common good—as lending themselves to a peaceful integration, but rather as prone to an explosive conflict, which the transcription of Tacitus rendered in a stylistically effective manner, since one was founded on the exclusive advantage of "single persons," the other on a value that transcended this point of view to attain the higher perspective of the community, of the whole, of organicity, which might not coincide with the sum of particular interests.

Once the contradiction had manifested itself, there was no option other than to choose. And it was precisely this duty to take sides that Cassius wished to emphasize. If he was admitting that his decision contained a certain degree of unfairness, it was because he was aware of a principle of equity inspired by not insignificant reasons. But it was a criterion that could be derogated: it did not represent the highest point of the legal assessment. Law was no place for the exclusive interest of single persons; it had been established above all for the common good, so that the multitude could be transformed (as Cicero had already said)[43] into an organic body, into a totality, into a *res publica;* and the absence, in ancient culture and society, of a strong "individualistic" alternative made the position particularly convincing: "private" singularity was a prerequisite of citizenship, not the foundation of inviolable rights; and here, what's more, the question regarded slaves. Keeping the social body intact sometimes required "great examples," where fairness could not be the overriding concern. There was no room for compromise when it came to the slave-owning basis of the community. Its defense, however unfair, was obligatory if what was at stake was the very survival of the institution.

With whom was Cassius engaging in particular? It would seem a direct attack on Nero can be ruled out: though the latter was probably not averse to an act of clemency, he must have taken what appeared to be a fairly discreet stance, and this certainly allowed some space for debate. A more likely candidate is the other leading jurist of the time, Proculus, who might have been present in the senate, and who did not dare to take the floor (as far as we know), but acquiesced, as for that matter did Nero, in allowing the intransigent line to prevail. And together with Proculus, we should also look to Seneca himself.[44]

In the vocabulary of the philosopher—who was anything but ignorant of legal culture—the use of the notion of equity was very frequent, and in a text of the *De clementia* we find a significant reference to "judging not according to a text, but in the name of the good and the fair," which takes us back to the earlier praetorian elaboration;[45] and we can safely say that in the philosophy of law that Seneca integrated into his model of the moderate exercise of power, the proposal of a flexible *ius,* built to measure for the needs of single people, played a major role: a theme that would later reemerge with Celsus as one of the major motifs of Hadrian's legal humanism.[46]

As for Proculus, he was probably Seneca's (and, up to a certain point, Nero's) jurist in the years when the philosopher was the intellectual most in the public eye, and a magnet for anyone trying to jostle for position in the power plays surrounding the imperial court, or at least to keep afloat:[47] his references to fairness probably also had a Senecan influence.[48] He certainly annotated writings by Labeo: possibly the *Posteriores,* possibly other works;[49] and he can justifiably be considered the protagonist of the detachment of the Labeonian conceptual picture from the anti-Augustan ideological frame within which it had come into being. There can in fact be no question about Proculus' scientific Labeonism. His *Epistulae*—which may have taken Seneca's letters as their literary model, even if a further influence from Labeo cannot be excluded[50]—should be read from this perspective: the continuation of the work of the *Pithana* and the *Posteriores* (and before those, of Servius and Alphenus); and the jurist was also a firm supporter of Labeo's theories on contracts (which must have reached him through the filtering influence of Nerva), as we learn from a citation from Ulpian that should be compared with Paulus' account of the difference between sale and barter.[51]

But Proculus' political prudence is equally unquestionable, as was that of Nerva the Younger, a jurist like his father, and praetor designate for the year 65:[52] those dark years continued in an atmosphere of fear and caution that seemed devoid of hope.

And yet there were presages of new times. The thinking of Seneca, as gathered by Proculus and Pedius, in some sense foreshadowed them: even if it drew on ideas typical of the Roman tradition, it was still capable of repositioning them in an original way around the question of the relationship between intellectuals and the power of the *princeps,* which would later be the focus of interest for the Antonine and Severan jurists.[53]

By contrast, Cassius' uncompromising stance was not destined to attract a broad consensus. But both positions—of Cassius and Proculus—reflected the effort, albeit through the use of different instruments, to direct and channel the power of an institution, the new "principate," only recently established but already in danger of coming catastrophically adrift, and which

threatened to compromise the solidity and prestige of branches of knowledge—law, philosophy—that aspired to enlighten the uppermost circles of
the empire.

3.

Over the same period, from the last decades of the republic to the age of
Tiberius, there was also, again in relation to the outcomes of the revolution
of formalism, another phenomenon of great importance in the history of
ius. The two great blocs that had until then constituted the fabric of the Roman legal experience—civil law and the edicts of the praetors—lost both fluidity and mobility, exhausting, as it were, their evolutionary impulse, and
crystallizing into more defined normative and conceptual forms, to a certain
extent already closed. But they did so without losing their vitality, without
being transformed, that is, into inert fossils, instead becoming fixed in paradigms and features capable of conditioning all later developments: the basis
of a continuity, immobile (or almost), destined to underpin and to orientate
everything new that would follow over time.

In this process of stabilization, legal thought played a decisive role, which
needs to be explained, beginning with the *ius civile*.

Already in Mucius' treatise, the relationship between the typification of
the case and the formulation of the maxim had attained a degree of elaboration never previously reached in Roman thought. In the Mucian lemmata
identifiable in Pomponius' commentary, as we have previously observed, the
conceptual isolation of the maxims from the description of cases is evident,
despite the interventions later overlaid upon them.[54] The result paved the way
for further development, and made it possible to capture perfectly the connection between the *Iuris civilis* books and the *Horoi:* the attempt to derive
from the exposition of the treatise a contained sequence of rules, capable of
expressing in the clearest possible fashion the exemplary value of the city's
ancient juridical tradition. Observed from this perspective, the *Horoi* seems to
be Mucius' early answer to the criticisms and impatience of Crassus in the *De
oratore.*

The *Horoi* should therefore be considered the intermediate link between
Mucius' *Iuris civilis* books and the three books by Sabinus, which marked the
conclusion of the itinerary. The concordance between the two jurists should

not be sought in the repetition of the same systematics, but in the shared quest for a reduction of the *ius civile* to maxims; in the effort to gather into a small cluster of formulations a centuries-old sapiential tradition that began with the pontifices and the Twelve Tables, saving it for the new times through the paradigms acquired with the formal revolution: diaeretic models, ontological figures, and an abstract construction of normativity.[55]

The identification of the Sabinian lemmata in the great commentaries of Pomponius, Paul, and Ulpian allows us to form a more than rough idea of Sabinus' working method: the coexistence of rules and cases was programmatically broken, as in the *Horoi*. But while in the short work by Mucius the exposition of the maxims must have had a purely exemplary value (its brevity makes this the only plausible conjecture), in Sabinus' text the goal is more ambitious. The field of the rules extended to the whole of the civil law tradition (we can be certain of this from the comments by Paul and Ulpian), which emerged completely transfigured from the new treatment.[56]

Confirmation that the books of Sabinus were perceived by the culture of the time in the terms we are describing is offered by some testimony from outside the world of law, which makes it all the more significant, because it reveals the rootedness of a view and of a judgment beyond specialist circles:

> And who is free if not he who can lead his life
> As he pleases?
> Once away from the praetor, and become my own with the wand,
> Why might I not do whatever my will commanded,
> Except if the rubric of Masurius forbade it?[57]

It is Persius—a contemporary of Masurius Sabinus—who in his fifth satire thus describes liberty from the point of view of someone who had once been a slave. And so the *Capita* (and the *Horoi*) of Mucius find a counterpoint in the "rubrics" of Sabinus. The word "rubric," in its narrowest meaning of "titulature in red," was not used frequently in juridical or literary Latin. It referred, as *caput,* to the writing of legislative texts: we find it again in a passage of the *Rhetorica ad Herennium*[58] and on just one occasion in Quintilian.[59] Among the jurists, it was used (as far as we know) only by Paul, on two occasions.[60] If Persius used it so confidently with reference to Sabinus, the only explanation is that it must have already belonged to the language and the composition of the work being recalled, and indeed that it was a key term whose use alone sufficed to identify it.

The implication is evident: a sequence of rubrics, that is, of titulatures that established the succession of topics, must have punctuated the whole of the Sabinian *ius civile*. In view also of the brevity of the composition, we are forced to deduce that the treated material was subjected to powerful pressure to compress it within the boundaries of an essential normative structure with the appearance of a legislative text. As had already happened for the Mucian *capita,* so too with the rubrics of Sabinus, the *lex* and its ordering model once again cast its intrusive shadow on the writing of the *ius civile.*

Let's move on a few years, and listen to the voice of Quintilian, in the twelfth book of his *Institutio oratoria:*

> But I should not like my advice about the development of moral attitudes and the study of law to be open to criticism on the ground that we know many people who became tired of the in-evitable labours of the would-be-orators and fled to these pur-suits as a safe haven for their idleness. Some of these went over to the praetor's *album* and the Rubrics, and chose to be "formular-ists" or "legal hacks," as Cicero calls them....[61]

The "album" and the "rubrics," but also, quite literally, the "white" and the "red," as the text suggests with an untranslatable semantic play on words. The first term—not used in any other instance by Quintilian—should cer-tainly be taken as a reference to the praetorian edict, as is further suggested by the corresponding use, immediately following, of the term *formularii*—"formularists"—which was likewise never again employed by Quintilian (and never used by Cicero at all). But what were the "rubrics" to which allusion was being made? The Ciceronian citation (from the first book of the *De ora-tore*)[62] does not help us to understand. Are they, generically, those of the legis-lative texts and—why not—of the edict, or are they perhaps, by antonomasia, those of the work by Sabinus, previously mentioned by Persius? This final possibility is intriguing, and is certainly not ruled out by the evidence (if Per-sius adopted a common way of indicating the books by Sabinus, why could Quintilian not have done the same thing just a short while afterwards, especially as he was certainly not unfamiliar with Persius?); this, however, is nothing more than a hypothesis.

But the fact remains that for Quintilian the forms of law were now the forms of its textuality; and of a textuality that was, so to speak, legislative: an assimilation that would have been unthinkable without the importance and the unified structure achieved by the praetorian edict, and without the transformation that, from Quintus Mucius to Sabinus, had condensed the ancient fluidity of the *ius civile* into a compact network in which a rigid surface of rules for specialists had replaced the uncertain waves of the previous tradition, entrusted to the civil expertise of the ancient political aristocracy.

We may therefore consider the process of textual consolidation carried out by Sabinus as a genuine crystallization of the *ius civile*. A text had imposed itself, but it immediately proved to be an immobile text. Thereafter, with the sole exception of the books of Cassius Longinus—which were not a successful work, and also for this reason are shrouded in an undispellable obscurity —no one would write a treatise on the *ius civile* except in the form of a commentary on Quintus Mucius or, especially, Sabinus. From the latter onwards, moreover, the normative and conceptual bloc of civil law would be fixed in place for all time: a North Star, a cross between a literary genre and a form of thought, yet developed with that freedom of construction that would always distinguish the civil law treatises from the corresponding works of commentary upon the edict.

Until the time of Julian, the influence of Sabinus would be rather discreet: the paths of jurisprudence between the Flavians and the Antonines took different directions. But after that it returned with impressive strength. In the major commentaries devoted to his work by Pomponius and later by Paul and Ulpian, he was considered the point of departure for what was now widely perceived, by the Severan jurists themselves, as one of the great lines of development of Roman law: a persistent thread to which successive conceptual and normative stratifications can be linked (the "Sabinism" of Gaius deserves a discussion apart).[63] In the civil law treatises by Paul and by Ulpian the polarity—still awaiting thorough exploration—between the Sabinian lemmata and the thinking of the author who wrote the commentary acquired the force of a descriptive paradigm capable of overwhelming any other constructive or demonstrative requirements.[64] The idea that the new should not be expressed except through the illustration of the ancient thus became, even more than a stylistic measure or a literary genre, the profound interiority of a branch of knowledge that had reached its peak: the expression of an oblique and indirect creativity, the heir to thought that from the very outset, in order to exist, had been obliged to invent a tradition for itself (remember the "mos est ritus").[65]

All the same, before Paul and Ulpian, Sabinus had not entirely replaced Quintus Mucius, who was still studied until the time of Pomponius. In particular, the latter was the only jurist to write commentaries on both Mucius and Sabinus. And his work on the ancient republican jurist must have served to mark a sort of beginning, from which it was clear that the authentic maturity of Roman thinking commenced with Mucius—confirmation of what had been stated in the *Enchiridion*. For that reason, Pomponius, in the lemmata he chose to transcribe in his commentary, tended to eliminate the references to earlier literature, which must have abounded in the original (the *caput* copied by Cicero, for instance). He wanted to distinguish the thought of the ancient master by presenting it in an exemplary (though historically fictitious) isolation, in order to accentuate the impression of a decisive turning point: it was from here—he wanted to say—that the historic time of his science first began.[66]

In the interpretation offered by Pomponius, alongside Mucius we find, like another solitary giant, the profile of Labeo, none of whose works had been commented upon by the Antonine author, but whom we know to have been the chief interlocutor in the composition of his vast *Ad edictum*. Wedged between the two, Pomponius tended to cast less light on the figure of Servius: the retrospective nature of his gaze enabled him to reconcile Labeo and Sabinus, but not Servius and Mucius, between whom he felt obliged to make a choice, reversing—and he must have been well aware of this—the one made by Cicero.

4.

Let's look now at the praetorian edict. The history of its formation, as we have said, is shrouded in darkness; and yet a stratigraphic analysis of the materials brought together in Otto Lenel's edition (derived largely from the Severan commentaries) might dispel at least some of the shadows.

There is good reason to suppose that in the period of its most impetuous development, between the second and first centuries B.C., the lines of the praetor's jurisdictional activity were not reflected in a preestablished and organic program. That in this early age there existed a unitary, though annual, text, endowed with its own level of intrinsic coherence, seems highly unlikely: the habit of using the plural—"edicts"—to indicate the normative activity of the magistrate is a sign of compositional fluidity pointing to the day-to-day urgency to regulate a society that had suddenly become imperial, yet was still unequipped with predetermined models.

But the trace of a change is definitely attested in a passage from Cicero's *De legibus* that we have already encountered, where what is striking is not so much the use of the singular as the comparison with the Twelve Tables: something quite unthinkable if the author were not already conscious of being in the presence of a complex of prescriptions so structured, and with such a capacity to delineate situations and relationships, if only from the point of view of the actions, as to suggest a comparison with a memorable and almost legendary document, recollection of which was bound up with the very origins of the republican community. [67] When Cicero was writing, the normative organization through which the jurisdiction of the magistrate was being delineated had therefore emerged from the magmatism of its nascent state, and had finally become something else: project, prediction, program.

This transformation would have been impossible without a decisive intervention from jurisprudence. And for that matter it was Cicero himself who provided an account, on more than one occasion, of the early sedimentation of assiduous interpretative labor conducted from the second into the first centuries around a number of clauses, relating for instance to the edict on violence, still remembered, much later, by Julian, Paul, and Ulpian:[68] a contribution that rescued the new prescriptions from their annual precariousness and entrusted them, through the reception of the jurists, to the much longer life of the city's regulative orders.

The era extending from 115–110 to 20–15 B.C. can thus be considered the great season of the edict, the time in which creative energy intertwined with stabilizing pressure, bringing about a combination that would never again be repeated; an age that began under the influence of Publius Rutilius Rufus and

Quintus Mucius Scaevola, both of whom were praetors (in 114 and in 98), and ended with the great commentary of Antistius Labeo, certainly consisting of more than thirty books, still extensively utilized by Pomponius, Paul, and Ulpian, and an authentic milestone in the history of that literary genre.

During this period there were two developments of particular significance: the Lex Cornelia of 67 B.C., and the work of Ofilius, which we have already had occasion to mention.

The exact normative content of the measure attributed to the tribune Gaius Cornelius—it was certainly a plebiscite—is unknown. What can be gleaned from Asconius and Dio Cassius does not permit an accurate reconstruction.[69] Certainly it touched on a delicate point: the discretional power of the magistrate—hitherto absolute—to modify, during his year in office, the framework of prescriptions accepted at the beginning of his term. It is highly probable that the intervention of the tribune, who presumably wished to hold the praetors to what they had established at the beginning of their year in office, betrayed a marked antisenatorial sentiment, and was inspired by ideas not far removed from those reflected in the Pompeian policies between 70 (the consulship of Pompey and Crassus) and 67 (the proposal by the tribune Aulus Gabinius for Pompey to be given extraordinary command in the war against the pirates, a decision also viewed with displeasure by the senate); and we may also suppose the existence of a direct link between Cornelius and Pompey.

It is equally plausible that the norm was never applied in a rigid fashion, to the extent that it was almost forgotten; the aristocracy and its jurists must have judged the intrusion to be partisan and demagogic, and they managed to ensure it was isolated and substantially rejected: an attitude that provides a good explanation for the silence surrounding the plebiscite on the part of the whole culture close to the legal world, from Cicero to Pomponius. But that does not mean the norm had no effect whatsoever, as it contributed to fixing the terms of a less fragile relationship between praetors and edicts—in response to a social demand that was probably quite widespread—and to inducing the magistrates to concentrate in a single document, at the beginning of their term of office, the innovations and changes they intended to make with respect to the preceding chain of edicts. The result was an early stabilization of the text, at least in the sense of accentuating its programmatic character, which it certainly acquired in the age of the principate: a sort of foreshadowing of the Lex Iulia, it too—we may safely believe—viewed without great favor by jurists like Labeo.[70]

The next step also concerned jurisprudence, and was linked, as we have said, to the work of Ofilius, rapidly described by Pomponius: "He [Ofilius] also was the first to thoroughly compile the praetor's edict on jurisdiction."[71] It is difficult to doubt that the jurist wrote a commentary on the edict: the citations by Ulpian demonstrate it, and allow us to assume the Severan master's direct familiarity with the corresponding work by Ofilius (nor should we forget, to complete the image of an Ulpian who read the jurist of Caesar, that he also cited in detail from Ofilius' *Libri iuris partiti*). We still need to explain, however, what Pomponius meant by the expression "compile the praetor's edict" (already used by Cicero),[72] which seems to refer more to an intervention on the structure of the text than to an activity of commentary.

It is possible that Pomponius intended to emphasize the aspect that struck him as most important about the object of his discussion. In contrast with all the later writings on the edict, Ofilius' work could not have taken the edictal text as an external and independent entity, enclosed in a clearly defined normative otherness, to be reproduced and interpreted lemmatically, but instead must, in a certain sense, have constructed the text itself while interpreting it (perhaps starting from the preliminary outline by Servius), aggregating and connecting in accordance with a preestablished sequence the disorderly and (relatively) chaotic series of magistral edicts, stratified over the period from the third to the first centuries, whose elusive fabric had until that point constituted the praetorian law. In other words, Pomponius must have seen Ofilius as the authentic founder of the edictal text, just as Publius Mucius, Brutus, and Manilius had been of the *ius civile* (after that, in the *Enchiridion,* there came, in the two parallel lines of history—of civil law and of the edict—respectively Quintus Mucius and Labeo);[73] and this primacy canceled the need to recall a body of interpretations that appeared to have been absorbed and dissolved in the new work.

We cannot say when Ofilius published his *Ad edictum,* but it would be elegant to imagine that—as has already been suggested—it was shortly before Cicero's *De legibus,*[74] so as to allow us to think that the idea of the comparison between the edict (in the singular) and the Twelve Tables had sprung to mind in the context of a freshly completed consolidation, capable finally of drawing from the welter of measures the profile of a unitary textuality, entrusted from then on no less to the normative practice of the magistrates than to the analysis and the science of the new jurists.

5.

The two blocs that solidified during the years around the principate of Augustus thanks to the work of jurisprudence—*ius civile* and the edict—would not undergo any further substantial modifications: political vicissitudes would never alter their basic outlines. The revolution of formalism and the new Labeonian science, which had been its epilogue, had constructed and deployed a network of concepts and analytical procedures that protected them behind an almost insurmountable shield, organizing the fabric of a great body of technical and specialized knowledge, without equal in the ancient world: its principles—the connection between case-based rationality and abstract thought, the choice of literary models capable of reflecting this duality, the ontological vocation—would never again be called into question. The continuity would not prevent the revision of a few noncentral aspects: for instance, a reduction in the use of diaeretic schemes. But certainly a deep structure of methods and paradigms—a common topical dialectic framework, we might say, sticking to an Aristotelian perspective—remained unchanged until the leading jurists of the third century.

From a more narrowly normative point of view as well, by the time of Labeo the picture was fairly stable: clustered around the primacy of a proprietary model that was expressed in the private exclusivity of the enjoyment of property, as an implicit presupposition of legal personality itself (and of citizenship). Long established, on its archaic foundations, was the recognition of the patriarchal and potestative character of the family, with the all-encompassing control of the *pater* over his children and wife, mitigated, however—for economic reasons linked to the dynamics of matrimonial exchanges—by the possibility of unions that left the woman out of this subjection. Also clearly defined was the regime of succession upon death, centering on the alternative system of civil law inheritance or the "possession of an estate" conceded by the praetor (the latter completed during the lifetime of Labeo). Similarly delineated were the specific forms of belonging (land, slaves, animals, equipment, or consumables, in the first place; but also houses and palaces in the city), through the structural and functional breakdown of the original situations of domination falling within *mancipium* ("that which one has in hand," "what one has at one's own disposal") and *usus* (de facto appropriation, not covered ritually by *ius*): the *dominium* (ownership of things, slaves included), the notion of which is found for the first time in Servius and Alphenus,[75] and its praetorian duplication, recently completed through the mechanism of the *actio Publiciana;* usufruct (the right to use an item of property and its fruits without being the owner)—invented for economic reasons tied once again to matrimonial exchanges—developed by the late-republican jurisprudence and then by Labeo; the configuration of the *possessiones* ("possessions": figures of material availability, distinct from ownership), likewise entirely sketched out in the same period.

The mechanism of the obligation as a purely legal bond had also already been conceived, and the typology of acts capable of constituting it articulated, establishing, alongside the forms that involved the exchange of ritual words or the handing over of something, the new Mediterranean schemes based on consensus; also started was the process directed toward the repression of fraud, violence, and threat: the formula *de dolo* dates from the 70s of the first century B.C, as does the interdict *de vi armata,* and not much later comes the *actio quod metus causa;* while discussion began, as we have seen, of the question of moving beyond contractual typicality: from the edict on pacts to the contribution of Labeo.[76] Lastly, the structure of the formulary procedure was already completed, from the Lex Aebutia to the Lex Iulia, and the network of interdictal procedures developed, allowing the Roman legal order to acquire once and for all its configuration as a law of cases and actions, oriented by magistrates and jurists, and set out to protect a horizontal network of patrimonial relations between heads of family subjected to absolute parity of treatment.

This imposing construction displayed, however, an intrinsically unilateral character, which the legal thought developed from Labeo to Ulpian would do nothing to correct, and in fact would only heighten, expanding it in the mirror of an extraordinarily effective conceptual apparatus. It increasingly presented itself as a legal order of property owners (of land and slaves) and merchants, not of producers; based on income and not on labor. As the law of a society in which capitalist accumulation, the result of the growth of trade under the empire (in its dimension, that is, of commercial capital), would never really take control of production or come into contact with organized human activity in the form of free, wage labor. This contact—the authentic crucible of modernity—would never take place, prevented by the overwhelmingly slave-based character of agriculture (and also, to a considerable extent, of manufacturing): an element that was at once both a condition for the preserving of that civilization and a barrier to any further progress.[77]

Legal historiography would do everything to ignore this fact, engrossed as it was by the individualistic and bourgeois utilization of Roman law, which would obscure its presence under the weight of an integration that tended to confuse and overlay ancient and modern elements.[78] And yet it can be seen, by a clear-eyed observer, with absolute clarity: through that lack, the whole of antiquity unveils its most distinctive trait: a world in which the transformation of nature and the material production of wealth were abandoned to the degraded sphere of slave labor, perceived as a dead zone in the progress of human civilization (only the jurists would attempt a different approach, as we have seen, and precisely in the years in question; but their efforts would not be sufficient).[79]

The revolution of formalism remained tied to this limitation, without being able to free any more than a small part of its potential: created by the concentration of power resulting from the conquest of the empire, as much as by the impulse of trade networks such as the societies of antiquity had never before seen, it was endowed with neither an adequate production base nor a culture—philosophical, ethical, or civil—capable of erecting a protective bulwark for the legal and social objectives it could have achieved, and which in some cases it came close enough to glimpse. It had power and markets, but not labor (except that of slaves) or technology. Enough to complete the invention of law. But not enough to take it to its furthest consequences. To do that, it would have been necessary to construct another history.

The same irreducibly dual nature of the Roman legal order in its phase of greatest creativity was an outcome of the same difficulty: it projected, on the level of an increasingly sophisticated construction, the intrinsic dualism of the society that had produced it, in which a relatively thin layer of development, almost on the threshold of modernity—opulent levels of consumption, robust trade networks, articulated social stratifications, a flourishing urban life, critical thought, and an advanced production logic, albeit within the limitations imposed by its slave-based character—coexisted with a quantitatively dominant base of shortcomings and of backwardness, both intellectual and material, thrusting the vast majority of the women and men of those times into a harsh state of nature, without hope and without mobility. From the retrospective view of the great jurisprudence of the principate, the polarity between civil and praetorian law would be seen as a providential sign of the talent of the ancestors, something that could easily be placed within the unitary framework of a conceptual architecture equal to the task—and that is how it would appear to the moderns. But instead it was the indicator of an unresolved fragility, not the revelation of a greatness: an adaptation to a state of affairs that could not be overcome, not the opening up of a new path.

In the modern age, the historically determined relation between capital and labor—between the entrepreneurial bourgeoisie and the working class— would underlie in economic and cultural terms the establishment of national civil societies, as loci for the construction of the diverse social subjectivities, of their needs, interests, and political projections. That is precisely what was lacking in the history of Rome: a space in which differences in personal status (between free men and slaves, first and foremost) could be transformed into differences of class within the context of a legal formalism capable of imposing its equality without limitation; where citizens could become producers either on the side of capital or on that of labor, and not remain just property owners (of land and slaves) or lumpen plebs.

That absence would have decisive consequences. Without the dynamics of an authentic civil society separate from the public sphere, the whole of Roman law, once its original connection with the republican community was broken, would find itself detached from a real political foundation. The legal order of strong and enterprising private elites, but unified only by their subordinate status to the emperor's will, and devoid of a genuine vision. And it would wind up revealing itself—to those who had not been captivated by the power of its concepts—as something trapped within a social model lacking a future, whose fate was nothing more than a progressive deterioration: irremediably unbalanced in favor of personal status (of father, mother, son, free man, freedman, and slave) with respect to the construction of authentic legal individualities; and of that of property, with respect to trade and contracts (despite all the elaborations of the jurists). Leaning toward the typicality of forms, as opposed to free will; without ever being capable of diffusing the formalism of its own equality from private relations to the terrain of politics. And it is for that reason that it never ceased to appear as something majestic and grandiose—a genuine ontological cathedral—but also, deep down, as something unmoving, immobile, statuelike: a completeness enveloped in closed forms—despite the conscious antisystematic vocation of a great deal of its literature. The congenital unilateralism of its structure would open directly onto the precocious myth of its petrified classicity.

And yet Roman law succeeded in expressing something of primary importance in the relationship between order and life, above and beyond the form in which life is played out: something similar to the primary foundation of a "juridical state" of soul. Above all, the very idea of the "private": the constitution of a space of nonpolitical sociality of human relations. Its ontology is an incomparable elementary syntax of proprietary subjectivity and of its system of needs, without which no modern individualism could ever have come into being. And then there is the idea of a rule excarnated from any sovereignty except its own: the pure form of the "ought-to-be," even if still a "private" ought-to-be; normativity as compliance with a procedure, whatever that might be, provided it was preestablished, and with an abstractly quantitative measurement, indifferent to the content, though tempered by the presence of fairness. Politics—the great invention of the Greeks—remained entirely outside this point of view. There was therefore something undeniably authentic in its exhibition of neutrality: once the transition had taken place from the aristocratic community of republican citizens to the status of subjects of the emperor, it would invent a new dialectic between powers that repelled and attracted one another with equal force—reciprocally independent, but obliged not to exclude one another.

Even more than a science, what had been formed was a mental style: and it was this that made the jurists a little bit all the same—that from then on would make the jurists of every era somewhat similar (in a sense, Valla and Savigny were not mistaken). But that did not prevent early divisions. Already in the years of Mucius and Servius, and even more so after Labeo, the ancient masters began to refute one another in their writings: often in a calm and

considered, even chilly manner, and at times harshly, progressively establishing the canon of an intense and closely reasoned colloquy, which extended
over and between generations and eras, binding together thought and studies
in a single fabric of problems, built on by the constant advancing of hypotheses, solutions, and new figures. Thus the specific historic time of Roman legal science was created, which tended, in the interplay of citations, references, and controversies, to erase the distances separating authors, dissolving
any sense of their chronological distance in a continuity of rules and doctrines.

19

Jurists and Emperors

I.

At the end of the first century A.D., Roman law, by now entirely detached from its republican foundations, was on its way to becoming the fully realized legal order of the principate and of its universalistic government. While the commentary on the edict written by Ofilius was above all an attempt to establish the unitary status of the praetorian text; and while the corresponding work by Labeo bore the imprint of a distinct separation between the role of jurisprudence and the tasks of the magistrate, and claimed an autonomous normative function for jurists and the possibility of critically reading the formulations and clauses examined, the *Ad edictum* by Sextus Pedius was inspired by the project to integrate and reconcile legal knowledge and the magistracy under the aegis of a shared acceptance of the new "material" constitution of the empire, and in many ways prepared the terrain for the imminent "codification" by Julian.

It was in any case an important book, and its author a protagonist of the first order—at least according to Paul and Ulpian.[1] Nevertheless, a veil seems to obscure the work and its writer from the view of contemporaries (with the possible exception of a note by Valerius Probus), as much as it does from ours. It is even difficult to pin down exactly when Pedius lived (his biography is entirely obscure), though the hypothesis of the period between Nero and the Flavians now appears to be the most probable. Julian, to the best of our knowledge, never cited him at all; nor do we have any references in Gaius and Pomponius.[2] On the other hand, he would be mentioned dozens of times by the Severan masters, who must have considered his writing to be the intermediate link between the commentary of Labeo and that of Pomponius (but whereas for Ulpian, Pomponius was of supreme importance, Paul may have placed Pedius and Pomponius on almost the same level):[3] the last phase of a lengthy intertwining between the history of the edictal text and the history of its interpretations, before the intervention of Julian.

Pedius was active at a time when the practice of post-Augustan government had not yet entirely extinguished the innovative power of the praetor to make way for the new legislation of the emperor; but the edict was already being fixed into a far less fluid structure than that of the late republic or even of the time of Labeo. And it is precisely in a context of this sort that we can place a methodological declaration by Pedius, reported by Ulpian, according to whom: "Whenever some particular thing or another has been brought within statute law, there is good ground to include other things which further the same interest through extension, whether this be done by interpretation [of jurists] or with certainty through jurisdiction [of the magistrates]."[4] It is unclear how we should understand the reference to "statute law": whether in the narrow sense of *lex publica* (fairly uncommon by the time of Pedius), or in a broader sense, inclusive both of the decrees of the senate and the new normative activity of the emperor, already of some significance by the end of the first century, and of the edictal norms themselves, by now cast into virtually immutable forms. But in any case it was an authentic integration between jurisprudence and jurisdiction that was being suggested, a far cry from the wholly political divergence—jurists on one side, magistracies controlled by the emperor on the other—implicit in Labeo's position: a model capable of ensuring a kind of constant analogical "extension" of the legal order (according to an originally Servian scheme), through the introduction of "useful" actions (the reference to the term *utilitas* is no accident), or *in factum,* or of the formulas *praescriptis verbis* employed by Labeo.

Pedius engaged deeply with Labeonian thought, orienting its original inspiration toward outcomes that were anticipatory (perhaps mindful of the

Senecan lesson), attentive, in the recognition of the validity of legal acts and their effects, to the intentional interiority of the subjects involved—to the inner landscapes of the mind—and with a greater concern to search for the reasons of fairness.[5] He was probably the protagonist of an important mediation in the field of contract doctrines, between the Mucian-Sabinian construction, accepted as a descriptive model in the ambit of typicality, but expanding within it the importance of consensus beyond just the relations of the *ius gentium,* and that of Labeo, taken not as a general definition of contract, but only as a scheme capable of allowing the analogical protection ("through interpretation") of new relationships, paving the way for the solutions of Aristo and, most importantly, of Ulpian.[6] This also explains the importance that the Severan master would place on the thought of Pedius: after his developments, the contrast between Labeo and Sabinus in the field of contracts would lose nearly all of its original significance, making it possible to produce a new and definitive synthesis.

Similarly, the work and life of Javolenus Priscus—who despite certain extravagances of behavior, perhaps due only to senility, had enjoyed a brilliant political career under Domitian, and finally wound up working closely with Trajan[7]—presaged the new developments of the second century. Following the crisis of the preceding decades, his example inaugurated a new chapter in the compromise between emperors and jurists, which began to take shape through a regular presence of jurists in the imperial council.[8]

Three of the four known texts by Javolenus are commentaries (lemmatic or in the form of epitomes) on works by earlier authors—Labeo, Cassius Longinus, Plautius—a genre new to Roman legal literature (if we exclude the Servian criticism of the *capita* by Quintus Mucius).[9] The choice revealed a precise intent: the reelaboration, with a polemical emphasis on their case-based character, of those works of first-century jurisprudence in which it was possible to detect a forerunner of this line: the Labeo of the *Posteriores*— whose core of prescriptive responses Javolenus attempted to highlight wherever possible—and not of the *Pithana;* the extensive books of Cassius and not the synthesis of Sabinus; the anthology (possibly the *Digesta*) by Plautius. Javolenus wanted to rediscover a style of analysis whose acceptance no longer struck him as unopposed, in the face of the great systematizing ontological wave.

But the reinvigoration of the case-based option in Javolenus was tinged with quite new shades, with which Pedius probably could not identify. In a passage of his *Libri epistularum*—the only work that was not a commentary on the writings of earlier authors, but was once again a collection of cases, quite distant, in literary and conceptual terms, from the *Epistulae* of Proculus—we read: "Every definition in civil law is dangerous; for it is rare that there is no possibility of it being overthrown."[10] Aside from the occasion that might have provoked such a statement, its general implications are beyond dispute. It was not just Labeo (the Labeo of the *Pithana* and the *Ad edictum*) who was being called into question;[11] the criticism extended to Sabinus and, with him, Quintus Mucius (at any rate, the Mucius of the *Horoi*). Rising to the surface was a descriptive empiricism that even had a skeptical hue previously unknown to jurisprudence, and certainly quite distant from the views of Pedius, but which also announced the climate of the new century.

2.

The jurists who, between the Flavians and the Antonines, forged a new alliance with the imperial power, belonged for the most part to the recent aristocracy of the Italic *municipia* or of the provinces of the west and of Dalmatia.[12] The years of Domitian probably represented a final period of difficulties, but the biographies and careers of Pegasus, Caelius Sabinus, and Juventius Celsus (the father of a much more important author of the same name from the age of Hadrian) show the depth and strength of the new relationships, besides what we have seen with Javolenus.[13]

Nonetheless it would only be with the jurisprudence undertaken between Nerva and Trajan—with Aristo and Neratius, both of whom had previously been cautiously hostile to Domitian—that legal science would rediscover, and then maintain throughout the century, the speculative force of the years between Quintus Mucius and Sabinus.[14] And it would be precisely from Aristo and Neratius onwards that this new beginning would acquire the features of an authentic renaissance: a genuine golden age for legal thought, which would accompany the great period of the principate, up to Marcus Aurelius

—the happiest age of mankind, according to the apologetic judgment of Gibbon.[15] The jurists, while never abandoning the detached and austere isolation
of their doctrine, would become the undisputed protagonists of the intellectual life of the empire, surrounded by a matchless prestige, which shone all
the brighter in a period of darkness and fragility for other traditions of study
such as literature, historiography, and philosophy.

This solitary primacy had deep-rooted causes. On the one hand, it reflected the further reinforcement of the epistemic paradigms, through to the
collective construction—culminating in the work of Julian—of a methodic
canon that was never explicitly formulated but was also never violated, centering on the specific demonstrative and noncontradictory character of legal
discourse (topical dialectic, as we have said), combined with the creation of a
great ontological "periodic table" of law extended to transcribe and cover,
with its parameters, symbols, and figures, the entire universe of private sociality, against the background of the public benevolence of the *princeps* and of
the Roman imperial peace.[16]

On the other hand, that supremacy found an explanation in the new tasks
assigned with increasing evidence to the jurists as a result of their collaboration in government, and which would ultimately transform the frame of references within which they worked. Until the time of Aristo and Neratius,
in fact (even though many things were already changing with them), legal
knowledge had remained to a substantial extent the thought of the aristocracy of a single city, though unequaled: the consciousness of the empire had
certainly proved decisive in its history, a worldwide diffusion of its disciplines
had certainly not been lacking, and it had had its institutional channels; but
all of this had not yet been transformed into the direct assumption of responsibility on a world scale. Later, with Celsus and especially with Julian, legal
thought crossed this threshold, and its protagonists acquired the attitude and
the traits of intellectual leaders entrusted with the historic task of orienting
a political power without limits, but which they sought to bring within the
bounds of a universal measure that could be accepted and shared in rational
no less than in ethical terms.

Aristo and Neratius were both Labeonian in spirit (the latter also by virtue of distant family ties):[17] a viewpoint that still dominated legal culture between the two centuries; the "Tacitism" of jurisprudence, which extended
until the time of Pomponius. Labeo was not only a figure of extraordinary

doctrinal standing, but also a master of moral rectitude. The rediscovery of his rationalism—now stripped of any meaning contrary to the principate, but not the antiautocratic nuances, and set forth in reference to a model of a quest for the truth and of persuasiveness that consciously drew on the paradigm of the *Pithana*—formed the basis for a theory opposed to that of Javolenus. In the work of Aristo, author of a *Digesta* known to both Pomponius and Paul[18]—the title used by Alphenus reappears, one century later, as if to emphasize the resumption of a long-interrupted program—there emerges a propensity for a *ius* that could be enclosed within a network of concepts capable of withstanding any "diversity of argumentations" (according to the words of a memorable portrait of the jurist sketched by Pliny):[19] two of them, among the most important, and also developed in connection with the thinking of Labeo, will be examined shortly.

But it was Neratius—a friend of the more elderly Aristo, with very close ties to Trajan, who may even have considered him as his possible successor in the principate, and for many years one of the most influential senators of the Italic aristocracy—in whom the Labeonism of the turn of the century was most fully embodied.[20] But now, in an altered cultural and political context, the revival of those motifs had a different appearance to when they had first been elaborated. In the years of the still-fluid establishment of the principate, close in time to the Caesarian projects and the debate on the tasks of legal knowledge that had involved, between Quintus Mucius and Cicero, ample sectors of the city's culture, the Aristotelian rationalism of Labeo had represented the most advanced possible outcome of the revolution of formalism. It prefigured an open normative universe, flexibly controlled by jurisprudence, whose *regulae iuris* were intended to mark the subsequent paths of development. But now that same option, weakened in its original points of reference, returned with an unequivocal closure and dogmatism; no longer open to the future, in opposition to the potential totalitarian ambitions of the emperor, but blocked in the past, establishing the boundaries of a *ius* perceived as having been entirely deployed, and in defense of a government, that of Trajan, which was finally restoring a traditionalist and prosenatorial practice.

Neratius wrote *Libri epistularum,* in keeping with a genre again dating back to Labeo (but also to Proculus and Javolenus), as well as *Libri regularum:* the latter were the first to bear such a title, in which the clear Labeonian echo became a specific constructive indication.²¹ In a passage from another of his works, the *Membranae* (a bizarre and contrived title, which would not be emulated by other authors),²² he stated, making a clear distinction between errors of fact and errors of law—inexcusable in any case—that *ius* could and should be considered as a "finite" whole. It is difficult to imagine that what Neratius had in mind here was a Sabinian kind of descriptive completeness. Rather he was carrying out a sort of superimposition or exchange between the logical predeterminability of *ius* in the mind of the interpreter (clearly a Labeonian and Servian motif) and its image as a structure already ontologically complete and perfect in and of itself, independent of the observer's analysis:²³ a dogmatic and paradoxically anti-Labeonian conclusion, indebted to a less creative, less confident rationalism, pessimistic and on the defensive. Law protected itself behind the walls of its finitude: shortly thereafter, the same would begin to be done, and not metaphorically, by the empire itself, having reached "the boundaries of the world."²⁴

For Neratius the past and present of law were above all a web of dogmatic certainties to be left untouched: "one should not delve deeply into the reasons for that which has been established; otherwise many certainties will be thus swept away," he wrote in another passage of the *Membranae:*²⁵ a firmly antirelativistic and positivist position, against the perils of an understanding of law that might reduce normative output to a fleeting measurement of the occasions that had determined it in one case or another, or that might annihilate such norms in a hypercritical analysis of their foundations.

Neratius lived long enough to see the central years of Hadrian's rule, and the new developments of his principate, though the scale of the change should not be exaggerated.²⁶ The alliance between the government and jurists was reinforced in any case on other grounds and with different content from those at the turn of the century, rendering possible and by now painless the emperor's decision to intervene with increasing frequency in matters of law, albeit through the ambiguous instrument of the rescript—a specific answer to a query from an official, a magistrate, or a private citizen, handwritten at the foot of a document bearing the question, and restricted to the case in question—midway between the power of law and a merely exemplary value, based on the authoritativeness of the emperor ("you, when you make a decision concerning single persons, bind everyone with your example," Cornelius Fronto would say, just a short while later, of Antoninus Pius).²⁷

Celsus and, later, Julian were the masterminds of this new organicity, which definitively deployed the jurists in the ranks of the imperial government: the former with a passionate vehemence quite foreign to the communicative style of jurisprudence;[28] the latter with the measured sobriety of an unrivaled classicity.

A pupil of Aristo and Neratius, summoned to become a member of Hadrian's council, Celsus also wrote books of *Digesta*,[29] from which emerged a wealth of themes and outlooks reflecting needs of various provenance. We shall have more to say about him presently, on a number of occasions, but it should be said straightaway that his departure from a number of Labeonian models never turned into a complete negation of the method based on definition. What dominated everything was an empiricist and antidogmatic outlook far removed from the world of his masters: the idea of a law receptive to transformation and change, a flexible instrument of contingent solutions, proportional to the subjects involved.[30] At the center of this approach lay a commitment to adapt the understanding of *ius* to the cultural climate of his own age, and to his own insistent approval of the development of a universal sociability that had never previously been experienced. This vision would become a point of reference for a sometimes radical critique (mindful of Javolenus) of a legal science—of Aristonian and Neratian derivation—that was distant from the requirements of the mature contemporary civilization, of a fullness of time perceived and exalted by all the intelligentsia under Hadrian. In the tension between the discovery of the possible inadequacy of tradition—never before expressed so openly by a jurist—and the elaboration of a *ius* which might freely reflect the orderly imperial cosmopolis and the refined sensibility of the new urban élites scattered from one end of the Mediterranean to another, there was taking shape the particular humanism of Celsus— which was able to do without all the harshness of a Neratius (to say nothing of a Cassius)—and which was the most visible meeting point between the jurist and the cultural setting of Hadrian's court.

But alongside Celsus, and with an even closer link, the enlightened *princeps* summoned to his side another intellectual, several years younger, who would soon become "his" jurist, as well as the major protagonist of the imperial council: Salvius Julianus.[31]

A pupil of Javolenus, like Aristo and Celsus he wrote *Digesta,* though they were far more substantial: ninety books, much used by Justinian's compilers, and in various respects the most significant work of Roman jurisprudence —according to a judgment that must already have been formed by Ulpian, and which was shared, after him, by the Byzantine scholars—unrivaled testimony of a case law built on a rigorous ontological foundation and stratified over centuries of history. Julian had a more prudent attitude toward tradition than Celsus, although it was far less rigid than that of a Neratius or an Aristo.[32] In a text from the fifty-fifth book, he reformulated Neratius' admonition not to "delve deeply into the reasons for that which has been established," proposing a softer and less dogmatically intransigent version: "It is not possible to find a rational explanation for everything which was settled by our forebears"; legal analysis, conducted in relation to what had been acquired by contemporary culture, could not help but exercise itself on the past as well. But this pursuit ran up against insuperable limits: tradition was not entirely explicable and resolvable in terms of the reason of the present. And yet we read, in another text from his *Digesta:* "We cannot obtain a rule of law in instances in which there has been a decision against the rationality of law:"[33] a prescription that could not be reduced to a rational parameter, even if it was consolidated in tradition, remained as an inert and extraneous body, upon which it was not possible to construct any analogical device.[34]

All of Julian's work was done under the influence of this counterpoint, which alternated respect for the past with the reforming power of the new times. With him there developed, attaining its most complete formulation, the particular rationalist historicism that is typical of the most mature Roman thought—not just legal—and which one of his pupils, Sextus Cecilius Africanus, would hold up, almost in the same years, in a dialogue reported by Gellius, in opposition to the discontinuist and excessively apologetic argumentation about the present and its independence advanced by the philosopher Favorinus ("the long passage of time has caused us to forget long-ago words and customs, but it is to these words and customs that the significance of the laws remains tied").[35]

The work of Julian also concluded and moved definitively beyond the debate between the empirical paradigm and the rationalistic and dogmatic one that had pitted Sabinus against Labeo, then Aristo against Javolenus, and Celsus against Neratius. And it was also for this reason that from Julian on it would no longer make sense (as Gaius and Pomponius were fully aware) to speak of divisions between "schools": Julian's model, more than a synthesis, actually overcame that polarity. Labeo, Sabinus, and Javolenus were used to the full, but in order to obtain from them a more advanced result, both in terms of the theoretical foundations and in those of the politics of law: a *ius* in which conceptual analysis and empirical assessment, analogical construction of "rules," and examination of the circumstances on the basis of fairness all became complementary and integrated tools for the achievement, through the alliance between the science of the jurists and the imperial legislation, of a "human" and "benign" legal order, an instrument well suited to the new universalistic monarchy celebrated by Favorinus and by Aelius Aristides.

The codification of the praetor's edict, which Julian carried out at Hadrian's behest, was likewise completed in the context of this common front. From then on, the text became unmodifiable for the magistrates, who were left only with the possibility of extending it analogically ("proceed by analogical reasoning," Julian would write, with reference to Pedius);[36] but we may assume that it had largely been so for some time, and that the aim of the intervention desired by Hadrian was not so much to fix this restriction as it was to undertake a definitive arrangement of the text, in accordance with an order that differed quite sharply from the one still known to Pedius. It was then handed over, in its new immobility, above all to the jurists, who made it the subject, with Pomponius, Paul, and Ulpian, of analytical commentaries, parallel to those regarding Sabinus, and together with the latter offering a recapitulation of the whole Roman legal tradition. But the edict was also consigned to the emperor, who would henceforth be able to adopt it as an integral element of his own normative activity. In the great design of Hadrian and Julian, legal science and imperial legislation were confirmed as pillars of the ecumenical regeneration of the principate. The new monarchy really could be enlightened, as long as it had the invaluable and irreplaceable jurists at its side, from then on authentic guardians, through the spread of their authoritativeness, not only of the private regulation of the whole imperial collectivity, but indirectly of the legitimacy of power itself, and of a legality that aspired to become a fully achieved measure of the world.

The figure of Julian would ultimately loom large over the entire century, and there was not a jurist between the ages of Hadrian and Septimius Severus who did not feel obliged to take him into account in one way or another: from Volusius Mecianus to Ulpius Marcellus; from Africanus to Cervidius Scaevola, Mauricianus, and Venuleius Saturninus; to say nothing of Gaius, who from his decentralized point of view as a teacher, probably far from Rome, considered him a solitary giant; or of Pomponius himself.[37]

Over the course of a few decades, Julian's model thus almost completely replaced that of Labeo. What established itself in the second part of the century was a paradigm of legal science that brought to fulfillment the Servian aspect more than the strictly Labeonian dimension of the revolution of formalism (Labeo was never an important author for Julian);[38] a science that emphasized the case-based aspect of its activities, with respect to a body of writing assembled around the great ordering blocks of tradition: the Sabinian *ius civile*, the edict as reorganized by Julian. Its literary genres would be, instead, the books of *Digesta, Responsa,* and *Quaestiones.*[39] It was a choice that fully delineated two paths, which ran through the whole of jurisprudence and cut across literary genres: one line that went from Servius to Julian, and then continued on to Papinian and Paul; and another from Labeo and Sabinus (the pairing is not paradoxical) to Pedius, Pomponius, and Ulpian. In the center of the first line was the case, perennially problematic; in the second the normative element, which originated in the sedimentation of the *ius civile,* in the jurisprudential rule or the edictal prescription.[40] It would be difficult to identify a substantial epistemological divergence between the two: rather, a diversity of accents and nuances, and a limited oscillation of interpretative paradigms.

Labeonism was not, however, entirely out of the picture. It still survived —above all as ideological nostalgia for an irretrievable period of complete autonomy of legal knowledge—in Sextus Pomponius, in the heart of the Antonine age. His commentary on the edict—immense in size, possibly comprising 150 books, greatly admired by Ulpian, who drew on it continually, perhaps less so by Paul[41]—was a real archeology of legal knowledge, dense with studied references to literature dating all the way back to republican times: a gold mine of ideas and doctrines, dominated by the importance accorded to Labeo's thought.[42] But it was the *Enchiridion* in particular, which we have frequently mentioned, that was entirely based on the theme of this revival. On the other hand, the extolling of republican models had now been completely absorbed within the symbolic and cultural horizon of the principate—markedly so from Trajan onwards—and indeed contributed to its defense (something vaguely similar would happen with the classicist republicanism of eighteenth-century England and France before the revolution, entirely reconciled with a complete loyalty to monarchism). That memory only indicated a recovery, somewhat polemical from the perspective of a criticism of customs, but certainly not subversive of the established power, of a model of civic virtue associated with the most authentic and precious kernel of the Roman character—with its genetic essence—completely stripped of all strictly constitutional significance. It had already been so for Cassius Longinus, Tacitus, and Pliny: Pomponius did nothing more than adopt the lesson.

3.

In the middle of the second century, then, jurisprudence was faced by a new framework for the production of law: on the one hand, the petering out of the *ius honorarium,* by now codified into an immutable text; on the other, an increasingly direct presence of provisions introduced by the emperor (constitutions) that in various forms established rules which could not be ignored. Admittedly, the jurists still often had a big say in them, because, as counselors (and before long as officials) of the emperor they were able to guide his normative decisions in a decisive manner. But even though the new and closer relationships with the imperial power did assign crucial tasks of supervision and oversight to legal expertise, the balance in relations between jurisprudence and the princes still tended inexorably to tip in the direction of politics and government.

This situation was reflected with great clarity in two passages from Gaius and Pomponius, which we may rightly consider as a symmetrical pair of snapshots that reproduce, from two different perspectives, what appeared to their authors as an overall picture of Roman law in their times.

The text by Gaius comes from the opening of his handbook of *Institutiones,* almost certainly written (at least in a first draft) during the final years of Hadrian's rule; a work intended for educational purposes, in all likelihood making use of Sabinian materials, well known to, but not (as far as we can ascertain) cited by, Severan jurisprudence, very popular in late antiquity and in the Byzantine schools, and which has survived to the present day almost entirely intact (thanks to a genuine stroke of historiographic luck) outside of Justinian's *Digesta*:[43]

> The laws of the Roman people consist of *leges* (comitial enact-
> ments), plebiscites, senatusconsults, imperial constitutions, edicts
> of those possessing the right to issue them, and answers of the
> learned.[44]

The writing takes the form of a list, with the characteristics of a genuine *partitio*. All of the *Institutiones*—beginning with the general scheme that guides them: the law of persons, things, and actions—are organized according to diaeretic patterns; they realized to some extent the project rejected more than two centuries earlier by Quintus Mucius and carried forward (we do not know how) by Cicero in *De iure civili* and by Ofilius in the *Iuris partiti* books: but this time it was just a manual, without excessive ambitions.

Immediately afterward Gaius went on to illustrate, one by one, with a scholastic monotony of style, the individual parts indicated: "a *lex* is . . . a plebiscite is . . . a senatusconsult is . . . an imperial constitution is . . . the right of issuing edicts is . . . the answers of the learned are . . ."[45]

Pomponius, in the *Enchiridion,* was more concise; he too composed a list, but he named and described at the same time, and with greater pace (his work was also a handbook, though shorter, and the intended readership may not have been only scholastic):

> Thus, in our city either there is the law laid down by statutes, or
> there is our own *ius civile,* which is grounded without writing in
> nothing more than interpretation by experts; or there are statu-
> tory actions at law, which contain the forms for taking legal pro-
> ceedings; or there is plebiscite law, which is settled without the
> advice and consent of the senate; or there is the magistrates'
> edict, whence honorary law derives; or there is a senatusconsult,
> which is brought in without statutory authority solely on the de-

cision of the senate; or there is an imperial constitution, in the sense that what the emperor himself has decided is to be observed as having statutory force.[46]

We can consider the two passages to be independent. We do not know whether there were any dealings between the two authors. There is just one mention in Pomponius of "our learned friend Gaius,"[47] but we cannot rule out the possibility that it was a reference to Gaius Cassius Longinus, well known to Pomponius; and, for that matter, there is no mention of Pomponius in Gaius.[48] Nor do we have sufficiently precise reconstructions of the chronologies of the two works to suppose on any factual grounds that one text might have been derived from the other.[49]

The outlooks of the two jurists were drastically divergent. The difference does not leap immediately to the eye, since it regards a point of extreme delicacy, about which it would have been unthinkable in those years to express a strong position. We must seek it out with care, always mindful that the communicative codes of ancient writing, whenever the need arose, did not shrink from dissimulation, disguise, and, if necessary (and here it was in particular), a studied reliance upon forms of Nicodemism.[50]

At first glance it might be tempting to reduce the difference between the positions to, as it were, a methodological distance: both jurists seem to have set out to exhaustively describe the phenomenology of the formation of *ius* in Roman history. But whereas Gaius made use of a unifying concept, modeled substantially on the notion of "public statutory law," taken as a paradigm to which to refer the plurality of normative experiences that had emerged over time—and thus operating on a systematic formalistic plane— Pomponius, working in tune with the overall structure of his little handbook, apparently chose a purely historical and continuist (one might even say stratigraphic) standpoint, limiting himself to setting forth the successive manifestations of *ius* in the city.[51]

This approach takes us in the right direction, but not the whole way. Let's try to look a little further, beginning once again with Gaius.

The first challenge facing us is to discover the origins of the scheme he presented. It is quite probable that it was a reelaboration of a previous Sabinian model, in turn dating to the description we encountered in Cicero's *Topica*, and even earlier, with some variants, in the *Rhetorica ad Herennium*: it was in fact precisely from the rhetorical tradition that Sabinus had in all likelihood taken his notion of "rule," and it was in that culture that the idea of a *partitio* of *ius* was first manifested, with a stylistic mode very similar to the one which would later surface in Gaius. Among the three versions—*Rhetorica, Topica, Institutiones*—there were certainly important differences, but the continuity of the approach, marked by a progressive "juridicization" of an original nucleus further removed from legal culture, seems unquestionable.[52]

In reality, the guiding thread of Gaius' discourse, more than the paradigm of statutory law as such, appears to be that of the subject hidden behind the (formalistic) screen of the *lex*: the "Roman people." And in fact the *"populus"* crops up in each of the definitions presented: directly in that of statutory law ("A *lex* is a command and ordinance of the *populus* . . .") and plebiscite ("A plebiscite is a command and ordinance of the *plebs*. The *plebs* differs from the *populus* ... which [a *Lex Hortensia*] provided that plebiscites should bind the entire *populus*. Thereby plebiscites were equated to *leges*");[53] and in an indirect way, through the deliberately ambiguous expression "has the force of *lex*," in the definitions of the senatusconsult ("it has the force of *lex*, though this has been questioned"),[54] of the imperial constitution (where Gaius took the connection with *lex*, and thus with the *populus*, as certain),[55] and, finally, of the edict, traced back to the concept of the people through the expression—charged with evocative value—"magistrates of the Roman people."[56] Only the definition of the responses seemed to be an exception, with respect to which neither people nor statutory law was mentioned; we shall return to this point shortly.

This list can now be compared with the reality of the legal order in Gaius' time. The *lex publica* had vanished. The same was true of the plebiscites; and indeed the sketchy account of their equivalence to laws—an ancient story—contributed to giving the reference the flavor of a distant memory. The decrees of the senate were fully operative as effective instruments of the emperor's will, but in quantitative terms they had had a relatively marginal value for *ius*. As for the edicts, by far the most important one, that of the urban praetor, explicitly recalled, was being fixed in those very years into an immutable text.[57] And so—if we continue to exclude for the moment the responses of the jurists—what was left? Nothing, to fill the scene of the current production of *ius*, except the constitution of the emperor, in its relationship of historical and ideological derivation from statutory law and, through it, from

the will of the people.[58] People, statutory law, and constitution—emperor
and people, then, in an extreme but very evident simplification, almost a conceptual and institutional short circuit: this is the real heart of Gaius' discourse,
with no other issue having more than a preliminary value.

And finally we come to the responses. Immediately striking is the use of
"authorized," around which the first part of the definition is constructed
("the answers of the learned are the decisions and opinions of those who are
authorized to lay down the law").[59] The verb recurs quite often in Gaius, and
its use always evokes the power that grants the concession.[60] But in our case,
who—or what—"authorizes" the jurists to "lay down the law"? In the logical
structure of the text it is precisely the presence of this power—implicit, even
if unnamed—that justifies the obtaining of the "force of *lex*" which immediately follows ("If the decisions of all of them agree, what they so hold has the
force of *lex*").[61] The entire description is constructed around the nexus—a
kind of circle—between these two poles of meaning: since certain jurists "are
authorized," they are capable of "laying down the law"; but the possibility for
them to do so exists from the moment in which their opinions, inasmuch as
they have been authorized (and are in conformity), have "the force of *lex*."
The power that allows the jurists to "lay down the law" is the same one allowing their responses to be tied back into the model of statutory law, and therefore of the people, and hence to fall within the general scheme constructed
by Gaius. The voice of the jurists—like that of all the other sources of *ius*—
therefore also speaks in the name of the people.

We have thus discovered the face of the subject both revealed and hidden
in the writing of the *Institutiones:* the only one capable of transmitting to the
force of the responses the value of statutory law. Standing out behind that
"authorized" is none other than the figure of the *princeps*, the profile of imperial power: it is only his concession of the faculty to "lay down the law"
through the *ius publice respondendi* that allows responses in the form of *sententiae* to share with the constitutions the same (ambiguous) assimilation
into statutory law. Since the *princeps* ("the emperor himself") received his investiture from a *lex*—albeit a rather particular one, the *lex de imperio*—and
therefore from the people, who represent the origin of his legality ("the emperor himself receives his *imperium* through a *lex*"), the acts based on his sovereign power—the constitutions every bit as much as the concession of the

ius respondendi—reflect the aura of that original derivation, and share its essence.[62]

In this image, where tradition has been completely overturned, jurisprudence now appears to be fully enmeshed in the web of imperial authority: a legal science that was certainly very lively and active, but whose most important function could be carried out only in the shadow of the *princeps*.

And in fact it is the emperor in person, in the shape of the great Hadrian, who appears in the announced conclusion of the discourse: "If they [the jurists who have the power to lay down the law] disagree, the judge [in a trial] is at liberty to follow whichever decision he pleases. This is declared by a rescript of the late emperor Hadrian."[63] It is the emperor, then, who even regulates how to evaluate the doctrinal controversies among jurists. There is already the typical air of late antiquity here: "authorized . . . has the force of *lex* . . . the late emperor Hadrian": an ineluctable crescendo. The jurists and the emperor were for Gaius the sole sources of *ius* still in existence in his time, but bound up in a relationship of unchangeable asymmetry, where the supremacy of the *princeps* and of his legislation must have appeared absolutely unquestionable.

4.

Let's move on now to Pomponius. The first part of his list recalled the Twelve Tables (and there was an allusion to them in the expression "laid down by law, that is by statute"),[64] the original nucleus of civil law (identified in the interpretation of the jurists), and finally the *legis actiones*.

This beginning was an exact reproduction of the scheme underlying the *Tripertita* of Sextus Aelius. What we have here is therefore a silent citation, as often happens in ancient literature: a tribute—for those capable of perceiving it—to the author of a work which Pomponius himself considered to contain "the cradle of law."[65] With a certain degree of awe, the structure of that ancient and precious piece of writing now became, in the construction of the *Enchiridion*, a guide for tracing the development of the forms of *ius* in the city. The description then continued by referring to the plebiscites, the edict, the senatorial decrees, and the constitutions of the emperor—elements also present in Gaius' version.

At first glance, it seems like a sequence with no perceptible center, in clear contrast with Gaius' treatment. And we can by no means rule out that it had roots in the distant past, and that already in the late-republican era there existed two archetypes of representation of *ius:* one more closely bound to a tradition within legal thought itself, and dating back to the *Tripertita;* and another, closer to rhetorical and philosophical culture, with ties to the *Rhetorica ad Herennium* and the *Topica,* and subsequently drawn on afresh in Sabinian circles.[66] Gaius followed the latter, readapting it, however, for his own purposes (the affirmation of the supremacy of the imperial constitution). Pomponius opted for the former: but like Gaius, he did so in a nonneutral way, because he in turn had an objective he wished to attain. Let's try to discover what it was.

In Pomponius' list there was a singular absence: the jurists. Their work was mentioned only in relation to the *ius civile,* at the beginning, in a counterpoint to the Twelve Tables (in keeping with a model that had already been employed elsewhere in the *Enchiridion*).[67] After that, nothing. How could this be, especially in a work that gave so much attention to jurisprudence? Let's read the following passage, which is generally not connected to the preceding text:

> After this study of the origin and development of law, the next thing to consider is the names and origin of the magistracies, because, as we have already shown, it is only through those who preside over jurisdiction that the final result is obtained. For how much is it worth that there be law [ius] in a civic body unless there be people able to administer the legal orders [iura]? Then after that we shall speak of the succession of authors, because law cannot exist unless there is some jurist who can improve it from day to day.[68]

There is unquestionably a gap (which is hard to attribute to the epitomist) in the discourse just concluded (nor does it make much of a difference if we suppose that the two passages were not contiguous in the original composition).[69] Once he had completed his description of *ius,* Pomponius went on to justify the expository choices of the *Enchiridion,* with the space devoted to the magistracies and to the jurists. And he did so with a calm, almost modest exordium, whose tone, however, immediately rose in timbre, through a rhetorical question, a little laborious but not ineffective. Talking about law without the magistrates would be meaningless, Pomponius explained: it was only through them that "the final result is obtained." What would *ius* amount to if there were no one capable of administering it? Then he turned his attention to the jurists—fittingly, since there can be no law if there is no one who improves upon that law day by day. And here they are at last: the jurists, but found—and this is the point—in their proper place, that is, not in a stratigraphy of the parts of *ius*. It was precisely this that Pomponius wanted to ensure would be clearly understood: the jurists were not in his estimation simply a part (a stratum) in the historical composition of law, an element among many, isolable alongside others; they were instead the preliminary condition—and therefore, in some way, outside the list presented earlier, inasmuch as they represented a prerequisite without which *ius* as a whole could never have existed.

But what law? All of it? Even that expressed by the imperial constitutions? Pomponius did not state this explicitly, but the conclusion, as things stood, was inescapable. The constitutions were a part of *ius,* but the jurists constituted the essential condition for the existence of the entire *ius.* And so, yes, even the law of the emperor, in order to have authentic effectiveness (the "effectus rei," as Pomponius had written) required their work.

We have reached the real heart of the *Enchiridion.* The force of the proposition demanded (and explained) the oblique prudence of its formulation. A direct declaration of the superiority of jurisprudence would have been out of the question in those years, when the design of a monarchic absolutism—"regulator of the world"—was already taking shape.[70] But the jurists were still on the scene, and the imperial power had to continue taking them into account. What could not be stated openly had to be suggested and allowed to be glimpsed: it was necessary to raise a hidden but perceptible barrier against the risks always associated with autocracy.

Rhetorically, Pomponius' strategy was focused entirely on the expedient of the break in the narrative: between what we read as two separate paragraphs, the landscape shifted, as did the subject of the discourse. But a sharp eye, observing the whole, could not miss the connection: first, the astonishing absence of jurists, with the mention of the imperial constitutions in last place, as if left hanging; then—barely disguised by the gap—they burst onto the stage, and they do so as the absolute protagonists, even though apparently in quite a different sense. Between the two crucial subjects (the emperor and jurisprudence), and avoiding a dangerous and excessively intimate contact which would have demanded a hierarchy quite different from what was being suggested, lay the pause in the narrative and the change of subject. Sufficient to protect, but not to conceal. The rest was left up to the mind of the reader: this too was part of ancient writing. And for that matter, in all of Pomponius' output the imperial constitutions occupy only a modest role: for him law is always an experience pertaining to magistrates and (especially) jurists.

What emerges fully is the distance from Gaius' point of view; not a cold difference of method—a formalistic as opposed to a historicizing approach—but instead a complete reversal of positions concerning a decisive issue in the politics of law: the relationship between jurisprudence and the *princeps* in the control of *ius*. For Gaius there was no doubt: the center of everything was the will of the emperor (though by now the appropriate term is "the sovereign"); the jurists had a role only to the extent that they were "authorized" to act. But for Pomponius it was still legal science that dominated the field, and the imperial constitutions, like any other source of *ius*, could not even exist ("constare non potest") unless they were integrated within the daily conceptualizing and interpretative labor of a class of intellectuals faithful to their own traditions.

Let's consider Pomponius a little further, to make a final check. Once again in the *Enchiridion,* toward the end of the section devoted to jurisprudence, and following the passages we have just examined, there is a brief sketch of the history of the *ius respondendi,* which we have already recalled. Let's look closely at the second part of this rapid account:

> It was the deified Augustus who, in order to enhance the authority of the law, first established that responses might be given [by jurists] under his authority. And from that time this began to be sought as a privilege. As a consequence of this, our most excellent emperor Hadrian issued a rescript on an occasion when some men of praetorian rank were petitioning him for permission to

give responses, saying that this thing could not be requested, but was to be earned and that he [the emperor] would accordingly be delighted if whoever had faith in his knowledge would prepare himself to respond to the questions of citizens.[71]

As we have previously noted, Pomponius outlined a history of the respondent activity of the jurists characterized by significant discontinuities.[72] The thread that made it possible to follow its course is identifiable in the varying success attributed to "faith in his knowledge" as a prerequisite for being able to issue responses (and this was, for Pomponius, a strongly self-centered perception: the recognition of one's own doctrine as an absolute value to which each jurist could associate both a role and an identity). Originally, in the republican era, wrote Pomponius in a part of the text not quoted here, the relationship was direct and immediate: "opinions were given by people who had confidence in their own studies."[73] Then matters became more complex, and Augustus intervened, introducing a new discipline; and thereafter the *ius respondendi* began to be requested as a privilege. In this conception, the prerequisite of "faith" lost force; what mattered was the imperial will, in a context of discretionality that outweighed all other evaluations. Finally, the Hadrianic present, enlightened by the episode of the rescript to "some men of praetorian rank," marked a return to the original situation. The idea of privilege was rejected ("could not be requested, but was to be earned"), and once again, what mattered was solely "faith in his knowledge." The *princeps* did no more than acknowledge a condition that the jurist must already have earned for himself; we are in the presence here of a sort of republican restoration.

Let's try now to compare the formulation "this thing could not be requested, but was to be earned" ("hoc non peti, sed praestari solere") with the expression "those who are authorized to lay down the law" ("quibus permissum est iura condere") in the text of Gaius: the contrast could not be more striking. On the one hand, in Gaius, what dominated was the image of the sovereign legislator, irradiating through his unchallengeable concession a part of his own power to the jurists, who were totally dependent on it. On the other hand, in Pomponius, there was taking shape the idea of an authentic regeneration of jurisprudential law, fully recognized by an imperial power that chose, after some wavering, to withdraw into the background.

The history of the magistracies and the history of jurisprudence are the two perspectives on which the whole of the *Enchiridion* (and all of Pomponius' work) is based. The justification of this choice (as we have just seen) was calm but quite firm: without magistrates and jurists it would not be possible to conceive of law. But praetors and jurisprudence had been the pillars of the republican legal order, the protagonists of what (again according to Pomponius' judgment) had been the golden age of Roman legal culture, the century extending from Publius Mucius to Labeo. That is how the "Tacitism" of Pomponius appears, a philorepublicanism that was by now combined with a political loyalism that we have no reason to question. All the same, this was more than innocuous nostalgia. Pomponius used the memory of that distant past to set it up decisively as an example for the political actions of the excellent emperor. In short, he was attempting to adroitly outline a model. And his idealization of the figure of Hadrian—the Hadrian of the rescript to men of praetorian rank, who chose to take a step back with respect to the knowledge of the jurists, as far as could be imagined from the Hadrian of the rescript recorded by Gaius, who had not even hesitated to establish a parameter against which to measure the debates of that science!—fitted perfectly into the framework of a similar reconstruction.

Was there something forced in this manner of presenting things, in this so markedly "republican" Hadrian? It is highly probable, but there is little point in asking whether the attentive Pomponius was aware of it. What mattered to the jurist was not to offer a realistic depiction of the politics of law under Hadrian; but to isolate a behavior of the emperor to the point of stressing its exemplary value, and to set it forth as a model that drew strength from its evocation of a luminous tradition, thus revived. The emperor who drew back in the presence of the jurists; the emperor who recognized that law—including what was enacted directly by him—was nothing unless integrated into the work of jurisprudence. This was Pomponius' nagging concern—the barely concealed motor of his writing.

Which of the two doctrines—that of Gaius or of Pomponius—would be destined to enjoy the greater success? Over the long term, unquestionably the Gaian one. As we have previously said: by irrevocably enclosing jurisprudence within the boundaries of the emperor's power, it was a bellwether of the experience of absolutism in late antiquity— and that is another of the reasons explaining the overwhelming and posthumous success of the master of the *Institutiones*.[74] Over a shorter period, however, it would be the ideas of Pomponius that attracted significant consensus. But that is another story, which takes us straight to the thinking of Ulpian.

II. The Government: Ulpian

20

The Great Systematization

I.

In the closing years of the second century Roman legal thought experienced the final metamorphosis in its history. The change took place against the backdrop of a remarkable occurrence: the establishment, following the crisis of Hadrian's model of government, of a full-fledged administrative machine to guide the empire. Bureaucratic and centralizing, it was unlike anything the ancient world had ever seen.

The network of local autonomies, which had prevailed since the Antonine age, was suddenly disintegrating. The long period of stagnation succeeding the end of the imperial expansion and the interruption of economic growth previously bloated by the spoils of war and the massive influx of slave labor, which had characterized the late-republican era, began to turn into a general systemic collapse.[1]

Through to the end of the Flavian era, the advantages stemming from the definitive agrarian–slave labor stabilization of the imperial economy and the ensuing development of a world dimension to mercantile activities—the contact between far-flung areas of production and the existence of a still-virtuous spiral between trade and tax revenues—continued to outweigh the costs that made them possible; the empire's accounts were still in order.[2] But over the second century the balance would be reversed, and the expenses of political unification—army, bureaucracy, transportation, communications—in the absence of technological innovations that might permit more than short-term savings or release new social energies, began to exceed the wealth being created. A massive shortfall developed that not even the political fueling of the economy (to borrow a Weberian formula) was capable of reversing.[3] At the edges of the empire, there were no further external resources to draw upon, or masses to enslave. Wars ceased to be an investment, and became purely defensive, with the sole exception of Trajan's—extremely costly —campaign in Dacia.[4]

In an attempt to mitigate the economic difficulties and ward off collapse, the imperial ruling groups—at this point mainly of provincial provenance—initiated, from the age of the Severans until the years of Diocletian and Constantine, between the third and fourth centuries, an unprecedented series of modifications to the structure of government and power, by now overwhelmingly militarized—in terms of ideology, social alliances, and methods of exercising sovereignty.[5] In other words, a new and dramatic "passive revolution" took place, albeit fragmentary and discontinuous, which did not hesitate in its later phases to seek the support of Christianity.[6]

But unlike the period of the first principate, the room for maneuver was virtually nonexistent: the imperial system had run through almost all its reserves. The crisis was at once productive, social, and financial, and had widespread cultural repercussions. While the army, the bureaucracy, and taxes all grew apace, the government began to intervene more and more directly in the economy, attempting to direct it from above, with a range of markedly centralized—though often rather approximate and empirical—planning instruments: redistributive fiscal programs; price freezes; and efforts to use far-reaching legislation to attain an adequate balance between liquidity, inflation, and a tendency to return to common practices of the natural economy (when Paul wrote his magnificent text about the difference between sale and barter, he was probably witnessing the first signs of these).[7] As always, the response was purely political: in the midst of its final and ultimate crisis, the ancient economy was unable to break away from its congenitally subaltern position.[8]

The effort was not successful, at least in the European West, though it sometimes seemed that the worst had been averted. But the situation and the destiny of the two parts of the empire were about to become uncoupled for good; the two histories started to separate again, as had not happened since the times of Polybius, with the East and Africa distant from the West and from northern Europe.⁹ The West began to move toward its final catastrophe (and then the late-medieval and modern regeneration); the East, toward the long continuity of Byzantium and the dazzling rise of Islam. The different nature of the crisis of late antiquity in these broad areas would establish two distinct styles of history, one pertaining to the regions where the rupture was sharpest, and the other to those where the transition was cushioned by the survival of Byzantium. Only the former would later experience the rebirth of modernity.¹⁰

The protracted resistance would nevertheless last long enough to completely transform the political organization of the empire. A new entity would emerge from the metamorphosis, at least in this part of the world: the almost complete form of a great absolutist State. Until then, in fact, it was only by adopting a questionable analogical approach that the Roman institutions could be described as a "State": and we have always avoided doing so. But now, out of the skeletal administration of the republican age and the early principate, capable with a handful of men and scanty resources—practically without a bureaucracy and with little more than a hint of apparatuses—of governing an empire extending from Mesopotamia to the North Sea, thanks to the development of a system of autonomies involving the exchange of consensus and legitimation for guarantees and integration, something completely unprecedented was emerging. Economic interventionism, the expansion of taxation, and the massive increase in the size of the army all contributed to the formation of a new set-up: the outline of a full-blown state structure, which emerged from the ruins of Hadrian's pluralism, and was soon destined to assume the autocratic and then Christianly paternalistic countenance of late-antique despotism.¹¹

It was the jurists—the last great generations, between Commodus and Alexander Severus—who led the change, and their marked presence would be clearly visible in all the subsequent developments, even within the military and bureaucratic mesh that soon came into being. Legalism, in fact—the decayed and threadbare product of the Severan legal culture—combined with economic centralization, fiscal voracity, the invasive presence of the army,

and the ethical and social regulation exercised through the far-reaching power
of the bishops, would become the dominant feature of the late-antique
State.[12]

The new configuration of government, already delineated during the principate of Septimius Severus, inexorably shifted the axis of jurisprudence to
within the orbit of the emperor's power. Just as the republican jurists had all
been magistrates of the Roman people, now all the leading scholars of law,
from Papinian onwards, would become top-level officials in the imperial administration: intellectual bureaucrats of an almost Hegelian kind, summoned
to manage directly a world-level government undermined by contradictions,
threats, and dangers, and devoured by an intrinsic autocratic vocation.

   In its time, jurisprudential law had come into being and developed as the
ius of a single city: only a restricted community without major difficulties in
communication or in managing its own institutions could so successfully
have entrusted its civil regulation to the collective knowledge of a circle of
experts, expressed without recourse to any public apparatus, and based on a
set of procedures that became increasingly delicate and fragile as it grew in
technical refinement. This model had managed to survive outside the boundaries of the republican polis, establishing itself at the heart of a worldwide
dominion, due exclusively to the creation of two conditions.

   The first had been the possibility of continuing to remain to some extent
the law of a single city—even though it was the mistress of the world—without ever being obliged to become the legal system of the entire empire,
thanks to the construction of an ample network of autonomies, which left
each community, whether city-based or tribal, its own traditions and rules
(the possibility of making "use of their own customs and their own laws," in
the words of Hadrian to the inhabitants of Italica).[13] Roman law did of course
have its own institutional channels for diffusion and emanation, but they reserved for the work of jurisprudence nothing more than an exemplary and
guiding role.

   The second condition was the shrewd compromise that, from the age of
Labeo onwards, the jurists succeeded in establishing with the new power, in a
reciprocal validation: recognition of their own role in exchange for a full and

total acceptance of the constitutional importance of the emperor and of his increasingly marked presence as a legislator, both through the prudent mechanism of the rescripts (customarily reserved for questions relating to *ius*) and the more incisive and direct one of the edicts.

But at the beginning of the third century, both of these premises began to crumble. On the one hand, the system of autonomies was dissolving completely, giving way to an unwieldy and convoluted political organization, which demanded a dense and uniform normative regulation that could never have been entrusted to the jurists alone, and had to appear as a direct emanation of the will of the sovereign ("living law"—the opposite of excarnation—in the autocratic outlook of late antiquity).[14] On the other hand, the old terms of both the Labeonian compromise and Julian's alliance between jurisprudence and imperial power proved spectacularly inadequate in the face of the overwhelming force of the new military-bureaucratic machine. By agreeing to occupy the top levels of the government and the administration, the jurists themselves surrendered what remained of their independence, perhaps aware, as they did so, that they were decreeing the death of jurisprudential law. But it enabled them to preside over the birth of the new State form of politics, and to try to project upon it a formal structure that took shape from the expansion of the categories of law from private regulation to administrative and constitutional organization. It was a path destined to be repeated and developed in the modern age, and which constructed, between the fifteenth and nineteenth centuries, its own "publicistic" orderings, deriving them from the conceptual framework of the Romanist tradition of private law, with significant consequences for the European political and juridical laboratory as a whole.

This led to the creation, from the end of the second century, of a new literary genre, which, beginning with Mecianus, Marcellus, and Venuleius, would find its definitive consecration in Ulpian's major treatise *De officio proconsulis*—one of the most widely read and distributed legal works, together with the *Institutiones* of Gaius, in late antiquity—which consolidated an original reflection combining political thought, administrative practice, and conceptualization of a more strictly juristic nature.[15]

Even when Ulpian was writing, in the years immediately following 210, the jurists and their literature could still be considered the linchpin of imperial law: their activity of interpretation and commentary served as the foundation of an irreplaceable normative continuity; and that is to say nothing about the fact that, by ceding to the legislation of the emperor a now inevitable supremacy in the production of new law, it was they themselves who once again had a say, as the counselors upon whom the legislating sovereign relied, and as the directors of the offices of the chancellery responsible for emanating the *constitutiones*.[16]

But this final equilibrium would last for only a short time; by the middle of the third century it would already have been irreversibly shattered: with the disappearance of every major figure, and with the exhaustion of the customary forms of a literary activity that had endured without a break since the time of Quintus Mucius, the whole world order was supported by the legislation of the emperor alone, and in the chancellery what dominated was the obscure labor of anonymous though far from incompetent bureaucrats: figures in whom it was no longer possible to distinguish an intellectual profile that did not coincide with the task demanded by their function. The Severan jurists had effectively forgone the future identity of their class in an attempt to impress upon the first form of the State in the West the seal of a legality with an openly ecumenical vocation, in which the limitless power of the sovereign, in the very act in which its absoluteness was definitively legitimized, could be softened and tempered in the design of a natural law that was at once pliant and rigorous, capable of shielding it from the temptations of an "oriental" and despotic future.

It was an arduous path, which did not open up great possibilities, at least in antiquity, but led only to that intertwining between bureaucracy and legalism, between the private claims of subjects and the public authority of the sovereign, which constituted so much of the history of the late-antique empire, and would later be interpreted with brilliant acumen by Godefroy, reader of the *Theodosian Code*.[17] But it was also a path paid for with their lives, in the space of little more than a decade, by two of the greatest jurists of the period: Papinian and Ulpian, both praetorian prefects, died in palace conspiracies in 212 and 223—the dark image of a legal science under attack, tragically drenched in its own blood. That policy, just like Labeo's attempts to oppose the will of Augustus, was destined over the short term to end in disaster. But precisely like the efforts of Labeo, it would leave a not insignificant trail—in the furrow of which a great deal of history would unfold.

2.

If Julian was the most luminous example of the jurist as "counselor of the *princeps*," Domitius Ulpianus was, to an even greater degree than his colleague (and probably rival) Julius Paul, that of the jurist as minister of the empire. His vast body of work, all concentrated in the space of a few years— probably between 212–13 and 218–19, after he left the office *a libellis* and before he assumed, in 222, the praetorian prefecture that would prove fatal to him[18]—used extensively by Justinian's compilers, and therefore legible to a degree unrivaled by any other author except Gaius,[19] has yet to be investigated in depth with truly reliable historiographical criteria.

Out of an old habit, when scholars of Roman law deal with Ulpian's writings, they generally consider them as a sort of neutral container, an almost inexhaustible—but not particularly interesting—reservoir of references and data from which to draw on as required: a doctrine of Pedius or Julian, an opinion from Pomponius or Labeo, a formula of the edict, and so on.[20]

This attitude, which reduced the work of Ulpian to an inert vehicle, is underpinned by a prejudice which may in part be justified by the great abundance of citations present in the jurist's texts: roughly 2,000, of which more than 1,000 are in the commentary on the edict alone.[21] It is an imposing mass: the whole of jurisprudence was evaluated and filtered in the composition of his prose, which often really does seem to step back, as if satisfied with the limited task of recording a memory spanning centuries.

And yet it gave expression to a precise and complex plan, in which the continual recourse to the history of jurisprudence was not determined by the need to offer a disinterested account of the depth of a tradition, but proved functional for the construction of a new and original synthesis, which unhesitatingly bent to its purposes the preceding literature, subjecting its memory to a consciously manipulative pressure.

In order to fully grasp this, we shall try to cast some light on a segment of great importance. The setting is the fourth book of the commentary on the edict, devoted to an exposition of the doctrine of contracts. We can thus pick up once again—and fully exhaust—the same theme found to be a privileged point of observation in the reconstruction of the thought of Mucius and Labeo, and which here too will prove to be particularly fruitful.

We are now no longer in the presence of the mercantile boom of the first century, in the aftermath of the great imperial conquests, with magistrates and jurists engaged in a feverish quest for hitherto-unexplored ways of disciplining the new reality; instead we find the mature requirements of a world economy already beyond its peak, and upon which Julian and Pomponius had already reflected at length.

The book was devoted almost completely to an elucidation of the fourth title of the edict (in Julian's edition), "On Pacts and Agreements," which we dealt with when we attempted to outline its genesis and original sense (in the commentary by Paul the same title was analyzed in the third book, while in Pomponius' far more extensive one, it must have been examined in books 6 to 8).[22]

The question that immediately springs to mind is why Ulpian chose this context—relating to the edict on pacts—to develop his more general discourse on contracts: neither Paul nor Pomponius (as far as we know) had done anything of the sort. A plausible response will emerge later. But for now, let's begin to read the text:

> This edict is grounded on natural equity. For what so accords with human faith as that which the parties have decided among themselves to observe? Moreover, "pact" (*pactum*) is derived from *pactio* (agreement) (the word "peace" comes from the same origin), and is the agreement and consent of two or more parties about the same thing. The word "agreement" has a general value, relating to everything agreed upon by those who perform an act [*agere*] for the purpose of contracting or transacting business; for just as those who are collected and come from different places into one place are said to come together, likewise those who, from different motions of the mind, agree on one thing, that is form one opinion.[23]

Ulpian's opening words ("this edict") referred to the rubric of the edictal title ("On Pacts and Agreements"), and the entire development of the discourse on contracts would appear as a lengthy commentary upon its formulation. The text proper, in Julian's version ("I will enforce pacts agreed between parties which have been made neither maliciously nor in contravention of a statute, plebiscite, senatusconsult, edicts or decrees of the emperor; nor as a fraud on any of these"), would, however, be quoted only later, after the jurist had completed the exposition of his own doctrine; and only from then on would it serve as a guide to the analysis conducted in the rest of the book.[24]

The exordium was categorical; it marked the resumption of the tendency to transcribe Roman law in natural-law terms that we saw forming between Cicero and Labeo, and which had found in the concept of "natural equity" one of its strong points.[25] In the books *Ad edictum,* Ulpian would make repeated use of such a paradigm, ultimately making it one of the cornerstones of his entire analytical framework. But the reproposal of the scheme should not deceive us. Concealed behind the apparent continuity was a drastic shift with respect to the late-republican point of view (after Labeo, still present in Gaius); Ulpian's doctrine of natural law had far different motivations and meanings, as we shall see later.[26]

Once the respect of pacts had been identified with reliability in civil relations, and the latter with a principle of natural human sociability (thus establishing a natural-law basis for what had been two fundamental notions of the Roman legal experience since republican times: the ideas of *fides* and *consensus*), Ulpian moved on to offer an interpretation of the two terms upon which the rubric was based: *pactum* and *conventio.* But by this point, after such a weighty incipit, the two words appeared to have been transfigured with respect to the stark edictal formulation: they had become the symbols of a kind of universal contractualism, understood as a constituent cell of human civilization.

Ulpian's elucidation followed different paths for the two terms. In the first case, it took the form of a rapid definition based on an evident reversal of the etymological genealogy, previously suggested in the Augustan age by Sinnius Capito (it is *pactio* that derives from *pax/pactum,* and not the other way round): by reproposing it in the fourth book of the *Disputationes,* Ulpian would completely forgo this etymological justification.[27] In the second case, he did no more than attribute an all-encompassing and general value to the word *conventio,* with a reach that would soon prove to have an ambitious ontological foundation.

At this point, however, the symmetry that the two terms preserved in the edictal text (the reflection of a substantial synonymy documented as far back as the age of Cicero, and which was certainly not unknown to Ulpian, who made mention of it in the passage of the *Disputationes*) was definitively broken. In the outlook adopted by the jurist the two words were being prepared for a completely different destiny. The notion of the pact was immediately abandoned, and only returned much later, and with a very specific meaning, linked to the particularly narrow legal scope that the edictal prescription in question had, as we know, long since assumed. In contrast, the concept of *conventio*, agreement, would dominate the whole of the subsequent analysis. It was made to coincide with the consensus of the parties, however manifested, and its overall meaning was effectively reiterated through the insistent sequence of the most commonly employed verbs of the Roman contractual lexicon (*contrahere, transigere, agere:* "those who perform an act [*agere*] for the purpose of contracting or transacting business [*transigere*]"; only *gerere* was absent).

For Ulpian, the entire legal phenomenology of economic exchange thus possessed an unmistakable consensualist base, which constituted a powerful unifying force. But the pinpointing of this principle referred, albeit perhaps in a more limited formulation, to the course of previous jurisprudence. The systematic and conceptual construction opened from within onto the horizon of the history of doctrines. Ulpian continued:

> Moreover, so true is it that the word "agreement" has a general significance that Pedius elegantly says that there is no contract, no obligation, which does not include agreement, whether it is achieved by the handing over of something or by the use of certain words. In fact, even a stipulation, which is made by the use of certain words, is void unless there is agreement.[28]

The citation of the earlier jurist reiterated an essential aspect of Ulpian's doctrine: in a sense it was as if it supported its entire weight, marking a turning point in the argumentation as a whole.

The Pedius transcribed by Ulpian likewise began—we cannot say whether he too was commenting on the same edictal title[29]—with a statement about the general value of the concept of agreement; it is highly probable, in fact, that the repetition of the same phrase, just a few lines apart, can be explained by the fact that at its second occurrence Ulpian was borrowing directly from

Pedius' commentary. There then followed a different justification, with respect to what had been said before, of the significance of the notion of agreement, which restricted in the terms of a rigorous conceptual foundation, in connection with the ontology of contracts alone, the broader and more all-encompassing ". . . relating to everything . . ." of the opening: as if the same principle were being enunciated from two distinct points of view: first, by Ulpian, in the terms of an all-inclusive consensualism with a natural-law background; then, through Pedius, with exclusive reference to the system of contracts. The formulation, in the style of Ulpian's transcription, acquired the tone of a full-fledged rule: "there is no contract, no obligation, which does not include agreement" (to be understood as a hendiadys: "no obligation contracted," that is, no obligation that arises from a contract; otherwise it would be a meaningless maxim, because it is obvious that the obligations from an illicit act—*delicta* in Gaius' systematization—had no agreement behind them).[30]

A rigid symmetry was thus established between contract and agreement, the conclusion of a long path in jurisprudence that had begun way back in the time of Mucius. In Ulpian's presentation, the end point and the guiding light of this trail was the doctrine of Pedius. Its "elegance" consisted in the concise brevity with which every possible residual element of the old ritualistic framework of the *ius civile* was rendered definitively obsolete in the name of a model of law where the investigation of the interiority of the agent—with a rejection of the pointlessly subtle analysis of the precise words used in favor of ascertaining the wishes of the subjects involved (as Pedius would write in a text reported by Paul)[31]—would become a lodestar in the work of the jurists.

As we have already seen, Pedius had subscribed to the Labeonian scheme of reciprocal obligation for recognizing contractual figures not foreseen by the edict.[32] But unlike Labeo, he also accepted an extended notion of contract—not restricted just to *synallagma*—that was clearly of Sabinian provenance (in keeping with a format later stabilized by Gaius).[33] Pedius in fact considered as obligations dependent upon a contract those achieved with words or through the handing over of a thing: and in particular he considered to be of contractual origin those deriving from a stipulation, as can be deduced from the final remarks with which Ulpian closed his citation. Even the ancient ritualism of the utterance of set phrases—of which the *stipulatio* was

an extreme example (and it is no accident that Pedius chose it), and its quintessence—could do nothing to undercut the power of the new rule: since the
notion of *conventio* included every obligation contracted, and the stipulation
was in fact a contract *verbis,* its regime could not elude the principle of the
indispensability of the consensual element.

3.

We now come to the end of Ulpian's crucial analysis:

> But the majority of agreements pass under some other name
> [in the sense of a specific edictal qualification], for example, sale,
> hire, pledge, or stipulation . . .
>
> There are three kinds of agreement. For they derive from either
> a public or a private cause, and a private agreement takes effect
> under either civil law or the law of nations. A public agreement is
> one made to conclude a peace or whenever leaders in war have
> agreed on specific terms . . .
>
> By universal law some agreements give rise to actions, some to
> exceptions. Those which give rise to actions do not remain in
> their name [that is, in their qualification as simple agreements]
> but pass under the proper name of a [typical] contract, such as
> sale, hire, partnership, loan of a movable, deposit, and the rest of
> such contracts. But even if the matter does not pass under the
> head of another contract and yet a cause exists, Aristo elegantly
> replied to Celsus that there is an obligation. Where, for example,
> I gave a thing to you so that you might give another [thing] to me,
> or I gave [something] so that you might do something, this is a
> *synallagma,* and hence a civil [-action] obligation arises. And there-
> fore I think that Julian was rightly reproved by Mauricianus in the
> following case: I gave the slave Stichus to you so that you would
> manumit [that is, free] the slave Pamphilus; you have manumit-
> ted; Stichus is then acquired by a third party with a better title
> [because evidently Stichus was not mine, and was claimed by the
> legitimate owner]. Julian writes that an *action in factum* is to be

given by the praetor. But Mauricianus says that a civil action for an uncertain amount, that is, *praescriptis verbis,* is available. There is in fact contract, what Aristo calls *synallagma,* from which this action arises . . . But when no cause exists, it is settled that no obligation arises from the agreement [alone]. Therefore a naked pact gives rise not to an obligation but to an exception [alone].[34]

Having concluded his citation of Pedius, Ulpian took the floor again, reiterating the nexus between agreement and contract. The two terms, however, were not identical in his view. In every contract there had to be an agreement, but not every agreement necessarily constituted a contract (otherwise the entire Roman contractual system would have become completely open: an inadmissible outcome). The idea he used to describe this relationship between genera (agreement) and species (contract) was that of movement, of the "passage" of (some) agreements outside the indistinctiveness implied by their essence—consensus in and of itself was not capable of fully substantiating an ontological figure—in order to achieve legal determinacy through their insertion into a form: a predefined multiplicity of contractual schemes, each with a specific denomination *(nomen).* Once the passage was made, the agreement underwent a metamorphosis; it was no longer directly recognizable in itself, but only as an indispensable (and sometimes exclusive) element of ontological structures that took it as a common reference: sale, hire, stipulation, pledge (a figure that developed in the republican age in the context of agrarian relations, to offer the owner of an estate a guarantee with respect to the buyer of the harvest (and later the tenant) who, in the event of non-payment of what was due, was obliged to hand over the tools and the slaves brought for the purpose—subsequently conceptualized by jurists as a "pledge agreement").

And precisely this transformation of agreements lay at the foundation of an initial classification introduced by Ulpian: not all of them, in fact, "passed under another name," but only "the majority" of them. The distinction would be of great importance later in the discourse; but for the moment it was dropped, and then another classification set alongside it, one no longer based on the "name," but on the "cause." In truth, we cannot rule out the possibility that at this point an entire part of the original text might have been lost when it was transcribed by Justinian's compilers. Still, even in the state in which we can read it today, the discourse is reasonably coherent, and the construction appears entirely justified.

The development of the second classification is more problematic. It begins with the statement that there are three kinds of agreements, but then appears to indicate only two: those founded on a "public" or "private" cause, with the latter subdivided into either "civil law" or *iuris gentium*. It is possible that the text was shortened, perhaps by a late publisher, and in that case we would have no alternative but to venture a conjecture, in order to recover the third species, since lost.[35] The most interesting and plausible solution would be to identify the agreements deriving from a "fiscal cause" as the missing category, eliminated to satisfy the exhaustiveness—typical of the legal culture of late antiquity, but by no means taken for granted in Ulpian's time—of the pairing of *ius publicum, ius privatum*.[36]

But it is possible—and probably preferable—to advance another interpretation, which accepts the text as it is. Examining the classification in the state in which we read it, it is conceivable that Ulpian wished, as it were, to count the pigeon-holes formed by his scheme. Scholastically speaking, he ought to have kept the two levels of the arrangement—the upper pair *(causa publica, causa privata)* and the lower pair (the civil law cause and the law of nations' cause)—separate. But in so doing he would have rendered less evident that the final outcome of his operation produced a sum of three *(conventiones ex causa publica; conventiones ex causa privata, legitimae; conventiones ex causa privata, iuris gentium)*. Yet this was precisely the result, in descriptive terms, that Ulpian wished to emphasize most. So what could be done? The answer was to fuse together the levels, indicating all the boxes as "species," in order to make it clear that their sum was in fact three—undoubtedly a rather lax solution from the standpoint of diaeretic orthodoxy, but impeccable with respect to the legal construction, and not without a certain direct communicative efficacy of its own. For someone who, like Ulpian, was accustomed to the liberty with which Roman legal thought had treated the Greek philosophical legacy for centuries, bending it without compunction to its own cognitive purposes, it would hardly have been a very surprising form of behavior.

In any case, whatever the original sequence might have been, the key to the classification is clearly found in the concept of "cause," to which Ulpian would return later in his analysis. The word was intrinsically polysemous, as we can see from its literary and legal uses as far back as the age of Cicero. In this context, it indicates the qualification of the relationship considered (let's also say its "sufficient reason" with respect to *ius*), both from the point of view of the subjects who had undertaken it and with respect to the normative plane that governed it.

And in fact the first difference established by Ulpian was between *causa publica* and *causa privata*. It did not, as we have suggested, coincide with the all-encompassing scheme of "public law, private law," especially if we are also to imagine a reference to a "fiscal cause." What emerges here is only the legal qualification of the authors of the agreement: the Roman people—through its delegates; the tax office (if we accept the integration); or simple private citizens; and thus the separate identification, the formal projection of a distinct predication with respect to the dynamics of consent, but which allowed its determination.

Exactly what is meant by a *conventio* deriving from a public cause is immediately explained. These were agreements that Ulpian restricted to the sphere of political and military treaties, entered into by the emperor or by commanders in the field; subjects who by virtue of their position in the constitutional order acted on the basis of a delegated power; their agreements were "public" because they reflected the will of the Roman people.

Symmetrically, the agreements deriving from a private cause were to be identified with those undertaken by private citizens. But these were immediately distinguished into two categories: *legitimae* and *iuris gentium*. The criterion is once again to be found in the notion of *causa* indicated above; but this time it refers not to the constitutional position of the subjects but to the denomination of the normative plane that defined the legal regime of the act: in the first case, a *lex publica*, a senatorial decree, an imperial constitution (by now, in Severan thought, a wholly accepted part of the notion of *lex*); the *ius gentium,* in the second case. But what exactly did Ulpian mean by this latter expression?

As can be seen from the examples given immediately afterwards, the jurist included agreements that fitted into the more traditional sphere of the *ius civile,* agreements protected by the *ius honorarium,* and finally consensualist schemes of the *ius gentium* in a more properly historical sense. In other words, he was adopting that approach of blending together sources for systematic or conceptual ends which was a long-established practice in Roman thought. The agreements *iuris gentium* were for him a composite set, within which there coexisted all the transactions among private parties whose normative qualification lay in the polarity between *ius civile* and the edict, as reelaborated through the filter of jurisprudence. The civil law tradition, the jurists, the edictal text: these were the points of reference that Ulpian wished to hold firm within the same parameter.

But why the name *ius gentium?* This choice is also explained in Ulpian's analysis. Bearing in mind the peculiar history of Roman consensualism, in which—starting with the jurisdiction reserved for foreigners, the first one capable of accommodating Mediterranean mercantile practices—the principle of the normative productivity of the will of the respective parties had first fully burst onto the Roman scene, it seemed to Ulpian that the name assigned for centuries to that original reception—*ius gentium*—was the only one capable of summarizing the discipline of a set of figures whose authentic core lay precisely in the element of consensuality. The *ius gentium* had established the genetic code of Roman consensualism: the memory of that name—further illuminated by the new light of natural law evoked at the beginning of the analysis—was now reproposed in a novel but correct ordering function, which appeared, if we can put it like this, at once genealogical and morphological.[37] Seemingly, we are in the presence of a harmonic convergence between a historic and a systematic perspective. But it was only so in appearance: in reality, the systematic perspective alone dominated the field. History was present, of course, but always contained within objectives and constructions that had little to do just with its narration. After all, this was the culture that Ulpian had inherited from his studies.

4.

The category of the agreements *iuris gentium* was, in its turn, broken down: we are at the final—and most significant—articulation of Ulpian's work. The viewpoint shifted, as was customary for the jurists, to the dynamics of trial procedure; the text was after all still a commentary on the edict, and in the edict what dominated was the interplay of *actiones*. There were, then, agreements protected by an action, that is to say, fully protected; and others capable only of producing an exception, meaning that they were defended only in an indirect and merely potential manner.

But the agreements capable of generating actions did not constitute a unitary whole. Ulpian further divided them into three categories (in a return to the "sum of three" classification that we encountered earlier): agreements with actions, which "pass under the proper name of a contract"; agreements with actions though without passing "under the head of another contract," provided that "a cause exists"; and agreements protected only by exceptions.

The apportionment intersected with the scheme presented at the beginning and then dropped, when Ulpian had divided the agreements into the groupings of "the majority," which passed "under another name," and "the rest," about which he had said nothing. Now, however, he could complete the discourse, and to do so he took up again the image of the "passage" and the ensuing metamorphosis. The "majority" of the agreements were nothing other than a part of those protected by actions, transformed into the contractual figures envisaged by the edict. It was the principle of Pedius, described, as it were, from the other end and according to a different development: if there was no contract that did not include an agreement, in turn agreements had to be able to encompass the entire system of contracts. And in fact Ulpian diligently lists "sale, hire, partnership, loan of a movable, deposit, and the rest of such contracts." Nothing was to be left out; and once again there emerged the acceptance of a broad notion of contract, Sabinian in origin, already acknowledged by Pedius and Gaius (though consensus now played a different role than in the *Institutiones*).

But the typical contracts did not cover all the agreements that could generate actions. Something very important still lay outside. And in fact, even if the agreement was not wrought into a contract with its "name," if its structure contained a recognizable *causa*, it was necessary in Ulpian's view to admit the existence of both obligation and action.

It was a decisive construction, which put an end to a debate lasting at least three centuries—from the issuing of the edict on pacts onward—by affirming in a definitive manner the possibility of getting round, through resort to an analogical mechanism, the restriction of the closed number in the legal forms of exchange. Once again it intertwined history and system; conceptual elaboration and the course of doctrines were integrated to the point of becoming indistinguishable, with a skill that has long been underestimated. But in the encounter, it was always the reasons of the system and of the concept that prevailed, that defined the style of the combination.

The point of arrival was the recognition that atypical agreements, without an edictal "name," could be qualified as contracts, through the development of a procedure enabling the interpreter (the magistrate who conceded the action, or the jurist who suggested it) to make this assimilation, once it had been reiterated that the agreement between the parties, as such, would never be accorded a full protection (the path fleetingly pursued at its time by the edict on pacts was by now closed off for good). In the light of this objective, the memory of the debate and disputes that had animated the jurisprudence constituted the underlying pattern that prepared the solution, echoing over time. The firm possession of a reliable conceptual key allowed Ulpian to bring some order to the past, to choose a thread, and to ignore the rest: in a certain sense, he did not recount, but judged.

Considered in terms of its essential mechanism, the solution was not original, and in fact the statement was immediately submerged by citations: Aristo, Celsus, Julian, Mauricianus, all authors from the second century, subsequent to Labeo, Sabinus, and Pedius. In the assemblage, the references were arranged in pairs: Aristo, Celsus; Julian, Mauricianus. But only in the second one was there any hint of a specific contrast (it is difficult to determine precisely whether Aristo's "reply" to Celsus was a reference to a didactic kind of response, following a question from the young Celsus, or if it alluded to a reply in a debate. And it is also hard to ascertain if this episode in the history of doctrines was pieced together by Ulpian point by point, on the basis of direct readings (as it might be more appropriate to believe), or if he had found it already sketched out elsewhere—for instance in the commentary of Pomponius—and considered it by now a sort of narrative stereotype. It is in any case likely that Ulpian used (reworking them to a certain degree) two blocks of writing: the first, by Aristo (possibly from his *Digesta,* and perhaps previously reproduced in the *Digesta* of Celsus); the second by Mauricianus, from his notes to Julian.[38]

What is certain is that Ulpian made all the citations revolve around the concepts of *synallagma* and *causa;* and the Greek term in particular, unusually repeated twice in the space of a few lines, figured as the symbol of the proposed solution. But it was not, as we know, an invention of Aristo. It had in fact formed part of Labeo's vocabulary; and Ulpian was perfectly aware of this, because it is to him that we are indebted for the particularly precise citation of the original Labeonian locus where it entered the formal apparatus of jurisprudence.

The point, however, was that from Labeo to Aristo the conceptual scope of the word had changed substantially. While the allusion to reciprocity had survived unaltered, its content had been modified; for Labeo, it was to be identified with the bilateral nature of obligations (and he had literally stated as much: *ultro citroque obligatio*), as happened in consensual contracts envisioned by the edict; for Aristo, on the other hand, the nexus was to be sought not in the correspondence of the obligations alone, but also in that of the performances, and the possibility of protection was triggered only when, once one party had complied with the terms of a transaction, it transpired that the other one had failed to do so.[39] The difference explains Ulpian's silence on Labeo: a reticence that would otherwise be incomprehensible. He was following Aristo, not the older jurist, and any mention of Labeo would only have disturbed the clarity of the proposed solution; he therefore sacrificed the citation, though not definitively, deferring it to a less crucial context: the definition of *gestum,* which perhaps is by no accident the only one of the "contractual" verbs that does not appear here.[40]

The sign of the change was the presence of the concept of *causa,* entirely absent from Labeo's scheme. Because for there to be a *synallagma,* there had to be a *causa* beneath it, as we read in Ulpian's transcription. What was Aristo saying here? The expression must be understood as meaning "sufficient reason," a "fact capable of provoking consequences," able to render effective the "synallagmaticity," that is, the material compliance of one of the contracting parties, which made necessary the performance of the other party.

In this way, Labeo's original concept was saved just as its scope was drastically restricted. For him, recognition of the objective bilaterality of obligations was in itself sufficient to make protection possible, without the necessity of compliance by one of the subjects involved; this meant that the validity of the atypical contract was attained with consensus alone, as was the case in sale, hire, and so forth. The analogy thus operated in its strongest mode, opening a wide and significant breach in the wall of typicality (or perhaps we should add that in this way the preservation of a vast space of atypicality was assured, after the recent restriction of the edict on pacts ensuing from the Lex Iulia).[41]

Aristo, for his part, though preserving the analytical structure of the Labeonian scheme—reciprocity as the nucleus of an analogical extension—shifted the symmetry from the plane of obligations to that of performance, and in doing so wound up introducing a further binding restriction, not required by Labeo: that there should be, in addition to consensus, compliance by one of the contracting parties. The conclusion was inevitable: protection was triggered not at the moment of the agreement, but only upon completion of a performance, as might once have happened for that consensualism destined then to be typified, at the time of its genesis.[42] The protection of these relations was therefore far less effective, the analogy with consensual contracts possessing a "name" weaker and more indirect—the space of atypicality was drastically restricted.

The axis of the new mechanism thus shifted from the nexus between agreement and *synallagma,* as it had been for Labeo, to that between *causa* and *synallagma.* It was in fact the existence of a *causa* (that is, of an event capable of triggering reciprocity) that determined in this context the recognizability of the *synallagma,* and therefore the inclusion of the figure in the ontology of the contract: the formal scheme thus introduced reiterated the presence of a lengthy series of consequences: from the "agreement" to the *causa,* to the *synallagma,* to the contract.

That this was the situation is further proven by the example illustrating the dispute between Julian and Mauricianus: "I gave the slave Stichus to you so that you would manumit the slave Pamphilus." In such a case, the possibility of the action originated in the moment of Pamphilus' manumission, which had been preceded by an invalid transfer of Stichus, later lost through eviction: it was linked, then, to the level of the correspondence of performances (failure to deliver Stichus as opposed to manumission of Pamphilus), and not that of the obligations. Julian and Mauricianus concurred that there should be protection for the party that manumitted Pamphilus without obtaining Stichus, but they differed on what form it should take: for Mauricianus, who recognized the contractual structure of the relationship, it was a civil action "for uncertainty" or with "prescribed words" (that is, the model used by Labeo); while for Julian, who evidently denied it, the only possibility was an action "in fact," not based that is on the legal qualification of the underlying relationship, but only on the existence of circumstances (the unjustified enrichment of one party at the expense of the other) such as to justify an extemporaneous intervention of the praetor.

In reality, Julian's position was complex.

He admitted the existence of contracts without an edictal name (". . . whenever contracts arise whose names were not instituted in civil law," we read in a brief fragment of his *Digesta*),[43] and envisioned for their protection an *agere praescriptis verbis* like the Labeonian model, which he also called *in factum civilis* (civil, because the formula was based on a specific legal qualification, stemming from the analogical extension of previously regulated figures; *in factum,* to emphasize its extraneity from the definitive text of the edict—all the more so after the codification—inasmuch as it was conceded on a case-by-case basis by the praetor through a decree). But at the same time he greatly restricted the possibility of recourse to this type of analogy, envisaging for all the other cases formulas that were *in factum* in the narrowest sense (called so not only because they were decretal, but also because they involved a structure "in fact" and not "in law," in which there was nothing more than a description of the circumstance warranting the praetor's extemporaneous intervention, outside of any legal qualification, leaving the quantification of the compensation up to the judge's discretion): a protection that was certainly fragile and unreliable. For Julian, a hypothesis like "I gave the slave Stichus to you so that you would manumit the slave Pamphilus" fell only into this last, residual category: a solution, however, that already appeared unacceptable to his pupil Mauricianus.

In the carefully considered construction of Ulpian, the doctrine of agreements, the doctrine of the contract, and the paradigm of the *synallagma* were combined into a single theory, capable of accounting for the entire phenomenology of the legal forms of exchange, and of representing it in an overview that was at once systematic and open-ended. It is quite possible that the jurist had already found in Pedius, and perhaps even in Aristo himself and in Julian, a nucleus of this synthesis; but certainly his work closed up, with a completion for which we have no other testimony, a division that had run through centuries of Roman thought. The ideas that made this reunification possible were, on the one hand, the recognition of the contractual pervasiveness of the agreement, and on the other the shift of the *synallagma* from the virtual plane of obligations to the material domain of performance, and its reduction from general form of contract to particular figure, present only in the schemes of typical consensualism, but sufficient through analogical extensions to breach, albeit through very narrow openings, the bond of typicality—which was reconfirmed as the authentic hidden god of the entire Roman experience of contracts, the ultimately insurmountable limit before which Ulpian's constructive fabric came to a halt. And indeed it was the reaffirmation of this principle that rounded off his discourse: "but when no cause exists . . .," that is, if there was no possibility of assigning the agreement either to an edictal category or to a synallagmatic scheme, then it inevitably fell within the ambit of agreements that generated only exceptions, because— and here is the statement of the rule—"it is settled that no obligation arises from the agreement."[44] There returned, then, to indicate this residual class of agreements without name and without cause, the word from which Ulpian had set out: "pact"—but in a technical and systematic sense, and not, as at the beginning, in a generic and almost metalegal one. "Therefore," he wrote, "a naked pact gives rise not to an obligation but to an exception":[45] a maxim that he would repeat with hammering insistence three times in just a few lines— "an action cannot arise from a pact"[46]—almost as a way of canceling with such emphatic reiteration (inexplicable, if it were a prescription that had never been denied) even the very memory of a time when things had been different, and when that word had carried a far different weight. The circle had by now been closed once and for all; in order to reopen it, it would first be necessary to form another world.

5.

In Ulpian's gray prose, devoid of twists and surprises, there was not merely and once again the expression of the collective voice of a class that had been moving forwards for centuries. Something more and different emerged: the tone and the program of an authentic Severan legislator—as if marking the return, after centuries (and how changed!), of the ancient design of Ofilius and Caesar—who now treated jurisprudence in the same way that Hadrian and Julian had the praetorian edict, trying to achieve a crystallization and a doctrinal consolidation that was the real final objective of a tradition.[47]

It would therefore be a mistake to think of Ulpian as merely a jurist among jurists. He was also the silent and tireless constructor of a new dimension for the Roman legal world, the inventor of a textuality that chose somehow to place itself outside the long course of history that had preceded it, having attained a vantage point perceived as superior. A perspective making it possible to embrace and order centuries of thought, and to repropose it within the canon of a definitive composure, ready for use by the nascent State of late antiquity, which no longer had any need for a jurisprudential law but was trying to avoid losing the foundation of an extraordinary past. Pomponius may have sought to do this earlier, but he was still unable to take a sufficiently "distant" view of his subject, and his vast commentary had little fortune. Ulpian instead had found an acceptable parameter, an authentic scripture of systematization, which dominates his commentaries and was destined to enjoy immense success: without its doctrinal and stylistic results, the work of Justinian's commissioners that led to the *Digesta* would have been inconceivable.

For a couple of decades, until roughly 230, the activity of the last great Severan authors—with Ulpian and Paul we should at least mention Callistratus, Tryphoninus, Marcianus, Macro, and Modestinus—seemed to maintain a miraculous equilibrium, in a period of intense intellectual fervor, which had begun when the century of crisis was already under way.[48] Even as it helped to create with its own choices the conditions for its disappearance, jurisprudence found the time and the strength to erect a monument to itself and its law—formalism as legal measurement of the world—however limited and dramatically contradictory its application might have been in the imperial society of the time, and prepared the path for all the subsequent actualizing recoveries, from that of Justinian through to the most important laboratories of modernity.

But prior to the epilogue, it would provide a last testimony of itself, one that summed up its entire history and was at the same time charged with future. To recount it, we must once again turn to the project of Ulpian.

21

The Custodians of Law

In the first book of his *Institutiones,* composed between 212 and 213, Ulpian wrote:

> For he who intends to devote himself to law (*ius*), first it is necessary to know from where the very name of law (*ius*) derives. It is called such from justice (*iustitia*). In fact, according to Celsus' elegant definition, law is the rational discipline of goodness and fairness, of which there are those who rightly call us the priests. And in fact we venerate justice and profess knowledge of what is good and fair, discriminating between fair and unfair, distinguishing lawful from unlawful, aiming to make men good not only through a fear of penalties but also indeed under allurement of rewards, and aspiring, if I am not deceived, to the true and not to the false philosophy.[1]

These words would have a great fortune, because, roughly three centuries later, Justinian's editors would select them for nothing less than the opening of their *Digesta.* It is highly probable that they also constituted, in turn, the introductory passage of the handbook from which they were quoted. Aside from considerations of style or content, what prompts us to believe this is a question of symmetrical correspondence. The incipit of the *Digesta* could not have consisted—in the rhetorical and compositional strategy of the Byzantine masters—of anything other than the incipit of the work used to begin the great mosaic.[2] And, for that matter, when, a few fragments later, and still in the first title of the first book, there was a citation of a passage from the *Institutiones* of Gaius, it too was a transcription of that work's opening words.[3]

The years 213–214 were very intense for Ulpian: it is reasonable to believe that in this time he completed books 6–31 of his commentary on the edict, as well as books 1 to 26 of his commentary upon Sabinus.[4] The *Institutiones*, therefore, reflect the thinking of a scholar who had already for some time been at the center of imperial power, in the first flourishing of his great literary creativity.[5]

Like every ancient author, when he composed the opening statements of this short text (consisting of just two books), Ulpian must have had certain models in mind, in stylistic terms if nothing else. One of them can be identified with a high degree of probability: the first lines of Gaius' commentary upon the Twelve Tables, also used by Justinian's compilers as the opening of the second title, again of the initial book of the *Digesta*.[6] The stylistic similiarities with Ulpian's exordium are unmistakable: the use, at the beginning, of the future participle, a fairly rare occurrence in Ulpian; the resemblance of Ulpian's formulation, "prius nosse oportet" ("ought first to know"), to Gaius' "necessario prius existimavi" (where "prius" is not—as Mommsen believed—an abbreviation of *populi Romani ius*); and finally, the identical use in the two passages of the formula *nisi fallor* ("if I am not deceived"), which was also unusual in the work of the Severan jurist.[7]

We may safely suppose that, besides the commentary on the Twelve Tables, Ulpian was also well aware of the *Institutiones* by Gaius, the only clearcut example of legal literature intended for teaching purposes that was available to him. This is not the place to consider the (very complex) problem of the relationship between the Gaian handbook and Ulpian's counterpart in terms of their expository structures;[8] certainly, however, beginning his own *Institutiones* with a clear echo of an incipit by Gaius, though not that of the corresponding work (the one on the Twelve Tables instead of on the *Commentarii*), has the air of being a kind of silent tribute to the (only) jurist who had preceded him in the same genre. In Ulpian, however, as we shall see, the stylistic imitation concealed a complete conceptual divergence: indeed, it became a carefully designed shell within which this distance manifested itself in all its vastness.

In our passage, as it is quoted in the *Digesta,* we must distinguish between two levels of writing, and three levels of meaning.

The former are, respectively, that of Ulpian, author of the text, and that of Celsus, quoted by Ulpian for a definition to which considerable importance is given ("according to Celsus' elegant definition"); while "goodness and fairness," the subject of the statement, later resurfaces as one of the guiding threads of the argumentation: "We . . . profess knowledge of what is good and fair, discriminating between fair and unfair."

The three levels of meaning, on the other hand, are, working chronologically backwards: first, the significance of the text for Justinian's compilers, who accorded it the supreme honor of opening the *Digesta,* thereby giving it an unrivaled visibility, which could hardly help but be matched by a great evocative value; next, the significance this piece of writing must have had for Ulpian himself, who had composed it inserting the quotation from Celsus; and finally, the significance that Celsus attributed to his statement about *ius* as *ars boni et aequi,* aside from (and prior to) the meaning it would acquire when integrated into Ulpian's design.

These levels should be considered, unless proved otherwise, as not coinciding; they derive from different milieux and have, so to speak, the right to be interpreted each in accordance with the order of the thoughts that produced them.

It is not necessary though to suppose that the Justinian level of meaning must have a corresponding autonomous layer of writing: to believe, that is, that the text was altered by the Byzantine editors (nor are there signs of any substantial interventions by pre-Justinian publishers: we have no reason to doubt that the copy of Ulpian's *Institutiones* used by the commissioners of the *Digesta* was an accurate edition of the original version). As will become clear, the masters of the compilation had no need in this case to modify what they were reading to bend it to their purposes: all they had to do was interpret it in the light of their world of values and ideas.

2.

Our point of departure is Ulpian, the author of the text, and the author of the quotation from Celsus.

In his discourse we can identify three nodes. The first—which under-pinned all the rest—consisted in the derivation of *ius* from *iustitia*. This was clearly a false etymology, or rather an etymological inversion. Ulpian had al-ready resorted to this method—and for fairly similar reasons—in his com-mentary on the edict on pacts.[9]

It was easy to see that the opposite was true: that *iustitia* derived from *ius*, and not the other way around. There is no need to attribute any particular lexicological expertise to Ulpian to suppose he was perfectly aware that the correct connection between the two words was the contrary of what he had claimed.[10] The reversal is all the more startling in that it was used to empha-size a word—*iustitia*—which, as we know, was a rarity in the language and the conceptual baggage of the jurists: apart from in this text, we find it only in two passages from Tryphoninus, in one from Modestinus, and in three other fragments from Ulpian, the first from the *Libri regularum,* the other two from the *Ad edictum* and from his commentary on the Lex Iulia *de adulteriis*.[11] Ulpian therefore began his *Institutiones* with a double *coup de théâtre*: a pat-ently groundless statement, and the foregrounding of a concept—that of *iustitia*—entirely alien to the tradition of Roman legal thought. What were his reasons for such a bold choice?

The etymological inversion can be easily explained. What we have here is a kind of deception practiced by the author on his readers, justified by the result he hoped to achieve (it should be borne in mind that we are in the opening lines of a handbook on institutions, destined therefore to remain im-pressed in the minds of complete or near beginners in legal studies; an audi-ence, in all likelihood, of apprentice functionaries of the Severan govern-ment apparatus, during the years of Caracalla). Moreover, ancient writing is often studded with astute devices of this sort. In its code of communication, an original and latent esoteric element was always active, never abandoned, which permitted the use of continuous dissimulations: strategies that might

[419]

even involve the apparent declaration of the contrary to what was believed, and which demanded, on the part of the reader, a corresponding capacity to interpret between the lines. They were designed to select a discerning élite, and could (as in our case) perform a pedagogic function: the literal meaning, perceptible at first glance, served only as a first step toward the attainment of a more complex and profound truth.[12]

In the words of Ulpian, the evident etymological confusion acted in fact as a medium for a very different message, both concealed and revealed therein, which was the real thought the jurist wished to communicate, namely, that there could be no law *(ius)* unless it was founded upon justice *(iustitia)*. The reversal in the lexical derivation—the false etymology—served only to demonstrate what was, in Ulpian's view, the true connection, the authentic genealogy—from the conceptual, not the lexicographic, point of view—between the two terms: the dependence of *ius* on the idea of justice. There was, then, a derivation: but it concerned the content, not the signs expressing it.

The combination nonetheless was presented (and this is the second part of the *coup de théâtre*), at least in appearance, as a leap outside the bounds of tradition. The link whose presence was declared in fact prevented *ius* from justifying itself by remaining solely within the formal isolation of its own constituent procedures, both jurisprudential and of other kinds (edicts, *leges,* emperor's constitutions), as had already been happening for centuries. On the contrary, in the perspective suggested by Ulpian, the substantive legitimation of the legal order wound up being dissociated from its formal legality, and could derive only from an external assessment, capable of taking law as the subject of a problematic judgment: a term of comparison, and not an absolute and self-referential certainty.

It was a strong position, and one that immediately posed a serious problem, which certainly could not have been grasped by a novice (who had, however, already been induced to comprehend—albeit by means of an expedient—the most important thing), but evident to a more expert reader. If law was to to be inspired by nothing other than justice, what was to be said of a *ius* that, as might well be the case, though correctly established by a power entitled to create it (and as Ulpian wrote, this role was increasingly filled by the emperor alone), still failed to correspond to its indispensable presupposition? And who held the keys to this decisive judgment of conformity? We will see shortly; for now, it is sufficient to point out that it was enough to take just a few steps to discover immediately the thinly veiled abyss, on which Ulpian's surprising opening centered: the foundation—albeit in hypothetical terms—of a (possible) critique of positive law, in years when—after the long and happy age of the Antonines—a well-tested dialectic of powers at the head of the empire, which had continued to leave a decisive role for jurisprudence, was breaking down into the new and worrying forms of a dangerous military autocracy with a tendency to concentrate into its own hands a legislative power that excluded all other production of *ius*.[13]

But what exactly did Ulpian mean by *iustitia*? We can leave the answer in abeyance for the moment, and move on to the second point of his discourse: the quotation from Celsus. The reference to the jurist of Hadrian's age developed entirely under the influence of the derivation presented immediately beforehand. The relationship, which was very close, was established by the expression "in fact," by the logical and syntactic power of the link. What was about to be quoted—that is, Celsus' definition—(said Ulpian) was to be understood as an explanation of what had just been stated: the dependence of *ius* upon *iustitia*. The former was based upon the latter precisely because it was the "rational discipline of goodness and fairness." For Ulpian, in other words, *iustitia* and *bonum et aequum* were the same thing.

Here then was already a first (though not conclusive) answer to the question formulated a moment earlier. But it must be said straight away that we have no reason to suppose the link held good for Celsus as well. Unfortunately, we cannot guess in what connection and context he had elaborated what Ulpian called a "definition"; nonetheless, we have not even the slightest clue to suggest the existence in his writing of the same relationship between *iustitia* and *bonum et aequum*. Ulpian behaved here with Celsus in much the same way that he was accustomed to do with the other authors he quoted: he surgically extracted fragments of thought from their original context, and blithely inserted them into the weft and weave of his own discourse.[14]

And yet we have seen that the equation established in the *Institutiones* had a lengthy past (though with a variant that for the moment we shall not attempt to evaluate), even if we are not authorized to include Celsus in it. The link in any case was by no means arbitrary, relating instead to an entire move-

ment of ideas between rhetoric and philosophy, which had enjoyed a significant development in the Ciceronian age.[15] Ulpian did not cite Cicero explicitly: a consolidated protocol of his scientific tradition prohibited him from
doing so;[16] but he did draw upon his thought as a well-assimilated resource,
grasping in full its natural law option, though for reasons (as we shall see)
that were completely different. For that matter, as we know, paradigms of
natural law had already been circulating for a while in Roman legal culture,
representing by this point one of its component threads (take Gaius or the
notion of "natural obligation");[17] even if we must guard against supposing
too close a symmetry between the technical construction of those frameworks, which developed with a certain degree of continuity in jurisprudential
thinking, and its ideological significance, in terms of the politics of law, which
each jurist instead tended to present in accordance with his own needs and
parameters.

Ulpian's reelaboration moved in two directions in particular. The first involved a firm reiteration of the late-republican tie between *iustitia, ius,* and
aequitas,[18] using without hesitation the expedient of a false etymology and
the licence of a subordination of *ius* to *iustitia.* This was a decisive point. In
fact the connection, implicit in the *Institutiones,* became immediate and direct
in the *Regulae,* where we read at the beginning (another incipit) that: "Justice
is the firm and enduring will to give to each his own right,"[19] thus allowing us
to discover, with the literal reuse of the motif of the *Rhetorica ad Herennium*
and of the *De inventione,* the missing link thus far, capable of connecting the
Severan master with his sources, and of explaining the significance he assigned to the word *iustitia:* the same that Cicero had applied to *aequitas:* a
universal principle of distributive and proprietary equilibrium, to which *ius*
could and should adhere.

In the second place, Ulpian developed a concept of natural equity parallel
to and entirely in keeping with his notions of law and justice, which he utilized as one of the keys to the natural-law interpretation of the foundations
of the praetorian edict (we have seen an example of this in his comment
about the title on pacts, and we can also find it in several passages by Paul,
though with a lesser strategic importance).[20]

For Ulpian, then, the assimilation between *iustitia, ius,* and *bonum et
aequum* could make sense only by bringing the *bonum et aequum* of Celsus' citation under the concept of natural equity, elaborated in accordance with

Cicero and Labeo (and probably of Gaius as well). He therefore used the words of Celsus, presenting them as perfectly capable of integration within the current of thought he had chosen to follow, the one begun by Cicero. In short, he saw Cicero, Labeo (perhaps), and Celsus as entirely interchangeable, and preferred to recall the jurist and not the philosopher, out of respect for an ancient custom of specialization: all of them (in his view), were expressions of a perspective that associated law with the sphere of natural equity. And indeed, this mode of understanding *bonum et aequum* in a natural law sense was common in the Severan age. To say nothing of other uses in Ulpian,[21] it appears clearly in a passage by Paul, in the fourteenth book of his commentary on Sabinus:

> Law is understood in different ways: in one way, when law is taken to mean what is always fair and good, as is natural law; in an other, as meaning what is in the interest of everyone, or a majority in each city, as is civil law.[22]

It was no accident that the compilers also used this passage in the opening title of the *Digesta,* in close proximity to the excerpt from Ulpian. Its content in fact seemed perfectly symmetrical with the discourse in the incipit (the chronologies we can hypothesize for the works from which the two texts derive would rather suggest a dependence on Ulpian's part).[23] There is, Paul said, a modality of law that identifies it with the *bonum et aequum* (and of the two possibilities, we must settle on one: either he was thinking directly of Celsus, as appears more likely—and in that case, he too was interpreting, as Ulpian would later do, Celsus' proposition in a natural-law way—or else he was alluding to the presence of Celsus in Ulpian's writing, which cannot entirely be ruled out). And this means—he concluded—speaking of *ius naturale,* bearing in mind the identification, which he took for granted, of *bonum et aequum* with natural equity (a concept which, as we have just said, he was familiar with and used frequently).[24]

But is that really how things stood? Were the two formulas—the *bonum et aequum* of Celsus, transcribed literally by Ulpian and recalled by Paul, and natural equity—really equivalent? Ulpian's assemblage does not betray the writing of Celsus only if we assume the two expressions to be perfectly synonymous. But were they ever truly so in the history of Roman legal and philosophical ideas, before the Severan age? We already know that they were not,[25] but for the time being let's suspend any observation on this point, refraining also from an assessment of the term *ars,* used in a significant way by Celsus (*ius est ars . . .*) and drawn on by Ulpian in his citation, and look instead at the third (and last) twist of the discourse that we are analyzing. "Of which there are those who rightly call us the priests," our text continues; and we must understand that "of which" as referring not only to the *ars boni et aequi* just mentioned (and hence to the *ius* identified with it), but also to *iustitia.* The jurists were, then, the "priests" of this intrinsic union between (natural) equity, law, and justice.

From a stylistic point of view, the "us" wedged in between the relative—"of which"—and the substantive—"priests"—is very strong. Us jurists, he meant; but the semantic wave of inclusion inevitably ended up including the listeners-readers as well, the intended recipients of the *Institutiones,* the audience of apprentice functionaries that was preparing to enter the machinery of the Severan government immediately after the *Constitutio Antoniniana,* which had just extended Roman citizenship to all the subjects of the empire.[26] It is as if Ulpian had said: all of you, inasmuch as you are experts in law, will be the guardians of a *ius* that cannot be based on anything other than natural equity and justice.

We may suppose that the recourse to the image of priesthood must have had an intense allusive value: perhaps not evident to everyone at first glance, but that mattered little; once again, different thresholds of comprehension were established. What Ulpian was now presenting as nothing more than a metaphorical exchange—the jurists in the guise of priests—had once been, at the origins of law and the city, a real fact: the first Roman experts of *ius* had really been nothing if not priests—the pontifices. Ulpian thus ideally completed a circle: that ancient past, the archeology of law, was symmetrically reproposed in the present—priests once, priests today (and for all time), albeit of a quite different religion, and facing another order of problems—and admittedly only through the literary invention of a play of analogies.[27]

And it was through the continuation of this metaphorical thread that Ulpian completed his discourse. Again he made use of "in fact" to express the nodes of consequentiality that punctuated the flow of his argument. He had already done so, as we saw, to connect the definition of Celsus to the concept of justice; he repeated it now ("and in fact we venerate justice"), in order to relate to the evoked image of this extraordinary secular priesthood the tasks of an ideal jurisprudence, worthy of its name.

"We venerate justice and profess knowledge . . .": first of all the intimate connection between justice and the *bonum et aequum* is reiterated, and not only from a theoretical point of view, but in the everyday practice of the jurists; while the use of the verb *colere* ("venerate") in relation to justice and law again recalls a Ciceronian stylistic element and, along with *profitemur* ("profess")—maintains—albeit in an attenuated manner, as if in a fade-out—the priestly image just evoked.[28] There then followed an insistent and conclusive sequence of participles, all of them governed by that initial "us" which enclosed within the circle of a single identification the author and his readers-listeners. The activities designated by the verbs describe what might be defined as Ulpian's model of the good jurist. The first two ("discriminating between fair and unfair," "distinguishing lawful from unlawful") should be considered as a further variant of the dominant theme: the relationship between experience of the law and actuation of the *bonum et aequum* (in the sense of natural equity). The third ("aiming to make men good"), with its counterpoint between reward and penalty, harked back to a classical idea in Greek moral philosophy (we find it, for instance, in the first book of Aristotle's *Rhetoric:*[29] Ulpian's writing preserves a number of Aristotelian traces; one can be found in another text from the first book of the *Institutiones*),[30] and it clearly served as a way of reinforcing with some emphasis what he presented as the ethical ground of his young readers' professional vocation. The fourth—"aspiring, if I am not deceived, to the true and not to the false philosophy"— deserves greater attention. It contains a radical proposition, in no way mitigated by the purely stylistic "if I am not deceived." The correct understanding and exercise of the law—Ulpian maintained—were to be considered as the authentic philosophy of the time, in opposition to the (false) one that simulated its appearance and name, but did not possess its substance and truth.

Perceptive analysts such as Paolo Frezza, Dieter Nörr, and Tony Honoré have all deciphered the intellectual background of this statement: the thinking of Origen and, going further back, the *Didascalicus* by Alcinous[31]—works that referenced the Platonic readings and interpretations typical of the Syrian urban elites in the years of the young Ulpian's education (though there is no evidence to suggest any personal dealings between Origen—a professor at Alexandria when the *Institutiones* were being composed—and our jurist: a possible contact through the mediation of Julia Mamaea, the mother of Alexander Severus and the daughter of a sister of Julia Domna, Septimius Severus' second wife, is too flimsy a hypothesis).[32] Appropriately, a comparison has also been made with the doctrines set forth at the beginning of the *Libri regularum:* "The basic principles of law are: to live honorably, not to harm any other person, to give to each his own. Jurisprudence is knowledge of matters divine and human, the science of the just and unjust,"[33] in which Ulpian borrowed from Alcinous (but may also have been mindful of a tradition dating back to Cicero) the definition of jurisprudence, which referred in the original to wisdom *(sophia)*.[34] In particular, it seems possible to glimpse in this statement an attempt to declare the primacy of the teaching of law over the schools of rhetoric and philosophy, which would, however, not be able to rise beyond the level of a somewhat dusty and mannered disputation.

That the background thus identified—let us say a Platonic context midway between theology and ethics—is the right one can hardly be doubted. And it also seems plausible to tie in, albeit with some effort and despite the lack of decisive proof, the scheme employed by Ulpian—true versus false philosophy—with a motif fluctuating in the tradition between Origen and Gregory Thaumaturge: all the same without forgetting that the comparison between (Greek) philosophy and (Roman) law was also already part of the thought of Cicero, and must have been even then well known to the jurisprudential tradition.[35]

But this result does not conclude the analysis, it is just the beginning. To identify the provenance of a certain conceptual material, with respect to the discourse that surrounds and in which we have found it, is never sufficient; the point is—once its origin has been established—to reconstruct its function and significance in the network of thoughts of the author (re)employing it.

Ulpian used the paradigm *vera, simulata philosophia* not in order to set law against philosophy (as we might be tempted to suppose at first glance, and as he must have been willing to allow his students to believe, who were thus induced to feel an early burst of professional pride), nor to undermine one philosophy in comparison with another (according to the use of this scheme in earlier tradition), but to achieve a different objective. That of solidly integrating legal science into philosophy, to place it, thus reclassified, in such an important position that it could be ascribed a privileged (if not entirely exclusive) mastery of the truth. He did not maintain that law was superior to philosophy, or even that it should be compared with philosophy (there were precedents along this line in the claims for an equal prestige with that science from other disciplines, such as medicine),[36] but that jurists were themselves directly philosophers, the true philosophers. This identification should be considered new and original, even if in its construction Ulpian had trodden a known path: Cicero had in his own time attempted to base Roman law *ex intima philosophia,* and Ulpian himself must have been well aware of that precedent; then, however, the attempt had been carried out by a philosopher elbowing aside the jurists, with a view to regenerating their knowledge and giving it a universalistic projection; in this later case, in contrast, it was a jurist who was attempting to assimilate his own doctrine to philosophy. We should ask ourselves why Ulpian felt the need to do so with such great emphasis, considering that, from Cicero onward, nearly three centuries of history had fully legitimized the autonomy of his discipline in the universe of ancient knowledge, and given that jurisprudence had become, from Julian onward, the science of the empire, and that the jurists, first in the emperor's council, and later occupying the highest levels of the government machinery, were making their own technique the principal instrument of administration, inventing a form of State, and becoming protagonists of a world power.

The only acceptable response is that, through the screen of the identification between jurists and philosophers, Ulpian really wanted to convey something even more significant and demanding: namely, the idea that there existed a profound and privileged relationship between the search for justice and the attainment of truth, and that jurists were the custodians par excellence of this bond. If law was to comply with justice, and if the latter was to be identified with that natural equity of whose practice only the jurists were the guardians, then their everyday work, with the whole legacy of technical specialization accumulated over time, became the sole guarantee that this proclaimed conformity could ever be achieved and preserved. And since the justice and law that derived from it were the truth—it was within this integrating of concepts, implicit but unequivocal, that all of Ulpian's thinking was concentrated—and philosophy was the search for truth (in compliance with the Platonic tradition: *vera philosophia* because it was a witness to the truth),[37] then it followed that the jurists, who sought justice, were nothing other than true philosophers. An insurmountable protective barrier was thus erected around the work of jurisprudence: it really was a sacralized process ("there are those who rightly call us the priests"; and the *civilis sapientia*—that is, jurisprudence—was defined as *sanctissima*—most holy—by Ulpian in a passage of *De omnibus tribunalibus,* probably written in the same years):[38] in his conceptual strategies there was revealed (and concealed) the essence of the action and the very lives of humans.

3.

But if the jurists were the true philosophers, whom should we identify as the false ones ("simulatam [philosophiam] affectantes")?

In the panegyric attributed to Gregory Thaumaturge and delivered in honor of Origen at Caesarea in the year 238 (Ulpian had been dead for about fifteen years), which we may safely consider an attentive and faithful illustration of numerous aspects of Origen's ideas, there was a rough outline of a theme destined, in the following decades and then for the whole of the fourth century, to enjoy considerable success: that of the philosopher's flight from the world.[39] Philosophy made it possible to live the true life, away from arms, public squares, and study of the laws: all occupations that distracted from the solitary contemplation of the *logos,* the sole activity worthy of being practiced.

These were not new motifs. At least since the middle of the second century, the return of a form of Platonism with mystical and esoteric shades, mixed with neo-Pythagorean contaminations (a not infrequent combination even among the Syrian elites during Ulpian's time), insistently suggested the retreat of the finer minds from the troubles and concerns of society in order to plunge into an inner life, in the truth of the "inner soul" (as Plotinus would later write),[40] or in the yearning for a nocturnal space in which to reestablish contact with a supernatural plane bringing magical salvation, the sole refuge against the anxieties of what were perceived as increasingly difficult times: a pursuit of shadows and fascinations ranging from Apuleius to Lucian, from Apollonius (as recounted by Philostratus) to Aelius Aristides, all the way through to Artemidorus and even Marcus Aurelius himself, who, however, was able to compensate them with quite different imperatives.[41]

It would only be later—after the death of Ulpian, and in the face of the open outbreak of the crisis—that these thoughts and attitudes would reach a peak. But already for some time there had crystallized around the practice of philosophy a full-fledged model, mental and behavioral, with a specific visual projection: the bearded philosopher, wrapped in a mantle, equipped with a sack and a stick, free of all restrictions, the only one able to think and speak freely: an image and a conduct capable of attracting admiration and consensus even outside the circle of the learned few. Herodian tells us that the emperor Macrinus, a few years after Ulpian's *Institutiones* are presumed to have been completed, made the inhabitants of Antioch laugh by growing a beard and speaking in public—he who was a rude illiterate at his ease only in military encampments—"so slowly and with such difficulty that often it was impossible to hear him because of his low voice," and attempting, in all this, to imitate the ways of a philosopher, in keeping with fashion.[42]

In the years of Ulpian, the philosophical and stylistic core—psychological and literary, but also gestural and visual—of this tendency was already fully formed, in part due to contributions from writers and currents associated with a Neoplatonism that hovered between paganism and early Christian thought, and was quite closely linked to Ulpian's milieux.

And it was precisely against this world that Ulpian launched his attack: in that adjective—*simulata,* false—to which the contested doctrine was nailed, there was the trace of an allusion to a way of acting, and not merely of thinking, to a form of behavior that feigned philosophy and its rigor, its love of the truth; but the more it believed it was reproducing it, the further it diverged, imitating nothing but its exterior shell. Ulpian wished to counteract the possible attraction that a refined message—at any rate one directed at more learned and well-to-do circles—of detachment and escapism might hold for young intellectuals who were still being instructed (especially in the cities of the East), opposing it with the superiority of the civil militia serving in the ranks of the empire. Only thus do his words have any meaning, really enabling us to place them in their own time. He was not comparing one set of ideas with another—he had no need to do so—but two ways of life, two models of virtuous conduct and of the pursuit of truth: that of the jurists (by

this point, government jurists, increasingly involved, over at least the two previous generations, in running the empire), engaged, through the exercise of
their techniques, in the quest for justice (concentrated in the flow of participles—*separantes*, *discernentes*, *cupientes*—is a powerful allusion to a ceaseless,
everyday toil), and thereby transfigured into authentic philosophers; and that
of those who usurped the name of philosophy ("simulatam philosophiam affectantes") in order to justify, with the icon of a disinterested scholarly attitude, an abdication, an abandonment that did not move closer to the truth
but just gave the illusion of doing so. The ethics of commitment and responsibility at the service of the empire (but of a just empire because it was enlightened by its jurists)—the primacy of practical reason, we might say—and
a flight from the world, in search of a private salvation in ascetic introspec-
tion and in the shadows of the "nocturnal men." Even a figure such as Marcus Aurelius, enclosed in his solitude, had managed in some way to hold together the two trails. Now it was becoming impossible to do so. Ulpian had
chosen his own path, and he was quite evidently and didactically pointing his
students in that direction.[43]

This conclusion also makes it possible to clarify another aspect that has
already been mentioned. The recovery of the natural-law motif of the identity of law, justice, and equity did not shift the center of gravity of *ius* from
legal thought to philosophy, as the "scandalous" derivation of *ius* from justice
might have led some to believe (or fear), nor did it entrust the judgment of
the substantive legitimacy of *ius* to a discipline (and a power) far removed
from juridical specialization. Thanks to the practice of natural equity, the jurists were transformed as such into philosophers, and became on their own
the guarantors and custodians of a normative order felicitously inspired by a
beneficent universal ethic. The autonomy of law was not undermined, provided it firmly incorporated a jurisprudence at once vigilant and well aware
that it was still playing a decisive role, despite being much changed. And yet,
something new was emerging in Ulpian's outlook, when compared with the
usual fabric of legal science: the quest—already begun with Papinian—for an
ethical foundation for law, which, though it did not break the discipline's tradition of isolation and separateness, engaged for the first time since Cicero
with an intellectual background in which there emerged the need to affirm
explicitly the existence of a privileged relationship between ethics and formalism, between legal construction and universal justice. It was as if the same

jurisprudence that was celebrating the attainment of the peak of its science were at the same time beginning to perceive its limits just as it was attempting to radiate its power in the process of the first construction of a world State. Its surprising moralism was a response to the crisis, not a betrayal of tradition.

4.

There was one great absent figure in Ulpian's exordium: the emperor, who when the jurist was writing had long since, and in full, become a sovereign legislator. Any discourse on *ius* in the Severan age—its definition, its vocation, its goals—could not have failed to take this protagonist into account. But before finding any mention of him, a certain distance has to be covered in the original course of the *Institutiones* (exactly how far we cannot say, though it was not vast, since we remain with the confines of the first book);[44] in the arrangement of Justinian's *Digesta*, we first come across him through the *Definitiones* of Papinian, then with the *Enchiridion* of Pomponius, then again with three fragments by Julian, Ulpian (but from another work), and Callistratus,[45] finally returning to the *Institutiones,* where we read:

> What the emperor has decreed has the force of statutory law. This is because the populace commits to him by a law supreme command and power. Therefore, whatever the emperor has determined by a letter, or with a response laid down as a footnote to a document, or has decreed when presiding in court or has pronounced outside of the court, or has prescribed by an edict, is undoubtedly law. These are what we commonly call constitutions.[46]

This is another famous passage, at least in its exordium—a short phrase, barely a line—that is of particular interest to us here. Its literal significance, limited and stripped down between the late Middle Ages and the early modern age by the interpretation of the canonists and the commentators whom they influenced, would be reproposed and emphasized throughout the seventeenth century in French, Spanish, and English milieux, which transformed it into a banner of modern absolutism, and was reiterated in many maxims of those legal and political cultures: "a Deo Rex, a Rege Lex," "Rex est Lex," "si veut le Roi, si veut la Loi," and so on.⁴⁷ We find an echo of it in Spinoza, in Hobbes, in Locke, and its shadow still hovers over the first pages of Leibniz's *Meditation on the Common Concept of Justice*⁴⁸—this takes us up to the turn of the eighteenth century (and we ought to add here that the influence of this declaration was shared with another graphic formulation by Ulpian— that of the *princeps legibus solutus,* of the sovereign not subject to the laws— taken from a brief passage in the commentary on the Lex Iulia et Papia, which also became a commonplace in political culture throughout the seventeenth century).⁴⁹

Such fleeting references should already be sufficient to plunge us into a major theme: that of the utilization of Roman legal materials—in particular from the period between the age of the Severans and that of Theodosius II— in the building of modern European statehood, its theory and its apparatuses: a problem addressed in recent years, and from a more specific point of view, by Quentin Skinner in the course of research that ought to be developed, and which in many cases deserves careful reexamination, both in terms of its methodological implications and the results attained.⁵⁰

We will forgo this challenging task here. All that is important for now is Ulpian's perspective, which we must separate, in its original profile, from the larger weft of successive reelaborations, well aware that—almost always— beneath the appearance of any continuity of sense or function between ancient elements and modern constructions lies the pitfall of an interpretative trap: and the recuperation of Roman forms winds up sooner or later betraying the presence of entirely new and distinctive contents, even where we might least expect to find them.

It is likely that Ulpian's original text underwent some later modification, but there are no reasons to suppose that it reflected a vulgarization of his thought by some less reliable pupil.⁵¹ Certainly, we can trace back directly to the jurist the constitutional paradigm delineated here: that in the hands of the emperor is concentrated a normative power presented as limitless ("What the emperor has decreed . . ."), and the acts issuing from him acquire the status and force of "statutory law," because it is through a *lex*—the *lex de imperio*—that the people, the original master, conferred such power upon the emperor. Thus was deployed a legitimizing model of imperial legislation in keeping with the traditional republican constitutionalism (in the sense that it was constructed according to republican parameters)—which Ulpian did not invent, but rather summarized in a conclusive manner—dating at least as far back as Hadrian's time, and which we have also found, though in different perspectives, in the thought of Gaius and of Pomponius.

The opening line—"What the emperor has decreed . . ."—certainly appears, in its conciseness, to be powerfully descriptive. In an attempt to contextualize its meaning, Paolo Frezza has subtly tried to reduce its scope to a statement that would only have value in connection with the normative decisions of the emperor in the course of a trial.[52] It is a line of reasoning that can only be followed with great difficulty.[53] Moreover, even if we admit that the attention of the jurist was here in some way attracted by the jurisdictional interventions of the emperor, this does not prevent us from believing that he consciously intended to give the beginning of his discourse a more general significance, axiomatically reaffirming for his students a point of departure that by now could be considered an incontrovertible fact.

In reality, this is not the right way to correctly place the statement we have before us, and to free it from the encrustations that the political thought of modern absolutism has deposited upon it. It is preferable instead to measure its weight and value by attempting to reconnect it to the order of ideas that originally produced it: that is to say, by comparing it with the discourse that began the *Institutiones,* concerning the importance of jurists as privileged custodians of the measure of goodness and truth.

If we do this, it becomes clear that the two texts evoke one another: the statement about *ius* and the jurists would be suspended in midair, if it were not tied to the figure of the emperor; and the acknowledgment of his normative power would be irremediably unilateral and unbalanced unless it were projected against the background of the achievements attained with regard to the first point.

Ulpian wished to affirm two principles with equal emphasis: the primacy of jurisprudence as the protagonist in the pursuit of a law based on justice and truth; and together, shortly afterwards (perhaps immediately so), with the same degree of importance, the fact that the emperor was to be considered as the sole possessor of a boundless legislative power, capable that is of binding to his will the conduct of the subjects of a vast empire.

Between the two doctrines there was undoubtedly a certain tension, in that they referred to each other strongly, and this reciprocal attraction fitted into Ulpian's program, independently of the distance that separated them in the textual space of the first book of the *Institutiones*. But there was no contradiction; rather, a studied and energetic integration. They expressed two different outlooks, each equally important, equally indispensable (for the jurist). We might define the second one (that of the emperor as legislator) as a need for positive legality; the first (that of the jurists as depositories of the truth) as a need for substantive legitimacy, with a clear grounding in natural law. Modern thought has accustomed us to consider these two points of view as alternatives (positivism *versus* the doctrine of natural law). Ulpian kept them together, along the thread of an elaboration begun long before him, from Cicero to Gaius, and he saw the full deployment of this nexus as both the "worldwide" fulfilment of Roman jurisprudential law, and the realistic acceptance of the political essence of his own time.

A government machine like that of the period after Hadrian, which grew incessantly and constructed increasingly elaborate structures (with respect to the parameters of antiquity)—and whose development already made it clear that the bureaucracy was the destiny of the empire—had a desperate need for positive legality—authority, uniformity, certainty—in order to be able to function. Legality, in this formal sense well known to the jurists, who had been the first to elaborate it, entirely detached from its content, would always be, in all circumstances from that time forward, the authentic mode of functioning of the bureaucracy.[54] The old jurisprudential law—upon which the imperial republic and the early principate had relied for centuries—was entirely unsuited for that purpose. It might have been the law of a single city—even of a city that ruled the world, for as long as it had managed to do so with a handful of men, and with hardly no administrative structures at all—but it could no longer represent the legal order of an empire that was obliged, first by stagnation and then by crisis, to adopt centralization and then the disproportion of apparatuses in order to survive. Between bureaucracy and the legislative form of the law (*ius*), an inevitable and irresistible circuit had by now been established. The sovereign legislator was invading the world of *ius* with a force still unknown in the age of the Antonines. The imperial chancellery—and no longer the jurists as a separate class of great specialists—became the authentic normative center of the empire. And yet jurisprudence, for Ulpian, had still not exhausted its task: even though it could no longer claim a function of direct legal production, it maintained a decisive role as the repository of a law based on natural equity—and therefore on the principles of a higher distributory and proprietory rationality ("to give to each his own")—to measure and configure the contents of legislation in reference to a universal criterion of justice. In short, legal science passed from the creation of *ius* (within a jurisprudential model) to its control (within a paradigm centered on the emperor's legislation). But in order to do this, formalism and its techniques were no longer sufficient. There was also a need to incorporate into them an ethics.

Between the jurists as custodians of a substantive legitimacy and the emperor as legislator, Ulpian imagined a relationship of active collaboration, but no longer as it had once been—external, as it were, between one power and another—but instead entirely internal, within the chancellery and the bodies of the State that was coming into being. By claiming a role of great importance for the government jurists, Ulpian certainly did not intend to dim the power of the sovereign. And yet, in the representation of law built up through the conjunction of the two texts we have just examined, the emperor's will, and autocratic instincts close to military despotism (a risk that always loomed dramatically large) appeared to have been challenged, limited, and circumscribed. The sovereign could pass laws as he pleased: his investiture, which covered and legalized the weight of the effective power relationships, gave him the faculty to do so. But control over whether his measures corresponded with truth and justice, and thus the substantive legitimacy of the empire, did not lie in his hands; it did not belong to him. It rested in the science, and the ethics, of the jurists, who had to be its jealous guarantors—its "priests." In this desired division of responsibilities there was no direct criticism of imperial absolutism: nothing could be more misleading than to imagine a "democratic" Ulpian, or even a republican-spirited one, in the style of Labeo or even Cassius Longinus. He tended only to defend the presence of a civil as opposed to an autocratic-military imprint on the government of the empire, to preserve a dialectic with some depth in the chancellery and in the government apparatuses, and to make the jurists—retaining for them a space that made it possible to exercise preventive control over the emperor's decisions—the force capable of tipping the balance on what might well prove to be crucial issues.

As we can see, the natural-law option—very differently to what had happened for Cicero—did not serve now to reduce the importance of jurisprudence and its specialization in the name of other cultures and vocations (philosophy, good administration), but, by transforming the jurists—with their whole body of expertise—directly into philosophers, it made them the ultimate depositories of the possibility of a just empire (world). The recovery of the same cultural motif revealed, at a distance of centuries, completely different vocations and attitudes.

Ulpian's choice represented a clear position, which to some extent picked up on and developed, adapting without rejecting, the line we previously saw to have been that of Pomponius, and not of Gaius, prematurely resigned to a subordinate status.[55] His jurists, described as authentic guardians of justice, engaged in an unremittingly demanding task, were in fact no different (even in the stylistic force of the image) from the Pomponian ones who, in the *Enchiridion,* "improve it [law] from day to day" with their hard work. And it was—for Ulpian much more than for Pomponius—a position not lacking in courage, even though it was presented, as we have seen, with great prudence. The times of Caracalla, after all, were not those of Antoninus Pius.

5.

Let's move on now to Celsus' plane of writing.

We have already said that unfortunately we are not aware of the context in which the jurist formulated what Ulpian called an "elegant definition." We cannot even identify the title of the work from which the citation was taken; and that it belonged to Celsus' *Digesta* remains nothing more than a hypothesis.[56]

The statement was composed, in Ulpian's transcription, of two distinct segments: the identification of *ius* as *ars* and the ensuing assimilation of the latter to the knowledge of *bonum et aequum.* In our analysis we shall reverse the sequence and concern ourselves first with *bonum et aequum.* And we will do so starting from a question which, after what has been said so far, is unavoidable: can we believe that for Celsus this expression had the same value of *aequitas naturalis* that Ulpian had attributed to it?

As we know, the two expressions reflected different histories. The one linked to the birth of the doctrine of natural law (in the line of Cicero-Labeo-Gaius-Ulpian) was the more recent, formed between the *Rhetorica ad Herennium* and Cicero, and marked, lexically, by the first appearance of the noun *aequitas*. The other, that of *aequum* and of *bonum et aequum,* related instead to a much more distant past, going all the way back to the heart of the republican era.[57]

After Labeo, both *aequitas naturalis* and *bonum et aequum* seemed to vanish from the language of the jurists. Certainly, our legacy of documents regarding post-Augustan jurisprudence is not particularly abundant, but we should not ignore the fact that while we are able to record an uninterrupted presence of *aequum/aequitas* over the course of the first century (we find them in Proculus, for instance, in two important texts from the fifth book of the *Epistulae,* while in a passage from the seventh book *benignius* is adopted for the first time[58]—the use probably also reflected Senecan influences—and almost certainly in Sabinus and Cassius, if we are to believe the account of Paul, in the sixth book *Ad Plautium,* as well as in Pedius),[59] there is no reference for the first two expressions. But it is an absence that we can explain.

We must start from the well-founded supposition that between the third and second centuries B.C., *aequum et bonum* had been a clause present in edictal structures and formulations, a reflection in turn of a movement of ideas that tended to restrict if not to overcome wherever possible the ritualism of the old *ius civile.*[60] This would account well for the early stereotypy of the expression, documented in various instances of literary testimony. In the thought of the first century we witness a cultural and lexical fracture: *aequum* took on a vaster and more complex significance, which led to the creation of the corresponding noun, *aequitas.* The two terms, also under the pressure of Greek influences—both Stoic and Aristotelian—became completely dominant, and express the whole of the history that had preceded them, as well as the meanings that had formed in it, by now reasonably stabilized, albeit with relatively fluctuating boundaries: one more closely linked to the Roman tradition of the struggle against archaic ritualism, the other more directly connected to elaborations of the nascent wave of natural law.[61] In the first im-

portant reordering of the edict carried out in the years of Ofilius (an undertaking, we can safely assume, that was not merely systematic in character,
but which also involved some terminological tidying up), *bonum et aequum*
disappeared and made way for *aequum* alone, a word that was already considered more cultivated, and which appeared to be capable of recapitulating the
entire original pair, thanks also to the work devoted to it by Cicero himself
and by Servius. When Labeo was writing, he was faced only with uses of
aequum and *aequitas;* and when Mela recorded the edictal formula of the *actio
iniuriarum,* reference was only made to *aequum.*[62] This situation extended—
from the lexical and conceptual point of view—throughout the first century
A.D.; it was subject to the elaborations of Proculus and Pedius, and it endured
until the age of Neratius.[63] The Labeonian scheme of *aequitas civilis, aequitas
naturalis* was no longer utilized: in it there was perhaps seen to be an excess
of systematizing conceptualization—corresponding what's more to Labeo's
idea of nature as a universal normative order—which interpretative practice
tended instead to obscure, overlapping the two notions. The field was occupied only by the pairing *aequum/aequitas,* with significances that included, in
a first approximation, both the values codified by Cicero and by Labeo.

But when Celsus came on the scene, things changed.

He decided to recover *bonum et aequum,* which probably no one had used
for a long time, from the republican tradition, and in a somewhat theatrical
touch (as was known to have been his style)[64] he inserted it, with an explosive
function, in at least two decisive contexts. The first was the definition of *ius*
that we are analyzing here. The second can be read thanks to the mediation
of Paul—the same Paul who, we should not forget, had already devoted attention to *bonum et aequum,* assimilating it to natural law—in the seventeenth
book *Ad Plautium:*

> Celsus the Younger writes that one who was dilatory in handing
> over Stichus whom he had promised could rectify the delay by of-
> fering him subsequently; [he writes] this being a question that re-
> lates to the good and fair, a genus in which more often than not
> ruinous errors are made under the authority of legal science.[65]

The passage cited by Paul probably belonged to the twenty-sixth book of
Celsus' *Digesta:*[66] the problem concerned the delay in discharging an obliga-

tion, and the way to resolve it *(purgatio morae)*. The full provision of what was promised (the slave Stichus), although subsequent to the established date, settled the *mora*. It was a problem, Celsus explained, that related to *bonum et aequum,* and then he went on to add his devastating critique: in such matters, legal science is often the cause of ruinous mistakes. The use of *genus* should not make us think of a rigorous *divisio,* in which there ought to be, among others (passed over in silence), a *quaestio de bono et aequo.* Celsus only wanted to say "in this kind of problem . . .," "in this sort of question . . ." The focus of his discourse lay elsewhere: in the more general contrast, which was his overriding concern here, between *bonum et aequum,* capable of putting the case on the path toward a solution, and *scientia iuris,* judged to be a dangerous dispenser of errors.

In republican culture we have already encountered something that recalls this contrast: there, too, *ius* and *bonum et aequum* stood against each other as separate and distinct entities. Celsus must have been well aware of this, and to some extent he even seems to refer to it. But now that ancient motif was adopted in a different form: no longer *ius,* but its science, even if the opposition appeared no less radical.

Undoubtedly, in the text by Paul, Celsus' reference to *bonum et aequum* has a far less extensive scope than in Ulpian's passage in the *Institutiones.* Still, this does not reveal a contradiction between the two positions, but rather a sort of crescendo. In Paul, the resolution of a particular case allows Celsus to make an observation that is already general in nature: the identification of the tension between *scientia iuris* (taken as a whole) and *bonum et aequum,* and the affirmation of the primacy of the latter over the former. In Ulpian, Celsus' view of *bonum et aequum* expands even further, and appears to be a criterion referable to *ius* in its entirety. In both texts, *bonum et aequum* tends to absorb for Celsus the *ius* against which it is measuring up: excluding a bad *scientia* in Paul; identifying directly with it in Ulpian.

We can therefore regard as clarified the significance Celsus attached to the expression: it could not be advanced again other than with the same value acquired in the earlier tradition; otherwise its rediscovery, and the use made of it in both texts, would not have made any sense. It was like a kind of citation, an invitation to rediscover an aptitude. Evidently, that of searching for flexible rules, measured against concrete cases, changeable over the course of time, suited to reestablishing the equilibrium broken by circumstances: a Roman capacity that was formed far from any conscious natural-law grounding (or at any rate relating to Greek thought). Celsus wished to reconnect explicitly with this style of thinking and of interpretative habits, and repropose it, technically updated, as the basis for a practice of giving responses suited to the problems requiring attention, avoiding at the same time the risk that his suggestion might be confused with the philosophical elaboration of equity conducted by Cicero and Labeo (and perhaps by Servius). That is not all: he also intended to use those ancient and (from his point of view) invaluable words as a symbol and as a weapon. But against whom, exactly? And what did *scientia iuris* mean to him? And why did he consider it to be so liable to deception?

In order to understand, we must attempt to contextualize the dispute. The rebirth of legal thought after the difficulties of the first century had taken place under the influence of different currents of ideas.[67] At least two major lines—the most important—can be identified with reasonable confidence. For both, the persistence of the case-based paradigm and the underlying achievements of the revolution of formalism were not in discussion. What divided them was the assessment of those accepted points: what weight should be given to ontological models and categories in the concrete elaboration of solutions? And within which conceptual framework should a case be deciphered? When Javolenus writes about how dangerous all definitions are, and when we discover Neratius affirming the dogmatic finitude of *ius,* we really can see two worlds colliding.[68] On one hand (that of Javolenus), the rejection of the *definitio* could not help but affect the entire conceptual structure of legal rationalism stemming from the revolution of formalism in the first century b.c.[69] On the other (that of Neratius) there emerged the foundations of a confident scientism, with genuinely restrictive dogmatic boundaries (extraneous even to Labeo).[70]

Celsus—though with several important distinctions—was on the side of Javolenus. The *scientia iuris* that led to "error" was the same one that elaborated "dangerous definitions": a jurisprudence devoted to concepts, rules, and rigid analogical constructions based on abstract quantifications. Protection against it could be provided by a legal knowledge capable of ignoring these excessively restrictive schemes, in the name of a practice guided by flexibility, by a return to the qualitative, and by a quest, unclouded by dogmatic prejudices, for the most appropriate solution in view of the interests at play. In order to indicate its essence, Celsus chose to recover the old expression that in its time had served as a standard banner of praetorian flexibility in opposition to the intolerable ritualism of the *ius civile*. Now, however, the verbal and gestural frames inherited from urban archaism were no longer the obstacle to be overcome. That was a battle that had by and large been won. The place of the ancient enemy had now been taken by another adversary, with a renewed capacity to do harm, to convert *ius* into *iniuria* ("incivile est . . ."—"it is entirely unlawlike"—wrote Celsus in an important passage of the ninth book of his *Digesta*):[71] the new conceptualism of the excessively unilateral heirs of Servius, Labeo, and, to some extent, of Cicero himself. It was this school of thought that Celsus was challenging (not directly Servius and Labeo, who had managed to temper the logical rigor of the abstractions with a pointed evocation of the reasons of *aequum*). Just as *bonum et aequum* had once served to undercut the ritualistic conditionings of the old *ius civile*—he seemed to be indicating—likewise the revival of its inspiring motifs could be used now to overcome the new restrictions of a legal science shackled by its definitions and formal structure.

The expression (*bonum et aequum*) recurred for a third and last time in Celsus (directly, not through the filter of a citation) in a passage of the sixth book of the *Digesta:* and this time it was used not to introduce a general principle, but just had an argumentative function with respect to the case in question.[72] All the same, it was not at odds with the first two texts. The passage presented an example of what could be called the case-related basis that allowed Celsus to make his general statements: the more the reference to *bonum et aequum* (or to *aequum* alone) emerges as a key theme in the jurist's method—a topos that runs through the whole of his *Digesta*[73]—the more those declarations of principle appeared to be justified. And this also helps to explain Celsus' propensity to use *aequum* instead of *aequitas,* a word that must have seemed to him to be too compromised by philosophical influences, and connoted with abstractly universalist values, not to have struck him as equivocal and ambiguous with respect to his perspective. As far as we know, Celsus used the noun in one text only, not to indicate the abstract category (which he rejected), but rather in the much more limited and concrete expression of *aequitas rei,* as equity inherent to the given situation *(res),* intrinsic to the facts.[74]

Ulpian did not accept the distinction made by Celsus. Instead, he merged, as it were, the two traditions: that of *bonum et aequum* and that of natural equity. He identified with the latter, which he brought to completion by fitting it into a very broad scheme of natural law. His writing completely overwhelmed Celsus' design, while still citing him faithfully: the original *bonum et aequum* was entirely reduced to the equation of *ius* and *iustitia;* its original significance—associated entirely with the contingencies and relativities of sociality and history—disappeared beneath a heavy cloak of natural law that transfigured it into a set of universal and immutable values. It was, furthermore, a way of proceeding used by Ulpian not only in the *Institutiones.* In a passage from the *Ad edictum* concerning a case about the possibility of attempting a *condictio indebiti* (a procedure for the restitution of a sum that had been wrongly paid out), the jurist observed, remarking on a decision by Celsus, that he had reached it "driven by natural equity."[75] But the comment was Ulpian's, and his alone: as was the category of natural equity. Nothing in the structure of the text suggests that such a reference was already to be found in Celsus' writings: the whole passage is a summary by Ulpian himself, and does not contain a single word attributable to the earlier jurist. Nor did the Severan master want his readers to believe otherwise: he was not falsifying, but interpreting, and, as in the *Institutiones,* it was an interpretation that destroyed the ideas of the author being cited. For Ulpian, *bonum et aequum, aequum,* and natural equity were the same thing. In the passage in the *Institutiones* he had literally summarized Celsus, allowing his words to survive, though he then inserted them into a context that wiped out their real meaning. In the *Ad edictum* he limited himself to commenting on the work of the earlier jurist, and he replaced in an entirely transparent fashion the original words with his own, which must have struck him as far more appropriate. Read correctly, the text constitutes the backstage to the incipit of the *Institutiones,* and shows with extraordinary clarity the pressure to which, on this topic, Ulpian systematically subjected the words (and the doctrine) of the author he was using.

6.

The time has come to return to the first part of Celsus' definition: "Ius est ars . . ."

The contact between the two words *(ius, ars)* must be considered an exceptional occurrence in the history of Roman jurisprudence. As far as we know, no jurist before him had ever proposed a similar juxtaposition, nor did anyone do so afterwards (if we exclude our text, where Ulpian unhesitatingly inserted the statement by Celsus into his own argument). Pomponius, in the *Enchiridion,* never used it.[76] Outside of jurisprudence, the situation was only slightly different: between the end of the first and the beginning of the second century A.D., we can only detect a few isolated traces. The idea of associating the knowledge of *ius* with *artes* appears, albeit fleetingly and in a conceptually marginal way, in two texts by Tacitus and by Gellius, both, oddly enough, referring to Labeo (there is perhaps an implicit reference to jurisprudence also in a passage from Livy);[77] while it is possible that in the general structure of an encyclopedic treatise whose second part has come down to us as the *De medicina* of Aulus Cornelius Celsus, jurisprudence featured in a list of *artes* alongside agriculture, the military disciplines, rhetoric, and philosophy.[78] And then, in this period of time, there is nothing.

Should we therefore take it to be an invention by Celsus? Absolutely not. Once again—as for *bonum et aequum*—the jurist was not inventing: he was borrowing and regenerating. The connection between *ius* and *ars* had in fact become some time earlier, as we well know, a symbol of Cicero's legal studies. When Celsus was writing, he could not have helped but think of him. In the years that separated them, there had been no significant development of that theme; it is impossible not to imagine a link. But of what kind?

In Cicero's intellectual programs, the necessity to transform the practice of *ius* into *ars* had been a point that was never disputed. In the learned language of the late republic, *ars* was a word that could take on different meanings. In the introductory remarks of the *Rhetorica ad Herennium* we can find a first important codification of the term, referring in fact to rhetoric but easily applicable to other disciplines (the first uses we are able to ascertain were by Plautus):[79] "*ars* is the doctrine that offers a certain rational method of eloquence."[80] From then on, its values shifted from that of "system" to that of "method," to that of "scientific mastery" (in the sense of the Aristotelian and

Stoic dialectic), to that of a "rationally organized discipline," and to "theory," and Cicero himself drew consciously on the polysemous flexibility of the term in his use of it. But in the range of these manifold connotations we can always find an underlying element in common, perfectly perceptible, and never obscured: *ars* invariably alluded to a body of knowledge structured according to intrinsically rational and universally valid rules, which was yoked to unity according to its own describable order; a knowledge endowed with a robust technical and theoretical specificity, and a powerful logical basis; to "that which is arranged in a connection and in an order . . . that makes it possible . . . to obtain a certain purpose."[81] In the Ciceronian project, the reduction of *ius* to *ars* was intended to mean the abandonment of the convoluted cognitive empirics of the jurisprudential tradition, in the name of a rigorous conceptual and definitory constructivism, both in the dialectic sense and (at least in an early phase) in a systematic diaeretic one: a qualitative leap which would be necessary to bring the practice of *ius* under the protective shadow of Greek philosophy, into the safe harbor of the typical sciences of Hellenistic encyclopedism.[82]

This conception did not outlive its author (except, perhaps, briefly, in a project of Ofilius).[83] The jurists—and Servius first of all, the same Servius whom Cicero so admired—chose another path: their revolution of formalism did not undermine the case-based rationality, but developed it; tradition was not eliminated, but reworked. The power of the concepts did not annul the logic of the response, but enhanced its potential. The *De iure civili in artem redigendo* disappeared from the scene; of *ius* as *ars*—at least in the weighty significance assigned to it by Cicero—no jurist ever spoke again. The word appeared too bound up with a project that had not been carried through. The association was only retained well away from legal thought, and in a marginal way, in connection with a weak and generic use of *ars* in the sense of knowledge, of subject.

What prompted Celsus to revive that contact?

In reality he did not subscribe to the implications at all. His idea of *ius* was completely different: a flexible law, pertinent to the situations to be regulated, guided by *aequum,* oriented toward an empirical evaluation of the circumstances, far removed from any conceptual rigidity. A *ius* reduced to *ars* in its strong Ciceronian sense would have fallen even more under the dominion of the "science" that was a perilous source of grave errors: the worst possible solution. So what was he doing?

We must accept the possibility that the two parts of the maxim *(ius est ars, ius est bonum et aequum),* taken literally, in the language and thoughts of Celsus, clashed irremediably. If *ius* was to be based on *bonum et aequum* (in his sense), it could not be identified at the same time with Cicero's notion of *ars* (which was the sole paradigm of this reduction of which Celsus and all his readers could think).

If we want to take this path, we might also suppose that Celsus was not contradicting himself. He was doing something different, which we know he liked to do. He was using the word *ars* in a polemical fashion, with an almost mocking tone, as was occasionally his wont, when swept up in the vehement defense of his own convictions.[84] He had constructed (from his point of view) a maxim on the verge of being an oxymoron. There were those who claimed—he said, compressing his reasoning into the flash of a single phrase —that *ius* must be *ars:* namely, system, theory, epistemological discipline, science (Cicero, as the unquestionable founder of this current, deserved the honor of the silent citation, but Celsus was clearly evidently speaking about the entire line of rationalist jurisprudence from Labeo to Neratius, which, though in a less unilateral and radical fashion, and without ever again using— as far we are able to determine—that compromised word, had continued to be inspired by it). And so—he continued—if *ius* really was "science" and "system," it would be the science and the system of that which it intrinsically could not be, of that which shunned by its essence any rigidity and any predetermined classification: it would be "the science, the doctrine, the system . . . of the good and fair." A witticism, certainly, but worthy of his style: at least for those able to grasp it.

The sole alternative hypothesis to this interpretation would be to give Celsus' use of *ars* a meaning that was, as it were, pre-Ciceronian, and far less binding, understanding it only in the sense of "ability," "talent," or "technique." The jurist might have used the word in polemical contrast with "science," to indicate a law entrusted to the profession of learned experts and not of rigorous theorists: a possible reading, though less suggestive than the first.

As for Ulpian, he was certainly not rescuing the thoughts of Celsus, however they may be interpreted. It is quite possible that his sharp gaze had been quite capable of capturing their nuances, but they were all covered by the vast weight of his writing and his communicative intentions (and it is worth specifying at this point that we stuck only to these in the translation of the text presented at the beginning of the chapter). Once *bonum et aequum* had

been transformed into natural equity, the disruptive sense of Celsus' evaluative empirics and the antidogmatic polemic contained therein vanished entirely; just as there vanished, as a consequence, the oxymoronic contrast (if it
existed) that had linked the two segments of the original maxim. And the
very identification of *ius* as *ars,* by now, at the turn of the third century, must
have appeared, although still fairly unusual, no longer truly surprising: the
encyclopedism of the Antonine culture had helped to make this assimilation
acceptable. Ulpian understood the word as a synonym of the *scientia* used by
Pomponius in the *Enchiridion* (and that is how it has been rendered in the
translation):[85] Celsus' entire statement now sounds like nothing more than an
acknowledgment that *ius* had to be identified with the authentic doctrine of
natural equity—a clear consecration of the natural-law perspective pursued
throughout the text.

We cannot determine with certainty whether Celsus had already described his statement as a "definition": it seems unlikely, even though he knew
the word, which, however, he used very rarely, and always in a context of a
negative judgment, along what we might call the line of Javolenus. ("Define,"
"definition" are used in two passages from Celsus, and in both they are linked
to an assessment of fallacy: in connection with the Catonian rule, presented
as "in some cases . . . misleading" in the thirty-fifth book of his *Digesta;*[86] and
when discussing the notion of *peculium* proposed by Tubero, in the sixth
book.)[87] In all likelihood it was Ulpian who chose that verb, to which he
was wont to resort,[88] and stressed its weight with an adverb—*eleganter*—that
he used frequently when he wished to emphasize the importance and the
conceptual dignity of his citation. To present it as a "definition" elaborated
with elegance must have seemed to him the most appropriate way to complete the transformation to which he had subjected the original thought of
Celsus: from a polemical topic, perhaps dense with sarcasm and echoes, to
the calm affirmation of a rule, capable of recapitulating and concluding a
lengthy history.

7.

Finally, a few quick observations need to be made on the value of the text for
Justinian's editors.

From the perspective of the Byzantine jurists the outlook of Celsus—of the Celsus outside Ulpian's treatment—appeared blurred and distant: a completely lost world. Less so that of Ulpian, of which they still discerned certain features. And the sequence they read in the opening of the *Institutiones*—law, justice, fairness (in the sense of natural equity, which they reconstructed through the Severan jurist himself)—had a very familiar flavor. It seemed almost to have been written by them: and that is why they selected it for the beginning of the *Digesta*.

The words endure longer than the concepts they express. Arranged as they were found, they appeared to lead directly to the heart of a typically Byzantine doctrine, and little did it matter whether in order to understand them thus it was necessary to cancel the thoughts they had originally been intended to voice. All that was required was an exchange, a shift in levels, which in the minds of Justinian's compilers must have presented itself nearly with the force of an automatic reflex. It was sufficient for Ulpian's rationalist doctrine of natural law to slide toward the colors and the forms of a theory of a theological and transcendent type, like that which was in the air in the libraries of Constantinople, and the change was complete. Evidently, Ulpian's project of a politics of law was entirely annihilated, but it had already been defeated by history. The thought that was its presupposition had completely failed to achieve its political objective; and it had ended in a far different way than that which would befall another elaboration of natural law, far more well-prepared and much closer to us, in the heart of modern Europe.

The reading of the Byzantines was facilitated moreover by the very structure of the text of the *Institutiones*. Was not (natural) equity a central category of legal thought and rhetoric in Justinian's time? And was not the same true of the concept of justice?

The masters of Constantinople must also have been pleased by that reference to the priesthood, to jurists as priests and as authentic philosophers, guardians of the truth. From their viewpoint, that metaphor no longer stood as a bulwark to limit the power of the sovereign, no longer helped to place the jurists once again in a privileged position with respect to the production of law. All this would have been unthinkable in the milieux of the Byzantine autocracy. But it helped to confer a sort of mystical and transcendent frame on legal knowledge, which must have been particularly in keeping with the sensibility of the times and the theological justification of imperial power. And that same "us"—so charged with effects in Ulpian—could now be interpreted in an entirely different way; it could change, so to speak, its implicit subject: no longer the jurists as a group, in an extreme and proud demand for space and intellectual independence, but the apparatus of the bureaucracy, with at its head the majesty of the emperor himself, supreme and direct custodian of an all-encompassing legality, which canceled out any other quest for legitimation. As was often the case, here too Justinian's editors had had no need to interpolate: all they needed to do was misunderstand.

22

Equality Ancient and Modern

I.

Ulpian was probably the only jurist of his time to pose the problem of transforming law and legal science into the overall ideology of the empire, the expression of a renewed political society, arising from the decision of Antoninus Caracalla to extend Roman citizenship to all the free subjects of the provinces: a choice that was in any case practically inevitable, and which completed a lengthy process of integration, even if in the shadow of a despotic rule. The jurist still imagined that the unification of the world might be achieved under the influence of the definitive affirmation of a science without equal, which had invented formalism and the very idea of order as legality, and was now attempting to shape the new state machinery making its debut in a dramatic era of crisis. When we found him writing, at the beginning of the *Libri regularum,* that "jurisprudence is knowledge of matters divine and human, the science of the just and unjust,"[1] we were right in the presence of this attempt. A traditional formula of philosophical scholastics was used, in reference to jurisprudence, to express entirely new content. Legal science *(iuris prudentia)* no longer appeared merely as the repository of highly specialized knowledge (this allusion was intrinsic to the semantic field of *prudentia,* and there was certainly no need to underscore it any further), but also as a knowledge capable of enclosing the understanding and the total significance of civilization ("divinarum atque humanarum rerum notitia"), and of offering a doctrine of justice ("iusti . . . scientia") in which legal technique, having now become moral commitment, might be transformed into a universal canon of conduct, into the ideology itself of the civilizing of the human race in the shadow of the empire.

It was the assumption of such an outlook that imposed upon the jurists—already with Papinian—a new relationship with ethics, obliging them to renew the connection pursued by Cicero to legitimize Rome's dominion over the Mediterranean, and from then on substantially rejected by a jurisprudence satisfied with its isolation and the formal power of its conceptual protocols. It was this change that dictated the transition from a law indifferent to questions of justice—which even when it talked of equity, as had been the case from Servius to Julian, did so within a horizon dominated by case-based fragmentation, only in order to avoid the risks of excessively rigid and abstractly consequential solutions—toward a law engaged in the quest for a just order, suspended between innatism and metaphysics.

Certainly, these models of ethicality were socially poor in effective prescriptive contents, unable to progress beyond the generic indications that Cicero had taken in his time from a Greek elaboration already centuries old: a few worn features of a patrimonialist and proprietary representation of the social tie—that world allowed nothing more. Roman thought had not made much progress in this field, and something resembling a public ethics, an authentic sense of the civic, had never developed, despite the exceptions of Seneca and Marcus Aurelius. However, that was not the point, but rather the perception that the formal isolation of law, its reduction to a purely reflexive relationship between an ontology immobilized in its completeness and an ought-to-be construed as a function "a priori" (in a Kantian sense), could no longer be sufficient. In fact, it was no longer faced by the private disciplining of a society already unified by the uncontested exercise of a political hegemony (as happened in republican times), but by the task of finding a rule and a measure in which a world on the brink of a devastating crisis, and a State whose disproportion with respect to the means of the era began to be equal to its impotence, might identify. The recovery in grand style of natural law, foreshadowed by the moralistic fervor of Papinian, was an attempt to respond to this problem, and makes it possible to evaluate the vast distance separating Hadrian's jurisprudence from the great authors who lived between the reigns of Septimius and Alexander Severus. Only a few decades had passed, and yet an abyss had opened up.

But what exactly were the uses and statutes of the natural-law option in Severan thought? To gain an understanding of this, we will evaluate how it functioned with regard to a delicate and revealing topic: the construction of the relationship between natural law *(ius naturale)* and the law of nations *(ius gentium),* through which the jurists came to consider the question, pregnant with future, of the universal equality of the human race.

We must, however, take a step back and return to Gaius, whose importance in the tradition of natural law we have already discussed. The text to look at is the opening of his *Institutiones:*

> Every people that is governed by statutes and customs observes partly its own peculiar law and partly the common law of all mankind. That law which a people establishes for itself is peculiar to it, and is called *ius civile* [civil law] as being the special law of that *ciuitas* [State], while the law that natural reason establishes among all mankind is followed by all peoples alike, and is called *ius gentium* [law of nations, or law of the world] as being the law observed by all mankind. Thus the Roman people observes partly its own peculiar law and partly the common law of mankind.[2]

We are immediately before the list of the parts of law examined previously in the comparison with Pomponius;[3] here we have the premise that underpinned the subsequent *partitio.* The scheme is evident: an expansion of the descriptive value of elements proper to the history of *ius,* in order to present them as a synthesis of the morphology of all human orderings. It begins with the division of law into two parts—into statutes and customs—typical of the Roman experience, but presented as a general characteristic; and then moves on to the distinction between *ius civile* and *ius gentium,* likewise peculiar to the development of the Roman legal order, and once again delineated as common to all peoples. In so doing, Gaius was moving along a consolidated line, that of the progressive delocalization and universalization of Roman law, which we observed earlier to be the chief objective of the late-republican doctrine of natural law, and which the new imperial legislation was now contributing to establish in a definitive manner. Even though here the jurist was not speaking literally of "natural law," it was the notion of *ius gentium*—and therefore a part of Roman positive law—that was identified directly with "natural reason," and thus incorporated within a model in which nature figured implicitly as a normative order: an idea that had been held by Labeo.[4] The description of the parts of the law outlined immediately afterwards, dating back as we know to a first nucleus that can be found in the *Rhetorica ad Herennium* and in Cicero's *Topica,* and then probably developed by the Sabinian tradition, had in its turn precociously inserted a reference to nature into its own catalogue.[5] Gaius omitted it, because he had presented it in an earlier and more important position: not as a segment among many others, but recognizing in natural reason the very origin of one of the two normative planes of the Roman legal order, complementary to civil law (the thread of this distinction would later work its way through to Papinian's *Definitiones* and even appear fleetingly in Paul, in the text on the multiple concepts of *ius* that we have already encountered, where for that matter the relationship between "utility" and civil law revealed another Ciceronian motif, taken up by Julian).[6]

2.

The Severan jurisprudence would shatter the essential part of this picture (even though we can still find traces of it in Paul).[7] The break would take place around the relationship between *ius gentium* and *ius naturale,* where it intersected with the formulation of a principle previously unknown to Roman legal thought: the explicit affirmation of equality in freedom as a "natural" characteristic of the human race, which the historical existence of slavery could not erase.

> Manumissions also belong to the *ius gentium.* "Manumission" derives in fact from the sending out of one's hand, that is, granting of freedom [...] . This thing originated from the *ius gentium,* since by the law of nature all men were born free; and manumission

was not heard of, as slavery was unknown. But after slavery came in by the law of nations, there followed the boon of manumission. And while by natural law men are all called by a single name, in the law of nations there came to be three classes: free men, and set against those slaves and the third class, freedmen, those who had stopped being slaves.[8]

As far as concerns the civil law slaves are regarded as not existing, not, however, in the natural law, because as far as concerns the natural law all men are equal.[9]

Slavery is an institution of the law of nations, whereby someone is against nature made subject to the ownership of another.[10]

. . . and indeed freedom is the condition of natural law and subjection the invention of the law of nations.[11]

Here we have three jurists who were working at the turn of the third century: Ulpian, once again (the first two texts, respectively from the first book of the *Institutiones* and from the forty-third book *ad Sabinum*), Florentinus (from the ninth book of his *Institutiones*), and Tryphoninus (from the seventh book of the *Disputationes*).[12] They all repeated, probably independently, the same doctrine: detaching slavery from the plane of the natural, and shifting its foundation to that of a unanimously accepted social convention, and, as a consequence, the identification of the natural condition with the freedom of men. What importance, however, ought we to give to this affirmation, which, taken literally, seems to open onto the very heart of modernity?

The abandoning of the naturalistic paradigm in order to justify slavery was not a recent one. That explanation had been staunchly defended by Aristotle in the *Politics,* where its most complete formulation can be found ("What the nature and power of a slave are is clear from these considerations. For anyone who, while a human being, does not by nature belong to himself but to another is by nature a slave").[13] But when the philosopher was writing, it was a conception contested by a not insignificant current of Sophistic thought ("But others think that to be a master is against nature, for they say it is by law that one person is a slave and another a master, whereas by nature there is no difference at all"),[14] mentioned by Aristotle himself, and by him implicitly rejected.[15] Cicero would later abandon it, in his *De republica*,[16] replacing it with a doctrine according to which the characteristic trait of slavery was no longer the placid mirroring of an unalterable qualitative difference inscribed in the nature of things ("ruler" and "ruled": obedient bodies in the presence of omnipotent minds),[17] but instead the coercive and repressive tendency of an entirely artificial regulation, harsh and severe, open to violence (this latter aspect was also already present in the thinking of the Sophists).[18] Whereas in Aristotle there was a polarizing insistence on the reference to *physis* (nature), reiterated to the point of redundancy, Cicero used the harsh vocabulary of surveillance and punishment: "tame," "castigate," "harry."[19] In this change—from nature to force—what came before any philosophical genealogy was the historical experience of Roman slaveholding and the problems that it had posed at the culmination of its spread across the Mediterranean.

In the face of the proliferation of tumultuous organizational and repressive forms whose outlines were still elusive, it is likely that the cold interpretation of the phenomenon proposed by Aristotle might have appeared, from the Roman point of view, to be weak and unfocused. It was necessary to develop more dynamic and realistic parameters, capable of accounting for an incandescent social issue, with an overwhelming need for a solid yet flexible network of prescriptions and operative modes that the classical Greek world had never known, and that the lack of legal specialization would in any case prevent it from elaborating. We have explored several references, found in the thinking of Servius and Alphenus,[20] both accustomed to an ethnic and social universe in which it was not only "barbarians" who were forced into slavery, but often men and women from more culturally developed environments than those of Rome, and in the presence of whom it would be difficult to speak of any "natural" inferiority.[21]

Cicero's variant attempted in fact to express the leap from nature to history; from slavery as a projection of being, to slavery as the ethical right and duty of masters: an idea that would survive through to American antiabolitionist literature in the years leading up to the Civil War.[22] The circle was thus closed. The ones in the right seemed to be the anonymous polemicists recorded in the *Politics* with cool detachment: slavery was "against nature," Florentinus would go so far as to say, translating literally the words with which Aristotle had summarized, in order to reject, the thinking of his interlocutors.[23]

The Severan jurists were certainly not hostile to the slave system: rather they were its last great interpreters (perhaps it is no accident that the concluding text of the *Digesta* contains a brief instruction by Paul on this topic),[24] and their statement no longer had any of the scandalously subversive tone that might have colored its first appearance, many centuries earlier, in Greek thought. In an entirely different context, they sought only to achieve a conceptual systematization of the functional and cultural peculiarities of the Roman form of chattel slavery; and it is not insignificant that both Ulpian and Tryphoninus expounded their assumptions about the figure of manumission: an institution that was entirely typical, in its more articulated developments, of the legislative and jurisprudential experience of republican society in the golden age of imperial slaveholding.[25] Nor was it possible for them to forget the lesson of the Stoics, reflected in a large number of philanthropic provisions introduced by Antonine legislation, intended to soften and mitigate the harshness of the servile condition, albeit without calling into question in any way its absolute legitimacy.

The splitting away of the law of nations from natural law was the mature fruit of this reality, and served to give greater depth of field to the jurists' vision, allowing them to articulate better their overall view in what we might call the "general doctrines" regarding personal statuses. It was no longer necessary for the delocalization of the Roman order to rest directly on a solely naturalistic foundation, as it had been for Cicero, and as Gaius still maintained, probably falling behind his own times. The long management of a boundless empire made timely a comparative historical outlook that had at first been unthinkable. Now it was possible to distinguish the various planes: that of historical processes and social conventions—of the common civilization of men—from that of ethics and philanthropy, and to make use of the latter not as a normative foundation in the narrowest sense (for those ends, the law of nations was sufficient), but as an ideal measure toward which the actions and designs of rulers ought to tend, within the historically possible limits: this was the "natural equity" that we found in Ulpian.

The confining of slavery in the *ius gentium* and the *ius civile*, far from natural law, thus emerged as the synthesis of two requirements, which until then had remained separate. On the one hand, the achievement of a historicized and sociologized idea of slavery, based on experience of a lengthy practice of repression and integration (through manumissions, which transformed, by the uncontestable decision of a private master, a prisoner devoid even of the right to life into a citizen of the community that ruled the world); on the other, the valorization of the ethical implications of Antonine humanism, which was pushing toward affirmations of great ideological impact, but of modest institutional scope.

Yet in doing this, what became of Gaius' "natural reason," once the horizon of history had been taken away from it? And how could its definition be reconciled with the doctrine of the "natural" equality of all men?

Let's listen to Ulpian one last time:

> Natural law is that which nature has taught to all animals; for it is not a law specific to mankind but is common to all animals— land animals, sea animals, and the birds as well . . .
>
> *Ius gentium*, the law of nations, is that which all human peoples observe. That it is not co-extensive with natural law can be grasped easily, since this latter is common to all animals whereas the law of nations is common only to human beings among themselves.
>
> The *ius civile* is that which neither wholly diverges from natural law and from the law of nations, nor follows the same in every particular. And so whenever to the common law we add anything or subtract anything from it, we make a law special to ourselves, that is *ius civile*, civil law.[26]

We should not be deceived by the apparent simplicity of the explanation and the links (sea animals and birds, and that mechanical "subtract" and "add"): we are still in the *Institutiones,* and it is appropriate to continue to suppose the presence of multiple levels of reading.[27]

The idea that Ulpian actually wanted to transmit was one of a natural law completely unhampered by human action and by the intervention of history. That is not how it had been in Gaius; for him, "natural reason" manifested itself entirely on the plane of historicity, albeit a universal historicity. Now instead it was shifting toward a kind of dogmatic innatism (there is perhaps a distant echo of Panaetius here) that saw nature as the place of a "teaching" ("docet") impressed above all upon the *tabula rasa* of animal behaviors.

3.

The retreat of natural law from the horizon of history immediately provoked a drastic regime change of its paradigm: reduced to representing a perspective devoid of any effective normative worth, but precisely for that capable of accepting maxims—such as that of equality among men—otherwise inconceivable for the legal culture of that world. Over longer spans of time, the change would open up the path to that sacral vision of nature and to its definitive theologization, destined to dominate so much of Christian thought, both Byzantine and that of the Western Middle Ages, and to survive almost intact, through the teachings of the Catholic church, right up to the present day.

The different possibility that Ulpian allowed to be glimpsed in the opening of his *Institutiones,* of a use of the natural-law perspective for a critique—at least potential—of a positive law that had stopped expressing values of justice and equity, was never a hypothesis pursued by the Severan jurisprudence, nor was it by the very master who had posited it, albeit with the caution which we have observed. This block has a profound explanation: the inability to transform the ancient theory of natural law into an authentic doctrine of human rights, even in the moment when it seemed closest to being attained.

What failed was something decisive: the connection between the theoretical elaboration of natural law as the site of justice and equality among men, and the construction, on the social prior even to the philosophical plane, of a strongly grounded individualism, capable of projecting itself fully onto the terrain of law and politics.

In the ancient world, an authentically individualistic conception of the person and of social subjectivity never effectively took root. When efforts in this direction did appear—from Epicurus to Zeno, and from Marcus Aurelius all the way up to the mystical tendencies of neo-Platonism in the third and fourth centuries—they always had a marginal and minority character.[28] They ended up suggesting nothing more than a retreat into the interiority of the soul, not the birth of an authentic emancipatory impulse. The competitive drive of the Roman aristocratic sociality had other foundations—citizenship, not individualism—and the Roman law constructed by the jurists was never, as we have seen, a law of individuals, but rather, a law first of citizens, who regulated through it the underlying patrimonial and family prerequisites of their civic condition, and then of propertied subjects, anchored to their own community or to the elite that governed the empire: and it was for this reason that it always remained centered more on property than on the contract; a law based on personal statuses and not on "economic" individuals who had placed labor at the heart of their lives. Only in modernity would it be interpreted in an individualistic sense, with a forcing of its original features—in part through the lesson of medieval Christian thought—to allow its bourgeois actualization.

The failure of ancient natural law theory cannot therefore be explained solely on the level of the history of doctrines. It is only the social history of ideas that can give us an adequate account. What Severan thought lacked was not the power of concepts. Rather, it was the absence—dating way into the past— of historical subjects capable of assuming and developing the implications of that thought, of making it the ideology of their own economic, civil, and intellectual growth; in other words, well beyond the narrow and now colorless circle of apprentice functionaries which formed the audience to whom Ulpian could hope to speak.

In the postmedieval West the advance of natural law would rub shoulders with the rise of the new bourgeoisie, in France, in England, and in America itself: it was the culture of a world that was taking shape, not the echoes of a dying empire. The contact would redefine the domain of politics (as Kant and Hegel knew perfectly well), and it would above all favor the start of that long and still far from complete process of the integration of politics into law—the foundation of the very idea of "human rights," unknown to the ancient world—from which modern democracy took form. In antiquity—where politics and a law that had always remained intrinsically "private" would never truly succeed in coming together after their separate births, respectively in Greece and Rome—that thinking would vanish without an outcome in the silence of the Byzantine libraries, and prior to that, in the indifference of a social universe that was not capable of grasping it. The maxim of the "natural" equality of men would remain a cold, dead letter, and that is how it was perceived even by the very authors who formulated it: a principle without any relationship to history, devoid of consequences; the recognition of an inert naturalness, entirely sterilized both politically and socially, which was unable to go beyond a book or a scholastic classification, and to become life, reality, and mass consciousness.

In the modern world the same principle would also be formulated by slaveowners: Thomas Jefferson probably owned no fewer than Ulpian. And in fact the decisive difference was not this but something else, namely that in the new situation it acquired the force of an explosive declaration, capable of unleashing energies, resources, and ideas—a dialectic of freedom built around social labor as a transforming power—which the ancient world was unable to produce.[29]

And yet, when expressed by the great Severan authors, that short phrase —"all men are equal"—was charged with resonances to which we must learn to be attuned. It was the furthest boundary of juridicality, in that world, the point of encounter, albeit shifted beyond the boundaries of history, between law and ethics: admittedly still referring to a *ius* that, though helpless in the prison of a "naturalness" incapable of becoming the foundation of an authentic civil society, still condensed not merely a philosophical doctrine filled with echoes, but above all the lesson of formalism, of that dissolution of social and economic power in the geometric order of a serial quantification, of legality as a procedure capable of measuring all magnitudes—truly an "order of the earth"—without which the individualism of the new Western world, projected out over the oceans and in space, could never have come into being.[30]

Certainly, embedded deep in the heart of modernity, that abstract way of being equal—irradiated so directly by the Roman experience—would often appear, and perhaps today even more than ever, incapable of grasping the contradictions of bare life, of forming a law truly capable of keeping pace with today's history—economics, technology, globalization, biopolitics; and therefore no longer as a final destination, but only as a point of departure, to attain other equilibriums, opening out onto new horizons. But the fact remains that, in the end, every time that we have attempted to go beyond and replace it with something more substantive, it has been necessary to accompany the experiment with such a degree of coercion, violence, and ethical overdetermination as to render its cost unsustainable. This must not prevent us from trying again; indeed, it is a fine thing to see in such an objective a guiding star of our future: the achievement of a totally modern way of being equal. But we must, however, recognize that the formalism of its law remains for now the destiny of the West; its civil soul; its only fully utterable public discourse. And it is about this—a far from small matter—that Roman law continues to speak to us: about the possibility of a historically determined relationship between form and power as the sole element upon which we can (thus far) rely for an order of the world that is at the same time both realistic and open to hope.

ABBREVIATIONS

NOTES

GENERAL INDEX

INDEX OF SOURCES

Abbreviations

ANRW *Aufstieg und Niedergang der römischen Welt. Geschichte und Kultur Roms im Spiegel der neueren Forschung,* ed. H. Temporini and W. Haase (Berlin, 1972–)

AUPA *Annali del Seminario Giuridico dell'Università di Palermo*

BIDR *Bullettino dell'Istituto di Diritto Romano*

Bremer F. P. Bremer, *Iurisprudentiae antehadrianae quae supersunt,* I, II.1, and II.2 (1896–1901; reprint, Leipzig, 1985)

CAF T. Kock, ed., *Comicorum Atticorum Fragmenta* (Leipzig, 1880)

CI *Codex Iustinianus,* ed. P. Krüger (Berlin, 1877) (ed. maior); *Corpus iuris civilis, II^{14},* ed. P. Krüger (Berlin, 1967)

CIL *Corpus Inscriptionum Latinarum* (Berlin, 1863)

Coll. *Collatio Legum Mosaicarum et Romanarum,* in FIRA, II, pp. 540–589

D. *Digesta Iustiniani Augusti,* ed. T. Mommsen (1870; reprint, Berlin, 1962–63) (editio maior); *Corpus iuris civilis* (1872), *I^{22}: Digesta,* ed. T. Mommsen and P. Krüger (Berlin, 1973)

DPR A. Schiavone, ed., *Diritto privato romano: Un profilo storico* (Turin, 2003)

EP O. Lenel, *Das Edictum perpetuum. Ein Versuch zu seiner Wiederherstellung,* 3d ed. (Leipzig, 1927)

F *Littera Florentina*

FgrHist F. Jacoby, ed., *Die Fragmente der griechischen Historiker,* 15 vols. (Berlin, 1923–1958)

FIRA *Fontes Iuris Romani Anteiustiniani,* S. Riccobono, J. Baviera, C. Ferrini, J. Furlani, V. Arangio-Ruiz, 3 vols. (editio altera) (Florence, 1940–1943; reprinted with appendix of vol. III, Florence, 1968)

Giuristi   A. Schiavone, *Giuristi e nobili nella Roma repubblicana. Il secolo della rivoluzione scientifica nel pensiero giuridico antico* (1987; reprint, Rome, 1992)

ILS   H. Dessau, ed., *Inscriptiones Latinae Selectae*, 3 vols. (1892–1916)

Iust.   Inst. *Institutiones in Corpus iuris civilis* (1872), ed. P. Krüger, *I²²* (Berlin, 1973)

JRS   *Journal of Roman Studies*

Leges publicae   G. Rotondi, *Leges publicae populi romani: Elenco cronologico con una introduzione sull'attivita legislativa dei comizi romani* (1912; reprint, Milan, 1990)

Linee   A. Schiavone, *Linee di storia del pensiero giuridico romano* (Turin, 1994)

Logiche   A. Schiavone, *Studi sulle logiche dei giuristi romani: Nova negotia e transactio da Labeone a Ulpiano* (Naples, 1971)

Origini   A. Schiavone, *Alle origini del diritto borghese: Hegel contro Savigny* (Rome, 1984)

Pal.   O. Lenel, *Palingenesia Iuris Civilis*, 2 vols. (1889; reprint, Rome, 2002); L. E. Sierl, *Supplementum* (Graz, 1960)

PG   J. P. Migne, ed., *Patrologia Graeca* (Paris, 1857–1866)

RE   *Paulys Realencyclopädie der classischen Altertumswissenschaft,* new ed. by G. Wissowa, W. Kroll, K. Mittelhaus, and K. Ziegler (Stuttgart, 1873–)

RHD   *Revue (Nouvelle revue) historique de droit français et étranger*

Roman Statutes   M. H. Crawford, *Roman Statutes,* 2 vols. (London, 1996)

SDHI   *Studia et Documenta Historiae et Iuris*

Storia   A. Schiavone, ed., *Storia del diritto romano e linee di diritto privato* (Turin, 2005)

Storia di Roma   A. Schiavone, ed., *Storia di Roma, I* (with A. Momigliano) (Turin, 1988), II.1 (1990), II.2 (1991), II.3 (1992), III.1 and III.2 (1993), and IV (1989)

Storia di Roma   A. Giardina and A. Schiavone, eds., *Storia di Roma* (Turin, 1999) (ed. minor)

Storia spezzata   A. Schiavone, *La storia spezzata: Roma antica e Occidente moderno* (1996), 4th ed. (Rome, 2002); in English as *The End of the Past. Ancient Rome and the Modern West,* trans. M. J. Schneider (Cambridge [Mass.], 2000)

SVF   I. von Arnim, *Stoicorum Veterum Fragmenta*, 3 vols. (1903–1905; reprint, Stuttgart, 1964)

T   *Tijdschrift voor Rechtsgeschiedenis* = *Revue d'histoire du droit*

TF   *Scaenicorum Romanorum Fragmenta, I: Tragicorum Fragmenta* (Munich, 1953)

TPSulp.   G. Camodeca, ed., *Tabulae Pompeianae Sulpiciorum: Edizione critica dell'archivio puteolano dei Sulpicii* (Rome, 1999)

ZSS   *Zeitschrift der Savigny-Stiftung für Rechtsgeschichte (Romanistische Abteilung)*

Notes

Translator's note:

The citations in English from Justinian's *Digesta* and the *Institutes* of Gaius are drawn respectively from *The Digesta of Justinian,* ed. and trans. A. Watson, rev. ed. (Philadelphia, 1998), 2 vols., and *The Institutes of Gaius,* part 1, trans. F. De Zulueta (1946; reprint, Oxford, 1951). In some cases the translations have been modified.

Preface

The words cited in the preface are from Foucault, "Nietzsche: La généalogie, l'histoire," in *Hommage à Jean Hyppolite* (Paris, 1971), pp. 145–172. In English as "Nietzsche, Genealogy, History," in *The Foucault Reader,* ed. P. Rabinow (New York, 1984), p. 81.

1. Roman Law and the Modern West

1. Procopius, *Historia arcana* 6.21; 9.51; 11.1–2; 13.20–23; 14.1.9–10; 14.1.20; 27.33; 28.9; 28.16; 29.15, concerning which: A. Cameron, *Procopius and the Sixth Century* (Berkeley, 1985), pp. 20, 63, 129, 228, 247, 255 ff.; E. Gibbon, *The Decline and Fall of the Roman Empire* (ed. Bury), II (London, 1898), chap. 35. See also Gibbon, *Memoirs of My Life* (ed. Radice) (1984; reprint, London, 1990), pp. 164–165 and 186.

2. *Corpus iuris civilis,* I^{22}, ed. T. Mommsen and P. Krüger (Berlin, 1973 [1st ed. Berlin, 1872]); II^{14}, ed. P. Krüger (Berlin, 1967 [1st ed. Berlin, 1877]); III^{8}, ed. R. Schöll and W. Kroll (Berlin, 1963 [1st ed. Berlin, 1895]).

3. F. Bluhme, "Die Ordnung der Fragmente in den Pandectentiteln. Ein Beitrag zur

Entstehungsgeschichte der Pandecten," *Zeitschrift fur geschichtliche Rechtswissenschaft*, 4 (1820): 257 ff. n. 3 (a classic still accorded considerable attention); F. Schulz, *Einführung in das Studium der Digesten* (Tübingen, 1916); F. Wieacker, "Zur Tecnick der Kompilatoren. Prämissen und Hypothesen," *ZSS*, 89 (1972): 293 ff.; D. Mantovani, *Digesto e masse bluhmiane* (Milan, 1987) (with bibliography). See also below, note 10.

4. L. Mitteis, *Reichsrecht und Volksrecht in den östlichen Provinzen des römischen Kaiserreichs. Mit Beiträgen zur Kenntniss des griechischen Rechts und der Spatrömischen Rechtsentwicklung* (Leipzig, 1891); E. Levy, "Westen und Osten in der nachklassischen Entwicklung," *ZSS*, 49 (1929): 230 ff.; Levy, *West Roman Vulgar Law: The Law of Property* (Philadelphia, 1951); and Levy, *Weströmisches Vulgarrecht. Das Obligationenrecht* (Weimar, 1956); F. Schulz, *History of Roman Legal Science* (1946; reprint, Oxford, 1953), pp. 278 ff.; F. Pringsheim, "Reichsrecht und Volksrecht," *Journal of Juristic Papyrology*, 7–8 (1954): 163 ff.; F. Wieacker, *Vulgarismus und Klassizismus im Recht der Spätantike* (Heidelberg, 1955); Wieacker, "Vulgarrecht und Vulgarismus, alte und neue Probleme und Diskussionen," now in *Ausgewählte Schriften*, I (Frankfurt am Main, 1983), pp. 240 ff.; Theo Mayer-Maly, "'Vulgo' und Vulgarism," *Labeo*, 6 (1960): 7 ff.; G. G. Archi, *Giustiniano legislatore* (Bologna, 1970), pp. 11 ff., 151 ff.

5. The fragments of the *Gregorianus* and of the *Hermogenianus* can be found in *Collectio librorum iuris anteiustiniani*, ed. P. Krüger, T. Mommsen, and G. Studemund, III (Berlin, 1890), pp. 221 ff. On the relationships between the *Gregorianus*, the *Hermogenianus*, and Justinian's codex (a work about which I shall have more to say later), still fundamental is *Leges publicae*, 110 ff. For the *Codex Theodosianus*, the edition customarily cited is that of T. Mommsen and P. M. Meyer, *Theodosiani libri XVI*, I.2, 2d ed. (Berlin, 1954). See T. Mommsen, *Prolegomena*, ibid., I.1, pp. 9 ff.; T. Honoré, "The Making of the Theodosian Code," *ZSS*, 103 (1986): 133 ff.

6. T. Honoré, *Tribonian* (London, 1978).

7. *CI*, 1.17.1; translation, with modifications, from *The Digesta of Justinian*, ed. and trans. A. Watson, rev. ed. (Philadelphia, 1998), vol. I, p.xliv.

8. From *digerere*: order, allot, register, distribute; but it was, as we shall see, a title that was widely used in Roman legal literature as far back as the late republican era.

9. See the *Index Florentinus*, in *Digesta Iustiniani Augusti, editio maior*, ed. T. Mommsen and P. Krüger, I (reprint, Berlin, 1962), pp. lii*–lvi*.

10. In addition to the works cited in note 3, mention can be made of: A. M. Honoré and A. Rodger, "How the Digest Commissioners Worked," *ZSS*, 87 (1970): 246 ff.; A. M. Honoré, "The Editing of the Digest Titles," *ZSS*, 90 (1973): 262 ff.; Honoré, *Tribonian*, pp. 139 ff.; *Justinian Digest: Work in Progress* (reprint, Oxford, 1983); D. J. Osler, "The Compilation of Justinian's Digest," *ZSS*, 102 (1985): 129 ff..

11. "paene annum confusum": *CI*, 1.17.1.5.

12. The three exceptions are books 30, 31, and 32.

13. "Let no one dare to compare that which belonged to antiquity with what we have introduced, because there are many important things that, for reasons of utility, have been transformed": *CI*, 1.17.2.10.

14. On the *Digesta*, see I nn. 2 *(ed. minor)* and 10 *(ed. maior)*; for the *Codex* and the *Novellae*, see II and III n. 2.

15. P. Stein, *Roman Law in European History* (Cambridge, 1999), esp. pp. 38 ff.; C. M. Radding and A. Ciaralli, "The *Corpus iuris civilis* in the Middle Ages," *ZSS*, 117 (2000): 247 ff.

16. This was an idea that dated back to Leibniz, *Nova methodus discendae docendaeque jurisprudentiae*, in *Samtliche Schriften*, VI.1 (1930; reprint, Berlin, 1971), pp. 297 ff. (and see also "Disputatio iuridica prior de conditionibus," ibid., pp. 101 ff.); *Origini*, pp. 72–73.

17. Friedrich Karl von Savigny, *Vom Beruf unserer Zeit für Gesetzgebung und Rechtswissenschaft* (1814), 3d ed. (1840; reprint, Hildesheim, 1967), pp. 28–29. The *Beruf* is available in H. Hattenhauer, ed., *Thibaut und Savigny. Ihre programmatischen Schriften* (Munich, 1973), pp. 95 ff.; and in J. Stern, ed., *Thibaut und Savigny. Ein programmatischer Rechtsstreit auf Grund ihrer Schriften* (1914; reprint, Darmstadt, 1959), pp. 69 ff. (the quotation is on p. 114 of the Hattenhauer edition).

18. Hattenhauer, *Thibaut und Savigny*: "We have demonstrated previously that, in our science, any success is based upon the mastery of the fundamental principles. And indeed it is precisely in this that we find the greatness of the Roman jurists: in the concepts and in the maxims of their science they do not see the fruit of their will, but real entities, whose existence and genealogy have become familiar through long acquaintance. It is for this reason that their way of proceeding possesses a confidence and certainty that cannot be found in any other field outside mathematics, as one might well say, without fear of exaggeration, that they calculate with their concepts." There is an important intuition in these statements: see Chapters 12, 17, and 22 in this volume.

19. Friedrich Karl von Savigny, *System des heutigen römischen Rechts*, 8 vols. (Berlin, 1840–1849; reprint, Aalen, 1981).

20. Henry Sumner Maine, *Ancient Law: Its Connection with the Early History of Society, and Its Relation to Modern Ideas*, 2d ed. (London, 1863), p. 7.

21. C. P. Sherman, *Roman Law in the Modern World*, 2 vols., 2d ed. (1922; reprint, Holmes Beach, Fla., 1994).

2. History Rediscovered

1. Although instead of *Aktualisierung* Savigny used *heutigen*—present-day—in his own title (*System des heutigen römischen Rechts*, 8 vols. [Berlin, 1840–1849; reprint, Aalen, 1981]).

2. There is a portrayal in D. R. Kelly, "Clio and the Lawyers: Forms of Historical

Consciousness in Medieval Jurisprudence," *Medievalia et Humanistica*, 5 (1974): 25 ff.; and Kelly, "The Rise of Legal History in the Renaissance," *History and Theory: Studies in the Philosophy of History*, 9 (1970): 174 ff., both now in Kelly, *History, Law and the Human Sciences* (London, 1984), chaps. 2 and 5.

3. *Codex Theodosianus cum perpetuis commentariis Iacobi Gothofredi* (1665), 6 vols. (Leipzig, 1736–1745).

4. G. B. Vico, *La scienza nuova giusta l'edizione del 1744 con le varianti dell'edizione del 1730 e di due redazioni intermedie inedite*, ed. F. Nicolini, 2 vols. (Bari, 1928), II, p. 245 (1348).

5. In a letter from the philosopher to Paul Yorck von Wartenburg, in 1884: G. Bowersock, "Rendering unto Caesar," *New Republic*, 16 December 1996, pp. 43–44. The text by Dilthey is in *Briefwechsel Wilhelm Dilthey und Graf Paul Yorck von Wartenburg* (Halle, 1923), pp. 39 and 43.

6. F. Schulz, *History of Roman Legal Science* (1946; reprint, Oxford, 1953), pp. 141 ff.

7. Friedrich Karl von Savigny, *Vom Beruf unserer Zeit für Gesetzgebung und Rechtswissenschaft* (1814), 3d ed. (1840; reprint, Hildesheim, 1967), p. 157.

8. In the preface to the third book of the *Elegantiae*, in *Prosatori latini del Quattrocento*, ed. E. Garin (Milan, 1952), pp. 607–609.

9. *Pal.*, I–II.

10. G. Pasquali, "Summum ius summa iniuria," *Rivista di filologia e d'istruzione classica*, n.s., 5 (1927): 231, reprinted in *Stravaganze quarte e supreme* (Venice, 1951) and again in *Pagine stravaganti*, II (Florence, 1968), p. 339.

11. F. Wieacker, *Textstufen klassischer Juristen* (1960; reprint, Göttingen 1975).

12. Ibid., pp. 93 ff.

13. See Wieacker, *Textstufen klassischer Juristen*, pp. 178 ff.; Schulz, *History of Roman Legal Science*, pp. 141 ff.

3. The Jurists in Rome

1. In the *Enchiridion* (on which see Chapter 8, sec. 3, and Chapter 19, sec. 3), in *D.* 1.2.2.13. I translate from a reading of "in melius produci"; but the reconstruction of the text is questionable, and there are those who prefer "in medium."

2. Also in the *Enchiridion*, in *D.* 1.2.2.47.

3. For example, in *De oratore* 1.42.191: see Chapter 8, sec. 4.

4. The expression comes from Carl Schmitt (who based it on Savigny), and it is used in reference to English law: *Die Lage der europäischen Rechtswissenschaft* (Berlin, 1958). See also W. W. Buckland and A. D. McNair, *Roman Law and Common Law*, ed. F. H. Lawson, 2d ed. (Cambridge, 1952).

5. F. Schulz, *History of Roman Legal Science* (1946; reprint, Oxford, 1953), p. 1. "Vocation" in the English text is rendered as "Beruf" in *Geschichte der römischen Rechtswissenschaft* (Weimar, 1961), p. 1.

6. *Storia,* p. 8 n. 1. The reference to Weber is present in the note in the German edition (pp. 1–2 n. 2) but absent from the corresponding note in the English edition. The latter, however, does mention the second edition of *Wirtschaft und Gesellschaft* in the works cited in the list of abbreviations (p. xvi).

7. Schulz, *History of Roman Legal Science,* pp. 6 ff., 60 ff., 102 ff., 124 ff., 267 ff.; M. Weber, *Wirtschaft und Gesellschaft,* ed. J. Winkelmann, 5th ed., 2 vols. (Tübingen, 1972), in English as *Economy and Society: An Outline of Interpretive Sociology,* trans. E. Roth (New York, 1968) I, pp. 207 ff.

8. Weber, *Economy and Society,* II, p. 809; translation modified.

9. Ibid., pp. 641 ff.

10. Schulz, *History of Roman Legal Science,* p. 39.

11. The relations between Schmitt and Weber should be studied in depth, if anything working from Schmitt's text analyzing the Weberian uses of "form," in *Politische Theologie. Vier Kapitel zur Lehre der Souveränität,* 2d ed. (Munich, 1934), in English as *Political Theology: Four Chapters on the Concept of Sovereignty,* trans. G. Schwab (Chicago, 2005), pp. 27 ff.

12. Syme's book was published in 1939. Momigliano's opinion is expressed in a more veiled manner in *JRS,* 30 (1940): 407 ff., esp. 415–416 (= *Secondo contributo alla storia degli studi classici* [Rome, 1960], pp. 407 ff.); and more directly in the introduction to the Italian translation of the book (Turin, 1962), pp. ix ff.

13. The German word is "Isolierung": *Prinzipien des römischen Rechts* (Munich, 1934), pp. 13 ff., in English as *Principles of Roman Law,* trans. M. Wolff (Oxford, 1936).

14. Aulus Gellius, *Noctes Atticae* 20.1.22–23.

15. Pliny the Younger, *Epistulae* 1.22. See Chapter 19, sec. 2 and note 19.

16. For example, on Labeo, Capito, and Cassius Longinus; see Chapter 17, sec. 1, and Chapter 18, sec. 2.

17. Plato, *Minos* 317d (defending the authenticity of the dialogue): see below, Chapter 12, note 13.

18. The theme of temporality as the destruction of order is already purely and clearly Platonic: *Republic* 8.3.546a (and see also *Laws* 3.1.676–677); the Heideggerian reformulation touches on the relationship between historicity and temporality: *Sein und Zeit,* 10th ed. (Halle, 1963).

19. F. Schulz, *Classical Roman Law* (Oxford, 1951), p. 2.

20. A. Momigliano, "Le conseguenze del rinnovamento della storia dei diritti antichi," in *La storia del diritto nel quadro delle scienze storiche* (Florence, 1966), pp. 21 ff.; later in *Terzo contributo alla storia degli studi classici e del mondo antico,* 2 vols. (Rome, 1966), I, pp. 285 ff.

21. F. F. Abbot and A. C. Johnson, *Municipal Administration in the Roman Empire,* 2d ed. (New York, 1968); R. Bernhardt, *"Imperium" und "Eleutheria." Die römische Politik gegenüber den freien Städten des griechischen Ostens* (Hamburg, 1971); L. Cracco Ruggini, "La città imperiale," in *Storia di Roma,* IV, pp. 201 ff.; P. Garnsey, "Aspects of

the Decline of the Urban Aristocracy in the Empire," in *ANRW*, II.1, pp. 229 ff., 252; J. Gascou, "La politique municipale de Rome en Afrique du Nord," ibid., II.10.2, pp. 136 ff.; D. Nörr, *Imperium und Polis in der hohen Prinzipatzeit*, 2d ed. (Munich, 1971); F. Grelle, *L'autonomia cittadina fra Traiano e Adriano: Teoria e prassi dell'organizzazione municipale* (Naples, 1972); F. Jacques, *Le privilège de liberté: Politique impériale et autonomie municipale dans les cités de l'Occident romain* (Rome, 1984). Also A. H. M. Hones, *The Cities of the Eastern Roman Empire*, 2d ed. (Oxford, 1971) (and even earlier: *The Greek Cities from Alexander to Justinian* [Oxford, 1940]); R. K. Sherk, *The Municipal Decrees of the Roman West* (New York, 1971).

4. Origins

1. See Chapter 7, sec. 3, and Chapter 8, sec. 3.
2. See Chapter 7, sec. 2.
3. A reliable portrayal of this orientation can be found in the contributions in vol. I of *Storia di Roma*.
4. See *Storia di Roma* (ed. minor), p. 5.
5. See A. Carandini, *La nascita di Roma: Dèi, lari, eroi e uomini all'alba di una civiltà* (Turin, 1997), p. 6.
6. G. de Sanctis, *Storia dei Romani*, 4 vols. (1907–1964; reprint, Florence, 1964–65); de Sanctis, *La leggenda della lupa e dei gemelli*, now in *Scritti minori*, III (Rome, 1972), pp. 457 ff.; A. Momigliano, "Rapporto provvisorio sulle origini di Roma" (1962), now in *Storia e storiografia antica* (Bologna, 1987), pp. 175 ff., in English as "An Interim Report on the Origins of Rome," *JRS* 53 (1963): pp. 95–121; E. Gabba, "Problemi di metodo per la storia di Roma arcaica" (1993), now in *Roma arcaica: Storia e storiografia* (Rome, 2000), pp. 11 ff.
7. B. G. Niebuhr, *Römische Geschichte*, 3 vols. (Berlin, 1874): A. Momigliano, "G. C. Lewis, Niebuhr e la critica delle fonti," in *Contributo alla storia degli studi classici* (Rome 1960), pp. 249 ff.
8. G. W. F. Hegel, *Vorlesungen über die Philosophie der Geschichte* (reprint, Leipzig, 1930), pp. 8, 175–176, 665, 687–688, 697–698, in English as *Lectures on the Philosophy of History*, trans. J. Sibree (London, 1894).
9. E. Gjerstad, *Early Rome*, 4 vols. (Lund, 1953–1973) (I subscribe to the views of Momigliano, "Interim Report"). Of considerable importance remains H. Müller-Karpe, *Vom Anfang Roms* (Heidelberg, 1959), esp. pp. 14 ff. We should also mention T. J. Cornell, *The Beginnings of Rome: Italy and Rome from the Bronze Age to the Punic Wars* (London, 1995), esp. pp. 48 ff.
10. Carandini, *La nascita di Roma*, p. 358.
11. A. Momigliano is right: "Le origini di Roma," now in *Roma arcaica* (Florence, 1989), pp. 35 ff.

12. E. Benveniste, *Le vocabulaire des institutions indo-européennes*, 2 vols. (Paris 1969), I, pp. 209, 217–218, 226, 257–258, 295, 309, 315–316; and II, p. 85. In English as Benveniste, *Indo-European Language and Society*, trans. E. Palmer (Coral Gables, Fla., 1973), pp. 169, 175 ff., 182, 206–207, 240–241, 252, 257–258; II, p. 368.

13. Momigliano, "Le origini di Roma," pp. 10 ff.; Carandini, *La nascita di Roma*, pp. 491 ff. (which together provide a fine example of the richness of Italian historiography). Also Cornell, *The Beginnings of Rome*, pp. 60 ff.

14. It is difficult to imagine that writing appeared in Latium before the late seventh century B.C., an age in which Latin was certainly spoken in Rome: Momigliano, "Le origini di Roma," p. 22. But it is not until at least the mid-sixth century B.C. that we find the first reliable surviving documentary evidence: the few words on the vase of Duenos and of the Lapis Niger in the Forum: see G. Colonna, "Duenos," *Studi etruschi*, 47 (1979): 163 ff.; A. E. Gordon, "Notes on the Duenos-Vase Inscription in Berlin," *California Studies in Classical Antiquity*, 8 (1975): 53 ff.; R. E. A. Palmer, *The King and the Comitium: A Study of Rome's Oldest Public Document* (Wiesbaden, 1969). Also dating from the sixth century are vases with Etruscan inscriptions found on the Palatine and Capitoline hills; but this evidence is not sufficient to cause us to suppose an archaic "bilingualism": Momigliano, "Interim Report," p. 98. Also Cornell, *The Beginnings of Rome*, pp. 41 ff. Review of archaic Latin inscriptions in G. Colonna, "L'aspetto epigrafico. Appendice: Le iscrizioni strumentali latine del vi e v secolo a.C.," in *Lapis Satricanus* (The Hague, 1980), pp. 53 ff.

15. It is impossible to follow the great French scholar and suppose with him the presence of a clearly recognizable Indo-European nucleus at the heart of archaic Roman thought (his position developed and was refined through considerable modifications). The most important points of reference remain G. Dumézil, *Jupiter Mars Quirinus*, 4 vols. (Paris, 1941–1948); Dumézil, *Les dieux des Indo-Européens* (Paris, 1952); Dumézil, *L'idéologie tripartie des Indo-Européens* (Paris, 1958); Dumézil, *Mythe et epopée*, 3 vols. (Paris 1968–1973; Dumézil, *La religion romaine archaïque*, 2d ed. (Paris, 1974), in English as *Archaic Roman Religion*, 2 vols., trans. P. Krapp (1970; reprint, Baltimore, 1996). See C. S. Littleton, *The New Comparative Mythology: An Anthropological Assessment of the Theories of Georges Dumézil*, 2d ed. (Berkeley, 1983); J.-P. Vernant, "Histoire et structure dans la religion romaine archaïque," in *Religions, histoires, raisons* (Paris, 1979); and Vernant, *Mythe et société en Grèce ancienne*, 2d ed. (Paris, 1981), in English as *Myth and Society in Ancient Greece*, trans. J. Lloyd (New York, 1990, pp. 241 ff.). But to reject this idea—and any other hypothesis (however it might be garbed) of a preestablished correspondence between genetic bases and cultural elaboration—need not signify a renunciation of any attempt to identify the long durations in the history of mental structures (or, worse, the abandonment of this task to ambiguous discoverers of archetypes), or to seek the elementary forms of their appearance, destined to survive, in more complex sys-

tems, as functional connections between self-renewing contents, and as a tendency to reelaborate in accordance with constant associative models the new experiences produced by the changed conditions of historical development. In this respect, I am intrigued by an interpretation that we might describe as "transcendental" by Dumézil (the Kantian metaphor, rough but effective, is proposed by C. Ginzburg, *Miti emblemi spie* [Turin, 1986], p. 220; and even earlier, Ginzburg, "Mythologie germanique et nazisme: Sur un ancien livre de Georges Dumézil," *Annales: Economies, sociétés, civilisations,* 40 [1985]: 695 ff.): see also C. Lévi-Strauss, "Réponse au discours de M. Georges Dumézil," in *Discours prononcés dans la séance publique tenue par l'Académie Française pour la réception de M. Georges Dumézil le jeudi 14 juin 1979,* ed. Institut de France, Académie Française (Paris, 1979), pp. 21 ff., esp. 30 ff. See also Chapter 5, sec. 2 and note 17.

16. Varro, *De lingua Latina* 5.9.55; 6.4.28; 9.49.86; Livy 1.31.4; Festus, p. 468 (Lindsay) (with the link between vestals and tribe); see also Plutarch, *Numa* 10.

17. Festus, pp. 474–476 (Lindsay). The word may refer to Labeo's commentaries *De iure pontificio:* Bremer, II.1, p. 79: F. Schulz, *History of Roman Legal Science* (1946; reprint, Oxford, 1953), p. 138.

18. I am reelaborating from L. Wittgenstein, "Bemerkungen über Frazers *The Golden Bough,*" *Synthese,* 17 (1967): 242: "eine Einkleidung eines formalen Zusammenhangs;" in English as *Remarks on Frazer's Golden Bough,* trans. A. C. Miles, ed. Rush Rhees (Retford, 1979), p. 9e.

19. J. Assmann, *Herrschaft und Heil. Politische Theologie in Altägypten, Israel und Europa* (Munich, 2000).

20. Polybius 6.56.6–15.

21. Cicero, *De natura deorum* 2.3.8 (and see also 1.42.117); translation from *Cicero, De Natura Deorum,* trans. H. Rackham, Loeb Classical Library (Cambridge, Mass., 1956).

22. Benveniste, *Le vocabulaire,* I, p. 184 (*Indo-European Language and Society,* pp. 145–148).

23. Almost all of these are fragments that have come down to us through some indirect channel in the successive republican tradition, and it is reasonable to imagine alterations to both the grammatical and orthographic elements and, in some cases, to the vocabulary itself: and this applies in particular to the most important text: the Twelve Tables (see Chapter 7, sec. 2). A very controversial problem is that of the Etruscan influence on archaic Latin; but it is certainly possible to compile a small list of Latin words of Etruscan derivation: among them are *populus* and possibly *par:* G. Devoto, "Nomi di divinità etrusche," *Studi etruschi,* 6 (1932): n. 6, pp. 243 ff.; and Devoto, *Storia della lingua di Roma,* 2d ed. (Bologna, 1969), pp. 78 ff. (but see Momigliano, "Interim Report," p. 98).

24. The monument is in the Louvre. At the top of the stele, in a relief, is a portrayal of the sovereign in the act of receiving the insignia of power from the god Mar-

duk: the linkage between divinity, royalty, and prescriptivity is upheld. The *editio princeps* of the text is in V. Scheil, *Textes élamites sémitiques,* II (Paris, 1902). A translation that is generally considered by specialists to be very good is that by A. Finet, *Le code de Hammurapi,* 2d ed. (Paris, 1983). See E. Szlechter, *Codex Hammurapi* (Rome, 1977); J. Bottéro, *Mésopotamie: L'écriture, la raison et les dieux* (Paris, 1987). J. Renger, "Noch einmal. Was war der 'Codex Hammurrapi' ein erlassenes Gesetz oder ein Rechtsbuch?," in *Rechtskodifizierung und soziale Normen im interkulturellen Vergleich,* ed. H. J. Gehrke (Tübingen, 1994), pp. 27 ff.; H. Neumann, "Recht im Antiken Mesopotamien," in *Die Rechtskulturen der Antike. Vom Alten Orient bis zum römischen Reich,* ed. U. Manthe (Munich, 2003), pp. 55 ff.

25. J. Zandee, *Der Amunhymnus des Papyrus Leiden I 344 verso,* III (Leiden, 1992), tables 9–10: Assmann, *Herrschaft und Heil,* pp. 180–181. See also S. Allam, "Recht im pharaonischen Ägypten," in Manthe, *Die Rechtskulturen,* pp. 15 ff.

26. M. Weinfeld, *Deuteronomy and the Deuteronomic School* (Oxford, 1972), esp. pp. 244 ff.; F. Crüsemann, *Die Thora. Theologie und Sozialgeschichte des alttestamentlichen Gesetzes* (Munich, 1992); Crüsemann, *Torah, Nomos, Ius. Abendländischer Antinomismus und der Traum vom herrschaftsfreien Raum,* ed. G. Palmer (Berlin, 1999); Assmann, *Herrschaft und Heil;* M. Liverani, *Oltre la Bibbia: Storia antica di Israele* (Rome, 2003), pp. 378 ff.; E. Otto, "Recht im antiken Israel," in Manthe, *Die Rechtskulturen,* pp. 151 ff.

27. According to Assmann, *Herrschaft und Heil.*

28. L. Gernet, *Anthropologie de la Grèce antique* (Paris, 1968), in English as *The Anthropology of Ancient Greece,* trans. J. Hamilton and S. J. and B. Nagy (Baltimore, 1981); also G. Thür, "Recht im antiken Griechenland," in Manthe, *Die Rechtskulturen,* pp. 191 ff.

29. There is in this sense an uncontrasted tradition in studies of Roman law, hypnotized by the ancientness and continuity of the term *ius.* And it is also in the wake of this (bad) habit that the word "law" is used in an inaccurate sense to describe ancient experiences of social regulation that had little to do with the Roman form: beginning with Gernet himself, all the way up to Bottéro and Assmann; and that is to restrict ourselves to scholars of the first rank. But in doing so we forgo the possibility of distinguishing, and interpreting for what they really are, the differences—in Greece, in Mesopotamia, in Egypt, in Israel—with respect to the peculiarities of Rome: a misunderstanding that makes impossible any authentic genealogical discourse. The justification attempted by Gernet for this abuse *(Anthropologie)* is very feeble, and nothing more than a petition of principle: it is taken for granted that an early common notion of law existed in Mediterranean societies, but that is precisely what needs to be demonstrated.

30. L. Gernet, "Droit et prédroit en Grèce ancienne," first published in *Année sociologique,* 3d ser., (1948–49): 21 ff., later in *Anthropologie.*

31. M. Ostwald, *Nomos and the Beginnings of the Athenian Democracy* (Oxford, 1969). Also L. Gernet, *Recherche sur le développement de la pensée juridique et morale en Grèce* (1917; reprint, Paris, 2001), pp. 257 ff. (admittedly, in an interpretative context to which I do not subscribe).

32. What is stated here presupposes, at least for the Greek aspect, L. Gernet, "Droit et ville dans l'antiquité grecque," in *Anthropologie;* J.-P. Vernant, *Les origines de la pensée grecque* (Paris, 1962), in English as *The Origins of Greek Thought* (Ithaca, 1982); C. Meier, *Die Entstehung des Politischen bei den Griechen* (Frankfurt am Main, 1980), translated by D. McLintock as *The Greek Discovery of Politics* (Cambridge, Mass., 1990, pp. 29 ff.); N. Loraux, *L'invention d'Athènes* (Paris, 1981), in English as *The Invention of Athens: The Funeral Oration in the Classical City,* trans. A. Sheridan (Cambridge, Mass., 1986); O. Murray, "Cities of Reason," *Archives européennes de sociologie,* 28 (1987): 325 ff.; E. A. Havelock, *Alle origini della filosofia greca. Una revisione storica* (Roma, 1996).

33. Dumézil, *La religion romaine archaïque* (*Archaic Roman Religion,* I, pp. 47 ff.).

34. H. Hubert and M. Mauss, *Essai sur la nature et la fonction du sacrifice* (1899), now in *Oeuvres,* vol. I (Paris, 1968), esp. p. 288.

35. R. Girard, *La violence et le sacré* (Paris, 1972), in English as *Violence and the Sacred,* trans. P. Gregory (Baltimore, 1979), pp. 274 ff.

36. For Varro: *Antiquitates rerum divinarum* (Cardanus), I, frs. 66, 78, 87; III, frs. 124–143. For Sarpi: "Pensieri sulla religione," in *Pensieri naturali, metafisici e matematici* (L. Cozzi and L. Sosio) (Milan, 1996), pp. 664–665. For Servius Grammaticus: *Ad Aen.* 2.141. On the *indigitamenta*: Dumézil, *La religion romaine archaïque* (*Archaic Roman Religion,* I, pp. 35–37).

37. A. Giardina, *L'Italia romana: Storie di un'identità incompiuta* (Rome, 1997), pp. 63 ff., with bibliography.

38. Festus, p. 424 (Lindsay). The text poses a very delicate problem, on which we need not linger here: why the killability of *homo sacer* ("qui occidit parricidi non damnatur") should be linked to the prohibition against making a ritual sacrifice of the same ("neque fas est eum immolari"). This topic—"the capacity to be killed but not sacrificed" of *homo sacer*—is the focus of a work by G. Agamben, *Homo sacer: Il potere sovrano e la nuda vita* (Turin, 1995), in English as *Homo Sacer: Sovereign Power and Bare Life,* trans. D. Heller-Roazen (Stanford, 1998), p. 71, which is a rare example of the integration of the history of Roman law into an interpretative context capable of extending beyond the narrow bounds of the specialization.

39. Girard, *La violence et le sacré* (*Violence and the Sacred,* pp. 99 ff., esp. p. 114).

40. Gernet, *Anthropologie.*

41. We need only mention R. Hirzel, *Themis, Dike und Vervandtes* (Leipzig, 1907), p. 51; P. de Francisci, *Arcana imperii,* III.1 (reprint, Rome, 1970), pp. 136 ff.; de Francisci,

Primordia civitatis (Rome, 1959), pp. 378 ff.; P. Noailles, *Du droit sacré au droit civil* (Paris, 1949), pp. 16 ff.; G. Devoto, *"Ius:* Di là dalla grammatica," *Rivista italiana di scienze giuridiche,* 3d ser., 2 (1948): 414 ff.; M. Kaser, *Das altrömische ius* (Göttingen, 1949), pp. 23 ff.; A. Guarino, *L'ordinamento giuridico romano,* 4th ed. (Naples, 1980), pp. 69 ff.; R. Orestano, *I fatti di normazione nell'esperienza romana arcaica* (Turin, 1967), pp. 102 ff.; G. Dumézil, *Idées romaines* (Paris, 1969, pp. 31 ff.); O. Behrends, "'Ius' und 'ius civile.' Untersuchungen zur Herkunft des 'ius'-Begriffs im römischen Zivilrecht," in *Sympotica Franz Wieacker* (Göttingen, 1970), p. 11.

42. Coarelli, *Il Foro romano,* pp. 178 ff., with bibliography. Also G. Dumézil, "Remarques sur la stèle archaïque du Forum," in *Hommages J. Bayet* (Brussels, 1964), pp. 172 ff.; Dumézil, *La religion romaine archaïque (Archaic Roman Religion,* I, pp. 84 ff.); Benveniste, *Le vocabulaire,* II, pp. 179 ff. (*Indo-European Language and Society,* pp. 379 ff.); Santalucia, *Diritto e processo penale,* pp. 2 ff. (and in *Storia di Roma,* I, pp. 430 ff.).

43. Benveniste, *Le vocabulaire,* II, pp. 133 (*Indo-European Language and Society,* pp. 407 ff.).

44. Ibid., pp. 111 ff., 168–169, 172–173 (*Indo-European Language and Society,* pp. 389 ff., 437, 440).

5. Kings, Priests, Wise Men

1. Festus, pp. 198–200 (Lindsay). "Maximus videtur Rex, dein Dialis, post hunc Martialis, quarto loco Quirinalis, quinto pontifex maximus. Itaque in soliis Rex supra omnis accumbat licet; Dialis supra Martialem, et Quirinalem; Martialis supra proximum; omnes item supra pontificem. Rex, quia potentissimus: Dialis quia universi mundi sacerdos, qui appellatur Dium; Martialis, quod Mars conditoris urbi parens; Quirinalis socio imperii Romani Curibus ascito Quirino; pontifex maximus, quod iudex atque arbiter habetur rerum divinarum humanarumque."

2. On the dating of Verrius Flaccus, see S. Mazzarino, *Il pensiero storico classico,* 2 vols. (Bari, 1966), II.2, pp. 175–176. It is possible that on this point he also drew on the books *De iure pontificio,* by Ateius Capito (for other links between Verrius and Capito: R. Reitzenstein, *Verrianische Forschungen* [Breslau, 1887], passim, all pointed out by W. Strzelecki, *C. Atei Capitonis Fragmenta* [Leipzig, 1967], pp. 28–56). See also Fabius Pictor, *De iure pontificio,* fr. 3 (= Bremer, I, pp. 10–11).

3. G. Dumézil, *La religion romaine archaïque,* 2d ed. (Paris, 1974) (*Archaic Roman Religion,* I, pp. 106, 109, 142–143); and Dumézil, *Idées romaines* (Paris, 1969). This text never left Dumézil's thoughts; it reappears in *Le moyenne noir en gris dedans Varennes* (Paris, 1984). See also T. J. Cornell, *The Beginnings of Rome: Italy and Rome from the Bronze Age to the Punic Wars* (London, 1995), p. 234.

4. A. Momigliano, "Le origini di Roma," now in *Roma arcaica* (Florence, 1989), p. 10.

5. Aulus Gellius, *Noctes Atticae* 15.27.5: the quotation is from the first book of Laelius Felix's commentary on Quintus Mucius (see Chapter 11, sec. 2 and note 26: the link for the reference is the idea of *comitia calata*, brought up in connection with an archaic type of will, evidently recorded by Mucius in the first book of his *Iuris civilis*, which was in fact devoted to this topic (see Chapter 12, note 26). The text by Dionysius of Halicarnassus is in 2.7.3.

6. Fundamentally exact were the intuitions of N. D. Fustel de Coulanges, *La cité antique*, 19th ed. (Paris, 1905); and J. Frazer, *The Golden Bough*, 12 vols. (1906–1915), abr. ed. (London, 1922), pp. 1 ff., 83 ff., 146 ff. We can accept the view set forth by Momigliano, "Le origini di Roma," pp. 43–44.

7. Also recorded by Gaius, *Institutiones* 1.112; see *CIL*, XIV, nn. 2089 and 2634: de Martino, *Storia della costituzione romana*, I, pp. 95, 102, 141, 215, 416–417; A. Momigliano, "Il *Rex Sacrorum* e l'origine della repubblica," now in *Roma arcaica*, pp. 165 ff.; Cornell, *The Beginnings of Rome*, pp. 232 ff.

8. The phenomenon of the attribution of magical powers to the royal function makes it possible to detect a long-enduring mental constant in European history, beneath the surface of changes in religious culture; and it is difficult to escape the idea that, despite everything, there is a very profound link between the myths of the forest of Nemi of Turner and Frazer (Strabo 5.3.12; Suetonius, *Cal.* 35; but probably Frazer in the renowned opening of his book overlays the images of two different paintings by Turner, now both at the Tate Gallery in London) with kings of medieval France and England, masterfully studied by Marc Bloch in *Les rois thaumaturges* ([1924; reprint, Paris, 1983], with a preface by J. Le Goff, pp. i–xxxviii, which points in the same direction that I am suggesting here); in English as *The Royal Touch: Monarchy and Miracles in France and England*, trans. J. E. Anderson (1961; reprint, New York, 1989). See also A. Magdelain, *De la royauté et du droit de Romulus à Sabinus* (Rome, 1995), pp. 17 ff.

9. J. Bayet, *Histoire politique et psychologique de la religion romaine*, 2d. ed. (Paris, 1969); Dumézil, *La religion romaine archaïque*, pp. 326 ff.

10. See Chapter 4, note 12.

11. Indications in this direction are found in Dumézil, *La religion romaine archaïque* (*Archaic Roman Religion*, I, pp. 32 ff.); and in J. Scheid, *La religione a Roma* (Rome, 1983), pp. 45 ff. In a text by Plutarch, *Quaest. Rom.* 111, the flamen of Jove is described as "a living statue," that is, a man petrified into a symbolic depiction of the deity.

12. Cornell, *The Beginnings of Rome*, pp. 103 ff.

13. Bayet, *Histoire politique et psychologique.*

14. Dumézil, *La religion romaine archaïque* (*Archaic Roman Religion*, I, pp. 161, 370 ff., 390 ff.).

15. A. Momigliano, "Premesse per una discussione su Georges Dumézil," *Opus:*

Rivista internazionale per la storia economica e sociale dell'antichità, 2 (1983): 329 ff., esp. 339–340; but see also Momigliano, "Georges Dumézil and the Trifunctional Approach to Roman Civilization," in *Ottavo contributo alla storia degli studi classici e del mondo antico* (Rome, 1987), pp. 135 ff. = *History and Theory: Studies in the Philosophy of History*, 22 (1984): 312 ff.; and in an earlier occurrence, "Interim Report," p. 113.

16. As Momigliano acknowledges with great honesty ("Dumézil and the Trifunctional Approach," p. 141), the big unanswered question (left unresolved by Dumézil) remains that of understanding and describing the relationships that must have been established between these imaginary representations (which, until proven otherwise, must be assumed to have a purely internal coherence) and the levels of reality—social, productive, and of power—involved, in keeping with a scale of possibilities that range from the simple ideal mirroring of a material form that was already established and solid in and of itself (essentially Dumézil's early position), to the complex integration between structures of thought and social bases in a multicentered system (this is the model of Marx in *Grundrisse der Kritik der politischen Ökonomie* [cited in Chapter 6, note 4], which I do not, however, believe that Dumézil ever read), up to and including the hypothesis of a disjunction and a noncorrespondence among the various levels: a sign of traumas and ruptures that had been almost completely cancelled. For further references, see Chapter 4, note 15.

17. It is again Dumézil who uses the adjective "mystical" ("mystique") in connection with the pairing of *rex flamen Dialis: La religion romaine archaïque (Archaic Roman Religion*, I, pp. 111, 152). On the characterization of the archaic Jove, we should also be aware of A. Momigliano, "*Thybris pater*," in *Terzo contributo alla storia degli studi classici e del mondo antico*, 2 vols. (Rome, 1966), II, pp. 609 ff., and esp. 613–614 (later in *Roma arcaica*, pp. 347 ff.).

18. Plautus, *Cistellaria* 1.1.20; Cicero, *Ad Atticum* 1.16.6 (and see also Livy 7.31.3).

19. In *D.* 1.1.10.2 (*Reg.* 1). See also Chapter 21.

20. Polybius 34.2.7 = Strabo 1.2.15, C24.

21. The "revolution" of the pontifices is hypothesized by K. Latte, *Römische Religionsgeschichte* (Munich, 1960), pp. 195 ff.; there are well-grounded criticisms by Dumézil, *La religion romaine archaïque (Archaic Roman Religion*, I, pp. 102 ff.).

22. *Storia di Roma*, I, pp. 53 ff. (M. Torelli) and 75 ff. (M. Menichetti).

23. Livy 10.8.9. translation from *Livy*, trans. B. O. Foster, Loeb Classical Library (1926; reprint, Cambridge, Mass., 1963). But this text proves nothing about the absence of *gentes* in the plebeian organization of kinship ties. In reality, Livy constructs the discourse of P. Decius Mus by attributing to him in this section a heavy dose of sarcasm: he does not set forth facts but rather, as it were, their patrician deforma-

tion: "semper ista audita sunt"—"from you we have heard always the same song" —"eadem penes vos auspìcia esse, vos solos gentes habere, vos solos iustum imperium et auspicium domi militiaeque: aeque adhuc prosperum imperium et auspicium fuitporroque erit." We must agree with Momigliano, "Le origini di Roma," p. 37 (other passages that are frequently cited in this connection—Gell., *Noct. Att.* 17.21.27; Ateius Capito, in Gell., *Noct. Att.* 10.20.5 = Strzelecki, *C. Atei Capitonis Fragmenta,* fr. 25; Livy 3.27.1 and 3.39.3—are equally inconclusive).

24. Momigliano, "Le origini di Roma," p. 35; also Cornell, *The Beginnings of Rome,* pp. 119 ff., 146–147. A long anthropological tradition has focused on this eventuality, from J. J. Bachofen, *Die Sage von Tanaquilla* (Heidelberg, 1870); to M. Harris, *Cannibals and Kings: The Origins of Cultures* (New York, 1977), pp. 119 ff. Even the name of the *curiae* was derived from feminine figures, the Sabine women ravished by the audacity of Romulus: Cicero, *De republica* 2.8.14; Livy 1.13.6; Festus, p. 42 (Lindsay).

25. On the hoplitic "reform" in the Mediterranean context we should also consider A. M. Snodgrass, "The Hoplite Reform and History," *Journal of Hellenic Studies,* 85 (1965): 110 ff., esp. 119 ff. (not always plausible); P. Cartledge, "Hoplites and Heroes: Sparta's Contribution to the Technique of Ancient Warfare," ibid., 97 (1977): 11 ff.; and J. Salmon, "Political Hoplites?," ibid., pp. 84 ff., esp. 93 ff., with reasonable observations. Also Cornell, *The Beginnings of Rome,* pp. 183 ff.

26. de Martino, *Storia della costituzione romana,* I, pp. 161 ff. (also in *Storia di Roma,* I, pp. 350 ff.).

27. The now-classic expression is by G. Pasquali, now in *Pagine stravaganti,* II (Florence, 1968), pp. 5 ff.: but the emphasis should not be exaggerated; I would rather subscribe to the balanced position of M. Musti in *Storia di Roma,* I, pp. 367 ff.

28. Cicero, *Pro Sestio* 58.123 (= Accius, *Brutus,* in *TF,* p. 367, 40 [Klotz]); Dion. Hal. 4.36; Tacitus, *Annales* 3.26.7.

29. Momigliano, "Interim Report," p. 119; C. Ampolo, "La città riformata e l'organizzazione centuriata," in *Storia di Roma,* I, pp. 218 ff.; Cornell, *The Beginnings of Rome,* pp. 179 ff.

6. Rituals and Prescriptions

1. The earliest Roman historians—Quintus Fabius Pictor and Cincius Alimentus— worked in the third century B.C. and wrote in Greek. It was not until the next century, with the *Origines,* composed at a late age by M. Porcius Cato, that a Latin-language historiography began to develop (see S. Mazzarino, *Il pensiero storico classico,* 2 vols. [Bari, 1966], II.1, pp. 59 ff.) which would go on to nourish late-republican culture. There existed in that period a precise relationship between the annalistic tradition and *ius pontificium,* involving such personalities as Cassius

Hemina and the annalist Fabius Pictor (not to be confused with his similarly named predecessor): Nonius Marcellus, p. 835, ll. 34–37 (Lindsay), fr. 3 Peter. Alongside the strictly historical thought there was also developing the aristocratic memory of the republic—I take the distinction, which we are not accustomed to making with respect to the history of Rome, from J. Assmann, *Das kulturelle Gedächtnis. Schrift, Erinnerung und politische Identität in frühen Hochkulturen* (Munich, 1992]: the work of Cicero, like that of all the "constructors" of the republican tradition (and "constructors" does not mean "falsifiers," as is incorrectly affirmed by A. Alföldi, *Early Rome and the Latins* [Ann Arbor, 1965], rightly criticized by Momigliano), is a remarkable mirror in which both these lines are reflected.

2. Festus, p. 346 (Lindsay).

3. G. Wissowa, *Religion und Kultus der Römer*, 2d. ed [München, 1992], pp. 503ff. (a classic in the tradition of Mommsen, which should not be forgotten); de Martino, *Storia della costituzione romana*, pp. 134 ff.; J. Bleicken, "Oberpontifex und Pontifikalkollegium," *Hermes* 85 (1957), pp. 345 ff.; Bayet, *Histoire politique et psychologique de la religion romaine.* See Livy 1.19.7, 1.20.5 and 7; Dionysius of Halicarnassus 2.25.2 and 73.2; Servius Grammaticus, *Ad Aen.* 1.31; Gaius, *Institutiones* 1.112; Aulus Gellius, *Noctes Atticae* 15.27.1 (and also 5.19.5 and 7.12.1). For more on the Roman calendar, see A. Kirsopp Michels, *The Calendar of the Roman Republic* (Princeton, 1967).

4. These are precisely the "divine presuppositions" ("göttliche Voraussetzungen") that Marx mentions in the *Formen die der kapitalistischen Produktion vorhergehen,* which allow a community to appropriate the objective conditions of life through the construction of family ties and the exploitation of the earth—the "great laboratory" ("das grosse Laboratorium") of that world: *Grundrisse der Kritik der politischen Ökonomie*, 3d ed. (Berlin, 1974), p. 376. It is, so to speak, the "function" of ideology in an archaic context, though in a different—yet not irreconcilable— sense with respect to what Dumézil proposed (see Chapter 4, note 15, and Chapter 5, note 14). There are also important observations in Girard, *La violence et le sacré* (*Violence and the Sacred,* pp. 89 ff.). See also L. Scubla, "Roi sacré, victim sacrificielle et victim émissaire," in *Qu'est-ce que le religieux? Religion et politique, Revue du MAUSS (Mouvement anti-utilitariste dans les sciences sociales)* 22 (2003), pp. 197 ff.

5. Hirzel, *Themis, Dike und Vervandtes*, pp. 7 ff.; Gernet, *Anthropologie de la Grèce antique*, p. 200.

6. W. J. Ong, *Orality and Literacy: The Technologizing of the Word* (London, 1982), pp. 16 ff. E. A. Havelock, *Preface to Plato* (Cambridge, Mass., 1963) can now be considered obligatory reading, esp. pp. 36, 87, 115. See also Havelock, *The Greek Concept of Justice from Its Shadow in Homer to Its Substance in Plato* (Cambridge, Mass., 1978), pp. 4 ff., 38 ff., 218 ff.; Havelock, "L'alfabetizzazione di Omero," in *Arte e comunicazione nel mondo antico,* ed. E. A. Havelock and J. P. Hershbell (Rome, 1981), pp. 3 ff.; W. V. Harris, *Ancient Literacy* (Cambridge, Mass., 1989), pp. 149 ff.; F. L. Müller,

Kritische Gedanken zur antiken Mnemotechnik und zum "Auctor ad Herennium" (Stuttgart, 1996), pp. 9 ff. A book that remains of great importance is F. A. Yates, *The Art of Memory* (London, 1966), pp. 1 ff., 6 ff. The reference to Plato involves, for instance, *Phaedrus* 275a and the contents of the *Seventh Letter,* esp. 343a–344d. See also G. Reale, *Platone: Alla ricerca della sapienza segreta* (Milan, 1998), esp. pp. 57 ff. and 75 ff., with criticisms of Havelock to which I frequently subscribe.

7. Still within Ciceronian memory, the pontifices were those "veteres illi, qui huic scientiae praefuerunt, optinendae atque augendae potentiae suae causa pervolgari artem suam noluerunt": *De oratore* 1.41.186. Those were the times when "erant in magna potentia qui consulebantur": *Pro Murena* 11.25. H. Drexler, "Potentia," *Reinisches Museum* 102 (1959), pp. 50 ff. Also important is S. Mazzarino, *Dalla monarchia allo stato repubblicano* (Catania, 1945), pp. 48 ff.

8. Pomponius, *Enchiridion,* in D. 1.2.2.6; Dion. Hal. 2.27.3. Schulz fails to understand this when he speaks of "clumsy and artificial rituals"; *History of Roman Legal Science* (1946; reprint, Oxford, 1953), p. 27.

9. This is a point to which we shall return in later chapters; for now, Cic., *Pro Mur.* 11.25–14.30; *De orat.* 1.43.191; 2.33.142; *De legibus* 2.47.

10. Still significant is A. Leroi-Gourhan, *Le geste et la parole,* II: *La mémoire et les rhythmes* (Paris, 1965); and also J. Assmann, "Inscriptional Violence and the Art of Cursing: A Study of Performative Writing," *Stanford Literature Review,* 9 (1992): 43 ff. See also Chapter 7, sec. 4 and note 50.

11. Cic., *De orat.* 1.28.128.

12. See Chaper 10.

13. See V. di Benedetto, *Il medico e la malattia: La scienza di Ippocrate* (Turin, 1986), esp. pp. 88 ff.; C. A. Viano, "Perché non c'era sangue nelle arterie: La cecità epistemologica degli anatomisti antichi," in *La scienza ellenistica,* ed. G. Giannantoni and M. Vegetti (Naples, 1984), pp. 297 ff.; C. A. Viano, *La selva delle somiglianze: Il filosofo e il medico* (Turin, 1985), pp. 169 ff.; M. Vegetti, "La scienza ellenistica: Problemi di epistemologia storica," in Giannantoni and Vegetti, *La scienza ellenistica,* pp. 427 ff. See also G. E. R. Lloyd, *Magic, Reason and Experience: Studies in the Origin and Development of Greek Science* (Cambridge, 1979), p. 126 ff.; and Lloyd, *Science, Folklore and Ideology: Studies in the Life Sciences in Ancient Greece* (Cambridge, 1983), p. 58 ff.; A. Momigliano, "La storia tra medicina e retorica," in *Tra storia e storicismo* (Pisa, 1985), pp. 11 ff. (= "History between Medicine and Rhetoric," in *Ottavo contributo alla storia degli studi classici e del mondo antico* [Rome, 1987], pp. 13 ff.); M. M. Sassi, *La scienza dell'uomo nella Grecia antica* (Turin, 1988), pp. 128 ff.; P. Butti de Lima, *L'inchiesta e la prova* (Turin, 1996), esp. pp. 85 ff.

14. W. Mommsen, *Römisches Staatsrecht,* II.1, 3d ed. (Leipzig, 1887), p. 44 ff.; Schulz, *History of Roman Legal Science,* pp. 16–17; Bretone, *Storia del diritto romano,* pp. 111–112.

15. See Chapter 8, sec. 3, and note 46. See Aristotle, *Metaphysica* 1.3.983a; 6.1.1025b; *Ethica Nicomachea* 6.5.1140a–b: M. Riedel, *Metaphysik und Metapolitik. Studien zu Aristoteles und zur politischen Sprache der neuzeitlichen Philosophie* (Frankfurt am Main, 1975).

16. I accept the interpretation of A. Momigliano, "Interim Report" (1962), *JRS* 53 (1963): p. 121.

17. *Storia di Roma,* I, pp. 263 ff. (L. Capogrossi Colognesi).

18. Q. Fabius Maximus Servilianus: Macrobius, *Saturnalia* 1.16.26 = fr. 4P; Bremer, I, p. 28, with doubts that I would recommend rejecting. Servius Sulpicius Rufus: discernable in Cicero, *Brutus* 42.156 (but see also *De orat.* 3.33.136). Servius later wrote at least two books *De sacris detestandis:* Gell., *Noct. Att.* 7.12.1; *Pal.,* II, col. 324; Bremer, I, pp. 224–225. Trebatius: nine or eleven books *De religionibus:* Bremer, I, pp. 404 ff.; *Pal.,* II, col. 343. Varro worked on the *ius pontificium,* particularly in the sixteen books of *Antiquitates rerum divinarum* (Cardauns): Bremer, I, pp. 123–124.

7. The Model of Statutory Law

1. The oligarchic stabilization was linked to the formation of the *nobilitas:* a process complete as early as the mid-fourth century. Still fundamental are the studies by M. Gelzer, *Die Nobilität der römischen Republik* (1912), later in *Kleine Schriften,* I (1962; reprint, Stuttgart, 1983), pp. 17 ff.; and A. Afzelius, "Zur Definition der römischen Nobilität in der Zeit Ciceros," *Classica et mediaevalia: Revue danoise de philologie et d'histoire,* 1 (1938): 40 ff.; and Afzelius, "Zur Definition der römischen Nobilität vor der Zeit Ciceros," ibid., 7 (1945): 150 ff.; also F. Cassola, in *Storia di Roma,* I, pp. 470 ff.

2. G. de Sanctis, *Storia dei Romani,* 4 vols. (1907–1964; reprint, Florence, 1964–65), I, pp. 228 ff.; also keep in mind H. Last, "The Servian Reforms," *JRS,* 35 (1945): 30 ff. (still important); and A. Momigliano, "Le origini di Roma," now in *Roma arcaica* (Florence, 1989), pp. 150 ff. See also Chapter 13, sec. 4.

3. The expression—very effective—used by Polybius is ἐ ἀντίπλοια: literally, "navigating against the stream" (6.10.7); through it he constructs the model of a constitution "according to nature"—of which the Roman one represented, in his view, the finest historical example—based on dynamics of contrasting powers, capable of compensating for excesses and disaggregating thrusts. This is the core of a paradigm that has been subjected to countless modern interpretations: E. Garin, *Machiavelli fra politica e storia* (Turin, 1993), pp. 3 ff. (where, however, not all his points are convincing: see *Storia spezzata,* pp. 215 and 260 [*The End of the Past,* pp. 209 and 266]. Still important is C. Nicolet, "Polybe et les institutions romaines," *Polybe, Entretiens Fondation Hardt,* 20 (1973): 255 ff.

4. See, for instance, Sallust, *Catilinae coniuratio* 28.4; and A. La Penna, *Sallustio e la*

rivoluzione romana (Milan, 1968), pp. 68 ff.; also P. A. Brunt, *"Nobilitas* and *Novitas,"* *JRS,* 72 (1982): 1 ff.

5. Pomponius' brief account is in the *Enchiridion,* in *D.* 1.2.2.4: see also Chapter 19, sec. 4. On what I call the "republican canon," an important work is T. J. Cornell, "The Formation of the Historical Tradition of Early Rome," in *Past Perspectives: Studies in Greek and Roman Historical Writing,* ed. I. Moxon, J. D. Smart, and A. J. Woodman (Cambridge, 1986), pp. 67 ff.

6. F. Wieacker, *Vom römischen Recht,* 2d ed. (Stuttgart, 1961), pp. 46 ff.; Wieacker, "Zwölftafelprobleme," *Revue internationale des droits de l'antiquité,* 3d ser., 3 (1956): 459 ff.; Wieacker, "Die XII. Tafeln in ihrem Jahrhundert," *Études d'archéologie classique,* 13 (1967): 291 ff.; Wieacker, "Solon und die XII. Tafeln," in *Studi Volterra,* III (Milan, 1971), pp. 757 ff.; Wieacker, *Römische Rechtsgeschichte* (Munich, 1988), pp. 287 ff.; A. Magdelain, *La loi à Rome: Histoire d'un concept* (Paris, 1978), esp. pp. 55 ff.; Magdelain, "Les XII tables et le concept de *ius,"* in *Zum römischen und neuzeitlichen Gesetzebegriff,* ed. O. Behrends and C. Link (Göttingen, 1987), pp. 13 ff.

7. I will limit myself to several references, although they are not convergent: P. Frezza, "Lex e *nomos,"* *BIDR,* 71 (1968): 1 ff., now in *Scritti,* 3 vols. (Rome, 2000), II, pp. 615 ff.; M. Ostwald, *Nomos and the Beginnings of the Athenian Democracy* (Oxford, 1969), esp. pp. 37 ff.; and Ostwald, *From Popular Sovereignty to the Sovereignty of Law: Law, Society, and Politics in Fifth-Century Athens* (Berkeley, 1986); J. Triantaphillopoulos, *Das Rechtsdenken der Griechen* (Munich, 1985), pp. 10 ff.; J. de Romilly, *La loi dans la pensée grecque* (1971), 2d ed. (Paris, 2001), esp. pp. 9 ff.; P. Cartledge, P. Millet, and S. Todd, eds., *Nomos: Essays in Athenian Law, Politics and Society* (Cambridge, 1990); O. Behrends and W. Selleret, eds., *Nomos und Gesetz. Ursprünge und Wirkungen des griechischen Gesetzesdenkens* (Göttingen, 1995); E. Stolfi, *"'Lex est . . . virorum prudentium consultum':* Osservazioni su (*Pap.* 1 def.) *D.* 1.3.1," *SDHI,* 70 (2004): 442 ff., esp. 457 ff.

8. The complete list of the texts is in Ostwald, *Nomos and Beginnings,* pp. 43 ff.; and in de Romilly, *La loi dans la pensée grecque,* pp. 15 ff. The doubt concerning Homer is dependent on how one reads the *Odyssey* 1.3: whether it is νόον or νόμον.

9. By Solon see esp. *Solonos Nomoi,* fr. 24 (Ruschenbusch); for Homer: *Odyssey* 9.215.

10. Herodotus 3.80.6. S. Mazzarino, *Fra Oriente e Occidente* (1947; reprint, Milan, 1989), pp. 296–297, sees in the "isonomic thrust" "the birth of the West" (p. 296).

11. Ostwald, *Nomos and Beginnings,* pp. 135 ff.; de Romilly, *La loi dans la pensée grecque,* pp. 17 ff.

12. Demosthenes 21.142–146: de Romilly, *La loi dans la pensée grecque,* pp. 146 ff.

13. Euripides, *Supp.* 429 ff.

14. The concept of "excarnation" that I use in the text is taken from J. Assmann, "Exkarnation. Zur Grenze zwischen Körper und Schrift," in *Raum und Verfahren,* ed. J. Huber and M. Müller (Zurich, 1993), pp. 133 ff., later reused by Assmann in

Herrschaft und Heil. Politische Theologie in Altägypten, Israel und Europa (Munich, 2000).

15. Livy 2.33.1; 2.33.3; 3.55.10; Dionysius of Halicarnassus 6.89.4; 11.55.3; Festus, p. 422 (Lindsay): de Martino, *Storia della costituzione romana,* I, pp. 340 ff., with bibliography.

16. This was in the second quarter of the sixth century: F. Coarelli, *Il foro romano,* I (Rome, 1983), pp. 178 ff. (and, in an earlier mention, "Il Comizio dalle origini alla fine della repubblica: cronologia e topografia," *La parola del passato,* 174 [1977]: 229 ff.); also R. E. A. Palmer, *The King and the Comitium: A Study of Rome's Oldest Public Document* (Wiesbaden, 1969).

17. The earliest documented appearance is that of Cassius Hemina in Pliny the Elder, *Naturalis historia* 32.20 = fr. 13 Peter = *FIRA,* I, p. 10. E. Gabba, "Studi su Dionigi di Alicarnasso, I: La costituzione di Romolo," *Athenaeum,* 48 (1960): 193 ff., esp. 200 ff.; and Gabba, "Considerazioni sulla tradizione letteraria sulle origini della Repubblica," *Études d'archéologie classique,* 13 (1967): 161 ff. (both now in *Roma arcaica: Storia e storiografia* [Rome, 2000], pp. 69 ff., 25 ff.).

18. Pomp., *Ench.,* in *D.* 1.2.2.2; Dion. Hal. 3.36.4; see also Festus, p. 260 (Lindsay).

19. There is a compendium of the documentation in *FIRA,* I, pp. 4 ff.

20. For Cassius Hemina see above, note 17; for Licinius Macer: Macrobius, *Saturnalia* 1.13.20 (and see also Cicero, *Pro C. Rabirio perduellionis reo* 4.15). For Granius Flaccus and Massurius Sabinus, a decisive document is Paul, *Ad l. Iul. et Pap.* 10, in *D.* 50.16.144.

21. For the edition of the *Annals,* see Chapter 10, sec. 3.

22. See also Chapter 19, sec. 3.

23. Cicero, *De officiis* 2.12.42, translation from *De Officiis,* trans. W. Miller, Loeb Classical Library (1913; reprint, Cambridge, Mass., 1968).

24. Pomp., *Ench.,* in *D.* 1.2.2.4.

25. Magdelain, *La loi à Rome,* p. 87.

26. Livy 3.31.8; 3.32.1; 3.33.5. Dion. Hal. 10.51.5; 10.52.4; 10.54.3; 10.55.5; 10.56.2; 10.57.5. Florus, *Epitoma* 1.24.1; Pliny the Younger, *Epistulae* 8.24.4. Ammianus Marcellinus, *Res gestae* 16.5.1 and 22.16.22. Symmachus, *Epistulae* 3.11.3. Augustine, *De civitate Dei* 2.16. Isidore of Seville, *Etymologiae* 5.1.3. Pomp., *Ench.,* in *D.* 1.2.2.4; Strabo 14.1.25, C642; Pliny, *Nat. hist.* 34.5.21: Wieacker, "Solon und die XII. Tafeln," pp. 757 ff.; M. Ducos, *L'influence grecque sur la loi des douze tables* (Paris, 1978), pp. 13 ff.; d'Ippolito, in *Storia di Roma,* I, pp. 398 ff.

27. A prejudice that runs throughout classical political thought, from Plato to Polybius, and clearly reflected in the theory of the forms of government and of their transformations: Herod. 3.80–82; Plato, *Politicus* 31.291d–e; Aristotle, *Politica* 3.7.1279a–b; Polybius 6.3–4 (but also 6.9 and 6.57): L. Canfora, "La tipologia costituzionale," *Quaderni di storia,* 37 (1993): 19 ff.; D. Hahm, "Kings and Constitutions:

Hellenistic Theories," in *The Cambridge History of Greek and Roman Political Thought*, ed. C. Rowe and M. Schofield (Cambridge, 2000), pp. 464 ff.

28. Quite clear, on the other hand, in the reconstruction of F. d'Ippolito, in *Storia di Roma*, I, pp. 405 ff., 409 ff.; and see also d'Ippolito, *Questioni decemvirali* (Naples, 1993), esp. pp. 57 ff., where there is a bibliography.

29. We may safely consider P. Jörs, *Römische Rechtswissenschaft zur Zeit der Republik*, I: *Bis auf die Catonen* (Berlin, 1888), pp. 66 ff., to have canonized this interpretation, which extends, in a quite implausibly extreme form, all the way up to W. Eder, "The Political Significance of the Codification of Law in Archaïc Societies: An Unconventional Hypothesis," in *Social Struggles in Archaic Rome*, ed. K. A. Raaflaub (Berkeley, 1986), pp. 262 ff.

30. Livy 2.44.9, translation from *Livy*, trans. B. O. Foster, Loeb Classical Library (1919; reprint, Cambridge, Mass., 1967).

31. Livy 3.32–33; Dion. Hal. 10.54–56: de Martino, *Storia della costituzione romana*, I, pp. 298 ff.

32. With the Canuleius plebiscite (though there is some doubt about the use of the term, and perhaps rightly so), dated traditionally around 445 B.C. (though the date is controversial as well): Livy 4.1–6: de Martino, *Storia della costituzione romana*, I, pp. 379–380.

33. With the Lex Poetelia Papiria, in 326: Livy 8.28.1–2; Valerius Maximus 6.1.9; Dion. Hal. 16.5.2–3.

34. de Martino, *Storia della costituzione romana*, I, pp. 300 ff.; Cornell, *The Beginnings of Rome*, pp. 274 ff.

35. The original was on wood or bronze. Livy 3.57.10, Dion. Hal. 10.57.7, and Diodorus Siculus 12.26.1 opt for bronze; Pomponius, *Enchiridion*, in *D.* 1.2.2.4, seems to point to wood (if we accept an emendation that is generally considered sound). One phase of the Aelian work on the ancient text is found in Cicero, *De legibus* 2.23.59: F. d'Ippolito, *I giuristi e la città: Ricerche sulla giurisprudenza romana della repubblica* (Naples, 1978), pp. 69–70; R. A. Bauman, *Lawyers in Roman Republican Politics: A Study of the Roman Jurists in Their Political Setting, 316–382 B.C.* (Munich, 1983), pp. 139 ff. For more on Sextus Aelius, see Chapter 8, sec. 3. His interpretative doubts would extend all the way up to Servius; see Chapter 14, notes 56 and 57.

36. Labeo: *Pal.*, I, col. 501; Bremer, II.1, pp. 81 ff.; Gaius: *Pal.*, I, cols. 242–246. The decemviral text was also closely read in the mid-second century by Sextus Cecilius Africanus and by Favorinus, as recounted by Gellius, *Noctes Atticae* 20.1, and it was still being cited as late as the fifth century: *ILS*, 8987: d'Ippolito, in *Storia di Roma*, I, p. 397. Also Cyprian, *Ad Donatum* 10 (= J. P. Migne, *Patrologia Latina* [Paris, 1844–1864], VI, p. 217); and Salvianus, *De gubernatione Dei* 8.5 (= *Patrologia Latina*, VIII, p. 158).

37. Cic., *De leg.* 2.23.59.

38. Ibid.: "Discebamus enim pueri XII ut carmen necessarium."

39. E. Norden, *Aus altrömischen Priesterbüchern* (Lund, 1939), pp. 254 ff.; D. Daube, *Forms of Roman Legislation* (Oxford, 1956), pp. 28–29, 57 ff., 105 ff. (an important book); M. Lauria, *Ius Romanum*, I.1 (Naples, 1963), pp. 21 ff. (rich in doctrine and ideas).

40. Livy 3.34.6: "fons omnis publici privatique est iuris"; translation from *Livy*, trans. B. O. Foster, Loeb Classical Library (1922, reprint, Cambridge, Mass., 1960); and see also 3.58.2 on Appius Claudius (the most important of the decemvirs).

41. Also in Livy 3.34.6: "in hoc immenso aliarum super alias acervatarum legum cumulo."

42. Cic., *De leg.* 3.4.11: "Cases in which the penalty is death or loss of citizenship shall be tried only before the greatest assembly": FIRA, I, p. 64 (tab. IX.1–2) = *Roman Statutes*, pp. 582, 696 ff.; E. Gabba, *"Maximus comitiatus,"* *Athenaeum*, 65 (1987): 203 ff., now in *Roma arcaica: Storia e storiografia*, pp. 245 ff.

43. Livy 3.34.3: "Se, quantum decem hominum ingeniis providendi potuerit, omnibus, summis infimisque, iura aequasse"; translation from *Livy*, trans. B. O. Foster, Loeb Classical Library (Cambridge, Mass., 1922, reprinted 1960); perhaps this judgment is also at the base of Tacitus, *Annales* 3.27.1: "finis aequi iuris."

44. Dion. Hal. 2.27.3; Pomp., *Ench.*, in D. 1.2.2.24: "ius quod ipse ex vetere iure in XII tabulas transtulerat," with reference to the work of Appius Claudius (see note 40).

45. See above, note 36.

46. Dion. Hal. 2.26.

47. FIRA, I, p. 35 (tab. IV.2) = *Roman Statutes*, pp. 580, 631–632. Also Gaius, *Institutiones* 4.79; and Papinian, *Collatio Legum Mosaicarum et Romanarum* 4.8.

48. "Si intestato moritur, cui suus heres nec hescit, adgnatus proximus familiam habeto. Si adgnatus nec escit, gentiles familiam [habento]": FIRA, I, p. 38 (tab. V.4–5) = *Roman Statutes*, pp. 580, 640 ff.

49. "Cum nexum faciet mancipiumque, uti lingua nuncupassit, ita ius esto": FIRA, I, p. 43 (tab. VI.1) = *Roman Statutes*, pp. 580, 652 ff.; Festus, p. 176, ll. 3–15 (Lindsay).

50. The formulaic words of the *sponsio* must originally have been accompanied by the ritual of libation: Benveniste, *Le vocabulaire*, II, pp. 209–210, 214–215 (*Indo-European Language and Society*, pp. 470–471); Gernet, *Anthropologie*. The notion of the "performative," by now fairly widespread among historians, draws on J. L. Austin, *How to Do Things with Words* (1962; reprint, Oxford, 1986), pp. 1 ff., 53 ff.

51. "Si aqua pluvia nocet": FIRA, I, p. 50 (tab. VII.8) = *Roman Statutes*, pp. 580, 673 ff.

52. FIRA, I, pp. 66–69 (tab. X.2–8) = *Roman Statutes*, pp. 582, 705 ff.

53. For example, *Antigone* 191 ff., 245 ff., 450 ff.

54. "Adsiduo vindex adsiduus esto; proletario civi quis volet vindex esto": FIRA, I, p. 27 (tab. I.4) = *Roman Statutes*, pp. 578, 588 ff.: see Gell., *Noct. Att.* 16.10.5: A. Pagliaro,

"Testo ed esegesi delle XII Tavole (I.4)," in *La critica del testo: Atti del secondo congresso internazionale della Società italiana di storia del diritto*, I (Florence, 1981), pp. 567 ff. The connection between *proletarius* and *proles* is later and "ideological": Cicero, *De republica* 2.22.40; Gell., *Noct. Att.* 16.10.12–13.

55. "Tertiis nundinis partis secanto. Si plus minusve secuerit, se fraude esto": *FIRA*, I, p. 33 (tab. III.6) = *Roman Statutes*, pp. 580, 625 ff.

56. "Si iniuriam [alteri] faxsit, viginti quinque poenae sunto": *FIRA*, I, p. 54 (tab. VIII.4) = *Roman Statutes*, pp. 582, 682 ff.; see Gell., *Noct. Att.* 20.1.12. Benveniste, *Le vocabulaire*, II, pp. 50, 252 (*Indo-European Language and Society*, pp. 340, 504–505).

57. "Si membrum rup[s]it, ni cum eo pacit, talio esto": *FIRA*, I, p. 53 (tab. VIII.2) = *Roman Statutes*, pp. 580, 680 ff.; see Gell., *Noct. Att.* 20.1.14.

58. This is the earliest emergence of the significance within the sphere of *ius* of an agreement between the parties, established without adherence to any particular rituals, a model that returns, with the same vocabulary, elsewhere in the Twelve Tables (*FIRA*, I, p. 28 [tab. I.6–7] = *Roman Statutes*, pp. 578, 592 ff.), as we shall see, with a considerable future ahead of it. See Chapter 17, sec. 3 and Chapter 20, sec. 2.

59. *FIRA*, I, p. 64 (tab. IX.4) = *Roman Statutes*, pp. 582, 696 ff., which mentions the "quaestores parricidii": see Pomp., *Ench.*, in *D.* 1.2.2.23; and Festus, p. 247, ll. 23–24 (Lindsay). The expression "par[r]icidas esto," reported by Festus, and attributed by him to a law by Numa, is very difficult to interpret: Y. Thomas, "*Parricidum*. 1: Le père, la famille et la cité," *Mélanges de l'Ecole Française de Rome: Antiquité*, 93 (1981): 659 ff.; G. MacCormack, "A Note on a Recent Interpretation of *Paricidas esto*," *Labeo*, 28 (1982): 43 ff.; A. Magdelain, "*Paricidas*," in *Du châtiment*, pp. 549 ff., later in Magdelain, *Jus Imperium Auctoritas: Études de droit romain* (Paris, 1990), pp. 519 ff.

60. Another term that is difficult to define—Livy 2.41; 6.20.12; 26.3—and which we are in fact unable to track down in the Twelve Tables: see Marc., *Institutiones 14*, in *D.* 48.4.3 = *FIRA*, I, p. 65 (tab. IX.5) = *Roman Statutes*, p. 703; A. Magdelain, "Remarques sur la '*perduellio*,'" *Historia*, 22 (1973): 405 ff., now in *Jus Imperium Auctoritas*, pp. 499 ff.

61. *FIRA*, I, p. 62 (tab. VIII.23): Gell., *Noct. Att.* 20.1.53.

62. *FIRA*, I, p. 31 (tab. II.3) = *Roman Statutes*, pp. 578, 621; see Festus, p. 262, l. 514 (Lindsay); and Gell., *Noct. Att.* 15.13.11.

63. *FIRA*, I, p. 56 (tab. VIII.10) = *Roman Statutes*, pp. 582, 689 ff.; see Gaius, *Ad l. XII tab. 4*, in *D.* 47.9.9.

64. "Qui fruges excantassit": *FIRA*, I, p. 55 (tab. VIII.8a) = *Roman Statutes*, pp. 582, 682 ff.; see Pliny, *Nat. hist.* 28.4.17–18.

65. *FIRA*, I, p. 56 (tab. VIII.9) = *Roman Statutes*, pp. 582, 684 ff.; see Pliny, *Nat. hist.* 18.3.12.

66. *FIRA*, I, p. 52 (tab. VIII.1) = *Roman Statutes*, pp. 580, 677 ff.; also from Pliny, *Nat. hist.* 28.4.18.

67. "Si nox furtum faxsit, si im occisit, iure caesus esto": *FIRA*, I, p. 57 (tab. VIII.12): see Macrob., *Sat.* 1.4.19.

68. *FIRA*, I, p. 59 (tab. VIII.14) = *Roman Statutes*, p. 582; see Gell., *Noct. Att.* 11.18.8; and also Gaius, *Inst.* 3.189. The text by Ulpian—"Nam et de furto pacisci lex permittit"—is from *Ad edictum* 4, now in *D.* 2.14.7.15, and centers upon a quotation from Labeo in *D.* 2.14.7.14.

69. That is, constructed around the mechanism—in fact, exquisitely political and traceable strictly to the republican order (despite Cic., *De rep.* 2.31.54)—of the *provocatio*, which paralyzed the magistrate's *coercitio*, performed in the name of the *mores*, replacing it with the comitial process: Pomp., *Ench.*, in *D.* 1.2.2.16.

70. This is the explanation offered by Gaius, *Inst.* 4.11, but it is not the only explanation possible.

71. Gaius, *Inst.* 4.26–29, relates the "legis actio per pignoris capionem" to the *mores* and not to the *lex*.

72. Gaius, *Inst.* 4.10–30.

73. Lex Silia, at the end of the third century: *Leges publicae*, p. 261; *Roman Statutes*, pp. 737 ff.

74. Gaius, *Inst.* 4.13–17.

75. "Per iudicis arbitrive postulationem," "per manus iniectionem," "per pignoris capionem," all present in the Twelve Tables (Gaius, *Inst.* 4.17; 4.21–25; 4.26–29), while the one "per condictionem" (Gaius, *Inst.* 4.17–20) had been introduced by the Lex Silia.

76. Gaius, *Inst.* 4.11; see also 4.30.

77. A. Watson, *Rome of the XII Tables: Persons and Property* (Princeton, 1975); d'Ippolito, *Questioni decemvirali*, pp. 3 ff.; also *Storia spezzata*, pp. 77 ff. [*The End of the Past*, pp. 70 ff.].

78. Which was already in part that of Cicero: *De oratore* 1.43.193. See also Chapter 19, sec. 2.

8. The *Logos* of the Republic

1. F. de Martino, *Storia della costituzione romana*, 2d ed., 4 vols. (Naples, 1972–1974), I, pp. 305 ff.

2. "Privilegia ne inroganto": *FIRA*, I, p. 64 (tab. IX.1–2) = *Roman Statutes*, pp. 696 ff.: Cicero, *De legibus* 3.4.11.

3. From Ateius Capito, in Gellius, *Noctes Atticae* 10.20.2 = W. Strzelecki, *C. Atei Capitonis Fragmenta* (Leipzig, 1967), fr. 24: "Lex—inquit—est generale iussum populi aut plebis rogante magistratu." See also below, note 52.

4. Valerius Maximus 2.5.2.; translation from *Memorable Doings and Sayings,* vol. 1, trans. D. R. Shackleton Bailey, Loeb Classical Library (Cambridge, Mass., 2000).

5. Livy 9.46.

6. There is mention, for instance, of an identification between knowledge (not merely legal) and the pontificate, even in the heart of the republican era, in *De oratore* 3.33.133–134. See also below, note 27.

7. Pomponius, *Enchiridion,* in D. 1.2.2.5 and 1.2.2.35 ("in latenti ius civile retinere cogitabant"); and see also Livy 6.1.

8. Gaius, *Institutiones* 2.102–103.

9. Livy 1.20.7: "Cetera quoque omnia publica privataque sacra pontificis scitis subiecit, ut esset quo consultum plebes veniret."

10. Polybius 6.11–18 and 6.57; see also above, Chapter 7, note 3.

11. G. W. F. Hegel, *Grundlinien der Philosophie des Rechts* (1820–21), in *Vorlesungen über Rechtsphilosophie 1818–1831. Edition und Kommentar in sechs Bänden* (unfortunately only the first four exist), ed. K.-H. Ilting (Stuttgart, 1973–74), II, pp. 65–66; in English as *Elements of the Philosophy of Right,* trans. H. Barr Nisbet, ed. Allen W. Wood (Cambridge, 1991), pp. 16–17 [translation modified]. This attack against the Historical School—there can be no question that there is a reference to Savigny—should be compared with what we can now read in the version not published in 1818–19 (text edited by a student, C. G. Homeyer) in the Ilting edition, I, pp. 232–233: *Origini,* pp. 5 ff. n. 7 and 47 ff.

12. *Origini,* p. 51.

13. Ibid., p. 49 n. 20.

14. W. W. Buckland and A. D. McNair, *Roman Law and Common Law,* 2d ed., ed. F. H. Lawson (London, 1952); and P. Stein, *Legal Institutions: The Development of Dispute Settlement* (London, 1984) and *Römisches Recht und Europa* (Frankfurt am Main, 1996).

15. "Urbanam militiam respondendi": *Pro Murena* 9.19.

16. E. S. Staveley, "The Political Aims of Appius Claudius Caecus," *Historia,* 8 (1959): 410 ff.; E. Ferenczy, "The Career of Appius Claudius Caecus after the Censorship," *Acta Antiqua Acad. Scient. Hungaricae,* 18 (1970): 71 ff.

17. Modern historiography has questioned the reliability of the report, transmitted by Pomponius, of the existence of this text and of its title (*Ench.,* in D. 1.2.2.36): "Post hunc Appius Claudius eiusdem generis maximam scientiam habuit: hic Centemmanus appellatus est, Appiam viam stravit et aquam Claudiam induxit et de Pyrrho in urbe non recipiendo sententiam tulit: hunc etiam actiones scripsisse traditum est primum de usurpationibus, qui liber non extat: idem Appius Claudius qui videtur ab hoc processisse, R litteram invenit, ut pro Valesiis Valerii essent et pro Fusiis Furii." See F. Schulz, *History of Roman Legal Science* (1946; reprint, Oxford, 1953), pp. 9–10. Good observations, which should be considered conclusive,

can be found in: A. Guarino, "Appio Claudio 'De usurpationibus,'" *Labeo*, 27 (1981): 7 ff.; R. A. Bauman, *Lawyers in Roman Republican Politics: A Study of the Roman Jurists in Their Political Setting, 316–382 B.C.* (Munich, 1983), pp. 21 ff.; F. Wieacker, *Römische Rechtsgeschichte* (Munich, 1988), p. 534; and R. Santoro, "Appio Claudio e la concezione strumentalistica del *ius,*" *AUPA*, 47 (2002): 293 ff.

18. Guarino, "Appio Claudio 'De usurpationibus,'" pp. 10 ff.; R. Santoro, "Actio in diritto antico," in *Poteri, negotia, actiones nella esperienza romana arcaica* (Naples, 1984), p. 206; F. d'Ippolito, *Giuristi e sapienti in Roma arcaica* (Rome, 1986), pp. 37 ff. Also J. G. Wolf, "Die literarische Überlieferung der Publikation der Fasten und Legisaktionen durch Gnaeus Flavius," *Nachrichten der Akademie der Wissenschaften in Göttingen, Philologisch-historische Klasse,* 1980, pp. 9 ff. n. 2.

19. Pomp., *Ench.*, in *D.* 1.2.2.6–7; Cic., *Pro Mur.* 11.25; *De orat.* 1.41.186; *Ad Atticum* 6.1.8; also Livy 9.46.1–15.

20. d'Ippolito, *Giuristi e sapienti*, pp. 57 ff., completing Guarino, "Appio Claudio 'De usurpationibus,'" p. 11.

21. D. Musti, in *Storia di Roma*, I, pp. 368 ff.

22. The difficulty is nicely illustrated by F. Cassola, *I gruppi politici romani nel iii secolo a.C.* (Trieste, 1962), pp. 128 ff., esp. 132 ff.

23. Livy 9.46.

24. Now considered classic is the study by C. Nicolet, *L'ordre équestre à l'époque républicaine (312–43 av. J.-C.),* 2 vols. (Paris, 1974).

25. d'Ippolito, *Giuristi e sapienti*, pp. 71 ff.

26. *Leges publicae*, p. 236.

27. Cic., *Pro Mur.* 11.25: "Inventus est scriba quidam, Cn. Flavius, qui . . . singulis diebus ediscendis fastos populo proposuerit et ab ipsis [his] cautis iuris consultis eorum sapientiam compilarit. Itaque irati illi, quod sunt veriti ne dierum ratione pervolgata et cognita sine sua opera lege agi posset, verba quaedam composuerunt ut omnibus in rebus ipsi interessent"; translation, with modifications, from *Cicero: In Catilinam 1–4. Pro Murena. Pro Sulla. Pro Flacco: B. Orations,* trans. L. E. Lord, Loeb Classical Library (Cambridge, Mass., 1967).

28. Cic., *De orat.* 1.41.186 (see also Chapter 11, sec. 3); *De rep.,* in a lost passage from the second book, as we can deduce from *Ad Att.* 6.1.8. (see also 6.1.18).

29. Fabius Pictor, *Historia graeca*, fr. 20 (Peter) = *FgrHist*, 809, F27 = Strabo 5.3.1, p. 228C: *Storia spezzata*, p. 64 [*The End of the Past*, p. 58].

30. Definitively sanctioned by the Lex Hortensia, probably in 287: Pliny the Elder, *Naturalis historia* 16.10.37; Gellius, *Noct. Att.* 15.27.4; Gaius, *Inst.* 1.3 (see also Chapter 19, sec. 3); Pomp., *Ench.*, in *D.* 1.2.2.8.

31. *Storia spezzata*, pp. 81 ff. [*The End of the Past*, pp. 74 ff]; Cassola, *I gruppi politici romani*, pp. 209 ff.

32. Pomp., *Ench.*, in *D.* 1.2.2.35: "Et quidem ex omnibus, qui scientiam nancti sunt,

ante Tiberium Coruncanium publice professum neminem traditur: ceteri autem ad hunc vel in latenti ius civile retinere cogitabant solumque consultatoribus vacare potius quam discere volentibus praestabant"; and 1.2.2.38: "Post hos fuit Tiberius Coruncanius, ut dixi, qui primus profiteri coepit: cuius tamen scriptum nullum exstat, sed responsa complura et memorabilia eius fuerunt."

33. See also the preceding note for *D.* 1.2.2.38, where his responses are defined as "long remembered"; the text by Pliny is in *Nat. hist.* 8.51, 77. See d'Ippolito, *Giuristi e sapienti*, pp. 27 ff.; Sini, *A quibus iura civibus praescribebantur*, pp. 81 ff.

34. Cicero, *Cato maior de senectute* 9.27.

35. d'Ippolito, *Giuristi e sapienti*, pp. 77 ff.; Sini, *A quibus iura civibus praescribebantur*, pp. 71 ff.

36. "Nihil Sex. Aelius tale, nihil multis annis ante Ti. Coruncanius, nihil modo P. Crassus, a quibus iura civibus praescribebantur"; *Cato maior* 9.27.

37. As we learn from Cic., *De leg.* 2.21.52.

38. "Quorum usque ad extremum spiritum est provecta prudentia": also from *Cato maior* 9.27.

39. P. Jörs, *Römische Rechtswissenschaft zur Zeit der Republik*, I: *Bis auf die Catonen* (Berlin, 1888), pp. 99 ff.; F. Wieacker, "Die römischen Juristen in der politischen Gesellschaft des zweiten vorchristlichen Jahrhundert," in *Sein und Werden im Recht. Festgabe von Lübtow* (Berlin, 1970), pp. 192 ff.; Bauman, *Lawyers in Roman Republican Politics*, pp. 121 ff.; Wieacker, *Römische Rechtsgeschichte*, pp. 290–291, 536–537, 570–571.

40. Bremer, I, pp. 13 ff.; *Pal.*, I, cols. 1–2.

41. Pomp., *Ench.*, in *D.* 1.2.2.38: M. Bretone, *Tecniche e ideologie dei giuristi romani*, 2d ed. (Naples, 1982), pp. 5 ff., 72 ff.; and also Bretone, "Sesto Elio e le XII Tavole," in *Per la storia del pensiero giuridico romano: Dall'età dei pontefici alla scuola di Servio*, ed. D. Mantovani (Turin, 1996), pp. 18 ff.; F. d'Ippolito, *I giuristi e la città: Ricerche sulla giurisprudenza romana della repubblica* (Naples, 1978), pp. 51 ff.; and also d'Ippolito, *Forme giuridiche di Roma arcaica* (Naples, 1997), pp. 191 ff., 219 ff.

42. In *D.* 1.2.2.7: "Postea cum Appius Claudius proposuisset et ad formam redegisset has actiones, Gnaeus Flavius scriba eius libertini filius subreptum librum populo tradidit et adeo gratum fuit id munus populo, ut tribunus plebis fieret et senator et aedilis curulis. Hic liber, qui actiones continet, appellatur ius civile Flavianum, sicut ille ius civile Papirianum: nam nec Gnaeus Flavius de suo quicquam adiecit libro. Augescente civitate quia deerant quaedam genera agendi, non post multum temporis spatium Sextus Aelius alias actiones composuit et librum populo dedit, qui appellatur ius Aelianum."

43. A. Watson, "*Ius Aelianum* and *Tripertita*," *Labeo*, 19 (1973): 26 ff.

44. Bretone, *Tecniche e ideologie dei giuristi romani*, pp. 224–225.

45. "Erant in magna potentia qui consulebantur": *Pro Mur.* 11.25.

46. The two terms alternate continuously in the vocabulary of Cicero, overlapping

with each other. The definition of jurists as *prudentes* is very frequent: in *De inventione* 2.53.160 there is a proposed tripartition of *prudentia*, distinguishing between *memoria, intellegentia, providentia* (and see also *Rhetorica ad Herennium* 3.2.3); in *De off.* 1.43.153 there is established an equation of *sapientia* with σοφία, and *prudentia* with φρόνησις: but in *Laelius de amicitia* 2.6 it is said of Lucius Acilius that he was known as a wise man *(sapientem),* because "prudens esse in iure civili putabantur." The node is conceptual, and not a matter of terminology: what Cicero was attempting to depict was the intertwining between the theoretical vocation and the practical application of legal knowledge: an ambiguity, as we shall see, charged with future.

47. Pomp., *Ench.,* in *D.* 1.2.2.12.

48. For example, in Cic., *De orat.* 1.42.191 (though it was still a very common expression); and here the accent fell chiefly on the theoretical, cognitive aspect.

49. Cic., *De orat.* 1.48.212; see also below, note 56.

50. The *De republica,* begun in 54 (*Ad Att.* 4.14.1 and 16.2), was completed in 51 (*Ad Att.* 5.12.2; 6.1.8; 6.2.3). As early as 53 it had not been possible to elect the magistrates; in January of 52 Annius Milo, candidate for the consulship, murdered Publius Clodius, candidate for the praetorship, in a brawl that erupted on the Appian Way: the urban plebs celebrated Clodius' funeral amidst indescribable rioting, resulting in the burning of the Curia Ostilia and the Basilica Porcia; at the end of February the senate voted to appoint Pompey sole consul ("consul sine conlega"): Plutarch, *Pompeius* 54.3; Appian, *Bella civilia* 2.23.84; Dio Cassius 40.50.4.

51. Cic., *De rep.* 1.2.2: "Nihil enim dicitur a philosophis, quod quidem recte honesteque dicatur, quod [non] ab iis partum confirmatumque sit, a quibus civitatibus iura discripta sunt. Unde enim pietas, aut a quibus religio? unde ius aut gentium aut hoc ipsum civile quod dicitur? unde iustitia fides aequitas? unde pudor, continentia, fuga turpi[tu]dinis adpetentia laudis et honestatis? unde in laboribus et periculis fortitudo? nempe ab iis qui haec disciplinis informata alia moribus confirmarunt, sanxerunt autem alia legibus"; translation, with modifications, from *De Re Publica,* trans. C. W. Keyes, Loeb Classical Library (1928; reprint, Cambridge, Mass., 1970).

52. "Philosophi autem Romanorum ipsi erant iurisconsulti" writes Vico in chap. 11 of *De nostri temporis studiorum ratione,* in *Opere,* I (ed. Gentile and Nicolini) (Bari, 1914), p. 101. See also chap. 85 of *De uno universi iuris principio et fine uno,* in *Opere,* II.1 (ed. Nicolini) (Bari, 1936), pp. 209 ff.

53. Cicero, *De natura deorum* 1.41.116.

54. *De rep.* 1.25.39, translation, with modifications, from *De Re Publica,* trans. C. W. Keyes, Loeb Classical Library (1928; reprint, Cambridge, Mass., 1970).

55. Gell., *Noct. Att.* 10.20.2 = Strzelecki, *C. Atei Capitonis Fragmenta,* fr. 24.

56. Cic., *De orat.* 1.48.211–212: "Qui quibus rebus utilitas rei publicae pareretur [et] augeretur teneret iisque uteretur, hunc rei publicae rectorem et consilii publici auc-

torem esse habendum; praedicaremque P. Lentulum principem illum et Tiberium Gracchum patrem et Q. Metellum et P. Africanum et C. Laelium et innumerabiles alios cum ex nostra civitate tum ex ceteris. Sin autem quaereretur quisnam iuris consultus vere nominaretur, eum dicerem, qui legum et consuetudinis eius, qua privati in civitate uteretur, et ad respondendum et ad agendum et ad cavendum peritus esset et ex eo genere Sex. Aelium, M. Manilium, P. Mucium nominarem"; translation, with modifications, from *De Oratore*, trans. E. W. Sutton, Loeb Classical Library (1942; reprint, Cambridge, Mass., 1967). Note the importance of the connection, which we have emphasized on a number of occasions, between jurisprudence and "private" subjectivity.

9. *Ius civile* and the Praetors

1. M. Kaser, *"Ius publicum* und *ius privatum,"* ZSS, 103 (1986): 1 ff.; J. Bleicken, *Lex publica. Gesetz und Recht in der römischen Republik* (Berlin, 1975); F. Casavola, in *Storia di Roma,* II.1, pp. 515 ff. There is a fairly precise calculation in F. Schulz, *Prinzipien des römischen Rechts* (Munich, 1934).

2. See Chapter 8, sec. 2 and note 15. The expression used by Cicero of which I speak in the text is: "Urbanam militiam respondendi."

3. *Leges publicae,* pp. 230–231, and Chapter 7, sec. 3.

4. *Leges publicae,* pp. 241–242 = *Roman Statutes,* pp. 723 ff.

5. *Leges publicae,* pp. 261–263 = *Roman Statutes,* pp. 741 ff.

6. *Leges publicae,* pp. 282–288.

7. Ibid., pp. 275–276.

8. Ibid., pp. 377–378.

9. Ibid., p. 438 = *Roman Statutes,* pp. 779 ff.

10. *Leges publicae,* pp. 304–305.

11. "Nimia subtilitas": Gaius, *Institutiones* 4.30.

12. M. Bretone, *Storia del diritto romano* (Rome, 1987), pp. 140–141. See also the extensive research done by T. Corey Brennan, *The Praetorship in the Roman Republic,* 2 vols. (Oxford, 2000), esp. I, pp. 58 ff., 79 ff.

13. Gaius, *Inst.* 4.30: "Effectumque est, ut per concepta verba, id est per formulas litig[e]mus." A significant point of reference remains M. Wlassak, "Die Litiskontestation in Formularprozess," in *Festschrift Windscheid* (Leipzig, 1888), pp. 53 ff. Less convincing are both G. Jahr, *Litis contestatio. Streitbezeugung und Prozessbegründung im Legisaktionen und im Formularverfahren* (Cologne, 1960); and J. G. Wolf, *Die litis contestatio im römischen Zivilprozess* (Karlsruhe, 1968).

14. See above, Chapter 7, note 75.

15. D. Daube, "The Peregrine Praetor," *JRS,* 41 (1951): 66 ff., now in *Collected Studies in Roman Law,* I (Frankfurt am Main, 1991), pp. 395 ff.; F. Serrao, *La "iurisdictio" del pretore peregrino* (Milan, 1954); Bretone, *Storia del diritto romano,* pp. 136 ff.

16. A. Giardina, *L'Italia romana: Storie di un'identità incompiuta* (Rome, 1997), pp. 68, 76–77; *Storia spezzata*, pp. 72–73 [*The End of the Past*, pp. 66–67].

17. Cicero, *De legibus* 1.5.17. See also below, Chapter 9, sec. 4, and Chapter 18, sec. 3.

18. *Storia spezzata*, pp. 95 ff. [*The End of the Past*, pp. 87ff.].

19. This is already a Ciceronian expression: see, e.g., *De republica* 1.2.2. P. Frezza, "*Ius gentium*," *Revue internationale des droits de l'antiquité*, 2 (1949): n. 2, pp. 259 ff. (now in *Scritti*, 2 vols. [Rome, 2000], I, pp. 615 ff.), remains a work worth reading. Also G. Lombardi, *Ricerche in tema di "ius gentium"* (Milan, 1946) and *Sul concetto di "ius gentium"* (Rome, 1947); M. Kaser, *Ius gentium* (Cologne, 1993).

20. See below, Chapter 18, sec. 5.

21. Marotta, "Tutela dello scambio," pp. 39 ff.

22. See E. Benveniste, *Le vocabulaire des institutions indo-européennes*, 2 vols. (Paris 1969), I, pp. 115 ff. (*Indo-European Language and Society*, pp. 94 ff.). The word forms part of an extensive constellation of terms through which the Roman intelligentsia in the third and second centuries B.C. depicted the connection between politics and civil ethics (see also below, Chapter 12, sec. 4): *concordia, salus, victoria, spes, honos, virtus, pietas*: W. V. Harris, *War and Imperialism in Republican Rome* (reprint, Oxford, 1992), p. 35. And as would be the case for *aequum* (see below, Chapter 9, sec. 5, Chapter 16, sec. 4, and Chapter 21, sec. 2) its connection with *bonum* for the formation of two stereotypes of the Roman legal lexicon *(bona fides, bonum et aequum)*, assignable to the same period, reveals a very precise origin: the reference to Nietzsche is to *Zur Genealogie der Moral, Eine Streitschrift* (Leipzig, 1887), in English as *On the Genealogy of Morality*, trans. C. Diethe, Cambridge, 1994. In Cic., *De rep.* 1.35.55, "aequitas et fides" appear significantly linked: see (admittedly in a different perspective) F. Pringsheim, "*Aequitas* und *bona fides*," in *Conferenze per il XIV centenario delle Pandette* (Milan, 1931), pp. 183 ff., now in *Gesammelte Abhandlungen*, I (Heidelberg, 1961), pp. 154 ff. See also E. Stolfi, *"Bonae fidei interpretatio": Ricerche sull'interpretazione di buona fede fra esperienza romana e tradizione romanistica* (Naples, 2004), esp. pp. 18 ff., with bibliography.

23. Gaius, *Inst.* 4.116: see also later in this section, in Chapter 16, sec. 4, and Chapter 21, sec. 2.

24. Terence, *Heautontimorumenos* 796.

25. Ibid., 795.

26. For Menander, *Epitrepontes* 218 (Sandbach) = *The Cairo Codex of Menander (P. Cair. J. 43227)*, ed. L. Koenen (London, 1977), 1; T. Kock, *Comicorum Atticorum Fragmenta* (Leipzig, 1880), III.2.635, p. 189. But he in turn could look back to Herodotus 3.53.4 and a significant Sophistic tradition (Gorgias: Diels-Kranz, 82B, fr. 6: F. Blass, *Die attische Beredsamkeit,* 3d ed., I (reprint, Hildesheim, 1979), p. 65. The doubt is already present in P. Jörs, *Römische Rechtswissenschaft zur Zeit der Republik*, I: *Bis auf die Catonen* (Berlin, 1888), p. 260 n. 1.

27. *De officiis* 1.10.33: Cicero does not claim credit for the formula *iam tritum sermone*

proverbium, but we have no other attestations of the maxim in these terms, either before or afterward, and it is very plausible that the author exerted stylistic pressure upon older materials.

28. Columella, *Res rustica* 1.7.2. All these texts have been studied in a well-known and frequently quoted and cited essay by J. Stroux, "*Summum ius summa iniuria*. Ein Kapitel aus des Geschichte der *interpretatio iuris*" (1926), in *Römische Rechtswissenschaft und Rhetorik* (Potsdam, 1949), pp. 7 ff.; but see also the review by E. Levy, in *ZSS*, 48 (1928): 668 ff., which still constitutes an excellent point of departure.

29. Gaius, *Inst.* 4.116a–b.

30. Cic., *De off.* 1.10.33; translation, with modifications, from *De Officiis*, trans. W. Miller, Loeb Classical Library (1913; reprint, Cambridge, Mass., 1968).

31. Ennius, *Annales* (ed. Vahlen, 2d ed. [reprint, 1963]), p. 143, l. 148 (with a correction that is unanimously accepted): see also Nonius Marcellus, p. 812, ll. 23–24 (Lindsay).

32. Ennius, *Annales* (Vahlen), p. 150, ll. 188–189.

33. Plautus, *Menaechmi* 580.

34. Plautus, *Stichus* 423.

35. Ter., *Heaut.* 642. See also Cicero, *Pro Caecina* 21.61 and 28.80.

36. There is a long history of discussion behind this, beginning with J. B. Hofmann, *Lateinische Umgangssprache*, 4th ed. (Heidelberg, 1978); G. Pasquali, *Lingua latina dell'uso*, now in *Pagine stravaganti*, II (Florence, 1968), pp. 329 ff.

37. Plaut., *Men.* 581–587.

38. Ibid., 587; "ubi dicitur dies" is at 585.

39. Ulpian, *Ad ed.* 57, in *D.* 47.10.17.2.

40. See A. Walde and J. B. Hofmann, *Lateinisches Etymologisches Wörterbuch*, I (Heidelberg, 1938), pp. 17–18.

41. Plautus: *Mostellaria* 682; *Persa* 399; *Curculio* 65; Terence: *Heaut.* 788; *Adelphi* 64 and 987; *Phormio* 451 and 637: and here we see the appearance of *bonum*: see below, Chapter 12, sec. 4, Chapter 16, sec. 4, and Chapter 21, sec. 2.

42. *Rhetorica ad Herennium* 2.13.19; and the *aequum bonum* returns again in 2.10.14 and 2.11.16, still in the same classificatory context (*lege, more, natura, bono et aequo fieri posse*): see below, Chapter 12, sec. 4, Chapter 16, sec. 4, and Chapter 21, sec. 2.

10. Orality and Writing

1. Polybius 1.3.4: ἀπὸ δὲ τούτων τῶν καιρῶν οἱονεὶ σωματοειδῆ συμβαίνει γίνεσται τὴν ἱστορίαν, συμπλέκεσθαί τε τὰς Ἰταλικὰς καὶ Λιβυκὰς πράξεις ταῖς τε κατὰ τὴν Ἀσίαν καὶ ταῖς Ἑλληνικαῖς καὶ πρὸς ἓν γίνεσθαι τέλος τὴν ἀναφορὰν ἁπάντων. *Storia spezzata*, pp. 88–89 [*The End of the Past*, p. 82].

2. "Cupiditas gloriae": Cicero, *De republica* 5.7.9; "cupido gloriae": Sallust, *Catilinae coniuratio* 7.3; W. V. Harris, *War and Imperialism in Republican Rome* (reprint, Oxford, 1992), pp. 17 ff.

3. "Semper enim fere bella gerebantur": *De officiis* 2.13.45.

4. A. J. Toynbee, *Hannibal's Legacy*, II (London, 1965), pp. 96, 190 ff.

5. *Storia spezzata*, pp. 113–114 [*The End of the Past*, pp. 66–67]. The words of the text also allude to the title of an important book by P. Veyne, *Le pain et le cirque: Sociologie historique d'un pluralisme politique* (Paris, 1976), in English as *Bread and Circuses: Historical Sociology and Political Pluralism*, trans. B. Pearce (Harmondsworth, 1992).

6. The textual problems linked to this work are examined in depth by M. Bretone, *Tecniche e ideologie dei giuristi romani*, 2d ed. (Naples, 1982), pp. 211 ff., with conclusions that strike me as definitive.

7. In *D.* 1.2.2.39: see sec. 2 of this chapter.

8. In *D.* 1.2.2.41: see Chapter 11, sec. 2.

9. *Enchiridion*, in *D.* 1.2.2.47: "Labeo ingenii qualitate et fiducia doctrinae, qui et ceteris operis sapientiae operam dederat, plurima innovare instituit." See Chapter 17, sec. 2.

10. *Storia spezzata*, p. 188. [*The End of the Past*, p. 180].

11. F. de Martino, *Storia della costituzione romana*, 2d ed., 4 vols. (Naples, 1972–1974), III, pp. 1 ff., 299 ff.

12. *Storia spezzata*, p. 200. [*The End of the Past*, pp. 193].

13. Ibid., pp. 191 ff. [p. 184].

14. Sallust, *Historiarum fragmenta* 4.69.18.

15. Aristotle, *Politica* 1.2.1252a: ἀνάγκη δὴ πρῶτον συνδυάζεσθαι τοὺς ἄνευ ἀλλήλων μὴ δυναμένους εἶναι, οἷον θῆλυ μὲν καὶ ἄρρεν τῆς γεννήσεως ἕνεκεν . . . ἄρχον δὲ φύσει καὶ ἀρχόμενον διὰ τὴν σωτηρίαν; see also 1.5.1254a.

16. *Storia spezzata*, pp. 198 ff. and 202 (with note on p. 258) [*The End of the Past*, pp. 190 ff. and p. 194 (with note on pp. 263–264)].

17. Ibid., p. 194.

18. A Quintus Mucius Scaevola—the first member of the family about whom we have reliable information—was praetor in 215 B.C. and *decemvir sacris faciundis* in 209: T. R. S. Broughton, *The Magistrates of the Roman Republic*, 3 vols. (New York, 1951–52), I, pp. 225 and 288. See M. Grant, *Roman Myths* (London, 1971), pp. 185 ff.

19. Broughton, *The Magistrates*, I, pp. 392 and 401; his brother Quintus was also praetor in 179 and consul in 174 (ibid., pp. 392 and 403).

20. Ibid., pp. 492 and 503. For the bibliographic references, see *Giuristi*, p. 193.

21. From the era of Quintus Mucius, praetor in 215 (see note 18) and mentioned by Pomponius, *Enchiridion*, in *D.* 1.2.2.37; the tradition continued with his son, the consul in 175, and father of our Publius: Cicero, *Brutus* 26.98; see R. A. Bauman,

Lawyers in Roman Republican Politics: A Study of the Roman Jurists in Their Political Setting, 316–382 B.C. (Munich, 1983), pp. 227 ff. See also Cicero, *De off.* 2.16.57; *De natura deorum* 3.32.80; *Laelius de amicitia* 1.1; *Pro S. Roscio Amerino* 12.33; *De oratore* 1.45.200.

22. Pomp., *Ench.,* in *D.* 1.2.2.39.

23. *Pal.,* I, cols. 755–756; Bremer, I, pp. 32–34.

24. Cic., *De orat.* 1.57.242; and Pomp., *Ench.,* in *D.* 1.2.2.39; "libri" instead, also in *De orat.* 1.56.240.

25. *Pal.,* I, cols. 125–126; Bremer, I, pp. 16–18; A. Guarino, "Catone giureconsulto," *Index,* 15 (1987): 41 ff.

26. Pomp., *Ench.,* in *D.* 1.2.2.39, accepting a generally agreed-upon emendation.

27. See Chapter 11, sec. 1 (Q. Mucius); Chapter 14, sec. 1 (Servius–Alphenus Varus); Chapter 17, sec. 1 (Labeo); Chapter 18, sec. 3.

28. The doubts about the contents of the Manilian opus (which Pomp., *Ench.,* in *D.* 1.2.2.39, called *monumenta*) are briefly summarized by Bretone, *Tecniche e ideologie dei giuristi romani,* p. 264 and n. 23: see Varro, *De re rustica* 2.3.5; 5.11 and 7; Cic., *De orat.* 1.58.246.

29. Plato, *Phaedrus* 275a; translation from *Phaedrus,* trans. H. N. Fowler, Loeb Classical Library (Cambridge, Mass., 1999). See also sec. 3 of this chapter.

30. There are important indications in E. Rawson, *Intellectual Life in the Late Roman Republic* (London, 1985), pp. 66 ff., 143 ff.; W. V. Harris, *Ancient Literacy* (Cambridge, Mass., 1989), pp. 149 ff., 175 ff.; D. Musti, "Il pensiero storico romano," in *Lo spazio letterario di Roma antica,* I: *La produzione del testo* (Rome, 1989), pp. 177 ff.; G. Cambiano, "I testi filosofici," ibid., pp. 241 ff.; E. Narducci, in *Storia di Roma,* II.1, pp. 885 ff.; E. S. Gruen, *Studies in Greek Culture and Roman Policy* (1990; reprint, Berkeley, 1996), pp. 79 ff., 158 ff.; and Gruen, *Culture and National Identity in Republican Rome* (Ithaca, N.Y., 1992), pp. 52 ff., 84 ff., 131 ff.; M. Citroni, *Poesia e lettori in Roma antica* (Rome, 1995), pp. 31 ff.

31. As we learn from Cic., *De orat.* 2.33.142: "video enim in Catonis et in Bruti libris nominatim fere referri, quid alicui de iure viro aut mulieri responderint"; the report was followed by a radical criticism of this way of proceeding. An interesting reference is in Plutarch, *Cato maior* 21.

32. Celsus, *Dig.* 35, in *D.* 34.7.1pr, and *Dig.* 39, in *D.* 50.16.98.1; Paul, *Ad Sab.* 12, in *D.* 45.1.14.1, and *Quaest.* 5, in *D.* 24.3.44pr; Ulpian, *Ad ed. aed. cur.* 1, in *D.* 21.1.10.1.

33. In *D.* 45.1.4.1 and 34.7.1pr.

34. *D.* 34.7.1pr: "Catoniana regula sic definit, quod, si testamenti facti temporis decessisset testator, inutile foret, id legatum, quandocumque decesserit, non valere."

35. Or else "Catonis regula," as we see in Ulpian, *Ad Sab.* 10, in *D.* 34.7.4 (but see also Ulpian, *Ad Sab.* 22, in *D.* 34.7.5). See Chapter 17, sec. 5.

36. The doubts expressed by P. Voci, *Diritto ereditario romano,* I (Milan, 1960), p. 236 n. 89, do not seem to me to be justified.

37. *Giuristi*, pp. 20 ff. See Chapter 11, secs. 1 and 3.

38. Broughton, *The Magistrates*, I, p. 480; and Bauman, *Lawyers in Roman Republican Politics*, pp. 238 ff.

39. We learn of the dialogic model from Cic., *De orat.* 2.55.223–224. See also *Pal.*, I, cols. 77–8; and Bremer, I, pp. 22–25.

40. F. Schulz, *History of Roman Legal Science* (1946; reprint, Oxford, 1953), pp. 93–94; F. Leo, *Geschichte der römischen Literatur*, I (Berlin, 1913), p. 348; Bretone, *Tecniche e ideologie dei giuristi romani*, p. 264; F. Wieacker, *Römische Rechtsgeschichte* (Munich, 1988), pp. 542–543, 572.

41. Cic., *De orat.* 2.33.142. The name of the son (Marcus) is at 2.55.224. It is possible, as claimed by Schulz, *History of Roman Legal Science*, pp. 92–93, that only the first three books took the form of dialogues.

42. Cic., *De orat.* 2.55.224.

43. Bretone, *Tecniche e ideologie dei giuristi romani*, pp. 263–264; also A. Watson, *Law Making in the Later Roman Republic* (Oxford, 1974), pp. 140–141.

44. Cicero: *Ad familiares* 7.22 (see Chapter 11, sec. 1); Labeo: from Gellius, *Noctes Atticae* 6.15.1; Gellius: *Noct. Att.* 17.7.3; Ulpian: *Ad Sab.* 17, in *D.* 7.1.68pr, *Ad Sab.* 28, in *D.* 18.2.13pr (with the mediation of Celsus), and *Ad ed.* 18, in *D.* 9.2.27.22–23; Paul: *Ad ed.* 54, in *D.* 41.2.3.3; Modestinus: *Reg.* 3, in *D.* 49.15.4.

45. Thus in *D.* 18.2.13pr (Mucius, Brutus, Labeo); in *D.* 41.2.3.3 (Brutus and Manilius); in *D.* 49.15.4 (Brutus and Scaevola); in Cicero, *Ad fam.* 7.22 (Sextus Aelius, Manilius, Brutus); in Gell., *Noct. Att.* 17.7.3 (Brutus and Manilius).

46. In *D.* 7.1.68pr and 9.2.27.22–23.

47. Cicero, *De finibus* 1.4.12.

48. *Pal.*, I, cols. 589–590; Bremer, I, pp. 25–27.

49. Varro, *De lingua Latina* 7.5.105: "Nexum Manilius scribit omne, quod per libram et aes geritur, in quo sint mancipia." The opinion of Aelius Gallus (whose dates we are unable to establish with any certainty: see in any case *Pal.*, I, cols. 1–2; Bremer, I, pp. 245–252) is reported by Festus, p. 160, ll. 32–35 (Lindsay).

50. See Chapter 12, sec. 2.

51. *Giuristi*, pp. 20 ff. Decisive for the dating of the work, no later than 139, is F. Bona, "Sulla fonte di Cicero, *De Oratore* 1.56.23940 e sulla cronologia dei '*decem libelli*' di P. Mucio Scevola," *SDHI*, 39 (1973): 425 ff., now in *Lectio sua*, II, pp. 615 ff.

52. Lex Atinia: Cic., *De leg.* 2.20.50; "partus ancillae": Cic., *De fin.* 1.4.12; *deditio* of Hostilius Mancinus: Pomponius, *Ad Quint. Muc.* 37, in *D.* 50.7.18; riots sparked by the death of Tiberius Gracchus: Javolenus Priscus, *Ex post. Lab.* 6, in *D.* 44.3.66pr.

53. Cicero, *Topica* 4.24: "P. Scaevola id solum esse ambitus aedium dixerit, quantum parietis communis tegendi causa tectum proiceretur, ex quo tecto in eius aedis qui protexisset, aqua deflueret, id tibi ius videri"; translation from *Topica*, trans. H. M. Hubbell, Loeb Classical Library (1949; reprint, Cambridge, Mass., 1976).

54. Cic., *De orat.* 1.56.239–240: "Quaero, igitur quid adiuverit oratorem in his causis

iuris scientia, cum hic iuris consultus superior fuerit discessurus, qui esset non suo
artificio, sed alieno, hoc est, non iuris scientia, sed eloquentia, sustentatus.
Equidem hoc saepe audivi: cum aedilitatem P. Crassus peteret eumque maior
natu et iam consularis Ser. Galba adsectaretur, quod Crassi filiam Gaio filio suo
despondisset, accessisse ad Crassum consulendi causa quendam rusticanum, qui
cum Crasso seduxisset atque ad eum rettulisset responsumque ab eo verum magis quam ad suam rem accomodatum abstulisset, ut eum tristem Galba vidit,
nomine appellavit quaesivitque, qua de re ad Crassum rettulisset; ex quo ut audi-
vit commotumque ut vidit hominem, 'suspenso' inquit 'animo et occupato Crassum tibi respondisse video,' deinde ipsum Crassum manu prehendit et 'heus tu,'
inquit, 'quid tibi in mentem veniat ita respondere?' Tum ille fidenter homo peritis-
simus confirmare ita se rem habere, ut respondisset, nec dubium esse posse; Galba
autem adludens varie et copiose multas similitudines adferre multaque pro
aequitate contra ius dicere; atque illum, cum disserendo par esse non posset—
quamquam fuit Crassus in numero disertorum, sed par Galbae nullo modo—ad
auctores confugisse et id, quod ipse diceret, et in P. Muci fratris sui libris et in Sex.
Aeli commentariis scriptum protulisse ac tamen concessisse Galbae disputationem
sibi probabilem et prope veram videri"; translation, with modifications, from *De
Oratore*, trans. E. W. Sutton, Loeb Classical Library (Cambridge, Mass., 1942, reprint 1967).

55. "Panetii auditor, prope perfectus in Stoicis": Cic., *Brut.* 30.114.

56. Pomp., *Ench.*, in D. 1.2.2.40, which attributes the opinion to Cicero; Bauman, *Lawyers in Roman Republican Politics,* pp. 303 ff.

57. See Chapter 16, sec. 4.

58. Cic., *De leg.* 2.19.47: "Saepe, inquit Publii filius, ex patre audivi pontificem bonum
neminem esse, nisi qui ius civile cognosset"; translation from *Laws*, trans. C. W.
Keyes, Loeb Classical Library (Cambridge, Mass., 1928, reprint 1970); *Giuristi*, pp.
18–19 and 197–198 n. 54.

59. As we learn from Cic., *De orat.* 2.12.52.

60. Varro, *De ling. Lat.* 5.5: B. W. Frier, "*Libri annales pontificum maximorum:* The Origins of the Annalistic Tradition," *Papers and Monographs of the American Academy
in Rome*, 27 (1979): 161 ff.; and Bauman, *Lawyers in Roman Republican Politics,* pp.
290 ff.

11. The Quest for Order

1. The political career of Quintus Mucius extended—according to a reliable hypothesis—from 109 B.C. (the likely year in which he was quaestor) to 94 B.C. (the most
probable date of his proconsulship in Asia). He may have been praetor in 98, with
the consulship in 95 (and we cannot rule out that the mission in Asia fell during

the interval between the last two offices): F. Münzer, "Mucius," in *RE*, XV.1, cols. 437 ff., with an indication of the sources; and also Münzer, *Römische Adelsparteien und Adelsfamilien*, 2d ed. (Stuttgart, 1963), pp. 207 ff., 216 ff., 257 ff.; T. R. S. Broughton, *The Magistrates of the Roman Republic*, 3 vols. (New York, 1951–52), I, pp. 546, 553, 575; II, pp. 4, 7, 11, 593; III, p. 42; W. Kunkel, *Herkunft und soziale Stellung der römischen Juristen*, 2d ed. (Graz, 1967), p. 18; a summary biography is in G. Lepointe, *Quintus Mucius Scaevola*, I: *Sa vie et son oeuvre juridique: Ses doctrines sur le droit pontifical* (Paris, 1926), pp. 9 ff., esp. 20 ff. Also R. A. Bauman, *Lawyers in Roman Republican Politics: A Study of the Roman Jurists in Their Political Setting, 316–382 B.C.* (Munich, 1983), pp. 340 ff. See also Chapter 13, sec. 1.

2. P. Krüger, *Index librorum*, s.v. "Q. Mucius Scaevola," in the *Additamenta* of the *editio maior* of the *Digesta* (and, of course, also the *Index Florentinus*, under the name of the jurist). *Pal.*, I, col. 713 n. 4, seems to presuppose the existence of a text by Q. Mucius devoted to pontifical law; but it is a hypothesis that cannot be proved.

3. *Pal.*, II, cols. 60–79.

4. *Pal.*, I, cols. 757–764.

5. *Pal.*, I, cols. 762–763.

6. Bremer, I, pp. 48 ff.

7. See below, Chapter 13, note 1.

8. Cicero, *Pro S. Roscio Amerino* 12.33; Appian, *Bella civilia* 1.88.403–404.

9. F. Wieacker, *Römische Rechtsgeschichte* (Munich, 1988), pp. 597 ff., 693 ff.

10. See sec. 2 of this chapter.

11. Beginning with Bremer, I, p. 65.

12. Cicero, *Ad familiares* 7.22: "Illuseras heri inter schyphos, quod dixeram controversiam esse possetne heres, quod furtum antea factum esse, furti recte agere. Itaque, etsi domum bene potus seroque redieram, tamen id caput ubi haec controversia est, notavi et descriptum tibi misi: ut scires id quod tu neminem sensisse dicebas, Sex. Aelium, M. Manilium, M. Brutum sensisse. Ego tamen Scaevolae et Testae adsentior"; translation from *Letters to His Friends*, trans. W. G. Williams, Loeb Classical Library (1929; reprint, Cambridge, Mass., 1983).

13. *D.* 1.2.2.47.

14. *Pal.*, I, col. 758; H. Fraenkel, "Some Notes on Cicero's Letters to Trebatius," *JRS*, 47 (1957): 66 ff., esp. 67–68, later adopted by P. de Francisci, "Cic. *Ad fam.* 7.22 e i libri *Iuris civilis* di Q. Mucio Scevola," *BIDR*, 66 (1963): 93 ff. See also R. Y. Tyrrell and L. C. Purser, *The Correspondence of M. Tullius Cicero*, 2d ed., V (1915; reprint, Hildesheim, 1969), pp. 360–361; P. Huvelin, *Études sur le furtum dans le très ancien droit romain*, I (1915; reprint, Rome, 1968), pp. 320 ff.; and F. Bona, "Sulla fonte di Cicero, *De Oratore* 1.56.23940 e sulla cronologia dei 'decem libelli' di P. Mucio Scevola," *SDHI*, 39 (1973): 472.

15. Cicero, *De lege agraria* 2.7.16 and 3.2.4. See, e.g., "Lex Antonia de Termessibus," in

FIRA, I, p. 137, 1.29 = *Roman Statutes*, I, p. 334, 1.29 = *CIL*, I.2.1, pp. 472–473 n. 589; "Lex Iulia agraria," in *FIRA*, I, pp. 138–139 = *Roman Statutes*, II, pp. 763–764.

16. Gellius, *Noctes Atticae* 4.1.20: Bremer, I, pp. 220 ff.

17. From de Francisci, "Cic. *Ad fam.* 7.22 e i libri *Iuris civilis*," p. 94.

18. See, e.g., *D.* 28.2.21 = *Pal.*, II, Pomponius, 221; *D.* 28.5.68 = *Pal.*, II, Pomponius, 224; *D.* 7.4.31 = *Pal.*, II, col. 233; *D.* 46.3.80 = *Pal.*, II, col. 239; *D.* 44.7.57 = *Pal.*, II, col. 316, all assignable to Quintus Mucius; and *D.* 34.2.10 = *Pal.*, II, col. 244; *D.* 24.1.51 = *Pal.*, II, col. 245; *D.* 33.1.7 = *Pal.*, II, col. 258; *D.* 34.2.34 = *Pal.*, II, col. 261; *D.* 40.7.29 = *Pal.*, II, col. 275; *D.* 8.2.7 = *Pal.*, II, col. 294, where the identification of the Mucian text is certain, because the name of the republican jurist was preserved by Justinian's compilers. Also important is Gell., *Noct. Att.* 6.15.2.

19. But perhaps Pomponius had yet to read them: M. Bretone, *Tecniche e ideologie dei giuristi romani*, 2d ed. (Naples, 1982), p. 263. Also D. Nörr, *Pomponius*, pp. 534 ff.; and Stolfi, *Studi sui libri ad edictum di Pomponio*, 2 vols. (Milan, 2001–02), I, pp. 309 ff.

20. I have previously made reference to this: the reconstructable fragments are in *Pal.*, II, cols. 323–324; and in Bremer, I, pp. 220–224.

21. *Pal.*, II, cols. 187–188; Bremer, I, pp. 383 ff. See Chapter 18, sec. 2.

22. All that survives of the work of Laelius Felix is a long Gellian citation of an antiquarian historical character, in *Noct. Att.* 15.27.1–3; as for Paul, he makes two mentions of a Laelius, in the books *ex Plautio*: *Pal.*, I, cols. 557–558; and F. Schulz, *History of Roman Legal Science* (1946; reprint, Oxford, 1953), pp. 204–205. We are informed of the existence of the commentary by Gaius only through a reference by Gaius himself, in *Institutiones* 1.188: Schulz, *History of Roman Legal Science*, p. 204. Of the work of Pomponius, on the other hand, the *Digesta* preserves 113 texts: above, note 3.

23. *D.* 1.2.2.41: "Post hos Quintus Mucius Publii filius pontifex maximus ius civile primus constituit generatim in libros decem et octo redigendo."

24. See Chapter 13, sec. 1.

25. Plato, *Sophist* 253d–e; translation from *Sophist*, trans. H. N. Fowler, Loeb Classical Library (1921; reprint, Cambridge, Mass., 1967). For the *Politicus*, see J. Stenzel, *Studien zur Entwicklung der platonischen Dialektik von Socrates zu Aristoteles*, 2d ed. (Berlin, 1931), esp. pp. 69, 72, 106–107.

26. C. A. Viano, "La dialettica in Aristotele," in *Studi sulla dialettica* (1958; reprint, Turin, 1969), pp. 38 ff. See also B. Mates, *Stoic Logic* (Berkeley, 1961), esp. pp. 58 ff.

27. Chrysippus: *SVF*, II, pp. 9 n. 16, 75 n. 224, 114 n. 317. Diogenes: *SVF*, III, pp. 215 n. 25, 233 n. 87.

28. D. Matthes, *Hermagoras Fragmenta* (Leipzig, 1962), pp. 8–56 nn. 2–23; M. L. Clarke, *Rhetoric at Rome* (London, 1953), pp. 7 and 24. For the *Rhet. ad Her.*, see below, Chapter 13, note 7.

29. Plutarch, *Aemilius Paul* 28; and Isidore of Seville, *Etymologiae* 6.5.1.

30. S. Mazzarino, *Il pensiero storico classico,* 2 vols. (Bari, 1966), II.1, p. 106.

31. See Gell., *Noct. Att.* 15.11.2; and Cicero, *De oratore* 3.24.93.

32. This, in substance, is the interpretation that became canonical from Schulz on: *History of Roman Legal Science,* pp. 38 ff.

33. Also ibid., pp. 62 ff.

34. Not even really overturned by J. Stroux, "Die griechischen Einflusse auf die Entwicklung der römischen Rechtswissenschaft gegen Ende der republikanischer Zeit," in *Atti Congr. dir. rom. Roma,* I (Pavia, 1935), pp. 111 ff. See also B. Schmidlin, "*Horoi, pithana* und *regulae.* Zum Einfluss der Rhetorik und Dialektik auf die juristische Regelbildung," in *ANRW,* II.15 (1976), pp. 101 ff.

35. Cic., *De orat.* 1.41.186–42.191: "Deinde, postea quam est editum, expositis a Cn. Flavio primum actionibus, nulli fuerunt, qui illa artificiose digesta generatim componerent; nihil est enim, quod ad artem redigi possit, nisi ille prius, qui illa tenet, quorum artem instituere vult, habet illam scientiam, ut ex eis rebus, quarum ars nondum sit, artem efficere possit. [187] Hoc video, dum breviter voluerim dicere, dictum a me esse paulo obscurius; sed experiar et dicam, si potero, planius . . . Omnia fere, quae sunt conclusa nunc artibus, dispersa et dissipata quondam fuerunt; ut in musicis numeri et voces et modi; in geometria lineamenta, formae, intervalla, magnitudines; in astrologia caeli conversio, ortus, obitus motusque siderum; in grammaticis poetarum pertractatio, historiarum cognitio, verborum interpretatio, pronuntiandi quidam sonus; in hac denique ipsa ratione dicendi excogitare, ornare, disponere, meminisse, agere, ignota quondam omnibus et diffusa late videbantur. [188] Adhibita est igitur ars quaedam extrinsecus ex alio genere quodam, quod sibi totum philosophi adsumunt, quae rem dissolutam divulsamque conglutinaret et ratione quadam constringeret. Sit ergo in iure civili finis hic: legitimae atque usitatae in rebus causisque civium aequabilitatis conservatio. [189] Tum sunt notanda genera et ad certum numerum paucitatemque revocanda. Genus autem id est, quod sui similis communione quadam, specie autem differentis, duas aut pluris complectitur partis; partes autem sunt, quae generibus eis, ex quibus manant, subiciuntur; omniaque, quae sunt vel generum vel partium nomina, definitionibus, quam vim habeant, est exprimendum; est enim definitio rerum earum, quae sunt eius rei propriae, quam definire volumus, brevis et circumscripta quaedam explicatio. [190] Hisce ego rebus exempla adiungerem, nisi apud quos haec haberetur oratio cernerem; nunc complectar, quod proposui, brevi: si enim aut mihi facere licuerit, quod iam diu cogito, aut alius quispiam aut me impedito occuparit aut mortuo effecerit, ut primum omne ius civile in genera digerat, quae perpauca sunt, deinde eorum generum quasi quaedam membra dispertiat, tum propriam cuiusque vim definitione declaret, perfectam artem iuris civilis habebitis, magis magnam atque uberem quam difficilem et obscuram. [191] Atque interea tamen, dum haec, quae dispersa sunt, coguntur,

vel passim licet carpentem et conligentem undique repleri iusta iuris civilis scientia"; translation, with modifications, from *De Oratore*, trans. E. W. Sutton, Loeb Classical Library (1942; reprint, Cambridge, Mass., 1967). This is a very well-known text.

36. Cicero, *Topica* 5.28: "Atque etiam definitiones aliae sunt partitionum aliae divisionum; partitionum, cum res ea quae proposita est quasi in membra discerpitur, ut si qui ius civile dicat id esse quod in legibus, senatus consultis, rebus iudicatis, iuris peritorum auctoritate, edictis magistratuum, more, aequitate consistat. Divisionum autem definitio formas omnis complectitur quae sub eo genere sunt quod definitur hoc modo: Abalienatio est eius rei quae mancipi est aut traditio alteri nexu aut in iure cessio inter quos ea iure civili fieri possunt."

37. Quintilian, *Institutio oratoria* 12.3.10; Gell., *Noct. Att.* 1.22.7; Charisius (Arcadius), *Ars grammatica,* p. 175, ll. 18–19B.

38. Cicero, *Brutus* 41.152–42.153: "Hic Brutus: ain tu? inquit: etiamne Q. Scaevolae Servium nostrum anteponis? Sic enim, inquam, Brute, existumo, iuris civilis magnum usum et apud Scaevolam et apud multos fuisse, artem in hoc uno; quod numquam effecisset ipsius iuris scientia, nisi eam praeterea didicisset artem, quae doceret rem universam tribuere in partes, latentem explicare definiendo, obscuram explanare interpretando, ambigua primum videre, deinde distinguere, postremo habere regulam, qua vera et falsa iudicarentur et quae quibus propositis essent quaeque non essent consequentia. Hic enim adtulit hanc artem omnium artium maxumam quasi lucem ad ea, quae confuse ab aliis aut respondebantur aut agebantur. Dialecticam mihi videris dicere, inquit. Recte, inquam, intellegis; sed adiunxit etiam et litterarum scientiam et loquendi elegantiam, quae ex scriptis eius, quorum similia nulla sunt, facillime perspici potest"; translation, with modifications, from *Brutus*, trans. G. L. Hendrickson, Loeb Classical Library (Cambridge, Mass., 1962). This too is a well-known text: Schulz, *History of Roman Legal Science,* pp. 68–69.

39. See Chapter 17, sec. 1.

40. See Chapter 16, sec. 2.

12. The New Paradigm

1. Gaius, *Institutiones* 1.188; and Paul, *Ad edictum* 54, in *D.* 41.2.3.23; reference to a *distinctio* of Mucius is also made by Ulpian, *Ad edictum* 18, in *D.* 9.1.1.1. We cannot rule out of course that other *divisiones,* of which there is evidence in the manual by Gaius, can be traced back to Quintus Mucius: thus, for instance, the *genera legatorum* (Gaius, *Inst.* 2.192), the *genera obligationum* (Gaius, *Inst.* 3.88: see sec. 2 of this chapter), the *genera actionum* (Gaius, *Inst.* 4.1), or the *genera societatis.*

2. W. D. Ross, *Aristotle* (London, 1923), pp. 21 ff.; and Ross, *Plato's Theory of Ideas* (Ox-

ford, 1951), pp. 11 ff., 104 ff., 213 ff.; A. C. Lloyd, "Plato's Description of Division," *Classical Quarterly*, 2 (1952): 105 ff.; M. Vanhoutte, *La méthode ontologique de Platon* (Louvain, 1956); A. R. Lacey, "Plato's *Sophist* and the Forms," *Classical Quarterly*, 9 (1959): 43 ff.; J. R. Trevaskis, "Classification in the *Philebus*," *Phronesis*, 5 (1960): 39 ff.; D. M. Balme, "*Genos* and *eidos* in Aristotle's Biology," *Classical Quarterly*, 12 (1962): 81 ff. G. E. R. Lloyd, *Polarity and Analogy: Two Types of Argumentation in Early Greek Thought* (Cambridge, 1966), pp. 421 ff.; and, from another point of view, B. Snell, *Die Entdeckung des Geistes. Studien zur Entstehung des europäischen Denkens bei den Griechen* (Hamburg, 1955), in English as *The Discovery of the Mind in Greek Philosophy and Literature*, trans. T. G. Rosenmeyer (Mineola, N. Y., 1982), pp. v ff.; and J.-P. Vernant, *Mythe et pensée chez les Grecs,* 3d ed. (Paris, 1990), pp. 373 ff., in English as *Myth and Thought Among the Greeks*, trans. J. Lloyd and J. Fort (New York, 2006). The Platonic dialectic in particular develops two procedures: a "generalizing synoptic" one and a "diaeretic" one, closely intertwined; thus G. Reale, *Platone: Alla ricerca della sapienza segreta* (Milan, 1998), p. 193. There are also important observations in H. G. Gadamer, *Wahrheit und Methode,* 3d ed. (Tübingen, 1972), in English as *Truth and Method*, (London, 1975), pp. 387 ff.

3. See Chapter 10, sec. 2. Quintus Mucius made an important change regarding *furtum usus*, as noted by Gellius, *Noctes Atticae* 6.15.2.

4. See Chapter 9.

5. See Chapter 4, sec. 4.

6. This is what I mean by genealogical reconstruction, in the sense of Nietzsche (above, Chapter 9, including note 22) and Foucault; see M. Foucault, *Naissance de la clinique: Une archéologie du regard médical* (Paris, 1963), in English as *Birth of the Clinic: An Archaelogy of Medical Perception* (New York, 1973) and *Surveiller et punir: Naissance de la prison* (Paris, 1975), in English as *Discipline and Punish: The Birth of the Prison* (New York, 1995).

7. Friedrich Karl von Savigny, *Vom Beruf unserer Zeit für Gesetzgebung und Rechtswissenschaft* (1814), 3d ed. (1840; reprint, Hildesheim, 1967): see Chapter 1, sec. 4, and note 17. On the Kantian formation of Savigny, G. Marini, *Friedrich Carl Von Savigny* (Naples, 1978), esp. pp. 66 ff.; *Origini,* pp. 40 ff.; D. Nörr, *Savignys philosophische Lehrjahre. Ein Versuch* (Frankfurt am Main, 1994), esp. pp. 15 ff.

8. Plato: *Republic* 7.14.534b–d; *Phaedo* 49.100b–e; Aristotle: *Physica* 2.3.194b–195b; *Metaphysica* 5.23.1013a–1104b; the Greek word for "abstraction" is ἀφαίρεσις; important works: E. A. Havelock, *Preface to Plato* (Cambridge, Mass., 1963), pp. 215 ff., 226 ff., 236 ff., 254; M. Riedel, *Metaphysik und Metapolitik. Studien zu Aristoteles und zur politischen Sprache der neuzeitlichen Philosophie* (Frankfurt am Main, 1975); and Reale, *Platone*, pp. 187 ff.; my interpretation is based on theirs.

9. Well described by Polybius 6.11–18. The relationship between knowledge and will in the juridical order has been analyzed by a significant tradition, from Thomas

Aquinas, *Summa Theologiae,* 2d ed. (Paul, 1988), q. 17, aa. 1 and 5; to M. Heidegger, *Parmenides* (Frankfurt am Main, 1982), in English as *Parmenides*, trans. A. Schuwer and R. Rojcewicz (Bloomington, 1992).

10. It is the same concrete-abstract-concrete circularity that we later find at the foundation of modern science: acute observations in G. della Volpe, *Logica come scienza positiva,* in *Opere,* IV (Rome, 1973), pp. 286 ff.; and in L. Colletti, *Il marxismo e Hegel* (Bari, 1969), pp. 35 ff. The centrality of the "case"—social materiality, nature, history—determined the intrinsically realistic and "positive" character of Roman legal thought—verging on materialism—despite the speculative and metaphysical vocation about which we are talking, always resolved in a sort of primacy of "practical reason": the case-based observation of the phenomenal multiplicity of life—inaugurated by Greek medical thought and (up to a certain point, independently of it) by Roman legal reflection, would ultimately underlie various major medieval and protomodern theological developments: a fine book on this subject is J.-C. Passeron and J. Revel, eds., *Penser par cas* (Paris, 2005), esp. pp. 9 ff. (J.-C. Passeron and J. Revel), 45 ff. (Y. Thomas), 95 ff. (A. Jonsen, S. Toulmin). See below, Chapter 14.

11. A. Pottage and M. Mundy, eds., *Law, Anthropology, and the Constitution of the Social* (Cambridge, 2004), esp. pp. 1 ff. (A. Pottage), 40 ff. (Y. Thomas), 73 ff. (B. Latour).

12. An intertwining similar to what I am describing is found in Riedel, *Metaphysik und Metapolitik;* and it is also evoked by Reale, *Platone,* pp. 187 ff., in his criticism of Havelock and when, while distinguishing the Platonic abstraction from its "modern" equivalent (p. 190), he connects it to the "very source of being" (ibid.), as inclined "always and exclusively to discover real things, not . . . mere thoughts" (p. 191). But the latter is implicit in Roman legal thought after the revolution of formalism: "that which is most universal is most real and that which is universal in the supreme sense is being in the supreme sense" (p. 193, also referring to Plato, and yet corresponding exactly with what Savigny said in connection with the working method of jurisprudence). It is also true, however, that the jurists were using the ontological schemes as "forms" of experience in a sense that approached the Kantian one, in order to construct a sort of synthetic knowledge a priori, in which the legal prediction (the rule of the case) managed to dominate becoming—bare life—because in it the occurrence of the event was anticipated as a preestablishment, through the universality of the concept, of what was, literally, still nothing (E. Severino, *Legge e caso,* 3d ed. [Milan, 1990], pp. 26 ff.; and see also, for the Kantian and Hegelian implications of my line of argument, K. Fischer, *Logik und Metaphysik oder Wissenschaftslehre* [1852], ed. H. G. Gadamer [Heidelberg, 1998], pp. 63 ff., 77 ff.): naturally, such a scheme always leaves open the possibility of a check, "of the irruption of something that displays itself as a new development that absolutely cannot be inserted in the context of the foreseen" (p. 30): this

is the liminal situation described by G. Agamben, *Stato di eccezione: Homo sacer*, II.1 (Turin, 2003), esp. pp. 68 ff., 95 ff., in English as *State of Exception*, trans. K. Attell (Chicago, 2005), esp. pp. 52 ff., 74 ff. The discussion that Carl Schmitt offers of the concept of form, between Weber and the neo-Kantians (*Politische Theologie. Vier Kapitel zur Lehre der Souveränität*, 2d ed. [Munich, 1934], in English as *Political Theology: Four Chapters on the Concept of Sovereignty*, trans. G. Schwab, [Chicago, 2005]) is a good starting point to take into account these paradigmatic oscillations in the analytical structure of Roman jurisprudence.

13. Plato, *Minos* 317d: Ὀρθῶς ἄρα ὡμολογήσαμεν νόμον εἶναι τοῦ ὄντος εὕρεσιν. Mention has already been made of this in Chapter 3, sec. 3 and note 17. This is a dialogue that many consider not to be authentic, but probably it is only an incomplete work that was discarded by the author (thus G. R. Morrow, *Plato's Cretan City: A Historical Interpretation of the Laws* [Princeton, 1960], pp. 35 ff.), and in any case put together with materials attributable to Plato (the date of composition may be prior to 350 B.C.): G. Reale, *Platone: Tutti gli scritti* (Milan, 2000), p. 1436. Here and elsewhere I speak of "legal ontology" and "social metaphysics" with reference to the ontological projections of the jurists: the idea of a "social metaphysics" is used by W. Dilthey, *Einleitung in die Geisteswissenschaften. Versuch einer Grundlegung für das Studium der Gesellschaft und der Geschichte* (1883), in *Gesammelte Schriften*, 6th ed., I (Stuttgart, 1966), p. 228: "dieser fundamentale Begriff der sozialen Metaphysik" (in English as *Introduction to the Human Sciences*, trans. R. J. Betanoz [Princeton, 1991]; and is later taken up again by Riedel, *Metaphysik und Metapolitik* (who prefers "metapolitics"), in connection with the Aristotelian apparatus of the *Nicomachean Ethics* and the *Politics* (while "social ontology" is already in its turn present in E. Husserl, *Soziale Ontologie und deskriptive Soziologie* (1910), now in *Zur Phänomenologie der Intersubjektivität. Texte aus dem Nachlass*, vol. I: *1905–1920*, ed. M. Nijoff (The Hague, 1973); and see P. di Lucia, ed., *Ontologia sociale: Potere deontico e regole costitutive* (Macerata, 2003), pp. 9 ff. (di Lucia) and 27 ff. (J. R. Searle); also P. Aubenaque and A. Tordesillas, eds., *Aristote politique: Études sur la "Politique" d'Aristote* (Paris, 1993), esp. the essays in secs. I, pp. 3 ff., and II, pp. 133 ff.; but in Aristotle the metaphysical structure did not directly hypostatize social contents to construct formal (universal) figures of prescriptivity, as the Roman jurists would later do, but rather served to incorporate into politics, through the concept of *physis*, "the doctrine of the principles of its metaphysics of substance" (Riedel, *Metaphysik und Metapolitik*, p. 104): it had, that is, a purely methodological value, or (though this is another matter entirely) a significance of a "naturalistic" foundation of a civil ethics (as in the *Nicomachean Ethics*: political theory as a "theory of the ethical institutions of the polis": J. Ritter, *Metaphysik und Politik. Studien zu Aristoteles und Hegel* (Frankfurt am Main, 1969). In a passage of G. B. Vico, *La scienza nuova seconda giusta l'edizione del 1744*, ed. F. Nicolini, 4th ed. (Bari, 1953), p. 506,

there is instead a discussion of "legal metaphysics"—an extraordinary intuition—precisely in connection with the Roman jurists; and even earlier, in a 1731 variant, in *La scienza nuova giusta l'edizione del 1744 con le varianti dell'edizione del 1730 e di due redazioni intermedie inedite,* ed. F. Nicolini, 2 vols. (Bari, 1928), I, p. 260 (1386), the philosopher wrote: "Thus the Roman jurisconsults, in the name of that jurisprudence, whose principles derived from divine providence, sensed what Plato, in the name of a sublime metaphysics, in which he demonstrated providence, understood of the eternal ideas: that, inasmuch as rights are modes of spiritual substance, therefore are they individual, because divisibility is proper to bodies, and therefore they are individual, they are thus eternal": this is the discovery of the theoretical and ontological vocation of Roman legal thought, destined to be buried ultimately under centuries of incomprehension (with the sole and partial exception of Savigny). Again, in the 1744 *Scienza nuova,* p. 486, Vico also wrote: "the cause that gave the Romans the wisest jurisprudence on Earth . . . is the same cause that gave them the greatest empire on Earth."

14. A world regulated by status more than by contracts: see H. Sumner Maine, *Ancient Law* (New York, 1861), pp. 164–165, 295 ff.; *Storia spezzata,* pp. 173 ff., esp. 180 ff. [*The End of the Past,* pp. 165 ff., esp. 172 ff.].

15. See Chapter 9, secs. 2 and 4. Also *Storia spezzata,* pp. 95 ff. [*The End of the Past,* pp. 87 ff.].

16. Paul, in *D.* 18.1.1pr: "Olim enim non ita erat nummus neque aliud merx, aliud pretium vocabatur, sed unusquisque secundum necessitatem temporum ac rerum utilibus inutilia permutabat": *Logiche,* pp. 103 ff.

17. Paul, in *D.* 19.4.1: "Sicut aliud est vendere aliud est emere, alius emptor, alius venditor, ita pretium aliud, aliud merx. At in permutatione discerni non potest, uter emptor vel uter venditor sit."

18. Paul, in *D.* 18.1.1pr: "Cum tu haberes quod ego desiderarem, invicem haberem quod tu accipere velles."

19. Pomponius, *Ad Quint. Muc.* 4, in *D.* 46.3.80: "Prout quidque contractum est, ita et solvi debet: ut, cum re contraxerimus, re solvi debet: veluti cum mutuum dedimus, ut retro pecuniae tantundem solvi debeat. Et cum verbis aliquid contraximus, vel re vel verbis obligatio solvi debet, verbis, veluti cum acceptum promissori fit, re, veluti cum solvit quod promisit. Aeque cum emptio vel venditio vel locatio contracta est, quoniam consensu nudo contrahi potest, etiam dissensu contrario dissolvi potest."

20. *D.* 34.2.34pr-2; *D.* 47.2.77.1; *D.* 33.1.7; *D.* 34.2.10; *D.* 24.1.51; *D.* 34.2.33 (correcting a paleographic error); *D.* 9.2.39; *D.* 40.7.29.1; *D.* 8.2.7; *D.* 18.1.66.2; *D.* 19.1.40; *D.* 8.3.15; *D.* 50.7.18 (the order followed is that used by O. Lenel in *Pal.,* I, cols. 757–762). Schulz, *History of Roman Legal Science,* p. 204; also E. Stolfi, *Studi sui libri ad edictum di Pomponio,* 2 vols. (Milan, 2001–02), I, pp. 312 ff.

21. Schulz, *History of Roman Legal Science,* p. 204.

22. The thirteen texts in which mention of the name of Mucius has been preserved are those indicated above in note 20. The attribution to Mucius, as far as *D.* 46.3.80 is concerned, was already made persuasively by P. Voci, *La dottrina romana del contratto* (Milan, 1946), pp. 80 ff.

23. Pomponius, *Enchiridion,* in *D.* 46.3.107: "Verborum obligatio aut naturaliter resolvitur aut civiliter: naturaliter veluti solutione aut cum res in stipulationem deducta sine culpa promissoris in rebus humanis esse desiit: civiliter veluti acceptilatione vel cum in eandem personam ius stipulantis promittentisque devenit."

24. Ulpian, *Ad Sab.* 48, in *D.* 50.17.35: "Nihil tam naturale est quam eo genere quidque dissolvere, quo colligatum est. Ideo verborum obligatio verbis tollitur: nudi consensus obligatio contrario consensu dissolvitur." See also the other Sabinian lemmata transcribed by Ulpian in the same book, in *D.* 46.2.2 and 46.4.8.3.

25. In the final phrase, "dissensu" should probably be corrected to "consensu."

26. Given the ratio between the size of the two works (the thirty-nine books of Pomponius versus the eighteen of Quintus Mucius), the fourth book of Pomponius (from which the text in question is taken) cannot correspond to a book beyond the third book of the work of Mucius. The fourth book of Pomponius is entirely *de legatis* (*Pal.,* II, cols. 62–63): A. Watson, *Law Making in the Later Roman Republic* (Oxford, 1974), p. 143, assigns to this topic the second, the third, and the first part of the fourth book of the text of Mucius (that Quintus Mucius in his second book dealt with the topic of legacies is moreover quite certain: it is proved by specific citations from Ulpian: *Pal.,* I, col. 757). But since the space that Pomponius dedicates to this argument extends to the ninth book, we should suppose that the fourth one corresponds to the beginning of Mucius' treatment: and therefore to the second book, or at the outside the beginning of the third. On the classification of the *genera legatorum,* see note 1 above. To maintain, as I do, that there were Mucian nuclei powerfully present in the fabric of Gaius' *Institutiones* (probably mediated in part through the tradition of Sabinus—see Stolfi, *Studi sui libri ad edictum di Pomponio,* II, pp. 32–33, with bibliography) does not mean supposing (as does Schulz, *History of Roman Legal Science,* pp. 94 ff., 156 ff., esp. 157–158) that the "systems" of Mucius, Sabinus, and Gaius had to be roughly identical (I have already spoken of the completely arbitrary nature of this thesis, in connection with the comparison of Q. Mucius and Gaius; for Sabinus, see the strong reservations of V. Arangio-Ruiz, *La società in diritto romano* [reprint, Naples, 1965], pp. 45 ff.). It only means underlining the undeniable existence of Mucian-Sabinian "blocks" in the composition of Gaius' *Institutiones,* arranged within a "system" that was certainly different from the original ones. In any case, it is an established fact that Quintus Mucius dealt in an original way with problems of succession. With regard to wills, he had to begin from the older comitial form, ultimately arriving at the more re-

cent figures, in accordance with a style of analysis that, as we shall see, would be typical of the books *Iuris civilis:* we can deduce this from Gell., *Noct. Att.* 15.27.1–3 (through the mediation of Laelius Felix: Arangio-Ruiz, *Società in diritto romano,* p. 44). Mucius also examined the *penus legata:* Ormanni, *"Penus legata,"* pp. 652 ff.; A. Watson, *The Law of Succession in the Later Roman Republic* (Oxford, 1971), pp. 134 ff.

27. But in *Pal.,* II, col. 63 n. 5, this possibility is postulated in relation to the commentary of Pomponius.

28. This is the earliest documented presence in the work of a jurist. Probably over a period of years not very distant from the time of Mucius, *contrahere* was also employed in the language of the edicts; for the list of clauses (naturally, of the Edict of Hadrian) in which it is possible to find it, see Voci, *La dottrina romana del contratto,* p. 15 n. 1. It is a very delicate problem to establish which of these clauses can be dated back to the age of Q. Mucius. In any case, it is very likely that the text of the edict known to Labeo already contained some use of *contrahere:* see Chapter 17, sec. 4.

29. Important testimony is offered by Varro, *De lingua Latina* 6.77–78. See also Chapter 17, sec. 4.

30. For Cicero see *Ad Brutum* 26 (1.18) 3. The definition that I discuss is that of *Iust. Institutiones,* 3.13pr: "Obligatio est iuris vinculum, quo necessitate adstringimur solvendae rei secundum nostrae civitatis iura."

31. See sec. 3 of this chapter.

32. Mucius' definition of *nexum* is in Varro, *De ling. Lat.* 7.5.105, and it is presented in opposition to that of Manilius (see above, Chapter 10, sec. 2).

33. On the latter part of the quotation in the text, Varro, *De ling. Lat.* 7.5.105: "Mucius quae per aes et libram fiant ut obligentur, praeter quom mancipio denture."

34. Cicero, *Pro Q. Roscio Comoedo* 5.14: "Haec pecunia necesse est aut data, aut expensa lata, aut stipulata sit."

35. See Chapter 9, sec. 5.

36. *D.* 50.17.73.4: "Nec paciscendo, nec legem dicendo nec stipulando quisquam alteri cavere potest." From *D.* 50.17.73 we obtain more than half (five of eight) of the definitions that we can read in Mucius' *Horoi:* we will find *horos* closer to the one we have just recalled (*D.* 50.17.73) in Chapter 13, sec. 3 and note 18. See Stein, *Regulae Iuris,* p. 38; also B. Schmidlin, *"Horoi, pithana* und *regulae.* Zum Einfluss der Rhetorik und Dialektik auf die juristische Regelbildung," in *ANRW,* II.15 (1976), pp. 108 ff.

37. See Chapter 11, sec. 1.

38. The text is divided into three parts by *Pal.,* I, col. 763, nn. 48–50.

39. *Rhet. ad Her.* 2.13.19: "Constat igitur ex his partibus: natura, lege, consuetudine, iudicato, aequo et bono, pacto."

40. *Pal.,* I, col. 758.

41. Watson, *Law Making*, p. 144; M. Bretone, *"Consortium e communio,"* Labeo, 6 (1960): 163 ff., esp. 177 ff.

42. *Linee,* esp. pp. 58 ff. See also the end of Chapter 11.

43. Gaius, *Inst.* 3.154–154a: we reconstruct this text through the fragments of Antinoe: Arangio-Ruiz, *Società in diritto romano,* pp. 3 ff.

44. The text is that found in *D.* 44.7.57, presented below in note 56 (see Arangio-Ruiz, *Società in diritto romano,* pp. 21–22; and F. Bona, *Studi sulla società consensuale in diritto romano* [Milan, 1973], p. 15 n. 23), and it is taken from the thirty-sixth book *ad Quintum Mucium,* which Lenel supposes, albeit with a degree of hesitation, to be devoted to the analysis of *societas* (*Pal.,* II, col. 77). In that case there would be a relationship between the fourteenth book of Mucius and the thirty-sixth book of Pomponius, and this would mean that the last part of Pomponius' commentary must have been much shorter than the preceding part, or that some of the arguments of the last books of Quintus Mucius were not included in the analysis of Pomponius.

45. Pomp., *Ad Quint. Muc.* 35, in *D.* 29.2.78. There is no doubt that the first part of the text reproduces a lemma by Mucius: a convincing demonstration of this point is in Bretone, *"Consortium e communio,"* pp. 201 ff. This is a case in which the linguistic evidence helps in our reconstruction of the original discourse of Mucius. See also Arangio-Ruiz, *Società in diritto romano,* p. 43.

46. Paul, *Ad ed.* 21, in *D.* 50.16.25.1. We have no reason to doubt the accuracy of the citation (mediated, in all likelihood, through the work of Servius).

47. F. Bona, "Contributi alla storia della *'societas universorum quae ex quaestu veniunt'* in diritto romano," in *Studi grosso,* I (Turin, 1968), pp. 402–403, now in *Lectio sua,* I, pp. 344 ff.; and *Studi sulla società consensuale,* pp. 20–21.

48. Bona, "Contributi," pp. 385 ff., esp. 400 n. 22, now in *Lectio sua,* I, pp. 342–343 n. 22.

49. We learn this through a citation by Ulpian, *Ad Sab.* 30, in *D.* 17.2.11 (the last very brief fragment of a passage broken up by the compilers into several texts: *Pal.,* I, col. 758, and II, cols. 1128–29).

50. Gaius, *Inst.* 3.149–150: "Magna autem quaestio fuit, an ita coiri possit societas, ut quis maiorem partem lucretur, minorem damni praestet. Quod Q. Mucius [contra naturam societatis esse existimavit. Sed Ser. Sulpicius, cuius] etiam praevaluit sententia, adeo ita coiri posse societatem existimavit, ut dixerit illo quoque modo coiri posse, ut quis nihil omnino damni praestet, sed lucri partem capiat, si modo opera eius tam pretiosa videatur, ut aequum sit eum cum hac pactione in societatem admitti." The integration is the one generally accepted on the basis of *Institutiones Iust.* 3.25.2.

51. Cicero, *De officiis* 3.17.70: "Q. quidem Scaevola, pontifex maximus, summam vim esse dicebat in omnibus iis arbitriis, in quibus adderetur 'ex fide bona,' fideique bonae nomen existimabat manare latissime, idque versari in tutelis, societatibus,

fiduciis, mandatis, rebus emptis, venditis, conductis, locatis, quibus vitae societas contineretur; in iis magni esse iudicis statuere, praesertim cum in plerisque essent iudicia contraria, quid quemque cuique praestare oporteret"; translation, with modifications, from *De Officiis,* trans. W. Miller, Loeb Classical Library (Cambridge, Mass., 1928).

52. It still strikes me as reliable to establish the year 94 as the date of the proconsulship of Mucius, accepting E. Badian, "Q. Mucius and the Province of Asia," *Athenaeum,* 34 (1956): 104 ff. A different view is held by B. A. Marshall, "The Date of Q. Mucius Scaevola's Governorship of Asia," ibid., 54 (1976): 117 ff.; and, even earlier, T. R. S. Broughton, *The Magistrates of the Roman Republic,* 3 vols. (New York, 1951–52), II, p. 7. See also D. Magie, *Roman Rule in Asia Minor,* 2 vols. (Princeton, 1950), I, pp. 173–176, and II, p. 1064. Cicero repeatedly praises the institutional policies of Mucius in Asia: see *Ad Atticum* 5.17.5; 6.1.15 (with a specific reference to *bona fides*); *In Verrem* 2.3.90.209; *Pro Plancio* 13.33. We know that the mission in Asia of the prestigious consul, already at that time a famous jurist, complied with specific requirements of the Senate's policies in those years: see E. Badian, "Q. Mucius and the Province of Asia," pp. 114 ff.

53. See, for example, Pomp., *Ad Quint. Muc.* 36, in *D.* 44.7.57, cited in sec. 4 of this chapter; while it is less certain to attribute to Mucius the references to *bona fides* that can also be found in Pomp., *Ad Quint. Muc.* 22, in *D.* 22.1.45 and *D.* 45.3.39; *Ad Quint. Muc.* 24, in *D.* 41.3.24pr.

54. Modern research into historical psychology focusing on the mental forms of republican governing groups in the age of their formation are still almost entirely lacking; mention can be made of some essays in the two volumes of *Wege der Forschung,* ed. H. Oppermann, vol. XVIII: *Römertum,* 3d ed. (1970), esp. pp. 11 ff., 35 ff., 87 ff., 155 ff.; vol. XXXIV: *Römische Wertbegriffe* (1967), esp. pp. 23 ff., 120 ff., 173 ff., 323 ff., 376 ff., 446 ff., 529 ff. But nearly all these studies show the marks of time and are quite questionable. See also W. V. Harris, *Restraining Rage: The Ideology of Anger Control in Classical Antiquity* (Cambridge, Mass., 2001), pp. 50 ff., 131 ff., 157 ff., 201 ff. A few useful ideas can be found in V. d'Agostino, "La *fides romana,"* *Rivista di studi classici,* 9 (1961): 73 ff., esp. 79–86. See also G. Dumézil, *Idées romaines,* 2d ed. (Paris, 1979), pp. 47 ff.; Lombardi, *Dalla fides alla bona fides,* pp. 165 ff.

55. A sketch of the history of Roman *fides* is in Gell., *Noct. Att.* 20.1.39–40; F. Wieacker, "Zum Ursprung der *bonae fidei iudicia,"* *ZSS,* 80 (1963), esp. pp. 40 ff. It is possible that Mucius was also aware of the Aristotelian elaborations of books 8–9 of the *Nicomachean Ethics:* see, e.g., 8.13.5–6.1162b, with a specific reference to πίστις, which fits into the same semantic field as *fides.*

56. Pomp., *Ad Quint. Muc.* 36, in *D.* 44.7.57: "In omnibus negotiis contrahendis, sive bona fide sint sive non sint, si error aliquis intervenit, ut aliud sentiat puta qui emit aut qui conducit, aliud quid cum his contrahit, nihil valet quod acti sit. Et idem in

societate quoque coeunda respondendum est, ut, si dissentiant aliud alio existim-
ante, nihil valet ea societas, quae in consensu consistit."

57. See sec. 2 of this chapter.

58. Bona, "Società universale e società questuaria generale," pp. 308–309, poses the
problem, albeit with what may be excessive prudence. More decisive is Arangio-
Ruiz, *Società in diritto romano*, p. 21.

59. In a stratigraphic reading of the text, I would attribute to Mucius: (a) the reference
to *bona fides*; (b) in relationship to the noncoincidence of the "feeling" in the contracting parties of an *emptio* or of a *locatio*; (c) the reference to the "societas quae
in consensu consistit"—this last was already a genuine relic in the time of Pomponius: I must agree with Arangio-Ruiz, *Società in diritto romano*, p. 22. We should
further emphasize the evident Stoic background of the doctrine concerning the
importance of inner feeling with respect to its mistaken manifestation: an element
that once again guides us toward a Mucian attribution, and which did not escape
the notice of M. Pohlenz, *Die Stoa. Geschichte einer geistigen Bewegung* (Göttingen,
1948), p. 263.

60. The trial in question is known as the *causa Curiana*: Schulz, *History of Roman Legal
Science*, pp. 79–80; F. Wieacker, "La *'causa Curiana'* e gli orientamenti della giurisprudenza coeva," *Antologia giuridica romanistica ed antiquaria*, 1 (1968): 111 ff.; Bona,
"Cicerone e i *'libri iuris civilis*,'" pp. 214 and 229 ff., now in *Lectio sua*, II, pp. 841 and
857 ff.; Bretone, *Tecniche e ideologie dei giuristi romani*, pp. 111 ff.; Cannata, *Storia
della scienza giuridica europea*, I, pp. 240 ff.

61. The texts that we have read thus far do not exhaust all our possibilities, albeit
within the context of an unquestionably very limited documentation, of tracking
down the presence of abstract forms within Mucius' analysis. If we wished to
conduct a complete research project, we would still need to take into consideration at the very least: (*a*) the conceptual picture that emerges in the definitions of
vis (Liber singularis horōn, in D. 50.17.73.2) and of *culpa* (reported by Paul, *Ad Sab.* 10,
in D. 9.2.31); (b) the defining procedure that Cicero, in connection with the notion
of *gentiles*, attributed to Mucius in *Topica* 6.29; (c) the structure of the *Horoi* concerning the interpretation of wills, in D. 50.17.73.4.

13. An Aristocratic Theology

1. On the date, see T. R. S. Broughton, *The Magistrates of the Roman Republic*, 3 vols.
(New York, 1951–52), II, p. 37. Certainly no earlier than the year 95, Mucius formed
part of the collegium of the pontifices: W. Kunkel, *Herkunft und soziale Stellung der
römischen Juristen*, 2d ed. (Graz, 1967), p. 18.

2. Augustine, *De civitate Dei* 4.27: "Relatum est in litteras doctissimum pontificem
Scaevolam disputasse tria genera tradita deorum: unum a poetis, alterum a phil-

osophis, tertium a principibus civitatis. Primum genus nugatorium dicit esse, quod multa de diis fingantur indigna; secundum non congruere civitatibus, quod habeat aliqua supervacua, aliqua etiam quae obsit populis nosse. De supervacuis non magna causa est; solet enim et a iuris peritis dici: superflua non nocent. Quae sunt autem illa, quae prolata in multitudinem nocent? 'Haec,' inquit, 'non esse deos Herculem, Aesculapium, Castorem, Pollucem; proditur enim ab doctis, quod homines fuerint et humana condicione defecerint.' Quid aliud? 'Quod eo-rum qui sint dii non habeant civitates vera simulacra, quod verus Deus nec sexum habeat nec aetatem nec definita corporis membra'"; translation, with modifica-tions, from *The City of God Against the Pagans*, trans. W. M. Green, Loeb Classical Library (Cambridge, Mass., 1963). This text has never been subjected to a careful and comprehensive reading. In the meantime see G. Lepointe, *Quintus Mucius Scaevola*, I (Paris, 1926), pp. 73–82. There is no more than a reference in F. Schulz, *History of Roman Legal Science* (1946; reprint, Oxford, 1953), pp. 80 ff. The essay by G. Lieberg, "Die *theologia tripertita* in Forschung und Bezeugung," in *ANRW*, I.4, pp. 63 ff., does not provide a great deal of help, but it does feature a further bibli-ography. See also G. Calboli, "La cultura romana imperiale tra letteratura e di-ritto," in *Per la storia del pensiero giuridico romano: Dall'età dei pontefici alla scuola di Servio*, ed. D. Mantovani (Turin, 1996), II, pp. 50 ff. There is no doubt that the "pon-tifex Scaevola" indicated by Augustine is Quintus Mucius and not his father, who was, as we know, also a pontifex: B. Cardauns, *Varros Logistoricus über Göttervereh-rung* (Würzburg, 1960), p. 35. In *De civ. Dei* 3.28, Augustine also mentions Quintus Mucius' tragic death in the temple of Vesta, "aram ipsam amplexus."

3. H. Hagendahl, *Augustine and the Latin Classics*, I: *Testimonia* (in collaboration with B. Cardauns), II: *Augustine's Attitudes* (New York, 1967), esp. II, pp. 602 ff.; T. Or-landi, "Sallustio e Varrone in Agostino, '*De civitate Dei*' I–VIII," *La parola del pas-sato*, 23 (1968), pp. 19 ff., esp. 34 ff. These are problems that were already well known to the historiography and the philology of the nineteenth century: H. Schwarz, "De M. Terentii Varronis apud sanctos patres vestigiis capita duo: Ac-cedit Varronis 'antiquitatum rerum divinarum' liber XVI," *Jahrbücher für classische Philologie*, suppl. 16 (1888): 405 ff., esp. 437 ff.; R. Agahd, *De Varronis "Rerum Divi-narum" libris I, XIV, XV, XVI ab Augustino in libris "De Civitate Dei" IV, VI, VII exscrip-tis. Dissertatio inauguralis* (Leipzig, 1896), reprinted, basically unmodified, in pp. 5–38 of "M. Terentii Varronis *Antiquitatum Rerum Divinarum* libri I, XIV, XV, XVI: Praemissae sunt quaestiones Varronianae," *Jahrbücher für classische Philologie*, suppl. 24 (1898): 1 ff., esp. 15 ff., 33–34; and, still earlier, L. H. Krahner, "Über das zehnte Buch der *Antiquitates rerum divinarum* des M. Terentius Varro," *Zeitschrift für die Altertumswissenschaft*, 10 (1852): nn. 49–52, cols. 385 ff., who was the first to set forth the hypothesis of the Curio, later criticized by Schwarz, "De M. Terentii Varronis apud sanctos patres," pp. 445 ff., but immediately adopted by O. Gruppe,

in *Wochenschrift für klassische Philologie*, 6 (1889): n. 19, cols. 513 ff.; and subsequently by Cardauns, *Varros Logistoricus*, pp. 12 ff. According to this reconstruction—which, however, failed to persuade Hagendahl, *Augustine and the Latin Classics*, II, p. 260—it was only in books 6 and 7 of *De civ. Dei* that Augustine directly consulted the *antiquitates*, while for book 4 we should suppose a chain of Varronian excerpta, save for the case of the citation in question, whose precision and accuracy would be explained by a reading of the Curio, with which Augustine demonstrates considerable familiarity in other passages (7.9; 7.34 and 35). As for the identification of the Mucian source, we cannot even discard the hypothesis that underlying the citation present in Varro there was no text by the pontifex at all, but instead merely a consolidated oral tradition around his theological thought. For other studies, see *Giuristi*, pp. 73 ff.

4. Dio Chrysostom 12.39–40 and 44; Plutarch, *Amatorius* 763B–C (but also D–F); Aëtius, *Placita* 1.6.9 (H. Diels, *Doxographi Graeci* [Berlin, 1929], p. 295 = *SVF*, II, pp. 299–300), probably to be linked with a doctrine of Posidonius (*SVF*, II, p. 299 n.; K. Reinhardt, *Poseidonios* [Munich, 1921], pp. 408 ff.; A. D. Nock, "Posidonius," *JRS*, 49 [1959]: 1 ff., later in *Essay on Religion and the Ancient World*, II [Oxford, 1972], pp. 853 ff.); Eusebius, *Praeparatio evangelica* 4.1.2 (but also 3.17). Important references include P. Boyancé, "Sur la théologie de Varron," *Revue des études anciennes*, 58 (1955): 57 ff. (later in *Études sur la religion romaine* [Rome, 1972], pp. 53 ff., but I shall always make reference to the journal); J. Pépin, "La 'théologie tripartite' de Varron: Essai de reconstitution et recherche des sources," *Revue des études augustiniennes*, 2 (1956): 265 ff., esp. 272 ff. (later in *Mythe et allégorie: Les origines grecques et les contestations judéo-chrétiennes* [Paris, 1958], pp. 276 ff., but I shall cite the journal). The most reliable hypothesis is that of a salvage—lexical and syntactic as well—of the original form of Mucius' discourse. In fact the entire citation of his thought is based on the use of twenty-five words, of which only two prove extraneous to late-republican Latin: *supervacuum* and *superflua*.

5. Pépin, "La 'théologie tripartite' de Varron," pp. 285–286, 288 ff.; and Boyancé, "Sur la théologie de Varron," pp. 58–59, with bibliography. An old hypothesis of A. Schmekel, *Die Philosophie der mittleren Stoa* (Berlin, 1892), p. 446, already called for a close link between the thought of Panaetius of Rhodes and the elaboration by Mucius, but the establishment of this nexus—although it is extremely important in terms of cultural genealogies—cannot overshadow the absolute originality of Mucius' thought, in the sense that I shall make clear in the text. See also M. van Straaten, *Panétius, sa vie, ses écrits, et sa doctrine* (Amsterdam, 1946), pp. 259 ff.; and J. M. Rist, *Stoic Philosophy* (Cambridge, 1969), pp. 178–179.

6. Boyancé, "Sur la théologie de Varron," pp. 58–59. On the original structure of the scheme, see also M. P. Nilsson, *Geschichte der griechischen Religion*, 2d ed., I (Munich 1961), pp. 281–282.

7. *Rhetorica ad Herennium* 2.20.31: "Duo genera sunt vitiosarum argumentationum: unum quod ab adversario reprehendi potest, id quod pertinet ad causam: alterum, quod tametsi nugatorium est, tamen non indiget reprehensionis"; translation from *Rhetorica ad Herennium*, trans. H. Caplan, Loeb Classical Library (Cambridge, Mass., 1954, reprint 1981). See G. Calboli, *Introduzione a Cornifici "Rhetorica ad Herennium"* (Bologna, 1969), pp. 241 ff.; Rist, *Stoic Philosophy*, p. 179. The last years of Mucius, those of his pontificate, overlap with the most likely dates for the publication of the *Rhetorica ad Herennium*. The connection between the pontifical experience of Mucius and his theological thought—which would allow us to refer the doctrine that we are examining to the years after 90—is less extrinsic than one might be tempted to believe at first glance: even though in fact nothing prevents us from believing that Quintus Mucius might have focused on the Roman religious tradition prior to his time as pontifex maximus, it is quite likely that only in that period did his thought on these themes attain the fullness of maturity, within a form (whether consigned to writing or handed down orally matters little) that was consolidated and widespread. These years are precisely the likely time of the composition of the *Rhetorica ad Herennium,* if we accept the traditional early dating of this work (88; 86–82: this is shared—slightly retouched by the hypothesis of a possible shift to a later date of the term *ad quem,* to around 75—by Calboli, *Introduzione a Cornifici "Rhetorica ad Herennium,"* pp. 12 ff., esp. 17, with ample critical discussion of the alternative hypotheses).

8. E. A. Havelock, *Preface to Plato* (Cambridge, Mass., 1963), pp. 3 ff.

9. Valerius Maximus 7.2.1: "Negotium populo Romano melius quam otium conmitti, non quod ignoraret quam iucundus tranquillitatis status esset, sed quod animadverteret praepotentia imperia agitatione rerum ad virtutem capessendam excitari, nimia quiete in desidiam resolvi"; translation from *Memorable Doings and Sayings: Vol. 2. C,* trans. D. R. Shackleton Bailey, Loeb Classical Library (Cambridge, Mass., 2000). See A. La Penna, *Sallustio e la "rivoluzione" romana* (Milan, 1968), p. 26; La Penna, "Aspetti e conflitti della cultura latina dai Gracchi a Silla," *Dialoghi di archeologia,* 4–5 (1970–71): 193 ff., now in *Fra teatro, poesia e politica romana* (Turin, 1979), pp. 105 ff.; and La Penna, "Potere politico ed egemonia culturale in Roma antica," now in *Aspetti del pensiero storico latino* (Turin, 1978), pp. 5 ff. The possible citation from Ennius would be from the *Iphigenia,* in a passage reported by Gellius, *Noctes Atticae* 19.10.12 (= A. Klotz, *Scaenicorum Romanorum Fragmenta,* I [Munich, 1953], p. 73, ll. 183–190): see J. M. André, *L'otium dans la vie morale et intellectuelle romaine* (Paris, 1966), pp. 17–18.

10. Pliny the Elder, *Naturalis historia* 7.43.139–140: "Q. Metellus in ea oratione, quam habuit supremis laudibus patris sui L. Metelli pontificis, bis consulis, dictatoris, magistri equitum, XV viri agris dandis, qui plurimos elephantos ex primo Punico bello duxit in triumpho, scriptum reliquit decem maximas res optimasque, in qui-

bus quaerendis sapientes aetatem exigerent, consummasse eum: voluisse enim primarium bellatorem esse, optimum oratorem, fortissimum imperatorem, auspicio suo maximas res geri, maximo honore uti, summa sapientia esse, summum senatorem haberi, pecuniam magnam bono modo invenire, multos liberos relinquere et clarissimum in civitate esse" (= E. Malcovati, *Oratorum Romanorum Fragmenta Liberae Rei Publicae*, 2 vols., 4th ed. [Turin, 1976, 1979], pp. 10–11, reading "primus" instead of "plurimos"). Translation, with modifications, from *Natural History*, trans. H. Rackham, Loeb Classical Library (Cambridge, Mass., 1942, reprint 1947), II. The text is analyzed in A. Lippold, *Consules. Untersuchungen zur Geschichte des römischen Konsulates von 264 bis 201 v. Chr.* (Bonn, 1963), pp. 75 ff., with bibliography.

11. *Storia spezzata*, pp. 95 ff. [*The End of the Past*, pp. 87 ff.]. We see once again that unmistakable aristocratic *bonum:* see above, Chapter 9, sec. 5 and note 22.

12. Gell., *Noct. Att.* 11.23: "Praeterea ex eodem libro Catonis haec etiam sparsim et intercise commeminimus: Vestiri—inquit—in foro honeste mos erat, domi quod satis erat. Equos carius quam coquos emebant. Poeticae artis honos non erat. Si quis in ea re studebat aut sese ad convivia adplicabat, grassator vocabatur" (= H. Iordan, *M. Catonis praeter librum "De re rustica" quae exstant* [1860; reprint, Stuttgart, 1967], p. 83, fr. 2); translation, with modifications, from *The Attic Nights of Aulus Gellius*, trans. J. C. Rolfe, Loeb Classical Library (Cambridge, Mass., 1927, reprint 1948), II. See André, *L'otium*, pp. 30–31; C. J. Préaux, "Caton et l' ars poetica," *Latomus*, 25 (1966): 710 ff., with bibliography. The text of Gellius in the Oxford edition edited by Marshall (vol. II, 1968), which I follow, features "crassator" instead of "grassator"; but on this point I prefer Iordan, *M. Catonis praeter librum "De re rustica,"* in agreement with Préaux, "Caton et l'ars poetica," p. 710 n. 1.

13. Gell., *Noct. Att.* 11.2.6: "Nam vita—inquit—humana prope uti ferrum est. Si exerceas, conteritur; si non exerceas, tamen robigo interficit. Item homines exercendo videmus conteri; si nihil exerceas, inertia atque torpedo plus detrimenti facit quam exercitio" (= Iordan, *M. Catonis praeter librum "De re rustica,"* p. 83, fr. 3); translation from *The Attic Nights of Aulus Gellius*, trans. J. C. Rolfe, Loeb Classical Library (Cambridge, Mass., 1927, reprint 1948), II.

14. Columella, *Res rustica* 11.1.26.

15. F. Cassola, *I gruppi politici romani nel iii secolo a.C.* (Trieste, 1962), esp. pp. 5 ff., 25 ff., 89 ff. The break in the ideal unity of the ruling group dating from the end of the third century, as a result of profound structural modifications, is documented in an exemplary manner by the disagreement over the policy of expansionism that developed from the years before the Second Punic War (consider, for instance, the clash between the Fabii and the Cornelii): see Cassola, *I gruppi politici romani,* pp. 400–401 and 424 ff.; and La Penna, *Sallustio e la "rivoluzione" romana,* pp. 235 ff., with further bibliography.

16. Plutarch, *Aemelius Paul* 28 (but see also 6.8). On relations between the Aemilii and the Scipiones from the third to the second centuries see Cassola, *I gruppi politici romani*, pp. 375 ff. See also Astin, *Scipio Aemilianus*, pp. 294 ff.

17. *Storia di Roma*, II.1, pp. 925–926 (M. Labate).

18. In *D.* 50.17.73.3: "Quae in testamento scripta sunt, ut intellegi non possint, perinde sunt, ac si scripta non essent." It is possible that the words *supervacua* and *superflua* are not Mucian: see above, note 4; and *Giuristi*, pp. 90–91.

19. On the debate between Trebatius and Labeo there is a trace in *D.* 32.30.5 (Labeo, *Post. a Iav. epit.* 2), in connection with a condition added to a legacy. The theme is taken up again by the Severan jurisprudence, with Ulpian (*Fideic.* 2, in *D.* 50.17.94: the statement in all likelihood referred in the original text to problems concerning the interpretation of fiduciary clauses), and with Paul (*Quaest.* 9, in *D.* 34.4.26.1). The passage from the *Pauli sententiae* is in 3.4a.10: "Plures quam septem ad testamentum adhibiti non nocent. Superflua enim facta prodesse iuri tantum, nocere non possunt." Even as late as the fourth century A.D. the maxim would surface again in a constitution of Arcadius and Honorius, dated 396, now in *CI*, 6.23.17 (= *Codex Theodosianus* [*Theodosiani libri XVI cum Constitutionibus Sirmondianis et Leges Novellae ad Theodosianum pertinentes*], ed. T. Mommsen and P. M. Meyer, I.1–2, II, 2d ed. [Berlin, 1954], 4.4.3pr, with some modifications). Undoubtedly, the hermeneutical canons of the *Horoi* and the *De civ. Dei* cannot be perfectly overlaid. All the same it strikes me that their composition suggests a single background. The interpretative problems of the acts *mortis causa* in any case aroused the interests of the earliest jurisprudence: see C. A. Maschi, *Studi sull'interpretazione dei legati: Verba e voluntas* (Milan, 1938), pp. 24 ff. Q. Mucius also dedicated himself to these questions in other contexts: in particular, concerning legacies, see ibid., pp. 27 ff.; A. Ormanni, *"Penus legata,"* in *Studi in onore di Emilio Betti*, IV (Milan 1962), esp. pp. 678 ff., with important observations; U. John, *Die Auslegung von Sachgesamtheiten im römischen Recht bis Labeo* (Karlsruhe, 1970), pp. 38 ff. and 97 ff.

20. Prodicus: H. Diels and W. Kranz, *Die Fragmente der Vorsokratiker*, 6th ed., II (reprint, Dublin, 1966), p. 317 (84B, fr. 5); Critias: ibid., p. 386 (88B, fr. 25).

21. μὴ[ἀπί]θανα ... φαίνεσται τὰ περὶ [τοῦ] τὰ τρέφοντα καὶ ὠφελοῦντα θεοῦς νενομισ[θα]ι καὶ τετειμῆσθ[αι] πρῶτ[ο]ν ὑπὸ [Προ]δίκου γεγραμμένα, μ[ε]τὰ δὲ ταῦτα του[ς εὑρ]όντας ἢ προφᾶσ ἢ [σ]κέπας ἢ τὰς ἄλλας τέχναζ [ὡς Δ]ήμητρα [κ]αὶ Δι[όνυσον] καὶ τού[ς] . . .: in *SVF*, I, p. 99 n. 448: see N. Festa, *I frammenti degli stoici antichi*, II (reprint, Hildesheim, 1971), p. 63.

22. Aëtius, *Placita* 1.8.1–2, in Diels, *Doxographi Graeci*, p. 307 (= *SVF*, II, p. 320 n. 1101).

23. Cicero, *De natura deorum* 1.42.118: Ferrero, *Storia del pitagorismo*, pp. 198 ff., esp. 211 ff.; Boyancé, "Sur la théologie de Varron," p. 271. It was against the Stoic thesis of the deification of heroes that Carneades, the most "scandalous" philosopher of the Athenian embassy to Rome, in 155, had leveled his polemic, to undermine the

entire Stoic theory of divinities. See also J. Scheid, *La religione a Roma* (Rome, 1983, pp. 119 ff.

24. Wissowa, *Religion und Kultus der Römer,* pp. 271 ff.; F. Altheim, *Griechische Götter im alten Rom* (Giessen, 1930), pp. 4 ff.; Bayet, *Histoire politique et psychologique;* Latte, *Römische Religionsgeschichte,* pp. 213 ff.; G. Dumézil, *La religion romaine archaïque,* 2d ed. (Paris, 1974), (*Archaic Roman Religion,* II, pp. 494 ff.); R. Palmer, "The Censors of 312 B.C. and the State Religion," *Historia,* 14 (1965): 293 ff.

25. Wissowa, *Religion und Kultus der Römer,* pp. 306 ff.; Bayet, *Histoire politique et psychologique;* Latte, *Römische Religionsgeschichte,* p. 173; Dumézil, *La religion romaine archaïque,* (*Archaic Roman Religion,* II, pp. 449–450).

26. Wissowa, *Religion und Kultus der Römer,* pp. 268 ff.; Bayet, *Histoire politique et psychologique;* Latte, *Römische Religionsgeschichte,* p. 173; Dumézil, *La religion romaine archaïque* (*Archaic Roman Religion,* II, pp. 484 ff.); R. Bloch, "L'origine du culte des Dioscures à Rome," *Revue de philologie, de littérature et d'histoire anciennes,* 34 (1960): 182 ff.; J. North, in *Storia di Roma,* II.1, p. 559.

27. In Cic., *De nat. deor.* 2.24.62: "Suscepit autem vita hominum consuetudoque communis ut beneficiis excellentis viros in caelum fama ac voluntate tollerent. Hinc Hercules hinc Castor et Pollux hinc Aesculapius." But it is in this direction that we should consider at least two other passages from book 3: 3.5.11 and 3.15.39.

28. Cicero, *De nat. deor.* 2.8.19: "Divos et eos, qui caelestes semper habiti, colunto et ollos, quos endo caelo merita locaverint, Herculem, Liberum, Aesculapium, Castorem, Pollucem, Quirinum"; translation from *Laws,* trans. C. W. Keyes, Loeb Classical Library (1928; reprint, Cambridge, Mass., 1970).

29. *Storia di Roma,* II.1, pp. 694–695 (E. Gabba).

30. P. Fraccaro, "I processi degli Scipioni," in *Opuscula* (Pavia, 1956), I, pp. 263 ff.; and R. A. Bauman, *Lawyers in Roman Republican Politics: A Study of the Roman Jurists in Their Political Setting, 316–382 B.C.* (Munich, 1983), pp. 192 ff. My interpretation accepts the traditional version, set forth with great insight by Cassola, *I gruppi politici romani,* p. 349, against certain critics (including H. H. Scullard, *Roman Politics, 220–150 B.C.,* 2d ed. [Oxford, 1973], pp. 110 ff.; and Kienast, *Cato der Zensor,* pp. 88 ff.), of a Cato who is a relatively consistent defender of the small landowners against the new oligarchy. In this line, it is perhaps not without significance that he should say nothing about the names of the characters in the *origines,* and especially those most closely linked, as if to quench the pride of the *duces* with respect to the collective effort of the *civitas:* Cornelius Nepos, *Cato* 3.4; and Pliny, *Nat. hist.* 8.5.11, concerning which Cassola, *I gruppi politici romani,* p. 354 (but the entire app. IX, dedicated to Cato, on pp. 347–355, should be read with attention). And in this context—in contrast with the Catonian orientation—it is also worth noting the establishment, in the last decades of the second century, of forms of "charismatic" autobiography: see A. La Penna, "Il ritratto 'paradossale' da Silla a Petronio," *Rivista*

di filologia e d'istruzione classica, 104 (1976), now in *Aspetti del pensiero storico latino,* pp. 209–210.

31. Q. Petilius was an urban praetor in 181 B.C., and a consul in 176: see Broughton, *The Magistrates,* I, pp. 384 and 400. We cannot be certain, however, of his identification with one of the two Petilii who accused P. Scipio, in the account in Livy 38.50 (we should also take into account Cassius Hemina's version of this episode, in Pliny, *Nat. hist.* 13.13.84–86 = fr. 37 Peter); but certainly, if not one of the two, he must have been a member of the same family, and therefore close to the positions of Cato: de Sanctis, *Storia dei Romani,* IV.1, pp. 577–578 n. 270; della Corte, *Catone Censore,* p. 182; Boyancé, "Sur la théologie de Varron," p. 62 and n. 3. On the discovery of the books of the Pseudo-Numa, see Ferrero, *Storia del pitagorismo,* pp. 231 ff.; Bayet, *Histoire politique et psychologique;* Dumézil, *La religion romaine archaïque,* (*Archaic Roman Religion,* II, pp. 460 ff.)

32. Livy 40.29.11–12. The reconstruction is by A. Delatte, "Les doctrines pythagoriciennes des livres de Numa," *Bulletin de l'Académie royale des sciences et belles-lettres de Bruxelles,* 22 (1936): 19 ff., esp. 29 ff.

33. Zeno: *SVF,* I, pp. 41 ff. nn. 152–177 and 61 n. 264 (a very radical criticism of the value of temples). Chrysippus: *SVF,* II, pp. 315–316 nn. 1076–77, on which see E. Brehier, *Chrysippe et l'ancien Stoicisme,* 2d ed. (Paris, 1971), pp. 198–199. See also Rist, *Stoic Philosophy,* pp. 178 ff. On Posidonius, also ibid., pp. 201 ff., with sources and bibliography; also M. Laffranque, *Poseidonios d'Apamée* (Paris, 1964); E. V. Arnold, *Roman Stoicism* (reprint, Freeport, N.Y., 1971), pp. 216 ff.; A. Grilli, "Lo Stoicismo antico: Zenone, Cleante, Crisippo," in *La filosofia ellenistica e la patristica cristiana: Dal 3. sec. a.C. al 5. sec. d.C.* (Milan, 1975), pp. 63 ff.

34. Delatte, "Les doctrines pythagoriciennes," pp. 34 ff.

35. Also in *De civ. Dei* 4.27: "Haec [the two Stoic theories] pontifex nosse populos non vult; nam falsa esse non putat."

36. Cassola, *I gruppi politici romani,* pp. 92 ff., 121 ff., 161 ff.; M. Dondin-Payre, "'Homo novus': Un slogan de Caton à Cesar?" *Historia,* 30 (1981): 22–23.

37. T. P. Wiseman, *New Men in the Roman Senate, 139 B.C.–14 A.D.* (London 1971), pp. 3 ff. See Cicero, *Orationes Philippicae* 9.2.4; and Velleius Paterculus 1.13.2. Also C. Nicolet, "Economie, société et institutions au ii siècle av. J. C.: De la lex Claudia à l'ager exceptus," *Annales: Economies, sociétés, civilisations,* 35 (1980): 871 ff.; *Storia spezzata,* pp. 77–78 [*The End of the Past,* pp. 70–71].

38. P. A. Brunt, *Italian Manpower, 225 B.C.–A.D. 14* (Oxford, 1971), pp. 61 ff., esp. 72, 269 ff.; F. de Martino, *Storia economica di Roma antica,* I (Florence, 1979), pp. 59 ff.; W. V. Harris, *War and Imperialism in Republican Rome* (reprint, Oxford, 1992), pp. 54 ff.; and the contributions to vols. II and III of *Società romana e produzione schiavistica,* ed. A. Schiavone (Rome, 1981); *Storia spezzata,* pp. 69 ff., 77 ff., 183 ff. [*The End of the Past,* pp. 63 ff., 70 ff., 175 ff.].

39. Ennius, *Annales* (ed. Vahlen, 2d ed. [reprint, 1963], p. 91, l. 500; and ibid., n. 37, information on the tradition of the text): P. Wülfing-von Martitz, "Ennius als hellenistischer Dichter," in *Ennius*, p. 281; and La Penna, *Sallustio e la "rivoluzione" romana*, p. 51.

40. Ibid., pp. 129 ff. and 189.

41. For that matter, the idea of the preservation of and the return to an older religion goes well beyond Q. Mucius: it was shared by Scipio Aemilianus and influential members of his "circle": E. Rawson, "Scipio, Laelius, Furius and the Ancestral Religion," *JRS*, 63 (1973): 161 ff., esp. 162 (where, in n. 8, there is a reference to Q. Mucius). That this aspiration to a return to some of the more archaic features of Roman religiosity might have had a political significance was clear within the context of those same cultural milieux, once again well beyond Q. Mucius.

42. Aug., *De civ. Dei* 6.5: "Deinde illud quale est, quod tria genera theologiae [Varro] dicit esse, id est rationis quae de diis explicatur, eorumque unum mythicon appellari, alterum physicon, tertium civile? . . . Deinde ait: 'mythicon appellant, quo maxime utuntur poetae; physicon, quo philosophi, civile, quo populi'"; translation, with modifications, from *The City of God Against the Pagans*, trans. W. M. Green, Loeb Classical Library (Cambridge, Mass., 1963). The text of Tertullian is in *Ad nationes* 2.8.11.

43. *De civ. Dei* 6.6: "Denique cum memoratus auctor civilem theologian a fabulosa et naturali tertiam quandam sui genera distinguere conaretur, magis eam ex utraque temperatam quam ab utraque separatam intellegi voluit. Ait enim ea, quae scribunt poetae, minus esse quam ut populi sequi debeant; quae autem philosophi, plus quam ut ea vulgum scrutari expediat"; translation, with modifications, from *The City of God Against the Pagans*, trans. W. M. Green, Loeb Classical Library (Cambridge, Mass., 1963).

44. Boyancé, "Sur la théologie de Varron," pp. 63 ff.; also Bauman, *Lawyers in Roman Republican Politics*, pp. 351 ff.

14. A Separate Reason

1. *Pal.*, II, cols. 321–334. We should also take into account the reports that can be derived from Pomponius' *Enchiridion*, in *D.* 1.2.2.42–44.

2. Gaius, *Institutiones* 1.88; 2.244; 3.149; 3.156; 3.183. Aulus Gellius, *Noctes Atticae* 4.1.17–20; 4.2.12; 4.3.2; 4.4.13; 7.12.1–3. Festus, pp. 174, 182, 210, 233, 321, 322, 376 (Lindsay). Quintilian, *Institutio oratoria* 10.1.22; 10.1.116; 10.7.30; 12.7.4; 12.10.11 (though these have more to do with Servius as orator than as jurist). For Cicero fundamental works are *Brutus* 41.151–42.155, and the entire *Orationes Philippicae* 9, to which we shall return. The dossier also includes a major collection of correspondence: two letters from Servius to Cicero (preserved in *Ad familiares* 4.5 and 4.12; see Chapter

15, sec. 1 and 2), and some from Cicero to the jurist (*Ad fam.* 4.1–4; 4.6). There are also references to Servius in Ciceronian letters not addressed to him, e.g., *Ad fam.* 10.28.3; 12.5.3; and 6.4.5.

3. *Pal.*, I, cols. 38–53.

4. F. Schulz, *History of Roman Legal Science* (1946; reprint, Oxford, 1953), pp. 205 ff. Further bibliography in E. Stolfi, *"Bonae fidei interpretatio": Ricerche sull'interpretazione di buona fede fra esperienza romana e tradizione romanistica* (Naples, 2004), p. 124 n. 7. See also C. Giachi, *Studi su Sesto Pedio: La tradizione, l'editto* (Milan, 2005), pp. 314–315.

5. C. Ferrini, "Intorno ai *Digesta* di Alfeno Varo," now in *Opere*, II (Milan, 1929), pp. 169 ff.; L. de Sarlo, *Alfeno Varo e i suoi "digesta"* (Milan, 1940), pp. 1 ff.; H.-J. Roth, *Alfeni Digesta. Eine spätrepublikanische Juristenschrift* (Berlin, 1999), pp. 1 ff. The Byzantine compilers utilized two different textual traditions to work back to the text of Alphenus Varus, which they may not have possessed in its original form: the first, which might seem direct but is not (*Pal.*, I, col. 37 n. 1; Schulz, *History of Roman Legal Science*, pp. 205 ff., esp. 206), consists of an anonymous summary of the original work. The order of exposition is that of the edict: but it is a model of the publisher. The second consists of an epitome by Paul, recorded by Justinian's compilers with two different inscriptions: up to D. 19.1, as *Paul libro . . . epitomarum Alfeni digestorum*, and then as *Alfenus libro . . . digestorum a Paulo epitomatorum*. Here the order followed is that of Alphenus (a sequence for which it is difficult to determine a criterion), and the problem arises of how to distinguish the presence of possible Pauline notes.

6. Pomp., *Ench.*, in *D.* 1.2.2.

7. F. Casavola, *Giuristi adrianei* (Naples, 1980), pp. 135 ff.; R. A. Bauman, *Lawyers in Roman Transitional Politics: A Study of the Roman Jurists in Their Political Setting in the Late Republic and Triumvirate* (Munich, 1985), pp. 66 ff. On the years spent in Cercina (an island of Syrtis Minor) there is a note by Pomponius (see *D.* 1.2.2.43); but it is not untainted by doubt: M. Bretone, *Tecniche e ideologie dei giuristi romani*, 2d ed. (Naples, 1982), p. 83 n. 62; Bauman, *Lawyers in Roman Transitional Politics*, p. 44.

8. Friedrich Karl von Savigny, *Vom Beruf unserer Zeit für Gesetzgebung und Rechtswissenschaft* (Heidelberg, 1814), 3d ed. (1840; reprint, Hildesheim, 1967), pp. 30–31, 126 ff.

9. *Pal.*, I, Alphenus 7 (= *D.* 9.2.52.3), 11 (= *D.* 15.3.16), 12 (= *D.* 18.6.12), 13 (= *D.* 19.1.26), 14 (= *D.* 44.1.14), 15 (= *D.* 19.2.27), 24 (= *D.* 6.1.57), 27 (= *D.* 19.2.29), 28 (= *D.* 39.4.15), 29 (= *D.* 50.16.203), 32 (= *D.* 41.3.34), 43 (= *D.* 8.3.29), 47 (= *D.* 46.3.35), 48 (= *D.* 5.4.9), 50 (= *D.* 10.3.27), 51 (= *D.* 17.2.71), 52 (= *D.* 18.6.15), 53 (= *D.* 19.1.27), 54 (= *D.* 19.2.30), 61 (= *D.* 8.3.30), 62 (= *D.* 18.1.40 and 50.16.205), 63 (*D.* 21.2.45), 71 (= *D.* 19.2.31). This is roughly 30 percent of all the Alphenian texts.

10. See Chapter 10, sec. 2.

11. The quaestorship of Servius is described as "negotiosa" by Cicero, *Pro Murena* 8.18: T. R. S. Broughton, *The Magistrates of the Roman Republic*, 3 vols. (New York, 1951–52), II, pp. 103, 109.

12. *Storia spezzata*, p. 104, with bibliography (pp. 239–240) [*The End of the Past*, p. 96, with bibliography (p. 240)].

13. See above, Chapter 11, sec. 1 and note 1.

14. *Storia spezzata*, pp. 69 ff., 77 ff., 95 ff. [*The End of the Past*, pp. 63 ff., 70 ff., 87 ff.].

15. Alphenus, *Dig. a Paulo epit.* 5, in *D.* 19.2.31: "In navem Saufeii cum complures frumentum confuderant, Saufeius uni ex his frumentum reddiderat de communi et navis perierat: quaesitum est, an ceteri pro sua parte frumenti cum nauta agere possunt oneris aversi actione. Respondit rerum locatarum duo genera esse, ut aut idem redderetur (sicuti cum vestimenta fulloni curanda locarentur) aut eiusdem generis redderetur (veluti cum argentum pusulatum fabro daretur, ut vasa fierent, aut aurum, ut anuli): ex superiore causa rem domini manere, ex posteriore in creditum iri. Idem iuris esse in deposito: nam si quis pecuniam numeratam ita deposuisset, ut neque clusam neque obsignatam traderet, sed adnumeraret, nihil aliud eum debere apud quem deposita esset, nisi tantundem pecuniae solveret. Secundum quae videri triticum factum Saufeii et recte datum. Quod si separatim tabulis aut heronibus aut in alia cupa clusum uniuscuiusque triticum fuisset, ita ut internosci posset quid cuiusque esset, non potuisse nos permutationem facere, sed tum posse eum cuius fuisset triticum quod nauta solvisset vindicare. Et ideo se improbare actiones oneris aversi: quia sive eius generis essent merces, quae nautae traderentur, ut continuo eius fierent et mercator in creditum iret, non videretur onus esse aversum, quippe quod nautae fuisset: sive eadem res, quae tradita esset, reddi deberet, furti esse actionem locatori et ideo supervacuum esse iudicium oneris aversi. Sed si ita datum esset, ut in simili re solvi possit, conductorem culpam dumtaxat debere (nam in re, quae utriusque causa contraheretur, culpam deberi) neque omnimodo culpam esse, quod uni reddidisset ex frumento, quoniam alicui primum reddere eum necesse fuisset, tametsi meliorem eius condicionem faceret quam ceterorum." See Roth, *Alfeni Digesta*, pp. 134 ff., where there is a bibliography.

16. G. de Santillana and H. von Dechend, *Die Mühle des Hamlet. Ein Essay über Mythos und des Gerüst der Zeit*, 2d ed. (Vienna, 1994), p. 304 (the original edition, G. de Santillana, *Hamlet's Mill: An Essay on Myth and the Frame of Time*, without the concluding observations by Dechend, which were added for the German edition, was published in Boston, 1969). See Chapter 21, note 12.

17. Plato, *Timaeus* 48a: μεμειγμένη γὰρ οὖν ἡ τοῦδε τοῦ κόσμου γένεσις ἐξ ἀνάγκης τε καὶ νοῦ συστάσεως ἐγεννήθη νοῦ δὲ ἀνάγκης ἄρχοντος τῷ πείθεν αὐτὴν τῶν γιγνομένων τὰ πλεῖστα ἐπὶ τὸ βέλτιστον ἄγειν, ταύτῃ

κατὰ ταῦτά τε δι᾽ ἀνάγκης ἡττωμένης ὑπὸ πειθοῦς ἔμφρονος οὕτω κατ᾽
ἀρχὰς συνίστατο τόδε τὸ πᾶν.

18. Alphenus, *Dig.* 2, in *D.* 9.2.52.2: "In clivo Capitolino duo plostra onusta mulae
ducebant: prioris plostri muliones conversum plostrum sublevabant, quo facil[e]
[ius] mulae ducerent: [inter] superius plostrum cessim ire coepit et cum muliones,
qui inter duo plostra fuerunt, e medio exissent, posterius plostrum a priore percussum retro redierat et puerum cuiusdam obtriverat: dominus pueri consulebat,
cum quo se agere oporteret. Respondi in causa ius esse positum: nam si muliones,
qui superius plostrum sustinuissent, sua sponte se subduxissent et ideo factum esset, ut mulae plostrum retinere non possint atque onere ipso retraherentur, cum
domino mularum nullam esse actionem, cum hominibus qui conversum plostrum
sustinuissent lege Aquilia agi posse: nam nihilo minus eum damnum dare, qui
quod sustineret mitteret sua voluntate, ut id aliquem feriret: veluti si quis asellum
cum agitasset non retinuisset, aeque si quis ex manu telum aut aliud quid immisis-
set, damnum iniuria daret. Sed si mulae, quia aliquid reformidassent, [recessissent]
et muliones timore permoti, ne opprimerentur, plostrum reliquissent, cum hominibus actionem nullam esse, cum domino mularum esse. Quod si neque mulae
neque homines in causa essent, sed mulae retinere onus nequissent aut cum coni-
terentur lapsae concidissent et ideo plostrum cessim redisset atque hi quo conversum fuisset onus sustinere nequissent, neque cum domino mularum neque cum
hominibus esse actionem. Illud quidam certe, quoquo modo res se haberet, cum
domino posteriorum mularum agi non posse, quoniam non sua sponte, sed per-
cussae retro redissent."

19. "Da mihi factum, dabo tibi ius."

20. *Leges publicae*, pp. 241–242 = *Roman Statutes*, pp. 723 ff.

21. Ulpian, *Ad ed.* 11, in *D.* 4.3.1.2; and Paul, *Ad ed.* 38, in *D.* 26.1.1pr.

22. *Pal.*, I, Alphenus 7 (= *D.* 9.2.52pr), 8 (= *D.* 10.3.26), 9 (= *D.* 44.7.20), 10 (= *D.* 11.3.16),
11 (= *D.* 15.3.16), 12 (= *D.* 18.6.12), 14 (= *D.* 44.1.14), 17 (= *D.* 40.1.6), 18 (= *D.* 40.7.14),
20 (= *D.* 33.8.14), 25 (= *D.* 40.1.7), 29 (= *D.* 50.16.203), 32 (= *D.* 41.3.34), 36 (= *D.*
35.1.28), 38 (= *D.* 50.16.204), 39 (= *D.* 32.60), 44 (= *D.* 33.7.16), 46 (= *D.* 33.8.15), 47 (=
D. 46.3.35), 49 (= *D.* 6.1.58), 50 (= *D.* 10.3.27), 54 (= *D.* 19.2.30.4), 59 (= *D.* 24.1.38), 62
(= *D.* 18.1.40.5), 69 (= *D.* 12.6.36), 73 (= *D.* 32.61): of course this series of texts
matches in many points that cited in note 9.

23. See Chapter 22, sec. 2; and *Storia spezzata*, pp. 142 ff., 173 ff. [*The End of the Past*, pp.
133 ff., 165 ff.].

24. *Storia spezzata*, p. 121 [*The End of the Past*, p. 112].

25. Ibid., pp. 194 ff. [p. 186 ff.].

26. *Storia spezzata*, p. 195 (and bibliography, p. 257) [*The End of the Past*, p. 187 (and bibliography, p. 263)].

27. Alphenus, *Dig.* 2, in *D.* 15.3.16: "Quidam fundum colendum servo suo locavit et

boves ei dederat: cum hi boves non essent idonei, iusserat eos venire et his num-
mis qui recepti essent alios reparari: servus boves vendiderat, alios redemerat,
nummos venditori non solverat, postea conturbaverat: qui boves vendiderat nummos a domino petebat actione de peculio aut quod in rem domini versum esset,
cum boves pro quibus pecunia peteretur penes dominum essent. Respondit non
videri peculii quicquam esse, nisi si quid deducto eo, quod servus domino debuisset, reliquum fieret: illud sibi videri boves quidem in rem domini versos esse, sed
pro ea re solvisse tantum, quanti priores boves venissent: si quo amplioris pecuniae posteriores boves essent, eius oportere dominum condemnari." See Roth,
Alfeni Digesta, pp. 66 ff., where there is a bibliography.

28. I employ the approach of K. Marx, *Das Kapital. Kritik der politischen Ökonomie,* III,
in K. Marx and F. Engels, *Werke,* XXV (Berlin, 1975), pp. 336 ff., upon which I overlay the formula of H. Sumner Maine "From Status to Contract," in *Ancient Law*
(1864; reprint, Tucson, 1986), p. 165.

29. Papinian, *Quaest.* 17, in *D.* 33.2.2: "Hominis operae legatae capitis deminutione vel
non utendo non amittuntur. Et quoniam ex operis mercedem percipere legatarius
potest, etiam operas eius ipse locare poterit, quas si prohibeat heres capi, tene-
bitur. Idem est si servus se locaverit."

30. Ulpian, in *D.* 9.3.5.12.

31. No later than the end of the second century B.C. or perhaps the turn of the first
century B.C. are the edicts *De exercitoria actione, De institoria actione, De peculio et de
in rem verso*—reported by Servius–Alphenus Varus in the text that we are analyzing—and *De tributaria actione,* all of which we can reconstruct indirectly through
the jurisprudential accounts of Julian's version of the edict—*EP,* pp. 257 ff.—in
which we find a delineation of the core of the legal discipline of the commercial
acivities run *per servos:* still a classic is W. W. Buckland, *The Roman Law of Slavery*
(1908; reprint, Cambridge, 1970).

32. *Peculium* is already a Plautine word: *Mostellaria* 253; *Asinaria* 541; *Rudens* 112; *Persa*
192; *Trinummus* 434: O. Karlowa, *Römische Rechtsgeschichte,* II (Leipzig, 1901), p. 113.

33. Ulpian, in *D.* 15.1.9.2: "Peculium autem deducto quod domino debetur com-
putandum esse."

34. *D.* 15.1.9.3: "Huic definitioni Servius adiecit et si quid his debeatur qui sunt in eius
potestate, quoniam hoc quoque domino deberi nemo ambigit."

35. *D.* 15.3.16: "Respondit non videri peculii quicquam esse, nisi si quid deducto eo,
quod servus domino debuisset, reliquum fieret."

36. Celsus mentions Tubero on other occasions in his *Digesta: D.* 32.43; 33.10.7.1–2;
45.1.72pr. Tubero began to work after 46 B.C.: the year is found in Pomp., *Ench.,* in
D. 1.2.2.46 (see also Quint., *Inst. or.* 5.13.20; 5.13.31; 10.1.23). For that matter, Celsus
himself, again in the sixth book of his *Digesta,* referring once again to the definition of Tubero (this time we have the text directly in Justinian's compilation, in *D.*

15.1.6, and do not need to rely upon the mediation of Ulpian), writes of a "definitio peculii quam Tubero exposuit," without therefore explicitly attributing the definition to him: as an expert of the republican authors (citations of republican jurists by Celsus can be found in Bretone, *Tecniche e ideologie dei giuristi romani*, p. 197 n. 10) he must have been well aware that the definition was not Tubero's, but Servius'.

37. Alphenus Varus, in *D.* 40.1.6 (see also Chapter 17, sec. 3 and note 40). We should also keep in mind an opinion of Servius' reported by Ulpian again in *Ad edictum* 29, in *D.* 15.1.17: A. Watson, *The Law of Obligations in the Later Roman Republic* (Oxford, 1965), p. 189; Horak, *Rationes*, pp. 144–145. See lastly the citation by Ulpian, *Ad Sab.* 27, in *D.* 40.7.3.2, while we ought to be more prudent in attributing to Servius two other texts that might concern our reconstruction, both from the Pauline epitome of Alphenus Varus, now in *D.* 46.3.35 and 41.3.34 (concerning the latter, it seems particularly difficult to choose between Servius, Alphenus Varus, or Paul himself: Bretone, *Tecniche e ideologie dei giuristi romani*, p. 95).

38. Javolenus Priscus, *Ex post. Lab.* 2, in *D.* 35.1.40.3: "Dominus servo aureos quinque eius legaverat: 'heres meus Sticho servo meo, quem testamento liberum esse iussi, aureos quinque, quos in tabulis debeo, dato.' Nihil servo legatum esse Namusa Servium respondisset scribit, quia dominus servo nihil debere potuisset." But Javolenus Priscus corrects Servius and adds: "ego puto secundum mentem testatoris naturale magis quam civile debitum spectandum esse, et eo iure utimur."

39. *Storia spezzata*, pp. 186 ff. [*The End of the Past*, p. 179 ff.].

40. Ibid., pp. 42–43 and 124–125 [*The End of the Past*, pp. 38–39 and 115–116].

41. Athenaeus 6.84.263c–d = *FgrHist*, 87, fr. 8 = Edelstein-Kidd, fr. 60; Diodorus Siculus 34–35.2.20, repeated in Athen. 12.59.542b = *FgrHist*, 87, fr. 7 = Edelstein-Kidd, fr. 59; Diod. Sic. 34–35.25.1 (also attributable to Posidonius); Athen. 6.91.266e–f = *FgrHist*, 87, fr. 38 = Edelstein-Kidd, fr. 51: K. Reinhardt, *Poseidonios* (Munich, 1921), pp. 19 ff., 31 ff.; and *Storia spezzata*, pp. 133 ff. [*The End of the Past*, pp. 124 ff.].

42. See Chapter 22, sec. 2.

43. See Chapter 18, sec. 2.

44. *Storia spezzata*, pp. 197–198 [*The End of the Past*, p. 190].

45. Pomponius, *Ad Q. Mucium* 9, in *D.* 34.2.34pr: "Scribit Quintus Mucius: si aurum suum omne pater familias uxori suae legasset, id aurum, quod aurifici faciundum dedisset aut quod ei deberetur, si ab aurifice ei repensum non esset, mulieri non debetur." See Amirante, "Ricerche in tema di locazione," *BIDR*, 62 (1959): 65 ff.

46. Ibid., pp. 65 ff.

47. Labeo's definition is reported by Paul, in *D.* 50.16.5.1.

48. Gaius, *Inst.* 3.149; Paul, *Ad Sab.* 6, in *D.* 17.2.30. See also Alphenus-Paul, in *D.* 17.2.71.

49. Gaius, *Inst.* 3.149: "Ut aequum sit" that "nihil omnino damni praestet, sed lucri partem capiat."

50. Gaius, *Inst.* 3.149: "Si modo opera eius tam pretiosa videatur."

51. Gaius, *Inst.* 3.149: "Saepe enim opera alicuius pro pecunia valet."

52. Gell., *Noct. Att.* 4.1.20.

53. *Pal.,* II, col. 323; Bremer, I, pp. 220 ff. Even if the structure of the model of late-republican "quaestorian partnership" (which Mucius and Servius debated) is certainly quite distant from the profile that it would later take on for the Severian jurisprudence, in the interpretation of Servius it already had an accentuated "mercantile" physiognomy.

54. This is supposed by Bremer, I, pp. 228–230. A more cautious approach is adopted by O. Lenel, in *Pal.,* II, cols. 325 n. 1 and 333 n. 1.

55. See Festus, pp. 180, 232, 426, 430, 516 (Lindsay). Also Ulpian, *Ad ed.* 18, in *D.* 9.1.1.4; and Gaius, *Ad l. XII tab.* 5, in *D.* 50.16.237.

56. Festus, pp. 180, 232, 426, 430, 516 (Lindsay): *Pal.,* II, col. 334.

57. The episode is in Gell., *Noct. Att.* 2.10.1–2: Bremer, I, p. 140; Schulz, *History of Roman Legal Science,* p. 93.

58. For example, a singular interpretation of the word *testamentum,* the sole relic of one of his works, *De sacris detestandis:* see the texts cited in note 55 above.

59. Gell., *Noct. Att.* 4.3.2 and 4.4.1–2; and Neratius, *Membranae* 2, in *D.* 12.4.8: Bremer, I, pp. 226–228; *Pal.,* II, cols. 321–322.

60. Gell., *Noct. Att.* 4.4.1–2: "in ea parte Italiae quae Latium appellatur: 'Qui uxorem—inquit—ducturus erat, ab eo, unde ducenda erat, stipulabatur eam in matrimonium datum iri; qui ducturus erat, ibidem spondebat. Is contractus stipulationum sponsionumque dicebatur sponsalia'"; translation from *The Attic Nights of Aulus Gellius,* 2 vols., trans. J. C. Rolfe (Cambridge, Mass., 1927, reprint 1948), I. An integration, by now considered a classic, by T. Mommsen, *Ad capita duo Gelliana,* now in *Gesammelte Schriften,* II (Berlin, 1905), pp. 87 ff. (accepted by Bremer, I, p. 226; and by O. Lenel, in *Pal.,* II, col. 322 n. 1), does not concern the point that we are examining here. Only three fragments of *De dotibus* can be reconstructed: *Pal.,* II, cols. 321–322. Aside from the citation of Neratius, it may be possible to track down an echo of the Servian text in Ulpian, *Lib. sing. de sponsalibus,* in *D.* 23.1.2, where the choice is in favor of the authenticity of the monograph: T. Honoré, *Ulpian,* 2d ed. (Oxford, 2002), pp. 122 ff.

61. Terence: *Hecyra* 633; Cicero, e.g.: *De oratore* 3.60.224; *De legibus* 3.14.31.

62. *Origini,* pp. 27 ff.

63. Gellius' account, in *Noct. Att.* 4.1.17, should be integrated with a citation by Ulpian of *Ad Sab.* 22, in *D.* 33.9.3pr.

64. Servius' thought has been handed down to us in a complex assemblage, along

with opinions by Tubero and Labeo, by Celsus, in book 19 of his *Digesta*, now in D. 33.10.7. But we also possess another text by Servius on the theme, transcribed in the third book (but it is probably an error, and it is really the second book: *Pal.*, I, col. 49 n. 3) of the Pauline epitome of Alphenus Varus, now in D. 33.10.6pr.

65. Casavola, *Giuristi adrianei* (Naples, 1980), pp. 116 ff., esp. 120.

66. Ulpian, *Ad ed.* 42, in *D.* 38.2.1.1–2: "Hoc edictum a praetore propositum est honoris, quem liberti patronis habere debent, moderandi gratia. Namque ut Servius scribit, antea soliti fuerunt a libertis durissimas res exigere, scilicet ad remunerandum tam grande beneficium, quod in libertos confertur, cum ex servitute ad civitatem Romanam perducuntur. Et quidem primus praetor Rutilius edixit se amplius non daturum patrono quam operarum et societatis actionem, videlicet si hoc pepigisset, ut, nisi ei obsequium praestaret libertus, in societatem admitteretur patronus. Posteriores praetores certae partis bonorum possessionem pollicebantur: videlicet enim imago societatis induxit eiusdem partis praestationem, ut, quod vivus solebat societatis nomine prestare, id post mortem praestaret." See A. Watson, *Law Making*, pp. 55–56.

67. As we learn from a citation of Venuleius (*Stip.* 15), in *D.* 46.8.8.2. See also Chapter 17, sec. 1.

68. See Chapter 10, sec. 3. The praetor Rutilius should in fact be identified as P. Rutilius Rufus, praetor probably in 118 B.C., consul in 105: Bremer, I, pp. 43–45; *Pal.*, II, col. 185 n. 1.

69. Here lies the source of the profound connection between jurisprudence and theology, which developed for at least four centuries of European thought, from the Middle Ages into the early modern period: a shared combination of case-based analysis and ontology, rendered uniform by Aristotelianism: M. Grabmann, "Forschungen überdie lateinischen Aristoteles-Übersetzungen des 13. Jahrhunderts," in *Beiträge zur Geschichteder Philosophie des Mittelalters*, XVII (Münster, 1916); F. Pelster, "Neuere Forschungen über die Aristoteles-Übersetzungen des 12. und 13. Jahrhunderts," *Gregorianum*, 30 (1949): 46 ff.

70. Alphenus Varus, *Dig.* 6, in *D.* 5.1.76: "Proponebatur ex his iudicibus, qui in eandem rem dati essent, nonnullos causa audita excusatos esse inque eorum locum alios esse sumptos, et quaerebatur, singulorum iudicum mutatio eandem rem an aliud iudicium fecisset. Respondi, non modo si unus aut alter, sed et si omnes iudices mutati essent, tamen et rem eandem et iudicium idem quod antea fuisset permanere: neque in hoc solum evenire, ut partibus commutatis eadem res esse existimaretur, sed et in multis ceteris rebus: nam et legionem eandem haberi, ex qua multi decessissent, quorum in locum alii subiecti essent: et populum eundem hoc tempore putari qui abhinc centum annis fuissent, cum ex illis nemo nunc viveret: itemque navem, si adeo saepe refecta esset, ut nulla tabula eadem permaneret quae non nova fuisset, nihilo minus eandem navem esse existimari. Quod si quis

putaret partibus commutatis aliam rem fieri, fore ut ex eius ratione nos ipsi non idem essemus qui abhinc anno fuissemus, propterea quod, ut philosophi dicerent, ex quibus particulis minimis consisteremus, hae cottidie ex nostro corpore decederent aliaeque extrinsecus in earum locum accederent. Quapropter cuius rei species eadem consisteret, rem quoque eandem esse existimari."

71. Schulz, *History of Roman Legal Science,* pp. 84–85, 206 n. 4.

72. See Chapter 15, sec. 1.

73. We find it in Cic., *Ad fam.* 4.5.1 and 2 (see Chapter 15, sec. 1); then also in other texts by Alphenus Varus, both in the anonymous epitome and in the Pauline epitome: *D.* 50.16.203; 32.60.2. And lastly it is a verb used to report Servian doctrines by Gaius (*Inst.* 3.149), by Celsus (*D.* 33.10.7.2), and by Ulpian (*D.* 43.17.3.11).

74. Alphenus, in *D.* 21.2.44 (text of the Pauline epitome). The idea of the "all" also returns in a Servian citation by Paul: *D.* 41.1.26pr.

75. Paul, *Epit. Alf.* 4, in *D.* 10.4.19: "Ad exhibendum possunt agere omnes quorum interest. Sed quidam consuluit, an possit efficere haec actio, ut rationes adversarii sibi exhiberentur, quas exhiberi magni eius interesset. Respondit non oportere ius civile calumniari neque verba captari, sed qua mente quid diceretur, animadvertere convenire. Nam illa ratione etiam studiosum alicuius doctrinae posse dicere sua interesse illos aut illos libros sibi exhiberi, quia, si essent exhibiti, cum eos legisset, doctior et melior futurus esset." The organization of the discourse ("consuluit," "respondit") is similar to that of the texts from the more faithful anonymous epitome. Here it seems that the comment must have recovered Alphenus' text, though perhaps with occasional elision; from "respondit" on, everything suggests that it is Servius speaking.

76. Cicero, *De officiis* 1.10.33: it may not be a specific reference (this would assume that the Servian response was very late), but instead merely a convergence of motifs. On Servius as orator, see Pomp., *Ench.,* in *D.* 1.2.2.43.

77. Bremer, I, pp. 230–237; *Pal.,* II, cols. 322–323; Schulz, *History of Roman Legal Science,* p. 91.

78. See Chapter 9, sec. 3.

15. Politics and Destiny

1. Servius was in Greece from the final months of 47 B.C. or the beginning of 46 until the summer of 45. In 48 he had been in Samos: F. Münzer, "Sulpicius Rufus," in *RE,* IV.A1 (1931), cols. 854–855; R. A. Bauman, *Lawyers in Roman Transitional Politics: A Study of the Roman Jurists in Their Political Setting in the Late Republic and Triumvirate* (Munich, 1985), pp. 48 ff. In the fall of 47 Servius may have made a short trip to Rome, probably to meet Caesar, who in October would assign the new offices in the provinces. And from there he went on to Achaea; see D. R. Shackleton Bailey,

Cicero, Epistulae ad Familiares, II (Cambridge, 1977), p. 416. See also P. Meloni, "Servio Sulpicio Rufo e i suoi tempi," *Annali della Facoltà di Lettere e Filosofia dell'Università di Cagliari,* 13 (1946): 183 ff. (on p. 187 n. 61, Meloni seems to state that Servius arrived in Greece directly from Samos; but I must agree with the "geographical" observation by Shackleton Bailey, in *Cicero, Epistulae ad Familiares,* II). Also by Shackleton Bailey see in *Classical Quarterly,* 54 (1960): 253–254 n. 7. P. Willems, *Le sénat de la république romaine,* II (Paris, 1883), p. 725 n. 2, believes that Servius' position in Achaea was that of *legatus Caesaris,* and not proconsul; but this is probably unfounded: T. R. Broughton, *The Magistrates of the Roman Republic,* 3 vols. (New York, 1951–52), II, pp. 299, 310. It might be that Servius left Athens for short trips around his province (once, right at the end of 46: Cicero, *Ad familiares* 6.4.5); but these were short absences. The plans for one of these trips are also in *Ad fam.* 4.12: which we shall read at the beginning of sec. 2 of this chapter, and in note 22 below. On the biography of Servius, see also C. Saunders, "The Political Sympathies of Servius Sulpicius Rufus," *Classical Review,* 37 (1923): 110 ff.

2. We do not have a date for his birth, but he was certainly the same or close to the same age as Cicero: the correct year could even be 105: Bremer, I, p. 139; Münzer, "Sulpicius Rufus," col. 851; Meloni, "Servio Sulpicio Rufo," p. 73. His mastery of Greek is implicit in the Ciceronian judgments of *Ad fam.* 4.3.3 and *Brutus* 42.153 (see Chapter 11, sec. 3); on his youthful journey to Greece, see Münzer, "Sulpicius Rufus," col. 852.

3. Cic., *Ad fam.* 4.1.1.

4. Cicero, *Ad Atticum* 10.14: this is the text upon which was based the youthful and possibly excessively harsh judgment of T. Mommsen, *Römische Geschichte,* III, 7th ed. (Berlin 1882), pp. 392–393.

5. Meloni, "Servio Sulpicio Rufo," pp. 183 ff.

6. Cic., *Ad fam.* 4.4.2.

7. From ibid.: "et nos, qui domi sumus, tibi beati videmur." See also 4.3.2.

8. Cic., *Ad fam.* 13.17–28a.

9. Cic., *Ad Att.* 5.4.1: Meloni, "Servio Sulpicio Rufo," pp. 149–150.

10. On the first, Broughton, *The Magistrates,* II, p. 197; on the second, ibid., p. 242.

11. When Cicero and Servius found themselves adversaries (Cicero was defending Lucius Licinius Murena, while Servius was his chief accuser): A. Bürge, *Die Juristenkomik in Ciceros Rede Pro Murena, Übersetzung und Kommentar* (Zurich, 1974), pp. 104 ff. (on which D. Nörr, in *ZSS,* 92 [1975]: 290 ff., now in *Historiae iuris antiqui,* ed. T. Chiusi, W. Kaiser, and H.-D. Spengler, II [Goldbach, 2003], pp. 947 ff.). Even so, the situation did not keep Cicero from calling Servius "sapientissimus atque ornatissimus"—without a hint of irony: we agree with M. Bretone, *Tecniche e ideologie dei giuristi romani,* 2d ed. (Naples, 1982), p. 79 n. 49.

12. Cic., *Ad Att.* 5.4.1 and 6.1.10.

13. Cic., *Ad fam.* 2.15.2 and 2.16.5; also 3.12.2: Shackleton Bailey, *Cicero, Epistulae ad Familiares,* II, p. 415. Details in P. Grimal, *Cicéron* (Paris, 1986).

14. Cic., *Ad fam.* 4.5: "Postea quam mihi renuntiatum est de obitu Tulliae, filiae tuae, sane quam pro eo ac debui, graviter molesteque tuli communemque eam calamitatem existimavi; qui, si istic adfuissem, neque tibi defuissem coramque meum dolorem tibi declarassem. Etsi genus hoc consolationis miserum atque acerbum est, propterea quia, per quos ea confieri debet, propinquos ac familiares, ii ipsi pari molestia adficiuntur neque sine lacrimis multis id conari possunt, uti magis ipsi videantur aliorum consolatione indigere quam aliis posse suum officium praestare, tamen, quae in praesentia in mentem mihi venerunt, decrevi brevi ad te prescribere, non quo ea te fugere existimem, sed quod forsitan dolore impeditus minus ea perspicias. Quid est quod tanto opere te commoveat tuus dolor intestinus? Cogita, quem ad modum adhuc fortuna nobiscum egerit; ea nobis erepta esse, quae hominibus non minus quam liberi cara esse debent, patriam, honestatem, dignitatem, honores omnis. Hoc uno incommodo addito quid ad dolorem adiungi potuit? aut qui non in illis rebus exercitatus animus callere iam debet atque omnia minoris existimare? An illius vicem, cedo, doles? Quotiens in eam cogitationem necesse est et tu veneris et nos saepe incidimus, hisce temporibus non pessime cum iis esse actum, quibus sine dolore licitum est mortem cum vita commutare! Quid autem fuit quod illam hoc tempore ad vivendum magno opere invitare posset? quae res, quae spes, quod animi solacium? ut cum aliquo adulescente primario coniuncta aetatem gereret? Licitum est tibi, credo, pro tua dignitate ex hac iuventute generum diligere, cuius fidei liberos tuos te tuto committere putares. An ut ea liberos ex sese pararet, quos cum fiorentis videret laetaretur, qui rem a parente traditam per se tenere possent, honores ordinatim petituri essent in re publica, in amicorum negotiis libertate sua usuri? Quid horum fuit quod non priusquam datum est ademptum sit? At vero malum est liberos amittere. Malum; nisi hoc peius sit, haec sufferre et perpeti. Quae res mihi non mediocrem consolationem attulit, volo tibi commemorare, si forte eadem res tibi dolorem minuere possit. Ex Asia rediens cum ab Aegina Megaram versus navigarem, coepi regiones circumcirca prospicere. Post me erat Aegina, ante me Megara, dextra Piraeus, sinistra Corinthus, quae oppida quodam tempore florentissima fuerunt, nunc prostrata et diruta ante oculos iacent. Coepi egomet mecum sic cogitare: 'Hem! nos homunculi indignamur, si quis nostrum interiit aut occisus est, quorum vita brevior esse debet, cum uno loco tot oppidum cadavera proiecta iacent? Visne tu te, Servi, cohibere et meminisse hominem te esse natum?' Crede mihi, cogitatione ea non mediocriter sum confirmatus. Hoc idem, si tibi videtur, fac ante oculos tibi proponas. Modo uno tempore tot viri clarissimi interierunt, de imperio populi Romani tanta deminutio facta est, omnes provinciae conquassatae sunt; in unius mulierculae animula si iactura facta est, tanto opere commoveris? Quae si

hoc tempore non diem suum obisset, paucis post annis tamen ei moriendum fuit, quoniam homo nata fuerat. Etiam tu ab hisce rebus animum ac cogitationem tuam avoca atque ea potius reminiscere, quae digna tua persona sunt, illam, quam diu ei opus fuerit, vixisse, una cum re publica fuisse, te, patrem suum, praetorem, consulem, augurem vidisse, adulescentibus primariis nuptam fuisse, omnibus bonis prope perfunctam esse, cum res publica occideret vita excessisse. Quid est quod tu aut illa cum fortuna hoc nomine queri possitis? Denique noli te oblivisci Ciceronem esse et eum, qui aliis consueris praecipere et dare consilium, neque imitare malos medicos, qui in alienis morbis profitentur tenere se medicinae scientiam, ipsi se curare non possunt, sed potius, quae aliis tute praecipere soles, era tute tibi subiace atque apud animum propone. Nullus dolor est, quem non longinquitas temporis minuat ac molliat. Hoc te expectare tempus tibi turpe est ac non ei rei sapientia tua te occurrere. Quod si qui etiam inferis sensus est, qui illius in te amor fuit pietasque in omnis suos, hoc certe illa te facere non vult. Da hoc illi mortuae, da ceteris amicis ac familiaribus, qui tuo dolore maerent, da patriae, ut, si qua in re opus sit, opera et consilio tuo uti possit. Denique, quoniam in eam fortunam devenimus, ut etiam huic rei nobis serviendum sit, noli committere ut quisquam te putet non tam filiam quam rei publicae tempora et aliorum victoriam lugere. Plura me ad te de hac re scribere pudet, ne videar prudentiae tuae diffidere. Qua re, si hoc unum proposuero, finem faciam scribendi: Vidimus aliquotiens secundam pulcherrime te ferre fortunam magnamque ex ea re te laudem apisci; fac aliquando intellegamus adversam. Quoque te aeque ferre posse neque id maius, quam debeat, tibi onus videri, ne ex omnibus virtutibus haec una tibi videatur deesse. Quod ad me attinet, cum te tranquilliorem animo esse cognoro, de iis rebus, quae hic geruntur, quemadmodumque se provincia habeat, certiorem faciam. Vale"; translation, with modifications, from *M. Tullius Cicero, Letters*, trans. E. S. Shuckburgh (New York, 1909–1914). Shackleton Bailey, *Cicero, Epistulae ad Familiares*, II, reads "at . . . credo" in place of "an caedo," and "peius est" instead of "peius sit." It is surprising to note the modest size of the bibliography on so important a text: a possible explanation and the few references are in *Giuristi*, pp. 141 and 230.

15. *Giuristi*, pp. 142–143.

16. A. La Penna, *Sallustio e la "rivoluzione" romana* (Milan, 1968), pp. 366 ff. Also R. Syme, *Sallust* (Berkeley, 1962), pp. 240 ff.; and A. D. Leeman, *Orationis ratio: The Stylistic Theories and Practice of the Roman Orators, Historians, and Philosophers* (Amsterdam, 1963).

17. Quintilian, *Institutio oratoria* 10.5.4: "Ac de carminibus quidem neminem credo dubitare, quo solo genere exercitationis dicitur usus esse Sulpicius."

18. Cicero, *Orationes Philippicae* 9.5.10.

19. Cic., *Ad fam.* 4.5.1.

20. Cic., *Ad fam.* 4.1.1 (above, note 3 and text).

21. Plutarch, *Cato minor* 68–71; I agree with E. Rawson, *Intellectual Life in the Late Roman Republic* (London, 1985), p. 95.

22. Cic., *Ad fam.* 4.12: "Etsi scio non iucundissimum me nuntium vobis allaturum, tamen, quoniam casus et natura in nobis dominatur, visum est faciendum, quoquo modo res se haberet, vos certiores facere. A.d.x. K. Iun. cum ab Epidauro Piraeum navi advectus essem, ibi M. Marcellum, conlegam nostrum, conveni eumque diem ibi consumpsi, ut cum eo essem. Postero die cum ab eo digressus essem eo consilio, ut ab Athenis in Boeotiam irem reliquamque iuris dictionem absolverem, ille, ut aiebat, supra Maleas in Italiam versus navigaturus erat. Post diem tertium eius diei cum ab Athenis proficisci in animo haberem, circiter hora decima noctis P. Postumius, familiaris eius, ad me venit et mihi nuntiavit M. Marcellum, conlegam nostrum, post cenae tempus a P. Magio Cilone, familiare eius, pugione percussum esse et duo vulnera accepisse, unum in stomacho, alterum in capite secundum aurem; sperari tamen eum vivere posse; Magium se ipsum interfecisse postea; se a Marcello ad me missum esse, qui haec nuntiaret et rogaret, uti medicos ei mitterem. Itaque medicos coegi et e vestigio eo sum profectus prima luce. Cum non longe a Piraeo abessem, puer Acidini obviam mihi venit cum codicillis, in quibus erat scriptum paulo ante lucem Marcellum diem suum obisse. Ita vir clarissimus ab homine deterrimo acerbissima morte est adfectus, et, cui inimici propter dignitatem pepercerant, inventus est amicus, qui ei mortem offerret. Ego tamen ad tabernaculum eius perrexi. Inveni duos libertos et pauculos servos; reliquos aiebant profugisse metu perterritos, quod dominus eorum ante tabernaculum interfectus esset. Coactus sum in eadem illa lectica, qua ipse delatus eram, meisque lecticariis in urbem eum referre ibique pro ea copia, quae Athenis erat, funus ei satis amplum faciendum curavi. Ab Atheniensibus, locum sepulturae intra urbem ut darent, impetrare non potui, quod religione se impediri dicerent, neque tamen id antea cuiquam concesserant. Quod proximum fuit, uti in quo vellemus gymnasio eum sepeliremus, nobis permiserunt. Nos in nobilissimo orbi terrarum gymnasio Academiae locum delegimus ibique eum combussimus posteaque curavimus, ut eidem Athenienses in eodem loco monumentum ei marmoreum faciendum locarent. Ita, quae nostra officia fuerunt pro collegio et pro propinquitate, et vivo et mortuo omnia ei praestitimus. Vale D.pr.K.Iun. Athenis"; translation, with modifications, from W. Roberts, *History of Letter-writing* (London, 1843), pp. 144–146. There are a few notes of commentary in R. Y. Tyrrell and L. C. Purser, *The Correspondence of M. Tullius Cicero,* V, 2d ed. (1915; reprint, Hildesheim, 1969), pp. 105–108; and in Shackleton Bailey, *Cicero, Epistulae ad Familiares,* II, pp. 421–423. See also Meloni, "Servio Sulpicio Rufo," pp. 199 ff.; and Bauman, *Lawyers in Roman Transitional Politics,* pp. 52–53.

23. Caesar was suspected of having ordered it, but in all likelihood unjustly so: E. G.

Hardy, *Some Problems in Roman History: Ten Essays Bearing on the Administrative and Legislative Work of Julius Caesar* (Oxford, 1924), pp. 126 ff.

24. "Vir bene litteratus," in Aulus Gellius, *Noctes Atticae* 2.10.1; "omnium doctrinarum studiosus" in the previously mentioned (above, note 2) *Ad fam.* 4.3.3; master of dialectic in *Brutus* 41.152–42.153, which we have explored (see Chapter 11; and see also *Ad fam.* 4.6.1). The intertwining of chance and nature (but from the point of view of the irresistible force of the elements) returns as well in two legal texts by Servius, which we can reconstruct through citations by Ulpian: now in *D.* 19.2.15.2 and 39.2.24.45.

25. For more on Mucius, see Chapters 12 and 13.

26. Esp. *Orationes Philippicae* 14.12.32–33.

27. Servius was in Rhodes in 78: Münzer, "Sulpicius Rufus," col. 852. Hipparchus died there in 125; Posidonius set up residence there around 95: between the two many ties were established. Rhodes was one of the places to which Roman culture was most deeply indebted in those years.

16. Legitimacy and Power

1. See Chapter 12, sec. 1.

2. Aristotle, *Politica* 1.3–5.1253b–1254a: S. Mazzarino, *Il pensiero storico classico*, 2 vols. (Bari, 1966), II.1, pp. 50–51; M. Maruzzi, ed., *La "politica" di Aristotele e il problema della schiavitù nel mondo antico* (Turin, 1988), pp. 25 ff.; G. Cambiano, "Aristotele e gli oppositori anonimi della schiavitù," in *La schiavitù nel mondo antico*, ed. M. I. Finley (Rome, 1990), pp. 27 ff., esp. 31 ff., 40 ff.

3. Thus was created an idea of order in which it was possible to begin thinking of law in the same form as life: a sort of "taking charge of life by power"—M. Foucault, *Il faut défendre la société* (Paris, 1997); in English as *Society Must Be Defended*, trans. D. Macey (New York, 2003), p. 253—as well as of a "private" construction of life, based on the personal character of the appropriation of wealth—note the penetrating observations in R. Esposito, *Bios: Biopolitica e filosofia* (Turin, 2004), pp. xiii, 18 ff., 59 ff., 65 ff., 96 ff.: modernity would later integrate it into the development of economic, political, and legal individualism: see Chapter 22 of this volume.

4. Romans 13.

5. See Chapter 6, sec. 2.

6. Aelius Aristides, *Orationes* 26.57: *Storia spezzata*, p. 8 [*The End of the Past*, p. 6].

7. See above, Chapter 1.

8. It was only with the "constitutio Antoniniana" (dating from 212 or 213 A.D.), which extended Roman citizenship to all (or nearly all) the subjects of the empire, eliminating the principle of the primacy of Rome as a city-state, that Roman law be-

came the law of the entire empire: Dio Cassius 77.9.4–5; Ulpian, in *D.* 1.5.17; C. Sasse, *Die Constitutio Antoniniana* (Wiesbaden, 1958).

9. The study of the relationships between legal thought and the construction of the empire—between legal elaboration and world domination—remains an unpardonable omission in modern historiography: in this book we try to fill it in some small part. On the cultural shift that came about in Rome as a consequence of the assumption of imperial responsibilities we begin, all the same, to have some good works: J.-L. Ferrary, *Philellénisme et impérialisme: Aspects idéologiques de la conquête romaine du monde hellénistique, de la seconde guerre de Macédoine à la guerre contre Mithridate* (Rome, 1988); E. Gabba, *Aspetti culturali dell'imperialismo romano* (Florence, 1993); C. Moatti, *La raison de Rome: Naissance de l'esprit critique à la fin de la République* (Paris, 1997).

10. See Chapters 12 and 22.

11. The criticism of Marx, from the *Economic and Philosophical Manuscripts,* to the *Grundrisse* and *Das Kapital,* if read in a nondeterministic way (as, indeed, sometimes his own formulations would seem to lead us to do), remains a fundamental chapter of modern historical understanding: in this sense, in truth, "we cannot say that we are not Marxists" (to paraphrase an old comment of Benedetto Croce). My position has changed considerably over the course of time, but without any radical reversals: the itinerary runs through my books—from *Storiografia* to *Origini* and through to *I conti del comunismo* (Turin, 1999), esp. pp. 18 ff. Today I believe we should be able to set alongside Marx both Weber and Foucault (and to a certain extent Nietzsche): the Weber of *Economy and Society*—legal rationalization as a characteristic of the West—and the Foucault of *Discipline and Punish,* the writings concerning "micro physics," and the unpublished works of the last years: the genealogical gaze on the morphologies and the pervasiveness of power; it would be more complex to tackle Nietzsche (on which see above, Chapter 9, note 22). I have attempted here to work in this direction, through concrete research and without pointless methodological pronouncements.

12. Cicero, *Pro Caecina* 25.70–75: "[70] Nam qui ius civile contemnendum putat, is vincula revellit non modo iudiciorum sed etiam utilitatis vitaeque communis; qui autem interpretes iuris vituperat, si imperitos iuris esse dicit, de hominibus non de iure civili detrahit; sin peritis non putat esse optemperandum, non homines laedit, sed leges ac iura labefactat. Quod vobis venire in mentem profecto necesse est, nihil esse in civitate tam diligenter quam ius civile retinendum. Etenim hoc sublato nihil est qua re exploratum cuiquam possit esse quid suum aut alienum sit, nihil est quod aequabile inter omnis atque unum omnibus esse possit. [71] Itaque in ceteris controversiis atque iudiciis cum quaeritur aliquid factum necne sit, verum an falsum proferatur, et fictus testis subornari solet et interponi falsae tabulae, non numquam honesto ac probabili nomine bono viro iudici error obici,

improbo facultas dari ut, cum sciens perperam iudicarit, testem tamen aut tabulas secutus esse videatur. In iure nihil est eius modi, reciperatores, non tabulae falsae, non testis improbus, denique nimia ista quae dominatur in civitate potentia in hoc solo genere quiescit; quid agat, quo modo adgrediatur iudicem, qua denique digitum proferat, non habet. [72] Illud enim potest dici iudici ab aliquo non tam verecondo nomine quam gratioso: 'iudica hoc factum esse aut numquam esse factum [creatum]; crede huic testi, has comproba tabulas'—hoc non potest: 'statuae cui filius agnatus sit, eius testamentum non esse ruptum; iudica quod mulier sine tutore auctore promiserit deberi.' Non est aditus ad huiusce modi res neque potentiae cuiusquam neque gratiae; denique, quo maius hoc sanctiusque videatur, ne pretio quidem corrumpi iudex in eius modi causa potest. [73] Iste vester testis qui ausus est dicere fecisse videri eum de quo ne cuius rei argueretur quidem scire potuti, is ipse numquam auderet iudicare deberi viro dotem quam mulier nullo auctore dixisset. O rem praeclaram, vobisque ob hoc retinendam, reciperatores! [26]. Quod enim est ius civile? Quod neque inflecti gratia neque perfringi potentia neque adulterari pecunia possit; quod si non modo oppressum, sed etiam desertum aut neglegentius adservatum erit, nihil est quod quisquam sese habere certum aut a patre accepturum aut relicturum liberis arbitretur. [74] Quid enim refert aedi aut fundum relictum a patre, aut aliqua ratione habere bene partum, si incertum est quae nunc tua iure mancipi sint, ea possine retinere, si parum est communitum ius [si] civile ac publica lege contra alicuius gratiam teneri non potest? Quid, inquam, prodest fundum habere, si, quae diligentissime descripta a maioribus iura finium, possessionum, aquarum itinerumque sunt, haec perturbari aliqua ratione commutarique possunt? Mihi credite, maior hereditas uni cuique nostrum venit in isdem bonis a iure et a legibus quam ab eis a quibus illa ipsa bona nobis relicta sunt. Nam ut perveniat ad me fundus testamento alicuius fieri potest; ut retineam quod meum factum sit sine iure civili fieri non potest. Fundus a patre relinqui potest, at usucapio fundi, hoc est finis sollicitudinis ac periculi litium, non a patre relinquitur, sed a legibus. Aquae ductus, haustus, iter, actus a patre, sed rata auctoritas harum rerum omnium ab iure civili sumitur. [75] Quapropter non minus diligenter ea quae a maioribus acceptis, publica patrimonia iuris quam privatae rei vestrae retinere debetis, non solum quod haec iure civili saepta sunt, verum etiam quod patrimonium unius incommodo dimittetur, ius admitti non potest sine magno incommodo civitatis"; translation from *The Orations of Marcus Tullius Cicero,* trans. C. D. Yonge (London, 1856).

13. B. Frier, *The Rise of the Roman Jurists: Studies in Cicero's Pro Caecina* (Princeton, 1985), esp. pp. xi ff., 97 ff.; S. D. Mühlhölzl, *Cicero Pro A. Caecina* (Aachen, 1997).

14. Cicero later joined *ius* and *lex* (the Twelve Tables, but also subsequent legislation) in accordance with the civilistic "canon" discussed in Chapter 8, sec. 4.

15. See Chapter 8, sec. 4.

16. Cicero, *Pro Murena* 11.25. See also H. Drexler, "Potentia," *Rheinisches Museum für Philologie*, 102 (1959): 50 ff.

17. Cicero, *De oratore* 1.42.188: "Sit ergo in iure civili finis hic: legitimae atque usitatae in rebus causisque civium aequabilitatis conservatio." See also sec. 4 of this chapter.

18. M. Pohlenz, "Nomos und Physis," now in *Kleine Schriften*, II (Hildesheim, 1965), pp. 341 ff.; O. Behrends and W. Sellert, eds., *Nomos und Gesetz. Ursprünge und Wirkungen des griechischen Gesetzesdenkens* (Göttingen, 1995); M. Gigante, *Nomos basileus* (1956; reprinted with app., Naples, 1993), esp. pp. 11 ff.; F. Heinimann, *Nomos und Physis. Herkunft und Bedeutung einer Antithese im griechischen Denken des 5. Jahrhunderts* (reprint, Darmstadt, 1987), pp. 170 ff.; E. Stolfi, "'Lex est . . . virorum prudentium consultum': Osservazioni su (*Pap.* 1 def.) D. 1.3.1," *SDHI*, 70 (2004), esp. pp. 461–462 n. 103, where there is further bibliography.

19. Heraclitus, in Diels-Kranz, 22B, fr. 123 (the source is Themistius, *Orationes* 5, p. 69 [Dindorf]) and fr. 54 (from Hippolytus, *Ref. contra omnes haereses* 9.9, p. 241 Wendland): G. Colli, *La natura ama nascondersi*, 2d ed. (Milan, 1988), esp. pp. 207–208 and 209.

20. What I say here presupposes *Storia spezzata*, pp. 157–158, 252 [*The End of the Past*, pp. 149 and 255]. The observation concerning Roman jurists is only a sketchy point. See also below, Chapter 21, note 20.

21. See below, note 35 and text. Also Heinimann, *Nomos und Physis,* esp. pp. 110 ff.; and J. Ritter, *Metaphisik und Politik. Studien zu Aristoteles und Hegel* (Frankfurt am Main, 1969).

22. See, e.g., Gigante, *Nomos basileus*, and note 35 below.

23. L. Gernet, *Droit et société dans la Grèce ancienne* (Paris, 1955), pp. 2 ff.; and Gernet, "Droit et prédroit en Grèce ancienne," now in *Droit et institutions en Grèce antique* (1968; reprint, Paris, 1982), pp. 7 ff.; J. W. Jones, *The Law and Legal Theory of the Greeks: An Introduction* (Oxford, 1956), pp. 68 ff.; J. de Romilly, *La loi dans la pensée grecque* (1971), 2d ed. (Paris, 2001), pp. 241 ff.

24. Antigone: D. Daube, *Civic Disobedience in Antiquity* (Edinburgh, 1972); R. Winnington-Ingram, *Sophocles: An Interpretation* (Cambridge, 1980), pp. 117 ff.; C. Segal, *Tragedy and Civilization* (Cambridge, Mass., 1981), pp. 152 ff.; S. Goldhill, *Reading Greek Tragedy* (Cambridge, 1986), pp. 88 ff.; and Goldhill, "Greek Drama and Political Theory," in *Greek and Roman Political Thought* (Cambridge, 2000), pp. 81 ff. Plato (and Socrates): A. D. Woozley, *Law and Obedience: The Arguments of Plato's Crito* (London, 1979); R. Kraut, *Socrates and the State* (Princeton, 1984).

25. I am referring to para. 357 of the *Grundlienen der Philosophie des Rechts*, in G. W. F. Hegel, *Vorlesungen über die Philosophie der Geschichte*, II (reprint, Leipzig, 1930), p. 814; in English as *Elements of the Philosophy of Right*, trans. H. Barr Nisbet, ed. Allen W. Wood (Cambridge, 1991), p. 379. For the reference to Seneca, P. Veyne, *Sénèque:*

Entretiens, Lettres à Lucilius (Paris, 1993), in English as *Seneca: The Life of a Stoic,* trans. D. Sullivan (New York, 2003), p. 17 ff.

26. See Chapter 21, sec. 2.

27. See Chapter 9, sec. 5.

28. *Rhetorica ad Herennium* 2.13.19: "Constat igitur ex his partibus: natura, lege, consuetudine, iudicato, aequo et bono, pacto."

29. Cicero, *Topica* 5.28, on which see Chapter 11, sec. 3 and note 36.

30. See Chapter 17, sec. 3.

31. Aristotle, *Rhetorica* 1.13.12.1373b and *Ethica Nicomachea* 5.7.1.1134b: this is one of the first direct points of contact between Greek thought and Roman conceptualizations. The author of the *Rhet. ad Her.* immediately afterward adds (again, in 2.13.19): "Natura ius est, quod cognationis aut pietatis causa observatur, quo iure parentes a liberis, et a parentibus liberi coluntur": this is the beginning of a thread that will extend to Gaius (see Chapter 22, sec. 1). The *aequum bonum* also returns in *Rhet. ad Her.* 2.10.14 and 2.11.16, again in the same classificatory context ("lege, more, natura, bono et aequo fieri posse").

32. See Chapter 21, note 17 and text.

33. See note 31 above.

34. Cicero, *De legibus* 1.5.17: "Non ergo a praetoris edicto, ut plerique nunc, neque a duodecim tabulis, ut superiores, sed penitus ex intima philosophia hauriendam iuris disciplinam putas?"; translation from *Laws*, trans. C. W. Keyes, Loeb Classical Library (1928; reprint, Cambridge, Mass., 1970). It is Atticus who is speaking.

35. Pindar, fr. 169a (Snell-Maehler); Herodotus 3.38.4 and 7.104.4; Plato, *Gorgias* 484b; Arist., *Pol.* 4.4.1292a; Chrysippus, *SVF,* III, p. 314 (= Marcianus, *Institutiones* 1, in *D.* 1.3.2): H. E. Stier, "Nomos Basileus," *Philologus,* 83 (1928): 225 ff.; H. Niedermeyer, "Aristoteles und der Begriff des Nomos bei Lykophron," in *Festschrift Koschaker,* III (Weimar, 1939), pp. 140 ff.; C. Schmitt, *Der Nomos der Erde im Volkerrecht des Jus Publicum Europaeum* (1950) (Berlin, 1974), pp. 42 ff., in English as *The Nomos of the Earth in the International Law of the Jus Publicum Europaeum,* trans. G. Ulmen (New York, 2003), pp. 67 ff., (with acute observations, on a questionable foundation); Gigante, *Nomos basileus;* Stolfi, "'*Lex est . . . virorum prudentium consultum,*'" pp. 464 ff.

36. Cic., *De leg.* 1.6.18–19: "Igitur doctissimis viris proficisci placuit a lege, haud scio an recte, si modo, ut idem definiunt, lex est ratio summa, insita in natura, quae iubet quae faccenda sunt, prohibetque contraria. Eadem ratio cum est in hominis mente confirmata et perfecta, lex est"; translation, with modifications, from *Laws,* trans. C. W. Keyes, Loeb Classical Library (1928; reprint, Cambridge, Mass., 1970).

37. Cicero, *De republica* 3.5.8–11.18.

38. Cicero, *Ad Quintum fratrem* 1.1.27–28: "Quod si te sors Afris aut Hispanis aut Gallis praefecisset, immanibus ac barbaris nationibus, tamen esset humanitatis tuae con-

sulere eorum commodis et utilitati salutique servire: cum vero ei generi hominum praesimus, non modo in quo ipso sit, sed etiam a quo ad alios pervenisse putetur humanitas, certe iis eam potissimum tribuere debemus, a quibus accepimus. Non enim me hoc iam dicere pudebit, praesertim in ea vita atque iis rebus gestis in quibus non potest residere inertiae aut levitatis ulla suspicio, nos ea quae consecuti sumus iis studiis et artibus esse adeptos quae sint nobis Greciae monumentis disciplinisque tradita. Quare praeter communem fidem quae omnibus debetur, praeterea nos isti hominum generi praecipue debere videmur ut, quorum praeceptis sumus eruditi, apud eos ipsos quod ab iis didicerimus velimus expromere"; translation, with modifications, from *M. Tullius Cicero, Letters*, trans. E. S. Shuckburgh (New York, 1909–1914).

39. Cic., *De rep.* 3.25.37: "Sic regum, sic imperatorum, sic magistratuum, sic patrum, sic populorum imperia civibus sociisque praesunt ut corporibus animus"; translation, with modifications, from *The Treatises of M. Tullius Cicero*, ed. and trans. C. D. Yonge (London, 1853).

40. *Rhet ad Her.* 3.2.3: "Iustitia est aequitas ius uni cuique retribuens pro dignitate cuiusque."

41. Terence, *Heautontimorumenos* 646.

42. See Chapter 9, sec. 5.

43. Cicero, *De inventione* 2.53.160; *De rep.* 3.11.18; *De officiis* 1.5.15, 2.22.78, 3.10.43. See also *De leg.* 1.6.19 (note 36 above); *De finibus* 5.23.65; and *De natura deorum* 3.15.38.

44. See Chapter 21, sec. 1.

45. Arist., *Rhet.* 1.15.6.1375a: καὶ ὅτι τὸ μὲν ἐπιεικὲς ἀεὶ μένει καὶ οὐδέποτε μεταβάλλει. See also *Eth. Nic.* 5.10.1–8.1137a–1138a; 6.11.1.1143a (and also 5.7.1–5.1134b–1135a); *Rhet.* 1.13.1–13.1373b–1374a, all of which are of highly complex interpretation.

46. *Rhet. ad Her.* 2.13.20: "Ex eo vel novum ius constitui convenit ex tempore et ex hominis dignitate."

47. *SVF*, I, pp. 85–86, n. 374; III, nn. pp. 125, 262–264, 266, 280: M. Pohlenz, *Die Stoa. Geschichte einer geistigen Bewegung* (Göttingen, 1959), I, pp. 125, 132, and II, pp. 71–72, 74.

48. Cicero, *Pro Caecina* 23.65: "Si contra verbis et litteris et, ut dici solet, summo iure contenditur, solent eius modi iniquitati aequi et boni nomen dignitatemque opponere."

49. Cicero, *Brutus* 38.143: "Cum de iure civili, cum de aequo et bono disputaretur, argumentorum et similitudinum copia"; translation from *Cicero, Brutus*, trans. G. L. Hendrickson, Loeb Classical Library (Cambridge, Mass., 1939).

50. Cic., *Topica* 5.28 (also mentioned in note 29 above): "ut si quis ius civile dicat id esse, quod in legibus, senatus consultis, rebus iudicatis, iuris peritorum auctoritate, edictis magistratuum, more, aequitate consistat."

51. See Chapter 19, sec. 3.

52. Cic., *Top.* 2.9: "Ius civile est aequitas constituta eis qui eiusdem civitatis sunt ad res suas obtinendas."

53. Cicero, *De orat.* 1.42.188: "Sit ergo in iure civili finis hic: legitimae atque usitatae in rebus causisque aequabilitatis conservatio."

54. Cicero, *Partitiones oratoriae* 37.129–130.

55. Cic., *De inv.* 2.53.160.

56. Cic., *Part. or.* 37.130.

57. Cic., *De leg.* 1.6.19.

58. Cic., *Top.* 23.90: "Cum autem de aequo et iniquo disseritur, aequitatis loci conligentur. Hi cernuntur bipertito, et natura et instituto. Natura partes habet duas, tributionem sui cuique et ulciscendi ius. Institutio autem aequitatis tripertita est; una pars legitima est, altera conveniens, tertia moris vetustate fermata."

59. Pomponius, *Enchiridion,* in *D.* 1.2.2.43. The detail of Cercina is reported by Pomponius only because it concerns the life of Servius, about whom he was talking. The acceptance by jurists of the concept of *aequitas* was certainly also encouraged by the influence of the great oratory of those years: an important example of this (referring to Mark Antony) is in Cic., *De off.* 3.16.67.

60. Cic., *Pro Caec.* 27.78: "Quapropter hoc dicam, numquam eius auctoritatem nimium valere cuius prudentiam populus Romanus in cavendo, non in decipiendo perspexerit, qui iuris civilis rationem numquam ab aequitate seiunxerit."

61. This too can be gleaned from the recollections of Cicero, *De off.* 3.14.60: "Aliud simulatum, aliud actum."

62. Servius followed the same line, as we learn from Ulpian, *Ad ed.* 11, in *D.* 4.3.1.2. Labeo seemingly then extended and complicated the picture (see the text by Ulpian).

63. Cicero, *Orationes Philippicae* 9.5.10–11: "Nec vero silebitur admirabilis quaedam et incredibilis ac paene divina eius in legibus interpretandis, aequitate explicanda scientia. Omnes ex omni aetate, qui in hac civitate intellegentiam iuris habuerunt, si unum in locum conferantur, cum Ser. Sulpicio non sint comparandi. Nec enim ille magis iuris consultus quam iustitiae fuit. [11] Ita ea quae proficiscebantur a legibus et ab iure civili, semper ad facilitatem aequitatemque referebat neque instituere litium actiones malebat quam controversias tollere"; translation, with modifications, from *Philippics,* trans. W. C. A. Ker, Loeb Classical Library (1926; reprint, Cambridge, Mass., 1963).

64. See Chapter 21, sec. 1.

65. Gaius, *Institutiones* 3.149: see Chapter 14, sec. 4.

66. Paul, *Ad ed.* 9, in *D.* 3.5.20pr: "Nam et Servius respondit, ut est relatum apud Alfenum libro trigensimo nono digestorum: [the precision of the reference is explained by the fact that Paul had epitomized the *Digesta* of Alphenus Varus] cum a

Lusitanis tres capti essent et unus ea condicione missus, uti pecuniam pro tribus adferret, et nisi redisset, ut duo pro eo quoque pecuniam darent, isque reverti noluisset et ob hanc causam illi pro tertio quoque pecuniam solvissent: Servius respondit aequum esse praetorem in eum reddere iudicium."

67. Alphenus Varus, *Dig.* 2, in *D.* 44.1.14: "Filius familias peculiarem servum vendidit, pretium stipulatus est: is homo redhibitus et postea mortuus est. [et] pater [eius] pecuniam ab emptore petebat, quam filius stipulatus erat. Placuit aequum esse in factum exceptionem eum obicere: 'quod . . .'": D. Daube, "Novation of Obligations Giving a *'bonae fidei iudicium,'" ZSS,* 66 (1948): p. 101 (= *Collected Studies in Roman Law,* I [Frankfurt am Main, 1991], pp. 243–244). It is perhaps possible to discover in Servius the earliest traces of a naturalistic paradigm along the lines of the one later developed by Labeo (see Chapter 16, sec. 4, and Chapter 22, note 4): one significant text is Alphenus, *Epit.* 2, in *D.* 48.22.3, if it reports—as I believe it does— the thought of Servius.

68. Ulpian, *Ad ed.* 38, in *D.* 47.4.1pr-1: "Si dolo malo eius, qui liber esse iussus erit, post mortem domini ante aditam hereditatem in bonis, quae eius fuerunt, qui eum liberum esse iusserit, factum esse dicetur, quo minus ex his bonis ad heredem aliquid perveniret: in eum intra annum utilem dupli iudicium datur. Haec autem actio, ut Labeo scripsit, naturalem potius in se quam civilem habet aequitatem [si quidem civilis deficit actio: sed] <nam> natura aequum est non esse impunitum eum, qui [hac spe] audacior factus est, quia neque ut servum se coerceri posse intellegit spe imminentis libertatis, neque ut liberum damnari, quia hereditati furtum fecit." In this section of the text I do not see any significant modifications, aside from those noted over the years, which I have enclosed in brackets; but what follows, not transcribed here, has all the earmarks of a clumsy reworking.

69. The concept of *aequitas civilis* would have considerable importance in the doctrine of modern natural law, underlying a (brilliant, as elsewhere) misunderstanding by G. B. Vico, *Scienza nuova seconda giusta l'edizione del 1744,* ed. F. Nicolini, 4th ed. (Bari, 1953), p. 114 (CX): this is reconstructed well by G. Crifò, "Ulpiano: Esperienze e responsabilità del giurista," in *ANRW,* II.15 (1976), p. 781 and n. 459.

17. Hermeneutics and the Politics of Law

1. A. Pernice, *Marcus Antistius Labeo. Das römische Privatrecht im ersten Jahrhunderte der Kaiserzeit,* I (Halle, 1873), pp. 7 ff.; P. Jörs, in *RE,* I, cols. 2548 ff.; W. Kunkel, *Herkunft und soziale Stellung der römischen Juristen,* 2d ed. (Graz, 1967), p. 114; R. A. Bauman, *Lawyers and Politics in the Early Roman Empire: A Study of Relations between the Roman Jurists and the Emperors from Augustus to Hadrian* (Munich, 1989), pp. 25 ff.

2. Appian, *Bella civilia* 4.17.135; and R. A. Bauman, *Lawyers in Roman Transitional Politics: A Study of the Roman Jurists in Their Political Setting in the Late Republic and Tri-*

umvirate (Munich, 1985), pp. 109–110. On Labeo's milieu, M. Bretone, *Tecniche e ideologie dei giuristi romani,* 2d ed. (Naples, 1982), pp. 129 ff. On his confrontation with Augustus on the occasion of the *lectio senatus* in 18 B.C., Suetonius, *Divus Augustus* 54; and Dio Cassius 54.15.7.

3. R. Syme, *The Augustan Aristocracy* (London, 1986).

4. See Chapter 19, sec. 4.

5. Tacitus, *Annales* 3.75.2: "Namque illa aetas duo pacis decora simul tulit: sed Labeo incorrupta libertas et ob id fama celebratior, Capitonis obsequium dominantibus magis probatur."

6. See Chapter 14, sec. 4.

7. Aulus Gellius, *Noctes Atticae* 13.12.1–2: "In quidam epistula Atei Capitonis scriptum legimus Labeonem Antistium legum atque morum populi Romani iurisque civilis doctum adprime fuisse. Sed agitabat—inquit—hominem libertas quaedam nimia atque vecors usque eo, ut divo Augusto iam principe et rempublicam obtinente ratum tamen pensumque nihil haberet, nisi quod iussum sanctumque esse in Romanis antiquitatibus legisset"; translation, with modifications, from *The Attic Nights of Aulus Gellius,* 2 vols., trans. J. C. Rolfe, Loeb Classical Library (1927; reprint, Cambridge, Mass., 1948), II.

8. Gell., *Noct. Att.* 13.12.3–4: "Ac deinde narrat, qui idem Labeo per viatorem a tribunis plebis vocatus responderit: 'Cum a muliere—inquit—quadam tribuni plebis adversum eum aditi [in] Gallianum ad eum misissent, ut veniret et muliebri responderet, iussit eum, qui missus erat, redire et tribunis dicere ius eos non habere neque se neque alium quemquam vocandi, quoniam moribus maiorum tribuni plebis prensionem haberent, vocationem non haberent; posse igitur eos venire et prendi se iubere, sed vocandi absentem ius non habere'"; translation, with modifications, from *The Attic Nights of Aulus Gellius,* 2 vols., trans. J. C. Rolfe, Loeb Classical Library (1927; reprint, Cambridge, Mass., 1948), II. From 23 B.C. onwards, Augustus was given the *tribunicia potestas* for life: Dio Cass. 53.32.5: F. de Martino, *Storia della costituzione romana,* 2d ed., 4 vols. (Naples, 1972–1974), IV.1, pp. 168 ff.

9. Still important is R. Syme, *The Roman Revolution* (London, 1939). In the last years of his rule, it seems that the emperor offered the jurist—by now old—the consulship, in a gesture of reconciliation: but his offer was met with rejection: Pomponius, *Enchiridion,* in *D.* 1.2.2.47: N. Horsfall, "Labeo and *Capito,*" *Historia,* 23 (1974): 252 ff. Dubious about the episode is R. Syme, "Fiction about Roman Jurists," *ZSS,* 97 (1980): 102 ff.; see also Bretone, *Tecniche e ideologie dei giuristi romani,* p. 360.

10. Pomp., *Ench.,* in *D.* 1.2.2.44–45. See also below, note 18.

11. Suetonius, *Divus Iulius* 44.1–4; Isidore of Seville, *Etymologiae* 5.13. We should also keep in mind Pomp., *Ench.,* in *D.* 1.2.2.44.

12. See Chapter 11, sec. 3.

13. Bremer, I, pp. 345 ff.; and *Pal.*, I, col. 798.

14. *Ench.*, in *D.* 1.2.2.44.

15. Mentioned by Quintilian, *Institutio oratoria* 12.3.10; Gell., *Noct. Att.* 1.22.7; and, much later, by the grammarian Charisius, p. 175, ll. 18–19B; and probably read by Pomponius.

16. See sec. 4 of this chapter.

17. Bremer, I, pp. 351 ff.; *Pal.*, I, cols. 798–799.

18. Both are the focus of fairly recent studies: Bauman, *Lawyers in Roman Transitional Politics*, pp. 89 ff.,123 ff.; F. Wieacker, *Römische Rechtsgeschichte* (Munich, 1988), I, pp. 607 ff., p. 613.

19. Pomp., *Ench.*, in *D.* 1.2.2.47: "Et totum annum ita diviserat, ut Romae sex mensibus secederet et conscribendis libris operam daret."

20. The comparison of Sallust and Cicero is already in A. La Penna, *Sallustio e la "rivoluzione" romana* (Milan, 1968), pp. 29 and 31. See also E. S. Gruen, *The Last Generation of the Roman Republic* (Berkeley, 1974).

21. The reference to the human sciences is in I. Berlin, "The Birth of Greek Individualism," now in *Liberty* (Oxford, 2002) (see also Chapter 22). For Rome, see *Storia spezzata*, pp. 201 ff. [*The End of the Past*, pp. 193 ff.].

22. A significant text is Cicero, *Ad Atticum* 6.1.15. Another situation to bear in mind is that illustrated by the "tabula Contrebiensis": P. Birks, A. Rodger, and J. S. Richardson, "Further Aspects of the *Tabula Contrebiensis*," *JRS*, 74 (1984): 45 ff.

23. *Ench.*, in *D.* 1.2.2.47: "Labeo ingenii qualitate et fiducia doctrinae, qui et ceteris operis sapientiae operam dederat, plurima innovare instituit."

24. See Chapter 12, sec. 2.

25. *Storia spezzata*, pp. 188 ff. [*The End of the Past*, pp. 180 ff.].

26. As would happen in modern European law, precisely through the reelaboration of Roman schemes in a direction that they allowed and had prepared but never truly pursued.

27. For the text by Paul, see above, Chapter 12, sec. 2 and notes 16 and 17.

28. We can detect Marx and Weber behind this method of interpretation: the *Grundrisse* just as much as *Wirtschaft und Gesellschaft*: an essential hybrid when it is necessary to construct explanations capable of taking into account the connections between economic structures and cultural or institutional developments: I have already mentioned, from another point of view, the importance of considering the two authors together, in *Storia spezzata*, p. 232 [*The End of the Past*, pp. 229–230]; now I am doing nothing more than continuing the same discourse on a different terrain. See also above, Chapter 16, note 11.

29. The research of A. Magdelain, *Le consensualisme dans l'édit du préteur* (Paris, 1958), strikes me increasingly as brilliant and ahead of its time.

30. *Storia spezzata*, pp. 77 ff. [*The End of the Past*, pp. 70 ff.].

31. See Chapter 20, sec. 2.

32. Ulpian, *Ad ed.* 4, in *D.* 2.14.7.7, transcribes from Julian's edict: "Ait praetor: 'pacta conventa, quae neque dolo malo, neque adversus leges plebis scita senatus consulta decreta edicta principum, neque quo fraus cui eorum fiat, facta erunt, servabo'": *EP,* pp. 64–65. In order to work back to the original tone we must rule out all references to the normative activity of the *princeps* (as has been done in the translation), evidently inserted at a later date. The conjecture about the reference to violence develops out of the parallelism between this edict and that of *quod metus causa,* already proposed by O. Lenel, in *EP,* p. 20 n. 1, as well as the content of *De officiis* 3.24.92, for which see below, note 37. See also note 42.

33. The observation develops out of one in *EP,* p. 20 n. 1.

34. For the texts, see Chapter 16, sec. 3 and note 28.

35. Cicero, *Pro Caecina* 18.51: "Quae lex, quod senatus consultum, quod magistratus edictum, quod foedus aut pactio, quod—ut ad privatas res redeam—testamentum, quae iudicii aut stipulationis aut pacti et conventi formula non infirmari ac convelli potest, si ad verba rem deflectere velimus, consilium autem eorum qui scripserunt et rationem et auctoritatem relinquamus?"; translation from *The Treatises of M. Tullius Cicero,* ed. and trans. C. D. Yonge (London, 1853).

36. Cicero, *De inventione* 2.22.68: "Pactum est, quod inter quos convenit ita iustum putatur, ut iure praestare dicatur."

37. Cic., *De off.* 3.24.92: "Pacta et promissa semperne servanda sint, quae nec vi nec dolo malo, ut praetores solent, facta sint"; translation from *Cicero, De Officiis,* trans. C. D. Yonge, Loeb Classical Library (Cambridge, Mass., 1990). It is above all on the basis of this testimony that the original text of the *edictum de pactis* should be integrated with the reference to fraud: see above, note 32.

38. Cicero, *Partitiones oratoriae* 37.130: "Scriptorum autem privatum aliud est, publicum aliud. Publicum lex, senatus consultum, foedus; privatum tabulae, pactum conventum, stipulatio."

39. Cic., *Ad Att.* 6.3.1: "Pomptinus, enim ex pacto et convento (nam ea lege exierat) iam a me discesserat"; translation from *Cicero, Letters to Atticus,* trans. E. O. Winstedt, Loeb Classical Library (Cambridge, Mass., 1970).

40. Alphenus, *Dig.* 4, in *D.* 40.1.6: (see also Chapter 14, note 37 and text): "Servus pecuniam ob libertatem pactus erat et eam domino dederat."

41. Seneca (the Elder), *Controversiae* 9.3: "Per vim metumque gesta ne sint rata. Pacta conventa legibus facta rata sint": once again with the parallelism between the *edictum quod metus causa* and that of the *de pactis:* see above, note 32. On the dating of the materials utilized in the *Controversiae,* see *Praef.* 2–3.

42. In particular Cic., *De inv.* 2.22.68, and Sen., *Controv.* 9.3, leave no doubts on the matter.

43. See *Pro Caec.* 18.51, quoted above, note 35.

44. It is impossible not to connect such a recognition to the admittedly limited and contradictory construction of a subjectivity of the slaves involved in commercial enterprises, which emerged in the analysis of Servius' thought: this small group of edicts, all issued over a few decades (*de pactis, de peculio, de in rem verso,* and on the actions *exsercitoria, tributoria, institoria,* and *quod iussu:* see above, Chapter 14, sec. 3), supported and accompanied by the interpretations and conceptualizations of Quintus Mucius and Alphenus, represents the forwardmost limit attained by the Roman order in the attempt to work around the two great structures that were acting at the same time as conditions of its own existence and as obstacles to any further development: the slave-based nature of production—with the linked fragility and limitations of mercantile circulation—and the "patrimonial" and "civic," as opposed to a directly "individualistic," nature of the private fabric of social life: see also Chapter 18, sec. 2.

45. *Storia spezzata,* pp. 196 ff., 209–210 [*The End of the Past,* pp. 188 ff., 202–203].

46. Those are the dates: it is difficult to think of an *edictum de pactis* issued before the turn of the first century, discernably later than the definitive acknowlegment of the purely consensual character of the schemes of the *ius gentium;* and on the other hand it was certainly well known to the master of the *Rhetorica ad Herennium;* let us venture, then, between 100 and 85 B.C.: the years of Mucius.

47. *Storia spezzata,* pp. 191 ff. [*The End of the Past,* pp. 184 ff.].

48. *Leges publicae,* pp. 448 ff. = *Roman Statutes,* pp. 787 ff.

49. *Storia spezzata,* pp. 198 ff. [*The End of the Past,* pp. 190 ff.].

50. In *D.* 50.16.19: "Labeo libro primo praetoris urbani definit, quod quaedam 'agantur,' quaedam 'gerantur,' quaedam 'contrahantur': et actum quidem generale verbum esse, sive verbis sive re quid agatur, ut in stipulatione vel numeratione: contractum autem ultro citroque obligationem, quod Graeci συνάλλαγμα vocant, veluti emptionem venditionem, locationem conductionem, societatem: gestum rem significare sine verbis factam."

51. Still useful: A. Pernice, "Ulpian als Schriftsteller," *Sitz.-Ber. Akad. Berlin., Philos.-Hist. Klasse* (1885): 462 ff. (reprinted in *Labeo,* 8 [1962]: 369 ff.); P. Jörs, in *RE,* V, cols. 1439 and 1441; T. Honoré, *Ulpian,* 2d ed. (Oxford, 2002), pp. 131 ff. Of the 173 fragments that make up Lenel's palingenesis of Pomponius' *Ad ed.* (*Pal.,* II, cols. 15 ff.: the work was not utilized by Justinian's compilers, and we can reconstruct it solely through the citations of the Severan masters: Stolfi, *Studi sui libri ad edictum di Pomponio,* esp. I, pp. 10 ff.), more than 100 consist of Pomponian citations from the first thirty books of Ulpian's *Ad ed.* The rest are taken from the surviving remains of Ulpian's *Ad edictum,* from the *Ad edictum* of Paul, from Marcianus, *Ad form. hypoth.* (a fragment), and from Cervidius Scaevola, *Quaest.* 1 (a fragment): there is no mistaking the disproportion. In *Ad ed.* 11, Ulpian cites Pomponius 32 times, in texts that were all utilized by O. Lenel to reconstruct Pomponius' *Ad ed.:* see Stolfi,

Studi sui libri ad edictum di Pomponio, I, pp. 215 ff., and II, pp. 259 ff. All the citations in which Ulpian mentions the book from which they were taken prove to be from book 28. We can therefore establish with some degree of confidence: Ulpian, *Ad ed.* 11 = Pomponius, *Ad ed.* 28, with an equation that roughly respects in its values the relationship between the different dimensions of the two bodies of work (83 books of Ulpian, as against the 150 books of Pomponius; but now see Stolfi, *Studi sui libri ad edictum di Pomponio,* I, pp. 29 ff., 205 ff.). The first thirty books of Ulpian correspond to the first two "segments" of composition in the analysis of Honoré, *Ulpian,* pp. 172 ff. The palingenesis of Pomponius contains no fewer than fifty-two citations of Labeo, and we are certain that he was the most significant reference for Pomponius: see T. Honoré, *Gaius* (Oxford, 1962), p. 170; Bretone, *Tecniche,* pp. 236 ff.; but now new light is cast on this relationship by Stolfi, *Studi sui libri ad edictum di Pomponio,* I, pp. 327 ff. The intertwining of texts between Labeo, Pomponius, and Ulpian is rendered clearly by certain passages of the *Ad edictum* by the Severan jurist: "et refert [Pomponius] Labeonem existimare"; "idem Pomponius refert Labeonem existimare"; "Pomponius quoque libro vicensimo octavo scribit Labeonem existimasse," all from *Ad ed.* 11, now in *D.* 4.2.9pr; 4.3.1.6; 4.4.13.1. In other texts Ulpian's reference is introduced in terms such that they leave no doubt about a direct reading: "apud Labeonem autem invenio relatum," or "apud Labeonem memini tractatum libro posteriorum" (*Ad ed.* 35, in *D.* 39.3.1.20; and *Ad Sab.* 17, in *D.* 7.8.2.1). Note the disconcerting statement by F. Schulz, *History of Roman Legal Science* (1946; reprint, Oxford, 1953), p. 198, where, after correctly stating the problem of the Pomponian mediation in the sources of Ulpian's *Ad ed.,* the author concludes that "the answer is a matter of complete indifference." Ulpian cites Labeo eleven times, ending each reference with an indication of the book. Three citations (including the text in question) are from the *Ad edictum* of the Augustan jurist: T. Honoré, *Ulpian,* 2d ed. (Oxford, 2002), p. 132. The relationship of Ulpian with Pedius has now been thoroughly investigated by Giachi, *Studi su Sesto Pedio,* pp. 127 ff.

52. In *D.* 21.1.17.14: "Erronem ita definit Labeo pusillum fugitivum esse, et ex diverso fugitivum magnum erronem." For this and other texts in which it is said of Labeo that "definit," Stolfi, *Studi sui libri ad edictum di Pomponio,* I, pp. 79–80 and n. 148.

53. In *D.* 43.8.3.2: "Publici loci appellatio quemadmodum accipiatur Labeo definit, ut et ad areas et ad insulas et ad agros et ad vias publicas itineraque publica pertineat."

54. In *D.* 4.3.1.2: "Itaque ipse (Labeo) sic definit dolum malum esse omnem calliditatem fallaciam machinationem ad circumveniendum fallendum decipiendum alterum adhibitam."

55. In *D.* 47.10.15.16: "et ita comitem Labeo definit qui frequentandi cuiusque causa ut sequatur destinatus in publico privatoque abductus fuerit."

56. In *D.* 50.16.38: "Ostentum Labeo definit omne contra naturam cuiusque rei genitum factumque."

57. See Chapter 18, sec. 4, Chapter 19, sec. 2, and note 51 above.

58. For Ulpian: *Pal.,* I, cols. 501–528 nn. 4–6, 8, 9, 11–13, 15, 18, 20–24, 26, 28–36, 38–42, 46, 48, 49, 51–54, 56–60, 63, 65–71, 73–85, 87, 89, 90, 91, 92, 93, 94–96, 99–102, 104, 105, 107–109, 111, 113–120, 122, 124, 125, 127–135, 137–144, 146–163, 165, 166, 168–173, 175, 176, 178, 179, 181, 182, 184, 185, 186–191; for Paul: ibid., nn. 10, 14, 16, 17, 19, 25, 27, 37, 45, 47, 50, 55, 61, 62, 64, 72, 75, 88, 97, 103, 121, 123, 126, 136, 145, 164, 188; for Neratius: ibid., n. 110; for Celsus: ibid., n. 86; for Cervidius Scaevola: ibid., n. 106; for Terentius Clemens: ibid., n. 112; for Venuleius: ibid., nn. 167, 174, 177, 180, 183, 187; for Papinian: ibid., n. 98; for Callistratus: ibid., nn. 43, 44; for Gellius: ibid., nn. 1, 2, 3, 7, 397, 398, 399; for Gaius: ibid., nn. 389–394.

59. As regards the dates of the *Ad edictum* and, in general, all of Labeo's known output, we are not today much further advanced than Bremer, II.1, p. 12, who observed that "Quo tempore Labeonis opera singula conscripta sint, de paucis accuratius explorari potest." Nor do we seem to have much help from the available biographical information on the life of the jurist. Concerning the *Ad edictum* we are still faced with the problem of the number of books, with reference to the relationship among the books *Ad ed. praetoris urbani* and the books *Ad ed. praetoris peregrini*: *Pal.,* I, cols. 501–502 n. 2.

60. *Pal.,* II, col. 460.

61. See Chapter 14, sec. 4.

62. We may likewise be able to assign to Servius–Alphenus the use of *contrahere* in *D.* 46.3.35 and *D.* 19.2.31 (see Chapter 14, sec. 4).

63. See Chapter 12, sec. 2.

64. There can be no doubt that Labeo was thoroughly familiar with Servius' work. He also cites Quintus Mucius on a number of occasions: see *D.* 32.29.1 and 40.7.39pr. The latter's *Iuris civilis* must have been a milestone in any legal education in the Augustan age: it is therefore certain that his approach to the *quaedam contrahantur* was conditioned by the texts that we have just read.

65. See Chapter 14, sec. 4.

66. As we learn from Ulpian, *Ad ed.* 4, in *D.* 2.13.6.3: "Rationem autem esse Labeo ait ultro citro dandi accipiendi, credendi, obligandi solvendi sui causa negotiationem."

67. *Pal.,* I, Lab., n. 10 (= *D.* 50.16.5.1), 124 (= *D.* 47.8.4.2), 126 (= *Collatio Legum Mosaicarum et Romanarum* 2.5.1), 159 (= *D.* 43.17.3.7), 364 (= *D.* 41.2.1pr), and in the first case the Greek term is introduced by the same stylistic element that we find in our text: "quod Graeci . . . vocant" (see note 72 below, and text). This list however does not take into account the Greek words that are found in the epitome of Javolenus on the *Posteriores* of Labeo, and which may also certainly be assigned to the Au-

gustan jurist: see, e.g., *D.* 28.7.20pr and *D.* 32.100. The rejection of an uncontrolled use of Graecisms is in Cicero, *Orator ad M. Brutum* 49.164 and *De off.* 1.31.111.

68. Aristotle, *Ethica Nicomachea* 5.2.12–13.1130b–1131a: τῆς δὲ κατὰ μέρος δικαιοσύνης καὶ τοῦ κατ'αὐτὴν δικαίου ἐν μέν ἐστιν εἶδος τὸ ἐν ταῖς διανομαῖς τιμῆς ἢ χρημάτων ἢ τῶν ἄλλων ὅσα μεριστὰ τοῖς κοινωνοῦσι τῆς πολιτείας (ἐν τούτοις γὰρ ἔστι καὶ ἄνισον ἔχειν καὶ ἴσον ἕτερον ἑτέρου), ἐν δὲ τὸ ἐν τοῖς συναλλάγμασι διορθωτικόν. τούτου δὲ μέρη δύο· τῶν γὰρ συναλλαγμάτων τὰ μὲν ἑκούσιά ἐστι τὰ δ'ἀκούσια, ἑκούσια μὲν τὰ τοιάδε οἷον πρᾶσις ὠνὴ δανεισμὸς ἐγγύη χρῆσις παρακαταθήκη μίσθωσις (ἑκούσια δὲ λέγεται, ὅτι ἡ ἀρχὴ τῶν συναλλαγμάτων τούτων ἑκούσιας), τῶν δ'ἀκουσίων τὰ μὲν λαθραῖα, οἷον κλοπὴ μοιχεία φαρμακεία προαγωγεία δουλαπατία δολοφονία ψευδομαρτυρία, τὰ δὲ βίαια, οἷον αἰκία δεσμὸς θάνατος ἁρπαγὴ πήρωσις κακηγορία προπηλακισμός. The ethical corpus of Aristotle is, taken as part of the philosopher's entire surviving output, the segment that presents, along with the *Metaphysics,* the greatest textual problems. In particular, what closely pertains to our discourse is the fact that the central books of the *Nicomachean Ethics* (including the fifth) are repeated in their entirety in the *Eudemian Ethics* (*Eth. Nic.* e–h = *Eth. Eud.* d–z). It is possible to identify five original blocks underlying the ethical works of Aristotle (leaving aside the *Magna Moralia*): (1) a primitive *Eth. Nic.* in five books instead of ten (*Eth. Nic.* a, b, g, d, k); (2) a primitive *Ethica Eudemia* in three books instead of eight—it is in fact generally accepted by now that the last three chapters of *Eth. Eud.* h should be considered an autonomous book q (*Eth. Eud.* a, b, g); and then a group of πραγματεῖαι composed by Aristotle in the form of notes, and which included: (3) *Eth. Eud.* h–q; (4) the three "common" books repeated in *Eth. Eud.* d, e, z and in *Eth. Nic.* e, z, h; (5) the little treatise περὶ ἀλίας later added to the *Eth. Nic.* Of these parts, the oldest would be the *Eth. Eud.*; then the notes of the "common book"; and last of all the five books of the *Eth. Nic.,* the product of the philosopher's more mature reflections. It was only from the period of Andronicus that these notes would be added to the *Eth. Nic.,* along with those of the περὶ ἀλίας. This reconstruction has the advantage of taking into account the systematic discontinuities, not to mention those of theoretical outlook, of the present composition of the *Eth. Nic.* and a certain degree of discursive confusion in the three "common books," without necessarily falling back on nonconservative hypotheses. On these problems see the comment of F. Dirlmeier, *Aristoteles, Nikomachische Ethik* (Berlin, 1956), pp. 243 ff.; and J. Ritter, "Naturrecht bei Aristoteles," in *Metaphisik und Politik. Studien zu Aristoteles und Hegel* (Frankfurt am Main, 1969). While the *Eth. Eud.* manifestly reveals a powerful presence of Platonic influences, the *Eth. Nic.* betrays a break with this orientation, with a shift toward a social and more worldly ethics. In the change of perspective, the "common books" mark an intermediate point: on the one hand we see in them a renunciation of a model

dominated by metaphysics, and a move towards a problematic horizon focused around the human subjectivity of the τυχὼν ἀνήρ, the empiricism of ἐθισμός, and practical wisdom. On the other hand, there is still the rigor of the moral imperative. In the text in question, in particular, it strikes me that there is already a presence of the descriptive method that is typical of the first four books of the *Eth. Nic.* That the entire fifth book of the *Eth. Nic.* should be read in that context is maintained by M. Finley, "Aristotle and Economic Analysis," *Past and Present,* 47 (1970): 3 ff. (= *Studies in Ancient Society* [London, 1974], pp. 26 ff.), who believes that the part concerning "corrective" (or "normative") justice is the only work of Aristotle, along with a section of book 1 of the *Politica,* in which we can detect a genuine "economic analysis": but this is an excessive judgment: see *Storia spezzata,* pp. 38–39 [*The End of the Past,* pp. 34–35].

The scope of the Aristotelian use of συνάλλαγμα has not yet been studied with sufficient thoroughness: bibliographic indications in *Giuristi,* pp. 169 ff. and 236–237. Of some utility might be a comparison of the Aristotelian significance of συνάλλαγμα with those found in Demosthenes 30.21; 24.212–213; 33.12; and in a text of the Hippocratic corpus, *De medico* 1 (Bensel, "Hippocraticus qui fertur 'De Medico' libellus ad codicum fidem recensitus," *Philologus,* 78 [1922]: 120 ff.): *Giuristi,* pp. 167 ff. Of minor interest is the connection with Plato, *Republic* 8.556a–b and *Laws* 9.861b (F. Pringsheim, *The Greek Law of Sale* [Weimar, 1950], p. 36 and n. 6): in the former there is only a passing mention of ἑκουσίων συμβολαίων; in the second there exists a classification according to the scheme τὰ μὲν ἑκούσια, τὰ δὲ ἀκούσια, but in reference to the δύο εἴδη τῶν ἀδικημάτων. Nor can we determine much more from the other Aristotelian uses of συνάλλαγμα, devoid of any particular conceptual value: *Eth. Nic.* 2.1.7.1103b; 5.4.1.1131b; 5.8.10.1135b; 7.10.19.1243a; 10.8.1.1178a; *Rhetorica* 1.1.1354b; 1.15.1376b; *Politica* 4.16.1300b; 6.8.1322b.

69. I have developed in a direction that he failed to consider a point of view first pursued by M. Riedel, *Metaphysik und Metapolitik. Studien zu Aristoteles und zur politischen Sprache der neuzeitlichen Philosophie* (Frankfurt am Main, 1975).

70. P. Moraux, *Der Aristotelismus bei den Griechen von Andronikos bis Alexander von Aphrodisias,* I: *Die Renaissance des Aristotelismus in I. Jh. v. Chr.* (Berlin, 1973), pp. 36 ff., 45 ff., 56 ff.

71. Ciceronian references to other Roman libraries that must have contained Aristotelian works: *Ad. Att.* 4.10.1 and *De finibus* 3.2.7 and 3.3.10. The anecdote is in *Topica* 1.1–5. The judgment ("Ofilius utroque doctior") of Cascellius and of Trebatius is in Pomp., *Ench.,* in *D.* 1.2.2.45.

72. Paul, *Ad ed.* 2, in *D.* 50.16.5.1: "'Opere locato conducto': his verbis Labeo significari ait id opus, quod Graeci ἀποτέλεσμα vocant, non ἔργον, id est ex opere facto corpus aliquod perfectum."

73. Ἀποτέλεσμα is a little-used word; one of its rare applications is in an apocryphal

work from the Aristotelian corpus: *De mundo* 5.397a. More frequent is the verb
ἀποτελεῖν. The first text in *Eth. Nic.* is 2.6.2.1106a: ῥητέον οὖν ὅτι πᾶσα ἀρετή,
οὗ ἄν ᾖ ἀρετή, αὐτό τε εὖ ἔχον ἀποτελεῖ καὶ τὸ ἔργον αὐτοῦ εὖ εὖ' ἀποδίδ-
ωσιν.

74. Arist., *Eth. Nic.* 6.12.6.1144a: ἔτι τὸ ἔργον ἀποτελεῖται κατα τὴν φρόνησιν καὶ
τὴν ἠθικὴν ἀρετήν.

75. Ulpian, *Ad ed.* 11, in *D.* 4.2.5: "Metum accipiendum Labeo dicit non quemlibet
timorem, sed maioris malitatis."

76. Arist., *Eth. Nic.* 3.1.4.1110a: ὅσα δὲ διὰ φόβον μειζόνων κακῶν πράττεται
ἢ διὰ καλόν τι, οἷον εἰ τύραννος προστάττοι αἰσχρόν τι πρᾶξαι κύριος
ὢν γονέων καὶ τέκνων, καὶ πράξαντος μὲν σώζοιντο μὴ πράξαντος
δ'ἀποθνήσκοιεν, ἀμασβήτησιν ἔχει πότερον ἀκούσιά ἐστιν ἢ ἑκούσια.
On the basis of an old prejudice, the Labeonian passage was suspected of having
been an interpolation, precisely because of its connection to the Aristotelian *Ethics*, by F. Schulz, *Prinzipien des römischen Rechts* (Munich, 1934), in English as *Principles of Roman Law*, trans. M. Wolff (Oxford, 1936).

77. Since in that context there was no clear evidence of the scheme of the *ultro citroque obligatio: Giuristi*, pp. 176 and 238 n. 69. See also A. Watson, "The Evolution
of Law: The Roman System of Contracts," *Law and History Review*, 2 (1984): 1 ff.

78. See Chapter 14, sec. 4.

79. Labeo, *Post a Iav. epit.* 5, in *D.* 18.1.80.3: "Nemo potest videri eam rem vendidisse,
de cuius dominio id agitur, ne ad emptorem transeat, sed hoc aut locatio est aut
aliud genus contractus." See also Javolenus, *Ex Post. Lab.* 5, in *D.* 18.1.79; *D.* 19.5.17.1
(Ulpian, *Ad. ed.* 28), which reports Labeonian thought; and *D.* 4.3.9.3 (Ulpian, *Ad.
ed.* 11), likewise with a precise Labeonian citation from the *Posteriores*.

80. In particular we should point out that of the fragments in the "Labeo series," to
which ours belongs, the only one in which it is possible to identify with confidence the presence of Javolenus, is *D.* 40.12.42: for the others, barring new evidence to the contrary, we should assume that they reflect the thought of Labeo.
For that matter, it is not conceivable that the passage in *D.* 18.1.80.3 (which is of
particular significance to us here) could be by Javolenus, because it clashes with
what must have in all likelihood been a consolidated non-Labeonian orientation
of the jurist (*Logiche*, p. 148: see Chapter 19, sec. 1). Nor does the passage present
signs of editing, either by pre-Justinian editors or by the compilers, confirmation
of the observation that in the fragments of the "Labeo series," "Pre-Justinian additions appear to be present . . . only to a small degree" (thus Schulz, *History of
Roman Legal Science*, p. 208).

81. Ulpian, *Ad ed.* 31, in *D.* 19.5.19pr: "Rogasti me, ut tibi nummos mutuos darem: ego
cum non haberem, dedi tibi rem vendendam, ut pretio utereris. Si non vendidisti
aut vendidisti quidem, pecuniam autem non accepisti mutuam, tutius est ita

agere, ut Labeo ait, praescriptis verbis, quasi negotio quodam inter nos gesto proprii contractus."

82. In *D.* 19.3.1, where there is a description of how the *actio de aestimato* was proposed "tollendae dubitationis gratia," at the end of a long disputation about the type of action to be conceded "propter aestimationem . . . utrum ex vendito . . . an ex locato . . . an ex conducto . . . an mandati," on the basis of the substantial recognition of a new contractual figure.

83. Gaius, *Institutiones* 4.131, speaks of an "uncertain formula," or "qua incertum petimus": *EP,* pp. 151 ff. and 156 ff.

84. Cic., *De fin.* 2.1.3; and *TPSulp.* 34. See also Gaius, *Inst.* 1.132.

85. See Chapter 20, sec. 4.

86. Ulpian, *Ad ed.* 11, in *D.* 18.1.50.3: "Labeo scribit, si mihi bibliothecam ita vendideris, si decuriones Campani locum me vendidissent, in quo eam ponerem, et per me stet, quo minus id a Campanis impetrem, non esse dubitandum, quin praescriptis verbis agi possit. Ego etiam ex vendito agi posse puto quasi impleta condicione, cum per emptorem stet, quo minus impleatur."

87. P. Stein, *Regulae Iuris: From Juristic Rules to Legal Maxims* (Edinburgh, 1966), pp. 54–55, where there is a bibliography.

88. Stein, *Regulae Iuris,* pp. 65–66.

18. The Definition of Characteristics

1. Pomponius, *Ad Sab.* 30, in *D.* 41.3.30.1 (*Pal.,* I, col. 528 and n. 1) for the books *Epistularum;* and Ulpian, *Ad ed.* 18, in *Collatio Legum Mosaicarum et Romanarum* 12.7.3 (*Pal.,* I, cols. 536–537), for the books *Responsorum.*

2. Pomponius, *Enchiridion,* in *D.* 1.2.2.47.

3. See Gellius, *Noctes Atticae* 1.12.18; 6.15.1; 20.1.13.

4. *Pal.,* I, cols. 528–534.

5. *Pal.,* I, cols. 534–536: see also above, Chapter 17, sec. 5.

6. See Chapter 17, note 87.

7. See Chapter 12, sec 1.

8. F. Schulz, *History of Roman Legal Science* (1946; reprint, Oxford, 1953), pp. 1125 ff.; R. A. Bauman, *Lawyers and Politics in the Early Roman Empire: A Study of Relations between the Roman Jurists and the Emperors from Augustus to Hadrian* (Munich, 1989), pp. 1 ff. Also see below, Chapter 19, sec. 4.

9. Tacitus, *Annales* 6.26.1: "Haud multo post Cocceius Nerva, continuus principi, omnis divini humanique iuris sciens, integro statu, corpore inlaeso, moriendi consilium cepit. Quod ut Tiberio cognitum, adsidere, causas requirere, addere preces; fateri postremo grave coscientiae, grave famae suae, si proximus amicorum nullis moriendi rationibus vitam fugeret. Aversatus sermonem Nerva abstinentiam cibi

coniunxit. Ferebant gnari cogitationum eius, quanto propius mala rei publicae viseret, ira et metu, dum integer, dum intemptatus, honestum finem voluisse"; translation, with modifications, from *The Annals of Tacitus*, trans. G. Ramsay (London, 1904).

10. Suetonius, *Caligula* 34.2: "De iuris quoque consultis, quasi scientiae eorum omnem usum aboliturus [Caligula] saepe iactavit se 'mehercule effecturum, ne quid respondere possint praeter eum.'"

11. Seneca, *Apocolocyntosis* 12.2: "Iurisconsulti e tenebris procedebant, pallidi, graciles, vix animam habentes, tamquam qui tum maxime revivescerent."

12. Pomp., *Ench.*, in *D.* 1.2.2.51–52: "Hic consul fuit cum Quartino [Surdino] temporibus Tiberii, sed plurium in civitate auctoritatis habuit eo usque, donec eum Caesar civitate pelleret. Expulsus ab eo in Sardiniam, revocatus a Vespasiano, diem suum obit."

13. Pomp., *Ench.*, in *D.* 1.2.2.49: "Et ex illo tempore peti hoc pro beneficio coepit." We can also add what Juvenal, 4.77–81, writes about Pegasus, another jurist of some importance (Bremer, II.2, pp. 199–210; *Pal.*, II, cols. 9–12; and, below, Chapter 19, esp. note 13), prefect of the city during the reign of Domitian: "interpres legum sanctissimus omnia, quamquam temporibus diris, tractanda putabat inermi iustitia"—"despite the ferocity of the time, he believed that he could treat all matters with an unarmed justice."

14. *Pal.*, I, cols. 787–790: fourteen citations by Ulpian, and twelve by Paul; but Nerva was also cited by Julian, Pomponius, and Gaius.

15. See Chapters 21 and 22.

16. This is, in substance, the thesis of Stolfi, "Il modello delle scuole," pp. 1 ff., esp. 7 ff., 68 ff., which articulates and demonstrates an old idea of mine (*Linee*, p. 199).

17. Stolfi, "Il modello delle scuole," p. 100.

18. Bremer, II.1, pp. 313 ff.; *Pal.*, II, cols. 187–216 (also by O. Lenel, *Das Sabinussystem* [Strasbourg, 1892], now in *Gesammelte Schriften*, ed. O. Behrends and F. d'Ippolito, II [Naples, 1990], pp. 3 ff.—a pioneering work); F. Schulz, *Sabinus-Fragmente in Ulpians Sabinus-Commentar* (Halle, 1906), reprinted in *Labeo*, 10 (1964): 50 ff., 234 ff.

19. Pomp., *Ench.*, in *D.* 1.2.2.50.

20. Paul, *Ad ed.* 40, in *D.* 38.1.18: *Pal.*, II, col. 187.

21. Recalled by Paul, *Ad l. Iul et Pap.* 10, in *D.* 50.16.144; *Pal.*, II, col. 189; Bremer, II.1, pp. 367 ff.

22. Paul, *Ad Plaut.* 16, in *D.* 50.17.1.3: "Regula est, quae rem quae est breviter enarrat: non ex regula ius sumatur, sed ex iure quod est regula fiat. Per regulam igitur brevis rerum narratio traditur, et, ut ait Sabinus, quasi causae coniectio est, quae simul cum in aliquo vitiata est, perdit officium suum."

23. But commented on by Javolenus Priscus, Neratius, Pomponius, and Paul; *Pal.*, II, cols. 13–14; Bremer, II.2, pp. 218–236.

24. Bauman, *Lawyers and Politics,* pp. 62 ff.

25. Ibid., pp. 76 ff.; *Pal.,* I, cols. 109–126; Bremer, II.1, pp. 9–261.

26. Bauman, *Lawyers and Politics,* pp. 87 ff.

27. Tac., *Ann.* 14.42–44: *Storia spezzata,* pp. 117 ff. [*The End of the Past,* pp. 108 ff.].

28. Plato, *Laws* 6.19.777b–c: δῆλον ὡς ἐπειδὴ δύσκολόν ἐστι τὸ θρέμμα ἄνθρωπος, καὶ πρὸς τὴν ἀναγκαίαν διόρισιν, τὸ δοῦλόν τε ἔργῳ διορίζεσθαι καὶ ἐλεύθερον καὶ δεσπότην, οὐδαμῶς εὔχρηστον ἐθέλειν εἶναι τε καὶ γίγνεσθαι φαίνεται, [777c] χαλεπὸν δὴ τὸ κτῆμα . . .; translation from *Laws,* trans. R. G. Bury, Loeb Classical Library (1926; reprint, Cambridge, Mass., 1967).

29. Ulpian, *Ad ed.* 50, in *D.* 29.5.1pr. See Dalla, *Senatus consultum Silanianum,* pp. 2–3.

30. Ulpian, in *D.* 29.5.1.26–27. See Dalla, *Senatus consultum Silanianum,* pp. 68 ff.

31. "Quidam insontes": *Ann.* 14.44.4.

32. Tac., *Ann.* 14.45.1–2.

33. Seneca, *Epistulae* 5.47.

34. Tac., *Ann.* 14.43.1: "Saepe numero, patres conscripti, in hoc ordine interfui, cum contra instituta et leges maiorum nova senatus decreta postularentur; neque sum adversatus, non quia dubitarem, super omnibus negotiis melius atque rectius olim provisum et quae converterentur [ad] deterius mutari, sed ne nimio amore antiqui moris studium meum extollere videtur"; translation from *Annals,* trans. J. Johnson, Loeb Classical Library (1937; reprint, Cambridge, Mass., 1963). Tacitus was an admirer of Cassius, as can clearly be seen in *Ann.* 11.12.

35. See Chapter 17, sec. 1.

36. See Chapter 19, sec. 2.

37. As we learn from Paul, *Ad Sab.* 33, in *D.* 18.1.1pr-1 (see also Gaius, *Institutiones* 3.141), and from Sabinus in Paul, *Ad ed.* 2, in *D.* 18.5.6.

38. Stolfi, "Il modello delle scuole," pp. 81–82.

39. Tac., *Ann.* 14.44.4: "At quidam insontes peribunt nam et ex fuso exercitu cum decimus quisque fusti feritur etiam strenui sortiuntur habet aliquid ex iniquo omne magnum exemplum, quod contra singulos utilitate publica rependitur"; translation from *Annals,* trans. J. Johnson, Loeb Classical Library (1937; reprint, Cambridge, Mass., 1963).

40. See Bauman, *Lawyers in Roman Republican Politics,* pp. 100 ff., with a rapid overview of the occurrences of *utilitas publica* in Tacitus (where I believe the expression is found for the first time—and we may well think of a Cassian derivation) and in the legal literature successive to Cassius Longinus. The notion of *utilitas* as an interpretative criterion, on the other hand, is already Ciceronian: e.g., *De legibus* 1.15.42. For the reference to Capito, I am thinking of the conceptual background of his definition of *lex,* previously mentioned above in Chapter 8, sec. 1 and note 3.

41. See Chapter 9, sec. 5.

42. We learn this from a citation of Paul, *Ad Plaut.* 6, in *D.* 22.1.38.7: ". . . Sabinus et Cassius . . . ex aequitate . . . fructus . . . praestandos putant . . ."; see also Chapter 21, sec. 5.

43. See Chapter 8, sec. 4.

44. *Storia spezzata*, pp. 119–120 [*The End of the Past*, pp. 110–111]; Bauman, *Lawyers and Politics*, p. 126.

45. Seneca, *De clementia* 2.7.3: "Clementia liberum arbitrium habet; non sub formula, sed ex aequo et bono iudicat"; another reference to *bonum et aequum*—an expression that as far as we are able to determine was not used in those years, is again in *De clem.*, at 1.4. See Chapter 9, sec. 5, and Chapter 21, sec. 2.

46. *Aequum/aequitas* both recur repeatedly in Seneca: e.g., *Epistulae* 30.11; 63.7; 86.2; 93.1; 94.11; 95.52; 107.6; 113.32; 123.16; *De brevitate vitae* 18.5; *Ad Polybium de consolatione* 14.1; 16.4. The philosopher's thinking verges on numerous occasions on an outlook resembling individualism, without ever succeeding in fully developing it, as was the case later with Marcus Aurelius, in his meditations: see Chapter 22, sec. 3.

47. See esp. T. Honoré, "Proculus," *T,* 30 (1962): 490–491; also Bauman, *Lawyers in Roman Republican Politics*, pp. 119 ff.

48. See Chapter 21 in sec 5; note 46 above, and Chapter 21, note 63.

49. *Pal.,* II, cols. 166–169; Bremer, II.2, pp. 130–138.

50. Honoré, "Proculus," pp. 472 ff.

51. The text of Paul, *Ad Sab.* 33, in *D.* 18.1.1pr-1, is the same one cited in connection with the thought of Cassius; that of Ulpian is in *Ad ed.* 26, in *D.* 12.4.3.3–4.

52. Proculus and Nerva the Younger do not receive even a mention from Tacitus: from the point of view of an entirely "political" historiography that shadow of caution—not worthy of attention—was the only distinguishing tone of these characters. For Nerva the Younger, see Bauman, *Lawyers and Politics*, pp. 43–44, 53–54, 119–120, 126–127.

53. See Chapter 19, sec. 4.

54. See Chapter 11, sec. 1 and note 18.

55. See Chapter 12, sec. 1.

56. For Paul: *Pal.,* I, cols. 1251–93; for Ulpian: *Pal.,* II, cols. 1019–98: see also above, note 18.

57. Persius 5.88–90: "Vindicta postquam meus a praetore recessi, / cur mihi non liceat, iussit quodcumque voluntas, / excepto si quid Masuri rubrica vetavit?" In his turn, Gellius, *Noctes Atticae* 11.18.21, writes "alio capite" in reference to the books of Sabinus, using the same words that Cicero applied to Mucius' *Iuris civilis:* the image is still that of the *lex,* of a writing that directly becomes normative canon.

58. *Rhetorica ad Herennium* 3.37. See also *Lex Municipii Salpensiani*, in *FIRA*, I, pp. 204 ff. = *CIL*, II, p. 253 n. 1963.

59. See note 71 below.

60. Paul, *Ad ed.* 63, in *D.* 43.1.2.3; and *Vaticana Fragmenta* 227 (also referring to Paul, but the word is actually from the editor of the *Fragmenta*).

61. Quintilian, *Institutio oratoria* 12.3.11: "Verum ea, quae de moribus excolendis studioque iuris praecipimus, nonne quis eo credat reprendenda, quod multos cognovimus, qui taedio laboris, quem ferre tendentibus ad eloquentiam necesse est, confugerint ad haec deverticula desidae? Quorum alii se ad album ac rubricas transtulerunt et formularii vel, ut Cicero ait, legulei quidam esse maluerunt"; translation from *The Orator's Education,* trans. D. A. Russell (Cambridge, Mass., 2001).

62. Cicero, *De oratore* 1.55.236.

63. See Chapter 19, sec. 3.

64. The legal literature of the principate would always privilege, among its various communicative modules, that of the commentary. From Cassius Longinus onwards, all the treatises of the *ius civile* would take the form of commentaries on the books of Quintus Mucius or Sabinus: thus for Gaius (*Pal.,* I, col. 251), for Pomponius (*Pal.,* II, cols. 60–79), for Paul (*Pal.,* I, cols. 1251–93), and for Ulpian (*Pal.,* II, cols. 1019–1198). In its turn, the commentary on the edict (urban and provincial) would become a successful literary genre: from Ofilius (*Pal.,* I, cols. 795–804) to Labeo (*Pal.,* I, cols. 501–528), to Pedius (*Pal.,* II, cols. 1–10), and Pomponius (*Pal.,* II, cols. 15–44), as well as Paul (*Pal.,* I, cols. 966–1098) and Ulpian (*Pal.,* II, cols. 421–898). And similarly in the major anthologies of legal opinions on cases and issues—in the *Digesta* of Julian (*Pal.,* I, cols. 318–484), as well as in those of Marcellus (*Pal.,* I, cols. 589–632), it was still the commentary—upon edictal titles, *leges,* and *senatusconsulta*—that punctuated the pattern of the entire composition; to say nothing of the notes and the comments which, beginning with the Servian *Reprehensa* themselves, would succeed one another for centuries, following the writings of Alphenus-Servius (notes or epitomes: *Pal.,* I, cols. 38–45, 45–53), Labeo (*Pal.,* I, cols. 528–534, 299–315, 536), and Julian (*Pal.,* I, col. 692 nn. 2 and 3). So vast a presence can be no accident. The diffusion of the literary genre betrays the underlying persistence of a form of thought. We might define it as the peculiar continuism of Roman legal science, or even (to state it from another point of view) the existence of a relationship, in the mental procedures of the jurists, between the technique of the commentary and the search for the truth, as a projection of the nexus between prescription and duration, between norm and time: in short, the magnetism of the past. In the work of the jurists from the first century A.D. onwards, the polarity between the reproposition of an older text—a *lex,* a *senatusconsultum,* a

well-established edictal title, a *caput,* or a *rubrica* of the Mucian or Sabinian *ius civile*—taken as a point from which to begin—and the power of the commentary itself, in which all possible intellectual creativity was obliged to pass through the filter of the literary form employed, imposed a certain uniformity upon the preceding text; it determined a particular curvature in the relationship between tradition and innovation, and the equilibrium between memory and change, so that every new development, even the most transformative, was inevitably obliged to blaze a path under the mitigated form of a reelaboration of the ancient. When medieval and modern legal thought—from Irnerio to Savigny—would imagine itself as an extension of classical science, it was doing nothing more than unconsciously retrieving a paradigm that the Roman jurists of the mature period had already used to construct their own relationship with the past: the commentary was for the latter—just as the interpretation of Justinian's *Digesta* would be for the moderns—not a restriction blocking the birth of the new, but a key to gain access to the specific temporality of their knowledge, and to the network of the logical and textual genealogies that supported and justified it: in order to gain access to that "dialogue between great authors" (I take the expression from L. Lombardi, *Saggio sul diritto giurisprudenziale* [Milan, 1967], p. 57—a book that still bears reading), which represented the very essence of their knowledge.

65. See Chapter 6, sec. 1.

66. In the entire commentary of Pomponius on Quintus Mucius there are no citations of pre-Mucian authors, except for the mention of Publius Mucius in *D.* 50.7.18 (there is however a reference to two episodes of republican history: the "postliminium" of Attilius Regulus, and the episode of Hostilius Mancinus and the Numantini, respectively in *D.* 49.15.5.3 and 50.7.18), while in the fragments of the *ius civile* of Ciceronian and Gellian provenance (*Noc. Att.* 17.7.1–3, to which we might add the reference to Brutus in 6.15.1), these references occupy a substantial space (we should also take into account a text from the third book of the *Regulae* of Modestinus, in *D.* 49.15.4, where the joint reference to Mucius and to Brutus allows us to think confidently of a Mucian citation of the earlier author, and a passage from Ulpian, *Ad Sab.* 28, in *D.* 18.2.13pr, from which we learn of a joint citation, made by Celsus, of Mucius, Brutus, and Labeo, allowing us to presume that it too is another Mucian reference to Brutus). An acceptable reconstruction of the original structure of the Mucian writing is in Bremer, I, p. 65 (correcting no fewer than three errors in a few lines: *D.* 47.22.77.1 should be read as 47.2.77.1; *D.* 9.1.1.1 as 9.1.1.11, and *D.* 49.15.5 as 49.15.4).

67. See Chapter 9, sec. 3.

68. Cicero, *Pro Caecina* 15.42; 16.47; 17.49; 19.55; 20.56–57; 21.59–60; 22.62, compared with Julian, *Dig.* 44, in *D.* 41.3.33.2; with Ulpian, *Ad ed.* 69, in *D.* 43.16.1.29; 43.16.3.1–4; *Ad ed.* 56, in *D.* 47.8.2.12 and 47.8.2.7; and with Paul, *Ad ed.* 7, in *D.* 48.6.9.

69. Asconius, *In Cornelianam* 1.59 (Clark) = 48 (Stangl); Dio Cassius 36.40.1–2. On C. Cornelius, T. R. S. Broughton, *The Magistrates of the Roman Republic,* 3 vols. (New York, 1951–52), II, pp. 44–45.

70. See Chapter 17, sec. 4.

71. Pomp., *Ench.,* in *D.* 1.2.2.44: "De iurisdictione idem edictum praetoris primus diligenter composuit."

72. Ulpian: *Pal.,* I, col. 798 (*D.* 32.55.1.4–7); Cicero: *Ad familiares* 3.8.3.

73. It should be remembered that *diligenter* is a *hapax* in the *Enchiridion;* its solitary use betrays a certain emphasis or, at the very least, a kind of particular underscoring (the adverb occurs on only two other occasions in the entire Pomponian corpus, in contexts that are completely different: *Ad Sab.* 5, in *D.* 40.4.8; and *Ex Plaut.* 7, in *D.* 40.7.21pr). And Pomponius in fact uses *fundare* in reference to Ofilius, although we are not certain that we can link the expression to the work on the edict ("et qui omnem partem operis fundarent reliquit," also in *D.* 1.2.2.44): as was the case for Brutus, Manilius, and Publius Mucius in *D.* 1.2.2.39 (see Chapter 10, sec. 1).

74. Bremer, I, p. 341.

75. The text of Servius-Alphenus is in Paul, *Epit. Alf. dig.* 4, in *D.* 8.3.30, which restores the original structure of a Servian response.

76. See Chapter 17, sec. 3.

77. *Storia spezzata,* pp. 183 ff. [*The End of the Past,* pp. 175 ff.].

78. See sec. 2 of this chapter and Chapter 22, sec. 3.

79. I have already touched on this point in *Storia spezzata,* p. 186. [*The End of the Past,* pp. 178].

19. Jurists and Emperors

1. *Pal.,* II, cols. 1–10; Bremer, II.2, pp. 79–99: C. Giachi, *Studi su Sesto Pedio: La tradizione, l'editto* (Milan, 2005), pp. 29 and 108 ff.; also T. Honoré, *Ulpian,* 2d ed. (Oxford, 2002), pp. 130, 140.

2. In the texts by Pomponius that have survived, Pedius is never mentioned; but it seems impossible to imagine that Pomponius' *Ad edictum* did not contain any citations from him. Traces of these presences are still perceptible in the writings of Ulpian: Bremer, II.2, pp. 80, 83; E. Stolfi, *Studi sui libri ad edictum di Pomponio,* 2 vols. (Milan, 2001–02), I, pp. 503 ff.; Giachi, *Studi su Sesto Pedio,* pp. 18 ff.

3. Giachi, *Studi su Sesto Pedio,* pp. 183 ff.

4. Ulpian, *Ad ed. aed. cur.* 1, in *D.* 1.3.13: "Nam, ut ait Pedius, quotiens lege aliquid unum vel alterum introductum est, bona occasio est cetera, quae tendunt ad eandem utilitatem, vel interpretatione vel certe iurisdictione suppleri."

5. Two important texts are Paul, *Ad ed.* 32 (but 33 according to O. Lenel, *Pal.,* I, col.

304 n. 2), in *D.* 19.4.1.2–3; and Ulpian, *Ad ed.* 27, in *D.* 13.5.3.2. For Pedius' use of *aequum*, see, e.g., Ulpian, *Ad ed.* 70, in *D.* 43.19.3.2; Ulpian, *Ad ed. aed. cur.* 1, in *D.* 21.1.25.4; Paul, *Ad ed.* 45, in *D.* 47.10.16.

6. See Chapter 20, sec. 4.

7. R. A. Bauman, *Lawyers and Politics in the Early Roman Empire: A Study of Relations between the Roman Jurists and the Emperors from Augustus to Hadrian* (Munich, 1989), pp. 165 ff.

8. J. Crook, *Consilium principis: Imperial Council and Counsellors from Augustus to Diocletian* (Cambridge, 1955), remains an important book.

9. See Chapter 18, note 64. The texts by Javolenus are in *Pal.,* I, cols. 299–315 (commentary on Labeo's *Posteriores*), 277–285 (from Cassius), 297–299 (from Plautius).

10. Proculus, *Epistulae* 2, in *D.* 50.17.202: "Omnis definitio in iure civili periculosa est: parum est enim, ut non subverti potest."

11. P. Stein, *Regulae Iuris: From Juristic Rules to Legal Maxims* (Edinburgh, 1966), p. 70.

12. W. Kunkel, *Herkunft und soziale Stellung der römischen Juristen,* 2d ed. (Graz, 1967), pp. 90 ff., 141 ff.

13. Bauman, *Lawyers and Politics,* pp. 142 ff. (on Caelius Sabinus), 146 ff. (on Pegasus; see above, Chapter 18, esp. note 13.)

14. Bauman, *Lawyers and Politics,* pp. 193 ff.

15. E. Gibbon, *The Decline and Fall of the Roman Empire* (ed. Bury), I (London, 1898), p. 78; *Storia spezzata,* pp. 19 ff. [*The End of the Past,* pp. 16 ff.].

16. The regulation of this private fabric, disconnected from its original integration in republican sociality, and reduced solely to dependence upon the arbitrary will of the *princeps,* would make an impression on G. W. F. Hegel, *Grundlinien der Philosophie des Rechts* (1820–21), in *Vorlesungen über Rechtsphilosophie 1818–1831. Edition und Kommentar in sechs Bänden* (unfortunately only the first four exist), ed. K.-H. Ilting (Stuttgart, 1973–74), II, p. 814 (para. 357), translated by Hugh Barr Nisbet in *Elements of the Philosophy of Right,* ed. Allen W. Wood (Cambridge, 1991), (but imperial despotism was already perfectly clear to Gibbon, despite his apologetic judgments: *Decline and Fall,* I, p. 78). In his scandalized reaction we see the distance separating the ancient world from European legal modernity, where the formalism of private law and its science would immediately encounter the State-constructing processes that opened out onto an array of quite different horizons and protagonists (mention has already been made of Hegel's text: see Chapter 8, sec. 1 and note 11; also Chapter 21, note 43).

17. Kunkel, *Herkunft und soziale Stellung,* pp. 144–145.

18. As we learn from Paul, *Quaest.* 5, in *D.* 24.3.44pr: *Pal.,* I, col. 61.

19. Pliny the Younger, *Epistulae* 1.22.3.

20. The report on the succession after Trajan is in *Scriptores Historiae Augustae, Vita Hadriani* 4.8.

21. *Pal.*, I, cols. 763–765 and 774–775.

22. *Pal.*, I, cols. 765–774.

23. Neratius, *Membranae* 5, in *D.* 22.6.2: "In omni parte error in iure non eodem loco quo facti ignorantia haberi debebit, cum ius finitum et possit esse et debeat, facti interpretatio plerumque etiam prudentissimos fallat."

24. *Storia spezzata,* pp. 211 ff. [*The End of the Past,* pp. 204 ff.].

25. Neratius, *Membr.* 6, in *D.* 1.3.21: "Et ideo rationes eorum, quae constituuntur, in-quiri non oportet: alioquin multa ex his quae certa sunt subvertuntur."

26. B. d'Orgeval, *L'empereur Hadrien: Oeuvre législative et administrative* (Paris, 1950), pp. 40 ff., is a good starting point. H. Vogt, "Hadrians Justizpolitik im Spiegel der römischen Reichsmünzen," in *Festschrift F. Schulz,* II (Weimar, 1951), pp. 198 ff., is useful though dated. A. d'Ors, "La signification de l'oeuvre d'Hadrien dans l'histoire du droit romain," in *Les empereurs romains d'Espagne* (Paris, 1965), pp. 149 ff., is brilliant, though questionable on some points. See also H. Hübner, "Zur Rechtspolitik Kaiser Hadrians," in *Festschrift E. Seidl* (Cologne, 1975), pp. 61 ff.; and *Storia di Roma,* II.3, pp. 100 ff.

27. Fronto, *Epistulae ad Marcum Caesarem* (Van den Hout²), I.6.2: "Tu ubi quid in sin-gulos decernis, ibi universos exemplo adstringis . . ."

28. Pliny, *Ep.* 6.5, offers a vivid portrait: F. Wieacker, "*Amoenitates Iuventianae.* Zur Charakteristik des Juristen Celsus," *Iura,* 13 (1962), esp. 2 ff.

29. *Pal.*, I, cols. 127–169.

30. See Chapter 21, sec. 5.

31. A curious "character-based" point of contact between Celsus and Hadrian can perhaps be found in *Script. Hist. Aug., Vita Hadr.* 15.10.

32. In Ulpian it is possible to count no fewer than 172 citations from Julian with the precise indication of work and book: more than twice as many as those devoted to Pomponius, whose *Ad edictum* was nonetheless a major point of reference for him: Honoré, *Ulpian,* pp. 128 ff.

33. Julian, *Dig.* 55, in *D.* 1 3.20: "Non omnium, quae a maioribus constituta sunt, ratio reddi potest."

34. Julian, *Dig.* 28, in *D.* 1.3.15: "In his, quae contra rationem iuris constituta sunt, non possumus sequi regulam iuris."

35. Gellius, *Noctes Atticae* 20.1. See also above, Chapter 7, note 36.

36. Julian, *Dig.* 15, in *D.* 1.3.12: "Non possunt omnes articuli singillatim aut legibus se-natus consultis comprehendi: sed cum in aliqua causa sententia eorum manifesta est, is qui iurisdictioni praestet ad similia procedere atque ita ius dicere debet."

37. Volusius Mecianus: *Pal.*, I, cols. 575–588; Ulpius Marcellus: *Pal.*, I, cols. 589–638; Africanus: *Pal.*, I, cols. 1–36; Cervidius Scaevola: *Pal.*, II, cols. 215–322; Mauricianus: *Pal.*, I, cols. 689–692; Venuleius Saturninus: *Pal.*, II, cols. 1207–23. For Gaius see be-low, note 43.

38. Only two citations can be tracked down: see T. Honoré, *Gaius* (Oxford, 1962), p. 156.

39. P. Frezza, "'*Responsa*' e '*quaestiones*': Studio e politica del diritto dagli Antonini ai Severi," *SDHI*, 43 (1977): 303 ff. (now in *Scritti*, 3 vols. [Rome, 2000], III, pp. 351 ff.).

40. It is rather risky to place Paul in the first of these orientations; he is more properly somewhere in the middle: he wrote great commentaries *Ad edictum* and *Ad Sabinum*, like Pomponius and Ulpian, but he was much less "systematic" than they were, and in contrast with Ulpian, he had no ambitions to undertake a wholesale "restatement" (see also Chapter 20, sec. 2): he cited much less extensively than Ulpian (Honoré, *Ulpian*, p. 153), and in this he perhaps resembled Julian; he also commented on Plautius (*Pal.*, I, cols. 1147–77), and he dedicated himself to a monographic output not to be found in the other great Severan jurist.

41. *Pal.*, II, cols. 15–42; of the 173 fragments that make up Lenel's palingenesis of Pomponius' books *Ad edictum*, as we have said, more than 100 consist of Pomponian citations taken from the first thirty books of Ulpian's *Ad edictum*. This work has now been thoroughly studied, with innovative methods and important results, by Stolfi, *Studi sui libri ad edictum di Pomponio*.

42. Stolfi, *Studi sui libri ad edictum di Pomponio*, I, pp. 338 ff.

43. On Gaius there is a vast bibliography, but no adequate reconstruction of his intellectual profile (an incredible gap given the huge advantage provided by the discovery of the Veronese manuscript of the *Institutiones* by Niebuhr, in 1816. The text is in *FIRA*, II, pp. 3–228). A fascinating book that attempts to fill this gap is Honoré's *Gaius*. See also sec. 4 of this chapter, Chapter 21, sec. 1, and Chapter 22, sec. 1.

44. Gaius, *Institutiones* 1.2: "Constant autem iura populi Romani ex legibus, plebiscitis, senatusconsultis, constitutionis principum, edictis eorum, qui ius edicendi habent, responsis prudentium."

45. Gaius, *Inst.* 1.3–7: "lex est . . . plebiscitum est . . . senatusconsultum est . . . constitutio principis est . . . edicta sunt . . . [adopting a universally accepted integration] responsa prudentium sunt . . ."

46. Pomponius, *Enchiridion*, in *D.* 1.2.2.12: "Ita in civitate nostra aut iure, id est lege, constituitur, aut est proprium ius civile, quod sine scripto in sola prudentium interpretatione consistit, aut sunt legis actiones, quae formam agendi continent, aut plebi scitum quod sine auctoritate patrum est constitutum, aut est magistratum edictum, unde ius honorarium nascitur, aut senatus consultum, quod solum senatu constituente inducitur sine lege, aut est principalis constitutio, id est ut quod ipse princeps constituit pro lege servetur." There is certainly some degree of disorder in this text, which can be attributed to a number of different authors: the epitomist of the Pomponian original (see M. Bretone, *Tecniche e ideologie dei giuristi romani*, 2d ed. (Naples, 1982), pp. 211 ff.); Justinian's compilers, who may have edited the work of the epitomist; at some points, perhaps even the manuscript tradi-

tion of the *Digesta*. Certainly jumbled is the opening phrase, "aut iure, id est lege, constituitur," for which I would choose the emended version proposed by V. Scialoja, "aut est ius, quod lege constituitur" (in his edition of the *Digesta* [Milan, 1908], *Ad h. l.*), which strikes me as preferable to the one proposed by Bretone, "aut est ius legitimum, id est quod lege constituitur" (*Tecniche e ideologie dei giuristi romani*, p. 226). But in both cases the substance does not change: Pomponius was referring to the Twelve Tables: the link is already present in L. Mitteis, *Römisches Privatrecht bis auf die Zeit Diokletians*, I (Leipzig, 1908), p. 33 n. 11. Nor is the conclusion acceptable: "id est . . . pro lege servetur," where, however, there clearly emerges the thought of the author, who intended to assimilate the *constitutio principis* to the *lex publica*. Moving from points of this kind to a general doubt about the authenticity of the conceptual content of the entire text strikes me as inadmissible: this was done, at a certain point, and on the sole basis of caution, by F. Schulz, *History of Roman Legal Science* (1946; reprint, Oxford, 1953), p. 74 n. 2 (contradicted, however, by what is stated on p. 115 n. 4). The arguments proposed by Bretone, *Tecniche e ideologie dei giuristi romani*, pp. 227 ff., against this approach strike me as sufficient to eliminate any reasonable concerns.

47. Pomponius, *Ad Q. Mucium* 22, in *D*. 45.3.39: "quod Gaius noster dixit."

48. See Honoré, *Gaius*, pp. 142 and 145 ("tabulae laudatoriae").

49. Even if I am inclined to believe that a first version of the *Institutiones* was already available in the age of Hadrian, and therefore very roughly in the same (presumable) years as the *Enchiridion*: Honoré, *Gaius*, pp. 46 ff., 55, 58 ff., 61, 69, which I consider reliable.

50. See below, Chapter 21, note 12.

51. Thus, in brief, Bretone, *Tecniche e ideologie dei giuristi romani*, pp. 209 ff. (but the reconstruction appeared for the first time in *Labeo*, 11 [1965]: 7 ff., in an essay titled "Motivi ideologici dell'Enchiridion di Pomponio").

52. The texts are in Cicero, *Topica* 5.28, and in *Rhetorica ad Herennium* 2.13.19 (see Chapter 11, sec. 3 and note 36). The "original nucleus" of which I speak is the one that is present in *Rhet. ad Her.*: the idea of applying the paradigm of a *partitio* to *ius* taken as a whole is precisely the one that—almost in the same years—Quintus Mucius, while making broad use of diaeretic modules, rejected as a criterion for the ordering of his *Iuris civilis* (see Chapter 11, sec. 3); the individual parts conceived by the master of the treatise blend together, in a juxtaposition that is not sufficiently elaborated, Greek tradition (the opening pairing of law/nature); the novelty of the edict, flourishing in those years (pact and *bonum et aequum*); and two inevitable references to *consuetudo* (the Roman specificity) and the *res iudicata* (in the "lawyerly" point of view of an orator). In the transition to Cicero something changes, and the point of view becomes more definitely technical and specialist-oriented (in the sense of the culture of law): nature vanishes; the praeto-

rian *bonum et aequum* becomes the *aequitas* of the great contemporary legal debate (that between Cicero himself, Servius, Aquilius Gallus, and later Labeo, incorporating within it, and "juridicizing," the reference to nature: see Chapter 16, sec. 4); the *lex*, named alongside the *senatusconsulta*, acquires greater institutional exactitude; jurisprudence appears in a more definite manner: we sense an air that could already be described as Ofilian (that of the *Iuris partiti*: see Chapter 17, sec. 1, and Chapter 18, sec. 4) and a proximity to the Gaian approach—not only that of 1.2–7, but also with respect to the more general framework of *Inst.* 1.1 ("omne ius quo utimur vel ad personas pertinet, vel ad res, vel ad actiones"), becomes evident. See also Chapter 22.

53. Gaius, *Inst.* 1.3: "Lex est quod populus iubet atque constituit . . . plebiscitum est quod plebs iubet atque constituit. Plebs autem a populo eo distat . . . ut plebiscita universum populo tenerent." Even the stylistic arrangement, with the separate explanation of each element—after the initial list—is reminiscent of *Rhet. ad Her.*

54. Gaius, *Inst.* 1.4: "Legis vicem optinere" ("idque legis vicem optinet, quamvis fuerit quaesitum"). See Honoré, *Gaius*, pp. 120–121.

55. Gaius, *Inst.* 1.5: "Nec umquam dubitatum est, quin id legis vicem optineat, cum ipse imperator per legem imperium accipiat."

56. Gaius, *Inst.* 1.6: "Ius autem edicendi habent magistratus populi Romani."

57. See Chapter 8, sec. 4.

58. The point of connection—as it were, entirely ideological—is the *lex de imperio;* through it there was established a sort of syllogism: the law is the will of the people ("iussum populi, quod populus iubet," from Capito [above, Chapter 8, sec. 1] to Gaius); but the people has transferred its power into the hands of the *princeps* through the investiture of the lex de imperio ("per legem imperium accipiat"); therefore the will of the *princeps* has the force of law; through an epigraph (*CIL*, VI.1, n. 930 = *FIRA*, I, pp. 154–156) we can read the *lex de imperio Vespasiani:* F. de Martino, *Storia della costituzione romana*, 2d ed., 4 vols. (Naples, 1972–1974), IV.1, pp. 462–463. In reality it appears that we must conclude that power was conferred through a deliberation of the senate, and that the comitial *rogatio* had no more than a symbolic value.

59. *Inst.* 1.7: E. Stolfi, "Per uno studio del lessico e delle tecniche di citazione dei giuristi severiani: Le *sententiae prudentium* nella scrittura di Papiniano, Paolo e Ulpiano," *Rivista di diritto romano*, 1 (2001): 385 ff., where there is a bibliography.

60. For example, in *Inst.* 1.23 ("Nec tamen illis permittit Lex Iunia . . . testamentum facere") or in 1.38 ("Item eadem lege . . . minori . . . non aliter manumittere permittitur"), referring to a *lex;* or in 1.68 ("Sed ex senatusconsulto permittitur . . ."), or in 2.112 (". . . senatusconsultum factum est, quo permissum est . . .") in connection with a *senatusconsultum.*

61. *Inst.* 1.7: "Quorum omnium si in unum sententiae concurrunt, id, quod ita sentiunt, legis vicem optinet."

62. This is a further application of the model of reasoning described above, note 58.

63. *Inst.* 1.7: "si vero dissentiunt, iudici licet quam velit sententiam sequi: idque rescripto divi Hadriani significatur."

64. Pomp., *Ench.*, in *D.* 1.2.2.12.

65. Pomp., *Ench.*, in *D.* 1.2.2.38: "Cunabula iuris."

66. See Chapter 16 in sec. 3. Sabinus' polemic against the Labeonian *regula* (see Chapter 18, sec. 2) might fit into this context, if we have interpreted it properly: the definitions did not need to have a normative character, but only to describe and explain, in potential connection with classificatory *partitiones*.

67. Pomp., *Ench.*, in *D.* 1.2.2.6: "et ita eodem paene tempore haec tria iura nata sunt: lege duodecim tabularum, ex his fluire coepit ius civile, ex isdem legis actiones compositae sunt": the reference to the *tria iura* is a further unmistakable reference to the structure of Aelius' *Tripertita*.

68. Pomp., *Ench.*, in *D.* 1.2.2.13: "Post originem iuris et processum cognitum consequens est, ut de magistratuum nominibus et origine cognoscamus, quia, ut exposuimus, per eos qui iuri dicundo praesunt effectus rei accipitur: quantum est enim ius in civitate esse, nisi sint, qui iura regere possint? Post hoc dein[de] de auctorum successione dicemus, quod constare non potest ius, nisi sit aliquis iuris peritus, per quem possit cottidie in melius produci" (I also prefer "in melius produci" instead of "in medium perduci," as I mentioned above, in Chapter 3, note 1).

69. In the Pomponian version, the caesura probably marked the transition from one section to another of the manual (from the section on the *origo et processus iuris* to the one on the *nomina et origo magistratuum*, which comes right before the last section on the *successio auctorum*: likewise between *D.* 1.2.2.34 and 35 there is a similar break); the text that I am commenting on was certainly the *incipit* of the second part, but it is possible that the first part did not end with the passage that we now find in *D.* 1.2.2.12.

70. Thus concerning himself Antoninus Pius—reported by Mecianus, *Ex lege Rhodia*, in *D.* 14.2.9: ἐγὼ μὲν τοῦ κόσμου κύριος· ample discussion in V. Marotta, *Multa de iure sanxit: Aspetti della politica del diritto di Antonino Pio* (Milan, 1988), pp. 73 ff.

71. Pomp., *Ench.*, in *D.* 1.2.2.49: "Primus divus Augustus, ut maior iuris auctoritas haberetur, constituit, ut ex auctoritate eius responderent: et ex illo tempore peti hoc pro beneficio coepit. Et ideo optimus princeps Hadrianus, cum ab eo viri praetorii peterent, ut sibi liceret rispondere, rescripsit eis hoc non peti, sed praestari solere et ideo, si quis fiduciam sui haberet, delectari se populo ad respondendum se praepararet." I too think it best to insert "consultorum" after "iuris" in the first sentence: Bretone, *Tecniche e ideologie dei giuristi romani*, pp. 243–244 (whose bril-

liant exegesis, pp. 241 ff., remains a point of reference here). The first part of the text has already been cited: see above, note 10.

72. See Chapter 18, sec. 1.

73. Pomp., *Ench.*, in *D.* 1.2.2.49: "Ante tempora Augusti publice respondendi ius non a principibus dabatur, sed qui fiduciam studiorum suorum habebant, consulentibus respondebant."

74. Honoré, *Gaius,* pp. 129–130; A. Watson, "The Law of Citations and Classical Texts in the Post-Classical Period," *T,* 34 (1966): 402 ff.; O. Stanojevic, *Gaius noster* (Amsterdam, 1989), pp. 116 ff., where there is a bibliography.

20. The Great Systematization

1. *Storia spezzata,* pp. 183 ff. [*The End of the Past,* pp. 175 ff.].

2. Ibid., pp. 203 ff. [*The End of the Past,* pp. 196 ff].

3. In M. Weber, "Agrarverhältnisse im Altertum" (1898 and 1909), now in Weber, *Gesammelte Aufsätze zur Sozial- und Wirtschaftsgeschichte* (Tübingen, 1924); in English as *The Agrarian Sociology of Ancient Civilizations* (London, 1976; reprint 1998), p. 365.

4. *Storia spezzata,* p. 206 [*The End of the Past,* p. 199].

5. Ibid., pp. 207 ff. [pp. 200 ff.].

6. See *Il mondo tardoantico,* esp. pp. 55 ff.

7. In *D.* 18.1.1: see Chapter 12, sec. 2 and note 16.

8. *Storia spezzata,* pp. 37 ff. [*The End of the Past,* pp. 33 ff.].

9. I am referring to Aristotle, *Politica* 1.3–4; see above, Chapter 16, note 2.

10. *Il mondo tardoantico,* pp. 60 ff.

11. Bibliographic references in *Storia spezzata,* pp. 258–259 [*The End of the Past,* pp. 264–265].

12. A useful portrayal is in G. W. Bowersock, P. Brown, and O. Grabar, *Late Antiquity: A Guide to the Post-classical World* (Cambridge, Mass., 1999); and, naturally in the research of Brown, *The World of Late Antiquity;* Brown, *Society and the Holy in Late Antiquity* (London, 1982); and P. Brown, *The Rise of Western Christendom* (Oxford, 1995). There is further bibliography in *Il mondo tardoantico.*

13. "Suis moribus legibusque uti," in Aulus Gellius, *Noctes Atticae* 16.3.4.

14. *Novellae Iustiniani* 105.2.4.

15. Ulpian's *De off. proc.* is the focus of the major work by V. Marotta, *Ulpiano e l'impero,* 2 vols. (Naples, 2000), esp. I, pp. 165 ff., and II, pp. 11 ff., esp. 111 ff. and 165 ff. Also keep in mind D. Mantovani, "Il bonus praeses secondo Ulpiano: Studi su contenuto e forma dei libri de officio proconsulis," *BIDR,* 96–97 (1993–94): 203 ff.

16. T. Honoré, *Emperors and Lawyers* (Oxford, 1981), pp. 54 ff.

17. *Codex Theodosianus cum perpetuis commentariis Iacobi Gothofredi* (1665), 6 vols. (Leipzig, 1736–1745).

18. Honoré, *Ulpian*, pp. 1 ff. and 177 ff.

19. *Pal.*, II, cols. 379–1200.

20. A prejudice that we find again, though greatly attenuated, in F. Schulz, *History of Roman Legal Science* (1946; reprint, Oxford, 1953), pp. 99 ff. and 196 ff.; and, more clearly, in V. Arangio-Ruiz, *Storia del diritto romano* (Naples, 1957), p. 276.

21. These figures take into account Honoré, *Ulpian*, pp. 128 ff.

22. See Chapter 17, sec. 3; *Pal.*, I, cols. 971–974 (for Paul), and II, cols. 15–16 (for Pomponius). See also below, note 24.

23. Ulpian, *Ad edictum*, in *D.* 2.14.1pr-3 (= *Pal.*, II, Ulpian, 240): "Huius edicti aequitas naturalis est: quid enim tam congruum fidei humanae, quae ea quae inter eos placuerunt servare? Pactum autem a pactione dicitur (inde etiam pacis nomen appellatum est) et est pactio duorum pluriumve in idem placitum et consensus. Conventionis verbum generale est ad omnia pertinens, de quibus negotii contrahendi transigendique causa consentiunt qui inter se agunt: nam sicuti convenire dicuntur qui ex diversis locis in unum locum colliguntur et veniunt, ita et qui ex diversis animi motibus in unum consentiunt, id est in unam sententiam decurrunt."

24. Ulpian, *Ad ed.*, in *D.* 2.14.7.7 = *Pal.*, II, Ulpian, 243: "Pacta conventa, quae neque dolo malo, neque adversus leges plebis scita senatus consulta decreta edicta principum, neque quo fraus cui eorum fiat, facta erunt, servabo" (but we should invert the sequence between "decreta" and "edicta," as O. Lenel rightly supposes; see above, Chapter 17, sec. 3 and note 32; and *EP*, p. 65 and n. 3). In the whole of Ulpian's corpus, the fourth book of the commentary *Ad edictum* is the most important piece of writing—even if it is certainly not the only one—devoted to the exposition of contract doctrines (suffice it to think of Ulpian's citation from Labeo in *Ad ed.* 11, already analyzed in sec. 4 of Chapter 17). In Paul's commentary *Ad edictum* the same edictal title is examined (from a perspective that has several points of convergence with Ulpian's) in the third book (*Pal.*, I, cols. 971–974); in the commentary of Pomponius (as we know, not utilized by the compilers) the same examination took place in the sixth book, and was probably continued in the seventh and eighth (*Pal.*, II, cols. 15–16 and 43).

25. See Chapter 16, sec. 3. It is plausible that Ulpian might have already found in Pomponius a nucleus of natural-law ideas that linked it to the late-republican and Augustan elaboration.

26. See Chapter 21, sec. 1.

27. Ulpian, *Disputationes*, in *D.* 50.12.3: "Pactum est duorum consensus atque conventio . . ." The reference to Sinnius Capito is in Festus, p. 260, l. 13 (Lindsay).

28. In *D.* 2.14.1.3 (= *Pal.,* II, Ulpian, 240): "adeo autem conventionis nomen generale est, ut eleganter dicat Pedius nullum esse contractum, nullam obligationem quae non habeat in se conventionem, sive re sive verbis fiat: nam et stipulatio quae verbis fit, nisi habeat consensum, nulla est."

29. O. Lenel, in *Pal.,* II, col. 1 and n. 2, seems to think he was, albeit with extreme and justified caution. The sequences of Pedius' *Ad edictum* also depend on the order of the edictal texts prior to Julian.

30. See Gaius, *Institutiones* 3.88 and 3.182.

31. Paul, *Ad Vit.* 2, in *D.* 33.7.18.3.

32. See Chapter 19, sec. 1.

33. In Gaius, *Inst.* 3.88–89: *DPR*, pp. 342 ff.

34. *D.* 2.14.1.4; 2.14.5; 2.14.7pr-4 (= *Pal.,* II, Ulpian, 240–242): "Sed conventionum pleraeque in aliud nomen transeunt: veluti in emptionem, in locationem, in pignus, vel in stipulationem . . . Conventionum autem tres sunt species; aut enim ex publica causa fiunt aut ex privata: privata aut legitima aut iuris gentium; publica conventio est, que fit per pacem, [aut] quotiens inter se duces belli quedam paciscuntur . . . Iuris gentium conventiones quaedam actiones pariunt, quaedam exceptiones. Quae pariunt actiones, in suo nomine non stant, sed transeunt in proprium nomen contractus: ut emptio venditio, locatio conductio, societas, commodatum, depositum et ceteri similes contractus. Sed et si in alium contractum res non transeat, subsit tamen causa, eleganter Aristo Celsus respondit esse obligationem. Ut puta dedi tibi rem ut mihi aliam dares, dedi ut aliquid facias: hoc συνάλλαγμα esse et hinc nasci civilem obligationem. Et ideo puto recte Iulianum a Mauriciano reprehensum in hoc: dedi tibi Stichum, ut Pamphilus manumittas: manumisisti: evictus est Stichus. Iulianus scribit in factum actionem a praetore dandam: ille ait civilem incerti actionem, id est praescriptis verbis sufficere: esse enim contractum quod Aristo συνάλλαγμα dicit, unde haec nascitur actio . . . Sed cum nulla subest causa, propter conventionem hic constat non posse constitui obligationem: igitur nuda pactio obligationem non parit, sed parit exceptionem."

35. *Linee,* p. 228.

36. Cerami, "*D.* 2.14.5: Congetture sulle 'tres species conventionum,'" pp. 135 ff., 188 ff., 211.

37. It is worth bearing in mind the observations of Cerami, "*D.* 2.14.5: Congetture sulle 'tres species conventionum,'" p. 177.

38. *Pal.,* I, cols. 691–692.

39. On the position of Aristo, see also Paul, *Ad Plaut.* 5, in *D.* 19.4.2: Santoro, *Il contratto nel pensiero di Labeone,* pp. 224 ff. In this text Aristo again, and once again on the topic of the identification of a contractual type, makes use of the category of *causa* ("Aristo ait, quoniam permutatio vicina esset emptioni, sanum quoque fur-

tis noxisque solutum et non esse fugitivum servum praestandum qui ex causa daretur"): with a meaning, as can be seen, entirely similar to that which we hypothesized in Ulpian's citation.

40. In the Labeonian construction the narrowness of the notion of *contrahere* is also justified by its placement alongside *agere* and *gerere*, which Ulpian also defined in *Ad ed.* ii, in *D.* 4.4.7pr: "Ait praetor: 'gestum esse dicatur': gestum sic accipimus qualiterqualiter, sive contractus sit, sive quid aliud contigit."

41. See Chapter 17, beginning of sec. 4.

42. See Chapter 9, sec. 5.

43. Julian, *Digesta* 14, in *D.* 19.5.3: "quotiens contractus existunt, quorum appellationes nullae iure civili proditae sunt."

44. In *D.* 2.14.7.4, quoted above, note 34.

45. Also in *D.* 2.14.7.4.

46. "Ne ex pacto actio nascatur" (or "nascatur actio"): in *D.* 2.14.7.5.

47. Schulz, in *History of Roman Legal Science*, p. 198, showed good insight when he spoke, in connection with Ulpian's work, of "a codification in the form of restatement."

48. On Tryphoninus see also Chapter 22, sec. 2 and notes 11 and 12.

21. The Custodians of Law

1. Ulpian, *Institutiones*, in *D.* 1.1.1pr-1: "Iuri operam daturum prius nosse oportet, unde nomen iuris descendat. Est autem a iustitia appellatum: nam, ut eleganter Celsus definit, ius est ars boni et aequi. Cuius merito quis nos sacerdotes appellet: iustitiam namque colimus et boni et aequi notitiam profitemur, aequum ab iniquo separantes, licitum ab illicito discernentes, bonos non solum metu poenarum, verum etiam praemiorum quoque exhortatione efficere cupientes, veram nisi fallor philosophiam, non simulatam affectantes." We have no reason to doubt that the copy of Ulpian's *Institutiones* used by the editors of the *Digesta* was a good version of the original edition. F. Wieacker, *Textstufen klassischer Juristen* (1960; reprint, Göttingen 1975), pp. 206 ff., 213–214, compares the edition employed by the editors of the *Institutiones Iustiniani* with the one adopted by the compilers of the *Digesta:* but I see no reasons sufficient to claim that the *Institutiones Iustiniani* is older than the *Digesta;* and the idea that both of them underwent substantial alterations remains—as almost always—a petition of principle (some further observations can be found in A. Schiavone, "Il testo e la storia," *Quaderni fiorentini per la storia del pensiero giuridico moderno*, 24 [1995]: 587 ff.): the comparisons merely make clear the relative importance of the variants from the point of view of the conceptual contents, by and large stable in both versions. In the case in question, Ulpian's incipit in *D.* 1.1.1pr has no counterpart in *Inst. Iust.* (but already *D.* 1.1.1.2 = *Inst. Iust.*

1.1.4, with some variants): the visibility linked to the opening of the *Digesta* evidently militated against a twofold utilization.

2. The identification of the exordium of Justinian's *Digesta* with that of the *Institutiones* of Ulpian is already in F. P. Bremer, *De Domitii Ulpiani Institutionibus* (Bonn, 1863), p. 48. The Gaian incipit is reproduced, with a few variants from the Veronese manuscript, in *D.* 1.1.9 (= *Inst. Iust.* 1.2.1).

3. In *D.* 1.1.9 = Gaius, *Institutiones* 1.1 (with a few minor variants).

4. The dating of the segments of the *Ad edictum* and of the *Ad Sabinum* is that proposed by T. Honoré, *Ulpian,* 2d ed. (Oxford, 2002), pp. 158 ff. Before those years, Ulpian had written very little. The beginnings of his career (he was born in Tyre around 170) are uncertain (but R. Syme is too skeptical, though brilliant as always: "Three Jurists," in *Roman Papers,* II [Oxford, 1979], pp. 790 ff., 794 ff.; and "Lawyers in Government: The Case of Ulpian," in *Roman Papers,* III [Oxford, 1984], pp. 863 ff.). He was close to Papinian and to the imperial family; had been secretary *a libellis,* probably from March 202 to the fall of 209; and had accompanied Septimius Severus and Caracalla on their campaign in the north of Britain in 209–210: T. Honoré, "The Severan Lawyers: A Preliminary Survey," *SDHI,* 28 (1962): 166–167, 189, 207 ff. (with different dates from those proposed in subsequent works); *Emperors and Lawyers* (Oxford, 1981), pp. 61 ff.; *Ulpian,* pp. 1 ff. Also keep in mind P. Jörs, in *RE,* V.1, cols. 1439 ff.; W. Kunkel, *Herkunft und soziale Stellung der römischen Juristen,* 2d ed. (Graz, 1967), pp. 245 ff.; and G. Crifò, "Ulpiano: Esperienze e responsabilità del giurista," in *ANRW,* II.15 (1976), pp. 737 ff. See also Chapter 16, sec. 1.

5. Honoré, *Ulpian,* pp. 158 ff., 177 ff.

6. Gaius, *Inst.,* in *D.* 1.2.1: "Facturus legum vetustarum interpretationem necessario prius ab urbis initiis repetendum existimavi, non quia velim verbosos commentarios facere, sed quod in omnibus rebus animadverto id perfectum esse, quod ex omnibus suis partibus constaret: et certe cuiusque rei potissima pars principium est. Deinde si in foro causas dicentibus nefas ut ita dixerim videtur esse nulla praefatione facta iudici rem exponere: quanto magis interpretationem promittentibus inconveniens erit omissis initiis atque origine non repetita atque illotis ut ita dixerim manibus protinus materiam interpretationis tractare? namque nisi fallor istae praefationes et libentius nos ad lectionem propositae materiae producunt et cum ibi venerimus, evidentiorem praestant intellectum": see esp. B. Albanese, "Sull'introduzione di Gaio al suo commento delle XII Tavole," in *Brevi studi di diritto romano,* II (extract from *AUPA,* 43) (Palermo, 1995), pp. 11–12, 13–14 (regarding the refusal to dissolve *prius:* but the entire essay merits a close examination. See also his useful observations in *Premesse allo studio del diritto privato romano* [Palermo, 1978], pp. 79 ff.).

7. The conjecture on *prius* was advanced in T. Mommsen, "Gaius ein Provinzialjurist" (1859), in *Gesammelte Schriften,* II: *Juristische Schriften* (Berlin, 1905), p. 33

n. 15; and, in a doubtful form, in *Digesta* (ed. Mommsen) *Ad h. l.*; and was followed by F. Schulz, *Einführung in das Studium der Digesten* (Tübingen, 1916), p. 18; and by M. Bretone, *Storia del diritto romano* (Rome, 1987), p. 63 n. 79. But that possibility was rejected by Bremer, *De Domitii Ulpiani Institutionibus*, p. 48 n. 1. The text— quite important, and certainly Gaian, deserves an in-depth analysis, which we cannot attempt here. Interesting observations can be found in T. Honoré, *Gaius* (Oxford, 1962), pp. 105–106.

8. That the works of Gaius circulated in the Severan age seems unquestionable, despite the silence that surrounds the name of the jurist: the *Institutiones* were present, for instance, in third-century Egypt (A. S. Hunt, *Oxy. Pap.*, XVII [London, 1927], pp. 173 ff. n. 2103; concerning which E. Levy, "Neue Juristenfragmente aus Oxyrynchos," *ZSS*, 48 [1928]: 532 ff. = *Gesammelte Schriften*, I [Cologne, 1963], pp. 31 ff.; see *FIRA*, II, pp. 167–168 = Gaius, *Inst.* 4.72–72a). Honoré, *Ulpian*, p. 137, believes that he can identify clearer traces of a direct Gaius-Paul relationship than he can of a Gaius-Ulpian one (the Gaius of Ulpian is, on this view, mediated by Paul); but the reasons for this preference are weak. See also H. Fitting, *Alter und Folge der Schriften römischer Juristen von Hadrian bis Alexander,* 2d ed. (1908; reprint, Osnabrück 1965), pp. 52–53; and W. W. Buckland, "Did Ulpian Use Gaius?," *Law Quarterly Review,* 38 (1922): 38 ff. Ulpian wrote his *Institutiones* immediately after the *constitutio Antoniniana*, probably with the intention of replacing the Gaian handbook in the didactic Sabinian model (P. Frezza, "La persona di Ulpiano," *SDHI*, 49 [1983]: 418, now in *Scritti,* 3 vols. [Rome, 2000], III, p. 533). He therefore had in mind (and before his eyes) the work of Gaius, for which he must have felt—aside from any doctrinal disagreements—consideration and respect (even though he never explicitly cites him, in accordance with a protocol that may have been inaugurated by Pomponius); he chooses, then, to pay him a tacit tribute, but to begin by borrowing the opening of the work that he intended to replace must have struck him as inappropriate: and so we see that he turns to the commentary on the Twelve Tables, which opened with a solemnity entirely in keeping with his compositional plan.

9. See Chapter 20, sec. 2.

10. From the lexicographic point of view, moreover, Ulpian was anything but unskilled, and he was certainly of an inquiring mind, though with the limitations of the instruments and the sensibility of antiquity: see, for example, *Inst.* 1, in *D.* 1.1.4; *Ad Sab.* 22, in *D.* 34.2.22; *Ad Sab.* 44, in *D.* 34.23.1–2 and *D.* 34.2.25.10; *Ad ed.* 6, in *D.* 47.15.1pr = *D.* 3.2.4.4; *Ad ed.* 18, in *D.* 50.16.31; *Ad ed.* 28, in *D.* 14.3.3; *Ad ed.* 59, in *D.* 42.4.7.8; *Ad ed.* 68, in *D.* 43.12.1.13 and *D.* 50.16.59; *Ad ed.* 71, in *D.* 43.23.1.4; *Ad ed.* 77, in *D.* 47.10.15.4. Keep in mind Crifò, "Ulpiano," pp. 727 ff.

11. Tryphoninus: *Disp.* 9, in *D.* 16.3.31.1 (in a context that also features recurring references to *aequitas* and to the Ciceronian-Ulpianic definition of *iustitia*, about which

I shall have more to say later), and *Disp.* 1, in *D.* 11.4.5 (but the word—here in a fairly insignificant meaning—might have been used by Antoninus Pius). Modestinus: *Pandect.* 8, in *D.* 4.1.3 ("scilicet ut iustitiam earum causarum examinet"). Ulpian: *Ad ed.* 56, in *D.* 47.10.1pr (". . . quod iure et iustitia caret": very significant, in connection with the definition of *iniuria*); and *Ad leg. Iul. de adult.* 2, in *D.* 48.5.18.6 ("vel gratia vel iustitia vel legis auxilio"): see Gallo, "Diritto e giustizia," p. 15, now in *Opuscula,* pp. 623–624.

12. I follow A. Kojève, *L'imperatore Giuliano e l'arte della scrittura* (Rome, 1998), pp. 25 ff. (an essay that appeared for the first time in *Ancients and Moderns: Essays on the Tradition of Political Philosophy in Honour of Leo Strauss* [New York, 1964], pp. 209 ff.). Likewise quite important is L. Strauss, *Persecution and the Art of Writing* (1952; reprint, Chicago, 1988), pp. 7 ff., 22 ff. See also P. Zagarin, *Ways of Lying: Dissimulation, Persecution and Conformity in Early Modern Europe* (Cambridge, Mass., 1990), pp. 1 ff., 15 ff. Of great importance is the testimony gathered by Clement of Alexandria, *Stromata* 5.8.50 (Stahlin, p. 360): H. von Dechend, in G. de Santillana and H. von Dechend, *Die Mülhe des Hamlet. Ein Essay über Mythos und des Gerüst der Zeit,* 2d ed. (Vienna, 1994), p. 320 (the original edition, G. de Santillana, *Hamlet's Mill: An Essay on Myth and the Frame of Time,* without the concluding observations by Dechend, which were added for the German edition, was published in Boston, 1969). But a "stratigraphic" theory of the reading—which assigned a degree of truth to each level of understanding of the text—already belonged to the theoretical-Gnostic core of the culture of Origen, who, as we shall see, was probably part of Ulpian's world.

13. The years in which Ulpian's output is concentrated—between 212–213 and 218–219—after he left the office *a libellis,* and before assuming, in 222, the praetorian prefecture that would prove fatal to him—are difficult to decipher from the biographical point of view: that he was close to the court remains unchallenged, and it would be reckless to imagine any immediate difficulties for him: but certainly his career, which probably suffered an interruption, and his life—like that of many other prominent characters of that period—followed a thin line through highly fragile equilibriums (the insistence of the senate on the issue of *concordia* betrays the disquiet of the time, following the death of Septimius Severus: Dio Cassius 77.1.4–5. Julia Domna, who was very close to the jurist, and was proclaimed *mater senatus et patriae,* must have appeared as a figure of stabilizing continuity: H. W. Benario, "Iulia Domna Mater Senatus et Patriae," *The Phoenix,* 11 [1958]: 67 ff., with a reexamination of *CIL,* VI, no. 1035 = H. Dessau, ed., *Inscriptiones Latinae Selectae,* 3 vols. [1892–1916], p. 426). That the history of the empire had entered a new and dangerous phase filled with transformations—though one not entirely devoid of hope and prospects—must have been Ulpian's guiding thought, which would accompany him both in his period of study and writing,

during the synoptic composition of the great triptych—the *Ad ed.*, the *Ad Sab.*, and the *De off. proc.*—and of the *Institutiones,* and in his program of government. And there is no need to overinterpret the significance of his tragic death—assassinated by the Praetorian Guard, before the eyes of the young emperor, in the late summer of 223—to see that his commitment to the defense of a "civil" (and legal) presence at the highest levels of the empire, in opposition to the steady drift toward military might ("enrich the soldiers and pay no heed to anyone else"—these are said, according to Dio Cass. 76.15.2, to have been the last words of Septimius Severus) should be considered to be the common thread of his political and intellectual choices: there is a good reconstruction in C. Letta, in *Storia di Roma,* II.2, pp. 690–691. One important observation in D. Nörr, *Rechtskritik in der römischen Antike* (Munich, 1974), p. 60 (and see also p. 87), concerning which we should keep in mind the review by M. Talamanca, "Per la storia della giurisprudenza romana," *BIDR,* 80 (1977): 406 ff. See also Chapter 20, sec. 1.

14. For the citations by Pedius and by Pomponius we now have the research of E. Stolfi, *Studi sui libri ad edictum di Pomponio,* 2 vols. (Milan, 2001–02), esp. I, pp. 59 ff.; and of C. Giachi, *Studi su Sesto Pedio: La tradizione, l'editto* (Milan, 2005), esp. pp. 127 ff., 180 ff.

15. See Chapter 9, sec. 5, and Chapter 16, sec. 4.

16. The jurists cite almost exclusively only other jurists; but in one case Ulpian mentions Cicero (a work that is now lost): *Ad ed.* 59, in *D.* 42.4.7.4. See D. Nörr, "Cicero—Zitate bei den klassichen Juristen," in *Ciceroniana III: Atti III colloquium Tullianum* (Rome, 1978), pp. 111 ff., now in *Historiae iuris antiqui,* ed. T. Chiusi, W. Kaiser, and H.-D. Spengler, II (Goldbach, 2003), pp. 1187 ff.

17. The keystone of the Gaian natural-law architecture, which extends throughout the *Institutiones,* is the category of *naturalis ratio* as the founding element of the *ius gentium,* in *Inst.* 1.1. And what about before Gaius? One important passage may have been the thinking of Labeo (see Chapter 22 and the end of Chapter 16). Even earlier, P. Frezza ("La cultura," p. 363, now in *Scritti,* II, p. 645; and Frezza, *Corso di storia del diritto romano,* 3d ed. [Rome, 1974], p. 372) thought of Quintus Mucius, on the basis of Augustine, *De civitate dei* 4.27, 6.8, and 7.5: it would certainly be an intriguing hypothesis to link Gaius' doctrine of natural law to a distant Mucian foundation, but it strikes me as reckless to attribute to the republican jurist the *naturales rationes* of 6.8; this concept can at the outside be attributed to Varro, based on the account of *De civ. Dei* 6.5. On the theology of Quintus Mucius see above, Chapter 13. Still useful is E. Levy, "Natural Law in Roman Thought," *SDHI,* 15 (1949): 1 ff. (= *Gesammelte Schriften,* I, pp. 3 ff.); while the old M. Voigt, *Das ius naturale, aequum et bonum und ius gentium der Römer,* 4 vols. (Leipzig, 1856–1875), has lost its usefulness.

18. See Chapter 16, sec. 4.

19. Ulpian, *Libri Regularum*, in *D.* 1.1.10pr: "Iustitia est constans et perpetua voluntas ius suum cuique [tribuendi] <tribuens>." I correct on the basis of *Inst. Iust.* 1.1pr, closer to the first formulation of the *Rhetorica ad Herennium* (see also Cicero, *De inventione* 2.53.160: see Chapter 16 at note 55) and stylistically sharper: previously thus F. Hotman, *Commentarius de verbis iuris* (Lyons, 1569), p. 203.

20. Ulpian, *Ad ed.* 4, in *D.* 2.14.1; *Ad ed.* 11, in *D.* 4.4.1; *Ad ed.* 26, in *D.* 12.4.3.7 (see also below, note 75); *Ad ed.* 27, in *D.* 13.5.1pr; *Ad ed.* 40, in *D.* 37.5.1pr; *Ad ed.* 71, in *D.* 43.26.2.2; *Ad Sab.* 12, in *D.* 38.16.1.4. Paul: *Ad edictum* 71, in *D.* 44.4.1.1 (very important); *Ad Sabinum* 16, in *D.* 49.15.19pr. See also *Quaestiones* 6 (this work is certainly authentic, and less the product of reworking by the editors of late antiquity, than Schulz, *History of Roman Legal Science*, pp. 238–239, seemed to believe; see also Wieacker, *Textstufen klassischer Juristen*, pp. 375 ff.) in *D.* 50.17.85. A natural-law line of thought that links Labeo and Ulpian is fleetingly presupposed in M. Bretone, *I fondamenti del diritto romano: Le cose e la natura*, 3d ed. (Rome, 1999), p. 102, which is followed, pp. 103 ff., by a reading of the Labeonian citation in Ulpian, *Ad ed.* 53, in *D.* 39.3.1.22–23: an important text for understanding the characteristics of the "materialism" of the Augustan jurist (see Chapter 16 at beginning of sec. 3).

21. Ulpian everywhere overlays the sense of *aequitas naturalis* upon the earlier meaning of *bonum et aequum* (see the end of Chapter 16). See *Ad ed.* 41, in *D.* 30.71.2; *Ad ed.* 74, in *D.* 2.11.2.8. Less evident, but equally perceptible, in *Ad ed.* 23, in *D.* 9.3.5.5; *Ad ed.* 25, in *D.* 11.7.14.6; *Ad ed.* 31, in *D.* 17.1.12.9; *Ad ed.* 36, in *D.* 27.7.4.2; in *Ad ed.* 57, in *D.* 47.10.11.1.

22. Paul, *Ad Sab.*, in *D.* 1.1.11.

23. The passage is read with great perception by C. A. Maschi, "La conclusione della giurisprudenza classica all'età dei Severi. Iulius Paul," in *ANRW*, II.15 (1976), pp. 694 ff. (and, even earlier, see Maschi, *La concezione naturalistica del diritto e degli istituti giuridici romani* [Milan, 1937], pp. 179 ff.). Observations concerning his analysis in Talamanca, "Per la storia della giurisprudenza romana," pp. 231 ff. It is a hypothesis with some foundation that the commentaries of Paul *Ad edictum* and *Ad Sabinum* are earlier, if only by a slight margin, than Ulpian's, and served as a constant point of reference for him (firmly convinced of this is Honoré, *Ulpian*, pp. 135 ff. For a dating of the *Ad Sabinum*, which would place its publication in the years of Septimius Severus, see also P. Krüger, *Geschichte der Quellen und Literatur des römischen Rechts*, 2d ed. [Leipzig, 1912], p. 231 and n. 32 [but *Ad Sab.* 6, in *D.* 17.2.25, does not strike me as decisive; better *Ad Sab.* 7, in *D.* 24.3.15.1], accepted—albeit with some hesitation—by O. Lenel, *Pal.*, I, col. 1251 n. 2). If this were the case, we would have to read the text of Paul as the (hidden) trace of Ulpian's discourse: the place where he found his suggestion for equating *ius* and *bonum et aequum* (understood as *aequitas naturalis*: but Paul distinguished the *ius* based on the *aequitas naturalis* from the *ius civile*, as we can also determine from the previously mentioned *Ad ed.*

71, in *D.* 44.4.1.1, while Ulpian tended to totalize)—and we cannot doubt that Paul, while he was writing, had Celsus in mind: there is too tight a correspondence in his comparison of *ius* and *bonum et aequum* (which he could not have found elsewhere) to think otherwise. For that matter, Paul was a reader of Hadrian's jurist: we shall analyze one important example later; moreover Celsus is one of the few authors cited in the *Ad Sabinum* (see *Ad Sab.* 7, in *D.* 24.1.28.7; and *Ad Sab.* 8, in *Vaticana Fragmenta* 1 [accepting O. Lenel's attribution]). But I would not go so far as to exclude the opposite hypothesis: that here it was Paul who borrowed from Ulpian's *Institutiones* (imagining a slightly later dating of the *Ad Sabinum*—a conjecture that is not entirely unreasonable): and in that case we would be obliged to consider his writing as a note and a summary of the statement of the *Institutiones*. I would, however, rule out the idea of two autonomous texts: there are too many coinciding passages to deny the evident nexus, whether in one direction or the other. The relationship between the two passages was already discussed by Irnerio, *Questiones de iuris subtilitatibus* (ed. Fitting) (Berlin, 1894), pp. 54–55. A. Mantello, *Il sogno, la parola, il diritto: Appunti sulle concezioni giuridiche di Paolo* (Macerata, 1993), also in *BIDR*, 33–34 (1991–92): 351 ff., subjects the passage in question to an in-depth examination, with some interesting observations, in a search for its points of reference, even the most distant ones. I do not agree, though, with the effort to make a distinction between Paul's position and that of Ulpian, with arguments that strike me as less than conclusive (Mantello captures nicely, if fleetingly, the relationship between Ulpian and Celsus, about which I shall have more to say; but he hypothesizes a distinction between the two Severan jurists that winds up becoming instead a confirmation of the absolute close proximity of their positions). Invaluable observations, albeit noted in passing, faintly, on the figure of Paul can be found in Syme, "Lawyers in Government," in *Roman Papers*, III [Oxford, 1974], p. 863). Ulpian, on the other hand, also defined *ius naturale,* and it was also in the first book of the *Inst.*, immediately after the text that we are examining: *D.* 1.1.1.3 (= *Inst. Iust.* 1.2.1, with some variants): see Chapter 22, sec. 2 and note 26.

24. See above, note 20.

25. See above, Chapter 16.

26. See Chapter 22, sec. 1.

27. See above, Chapters 3–6. Observations worth taking into account, though not entirely in line with the approach I advocate, can be found in D. Nörr, "Iurisperitus sacerdos," in *Xenion. Festschrift Zepos,* I (Athens, 1973), pp. 555 ff., now in Chiusi, Kaiser, and Spengler, *Historiae iuris antiqui,* II, pp. 851 ff., with a solid defense of the authenticity of this section of the passage (I wonder whether this major scholar, in his justifiable attempt to contextualize Ulpian's thinking, has not ventured beyond the proper bounds, and might not have been influenced to some degree by E. Kantorowicz, *The King's Two Bodies: A Study in Mediaeval Political Theology*

[Princeton, 1957], pp. 119 ff., 124 ff., 132 ff., 138–139; and see also "Synthronos Dike," in *American Journal of Archaeology,* 57 [1953]: 65 ff.). Underlying the reference to the priesthood it strikes me that there is, in the overall economy of Ulpian's discourse, more an old motif internal to the legal tradition—the reproposal of the image of the pontifices as figures of memory (and of the Roman myth of law), prior even to being of history itself (I am employing the scheme of J. Assmann, *Moses the Egyptian: The Memory of Egypt in Western Monotheism* [Cambridge, Mass., 1997]; and see also Assmann, *Das kulturelle Gedächtnis. Schrift, Erinnerung und politische Identität in frühen Hochkulturen,* 2d ed. [Munich, 1999])—than the adoption of more recent cultural notions. Having said this, I would not exclude, in the statement of Ulpian, the presence of a "mystical" element, linked to the theme of the *sacerdotes iustitiae,* to the idea of an "Eintritt in die 'Rechtsschule' als initiatio in ein Mysterium" (thus Nörr, "Iurisperitus sacerdos," p. 559 = Chiusi, Kaiser, and Spengler, *Historiae iuris antiqui,* II, p. 855). This would be basically the same "mysticism" that a lengthy Western tradition links to the pairing of *rex-sacerdos* (in fact the one that Kantorowicz investigated) and the "magical" royalty of the kings of France and England—as featured in the renowned book by Marc Bloch on the divine touch of the kings. Moreover, if this were so, we would have a clear explanation as well of "quis nos . . . appellet": Ulpian seems to place in the present those who call jurists priests—and therefore appears to be referring to cultural and emotional currents set in his own time. Probably—if the truth is in the intertwining—he made use of this more current approach only as a key to the introduction of the theme of the jurist-priest, charged, in the tradition of jurisprudence (for those capable of representing it—and once again we are faced with a problem of levels of reading), with an evocative power that touched deeper and more-distant layers of consciousness and sensibility.

28. See Cicero, *Pro Archia* 1.7.16 ("colere virtutem"); *De officiis* 1.2.5 ("colere amicitiam, iustitiam, liberalitatem"), 1.41.149 ("colere affectos"); *Brutus* 91.315 ("cultum philosophiae"), 31.117 ("colere disciplinam"), etc.

29. Aristotle, *Rhetorica* 1.13.11–12.1374a; 1.14.7.1375a.

30. Ulpian, *Inst.,* in *D.* 1.1.6.1: "Hoc igitur ius nostrum constat aut ex scripto aut sine scripto, ut apud Graecos τῶν νόμων οἱ μὲν ἔγγραφοι, οἱ δὲ ἄγραφοι." The comparison is with *Rhet.* 1.13.2.1373b, even though the expression is not Aristotelian, but should rather be attributed to later lexical customs: Frezza, "La cultura," p. 370 (= *Scritti,* II, p. 652). Another case is offered by Ulpian, *Ad Sab.* 30, in *D.* 19.5.4: "Natura enim rerum conditum est, ut plura sint negotia quam vocabula," to be read with Aristotle, *Sophistici elenchi* 1.165a.

31. Frezza, "La cultura," pp. 367 ff. (= *Scritti,* II, pp. 649 ff.); and see also Frezza, "La persona di Ulpiano," pp. 416–417 (= *Scritti,* III, pp. 531–532); Nörr, "Iurisperitus sacerdos," pp. 555 ff.(= Chiusi, Kaiser, and Spengler, *Historiae iuris antiqui,* II, pp. 851

ff.); Honoré, *Ulpian,* pp. 76 ff., 79 ff.; and Falcone, "La 'vera philosophia' dei 'sacerdotes iuris,'" pp. 3 ff., with many interesting observations on Ulpian's cultural background. For the ancient authors cited, see below, notes 34–35. Frezza attributes the *Didascalicus* to Albinus, in keeping with the beliefs of the time, still argued by J. H. Dillon, *The Middle Platonists: A Study of Platonism, 80 B.C. to A.D. 220* (1977; reprint, London, 1996), pp. 268 ff. (but see also the afterword to the 1996 edition, pp. 445 ff., with bibliography). See also H. Tarrant, *Plato's First Interpreters* (Ithaca, N.Y., 2000), pp. 88–89; and J. H. Dillon, *Alcinous: The Handbook of Platonism* (Oxford, 1993), pp. ix ff.; as well as the excellent T. Göransson, *Albinus, Alcinous, Arius Didymus* (Göteborg, 1995), pp. 105 ff.

32. Dio Cass. 76.15.6–7; Philostratus, *Vitae sophistarum* 2.30.622; Eusebius, *Praeparatio evangelica* 6.21.3–4. Frezza, "La cultura," p. 369 (= *Scritti,* II, p. 651); G. W. Bowersock, *Greek Sophists in the Roman Empire* (Oxford, 1969), pp. 101 ff.; D. Nörr, "Etik von Jurisprudenz in Sachen Schatzfund," *BIDR,* 75 (1972): 11–12, 20–21 (and n. 58), 28 ff. (= Chiusi, Kaiser, and Spengler, *Historiae iuris antiqui,* II, pp. 897–898, 906–907, 914 ff.); Crifò, "Ulpiano," pp. 734 ff., where there is a bibliography.

33. Ulpian, *Libri regularum,* in D. 1.1.10.1–2: "Iuris praecepta haec sunt: honeste vivere, alterum non laedere, suum cuique tribuere. Iuris prudentia est divinarum atque humanarum rerum notitia, iusti atque iniusti scientia." Only prejudices are to be found in Schulz, *History of Roman Legal Science,* pp. 135–136. Naturally it is possible that in Ulpian's original the three paragraphs of the current version were arranged in a different context, and that the sequence that we read today is the product of a stitching together by subsequent editors.

34. Alcinous, *Didascalicus* 1 (= Whittaker-Louis p. 1 = Hermann p. 152, ll. 5–6). See H. Dorrie and M. Balthes, *Die philosophische Lehre des Platonismus,* IV (Stuttgart, 1996), 102, 2. Keep in mind Seneca, *Epistulae* 89.5: "Sapientiam quidam ita finierunt ut dicerent divinorum et humanarum scientiam"; Ussani, *L'ars dei giuristi,* pp. 137 ff. and nn. 103, 104; and Falcone, "La 'vera philosophia' dei 'sacerdotes iuris,'" pp. 81 ff., which refers to Cicero, *De legibus* 1.22.58–23.61 (but it is a problematic contact).

35. Frezza, "La cultura," p. 368 (= *Scritti,* II, p. 650); and Frezza, "La persona di Ulpiano," p. 417 (= *Scritti,* III, p. 532), contradicts himself, though sticking to his point of view (and in the second work also qualifies in an imprecise manner as "youthful" Ulpian's thinking in the *Institutiones*). The possible links along the path indicated by Frezza (and followed substantially, but with useful details, by Mantello, "Un illustre sconosciuto," pp. 982–983) are with Origen, *In genesim homiliae* 11.2 (Baehrens) [= *PG,* 12.222–223]—*Vera philosophia Christi*—and *Epistula ad Gregorium* 1 (Crouzel) [= *PG,* 11.88]; and with Gregory Thaumaturge, *Oratio Panegyrica in Origenem* 1.1–7 (Crouzel) [= *PG,* 10.1052–53]; and see also Justin Martyr, *Apologia* 1.2 and 1.4 (Marcovich). But in reality the theme of the true philosophy extends throughout the culture of the second century: a good reconstruction is provided

by V. Marotta, *Multa de iure sanxit: Aspetti della politica del diritto di Antonino Pio* (Milan, 1988), pp. 122 ff. See also Schermaier, "Ulpian als 'wahrer Philosoph,'" pp. 303 ff.; and W. Waldstein, "Zum Problem der 'vera philosophia' bei Ulpian," pp. 607 ff. Let us not forget that the engagement between philosophy (Greek) and law (Roman) is already found in Cicero, as we can see clearly in *De republica* 1.2.2: see above, Chapter 8, note 51 and text.

36. On relations between Galen and Ulpian, G. Lanata, *Legislazione e natura nelle novelle giustinianee* (Naples, 1984), pp. 214 ff., with an opportune reference to Ulpian, *De omnibus tribunalibus* 8, in *D.* 50.13.1.4 (see also below, note 85).

37. Again Alcinous, *Didasc.* 1 (= Whittaker-Louis p. 1 = Hermann p. 152, ll. 2–4): "Philosophy is . . . the freeing and turning around of the soul from the body, when we turn towards . . . what truly is"; translation from Dillon, *Alcinous,* p. 3 (see Plato, *Phaedo* 12.67c–d, 29.80d–81a; *Republic* 7.6.521c—and here we are probably at the origins of the motif of "true philosophy" in Greek thought). See Dillon, *Alcinous,* pp. 51–52. I agree with Mantello, "Un illustre sconosciuto," pp. 984 ff. and n. 40, that in the text in question, *affectare* means "to tend towards"; but this does not weaken—as it seems to me that he supposes—the identification of the jurists as true philosophers: true philosophy is a testimonial to the truth; and a continual quest for it *(affectantes)* is the proper stance of authentic philosophers.

38. In *D.* 50.13.1.4–5. For the dating (probably 215), Honoré, *Ulpian,* pp. 184, 196–197.

39. *Or. pan. in Orig.* 6.73–79 (Crouzel) (= *PG,* 10.1068–69). For that matter, these are common motifs in the Platonism of the second and third centuries: Dillon, *The Middle Platonists,* pp. 298 ff.; and esp. M. Rizzi, in Gregory Thaumaturge, *Encomio di Origene* (Milan, 2002), pp. 9 ff.

40. The text of Plotinus is in *Aenneades* 3.2.15.

41. *Storia spezzata,* pp. 11 ff. [*The End of the Past,* pp. 9 ff.].

42. Herodian, *Ab excessu divi Marci* 5.2.3. P. Brown, *Power and Persuasion in Late Antiquity: Towards a Christian Empire* (Madison, Wis., 1992), pp. 62–63; and in *Storia di Roma,* III.1, pp. 878 ff.; J. Hahn, *Der Philosoph und die Gesellschaft. Selbstverständnis, öffentliches Auftreten und populäre Erwartungen in der hohnen Kaiserzeit* (Stuttgart, 1989), pp. 9 ff., 33 ff., 54 ff., 165 ff.; R. J. Penella, *Greek Philosophers and Sophists in the Fourth Century A.D.: Studies in Eunapius of Sardis* (Leeds, 1990), pp. 75 ff. Also G. Fowden, "The Pagan Holy Men in Late Antique Society," *Journal of Hellenic Studies,* 102 (1982): 33 ff., 51 ff.; and R. R. Smith, "Late Roman Philosophers' Portraits from Aphrodisias," *JRS,* 80 (1990): 144 ff.

43. His reflection represents the culmination of that tradition of imperial "public ethics," from Cicero himself to Seneca and Marcus Aurelius, whose intrinsic fragility in the wake of the collapse of the republican model of citizenship I have already indicated (see Chapter 16, sec. 3), but whose importance we should definitely not underestimate with respect to the formation of the Mediterranean governing

NOTES TO PAGES 431–432

elites: certainly incomparably weaker when compared with the forceful diffusion of legal thought and its paradigms, but nonetheless not superficially nourished on Stoic doctrines reelaborated through the experience of world domination; the only one able, despite all its limitations, to update the terms of a debate of moral philosophy that Greek thought had otherwise rendered rigid as far back as the Hellenistic period in a scholasticism incapable of any authentic renewal and a strong relationship with its own time. This too lies behind the moralism of the Severan jurists—and not only the Ulpian of the *Institutiones* and the *Regulae,* but also Papinian (with greater vehemence and rhetoric) and even Paul: the attempt to combine faithfulness to a specialization that had succeeded in endowing itself with protocols which were ironbound but enclosed in the impenetrability of their formalism—the omnipotent solitude of law—with the demand for a regeneration of the public spirit of the governing groups, put to harsh trial by a political abso-lutism that neither left a way out nor opened up perspectives: and once again we return to the intuition of Hegel, previously mentioned (see Chapter 8, sec. 1 and note 11; Chapter 16, sec. 3 and note 25; and Chapter 19, note 16). Mantello, "Un il-lustre sconosciuto," pp. 984–985, supposes that Ulpian intended to launch a po-lemic concerning the essence and collocation of truth with "Judaeo-Christian cur-rents and, particularly, with Origen": it is an intriguing hypothesis, but the clues are weak at best, although subtly analyzed; and it strikes me as unlikely—though not impossible—that a pointed (though veiled almost to the verge of conceal-ment) anti-Christian stance might form part of the program for the incipit of a handbook for legal institutions, even at the turn of the third century. Similarly doubtful: Bretone, *Storia del diritto romano,* p. 272.

44. *Pal.,* II, cols. 926–928.

45. Papinian, *Definitiones* 2, in *D.* 1.1.7pr; Pomp., *Ench.,* in *D.* 1.2.2 (more than once: e.g., 1.2.2.12 and 1.2.2.49); Julian, *Dig.* 90, in *D.* 1.3.11; Ulpian, *Ad l. Iul. et Pap.* 13, in *D.* 1.3.31; Callistratus, *Quaestiones* 1, in *D.* 1.3.38.

46. Ulpian, *Inst.,* in *D.* 1.4.1pr-1: "Quod principi placuit, legis habet vigorem: utpote cum lege [regia], quae de imperio eius lata est, populus ei [et in eum omne suum] imperium et potestatem conferat. Quodcumque igitur imperator per epistulam et subscriptionem statuit vel cognoscens decrevit vel de plano interlocutus est vel edicto praecipit, legem esse constat. Haec sunt quae vulgo constitutiones appella-mus." For the restitution of the text that I propose, see below, note 51.

47. Kantorowicz, *The King's Two Bodies,* pp. 133 ff. and n. 148, 145 ff., 151–152, 414–415 and n. 335.

48. Spinoza: *Tractatus Theologico-Politicus,* in *Opera,* III (ed. Gebhardt) (Heidelberg, n.d.), pp. 189 ff.; Hobbes: *Leviathan* (ed. Tuck) (Cambridge, 1991), pp. 138 ff.; Locke, *The Second Treatise on Government* (ed. Gough) (Oxford, 1966), pp. 67 ff.; Leibnitz, *Méditation sur la notion commune de la justice,* in *Rechtsphilosophisches aus Leibnizens*

ungedruckten Schriften (ed. Mollat) (Leipzig, 1885), pp. 56 ff. (for the dating, see V. Mathieu, ibid., p. 67).

49. Ulpian, *Ad l. Iul. et Pap.* 13, in *D.* 1.3.31: "Princeps legibus solutus est: Augusta autem licet legibus soluta non est, principes tamen eadem illi privilegia tribuunt, quae ipsi habent." The theme had already been extensively developed by medieval thinkers: e.g., Thomas Aquinas, *Summa Theologiae,* q. 96, a. 5: "Praeterea, iurisperitus dicit quod princeps legibus solutus est. Qui autem est solutus a lege, non subditur legi. Ergo non omnes subiecti sunt legi"; and John of Salisbury, *Policraticus* 4.2 (ed. Webb) (Oxford, 1909), 515a = *Opera Omnia,* III (1848; reprint, Leipzig, 1969), p. 221: "Princeps tamen legis nexibus dicitur absolutus, non quia ei iniqua liceant, sed quia is esse debet, qui non timore poenae, sed amore iustitiae aequitatem colat, rei publicae procuret utilitatem, et in omnibus aliorum commoda privatae praeferat voluntati."

50. I am thinking especially of Q. Skinner, *Liberty before Liberalism* (Cambridge, 1998), pp. 38 ff.; but see also Skinner, *The Foundations of Modern Political Thought,* 2 vols. (Cambridge, 1978), I, pp. 84 ff., 207–208, and II, pp. 269–270.

51. As still believed by Frezza, "La persona di Ulpiano," pp. 419 ff. (= *Scritti,* III, pp. 534 ff.), drawing upon an observation by W. Mommsen, *Römisches Staatsrecht,* 3d ed. (reprint, Basel, 1952), II.2, pp. 876–877 n. 2. The elimination of "regia" is now commonly accepted. That matter aside, I agree with the proposal of A. Steinwenter, "Zur Lehre vom Gewohnheitsrechte," in *Studi Bonfante,* II (Milan, 1930), pp. 423–424, which strikes me as conservative and elegant, to exclude only the words "et in eum omne suum." The text of Ulpian is repeated in *Inst. Iust.* 1.2.6, with a few variants that do not affect the substance (see Wieacker, *Textstufen klassischer Juristen,* pp. 207–208). In general, in this case too I see no reason to prefer the version of *Inst. Iust.* over that of *D.* Disagreement on this point in P. Frezza, *Corso di storia del diritto romano,* 3d ed. (Rome, 1974), p. 436 and n. 11. The attention of the critics was attracted by "vulgo," present in *D.* but omitted in *Inst. Iust.:* this is, however, a word used extensively by Ulpian (see, e.g., *Ad ed.* 18, in *D.* 4.9.7.2; *Ad ed.* 23, in *D.* 9.3.1.2; *Ad Sab.* 18, in *D.* 7.1.13.8; etc.), and which belongs to the vocabulary of the jurists, in particular the Severan ones.

52. Frezza, "La persona di Ulpiano," pp. 418 ff. (= *Scritti,* III, pp. 533 ff.), in disagreement with Honoré, *Ulpian,* p. 241 (from the 1st ed., Oxford, 1982: I don't find the reference in the 2d ed.), who I believe is right, however.

53. It strikes me as arbitrary to cancel the reference to the *edicta* solely on the basis of its place in the list: not even Gaius began with them, but rather with the *decreta,* in *Inst.* 1.5; the first beginning from the *edicta* was to be found in Julian's version of the edict: *EP,* 4.10 and 6.16, pp. 64–65, 77; and it is quite possible that Ulpian chose to construct a sort of sequence (from the point of view of the occasion at the origin of the normative act: *subscriptiones, decreta (pro tribunali), de plano interlocutiones* (not *pro tribunali),* and *edicta.*

54. I presuppose of course M. Weber, *Wirtschaft und Gesellschaft,* ed. J. Winkelmann, 5th ed., 2 vols. (Tübingen, 1972), I, pp. 125 ff., in English as *Economy and Society: An Outline of Interpretive Sociology,* trans. E. Roth (New York, 1968) I, pp. 217 ff.

55. See the last pages of Chapter 19.

56. Lenel does not take a position, and prudently places the text among the fragments of uncertain provenance: *Pal.,* I, col. 170.

57. See Chapter 9, sec. 5 and Chapter 16, sec. 3.

58. The passages from Proculus are in *D.* 17.2.76; 46.3.82; and 12.6.53 (see Chapter 18, sec. 2, and below, note 63). Consider also Honoré, "The Severan Lawyers," p. 180. For the Senecan traces, see Chapter 18, sec. 2. See also T. Honoré, "Proculus," *T,* 30 (1962): 472 ff., 490–491.

59. In *D.* 22.1.38.7: "tunc Sabinus et Cassius ex aequitate fructus quoque post acceptum iudicium praestandos putant": though we cannot entirely rule out the possibility that the use of the substantive is a choice of Paul, and that Sabinus and Cassius spoke only of *aequum.*

60. See Chapter 9, sec. 5.

61. See Chapter 16, sec. 3.

62. See Chapter 9, sec. 5 and note 39.

63. After Labeo (who used it extensively: see, for example, all those due to the mediation of Ulpian's *Ad edictum, D.* 2.14.7.10; 3.5.3.9; 4.4.13.1; 4.9.3.1; 14.4.5.13; 15.1.3.12; 47.9.3.2; 42.8.6.6; 43.12.1.12; 44.4.4.7; 44.4.4.13; 39.2.24.4; while we are indebted to Pomponius for the mention in *D.* 10.4.15; and finally, thanks to the epitome of Javolenus Priscus to the *Posteriores, D.* 24.3.66.7 and 19.1.50, the use of *aequum/aequitas* becomes rarer, as we have previously noted, in the jurisprudence of the first century, with the sole exceptions of Proculus and Pedius (for the latter, see also Chapter 19, sec. 1 and note 5). But we should not add Proc., *Epist.* 5, in *D.* 17.2.80 to the passages mentioned in note 58, as seems to be the view of Honoré, "The Severan Lawyers," p. 180 (to be kept in mind for a rapid overview of the quantities, albeit in an interpretative context I do not share). In Livy, in the presence of a very frequent use of *aequum, aequum et bonum* occurs only once (in 42.41.14). It then reappears in two passages from Seneca, *De clementia* 2.7.3 and 2.1.4, which we have already considered (see Chapter 18, sec. 2 and note 45).

64. The "temperament" of Celsus had not even escaped the notice of ancient observers who were not legal scholars: Pliny the Younger, *Epistulae* 6.5.4–7, with an elegant and very vivid portrayal, the obligatory point of departure (though largely overlooked) for those who wish to reconstruct the character of the jurist, as are his texts that feature the clause (highly uncommon in legal vocabulary) "ridiculum est" (*Dig.* 5, in *D.* 28.1.27, which also contains a memorable "valde stulta"; *Dig.* 12, in *D.* 47.2.68.2; *Dig.* 23, in *D.* 41.2.18.1), or his probable status as an enemy of Julian, who ignores him (we find a single citation in Iul., *Dig.* 29, in *D.* 28.2.13pr, concerning which, however, there are serious suspicions—Wieacker, *Textstufen klas-*

sischer Juristen, p. 388 n. 309). See also below, note 84. Research that should not be overlooked includes F. Wieacker, *"Amoenitates Iuventianae.* Zur Charakteristik des Juristen Celsus," *Iura,* 13 (1962): 1 ff.; and Bretone, *Tecniche e ideologie dei giuristi romani,* pp. 191 ff., 205 ff. But we are now begining to know more about the whole of Celsus' thought, thanks above all to the contributions of the school of Palermo (which has been studying Celsus since Riccobono, "La definizione del 'ius,'")—B. Albanese, *Tre Studi celsini* (Palermo, 1973) (extract from *AUPA,* 34 [1973]); and Cerami, "La concezione celsina del *ius,*" pp. 5 ff.—by V. Scarano Ussani, *Valori e storia nella cultura giuridica fra Nerva e Adriano* (Naples, 1979), pp. 101 ff.; and F. Casavola, *Giuristi adrianei* (Naples, 1980), pp. 34 ff., 107 ff.; while not much is found in H. Hausmaninger, "Publius Iuventius Celsus. Persönlichkeit und juristische Argumentation," in *ANRW,* II.15 (1976), pp. 399 ff. Outside the field of juridical thought, aside from the cases of Livy and of Seneca, *De clementia* 2.7.3 and 2.1.4, we find a trace of the *bonum et aequum* in Quintilian, *Institutio oratoria* 1, proem. 16; 12.1.8; 12.2.3, in reference to a traditional variety of oratory ("de aequo ac bono")—and we may imagine the survival of a classificatory stereotype.

65. Paul, *Ad Plaut.* 17, in *D.* 45.1.91.3: "et Celsus adulescens scribit eum, qui moram fecit in solvendo Sticho quem promiserat, posse emendare eam moram postea offerendo: esse enim hanc quaestionem de bono et aequo: in quo genere plerumque sub auctoritate iuris scientiae perniciose, inquit, erratur." It is very likely that in the books *Ad Plautium* the citations of jurists earlier than the end of the first century A.D. (Labeo, Sabinus, Cassius, Proculus, et al.) should be attributed to the text being commented on, while those of later authors (Celsus, Julian, Pomponius) can be thought to reflect only the choices of Paul: see *Pal.,* I, col. 1147 n. 1. The *adulescens* must be understood as "the Younger," to distinguish the jurist from his father, "Celsus pater," in the identification given by Neratius, *Membr.* 7, in *D.* 17.1.39: T. Honoré, "Julian's Circle," *T,* 32 (1964): 4 n. 28.

66. As a comment upon the edictal title *de stipulationibus praetoriis,* in keeping with the correct conjecture of O. Lenel, in *Pal.,* I, col. 161.

67. See Chapter 19, sec. 1.

68. See Chapter 19, sec. 2.

69. See Chapter 19, sec. 2. What emerged was the radical belief in the rightness of the ideas of a cognitive empiricism—which did not even exclude hints of skepticism —hitherto alien to the culture of the jurists. And the literary choices of Javolenus confirm his case-based radicalism. Already the *Epistulae*—a tribute to Proculus?— reveals—beginning with the absence of any ordering criterion—his general vocation: *Pal.,* I, col. 285 n. 7, even in this repeating a choice of Proculus (*Pal.,* II, col. 159 n. 2). Javolenus probably worked in the context of the civilistic tradition—and was in any case the only one to comment on the books *Iuris civilis* by Cassius Longinus: Pomponius, after him, chose instead to comment on Sabinus (and was the first to do so): Stolfi, *Studi sui libri ad edictum di Pomponio,* pp. 477 ff. Javolenus

also commented on Plautius, whose work—according to Schulz, *History of Roman Legal Science,* p. 228, "a collection of problemata"—is shrouded in mystery. No more than a hypothesis is that of *Pal.,* I, col. 1147 n. 1, on which Paul commented, juxtaposing not one but several texts by this jurist.

70. See Chapter 19, sec. 2.

71. Celsus, *Digesta* 9, in *D.* 1.3.24: "Incivile est nisi tota lege perspecta una aliqua particula eius proposita iudicare vel respondere."

72. The text is in *D.* 12.1.32: "Si et me et Titium mutuam pecuniam rogaveris et ego meum debitorem tibi promittere iusserim, tu stipulatus sis, cum putares eum Titii debitorem esse, an mihi obligaris? Subsisto, si quidem nullum negotium mecum contraxisti: sed propius est, ut obligari te existimem, non quia pecuniam tibi credidi (hoc enim nisi inter consentientes fieri non potest): sed quia pecunia mea quae ad te pervenit, eam mihi a te reddi bonum et aequum est" (with *Pal.,* I, col. 134 n. 2, I correct the "quinto" of the *inscriptio* according to F to "sexto"). Celsus cites both Servius and Labeo repeatedly; and Labeo is the jurist whom Celsus mentions most frequently, along with Proculus and Tubero, though in some cases in the context of a harsh polemic (see, e.g., Ulpian, *Ad ed.* 10, in *D.* 3.5.9.1; and Celsus, *Dig.* 6, in *D.* 15.1.6).

73. To the texts previously mentioned, we should add *Dig.* 11, in *D.* 27.8.7 ("aequius esse existimo"); *Dig.* 12, in *D.* 38.1.30pr ("quam si aequum arbitratus sit"); and *Dig.* 17, in *D.* 22.3.12 ("prima fronte aequius videtur").

74. *Dig.* 10, in *D.* 37.6.6: "Dotem, quam dedit avus paternus, an post mortem avi mortua in matrimonio filia patri reddi oporteat, queritur. Occurrit aequitas rei, ut, quod pater meus propter me filiae meae nomine dedit, perinde sit atque ipse dederim."

75. Ulpian, *Ad ed.,* in *D.* 12.4.3.7: "Sed si servus, qui testamento heredi iussus erat decem dare et liber esse, codicillis pure libertatem accepit et id ignorans dederit heredi decem, an repetere possit? Et refert patrem suum Celsum existimasse repetere eum non posse; sed ipse Celsus naturali aequitate motus putat repeti posse. Quae sententia verior est . . .": Ulpian was probably quoting from the sixth book of the *Digesta* of Celsus, where the jurist reported his father's opinion: *Pal.,* I, col. 135.

76. In the *Enchiridion* the word used is always *scientia.* Scholars of Roman law have also discussed the significance of the term *ius* for Celsus (and Ulpian): whether it should be taken in the sense of "ordering" or rather that of "legal science." But it is worth noting the observation of Cerami, "La concezione celsina del *ius,*" p. 8 and nn. 9 and 10 (where there is also a bibliography), concerning the questionable applicability of the distinction—at least in its modern terms—to the Roman legal experience until the third century. For Celsus (and for Ulpian, who takes it up as well) the term *ius* contains intrinsically—thanks to a very peculiar historical development—a twofold and indivisible allusion: both to the Roman legal order, and to

jurisprudence as a positive and specialized body of knowledge, which had played a fundamental role in the construction of that order.

77. Livy 9.42.4; Tacitus, *Annales* 3.75 (here the reference is not exactly to the *ius*, but to the *studia civilia* mentioned immediately before in reference to Ateius Capito: "ut Labeonem Antistium isdem artibus praecellentem": see Chapter 17, sec. 1); and Gellius, *Noctes Atticae* 13.10.1 (in an even more indirect and fleeting manner: "Labeo Antistius iuris quidem civilis disciplinam principali studio exercuit . . . [set] ceterarum quoque bonarum artium non expers fuit"). In Livy there is generic mention of *urbanae artes* in reference to the civil engagement of Appius Claudius. Irrelevant, however, is Suetonius, *Galba* 5.1.

78. A great deal depends on how we interpret Quint., *Inst. or.* 12.11.23–24.

79. Plautus, *Mostellaria* 151 *(ars gymnastica); Epidicus* 450 *(ars duellica).*

80. *Rhet. ad Her.* 1.2.3: "ars est praeceptio, quae dat certam viam rationemque dicendi."

81. For Cicero, see Chapter 11, sec. 3. Also in Quintilian we find a definition of *ars,* in *Inst. or.* 2.17.41 ("artem constare ex perceptionibus consentientibus et coexercitatis ad finem utilem vitae"), derived from Cleanthes (*SVF,* I, p. 110, n. 490). But Quintilian himself, when he speaks specifically of legal knowledge, also uses *scientia,* and not *ars:* "Iuris quoque civilis necessaria huic viro scientia est"; *Inst. or.* 12.3.1. The quotation in the text is from E. Severino, *Destino della necessità,* 2d ed. (Milan, 1999), p. 265; see esp. ibid., pp. 263–287.

82. See Chapter 11, sec. 3.

83. See Chapter 17, sec. 1.

84. To the texts listed above, note 64, we should add at least *Dig.* 11, in *D.* 16.3.32 ("Quod . . . Proculo displicebat, mihi verissimum videtur"); *Dig.* 18, in *Vat. Frag.* 75.5 ("Quam sententiam ipse, ut stolidam reprehendit"—thanks to the mediation of Ulpian, *Ad Sab.* 17; *Dig.* 1 (thanks to Ulpian, *Ad ed.* 10), in *D.* 3.5.9.1 ("istam sententiam Celsus eleganter deridet"), as earlier, cited in note 72.

85. It may have influenced him to see how Galen, *Adhortatio ad artes addiscendas* 14 (1.39 Kühn) and *De propriorum animi cuiusque affectum dignotione et curatione* 7 (5.103 Kühn), by now included without concern jurisprudence among the τέχναι λογικαί.

86. Celsus, *Dig.* 35, in *D.* 34.7.1pr.

87. Celsus, *Dig.* 6, in *D.* 15.1.6: "Definitio peculii quam Tubero exposuit, ut Labeo ait, ad vicariorum peculia non pertinet, quod falsum est," to be compared with Ulpian's citation in *Ad ed.* 29, in *D.* 15.1.5.4: "Peculium autem Tubero quidem sic definit, ut Celsus libro sexto digestorum refert, quod servus domini permissu separatum a rationibus dominicis habet, deducto inde si quid domino debetur." *D.* 15.1.6 has already been mentioned, above, note 72.

88. It is necessary to do no more than leaf through the *Vocabularium Iurisprudentiae Romanae* for the entries "definio" and "definitio," to realize this.

22. Equality Ancient and Modern

1. Ulpian, *Libri regularum,* in *D.* 1.1.10.1–2. See Chapter 21, note 33 and text.

2. Gaius, *Institutiones* 1.1: "Omnes populi qui legibus et moribus reguntur, partim suo proprio, partim communi omnium hominum iure utuntur; nam quod quisque populus ipse sibi alius ius constituit, id ipsius proprium est vocaturque ius civile, quasi ius proprium civitatis: quod vero naturalis ratio inter omnes homines constituit, id apud omnes populos custoditur vocaturque ius gentium, quasi quo omnes gentes utuntur." An important work is Y. Thomas, *"Imago naturae:* Note sur l'institutionnalité de la nature à Rome," in *Théologie et droit dans la science politique de l'état moderne* (Rome, 1991), pp. 201 ff.

3. See Chapter 19, sec. 3.

4. See Chapter 16, sec. 4. There are two important citations from Labeo: in Ulpian, *Ad edictum* 53, in *D.* 39.3.1.22–23; and in Paul, *Ad edictum* 49, in *D.* 39.3.2.6.

5. See Chapter 16, sec. 4.

6. Papinian, *Definitiones* 2, in *D.* 1.1.7. For Cicero, see above, Chapter 16, sec. 4.

7. The distinction between *ius naturale* and *ius gentium* is less clear-cut in Paul than in Ulpian: see *Ad ed.* 33, in *D.* 18.1.34.1; and *Quaestiones* 3, in *D.* 50.17.84.1 (and keep in mind as well *Ad ed.* 21, in *D.* 6.1.23pr and *D.* 18.1.51; *Ad ed.* 33, in *D.* 18.1.1.2; *Ad sen. Turp.,* in *D.* 23.6.68).

8. Ulpian, *Institutiones* 1, in *D.* 1.1.4 (= *Institutiones Iustinianae* 1.5pr): "Manumissiones quoque iuris gentium sunt. Est autem manumissio de manu missio, id est datio libertatis . . . quae res a iure gentium originem sumpsit, utpote cum iure naturali omnes liberi nascerentur nec esset nota manumissio, cum servitus esset incognita: sed posteaquam iure gentium servitus invasit, secutum est beneficium manumissionis. Et cum uno naturali nomine homines appellaremur, iure gentium tria genera esse coeperunt: liberi et his contrarium servi et tertium genus liberti, id est hi qui desierant esse servi."

9. Ulpian, *Ad Sabinum* 43, in *D.* 50.17.32: "Quod attinet ad ius civile, servi pro nullis habentur: non tamen et iure naturali, quia, quod ad ius naturale attinet, omnes homines aequales sunt."

10. Florentinus, *Institutiones* 9, in *D.* 1.5.4.1 (= *Inst. Iust.* 1.3.3): "Servitus est constitutio iuris gentium, qua quis dominio alieno contra naturam subicitur."

11. Tryphoninus, *Disputationes* 7, in *D.* 12.6.64: ". . . ut enim libertas naturali iure continetur et dominatio ex gentium iure introducta est."

12. F. Schulz, *History of Roman Legal Science* (1946; reprint, Oxford, 1953), p. 234, with unjustified doubts about authenticity.

13. Aristotle, *Politica* 1.4.1254a; in English in *The Politics of Aristotle,* trans. P. Simpson (Chapel Hill, 1997), p. 14.

14. *Pol.* 1.3.1253b; in English in *The Politics of Aristotle,* trans. P. Simpson (Chapel Hill, 1997), p. 13.

15. *Storia spezzata,* pp. 47 and 228 [*The End of the Past,* pp. 43 and 224].

16. Cicero, *De republica* 3.25.7: Cavallini, "Legge di natura," pp. 175 ff.; J.-L. Ferrary, *Philellénisme et impèrialisme* (Rome, 1988).

17. Arist., *Pol.* 1.5.1254a.

18. Again, according to Arist., *Pol.* 1.3.1253b.

19. Cicero, *De Re Publica,* 3.25.7: "Sed et imperandi et serviendi sunt dissimilitudines cognoscaendae. Nam ut animus corpori dicitur imperare, dicitur etiam libidini, sed corpori ut rex civibus suis et parens liberis, libidini autem ut servis dominus, quod eam coercet et frangit, sic regum, sic imperatorum, sic magistratuum, sic patrum, sic populorum imperia civibus sociisque praesunt ut corporibus animus, domini autem servos ita fatigant, ut optima pars animi, id est sapientia, eiusdem animi vitiosas imbecillasque partes, ut libidines, ut iracundias et perturbationes ceteras": see Chapter 16, sec. 3 (but from another point of view).

20. See Chapter 14, sec. 3.

21. As Aristotle says, *Pol.* 1.3.1253b; 1.5.1254a.

22. *Storia spezzata,* pp. 121 ff., 142 ff. [*The End of the Past,* pp. 112 ff. and 132 ff.].

23. "Contra naturam" in Fiorentino (D. 1.5.4.1) and παρὰ φύσιν in Arist., *Pol.* 1.3.1253b.

24. Paul, *Ad ed.* 69, in D. 50.17.211.

25. A. Watson, *The Law of Persons in the Later Roman Republic* (Oxford, 1967), pp. 173 ff. and 185.

26. Ulpian, *Inst.* 1, in D. 1.1.1.3–4 and D. 1.1.6pr: "Ius naturale est, quod natura omnia animalia docuit: nam ius istud non humani generis proprium, sed omnium animalium, quae in terra, quae in mari nascuntur, avium quoque comune est . . . Ius gentium est, quo gentes humanae utuntur. Quod a naturali recedere facile intellegere licet, quia illud omnibus animalibus, hoc solis hominibus inter se commune sit. Ius civile est, quod neque in totum a naturali vel gentium recedit nec per omnia ei servit: itaque cum aliquid addimus vel detrahimus iuri communi, ius proprium, id est civile efficimus." Lenel separates the texts: *Pal.,* II, Ulpian, nn. 1909, 1910, 1916. My unified reading is not meant as a palingenetic proposal (at least for the moment).

27. See above, Chapter 21.

28. Well interpreted, albeit with some limitations, by I. Berlin, "The Birth of Greek Individualism," now in *Liberty* (Oxford, 2002). Modern individualism is the result of the philosophy of the Renaissance, of Descartes, of Locke, and of the bourgeois economic takeoff that led to the Industrial Revolution: there was nothing similar in the ancient world. Modern historians—even the best, from J.-P. Vernant to M. Foucault—tend to make no distinction between the discovery of the interiority of the ego—which was unquestionably a Greek achievement, from Heraclitus on (*Storia spezzata,* pp. 161 and 252 [*The End of the Past,* pp. 152 and 256])—and

the individualistic construction of the "social self," which presupposes the laboratory of the modern "homo oeconomicus," and the theory of the naturalistic foundation of the irrepressibility of "human rights": the path that leads to Rousseau and to Kant—M. Riedel, *Metaphysik und Metapolitik. Studien zu Aristoteles und zur politischen Sprache der neuzeitlichen Philosophie* (Frankfurt am Main, 1975)—and on from there to the great apparatuses of bourgeois law. But on the right track is P. Veyne, "Mythe et réalité de l'autarchie à Rome," *Revue des études anciennes,* 81 (1979), esp. pp. 264, 269 ff.: the Roman (and also the Greek) model is built around the self-sufficiency of the property-owner, excluding the "system of needs" guaranteed by the "invisible hand" of the market (thus, from Smith to Ricardo and Hegel)—the economic premises of modern individualism. Naturally nothing prevents us from continuing to use the word "individualism" in relation to ancient phenomena as well—for instance, to describe the competitiveness that characterized the aristocracies, especially those of the city (the *cupido gloriae* to which we have already made reference): and I believe that I have done it myself in *Storia spezzata;* but it is important to be clear on the difference between these forms and those of modernity. See Chapter 21, sec. 3.

29. *Storia spezzata,* pp. 165–166, 173 ff. [*The End of the Past,* pp. 157–158 and 165 ff.]. On the integration of politics into law as a foundational basis for modern democracy, there are important observations in J. Habermas, *Faktizität und Geltung. Beiträge zur Diskurstheorie des Rechts und des demokratischen Rechtsstaats* (Frankfurt am Main, 1992).

30. The interplay between *terra* (land) and *mare* (sea) is echoed by C. Schmitt, *Der Nomos der Erde im Volkerrecht des Jus Publicum Europaeum* (1950) (Berlin, 1974), in English as *The Nomos of the Earth in the International Law of the Jus Publicum Europaeum,* trans. G. Ulmen (New York, 2003), pp. 42 ff.: the Roman Mediterranean is a "terrestrial" sea, as its very name clearly states, although that name does not appear until the third century A.D., with Julius Solinus, *Collectanea rerum memorabilium* 18.1 (ed. Mommsen)—"mediterranea maria"—and it is taken up again by Isidore, *Etymologiae* 13.16.1.

General Index

Absolutism, 385, 389, 395, 431, 435

Abstraction, 48, 197, 202, 210; diairesis and, 212, 220, 245; expansion of realm of, 198; legal science and, 203

Actiones, 141, 142–143, 408

Actualization, 21, 22

Adoption, 107

Adultery, 329

Advising, 123

Aelius, Sextus, 46, 96, 119, 122, 126, 165, 167–168; aristocratic tradition and, 127; cited in Roman legal literature, 182–183; Quintus Mucius' writings and, 180

Aemilius Paulus, 185

Aesculapius (hero-god), 227, 234, 235

Africa, 7, 138, 154, 270, 395

Africanus, Sextus Caecilius, 263, 375

Agere, 123, 127, 326, 327, 328, 402

Agere praescriptis verbis, 334, 335, 413

Agreements, 216, 322, 402; performance and, 412; pledge agreements, 405; symmetry with contracts, 403, 404; types of, 404–405, 409. See also *Conventio*

Agriculture, 67, 103, 142, 240, 363, 443

Alcaeus, 88

Alphenus Varus, 164, 247, 248, 250, 304, 315; last generation of republican jurists and, 313; legal issues involving slaves and, 254, 255, 256

Ambitus aedium, 197

America and American law, 12, 14, 17, 32, 110, 454, 458

Amun (Egyptian deity), 56

Ancestors, customs of, 74

Ancient Law (Maine), 17

Ancus Marcius (legendary king), 66

Annales maximi, 174

Annalistic tradition, 87

Anthology model, 7, 8, 9, 21, 23, 25, 33

Anthropology, 3, 48, 50, 53, 298

Antigone, 99

Antiquarianism, 53, 87, 96, 262, 338

Antonine age, 146, 356, 370, 393, 421

Antoninus Pius, 373, 436

Apollonius, 428

Appius Claudius Caecus, 86, 98, 114–115, 116, 165, 229, 234

Apuleius, 38, 428

Aquilius Gallus, 303

Arangio-Ruiz, V., 27

Archeology, 47, 48, 50, 52, 70, 204

Archilochus, 88

Fraccaro, P., 47

France, 14, 17, 20; absolutism in, 431; classicist republicanism in, 378; Enlightenment in, 15; formation of nation-state, 108; Napoleon's codification of law, 32; natural law in, 458; revolution in, 12, 111

Francisci, Pietro de, 27

Fraud, 202, 254, 362

Frazer, James, 66

Frezza, Paolo, 425, 433

Fronto, Cornelius, 373

Funerals, 91, 99

Gabba, E., 47

Gabinius, Aulus, 359

Gaius, 96, 344, 376, 388, 455; "classical law" and, 144; emperor (sovereign) and, 383, 386, 387; on "excessive technicality," 136–137; on fairness *(aequum)*, 146–147, 148, 149; historicism and, 263; *Institutiones*, 382, 397, 409, 417, 451; Julian and, 377; on *lex (leges)*, 379, 381, 382; natural law and, 437, 456; *obligatio* concept and, 210; on partnership, 217, 219, 261; public statutory law and, 380; Quintus Mucius and, 179, 183, 196, 219, 261; Sabinian tradition and, 301, 356, 384, 409, 452; Servius and, 247; Twelve Tables commentaries by, 98, 101; Ulpian and, 401, 403, 417–418, 433, 434, 436; on value of services, 262

Galba, Servius Sulpicio, 171, 172, 173

Gellius (Alus Gellius), 38, 119, 168, 181, 375; on archaic society, 65; Capito and, 312, 313; Labeo and, 327, 338, 443; on poets, 230–231; Publius Mucius and, 163; Quintus Mucius and, 179; Servius and, 247, 262–263

Genera legatorum, 209

Genesis, interdiction of, 52, 53

Gens [pl. *gentes*] (clan structures), 51, 82, 114; "lockout" of patriciate and, 85–86; pon-

tifices selected from ranks of, 69; republican culture and, 81; tribes and, 54

Geopolitics, 40

Gerere, 209, 326, 327, 328, 402

Germany, 14, 15, 16, 17, 22, 111

Gernet, L., 57

Gibbon, Edward, 4, 20, 371

Globalization, 459

Global law, 17

Gnaeus Flavius, 114–115, 119, 187

Gnaeus Ogulnius, 116

Gnoseology, 189, 192

Godefroy, Jacques, 20, 398

Good faith *(bona fides)*, 151, 202, 221, 222, 320, 334–335; extensive application of, 221; intentionality and, 224; Mediterranean trade and, 146

Goods, circulation of, 135, 205–206, 321

Gracchi, 86, 160, 259

Granius Flaccus, 92

Greece and Greek culture, 3, 52, 85, 93, 112, 281; archaic period, 56, 57; collapse of western Roman empire and, 10; constitutional models of, 108; democracy and, 86, 94, 99; ethics and, 295; funerals, 99; legislation as political command, 84; *lex* paradigm and, 87, 88; medical wisdom, 79; Mediterranean trade relations and, 141; natural law in, 297; oracular priest-king in, 76; origins of, 52; people's juries, 105; *phratria*, 65; political paradigm of, 11; politics and philosophy linked, 72, 73; public space in, 12; religiosity in, 56, 58; Roman occupation of, 154; science, 251. *See also* Athens; Philosophy, Greek

Greek language, 13, 45, 46, 90, 184, 270

Gregory Thaumaturge, 426, 428

Guardianship, 135, 194, 196, 202, 221, 254

Hadrian, 6, 31, 96, 156; absolutist state and, 395; codification of praetor's edict and, 376; council of, 374; on customs and

Hadrian *(continued)*
laws, 396; edict on pacts and, 322; intel-
lectuals in time of, 103, 157; jurispru-
dence of, 451; jurists and, 342; legal hu-
manism of, 352; rescript of, 383, 386, 387,
388
Hammurabi, 56
Hannibal, 240
Hegel, G. W. F., 39, 294, 458; on jurists as
oligarchy, 125–126; Niebuhr's dispute
with, 47–48; on statutory law, 108–110
Heidegger, Martin, 39
Hercules (hero-god), 227, 234, 235
Hermagoras, 184, 185, 198
Hermodorus of Ephesus, 93
Hermogenian Code, 6
Hesiod, 88
Hipparchus, 282
Hiring, 145, 207, 221, 320; contract and, 409;
ius gentium and, 248; in Ulpian, 405
Historians, 3, 20, 30, 38, 56; incomplete cul-
tural transmissions and, 33; "interdiction
of genesis" and, 52, 53; origins of Roman
legal experience and, 45
Historical School, 21, 109
Historicism, 21, 25, 39
Historiography, 20, 22, 25, 33, 157, 293, 342;
of Augustan age, 54; debates, 47; end of
legal historiography, 39; flawed, 27; fra-
gility of, under empire, 371; Hellenistic
wave and, 165; Justinian's perspective on
Roman law and, 35; modern, 94; political, 344; "republican canon" and, 87; Romanist tradition and, 38; universal, 154
History, 3, 10, 21, 37, 297, 456; anthropology
and, 53; disorderly quality of, 8, 24; law
distanced from, 38; religious, 47; Romanist studies and, 22
History of Roman Legal Science (Schulz), 35,
36–37
Hobbes, Thomas, 14, 432
Honoré, Tony, 425
Hoplite system, 70

Hugo, Gustav, 20
Huizinga, Johan, 35
Humanism, legal, 20, 305, 352
Humanists, Italian, 15
Human rights, 457, 458

Imperium (authority), 97, 102, 134
Imprisonment, 329
Individualism, 17, 365, 457, 459; bourgeois,
16, 320, 363, 458; Fascist and Nazi opposi-
tion to, 22
Industrial Revolution, 14
Inheritance, 202, 361
Injustice, law as, 146–148
Institutiones (Ulpian), 416, 418, 419, 421, 425,
429, 434; on *bonum et aequum,* 439; Byzan-
tine jurists and, 447; on jurists, 433; on
role of emperor, 431; on slavery, 453
Institutions, 4, 17, 45, 53
Intellectuals, 103, 114, 157, 316, 343, 352, 429
Interim Report (Momigliano), 47
Iron Age, first, 55
Islam, 395
Isonomia, 89, 93, 95, 103
Israel, ancient, 62
Italy, 4, 14, 18, 40, 139; authoritarian state in,
111; codification of law (1865), 32; *comuni,*
15; expansion of republic throughout,
160; Fascist, 22, 37; Greek-colonized
south of, 117; legal humanism, 20; medieval, 13; military reconquest of, 5; Roman expansionism and, 154; slave population of, 255, 259
Iuris civilis (Quintus Mucius Scaevola), 167,
178, 179, 187, 190, 194, 296; abstraction
and diairesis in, 212, 215, 245; on good
faith, 224; *Horoi* linked to, 353; obligation
in, 210; on partnership, 216–220; Pomponius' commentary on, 178, 179–180, 182,
183, 206–207, 216, 217, 223; triadic structure of, 227
Ius, 46, 57, 92, 267, 283, 286, 373; abstraction

and, 199, 200; aristocratic hegemony and, 313; as *ars*, 418, 424, 436, 443, 444–446; case-based character of, 197; ceremonial practices and, 60; disciplining function of, 199–200; divine and, 54, 55, 62; equality and, 97–98; etymology of, 60–61; expert knowledge associated with, 113; fairness *(aequum)* and, 149–151, 153, 299; first texts on, 114; hegemony of *nobilitas* and, 135; imperial constitutions and, 385; interaction with politics and religion, 82; *ius prudentia*, 73; Jove and, 68; knowledge of, 239, 241; *lex* compared with, 88, 93, 95, 134–135, 145; as *logos* of the republic, 124, 189; magic and, 102; mercantile practices and, 143; naturalization of, 292; natural law and, 297; ontology and, 202, 225, 265; origins of, 136, 174, 416; *pactum* and, 322; *patres* identified with, 55; patrician–plebeian conflict and, 87; phenomenology of formation of, 380; philosophy and, 430; as product of civil knowledge, 72; punishment of crime, 100; *responsa* and, 77, 106, 107; Roman specificity of, 90; as science, 445; secrecy of, 93, 118; slavery and, 256, 257, 259; social tensions and, 84; supremacy of emperor *(princeps)* and, 383; as tradition *(mos)*, 75, 79; transformation from will to knowledge, 287; universalistic monarchy and, 376

Ius Aelianum, 119

Ius civile, 45, 83, 125, 178, 225; abstraction and, 198; Cato's books on, 164; complete exposition of, 246; consolidation of, 167; continuist historiography and, 94; dualism with *aequum et bonum*, 301; equity and, 301; erosion of ritualism and, 152; fairness *(aequum)* and, 146, 153; injustice and, 146, 148; *ius gentium* and, 451; *ius honorarium* in dialectic with, 144–145; jurists and, 159; *lex* and, 136; Lex Aquilia and, 254; liability, 213; natural law and,

294; patrimony of, 217; property ownership and, 142; in Quintus Mucius, 179–180, 181, 196; restrictions on everyday behavior, 123; rigidity of, 61; ritualism of, 299, 441; Sabinian, 344, 355, 377; slavery and, 455; social disciplining of city and, 133; specialists and, 356; textuality and, 177–178; trade relations and, 138; transformation of, 214; Ulpian and, 407; verbalistic framework of, 223–224. *See also* Civil law

Ius civile (Sabinus), 208

Ius civitatis, 300

Ius edicendi, 137

Ius Flavianum, 114–115

Ius gentium, 125, 142–143, 249, 320, 325, 369; agreements in, 406; Alphenus and, 248; consensual contracts and, 217; contractual paradigms of, 260, 324; manumission and, 452–453; natural law and, 451, 452; slavery and, 455; in Ulpian, 407–408; *ultro citroque obligatio* and, 331, 335. *See also* Nations, law of

Ius honorarium, 144–145, 153, 378, 407

Ius Papirianum, 91

Ius respondendi, 312, 341, 342–345, 382, 386, 387

Iustitia, 125

Javolenus Priscus, 258, 333, 369–370, 372, 440

Jefferson, Thomas, 458

Jhering, Rudolf von, 22, 37

Jove (deity), 54, 65, 67, 68

Judges, 4, 9, 139, 291; citizens serving as, 102; error by, 289; fairness *(aequum)* and, 150–151; in Middle Ages, 13; in modern world, 108

Julian, 178, 339, 356, 368, 375–377; on contracts, 412–413; edict on violence and, 358; jurisprudence allied with imperial power, 397; organicity and, 374; Ulpian edition of, 400–401

76, 91, 361; betrothal contracts, 262–263; *connubium* prohibition, 96; *ius civile* and, 123

Mars (deity), 54, 64, 65, 67

Marx, Karl, 23, 39

Massurius Sabinus, 92

Mathematics, social, 16

Mauricianus, 377, 412

Mauss, Marcel, 58

Mazzarino, S., 20

Mecianus, Volusius, 377, 397

Medicine, 33, 79, 427

Mediterranean region, 5, 55, 90; city and politics in, 50; Hellenism in, 178; *lex* paradigm in, 87; mercantile practices of, 222; origins of civilizations in, 52, 54; population density in, 49; prosperity and growth in, 51; religious practices, 56; Roman hegemony in, 205, 239, 450; Roman trade with, 138, 140; royalty and sacrality in, 66; slavery in, 254, 454; theologization of divine wrath in, 55; trade relations in, 141, 142, 146, 248, 249

Memory, 122, 127, 188

Merchants, 142, 230, 249–250, 362; foreign, 138, 141, 142; modern bourgeoisie compared with, 325

Mesopotamia, 55, 90, 395

Metaphysics, 202, 204, 450

Metellus, Quintus Caecilius, 230

Middle Ages, 13, 19, 108, 431, 457

Military forces (army), 70–71, 113, 395; hero-gods and, 236; hoplite system, 70; organization of, 118; political rationality of, 82; professionalization of, 236; social mobility and, 160; wars of empire, 394

Minerva (deity), 67

Minor, Gaius Marius, 179

Mitteis, Ludwig, 27

Modernity, 3, 16, 112, 203, 263, 415; free wage labor and, 363; idea of the West and, 11; rebirth of, 395

Modestinus, 168, 415, 419

Momigliano, Arnaldo, 37, 39, 47, 65, 67

Mommsen, Theodor, 20, 417

Monarchy, 71, 81, 85

Money, 205, 206, 240, 249; depositaries of, 251; quantification of, 265; as universal equivalent, 321

Mores, 93, 120, 265, 296; archaism in interpretation of, 113, 320; jurists and, 159

Mos (ancestral customs), 74, 75, 79, 88, 98

Mucianus, Publius Licinius, 172, 173, 183

Mucii, 163, 168, 171, 173, 185

Murder, 99, 100, 198, 329

Mussolini, Benito, 37

Myths, 58–59, 67

Namusa, Aufidius, 258, 313

Napoleon I, 32, 109

Nations, law of, 124, 404, 406, 451, 455. See also *Ius gentium*

Natural law, 15, 289, 293, 296, 297, 430, 450; absolutism and, 398; *bonum et aequum* and, 437, 438, 442; Byzantine jurists and, 447; equity *(aequitas)* and, 303, 305, 306; fairness and, 295; history and, 456–457; *ius gentium* and, 408; law of nations and, 451, 455; positivism opposed to, 434; Roman law transcribed in, 401; slavery and, 453–454; in Ulpian, 422. *See also* Law

Nazism, 22, 36

Neoplatonism, 8, 429, 457

Neratius, 263, 327, 349, 370; as Labeonian, 371, 372–373; scientism and, 440; works of, 372–373

Nero, 342, 343, 346, 347, 348, 351, 352

Nerva, 341, 343, 344, 346, 349

Nerva the Younger, 352

Nexum (debtor's servitude), 76, 99, 101, 169; abolition of, 96, 135; definitions of, 197, 211. *See also* Debts and debtors

Nicodemism, 380

Niebuhr, Barthold Georg, 20, 47–48

Nietzsche, Friedrich, 146

Public sphere, 364
Puchta, Georg Friedrich, 21
Punic Wars, 138, 141, 154, 230
Purchasers, obligations of, 33, 203

Quintilian, 38, 247, 275, 354, 355–356
Quirinus (deity), 54, 64, 65, 67, 235

Ramnes (tribe), 54
Ranke, Leopold von, 35
Rationalism, 62–63, 189, 233, 335, 373
Rationality, 118, 173; aristocratic, 239, 241,
    249, 268, 282, 316; case-based, 314, 361;
    law as separate kind of, 288–289; quanti-
    tative, 199
Reciprocity, 146, 320, 328, 334, 411
Regula, 166, 169
Religion, 4, 14, 56, 120, 200; anthropomor-
    phism in crisis, 237, 238; civic ordering
    and, 134; construction of the city and,
    68; ethics and, 294; fossilization of, 62;
    historic connections with law, 125; juris-
    prudentialization of, 83; origins of
    Rome and, 50; political rulers and, 238;
    republican, 234; secular influence of pol-
    itics and, 71–72; shift to politics from, 113;
    structural versus diachronic interpreta-
    tion of, 53; "tragedifying" of Roman reli-
    gion, 55. *See also* Christianity; Cults and
    cultic experience; Deities (gods); Theol-
    ogy
Renaissance, 4, 108
"Republican canon," 87, 94, 97, 115, 126
Res iudicata, 296
Res locata ("thing hired"), 256, 260–261
Respondere, 123, 127
Responsum (pl. *responsa*), 76, 78, 88, 92–93,
    97, 102, 164; *actiones* and, 144; as aristo-
    cratic prerogative, 112; Cato and, 166; *ius*
    and, 106, 107; *lex* and, 134–135; oral mem-
    orization of, 194; Publius Mucius

Scaevola and, 169; of secular experts,
    120, 121
Revolution, 111
Rhetoric, 33, 105, 165, 293, 301; fairness and,
    350; first school of, 185; jurisprudence
    versus, 105, 198; philosophical founda-
    tion for law and, 297
Rhetorica ad Herennium (Quintus Mucius),
    163, 184, 196, 198, 380–381; agreement in,
    216; on *ars,* 443; on civil law, 301; on "de-
    fective arguments," 229; diairesis and,
    315; equity *(aequitas)* and, 300, 302, 437;
    Gaius and, 384, 452; German philosophy
    and, 208; on justice, 299–300, 422; on na-
    ture and natural law, 295–297; *obligatio*
    concept absent from, 210; on *pactum,* 323
Rites and rituals, 58–59, 72, 136; *ius* and,
    200; memory of, 201; pontifices and, 69–
    70; public space and, 66; sacrificial, 66,
    69, 74; words prescribed for, 98. *See also*
    Bronze and scales
Robbery, 329
Roman empire, 61, 317; absolutist state of,
    395; bureaucracy of, 393; expansion of,
    373, 393; fall of western empire, 4, 395;
    outlying territories of, 40; trade under,
    363; two parts of, 395. *See also* Augustan
    age; Emperor *(princeps);* Principate
Romanist tradition, 19, 21, 34; Anglo-
    American law and, 32; Byzantine out-
    look perpetuated by, 27; "classical law"
    myth and, 34; dogmatics of law and, 23;
    German codification and, 26; historiog-
    raphy and, 38; myths of, 36; private law
    and, 397
Roman law, 3–4, 33, 288, 299, 460; bour-
    geois individualism and, 16, 320, 363;
    conservative apologia of, 21; as creation
    of jurists, 32; detached from republican
    community, 364, 367; diffusion of, 396;
    golden age of, 5; Greek philosophy and,
    426; historical understanding of, 21–22;
    Justinian and, 6; medieval interest in, 13;

Index of Sources

Literary Texts

Accius:
  Brutus (*TF*, Klotz):
    p. 367, fr. 40: chap. 5, n. 28
Aelius Aristides:
  Orationes (Keil):
    26.57: chap. 16, n. 6
Aëtius:
  Placita:
    1.6.9 (= p. 295 [Diels] = *SVF*, II, pp. 299–300 n. 1009): 199; chap. 13, n. 4
    1.8.1–2 (= p. 307 [Diels] = *SVF*, II, p. 320 n. 1101): 24; chap. 13, n. 22
[Alcinous]:
  Didascalicus:
    1(= p. 1 [Whittaker-Louis] = p. 152, ll. 24 [Hermann]): chap. 21, n. 37
    1(= p. 1 [Whittaker-Louis] = p. 152, ll. 56 [Hermann]): 369; chap. 21, n. 34
Ammianus Marcellinus:
  Res gestae:
    16.5.1: 81; chap. 7, n. 26
    22.16.22: 81; chap. 7, n. 26

Appian:
  Bella civilia:
    1.88.403–404: chap. 11, n. 8
    2.23.84: chap. 8, n. 50
    4.17.135: chap. 17, n. 2
Aristotle:
  Ethica Nicomachea (Bywater):
    2.1.7.1103b: chap. 17, n. 68
    2.6.2.1106a: 286; chap. 17, n. 73
    3.1.4.1110a: 286; chap. 17, n. 76
    5.2.12–13.1130b–1131a: 285; chap. 17, n. 68
    5.4.1.1131b: chap. 17, n. 68
    5.7.1.1134b: 255; chap. 16, n. 31
    5.7.1–5.1134b–1135a: chap. 16, n. 45
    5.8.10.1135b: chap. 17, n. 68
    5.10.1–8.1137a–1138a: chap. 16, n. 45
    6.5.1140a–b: chap. 6, n. 15
    6.11.1.1143a: chap. 16, n. 45
    6.12.6.1144a: 286; chap. 17, n. 74
    7.10.19.1243a: chap. 17, n. 68
    8.13.5–6.1162b: chap. 12, n. 55
    10.8.1.1178a: chap. 17, n. 68

1.5.15: 258; chap. 16, n. 43

1.10.33: 127 ff., 233; chap. 9, n. 27,
   n. 30; chap. 14, n. 76

1.31.111: chap. 17, n. 67

1.41.149: 368; chap. 21, n. 28

1.43.153: chap. 8, n. 46

2.12.42: chap. 7, n. 23

2.13.45: 134; chap. 10, n. 3

2.16.57: chap. 10, n. 21

2.22.78: 258; chap. 16, n. 43

3.10.43: 258; chap. 16, n. 43

3.14.60: chap. 16, n. 61

3.16.67: chap. 16, n. 59

3.17.70: 193 ff.; chap. 12, n. 51

3.24.92: 280; chap. 17, n. 32, n. 37

De republica:

1.2.2: 107 ff., 370; chap. 8, n. 51; chap.
   9, n. 19; chap. 21, n. 35

1.25.39: 108–109; chap. 8, n. 54

1.35.55: chap. 9, n. 22

2.8.14: chap. 5, n. 24

2.22.40: chap. 7, n. 54

2.31.54: chap. 7, n. 69

3.5.8–11.18: 257; chap. 16, n. 37

3.11.18: 258; chap. 16, n. 43

3.25.7: 393–394; chap. 22, n. 16

3.25.37: 257; chap. 16, n. 39

5.7.9: 134; chap. 10, n. 2

Laelius de amicitia:

1.1: chap. 10, n. 21

2.6: chap. 8, n. 46

Topica:

1.1–5: chap. 17, n. 71

2.9: 260; chap. 16, n. 52

4.24: 148; chap. 10, n. 53

5.28: 165, 255, 260, 330; chap. 11,
   n. 36; chap. 16, n. 29, n. 50; chap.
   19, n. 52

6.29: chap. 12, n. 61

23.90: 160; chap. 16, n. 58

Clement of Alexandria:

Stromata (Stahlin):

5.8.50: chap. 21, n. 12

Codex Theodosianus:

4.4.3pr: chap. 13, n. 19

Collatio Legum Mosaicarum et Romanarum:

2.5.1: chap. 17, n. 67

4.8: 85–86; chap. 7, n. 47

12.7.3: chap. 18, n. 1

Columella:

Res rustica:

1.7.2: 127; chap. 9, n. 28

11.1.26: 202; chap. 13, n. 14

Cornelius Nepos:

Cato:

3.4: chap. 13, n. 30

Corpus Iuris Civilis:

I. *Institutiones:*

1.1pr: chap. 21, n. 19

1.1.4: chap. 21, n. 1

1.2: 328 ff.; chap. 19, n. 61

1.2.1: chap. 21, n. 2, n. 23

1.2.6: chap. 21, n. 51

1.3.3: 393 ff.; chap. 22, n. 10

1.5pr.: 393 ff.; chap. 22, n. 8

3.13pr.: 184; chap. 12, n. 30

3.25.2: chap. 12, n. 50

II. *Digesta:*

1.1.1pr: chap. 21, n. 1

1.1.1pr-1: 361 ff.; chap. 21, n. 1

1.1.1.2: chap. 21, n. 1

1.1.1.3: chap. 21, n. 23

1.1.1.3–4: 395 ff.; chap. 22, n. 26

1.1.4: 363, 393 ff.; chap. 21, n. 10; chap.
   22, n. 8

1.1.6pr: 395 ff.; chap. 22, n. 26

1.1.6.1: 369; chap. 21, n. 30

1.1.7: 392; chap. 22, n. 6

1.1.7pr: 374; chap. 21, n. 45

1.1.9: 361–362; chap. 21, n. 2, n. 3

1.1.10pr: 366; chap. 21, n. 19

1.1.10.1–2: 367; chap. 21, n. 33; chap. 22,
   n. 1

1.1.10.2: 60; chap. 5, n. 19

1.1.11: 367, 392; chap. 21, n. 22

1.2.1: chap. 21, n. 6

Juvenal *(continued)*

IX.1–2 *(FIRA,* I, p. 64 = *RS,* pp. 582, 696
  ff.): 91; chap. 7, n. 42; chap. 8,
  n. 2

IX.4 *(FIRA,* I, p. 64 = *RS,* pp. 582, 696 ff.):
  chap. 7, n. 59

IX.5 *(FIRA,* I, p. 65 = *RS,* p. 703): chap. 7,
  n. 60

X.2–8 *(FIRA,* I, pp. 66–69 = *RS,* pp. 582,
  705 ff.): chap. 7, n. 52

Livy:

Ab urbe condita:

  1.13.6: chap. 5, n. 24
  1.19.7: chap. 6, n. 3
  1.20.5: chap. 6, n. 3
  1.20.7: chap. 6, n. 3; chap. 8, n. 9
  1.31.4: chap. 4, n. 16
  2.33.1: chap. 7, n. 15
  2.33.3: chap. 7, n. 15
  2.41: chap. 7, n. 60
  2.44.9: 83; chap. 7, n. 30
  3.27.1: chap. 5, n. 23
  3.31.8: 81; chap. 7, n. 26
  3.32.1: chap. 7, n. 26
  3.32–33: chap. 7, n. 31
  3.33.5: chap. 7, n. 26
  3.34.3: 85; chap. 7, n. 43
  3.34.6: 84; chap. 7, n. 40, n. 41
  3.39.3: chap. 5, n. 23
  3.55.10: chap. 7, n. 15
  3.57.10: chap. 7, n. 35
  3.58.2: chap. 7, n. 40
  4.1–6: chap. 7, n. 32
  6.1: 92; chap. 8, n. 7
  6.20.12: chap. 7, n. 60
  7.31.3: chap. 5, n. 18
  8.28.1–2: chap. 7, n. 33
  9.42.4: 384–385; chap. 21, n. 77
  9.46: 92; 100; chap. 8, n. 5, n. 23
  9.46.1–15: 99; chap. 8, n. 19
  10.8.9: 61; chap. 5, n. 23
  26.3: chap. 7, n. 60
  38.50: chap. 13, n. 31

40.29.11–12: 207; chap. 13, n. 32
42.41.14: chap. 21, n. 63

Macrobius:

Saturnalia:

  1.4.19: chap. 7, n. 67
  1.13.20: 80; chap. 7, n. 20
  1.16.26: 73; chap. 6, n. 18

Menander:

Epitrepontes (Sandbach):

  218 (= *Cod. Cair.,* 1; *CAF,* III.2.635,
    p. 189): 127; chap. 9, n. 26

New Testament: St. Paul of Tarsus:

Epistula ad Romanos:

  13:247; chap. 16, n. 4

Nonius Marcellus:

De compendiosa doctrina (Lindsay):

  p. 812, ll. 23–24: chap. 9, n. 31
  p. 835, ll. 34–37: chap. 6, n. 1

Origen:

Epistula ad Gregorium (Crouzel):

  1 (= *PG,* 11.88): 370; chap. 21, n. 35

In genesim homiliae (interprete Rufino)
    (Baehrens):

  11.2 (= *PG,* 12.222–223): 370; chap. 21,
    n. 35

Pauli Sententiae:

  3.4a.10: chap. 13, n. 19

Persius:

Saturae:

  5.88–90: 307; chap. 18, n. 57

Philostratus:

Vitae sophistarum:

  2.30.622: chap. 21, n. 32

Pindar:

Carmina (Snell-Maehler):

  fr. 169a: chap. 16, n. 35

Plato:

Gorgias:

  484b: chap. 16, n. 35

Laws:

  3.1.676–677: 36; chap. 3, n. 18
  6.19.777b–777c: 301; chap. 18, n. 28
  9.6.861b: chap. 17, n. 68

Epigraphs

.